PERSONALITY:
Inquiry and Application

(PGPS #74)

PERGAMON GENERAL PSYCHOLOGY SERIES

Editors: Arnold P. Goldstein, *Syracuse University*
Leonard Krasner, *SUNY, Stony Brook*

TITLES IN THE PERGAMON GENERAL PSYCHOLOGY SERIES
(Added Titles in Back of Volume)

The terms of our inspection copy service apply to all the above books. A complete catalogue of all books in the Pergamon International Library is available on request.

The Publisher will be pleased to receive suggestions for revised editions and new titles.

PERSONALITY:
Inquiry and Application

Mark Sherman

Pergamon Press

New York • Oxford • Toronto • Sydney • Frankfurt • Paris

Pergamon Press Offices:

U.S.A.   Pergamon Press Inc., Maxwell House, Fairview Park,
                         Elmsford, New York 10523, U.S.A.

U.K.   Pergamon Press Ltd., Headington Hill Hall,
                         Oxford OX3 0BW, England

CANADA   Pergamon of Canada Ltd., 150 Consumers Road,
                         Willowdale, Ontario M2J 1P9, Canada

AUSTRALIA   Pergamon Press (Aust) Pty. Ltd., P O Box 544,
                         Potts Point, NSW 2011, Australia

FRANCE   Pergamon Press SARL, 24 rue des Ecoles,
                         75240 Paris, Cedex 05, France

FEDERAL REPUBLIC   Pergamon Press GmbH, 6242 Kronberg/Taunus,
OF GERMANY   Pferdstrasse 1, Federal Republic of Germany

Library of Congress Cataloging in Publication Data

Sherman, Mark.
    Personality—inquiry and application.

    (Pergamon general psychology series: 74)
    1. Personality—Research. 2. Personality
assessment. 3. Personality. I. Title.
BF698.S5153 1979   155.2   78-13540
ISBN 0-08-019585-7

To Enid

Contents

viii   Contents

Foreword

In many ways, this book has been ten years in the making. It reflects what I have learned after a decade of teaching undergraduate *Personality* to over 3000 starry eyed and bleary eyed college students.

Personality: Inquiry and Application includes a carefully selected array of topics on personality assessment, research, and theory. The material chosen and its manner of presentation have been guided by an interest in reaching a middle ground on two pedagogical issues. First, an effort was made to cover an appropriate range of major topics. Presenting too many content areas in an academic semester creates confusion, while introducing too few denies the student the opportunity to gain a comprehensive sense of the overall picture. Thus, the selection of the particular personality assessment approaches discussed in Part II was dictated more by what is deemed important and representative than by an attempt to be exhaustive. Similar considerations influenced the organization of Part III. The personality theories presented therein reflect major trends which currently prevail in the field. The focus of each chapter is on the particular theorists who best exemplify the orientation in question, and their numbers have been kept to a minimum. Such a strategy allows the chosen theories to be presented in sufficient detail for the studious reader to become well informed.

The second concern, clearly related to the first, is that of difficulty level. The goal was to provide the student with an opportunity to confront successfully some of the complex core issues relevant to personality assessment, research, and theory. In order to assure mastery, material is frequently presented in considerable detail; the logic or conceptual underpinnings of a method or an idea is spelled out in stepwise fashion. In this way, a thorough, lasting understanding is established, instead of a soon-to-be-forgotten superficial acquaintanceship. This strategy was most important to the development of Part I, in which research design, interpretation, and ethics are presented with the degree of emphasis I believe they deserve in a broad band course in personality.

While I am the sole author of this text and therefore bear full responsibility for what follows, I do not presume to deserve complete credit. This "personality," willing and able to undertake the enterprise of textbook writing, was given its direction by caring, intelligent, creative, and responsible parents. I found similar qualities in my mentors at the University of Connecticut, particularly Amerigo Farina and Julian Rotter, who were highly influential in guiding my early development as an academician.

There are many I have come to know more recently who have been instrumental in helping me shape this book. My students, both undergraduate and graduate, who have asked the right questions and who have made insightful comments have been very important. I must especially single out Deborah Woodford, whose assistance in the role of researcher, proofreader, and reviewer was invaluable. The quality work of Leona Catlin and Lorna Ber, who typed the manuscript and indices into the night and on weekends, must be acknowledged as well.

I am also indebted to John G. Allen for his thorough reading of an earlier manuscript. His thoughtful suggestions concerning the form and substance of the book were of enormous benefit.

A sincere "thank you," one deeply felt, is directed to my most admired colleague and "best friend," Arnold P. Goldstein. He has been a constant source of help and inspiration — for this project as he has been for others before it and, will be, I hope, for others yet to come.

Anyone who labors countless hours on a serious task, no matter how devoted to it, must have his moments of pause and refreshment. My daughters, Cori and Julie, provided these blessed distractions. I only wish we could have been together more, for nothing can replace time away from a child growing up — which is indeed what they did while I was writing in my "dungeon."

Finally, no expression of gratitude to my wife, Enid, can adequately communicate what I feel. I could never have asked her to put up with what she did and come through it all, still my loving wife. If I failed her for not asking, or for putting her through it, she did not fail me. It is to her that this book is dedicated.

CHAPTER 1
Introduction

The purpose of this book is to provide the college undergraduate with an understanding of *personality* as a sub-area of psychology and to acquaint him with the principal methods of inquiry responsible for the acquisition of knowledge relevant to personality. This domain of study is sometimes referred to as *personology*. But what is it that personologists investigate? What is personality?

DEFINITION

Undoubtedly, we all have an intuitive sense of the meaning of *personality*. It has to do with people, the way they come across to others, the image they present, their social facade. In fact, the term "personality" derives from the word *persona*, which referred to the masks worn by actors in ancient Roman theater. These persona permitted audiences to identify easily the various roles enacted by the players and they facilitated understanding of the stage characters. Later, the roles themselves would be called persona. Of course, today people do not go around wearing masks in order to advertise their persona. Nevertheless, what a person is about — his personality — still is manifested to others through verbal and nonverbal behaviors. These expressions may lead others to characterize an individual's personality as "intellectual," "crude," or perhaps as "just plain great."

On a more formal level, in 1937 Gordon Allport presented a lengthy list of already-published definitions of personality. Since that time many more have been suggested, leading us to conclude, along with Allport, that "Everyone, it seems, knows what personality is, but no one can precisely define it." (1961, p. 22). Our own best effort is the following: *Personality is the characteristic pattern of behaviors, cognitions, and emotions which may be experienced by the individual and/or manifest to others.*

This definition specifies several essential points. It includes *behaviors* (actions), *cognitions* (thoughts), and *emotions* (feelings) as the basic content of personality. Behaviors, cognitions, and emotions may be collectively referred to as person-events.

1

Some personologists focus upon one class of person-events more than upon others. As we will see, Sigmund Freud spends considerable time discussing emotion; other workers, such as B.F. Skinner, emphasize behavioral phenomena; cognitively oriented personologists are well represented by Carl Rogers. Most personality theorists, however, talk about the complete human being and, in so doing, deal implicitly with all three classes of person-events.

The word *characteristic* in our definition suggests that person-events are specific to particular people. This specificity sets each individual apart from all others. Thus, *every* person acts, thinks, and feels somewhat differently. In addition, these characteristic person-events are not random occurrences but rather emerge in *patterns*; person-events are related to each other in that the presence of one event tends to be associated with the presence (or absence) of others. For example, we know that ideas of high self-esteem ("I'm a great person") are more likely associated with good feelings and smiling behaviors than are ideas of low self-esteem. Also, patterning has a temporal aspect in that person-events are related to other previous or subsequent events. Our knowledge that feelings of anger often precede aggressive behaviors is one example of such temporal patterning. These patterns and their repetitions make for the apparent stability of personality.

The word *may* in our definition implies three important things. First, some person-events *may* not be *experienced* by the person himself but are nevertheless *manifest* to others. That is, the individual may not consciously know the reasons for, or even the content, of his behavior. An example of this is the person others accurately perceive as hostile but who honestly does not think of himself in that way. Second, a person *may* indeed *experience* certain aspects of himself of which others are unaware; these are not *manifest* person-events. For instance, we often have evaluative thoughts about people ("She is one boring person") which we are loathe to reveal and can, in fact, successfully hide. Third, some person-events are neither *experienced* by the person himself, nor are they *manifest* to others. In this vein, Freud pointed out that humor may serve to conceal angry feelings. Neither the perpetrator of a practical joke nor the person who serves as its object may realize that their "playful" interaction really involves the expression of hostility in a disguised form.

METHODOLOGY

At an informal level, once we arrive at some initial definition of another's personality, we are prone to engage in a variety of inferential activities, many of them ill-founded. We speculate about why the person is the way he is and what we might expect from him in a given situation. Perhaps we even theorize about human nature in general.

In many respects, personologists do much the same thing. The main difference is that their inferential activities are presumably conducted in a manner which is acceptable to the scientific community. Unfortunately, scientific acceptability is as difficult to define as personality itself.

Some psychologists assert that personology could best be advanced by adopting a *nomothetic* orientation. This nomothetic approach dictates that relatively narrow aspects of large numbers of people be studied in the service of discovering general principles. Several research strategies, such as experimentation and correlational studies, are well suited to the nomotheticist's preferences. These will be discussed in later chapters. Other personologists argue that the most viable route to understanding personality is by way of intensive investigation and assessment of single cases — the *idiographic* approach. Probably the best exemplar of this school of thought was Freud who, on the basis of a relatively small number of individual psychotherapeutic encounters, developed a systematic statement about personality development and processes which he maintained was universally applicable.

Nomotheticists criticize the idiographic approach as being too "clinical" and insufficiently scientific. They claim that the idiographic position is one which, in practice, cannot be followed. The assertion is made that an in-depth assessment of a given personality can only be made if at least implicit normative comparisons are drawn. For example, nomotheticists say that it is impossible to judge someone as "sexually constricted" on the basis of an intensive personality analysis unless there is some normative standard held regarding the nature of sexual expression in general. The argument is further made that these normative standards ought to be explicitly acknowledged and used in the most rigorous, scientific fashion possible.

In actual practice psychologists tend to operate within both nomothetic and idiographic frameworks, with the approach being emphasized at a given time dependent on the psychologists' purposes. Clinical work usually demands a relatively idiographic examination of matters; research activity requires a more nomothetic perspective.

Regardless of whether a personologist chooses group (nomothetic) or individual (idiographic) investigative methods, the problems and goals remain fairly constant. Like the casual observer, personologists are interested in trying to understand the functioning of personality, to gain knowledge of its antecedents, and to acquire the capacity to predict accurately the way it will manifest itself on future, specified occasions.

PROSPECTUS

There are four basic methods of inquiry associated with personology. Three of these are research, individual personality assessment, and theory construction. Each of these strategies will be given primary attention.

Part I is devoted to a thorough examination of personality research. It is felt that an understanding of this area is crucial for an appreciation of personality as a scientific discipline. Experimentation, as one research method, is covered in two chapters. The first of these deals with basic experimental designs; the second discusses sources of error which may render the results of an experiment uninterpretable. Two chapters on non-experimental research present the design, assets, and liabilities of correlational, single subject, and case study investigations. Finally, the inclusion of a separate chapter on professional ethics accords this topic its due emphasis.

Part II covers personality assessment. Individual chapters are devoted to issues which transcend any particular procedure, such as interpersonal factors which interfere with the accurate assessment of others, and instrument characteristics which severely limit the usefulness of a test as a tool for the prediction and understanding of human behavior. Although attention is given to some of the statistical conceptions which underlie personality test construction and utilization, the material presented is designed for students who do not have prior coursework in statistics. A brief chapter which discusses the main dimensions of personality assessment procedures is followed by four chapters in which selected instruments and approaches are presented in detail.

Part III is concerned with the presentation of personality theories. The section begins with an overview in which the nature and criteria of adequate personality theory are presented. These criteria are then used to help evaluate each theory as it is presented. The next two chapters attend primarily to the personality theories of Freud and Rogers as representative of the psychodynamic and phenomenological viewpoints, respectively. This is followed by chapters in which the principles of classical and operant conditioning are detailed, and their application to human behavior acquisition, maintenance, and change reviewed. The final chapter reflects the current trend toward cognitive-learning personality theorizing. In particular, it contains descriptions and applications of the ideas of prominent psychologists in this movement. Bandura's socio-behavioristic approach with its emphasis upon observational phenomena, Rotter's Social Learning Theory, Mischel's cognitive reconceptualization of personality and transactional personality theory as elaborated by Endler and Magnusson are all examined.

The reader should be forewarned that this tripartite discussion is for instructional convenience only. In reality, the assessment, research, and theory-building enterprises are mutually interdependent. The particular aspects of personality one chooses to assess and the areas of research the personologist pursues are usually dictated by his theoretical understanding of personality. In turn, that theoretical understanding emerges in part from the findings of individual assessments and research.

Psychotherapy is a fourth important strategy of inquiry. While psychotherapy is typically thought of as being primarily concerned with treatment, it may well be the single most important source of ideas regarding the nature of personality. After all, no other vehicle permits one to gain such intimate knowledge about the behavior, ideas, and feelings of another human being. These insights may then serve as a basis for modifying and extending existing personality theory, as a focus of personality assessment and/or as an impetus for research. Because psychotherapy, in all its forms, is so entwined with the other inquiry strategies, no attempt has been made to deal with it separately. Instead, material relevant to clinical practice is discussed throughout, both in the context of it being a source of new knowledge and as a major endeavor to which personality assessment, research, and theory are applied.

PART I
Personality Research

CHAPTER 2
Personality Research: An Overview

THE NATURE OF SCIENCE

The purpose of science is to gain knowledge about our universe. This goal, of course, is not unique to scientific inquiry. A variety of vehicles have been proposed to obtain such knowledge. Plato said that the essence of an event is known prior to birth. If one wishes to discover what a tree is about, one must reflect upon what makes a tree a tree. In this way, accurate prenatal concepts regarding the essence of a tree will be captured. *Reminiscence,* then, was seen by Plato as the route to basic knowledge.

The sensory experiences associated with encountering specific events, vision and touch, were thought by Plato to be inferior ways of attempting to gain knowledge. This rejection of reliance upon direct observation was later advocated by Descartes and Spinoza who, as *rationalists,* believed that truth could be acquired through reason.

Modern scientific approaches to the acquisition of knowledge about the universe depend heavily upon *empiricism.* In this context, empiricism means a "reliance upon observation as opposed to dependence upon interpretation, speculation, and subjective judgement" (Shontz, 1965, p. 87). Thus, observation lies at the very core of empirical science.

The emphasis on observation as the route to knowledge holds with it a basic but often forgotten assumption. Namely, that what is observed exists apart from the observer. That is, the universe is assumed to be more than just the collection of an individual's perceptions. Events are thought to have permanency which transcends the act of perceiving them. Thus, the New World existed long before it was "discovered" by Columbus and continued to exist after he and his crew departed for home. Similarly, the observed behavior of a rat in a learning maze is more than just an awareness on the observer's part of his own visual sensations. There is a reality which consists of a real rat running through a real maze.

A basic requirement of empirical science is that its assertions about the nature of the universe correspond to the external reality which is assumed to exist. When scientific statements meet this standard, they are said to have *transcendent truth.* The lack of a correspondence between assertion and observed reality may mean that the

7

assertion is incorrect and must be modified. Alternatively, the assertion may correspond to objective reality (transcendent truth) but our observation of reality may be inaccurate. Recognizing the fallibility of unaided human observational processes, scientific inquiry employs whatever tools it can, from microscopes to intelligence tests in order to sharpen the precision of its observations.

There is a second kind of truth which scientific assertions must attain in order to be acceptable. This is *immanent truth,* the demonstration that assertions are logically interrelated and nowhere contradict each other. A formal science, such as mathematics, is required only to have immanent truth. However, an empirical science which concerns itself directly with understanding external reality must strive for both immanent and transcendent truth; the attainment of the former without the latter would render an empirical science trivial. For example, the importance of psychology depends upon the significance of the real world events to which its assertions correspond. The most influential figures in the history of psychology, men such as Pavlov, Freud, and Skinner, gained distinction on the basis of observing important events and generating assertions regarding what they observed. These assertions have transcendent truth. Not one of these scientists was a mathematician who set as a primary goal the establishment of immanent truth.

There are two additional assumptions, in addition to that having to do with the existence of a real external world, upon which scientific inquiry rests. First, it is assumed that what is observed occurs within a lawful, ordered context. That is, *every observation can be understood as the outcome of antecedent events.* For example, a light goes on because a switch is turned on; writing appears on paper because ink is spread over it by a pen point.

This notion of observed events as causal outcomes rather than capricious phenomena is known as *determinism.* Determinism must be accepted as an operating assumption of psychology in order for inquiry to proceed from a scientific perspective. It makes no sense to try to discover lawful relationships between observable events, a primary scientific enterprise, if the events themselves are assumed to be chance occurrences.

A second assumption relating to the nature of scientific observation and to the issue of determinism is that there are a limited number of antecedents relevant to the occurrence of an observed event. This is known as *finite causation* (Underwood, 1957, p. 6). The laughter of someone in Nebraska does not depend on another person coughing in India or a lemming drowning at sea; rather, a limited number of potentially discoverable factors are causally related to the Nebraskan's laughter. In the case of human behavior, the number of relevant antecedents may be quite large but it is still less than infinite. Indeed, Underwood points out, "science would be almost a hopeless undertaking if nature were so constituted that everything in it influenced everything else" (1957, p. 6).

We have stressed the importance of observation as the basis of empirical scientific inquiry. However, not all observation is scientific in nature. Only those observations which are replicable can serve as the basis of an empirical science. What this means is that the conditions under which observation occurs must be specifiable in terms which are precise. This enables another person, in another time and place, to duplicate the original conditions and observe the same phenomenon. For example, it is not sufficient for a scientist to report that a hungry pigeon can be trained to peck at a disc if he is given food pellets. One can provide unlimited amounts of food pellets to a hungry pigeon and observe nothing more than eating behavior. As an alternative, the original observer should have reported that he had taken a pigeon which had been deprived of food for 10 hours , put the pigeon in a container which — among its other specifiable measurements and characteristics — had a white disc mounted on a vertical wall at pigeon-eye level, dropped a food pellet into the container via a chute immediately after (and only after) the pigeon happened to peck at the disc, and recorded a dramatically higher rate of disc pecking by the pigeon as these operations were followed. These reported observations are scientifically useful because they define the observational conditions with sufficient clarity so that replication is possible. Personal observation thus becomes publicly available scientific evidence which is open to confirmation or refutation; anyone may test the accuracy of the observations.

The Scientific Method

The scientific method is not a single method per se. Rather it is an approach which scientists explicitly or implicitly adopt as they try to better describe, explain, and predict observations. Traditionally, the scientific method has been seen to involve a number of steps.

Observation. Observation is always the starting point. Observations are the empirical facts upon which the scientific method rests. Although the scientist may be geared up to observe certain phenomena, it has repeatedly been the case that important observations are made when least expected. An accidental discovery is referred to as "serendipity" (Cannon, 1945), recalling the tale of the three Princes of Serendip who traveled the world, never finding what they were seeking but discovering many things they had not sought.

Sidman (1960) reports that important discoveries relating to the etiology of ulcers were the product of serendipity. Joseph Brady (1958) was studying learning in monkeys at Walter Reed Laboratory under a variety of conditions, including shock avoidance. The animals were expected to learn to press a lever in order to avoid receiving a shock. An unexpectedly high number of animals died during the course of his research, much to the puzzlement of Brady. At about this time, R.W. Porter was assigned to the Walter Reed Laboratories as part of his obligatory military service. He had previously done research on ulcers and had conducted many post-mortem examinations on monkeys. When he heard of Brady's trouble, Porter asked if he could examine the deceased animals as they became available. Periodically, thereafter, Porter presented evidence to Brady in the form of an ulcerated section of monkey gut. Brady himself reports that a "message finally burst out in neon lights when he (Porter) remarked that out of several hundred monkeys which he had had occasion to examine in the past, not one had shown any sign of a normally occurring ulcer" (Sidman, 1960, p. 11).

Thus, an unexpectedly high mortality rate, coupled with the fortuitous assignment of a pathologist, led to a shift in Brady's research interests to an explanation for the development of the ulcers.

One of the schedules of shock avoidance which had been used in Brady's learning research was selected for the first ulcer studies. It consisted of six hours of shock avoidance followed by six hours of rest. Brady and Porter confined two monkeys in restraining chairs. One monkey (the executive) could avoid shock for both by pressing a bar. The non-executive monkey also had a bar, but it was functionless. When the animals were sacrificed, ulcers were found in the executive animals. The paired animals who had received precisely the same shocks, but who had no responsibility for preventing them, did not develop ulcers. The point here is that, while planned observation is usually considered to be a hallmark of science, accidental observation and the curiosity to follow up on what may at first appear to be unexplained confusion are equally important sources of discovery. The scientist must avoid being blind to anything. Although he may have preconceived ideas, he should always keep Skinner's advice in mind: "When you run into something interesting, drop everything else and study it" (1959, p. 81).

Empirical propositions. After a number of discrete observations are made, it may be possible to arrive at a general statement which summarizes and is descriptive of what has been noted. In Brady's monkey research, there came a time when he reached the tentative generalization that shock avoidance learning in monkeys is associated with the production of ulcers. This descriptive summarization is called an *empirical proposition*. Empirical propositions are arrived at by *induction,* the process of reaching general statements regarding a class of events on the basis of having made specific observations.

Hypotheses. Once an empirical proposition exists, the creative scientist is in a position to think about its implications. Given the empirical proposition that shock avoidant training is associated with the development of ulcers in monkeys (Brady, 1958), it is possible to predict that any monkey subjected to shock avoidant training will develop an ulcer. An expectancy regarding the individual case is arrived at through the application of a more general proposition. This is the process of *deduction.*

The specific expectancy, called a hypothesis, often takes the form of an if-then statement; *if* monkey X is subjected to shock avoidant training, *then* monkey X will develop an ulcer. By stating the deduced implication of an empirical proposition in the form of an if-then statement, the scientist is in a position to easily devise a situation in which the accuracy of the hypothesis may be tested. In this case it would be to subject monkey X to shock avoidant training, sacrifice the animal, and observe whether an ulcer has developed.

Very frequently, the implications of an empirical proposition are associated with selected dimensions related to the proposition. For example, one implication of Brady's empirical proposition is that brief rest periods between shock avoidant sessions are more conducive to the development of ulcers in monkeys than are long rest periods. The following hypothesis may thus be deduced: Monkeys will produce ulcers more rapidly with a six hour shock avoidant and two hour rest schedule than with a six hour shock avoidant and six hour rest schedule.

Research. One of the main purposes of research is to test the accuracy of hypotheses deduced from empirical propositions. Continuing to use the example provided by Brady's laboratory, the above hypothesis was evaluated by subjecting monkeys to the two schedules of shock avoidance and rest mentioned. Contrary to the expected outcome, the research demonstrated that the six hour avoidance and six hour rest was *more* productive of ulcers than any other schedule. Subsequent research in which the concentration of stomach acidity was monitored revealed that stronger concentrations began to occur about three hours into a rest period which followed a six hour shock avoidance period. The introduction of a second avoidance period after only two hours of rest precluded production of strong acid concentrations and ulcers failed to develop (Brady, 1958). It is interesting that the six hour avoidant and six hour rest schedule was first selected for reasons which were anything but scientific. Because of space limitations, the research had to be conducted in Porter's office. He believed that the six hour cycle would be least disruptive to his regular office routine. Thus, administrative concerns of Porter proved to have unexpected relevance to his research findings — another example of serendipity!

The most scientifically rigorous research is experimentation. The specific purpose and nature of experiments in psychology will be discussed in detail. There are circumstances in which other forms of research are employed. These non-experimental research procedures will also be carefully examined.

Theory Formulation. Research allows the scientist to observe new phenomena, usually under carefully defined conditions. After a number of studies have been conducted, each designed to test the validity of hypotheses deduced from empirical propositions, the process of induction may again become important. That is, the scientist may overview a set of experimental and non-experimental research findings and then arrive at some new general statements which tentatively account for the obtained data. These statements are *theoretical propositions*. They are less tightly related to direct observation than empirical propositions which are descriptive in nature.

Theoretical propositions are usually intended to be explanatory. As such, they may include references to hypothetical events or conditions which are not themselves directly observable or measurable. *Theoretical construct* is the term which refers to one of these hypothetical explanatory events or conditions. For example, one might observe that rats raised in a complex cage containing an assortment of wheels, bars, and cubes which can be manipulated and climbed over, under, and through, very quickly learn to run a maze as adults. Specifically, they are seen to acquire the ability to reach a food box at the end of a maze much more quickly than rats raised in an empty cage. The scientist may attempt to account for the observed co-variation between complexity of infantile environment and adult maze performance by invoking the theoretical construct "intelligence," defined as "problem solving ability." Notice that the capacity itself is never directly observed but is the hypothetical bridge which theoretically links the two related observations of the complexity of environment during infancy and the speed with which a maze is solved as an adult.

Just as an empirical proposition suggests implications which may be tested through research, so does a theoretical proposition. Thus the scientist may deduce hypotheses about the relevance to intelligence of antecedent factors other than that of infantile cage complexity, such as genetics and infantile nutrition. He may also raise questions regarding the relationship between the theoretical construct of intelligence and other behaviors, such as discrimination learning. This may lead to research which shows, for example, that both genetic and early nutritional factors are related to adult maze learning and discrimination problem solving. All of these empirical relationships can be accounted for by the theoretical construct of intelligence. In effect, the empirical relationships and theoretical explanatory construct of intelligence comprise a kind of miniature theory. The nature of theory in psychology, its purposes, and its limitations will be discussed in Chapter 16.

Observation, induction of empirical propositions, deduction of hypotheses, research, and theory formulation do not always follow one another in a neat manner. Theory formulation does not necessarily depend upon preceding research. Observations can be made and theories built in an attempt to explain those observations without ever resorting to research. Of course, until research is conducted which tests the accuracy of its propositions, the validity of a theory remains an open issue. In other words, it is often the case that theory prompts research instead of the other way around.

What the psychologist chooses to observe and the particular questions he tries to answer in his research are often defined by his initial theoretical leanings. The theory may be quite informal and, in the beginning, hardly more than a loosely formulated guess. Nevertheless, some system of ideas or a theory regarding the nature of people is usually responsible for causing the psychologist to observe this instead of that, to research one hypothesis instead of another. Probably the safest thing to conclude then is that, while their order of occurrence may at times vary, observation, research, and theory formulation are all indispensible components of the enterprise called science.

SUMMARY

This chapter began by describing the nature of science and noted that psychology, as a science, must seek to establish both transcendent and immanent truth. The assumption that psychological phenomena are the causal outcomes of a limited number of antecedent events was shown to be basic to a scientific perspective. Finally, the scientific method was explained as consisting of several interrelated steps, including observation, the generation of empirical propositions and hypotheses, the conduct of research, and the formulation of theory. In Chapter 3 we will begin to look at one of the many methods employed by psychologists in the conduct of research — experimentation.

TERMS TO KNOW

	Page No.		Page No.
deduction	10	induction	10
determinism	8	rationalism	7
empirical propositions	10	reminiscence	7
empiricism	7	scientific method	9
executive monkeys	10	serendipity	9
finite causation	8	theoretical construct	11
hypothesis	10	theoretical proposition	11
immanent truth	8	transcendent truth	7

CHAPTER 3
Experimentation

The general research strategy adopted by the empirically oriented investigator is referred to as a *method*. In this chapter we will consider the most powerful method in the researcher's arsenal for establishing causal relationships between events — the *experimental method*.

A Sample Experiment

After casually observing the behavior of psychiatric patients for some time, Braginsky and Braginsky (1967) were able to arrive at some general propositions. Most salient of these was the observation that many long-term psychiatric patients appeared to have a recreational orientation to the hospital rather than a therapeutic one geared toward their early discharge. By having patients complete questionnaires about various aspects of their hospitalization, Braginsky discovered that most long-term patients were quite aware of such information as the location and hours of the hospital coffee shop, swimming pool, and movie theater. They were much less well informed about the names and office locations of their psychiatrists, psychologists, and social workers. On the basis of these data, the Braginskys reasoned that many, if not most, long-term psychiatric patients remained in the hospital largely because they chose to do so. It was believed that, perhaps because of an insensitive, nagging spouse at home or some other reason, these patients had come to the conclusion that psychiatric hospitalization was a more acceptable alternative than living in the "real world." The authors further reasoned that, if this was so, such patients would be motivated to maintain a position within the hospital which would permit as pleasant a life style as possible. This would presumably include an open ward assignment, which allows patients the freedom to move around and have easy access to the hospital's recreational resources. Confinement to a locked ward, the usual placement of new patients who are under observation and severely disturbed patients who require constant supervision, would be considered much less attractive.

14

To test the validity of these ideas, Braginsky sought to experimentally determine whether patients who were given different information regarding the purpose of a psychiatric interview would vary the degree of psychopathology they communicated during their interviews. Specifically Braginsky hypothesized that long-term open ward patients who were thought to be motivated to remain hospitalized would present themselves as relatively sick when threatened with discharge, in order to guard against appearing healthy enough to be released. They would present themselves as relatively healthy when threatened with assignment to a locked ward, in order to guard against appearing sick enough to warrant confinement.

The experimental procedure consisted of bringing 30 patients who had been living on an open ward for more than two continuous years to a waiting room. The patients were then escorted, one at a time, to a second room in which they were to receive a "mental status interview." On the way to this interview, one-third of the patients were advised by their escort that the purpose of the interview was to find out who should be placed on a locked ward (group L). Ten additional patients were led to believe that the interview was to determine who was ready for discharge (group D). The last third of the patients was not provided with any specific information about the purpose of the interview other than that it was for mental status evaluation (group MS).

Upon entering the interview room, each patient was asked how he felt physically and mentally. The interviewer, who had no knowledge of what the patients had just been told, tape recorded these verbal exchanges which lasted about two minutes.

The tape recordings were then given to hospital psychiatrists who were unfamiliar with the nature of the experiment. The psychiatrists were asked to rate the patients' interview behavior on three dimensions: severity of psychopathology on a 5 point scale, amount of hospital control needed on an 8 point scale, and speech pattern peculiarities on an 8 point scale.

As predicted, the psychiatrists rated least psychopathological and least in need of hospital control those patients who believed the interview might lead to a locked ward assignment; those patients who were threatened with the prospect of the unpleasant restrictions associated with locked ward living came across as relatively healthy. This confirmed Braginsky's hypothesis that they would in no way want to suggest that restrictions were necessary in their case.

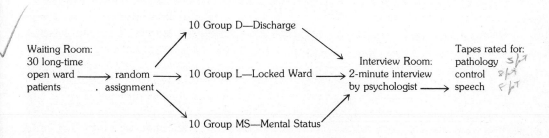

Figure 1. Schematic of the Braginsky and Braginsky (1967) experiment.

E bias - p 25

The patients who were told that discharge was a possible outcome of the interview were rated by psychiatrists as being both relatively sicker and in need of more control. This is also consistent with Braginsky's anticipation that long-term patients who desire to remain hospitalized will try to avoid appearing healthy when the prospect of discharge is imminent.

The patient group which was not provided with any pre-interview information behaved in a manner similar to the group threatened with discharge. This was expected since most mental status interviews would be geared toward psychiatric evaluation with respect to the issue of discharge. Thus, for the MS patients, the interview was probably understood to have a purpose similar to that made explicit to the D group.

Braginsky interprets his findings to mean that these schizophrenic patients are not necessarily irrational or ineffectual. Rather, they were shown to be quite active in systematically manipulating the interpersonal impression they created. The patients did this in an expected manner if one assumes that they, like all people, are goal-oriented, and act efficiently to attain their goals.

Braginsky points out an alternative explanation for these results in terms of actual severity of psychopathology. That is, instead of assuming that when anticipating discharge patients become motivated to appear sicker, is it possible that they actually become sicker? Did the D and MS conditions raise the anxiety levels of the patients to the point where they were more psychopathological and more in need of hospital control? Braginsky rejects this alternative explanation of his findings by pointing out that the psychiatric ratings on speech atypicalities were unaffected by the experimental manipulations. In fact, all patient groups were rated as sounding reasonably normal. Braginsky therefore reasons that judgments of psychopathology and need for hospital control were probably not based upon manifest symptoms. "Patients did not behave in a disturbed manner; rather, they told the interviewer how disturbed they were" (p. 547). A content analysis of the patient statements confirmed this idea. Ratings of psychopathology and need for hospital control were indeed strongly related to the frequency of positive and negative self-referent statements expressed. Also, patients tended to say either positive or negative things about themselves, indicating that their expressed self-evaluations were consistent, not random, in nature.

THE EXPERIMENTAL METHOD

The experimental method is characterized by the direct investigation of the effect one phenomenon has upon another. In the Braginsky (1967) research, this takes the form of exploring the effect which pre-interview information has upon within interview behavior.

Variables and Groups

The first mentioned event, pre-interview information, is regulated by the experimenter, and is called an *independent variable*. The independent variable in experimental research is what the experimenter manipulates or varies. For example, in an experiment exploring the impact of pain on performance, certain subjects may be exposed to a standard intensity of the independent variable, shock, while trying to solve a puzzle. The administration of shock is the *experimental treatment.* Subjects receiving this treatment are referred to as *experimental subjects* and, collectively, comprise the *experimental group.* Other subjects may be treated under conditions wherein the experimental treatment is withheld. In our example, then, they would not receive shock while trying to solve the puzzles. These are the *control subjects* and they constitute the *control group.* It may be useful to think of the two or more subject groups in an experiment as simply *comparison* groups rather than experimental (treatment) and control (no-treatment) groups. This is because many experiments do not have a strict no-treatment condition. They may, however, have two or more comparison groups, each of which receive a somewhat different form of treatment. For example, in the Braginsky experiment, the L and D treatment groups received explicit, although qualitatively different, information about the potential outcome of the interview. The MS group approximated a no-treatment control. Thus, the manipulation by the experimenters of the independent variable may involve either giving, modifying, or withholding a treatment to groups of subjects. The manipulations are conducted to determine their effects on the outcome. The outcome phenomenon of interest is called the *dependent variable.* It is the variable which can be observed or measured in some way. In the Braginsky experiment, it was patients' interview behavior which was of prime interest. The intent was to see whether interview behavior could be explained as a function of the independent variable, in this case pre-interview information, or, to put it alternatively, to predict interview behavior on the basis of pre-interview information.

Operational definitions

In order for an experiment to be replicable and, therefore, scientifically acceptable, both independent and dependent variables have to be carefully defined. It is not sufficient for the experiment to claim that when long-term open ward patients are threatened with discharge they tend to appear more psychopathological. The terms "threatened with discharge" and "psychopathological" require further clarification.

In research, this clarification takes the form of defining terms in an operational manner. *Operational definitions* spell out the actual procedures (or operations) associated with a given term in the experiment. Thus, "psychopathological" in the Braginsky study is operationally defined as "ratings made by psychiatrists along the three dimensions of severity of pathology, need for hospital control, and speech atypicalities. These three ratings are each referred to as a *dependent measure.*

The operational definition of "threaten with discharge" in Braginsky's research involves spelling out, word-for-word, what was said to the patients between the time they left the waiting room and entered the interview room. In this way, any reader would know exactly what is required to replicate Braginsky's threat to patients. The replicability of an experiment may be further enhanced if actual rating forms used as a dependent measure are included in the research report. When the dependent measurement involves the use of some equipment, a detailed description of it is usually appropriate, including manufacturer and model number. If the equipment is developed especially for a particular experiment, a schematic, dimensions, construction, and appearance details are either routinely reported or made readily available to interested parties.

Confounding

The defining of independent and dependent variables in operational terms is itself not sufficient for an experiment to be scientifically acceptable. Recall that the major purpose of any experiment is to permit the investigator to draw conclusions about the impact which an independent variable has upon a dependent variable. In order for clarity to exist on this crucial matter, the research must be designed so that the *only* factor operating which can conceivably produce dependent variable differences between comparison groups is the independent variables. Any other factors operating which have the capacity to produce between-group differences on the dependent variable are called *confounding variables*. An experiment is said to be *confounded* when such a variable exists and possibly influence results. When trying to interpret a confounded experiment, the researcher will not be able to determine if between-group differences on the dependent variable are attributable to the independent variable, to the confounding variable, or to both.

As an example of a confounded experiment, consider whether Braginsky's findings would have been easily interpretable if he had used a male interviewer in the D condition and a female interviewer in the L condition. The between-group differences on the dependent measures of psychopathology and amount of control needed would not then have been so clearly due to the independent variable of pre-interview information. Instead, the results could have been the product of a confounding variable, the sex of the interviewer. Male patients may be more open and willing to express negative self-referent statements to a male than to a female interviewer. Thus, the fact that there would have been more than one difference between the D and L treatments, pre-interview information *and* the sex of interviewer, would have confounded the experiment and rendered speculative, at best, the interpretation of group differences on the dependent measures.

Control

A well designed experiment is one in which events are so arranged that the confounding influences of variables other than the independent variable are effectively eliminated. Such arrangements are called *controls* and include a wide array of specific operations. An experiment which incorporates all necessary control procedures is said to be well-controlled; it is an experiment whose results are not open to alternative interpretations.

There are basically two sources of confounding in an experiment — the subjects themselves and the experimental situation. Regardless of the source, the impact of potentially confounding variables may be held to a minimum through the control procedures of *randomizing, manipulating,* or *holding constant.*

Randomization. This procedure is most often used in the assignment of subjects to treatment groups. True randomization in this sense requires that every subject has an equal chance of being assigned to any of the treatment groups. In a two-group experiment this might be accomplished by assigning subjects on the basis of a coin flip; "heads" are experimental, "tails" are control. Through this or some variant procedure an experimenter is able to assert that all subject variables, such as intelligence, age, maturation and cooperativeness have been equally distributed across the groups. Consequently, between-group differences on the dependent variable, the *experimental effect,* cannot be attributed to, for example, one group being more intelligent than the other. The experimental effect can then be seen more confidently as the product of the experimenter's manipulation of his independent variable.

If the assignment of subjects to groups is not done randomly, the assignment procedure and the resulting groups are referred to as *biased.* In this case, the term biased refers to a situation wherein groups are formed which systematically differ from each other on a confounding variable. If Braginsky had assigned the first 10 subjects who arrived at the waiting room to the lock ward treatment and the next 10 to the discharge condition, the result may well have been biased groups. One way in which bias might have been introduced in this way lies in the observation that early arrivers are more generally enthusiastic and that such enthusiasm may constitute a sign of psychological well-being. This alone might have been capable of producing the psychiatric ratings of greater health for subjects in the L than in the D condition. However, through random assignment, some early-arriving subjects end up in the D group, some in the L group. Enthusiasm is thus no longer a variable on which the groups systematically differ and, therefore, it cannot be a source of confounding.

Randomization as a control procedure can also be used to minimize confounding which may arise from situational factors. For example, it is not unusual in large sample experiments to enlist the services of more than one experimenter. While each may receive extensive training in how to conduct the experiment, a variety of subtle differences may exist in the way they actually run subjects. Consequently, it would not do to have each group led by a different experimenter. If that was the case, we would end up asking whether the experimental effect was due to the independent variable or to the experimenters. This particular problem was exemplified previously when we considered the confounding that would have resulted if, in Braginsky's experiment, the D group was interviewed by a male and the L group by a female. Such confounding can be circumvented by having subjects randomly assigned to interviewers as well as to treatments. The interviewer effect would then be equally distributed over groups.

There are some difficulties in relying only on randomization as a control procedure. With respect to subject assignment, for instance, it rarely results in equal-sized groups. One group typically ends up with more subjects than the other, a disadvantage when it comes time to statistically analyze the data from an experiment. Similarly, and especially when dealing with small numbers of subjects, random assignment may result in an uneven representation of subjects across groups with respect to some important personality characteristic. Thus, intelligence may be considered to be a variable which might affect performance on dependent measures. Pure random assignment of 20 subjects to two groups may, by chance, result in the brightest subjects ending up in the same group. This between-group inequality would constitute a source of confounding.

Manipulation. Because of these difficulties, randomization is frequently supplemented as a control procedure by *systematic manipulation* of variables. Systematic manipulation means that the experimenter intentionally arranges the levels or quality of a variable which exists within and/or between groups. In all cases, of course, the experimenter systematically manipulates his independent variable so that one level or quality of it is presented to one group and another level or quality to a second group. This assures that the experience of each group is different with respect to the independent variable.

In a similar fashion, the experimenter may systematically manipulate a variable to be certain that the several treatment groups are equated along the dimension it represents. For example, if "length of hospitalization" was thought by Braginsky to have been a particularly important variable to control, he may not have wanted to rely on randomization alone, which, by chance, may have assigned the three or four longest-term patients to the same treatment group. Instead he could have matched triads of subjects according to their having been hospitalized for approximately equal lengths of time. The members within each triad could then have been randomly assigned, one to each of the three treatment groups. Goldstein, Heller, and Sechrest refer to this control procedure as *within sample matching* (1966, p. 27). It is held to be an acceptable way to render treatment groups comparable on the matching variable through manipulation, while at the same time controlling for other sources of confounding through randomization.

It must be stressed that even the most skillfully executed matching is never an appropriate substitute for randomization. However, when randomization is impossible, matching may be the next best control procedure. This is very often the case in psychological, sociological, and educational research using already-intact and self-selected groups of people. For example, a researcher may wish to determine the impact of nursery school experience on first grade reading-readiness. Not being able to randomly assign subjects to nursery and no-nursery school treatments, the researcher may have to select subjects from samples of children who have and who have not attended nursery school. The subjects who are actually included for study may be equated on one or a number of relevant variables, such as age, sex, and IQ through *between sample matching* (Goldstein, Heller, and Sechrest, 1966, p. 28). This involves using a subject from one sample who can be matched with a subject from the other sample on the variable of concern, an easy procedure when one variable is used for matching, but cumbersome if not impossible when the number of matching variables exceeds more than two or three. In any case, no matter how precisely the matching is done, this control procedure does nothing to assure that the groups are equated on a myriad of other variables. The typical home atmosphere of children who attend nursery school may be more verbally oriented then that of non-attenders. This in itself could conceivably cause the nursery school group to score higher on reading-readiness once they reach the first grade. Home atmosphere would remain an uncontrolled and, therefore, viable alternative to nursery school experience as an explanation for group differences on reading readiness in the first grade. In fact, because of the weak controls over confounding variables in research using naturally intact groups, Campbell and Stanley (1963) refer to such designs as "pre-experimental" rather than truly experimental in nature.

Systematic manipulation of situational variables is also a common control practice. If subjects must be run individually, the actual procedure may change slightly from the time the experimenter sees his first subject to when he sees his 100th subject. If the data from one group are all gathered before the data from the second group, the order effect might well be an important source of confounding. Consequently, order as a variable is systematically manipulated and controlled through the use of schedules in which subjects are run in rotation; one subject from each group is run before the second subject from a group is seen.

Holding Constant. A third control procedure is that of holding a variable constant. Obviously, variables like order or time of day can be controlled if all subjects are run at the same time. In such cases there is no order, and the time is the same for all subjects, so these variables cannot possibly have confounding effects on the experiment. In similar fashion, Braginsky controlled for sex by using only males, thereby holding constant and eliminating sex as a potentially competing explanation for between-group differences. In general, the experimenter strives to hold constant across groups all variables except those intentionally manipulated or randomized. This would include the experimental instructions, procedures, and conditions under which the dependent measures are obtained.

Direct and Remote Control. Shontz (1965) conceptualized the three control procedures of randomizing, systematically manipulating, and holding constant variables in terms of their being either *directly* or *remotely* related to the variables of concern. A *direct control* deals with variables in a way which involves no assumptions. Thus, when Braginsky chose only to use male patients in his experiment he was exercising direct control over a potential source of confounding, the subjects' sex. A second personal characteristic which Braginsky sought to hold constant was that of "motive to remain in an open ward." However, this motive cannot be directly observed; its presence can only be inferred from other observations, such as the length of time a patient has been on an open ward. By selecting only long-term open ward patients, Braginsky sought to attain remote control over a motivational variable of interest. As a generalization, it can be said that direct control is impossible whenever an experimenter seeks to hold constant, randomize, or manipulate the impact of a central personality characteristic. At best, subjects are selected because they manifest peripheral features thought to be signs of the central characteristic.

Sometimes central characteristics are remotely influenced via direct enrironmental manipulation. As an example of this, consider an experiment in which subjects have to perform a task while in a high state of anxiety. Anxiety per se, as a central characteristic, cannot be directly controlled. One can, however, remotely manipulate the anxiety level in subjects by telling them that for the purposes of the experiment for which they have volunteered it will occasionally be necessary to give them a shock which might be momentarily painful.

Indirect Control. A third important way in which variables may be controlled in addition to direct and remote means is through *indirect procedures* (Shontz, 1965). While there are several indirect control procedures, the one which is most commonly used with the experimental method is that of including at least one control or comparison group within the overall research design. In fact, the inclusion of some sort of comparison group to which subjects are randomly assigned is often taken as a defining characteristic of the experimental method. The treatment to which control subjects are exposed most often is identical to that which the experimental subjects experience, except that active or essential treatment ingredients are withheld. In this way, the data from such a no-treatment control group provides a standard against which to judge the impact of the essential treatment ingredients. In order to illustrate various no-treatment control group designs we can consider research geared to investigate whether foreign language competency (French) can be facilitated by having an audio tape of vocabulary lessons play while the learner sleeps. We will call this treatment "nocturnal training."

The simplest research procedure would involve exposing one or a few sleeping subjects to an audio tape which is played repeatedly for several consecutive nights. This would be followed by a post-treatment evaluation of language skill, perhaps in the form of a written translation test. Campbell and Stanley (1963) called this design a *one shot case study*:

$$Subjects \longrightarrow Treatment \longrightarrow Post\ test$$

The subjects' test performances can only be compared to some implicit standard. That is, the researcher may believe that the subjects did unusually well and try to attribute the high quality of performance to nocturnal training. However, one cannot be certain that the subjects performed better than they would have had they not been exposed to the treatment. To put this another way, there are many variables, independent of the nocturnal training they received, which might be responsible for the seemingly good performance of the subjects. These might include a desire to work hard on the translation test, prior expertise in French translation, etc. Thus, these constitute uncontrolled competing factors which may account for the apparent findings. Because the one shot case study does nothing to eliminate competing explanations it is deemed to be a *pre-experimental design* by Campbell and Stanley. The design may be modified so that it is *truly experimental* if a no-treatment control group is added. This consists of subjects who do not receive the treatment but who are in all other ways equivalent to the treatment group. This equivalence is established on the basis of assigning subjects on a strictly random basis to either the experimental treatment or to the no-treatment control group. The design then becomes a *post-test only, control group design* (Campbell and Stanley, 1963) and can be diagrammed as follows:

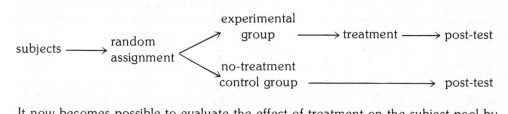

It now becomes possible to evaluate the effect of treatment on the subject pool by employing the data from the no-treatment control group as the standard. If the performance at post-test of the experimental group exceeds that of the no-treatment control group, this experimental effect can be attributed with confidence to the fact that one group of subjects received the treatment whereas the other did not. Most other potentially confounding variables such as prior language skill, age, intelligence, etc. can be eliminated as competing explanations because the two groups have been rendered equivalent in these respects on the basis of having been formed via random assignment.

A second pre-experimental way of evaluating the impact of nocturnal training on French translation proficiency would be to employ what Campbell and Stanley call the *one group pre-test post-test design:*

subjects ⟶ pre-test ⟶ treatment ⟶ post-test

This design is more sophisticated than the "one shot case study" in that the subjects serve as their own basis for comparison. It is, therefore, possible to judge whether apparently improved performance subsequent to treatment is, in fact, any better than the performance the subjects were capable of prior to treatment. However, as in other pre-experimental designs, too much remains uncontrolled. The one group pre-test post-test design in no way permits the researcher to assert, without qualification, that improvement from pre-test to post-test is due to the treatment. It is equally plausible, for example, that the French translation is superior on the post-test because of the practice afforded by the pre-test, or because subjects are more relaxed and efficient at post-test time. Again, in order to eliminate these and other competing explanations, a no-treatment control group to which subjects can be randomly assigned is required. The one group pre-test post-test design then evolves into the truly experimental *pre-test post-test control group design* (Campbell and Stanley, 1963):

experimental

subjects ⟶ random assignment ⟶ group ⟶ pre-test ⟶ treatment ⟶ post-test

no-treatment control group ⟶ pre-test ⟶ post-test

Because of practice effects, greater relaxation at post-test, daytime learning between pre- and post-test, even the no-treatment control group may show pre-test to post-test French translation improvement. It is, therefore, a comparative-standard group on which these variables are free to exert their effect on the dependent measure. If the improvement by the experimental treatment group exceeds the gains made by the no-treatment control group, one can be reasonably certain that the nocturnal training is having a real effect over and above the other operative variables. Practice effects, outside learning, etc. are eliminated as competing explanations for the experimental effect; they are indirectly controlled.

In passing, we might mention that random assignment of subjects to experimental treatment and control groups is the most preferred procedure for establishing equivalence between the groups on all potentially confounding variables. However, some researchers feel most comfortable when there is empirical confirmation of such equivalence on the dependent measure prior to treatment; in the case of our example, this would be French translation proficiency. The pre-test post-test control group design allows the researcher to document such equivalence by comparing the pretest translation scores of experimental and control subjects. If randomization has been successful the two groups should be about equal in translation competency at this point in the procedure.

The two true experimental designs described above may in themselves be insufficient to indirectly control for all potential sources of confounding. For example, we might choose to employ the pre-test post-test control group design in our exploration of nocturnal training, and with it discover greater improvement among experimental treatment subjects than among no-treatment control subjects. It is entirely possible that the experimental subjects do better not because they have actually profited from nocturnal training, but because they have high expectations that the treatment will be effective. Thus, differences in expectation between the treatment and no-treatment control groups may be a source of confounding and be responsible for the observed difference between groups on the dependent measure. In order to indirectly control this confounding, a comparison group is needed who shares the high expectations of the experimental subjects but who does not receive active treatment. These subjects receive inactive treatment and are referred to as an *attention control group*. In this case the inactive treatment may consist of telling subjects that they are to receive nocturnal training, fitting them with headphones while they sleep, but providing no auditory stimulation relevant to French translation competency. When an attention control treatment is intended to induce the same expectancy for treatment success, as in the active treatment condition, the attention control group may be referred to as an *expectancy control group*.

If such an attention control group also does better than the no-treatment control group and as well as the experimental treatment subjects, the experimental effect cannot be attributed to nocturnal training. Instead, it is probably due to the high expectancies for improvement shared by the experimental and attention control groups but not by the no-treatment control subjects. If the attention control group does better than the no-treatment control subjects but not as well as the experimental treatment group, we can conclude that expectations may exert a powerful effect on performance but that the active treatment has an impact beyond what high expectations can yield.

Internal Validity. The difference between pre-experimental and truly experimental designs can be summarized in terms of their relative degrees of *internal validity*. Research is internally valid when its findings are clearly interpretable, or, in other words, when the impact of the independent variable upon the dependent variable is separable from other sources of influence on the dependent variable. We saw that such separation was virtually impossible in the one shot case study. Similarly, in the one group pre-test post-test design, improvement or change due to treatment overlaps with the change attributable to such variables as outside learning, maturation independent of the experimental treatment, or the reactive effects of repeating testing.

In contrast, a well-controlled truly experimental design, in which subjects are randomly assigned to the several groups, is able to separate the effect of the independent variable upon the dependent variable from other sources of influence. In order to accomplish this, it is frequently necessary to construct control group procedures such as attention control groups which are more involved than no-treatment groups.

Experimenter Bias

In recent years, a special source of confounding which can seriously threaten the internal validity of an experiment has received widespread attention. The confounding is introduced by the experimenter who allows his own expectancies, hypotheses, or desires to have a differential impact upon the various groups within the research design. Confoundings attributable to these sources have been referred to by Rosenthal as *experimenter bias effects* (1966).

Rosenthal and Fode (1963) conducted an experiment which was designed to test whether the biases of experimenters can significantly affect the results of a given study. Their subjects were twelve undergraduate psychology students enrolled in an experimental laboratory course. The students were advised that they would be replicating previous animal learning research using "bright" and "dull" rats. Half the students were randomly assigned rats alleged to be bright, and were led to expect rapid learning. The remaining students were told they had been given dull rats which should show "very little evidence of learning." In fact, all the rats came from the same colony of animals and were very likely quite homogeneous with respect to brightness.

Each subject was instructed to run five rats through a simple maze ten times a day for five consecutive days. The rats were supposed to find their way to the darker of two platforms. Whether or not the animals succeeded was recorded by the experimenters who each kept a log of the 250 trials for which he was responsible.

Rosenthal and Fode report that the so-called "bright" animals averaged 2.3 correct maze solutions per day, whereas the "dull" animals had a mean of only 1.5 correct solutions. This experimental effect is of a significant magnitude and, Rosenthal asserts, is evidence that experimenter bias can be a powerful confounding variable.

Barber and Silver enumerate what they believe to be the eleven major factors mediating experimenter bias effects (1968, p. 58): "paralinguistic cues" such as voice tone; kinesic cues, including body movements and facial expressions such as frowning or smiling; "verbal reinforcements" such as praise in response to preferred subject behaviors; "misjudgment" of subject behaviors in the context of vaguely defined criteria; and the "misreading of data." Barber and Silver point out that these five factors may be either intentional or unintentional (the result therefore being ten mediating factors). The eleventh factor is blatant "fudging" of data.

The importance of Rosenthal's contribution does not lie in his assertion that premeditated biasing on the part of a researcher may seriously threaten the internal validity of an experiment. Rather, Rosenthal gained notoriety by calling the attention of the scientific community to the confounding effects which *unintentional* bias might have, even in the most well-meaning of experimenters. So suspicious did psychologists become of the operation of these effects that it was the rare doctoral student who did not have to defend his dissertation by explaining how he controlled for experimenter-bias effects.

Barber and Silver (1968) reviewed 31 studies which had been designed to test the efficacy of experimenter bias. Of these, only 12 revealed an experimenter-bias effect. The authors concluded that "the experimenter-bias effect appears to be more difficult to demonstrate and less pervasive than was implied" (1969, p. 58) by Rosenthal. In addition, Barber and Silver point out that 10 of these 12 studies did not exclude the possibility that the experimenter-bias effect was due to misjudging or misrecording of responses, easily avoidable and/or correctable problems, or to misjudging of data. Only two experiments clearly supported Rosenthal's claim that subtle paralinguistic or kinesic cues from the experimenter are sufficient to mediate a bias effect. Even in these two studies the designs were such that the subtle biasing cues could have been introduced intentionally. Thus, it appears that the initial concern over the issue of experimenter bias may have been overstated. Nevertheless it remains incumbent upon researchers to do what is reasonable to avoid this potential source of confounding. In most cases the problem can be circumvented if an experimenter is employed who is unfamiliar with, or "blind" to much of the experimental procedures, purposes, and predictions. For example, the interviewer in the previously-discussed experiment by Braginsky and Braginsky did not know what treatment the patients he was interviewing were receiving. Specifically, he was "blind" to what each patient had been told about the alleged purpose of the interview.

This procedure is called the *single-blind technique*. Quite often, in drug research, the *double-blind technique* is used. In this approach neither the researcher nor the patient knows whether the treatment being offered is the active or inactive one; the sugar pill and the real pill appear to be identical. In this way, expectancies for successful treatment by the person who dispenses the pills and by those who consume them are eliminated as potential sources of confounding. The research project is administered by a non-involved person who alone knows which patients are in which treatment groups.

SUMMARY

This chapter outlined some of the important features of the research method known as experimentation. We pointed out that the central purpose of an experiment is to determine what effect, if any, one variable (the independent variable) has upon another (the dependent variable). In order to arrive at unambiguous conclusions regarding the influence of the independent variable upon the dependent variable it is necessary for the researcher to design his experiment so that the impact of confounding variables upon the dependent variable is eliminated. In this way, if an experimental effect is found , it may be confidently concluded that it is caused by the intentionally different treatments to which the various comparison groups have been exposed. Such an experiment is said to have internal validity. Much of this chapter described control procedures available to the experimenter — specifically, randomization, systematic manipulation, and holding constant. We pointed out that these procedures can be seen as being either direct or remote in their control of potentially confounding variables. The use of comparison or control groups was described in terms of their being an indirect means of control. We illustrated how the addition of an appropriate control group can transform pre-experimental research designs into truly experimental designs. Finally, we looked at one confounding variable which has been considered an important threat to the internal validity of many experiments, experimenter bias. Single- and double-blind techniques were suggested as appropriate ways to minimize experimenter-bias effects.

In Chapter 4 we will continue our examination of experimentation. Our focus will shift to issues which have to do with the generalizability of experimental findings.

TERMS TO KNOW

CHAPTER 4
External Validity and Reliability

Obviously, if an experiment is poorly controlled, if variation on the dependent variable cannot be unequivocally attributable to manipulation of the independent variable, it is of little value. However, even research having all the design elements necessary for internal validity may yield essentially worthless findings. This happens when the experimental procedures are such that results cannot be generalized to the "real world."

EXTERNAL VALIDITY

One of the costs of designing a well-controlled study is that the experimental situation may depart dramatically from what we usually encounter in real life. For example, a researcher who wishes to study the effect of anxiety on learning may induce anxiety by exposing subjects to the threat of electric shock. The nature of this threat, however, is so unusual when we consider the routine sources of anxiety in our daily lives that one might question whether the learning which occurs in such a setting has implications for learning outside of the experimental situation. If it does not, the experiment lacks *external validity*.

Experiments are not either externally valid or externally invalid, instead they may manifest this quality to varying degrees. As a general rule, external validity is limited by any design aspects which render an experimental situation different from the setting to which the results are intended to apply. More specifically, limitations of generalizability can stem directly from the design of an experiment or, from subjects' reactions to the design.

Design limitations

A most frequent complaint heard over the years from critics of learning theory was that the research was too often conducted on animals. There was concern that an elaborate psychology of the white laboratory rat was being developed which had little relation to the psychology of people. More recently, similar objections have been raised over personality research which restricts itself to the captive Introductory Psychology student on college campuses. Of course, if one is interested in this population for its own sake, using it in research could not be more proper. Typically, however, the findings which emerge are couched in terms which suggest that they are applicable to other specific groups, or to people in general.

Baron and Bell conducted an experiment on the relationship between environmental temperature and physical aggression. They began their research report by noting that "tragic, instances of collective violence" may partly stem from the "long, hot summer" (1976, p. 245). The United States Riot Commission suggested "that high ambient temperatures may play an important role in the initiation of dangerous cases of civil disorder" (1968, p. 245). Baron and Bell go on to describe their procedure for testing their hypothesis and their conclusions. Their subjects were "35 undergraduate students (18 males and 17 females) enrolled in sections of Elementary Psychology at Purdue University who participated in the experiment in order to satisfy part of a course requirement" (p. 247). Briefly, the experiment involved a number of phases, all of which took place either in room temperatures in the 70s or in the 90s. There was an "affect induction phase" in which half the subjects received positive personal evaluation and half a negative evaluation ("insincere, immature, and below average in intelligence") from a confederate of the experimenter posing as another subject. This was followed by an aggression phase, in which subjects were told that the researcher was "concerned with the effects of temperature and humidity upon physiological reactions to electric shock" (pp. 247-248). The real subject was selected to administer 20 shocks to the confederate, and was free to vary both their intensity and their duration. The last experimental phase involved the administration of a post-questionnaire to subjects. This inquired into the subjects' perceptions of room warmth and their level of anger toward the confederate. These particular questions served as a check as to whether or not the subjects were experiencing the independent manipulations of temperature and communication in the way which was intended. There were three additional questions pertaining to the subjects' affect state along the dimensions of uncomfortable-comfortable, bored-enthusiastic, and irritated-relaxed.

The findings of this research indicate that high room temperatures increased aggression (shock) toward another person, but only when the aggressor had received a *favorable* and not an unfavorable personal evaluation. In the latter case, room temperatures in the 90s were associated with *less* aggressive behavior than temperatures in the low 70s. This confirmed earlier research which showed that high ambient temperatures serve to facilitate aggression, but only when other sources of negative affect (such as unfavorable personal evaluation) are absent. Baron and Bell suggest that high room temperatures *and* receipt of an unfavorable evaluation render subjects so unhappy that they are more interested in just escaping from an adverse situation than they are in aggressing. This explanation is consistent with the fact that subjects who were in the "high temperature-negative report" condition expressed having the most unpleasant affect on the post-questionnaire of all subjects.

Specific Populations. Do these experimental effects have anything to do with "tragic instances of collective violence" and "the long hot summer?" It might be argued that the experimental effects have little external validity with respect to the ghetto riots which began to plague our country in the early 1960s. A group of people (Purdue Introductory Psychology students) more different in background and outlook than the inner city rioters alluded to at the start of Baron and Bell's report can hardly be imagined. It might be somewhat more reasonable to use the reactions of Baron and Bell's college subjects as a vehicle for understanding the campus disorder which emerged somewhat later in the decade. Thus, the external validity of this experiment, like all others, must be evaluated with respect to *specific populations*. The findings of an experiment cannot be said to be "generalizable" without considering the group(s) to whom one wishes to generalize.

It has been suggested by Neale and Liebert that "the best solution to the problem of population generalization is to define and randomly sample directly from the population of ultimate interest" (1973, p. 181). This means that if one wishes to explore the adjustment problems of Vietnam draft evaders, one must procure subjects directly from that group in order for the research to have external validity. Alternatively, if one wishes to study adjustment problems of young male adults in general, Vietnam draft evaders would be a poor choice of subjects. Because of their uniqueness any generalization of findings from them to the general population of young men would be hazardous at best.

Specific Operations. A second group of design features which may limit external validity are those related to the *specific operations* employed by the experimenter to define his variables. For example, in the Baron and Bell experiment, aggression was assessed in terms of the intensity and duration of shocks which subjects administered to other students. While there is ample research testifying to the appropriateness of using shock as a behavioral measure of aggression in research, the legitimacy of generalizing from this experimental arrangement to violence in the streets is questionable. There are a number of substantial differences between the two circumstances. Within the laboratory there is an implicit message delivered to the subject that what he does is in the name of science, that the research is being conducted under the auspices of a prestigious university, and that a responsible researcher directly oversees the procedures. All this creates an atmosphere in which the administration of electric shock is acceptable. None of these factors operated in the steamy summer streets of Newark, Watts, or Chicago. In addition, the laboratory instructions make no explicit mention of aggression per se in the context of describing the use of shock. In civil disorder, on the other hand, the goal of destroying people and their property is clearly uppermost in the minds of the aggressors. Lastly, the Baron and Bell experiment ran subjects individually. Civil disorder is, by definition, a collective act in which the behavior of one individual has an impact on the behavior of others. Related to this point, Milgrim (1965) has clearly demonstrated within a laboratory setting that aggressive behavior (the administration of shock) is mediated by the presence or absence of cooperation and affirmation afforded by the aggressive behavior of others.

In summary, in order for research to have some measure of external validity, the experimental situation must be similar in substantive ways to the settings to which the researcher wishes to generalize his findings.

Reactivity

In addition to design features themselves limiting external validity, an experimental effect may have little in the way of external validity because it emerges from subjects who are aware of and sensitive to the fact that they are experimental participants. This in itself is sufficient to modify subject behavior so that it may be unrepresentative of what would occur outside of the laboratory. *Reactivity* is the general term which describes these changes in a person's behavior as a function of knowing that one is being observed and investigated.

In the 1930s a number of studies were conducted at the Hawthorne Western Electric Company to find ways of increasing worker productivity. A number of manipulations were attempted, including modifying working hours. To the investigator's surprise, all of the variations were followed by increased production. It has since been concluded that this favorable outcome was simply due to the workers awareness of special concern and attention, and was not the product of the specific manipulations of work conditions. This phenomenon has come to be known as the *Hawthorne effect.*

A similar effect is observed in psychiatric hospitals where the implementation of almost any treatment program seems to result in at least temporary patient improvement. This might be due to fresh enthusiasm on the part of the staff offering the treatment and/or to the renewal of hope in patients receiving it. It too, however, is independent of any specific treatment operations and is referred to as the *placebo effect,* a term which is essentially synonymous with Hawthorne effect. In psychotherapy or drug research the placebo effect may be indirectly controlled through the use of an *attention (placebo) control group* which has all of the expectations associated with receiving a new therapeutic treatment but receives, in fact, an inert or inactive program.

When Hawthorne or placebo effects are not controlled, the results of research cannot be generalized unhesitatingly to situations in which the treatment is to be eventually applied. Specifically, a treatment, whether it be the modification of work conditions or the imposition of a drug or psychotherapy, will probably be followed by a different outcome when routinely administered in the applied settings than when first tested on groups who were reactive to their participation in a special program.

Pre-testing. One common experimental design feature which tends to heighten reactivity is the use of *pre-testing* on some measure. Pre-testing was mentioned as a part of the truly experimental pre-test post-test control group design, a design which allows the researcher to record actual changes in his dependent variable. The pre-test however, may inform subjects of what the experimenter is interested in, the actual treatment then having a different effect than if the subjects had not been so sensitized.

One simple vehicle for circumventing this limitation is to avoid the use of pre-testing. Bell and Baron chose this tactic when they asked subjects about their affect states only at post-test. Had they questioned their subjects prior to the experimental manipulation many would have become sensitive to the experimenters' interest in comparing pre-test and post-test measures of affect. Some subjects might have decided to recall their earlier responses at post-test in an effort to show they were unaffected by their experimental experiences; others may have been motivated to be good subjects and manifest all sorts of changes. There are certainly many other subject response patterns which could possibly be manifested. However, any responses which are mediated by an awareness of the experimenter's focus, made possible through *pre-test sensitization,* will be something other than straightforward consequences of the experimental manipulation. As such, these responses may not be indicative of what would happen in the real, non-experimental world.

Sometimes an experimenter is very reluctant to give up pre-test measurement, perhaps because it is crucial to establish equivalence between groups on some variable. In such cases, a complex experimental design may be employed, this being a combination of the pre-test post-test control group design and the post-test-only control group design. The resulting design is known as the *Solomon four group design*:

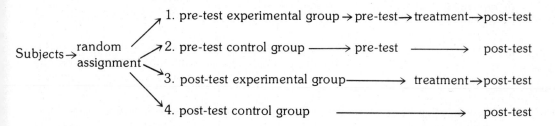

The strength of this design lies in its ability to compare the effect of pre-testing independent of the effects of treatment. Specifically, post-test differences between control groups 2 and 4 permit the investigator to establish the impact which a pre-test alone has upon post-test. In addition, the design allows for multiple comparisons which all bear on evaluating the impact of the experimental treatment. For example, if the pre-test and post-test measures assess adjustment and the treatment is some form of psychotherapy, the treatment may be deemed effective if: group 1 shows greater adjustment at post-test than pre-test; group 1 shows greater adjustment at post-test than group 2 at post-test; group 3 shows greater adjustment at post-test than group 4 at post-test; group 3 shows greater adjustment at post-test than both groups 1 and 2 at pre-test. If all of these findings emerge, a considerable degree of confidence may be accorded the reliability of the findings.

Demand Characteristics

Another major factor which limits the generalizability of experimental findings is that of *demand characteristics.* Orne and Schiebe have discribed these as "cues, both implicit and explicit, that communicate to the subject what is expected of him in the experimental situation" (1964, p. 3). As such, demand characteristics may be seen as experimental stimuli to which subjects are reactive and which pull subjects' behavior in a particular direction.

In order to illustrate the operation of demand characteristics in experimental settings, Orne and Schiebe (1964) investigated a phenomenon which had been receiving considerable attention —*sensory deprivation effects*. In the 1950s a number of studies demonstrated that subjects who are deprived of sensory input subsequently claim to have experienced bizarre visual imagery, manifest impairment on a variety of cognitive tasks, lose their spatial and temporal orientation, and have difficulty concentrating. The imposition of sensory deprivation treatments involved such procedures as having subjects detained for periods of time in isolation rooms wearing translucent goggles, cardboard arm and hand sleeves, and other restrictors of sensory input. Hebb wrote that "without physical pain, without drugs, the personality can be badly deformed simply by modifying the perceptual environment" (1958, p. 110).

Orne and Schiebe felt that at least some of these unusual sensory deprivation phenomena may be attributable not to sensory deprivation per se but to the demand characteristics operative within sensory deprivation experiments. For example, if sensory-deprived subjects are exposed to verbal or non-verbal cues which lead them to anticipate that they will have peculiar experiences, that anticipation itself may promote the experiences, or at least retrospective reports of having had them. Having subjects sign ominous-looking release forms, screening them for psychiatric and physical well-being prior to participating along with the presence of observation windows looking into the isolation room, and "panic buttons" available for pressing should the subject wish to terminate his isolation — all provide cues which, one way or another, communicate the message that something bad or unusual can be expected.

The question which Orne and Schiebe sought to explore experimentally was whether these kinds of demand characteristics alone are sufficient to promote sensory deprivation phenomena, i.e. reports of perceptual distortion. Twenty paid, male volunteers were randomly assigned to either the experimental or control group. The 10 experimental subjects were individually met by an experimenter dressed in a white medical coat. A medical history was taken in a room containing a tray of drugs and medicine labelled Emergency Tray. The subjects were advised that they would be spending an unspecified amount of time in deprivation chambers, under constant observation. They were encouraged to report, via a microphone, any "unusual feelings, difficulties in concentration, hallucinations, feelings of disorientation, or the like" (p. 5). The experimental subjects were advised that they could press an Emergency Alarm button in the isolation chamber if they became very "discomforted" and felt the need for immediate termination of the procedure. It was also stated that a physician was on hand should the need arise. A release form was then signed by subjects which relieved the institutional organization and personnel from legal responsibility for experimental consequences. It is noted by Orne and Schiebe that these instructions were a composite of those used in actual sensory deprivation research.

Prior to entering the isolation chamber, the subjects' blood pressure and pulse were taken and they were given 10 tests of perceptual, cognitive, and motor ability which previous research had reported to be sensitive to sensory deprivation effects.

The chamber itself consisted of a 6x7x8 room containing a desk, two chairs, good lighting, an observation window, the "Emergency Alarm," ice water, a sandwich, and about 2000 sheets of paper containing columns of numbers which the subjects could add if they so chose. There were no restrictions on movement within the room. In brief, this chamber was in no way a real sensory deprivation room.

After spending four hours in the chamber, experimental subjects were released, and again all of the tests taken prior to their sensory deprivation experience were administered.

Control subjects were exposed to the same chamber environment and the pre- and post-chamber tests were also administered. However, they worked with a less serious experimenter dressed in a business suit, and the medical aura was absent. These subjects were told they were part of a control group in a sensory deprivation experiment and that they would provide comparison data based upon "simply being left alone in a room for a period of time (p. 6)." They too were asked to freely report their experiences while in the room and were advised that they could prematurely end their control group participation by knocking on the window; there was no Emergency Alarm.

The 10 perceptual, cognitive, and motor tests yielded 14 separate scores. On all but one of these the experimental group performed more poorly than the control group, with substantial differences for 6 of the 14 scores.

Thus, Orne and Schiebe's experimental (but not sensory deprived) subjects did relatively poorly on a number of tasks previously shown to be sensitive to the alleged deterioration brought about by real sensory deprivation. An examination was also made of all subjects' reports of symptoms previously reported by real sensory deprivation subjects. These include perceptual aberrations, intellectual dullness, affective unpleasantness, anxiety, spatial disorientation, restlessness, and irritability. Orne and Schiebe report that all 10 experimental subjects, but only 5 of the 10 control subjects, reported having such symptoms. The total number of these sensory deprivation symptoms reported by the experimental group (46) was considerably greater than the number (18) reported by the control subjects. These results indicate that the subjective reports of the experimental subjects in the research became replete with symptomatic complaints, not unlike those previously reported by real sensory deprived subjects.

In summary, Orne and Schiebe were able to demonstrate that sensory deprivation phenomena could be observed in non-sensory deprived subjects under certain conditions. These conditions involved exposure to all of the cues (demand characteristics) which have surrounded the real sensory deprivation experiences to which subjects in other research had been exposed. Demand characteristics alone, then, could have been capable of inducing sensory deprivation effects in these other studies, causing subjects to become good sources of experimental group data for reasons other than the experimenter's manipulation of the independent variable (sensory deprivation) itself. Obviously, if this is the case, the research on sensory deprivation may have little external validity or generalizability to real world situations in which people might have to be subject to periods of sensory deprivation, but which lack the demand characteristics (panic buttons) found only in the laboratory research.

Increasing Generalizability

There is a frequently employed research strategy which is specifically intended to increase the external validity of experimental findings. The strategy tries to remove subjects from the reactive aspects of laboratory guinea pig experience. The goal is to observe and/or measure behavior under conditions which more closely approximate the real world.

Unobtrusive Measurement. Research data may be acquired in a way which does not interact with the phenomenon being observed. The measurement process, then, becomes totally non-reactive. Webb, Campbell, Schwartz, and Sechrest (1970) suggest that such non-reactive measurement may involve the use of physical traces, archives, and unobtrusive observation.

Physical traces. There may be two sorts of physical traces. First, there are *erosion measures.* This involves the assessment of differential "wear" as an index of behavior. Webb and his colleagues (1970, p. 36) suggest that a meaningful way to evaluate the popularity of museum exhibits is to keep track of the rate of floor tile replacement. For example, they report that the vinyl tiles around a chick-hatching display in the Chicago Museum of Science and Industry had to be replaced about every six weeks; those surrounding other exhibits went for years before replacement was necessary. This evidence was gathered from routine records on file in the museum's maintenance department. The behavior of viewers was thus evaluated by a method which was completely non-reactive because visitors did not know that their preferences were being monitored. Consequently, they could not engage in reactive behavior in order to impress an interviewer, such as saying they preferred sophisticated exhibits, when in fact it was the hatching chicks which really captured their interest. Similarly, expressions of interest in books or sections of books may be assessed by noting the degree of wear they exhibit. For example, library copies of older editions of D.H. Lawrence novels exhibit selected areas of particular wear around the more provocative sections. This may be taken as an index of adolescent interest, which might not have been admitted if preferential questions had been put directly to the readers of Lawrence's works.

A second kind of physical trace involves the "remnants of past behavior" (1970, p. 38) in the form of accumulations or deposits of materials. Webb and his co-authors refer to these traces as *accretion measures.* They point out that in addition to floor tile erosion an accretion measure may be employed as a non-reactive index of museum exhibit popularity. Specifically, the number of noseprints deposited on a glass display case each day serves this function. This particular measure has the added value of permitting an estimate of exhibit popularity as a function of the viewer's age, with age being grossly assessed in terms of the height of noseprints from the floor.

It is clear that physical-trace measurement circumvents the problem of reactivity by not requiring cooperation between subject and researcher. Nevertheless, erosion and accretion measures are often encumbered by problems of interpretation. While noseprints may be a valid index of enthusiasm toward an exhibit among the very young, older children may be less likely to engage in the infantile gesture of pressing their noses against glass regardless of their level of enthusiasm. Similarly, while the erosion measure of floor tile replacement may indeed be an index of interest in an exhibit, it may also be the product of routine stops by a tour guide and his entourage in front of the exhibit. In that case floor tile wear may be the result of the shuffling feet of bored, impatient listeners. Webb suggests that because the meaning of physical traces may be open to competing interpretations they might be best employed as supplemental indices, useful to confirm findings obtained from more direct measurement procedures.

Archival Data. The second major category of non-reactive measurement involves the use of *archival data* such as newspapers, voting records, and diaries. Historians and archeologists have long been forced to focus on archives as a main source of information. Psychologists, researching more contemporary issues, have only recently taken full advantage of the written record.

Barthell and Holmes (1968), in an exemplary use of archival data, sought to gain evidence pertinent to the frequently-heard notion that early social isolation is related to the later development of schizophrenia. Instead of resorting to the direct interrogation of the families and friends of schizophrenics, therefore having to depend upon notoriously unreliable retrospective verbal reports, Barthell and Holmes studied the high school yearbooks of hospitalized schizophrenic and neurotic patients. The recorded participation in social, service, and performance or athletic activities was noted. To provide a basis for comparison, control group data were gathered on the student whose picture followed that of each subject. If the next picture depicted someone of a race or sex different from the subject or had the same name (indicating possible family relationship), the following picture was selected. It was found that the average number of total activities in which the schizophrenics and neurotics participated differed markedly from that of the control sample. There was, however, little difference in participation level between the schizophrenics and neurotics while in high school. Specifically, the schizophrenics and neurotics participated in an average of only 3.75 and 4.00 activities, respectively, while the control sample had a mean of 6.95 activities.

Barthell and Holmes suggest that the surprising tendency of their sample of neurotics to have been almost as isolate in high school as were the schizophrenics may reflect the severity of their neuroses. Most psychoneurotics do not require institutional confinement; the hospitalized neurotics used in the study may have been, in general, more severely disturbed than neurotics in general and, therefore, unrepresentative.

When specific categories of activity were looked at, the trend in all cases was for the normal sample to have been more participatory than the schizophrenics. However, this difference was large only in the sphere of social activities, with the mean number for the schizophrenics being only 1.60 activities while the normal population participated in 2.83 activities. Thus, this specific finding lends support to the idea that the person who eventually becomes schizophrenic first passes through an adolescent period which is characterized by social isolation and introversion.

While not being necessarily critical of this general formulation, Schwarz (1970) did point to a methodological weakness in Barthell and Holmes' work. Schwarz cites research demonstrating that hospitalized schizophrenics most frequently come from the lowest social classes, and that long before schizophrenic symptoms emerge there is evidence of pre-schizophrenic intellectual inferiority during childhood and adolescence. Given this information, it is quite probable that the randomly selected control subjects used by Barthell and Holmes were from a relatively higher socio-economic background and were better off intellectually. These two factors themselves could easily account for the discovered differences between groups on the variable of high school isolation. Schwarz appropriately suggests that clarification could be attained if it were shown that participation in high school activities is independent of socio-economic background or of intelligence. The alternative would be to employ a control sample matched with the schizophrenics on these important personality and social variables. Thus, if schizophrenics could be shown to have been more isolate than non-schizophrenic students of similar intellectual and social background, stronger evidence would exist for asserting that high school social isolation uniquely characterizes the life style of a pre-schizophrenic.

Webb et al, (1970) indicates that there are two potential sources of bias which may be operative in any research utilizing archival data (p. 54). The first source of bias is *selective deposit.* Not all of the relevant data may find their way into the public, or even private, record. For example, it is quite probable that high school students participate in many social activities which are never noted in yearbooks. In fact, only those activities organized and sanctioned by the school are likely to be mentioned. This, of course, raises the question as to whether the archival information used by Barthell and Holmes is a reflection of social interaction in general or only of participation in organized school activities.

A less pervasive problem with the use of archives is that of *selective survival.* There is little doubt that certain records are more prone to be lost than others, the remaining data then imparting a distorted picture of the situation they purportedly describe. Selective survival is probably most relevant when trying to evaluate previous business or political activities and the people involved in those activities. Is it possible that files or recordings are destroyed because they may reflect poorly on their keeper's actions and intentions? This, and other less premeditated disposal procedures, may cause the surviving documents to leave a highly biased image.

In summarizing the worth of archival data, Webb reminds us that "the gnawing reality remains that archives have been produced for someone else and by someone else" (p. 84). Indeed, it is quite possible that the data contained in the archives were obtained originally under highly reactive circumstances. Not knowing the specifics of those circumstances, the archival researcher cannot compensate for subject reactivity in trying to draw conclusions. Lastly, the important matters of selective deposit and survival of archival material can bias the available record. This, in itself, becomes most damaging when the researcher is unaware that these biasing factors are operating.

Direct Observation. The third major category of unobtrusive measurement is that of *direct observation.* In many cases it is possible for an observer to gain important information simply by keeping track of the natural unfolding of human events. Ideally, in these circumstances, the subjects aren't aware that they are under scrutiny so that reactivity is eliminated. In addition, the observer in no way structures or renders the situation artificial. This serves to further insure non-reactivity and enhances the generalizability of findings.

Because of the volatile nature of the issues and the extreme self-consciousness of respondents, it is often difficult to gain valid information on racial opinions and beliefs. The need people have to publicly express attitudes of either a liberal or a conservative nature on these matters may greatly distort their true feelings. Consequently, unobtrusive observation of interracial behavior has frequently been resorted to as the best investigatory approach. Campbell, Cruskal, and Wallace (1966) were interested in finding out about racial attitudes. As their non-reactive index they used classroom seating patterns. They reasoned that when students are permitted to self-select their seats, clustering by race can be taken as a sign of the degree to which skin color determines interpersonal preferences. If natural segregation is observed it may be concluded that friendship patterns are primarily the product of racial issues; more interracial seating arrangements suggest that friendship patterns are established on bases independent of race. In fact, Campbell and his colleagues found significant racial segregation, with the degree of clustering varying with the school.

One of the great difficulties with simple observation is that one may not be sure of the meaning of what is being observed. This is because the conditions and events responsible for the naturally occurring behavior are frequently unknown. Certainty regarding the antecedents of behavior is increased if the situation is one which is arranged. In such cases, unobtrusive observation becomes less opportunistic and more controlled. A number of investigations on interracial behavior have been conducted, their designs illustrating what Webb refers to as *contrived observation*.

Some of this research was an outgrowth of the infamous Kitty Genovese case in which a young woman was brutally murdered in the presence of a number of apathetic bystanders. Piliavin, Rodin, and Piliavin (1969) explored the phenomenon of bystander apathy as a function of the victim's race and circumstances. Arrangements were made for a victim to collapse on a New York City subway train, either from apparent illness or drunkeness. The services of a black and a white college student were enlisted for this public display. Results indicated that the tendency for same-race helping to occur was restricted to the condition in which the victim was ostensibly drunk. In a somewhat less dramatic contrivance, West, Whitney, and Schnedler (1975) explored the effects of the sex and race of the victim and the racial composition of the neighborhood on the frequency with which passing travelers helped a motorist in distress. Sixty-four separate incidents were staged in a variety of neighborhoods in Tallahassee, Florida. Essentially, each incident consisted of a driver coasting to a stop by the side of the road. The victim would then raise the automobile hood and stand at the vehicle's rear, facing oncoming traffic. Two unobtrusive observers recorded the time elapsed from hood raising to offers of assistance. The race and sex of passing motorists were recorded as well as the race and sex of those stopping to provide aid. There were two substantive findings. First, on the average, female victims elicited help more quickly (mean = 3 min. 16 sec.) than did male victims (mean = 7 min. 13 sec.). Second, black victims were helped more quickly in black neighborhoods and whites more quickly in white neighborhoods. With respect to helper characteristics, it was found that while only 59% of the passing drivers were male, 92% of the people who stopped were male; and while 34% of the potential helpers were black, 94% of the aid accorded white victims came from white helpers and 97% of the aid for black victims was received from black helpers.

West and his co-authors tested the generality of these results by replicating their research in the proximity of predominantly black or white college campuses in Tallahassee, as well as in new non-college areas of the city. Contrary to their expectations, there was no evidence suggesting greater willingness to offer cross-racial assistance in the college areas frequented by presumably liberal citizens. In looking at their latency measure in this second research, they found that black victims were assisted more quickly near a white college than when in distress near a black university. This speedy aid was primarily imparted by black rather than by white students. This result is consistent with Braddock's (1972) finding that at mainly white Southern universities, the minority black students experience a high degree of comraderie. West suggests from this that "when these black students refer to other blacks as brothers and sisters, it is apparently more than mere rhetoric" (p. 696).

In conclusion, these contrived observational studies suggest that both black and white drivers are highly selective about whom they are willing to aid, with this selectivity apparently being dictated by racial considerations. College blacks appear especially predisposed to rescue motorists in distress if the victims are of their race and the breakdown occurred near a predominently white college campus.

There are some important advantages of contrived over simple observational research. Because one is able to plan the time and location of events, it becomes possible to utilize complex hardware in the service of procuring more accurate data. Specifically, audio or video tape recordings of reactions to the planned events may be surreptitiously made, allowing investigators to bypass the potentially unreliable record keeping of human on-the-spot observers.

Even more important, contrived observational research permits the systematic exploration of a variety of variables in subjects, such as sex or race. In the West, Whitney, and Schnedler (1975) studies, location of the contrived incident was also varied. Piliavin, Rodin and Piliavin (1969) chose to systematically manipulate the nature of victim's distress (illness or drunkeness). Because of the control exerted over independent variables, these studies approximate experimental designs which might be used in the psychology laboratory. They are known as *field experiments,* however, because the dependent measurement is taken directly within the situation of interest. When the measurement is done unobtrusively, field experiments may be seen as a kind of bridge between reactive laboratory experimentation and simple non-reactive observation of responses to uncontrolled natural events.

RELIABILITY OF EXPERIMENTAL EFFECTS

The term "reliable" connotes consistency with respect to experimental results. A difference between an experimental and a control group on some dependent measure is said to be reliable, or "significant," if it can be reasonably attributed to systematic, and, therefore, repeatable antecedent events rather than to unsystematic factors or chance. In practical terms, a significant experimental effect is one which is expected to recur if the experimental procedures are replicated on a new sample of subjects.

Chance is almost always a viable competing explanation for between-group differences. Whenever two groups are formed on the basis of random assignment, as are experimental and control groups, there will inevitably be at least some slight difference between the groups on whatever variable one might choose to assess. For example, two randomly selected groups of people will exhibit some average difference in height, weight, IQ, or on any other measured personality dimension. In the course of randomly assigning people, it just may happen that most of the tallest, or heaviest, or brightest people end up in a common group, thereby producing an average between-group difference on these variables.

The question then is how can a researcher be certain that an obtained experimental effect is real or, in other words, that it is attributable to systematic antecedent events, such as the manipulation of an independent variable. The answer is that one can't be certain but can only be confident at some level of probability. If a relatively small experimental effect is obtained, a researcher may believe that the probability it is due merely to chance is 50-50. However, if the experimental effect is of a large magnitude, the researcher may claim to be almost positive (perhaps 99% sure) that it is due not to chance but to the different treatments to which the groups had been systematically exposed.

Magnitude of Experimental Effect

In general, it can be said that, if all else is equal, the larger a between-group mean difference is, the less likely it is a chance occurrence and the more likely it is due to a systematic antecedent. Imagine an experiment concerned with the effect of an early home enrichment program on the IQs of pre-school, culturally deprived youngsters. The subjects in this hypothetical research could be selected from those children participating in project Head Start. The youngsters would be assigned on a random basis. Half would participate in a home enrichment (experimental) treatment in which college volunteer aides would go into the homes and assist parents in providing culturally enlightening experiences for their children. The other half would receive control treatment consisting only of the in-school Head Start experience. At the start of kindergarten all the children would be given an IQ test. Suppose that the mean IQ in both groups is found to be 95. Obviously then, the home enrichment effort did not have an impact — at least one measureable in terms of IQ scores. Let us say, however, that the experimental group is found to have a mean IQ of 97 and the control subjects prove to have a mean IQ of 95. One might then be tempted to conclude that the addition of a home-based enrichment experience augments the effectiveness of the Head Start program. Intuitively though, the group mean difference of only two IQ points is so small that it might reasonably be due to a few of the initially brighter youngsters having been assigned, by chance, to the experimental treatment group. If the results of this experiment were such that the difference between the experimental and control groups mean IQ was 15 points, with the former group mean being 110 and the latter only 95, an explanation in terms of chance appears less plausible. It is unlikely that a mean difference as large as 15 IQ points would occur only on the basis of chance. It is, therefore, probably a reliable difference due to some systematic source. If we assume the experiment is one which is well-controlled, the systematic source for the experimental effect would be the independent variable, the differential treatment programs to which the groups had been exposed.

Score Variability

The scores within an experimental or control group are rarely uniform; there is usually some amount of within-group variability evident. This variability can be expressed in terms of a statistic, called the variance (S^2), whose magnitude depends upon the degree to which individual scores deviate or are different from the group mean. The within-group variance (S^2 within) is referred to as *error variance* because it is due to uncontrolled and, usually unknown chance sources.

In addition to computing S^2 from differences between individual scores and the group mean, S^2 may be calculated from group mean differences. In this case it is known as S^2 between and expresses the degree to which individual group means tend to deviate from the overall mean. S^2 *between* is said to reflect *systematic variance* because between-group mean differences are supposed to be primarily due to systematic rather than chance sources, such as the exposure of several groups to differential experimental treatments.

When there is considerable error variance one may anticipate a larger between-group difference on the basis of chance than when error variance is minimal. Consequently, a given experimental effect will be deemed as less likely to be a chance occurrence and, therefore, more reliable when S^2 within is small. To illustrate this point, imagine that the researcher conducting the hypothetical experiment obtains the following data:

Experimental Group	Control Group
95	111
98	112
95	107
94	110
96	113
92	107
Sum = 570	Sum = 660
IQ mean = 95	IQ mean = 110

Overall IQ mean = 102.5

Notice that the variability of scores within each group is quite small; no IQ score deviates more than 3 points from its respective group mean. Relative to this, S^2 between is large, with each group mean deviating 7.5 IQ points from the overall mean. One way to conveniently express this is in terms of the ratio of systematic to error variance: S^2 between/S^2 within. As the magnitude of this ratio increases, so does confidence in the reliability of an experimental effect.

Now consider some alternative raw data:

Experimental Group	Control Group
60	55
90	135
65	90
135	110
95	170
125	100
Sum = 570	Sum = 660
IQ mean = 95	IQ mean = 110

Overall IQ mean = 102.5

Notice that the same group means emerge but there is considerably more within group variability; there is much more error variance. In this case, chance factors account for a greater degree of score dispersion than in our first illustration. In the experimental group one subject's score deviates by 40 IQ points from the group mean; among the control subjects there is one group mean individual score discrepancy of 60 points! Under these circumstances the S^2 between/ S^2 within ratio would have a relatively small numerical value and the experimental effect might well be construed as one which could reasonably have occurred on the basis of chance. In other words, even though the IQ mean of the experimental groups is 15 points higher than that of the control group, high confidence in this being the reliable outcome of systematic sources is probably unwarranted. Because the ratio of systematic to error variance is critical, most researchers design their experiments so as to maximize the former and minimize the latter. In practice, this means utilizing treatments which are powerful enough to induce score changes clearly discriminable from score variability due to chance factors. Thus, in our hypothetical experiment the researcher would impose a home enrichment program which was as intense and as lengthy as feasible. At the same time, S^2 within can be kept at a minimum by making sure that conditions are kept as constant as possible within each group. This may be translated into providing the same number of home visits to each subject in the experimental group, training home aides to provide uniform enrichment experiences to the subjects, and using the most reliable IQ measures available. In effect, the control procedures we have discussed are the vehicles for keeping error variance low.

Number of Subjects

There is a third factor which influences confidence in the reliability of an observed experimental-control group difference apart from the magnitude of that difference and the dispersion of scores within each group. This is simply the *number of subjects* (N) employed by the researcher. A given experimental effect will be judged more reliable if it is based upon a large as opposed to a small N. For example, in our hypothetical experiment, consider how you would intuitively react to the extreme case in which there is only one subject per group. Imagine that the subject who is exposed to the home enrichment program is ultimately found to have an IQ of 110 upon kindergarten entrance, while that of the control subject is 95. Here, the 15 point IQ difference might easily be due to the fact that the brighter child just happened, by chance, to be assigned to the experimental treatment. In an experiment in which 100 subjects are assigned to each treatment group, the same 15 IQ point mean-group difference would be seen as a much more reliable finding. When 200 subjects are assigned randomly to experimental and control groups, it is likely that the placement of some especially bright people in one group will be balanced by the assignment of some other bright individuals to the other group. Under these circumstances a group mean difference as large as 15 IQ points would be very unlikely to occur simply on the basis of random subject assignment. Thus, this magnitude of effect would probably be seen as due to systematic antecedents, such as the experimental and control procedures to which the respective group members had been exposed.

Even when there are a few especially bright (or dull) subjects who, by chance, end up in the same group, the impact of this will be less when the overall subject sample is large than when it is small. To see this more clearly, consider three subjects with IQs of 100, 95 and 105. The average, of course, is 100 for these three. The chance assignment of a fourth subject having an IQ of 140 raises the overall group mean IQ to 110, an increment of 10 points over what it was without the fourth deviant group member. Now observe what happens when that same 140 IQ subject is randomly assigned to a group of seven subjects having the following IQs:

$$
\begin{array}{r}
100 \\
100 \\
95 \\
100 \\
105 \\
95 \\
105 \\
\text{Sum} = 700 \\
\text{IQ Mean} = 100
\end{array}
$$

In this case the addition of the subject with an IQ of 140 has the effect of raising the group mean only 5 points, to an IQ of 105. Because such chance occurrences produce less extreme effects on large groups, a given group mean difference can be more confidently attributed to systematic antecedents when large samples are employed.

By way of summary, in order to evaluate the likelihood that an experimental effect is reliable and not due to chance, three factors are taken into consideration: the absolute magnitude of the average between group differences, the variability of scores within each group, and the number of subjects each group contains.

Statistical Significance

Rather than depending upon a casual "eye-balling" of data, psychologists employ an array of statistical procedures. These take into account precisely the above three factors and permit a researcher to find the probability that an obtained experimental effect is due to chance. By convention, when the results of a statistical analysis of data indicate that the experimental effect is one which would occur on the basis of chance only five times (or less) out of one hundred, the effect is said to be *statistically significant*. In other words, chance is shown to be such an unlikely explanation that the effect is acknowledged to be one which is reliable or real. Also, by convention, an effect of this magnitude is said to be "significant at the $p < .05$ level" (probability is less than 5 times in 100 that the effect is a chance occurrence). When an experimental treatment proves to be extremely potent, it may result in an experimental effect significant at the .01 level or even at the .001 level ($p < .01$ and $p < .001$, respectively). These high levels of statistical significance mean that the observed between-group difference, given the number of subjects involved and the within-group score variation, is so great that chance alone would produce it only one time out of a hundred or, in the second instance, once out of a thousand.

When an effect is shown to be statistically significant, whether it be at the .05, .01, or .001 level, the hypothesis that it is due to chance is rejected. This chance hypothesis is also known as the *null hypothesis*. Rejection of the null hypothesis implies that we are confident (at some probability level) that the experimental-control group difference is a real one. Whether we can attribute it to the manipulation of the independent variable depends upon whether the experiment is one which is internally valid. That is, even the highest level of statistical significance says nothing about whether or not it was brought about by confounding sources of influence.

Another point to be kept in mind about the nature of statistical significance is that we are always dealing with probabilities. If an effect proves to be significant at the .05 level, the researcher can be 95% certain about his rejection of the null hypothesis. However, this rejection will still be in error 5% of the time. In other words, the results just may have been one of those 5 times in 100 in which an effect as great as that obtained does occur on the basis of chance. In such a case the individual may believe erroneously in the reliability of his/her findings when they unfortunately happen to be nothing more than an unlikely chance phenomenon.

Obviously, by raising the probability level which must be attained before the null hypothesis is rejected, the likelihood of incorrectly believing in the reliability of an experimental effect is correspondingly lowered. Thus, if a researcher chooses not to accept any effect as statistically reliable unless significant at the .01 level, he will incorrectly reject the null hypothesis only 1% of the time.

Another issue which statistical significance per se does not address has to do with the meaningfulness of findings. It is here that a distinction is made between statistical and *psychological significance*. Consider once again our home enrichment program as a supplement to Head Start experience. It is possible that if a large enough sample of subjects was used, at least several hundred children in each of the experimental and control groups, even a very slight IQ mean difference may be found to be statistically significant. For example, a mean difference of only two IQ points may prove to be significant at the .05 level, assuming reasonably low levels of within group variability of IQ scores. However, while the effect may be statistically significant, is the production of an average IQ increment of two points *psychologically* significant? Is it important enough for school administrators to implement the very expensive process of affording home enrichment to all Head Start children? It is quite likely that when the modest IQ gain, no matter how statistically significant, is evaluated in terms of its implications for real-world behavior and in the context of the manpower/monetary resources necessary to produce such a score change, the research findings will be judged to be neither psychologically significant nor meaningful to life in the real world.

SUMMARY

In the first half of this chapter we introduced the notion of external validity as having to do with the generalizability of an experimental finding. It was shown that design limitations, such as using atypical populations or procedures, may render the experiment so different from real life that results may not be safely extrapolated to the world in general. Reactivity often produced by the pre-testing of experimental subjects was also said to place limits on the external validity of an experiment. The so-called Solomon four group design is a complex experiment in which the effects of reactivity induced by pre-testing (pre-test sensitization) are indirectly controlled. Demand characteristics is the third major factor limiting the generalizability of experimental findings. Various unobtrusive measurement procedures were described for the purpose of minimizing reactivity and maximizing the external validity of research.

The second section of Chapter 4 dealt with factors which are taken into account when trying to assess the reliability of an experimental effect. It was shown that, all else being equal, large group mean differences (a large experimental effect), small within-group variability, and a large number of subjects tend to facilitate the confidence one has in the reliability of experimental findings. Finally, the logic of the term statistical significance was discussed. We pointed out that, by convention, when an experimental effect is found to be so large that it would occur on the basis of chance only 5 times out of 100 ($p < .05$), the effect is said to be significant. In other words, it is accepted as having been due to systemic antecedents, such as the manipulation of the independent variable by the experimenter, and is not due to mere chance.

TERMS TO KNOW

CHAPTER 5
Correlational Research

In an experiment the random assignment of subjects to experimental and control treatments assures that exposure to different levels or intensities of the independent variable is unrelated to the myriad of personal characteristics which subjects naturally possess. This manipulation of the independent variable therefore creates multiple groups of subjects who are made to systematically differ in some important way (e.g., anxiety level) while, on the average, they are essentially equivalent in all other ways. The effect of this induced difference between groups upon the dependent variable is then observed and its reliability statistically assessed.

CORRELATIONAL DESIGNS

For a number of reasons a researcher may decide not to artificially create different kinds of subjects but instead choose to study the naturally occurring between-subject variation on some personality variable, such as intelligence, as it relates to some other variable, perhaps psychological adjustment. This general research strategy is referred to as *correlational*.

The most conceptually simple correlational personality research seeks to discover the empirical relationship between two or more variables. A statistic, known as the *correlation coefficient,* is calculated as a vehicle for describing the discovered relationship(s). It is crucial to understand the logic behind this statistic in order to appreciate the meaning of correlational research findings, and to understand some important issues relevant to personality assessment which will be presented in later chapters. For these reasons, the correlation coefficient will be discussed in some detail.

Correlation Coefficient

A correlation coefficient is a descriptive statistic which summarizes the degree of relationship or correspondence which exists between paired sets of scores, such as those depicted in Table 1. There are many formulas which can be used to compute a correlation coefficient. However, with rare exception, the value of the coefficient can range only from $+1.00$ through zero to -1.00. A correlation coefficient which has a positive value indicates that the pairs of scores tend to be *directly related* to each other. If one score is high, the other score comprising the pair also tends to be high; if one is low, the other score tends to be low as well. A coefficient having a negative value results when the scores which comprise the pairs tend to be *inversely related*; if one of the scores is high, the second score tends to be low, or vice versa. The more discrepant from zero the value of the correlation coefficient, the greater the degree of relationship, either direct or inverse, between the two sets of scores. A value of $+1.00$ or -1.00 indicates perfect direct and inverse relationships, respectively, while a value of zero means that the two sets of scores are unrelated.

TABLE 1 Illustrative Correlational Data: Subjects' Scores on Tests A and B

	TEST	
SUBJECT	A	B
1	80	83
2	91	88
3	67	73
4	60	58
5	85	85
6	96	90

Note: The two scores obtained for any given subject constitute a pair, e.g., the scores of 80 and 83 for student 1. The two columns of scores are each referred to as a set.

In order to illustrate these points, consider a two day investigation in which the researcher is interested in discovering whether IQ, test-anxiety and academic self-esteem are interrelated. His subjects are seven high school students. On the first day they are administered a standard IQ test, and are asked to answer a 10 item true-false test-anxiety questionnaire containing statements such as, "I sweat when I have to take an exam." On the second day the students fill out a 20 item true-false academic self-esteem questionnaire which might contain statements such as, "I'm probably among the dullest kids in this class." In addition, the opinion of the students' teacher regarding their test-anxiety is obtained by having him complete a 70 item questionnaire regarding each of the seven subjects. The data obtained from these four measurements are presented in Table 2.

A correlation coefficient which is based solely on the pairs of rankings earned by the students on the two anxiety questionnaires is found to be $+1.00$, the highest it could be. This reflects the perfect correspondence which exists between the rankings of students on these two questionnaires. The correlation coefficient based on rank orderings is called *rho*, after the Greek letter for r, ρ. A different computational formula may be used, yielding a *product moment correlation coefficient*, called r. It tends to be more precise because it takes into account the actual scores rather than mere ranks. In the case of the anxiety data presented in Table 2, the product moment correlation computes to be +.985. The fact that it is less than +1.00 indicates a less than perfect consistency between the two sets of scores and is reflective of the small discrepancies between the self-administered and teacher-administered scores for subjects C and F.

Turning attention now to just the events of the second day as depicted in Table 2, it can be seen that the student who was given the highest test-anxiety score by his teacher obtained the lowest score on the academic self-esteem scale; the second highest score on the teacher-completed test-anxiety scale was paired with the second lowest self-esteem score, and so on. In terms of ranks only, these data yield a perfect inverse relationship and a rho value of −1.00. The product moment correlation, which takes into account each score value, is computed to be −.977. Notice that the high negative correlation expresses about the same strong magnitude of relationship as did the high positive correlation computed from the two test-anxiety questionnaire data sets. The difference is that the relationship is now inverse rather than direct or positive.

TABLE 2 Data Obtained in Correlational Research

		DAY ONE		DAY TWO			
				ANXIETY (BY TEACHER)		ACADEMIC SELF-ESTEEM	
STUDENT	IQ	ANXIETY (BY SELF)					
		Score	Rank	Score	Rank	Score	Rank
A	131	10	1	10	1	6	7
B	105	9	2	9	2	7	6
C	99	8	3	7	3	9	5
D	148	6	4	6	4	11	4
E	115	5	5	5	5	14	3
F	108	3	6	4	6	17	2
G	120	1	7	1	7	20	1

Another point to be remembered is that any correlation is based upon scores alone, not upon what the scores may be measuring. In order to be aware of the psychological meaning of a correlation one has to know what high and low scores on each test indicate. In our illustrative research we will say that a high score on the test anxiety questionnaire reflects high levels of student anxiety and low scores are indicative of low anxiety. Similarly, on the self-esteem measure, a high score is produced by a student having high academic self-esteem. Thus, the negative correlation between test-anxiety and self-esteem scores indicates that low test-anxious students tend to have high academic self-esteem; those with low academic self-esteem are judged by their teacher to have considerable test-anxiety.

As a third illustration based upon Table 2, consider the relationship between academic self-esteem scores and the previously obtained IQ scores. Scanning the data reveals no clear trend. In fact, a correlation coefficient computed from ranks yields a rho value of +.072, and a product moment correlation based on actual scores is found to be −.035. Either way, it is very close to zero, indicating essentially that no relationship is present.

In addition to the presentation of a correlation coefficient, relationships between sets of scores may be expressed by using a *scatter plot* or *bivariable distribution*. Each subject's two scores are plotted with a single point against two axes, one representing each of the two test administrations. Figures 2, 3, and 4 illustrate the scatter plots which correspond to the three relationships discussed above. Notice that when each subject's two test-anxiety scores are appropriately represented on the scatter plot by a single point, the points line up from lower left to upper right. This trend becomes most linear in shape when a correlation coefficient approximates +1.00, as it does in this case. When the correlation coefficient departs somewhat from +1.00, when it is +.70, the direction of the trend depicted in the scatter plot remains the same, because the relationship is still positive or direct. However, the points fall on a more oval shape, as illustrated in Fig. 2 by the shaded area.

Figure 3 shows the scatter plot which corresponds to the −.977 product moment correlation computed from the teacher-administered test-anxiety questions and the academic self-esteem questionnaire. As they would in any strong negative relationship, the subjects' points fall along a line from upper left to lower right. Again, as a negative correlation coefficient departs further from −1.00, its corresponding scatter plot becomes more oval in shape, as illustrated in Fig. 3 by the shaded area.

Of course, the most extreme departure from a perfect direct or inverse relationship exists when a correlation coefficient computes to a value of zero. This was approximately the case when we found the product moment correlation between academic self-esteem scores and IQ to be −.035. The lack of a relationship between two variables finds depiction on a scatter plot in the form of a circular array of points, as illustrated in Fig. 4.

It should now be pointed out, if not already realized, that a +1.00 or −1.00 correlation allows for perfect prediction of one score based on the value of the other score. If there is perfect correspondence of ranks, as there was between those obtained using the two test-anxiety questionnaires, then by knowing a student's rank on one questionnaire it is possible to predict rank, without error, on the second. Similarly, by knowing which student has the highest rank on the test-anxiety questionnaire, because of its perfect inverse relationship with self-esteem scores, it is possible to predict without error that the student will have the lowest rank on the self-esteem questionnaire. As the correlation between sets of scores becomes less than perfect, prediction becomes more prone to error, until it finally reaches purely chance levels in the case of a zero correlation coefficient. For example, by referring back to Fig. 4, it can be seen that students who get middle range scores on the self-esteem measure have IQs which range from low to high. One cannot predict IQ from self-esteem scores. Alternatively, of course, self-esteem scores can't be predicted from IQ. Any level IQ student may obtain any level of self-esteem score.

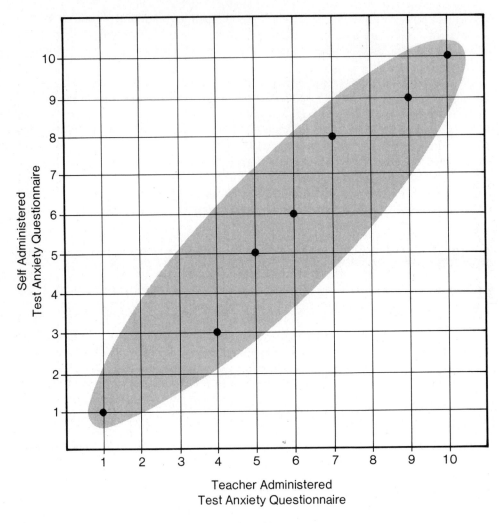

Figure 2. Scatter plot of hypothetical data from Table 2.

Correlation Magnitude and the Range of Scores

In order for two sets of scores to generate a correlation coefficient of any magnitude there must be an ample range of scores within each set. It is statistically impossible for a correlation coefficient to approach +1.00 or −1.00 unless some subjects who score at the extreme, either high or low, in the first set fall at one or the

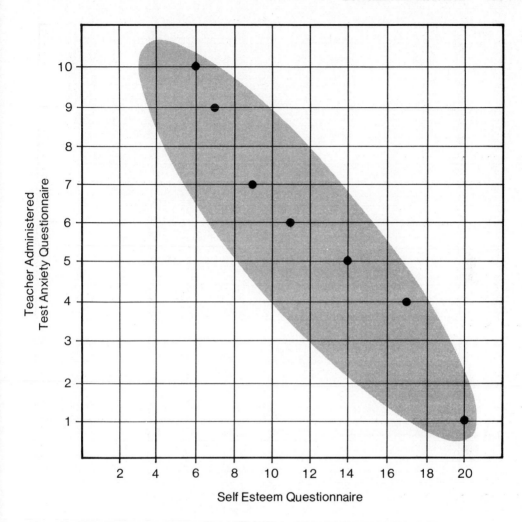

Figure 3. Scatter plot of hypothetical data from Table 2.

other extreme on the other set of scores. When there is no score variation within a set, there are, of course, no extremes.

Unless a researcher keeps this point in mind, he may erroneously conclude that two personality variables in which he is interested are unrelated. For example, imagine that you administer an intelligence test which is designed to yield IQ scores from 50 to 150. In order to establish the relationship between intelligence and social maturity, you also have each of the subjects complete a social maturity scale which yields social quotients (SQs) from 50 to 150. You request that your psychology professor allow his

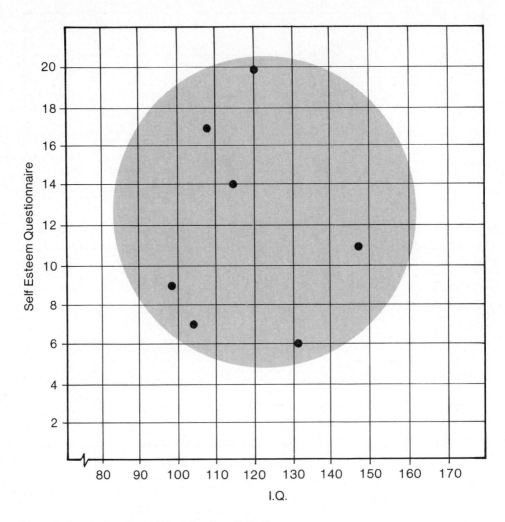

Figure 4. Scatter plot of hypothetical data from Table 2.

class to volunteer as subjects in your project. Your results yield a very low correlation coefficient and you conclude that general intelligence and social maturity are unrelated. Too bad, because it is quite possible the two personality variables are related and it was the subject sample which was at fault.

By way of explanation, consider Fig. 5, which is a scatter plot whose points represent scores on the IQ and SQ tests obtained from a representative sampling of the general population. The overall data would probably yield a correlation coefficient close to +.80. However, notice what would happen if instead of testing a sample

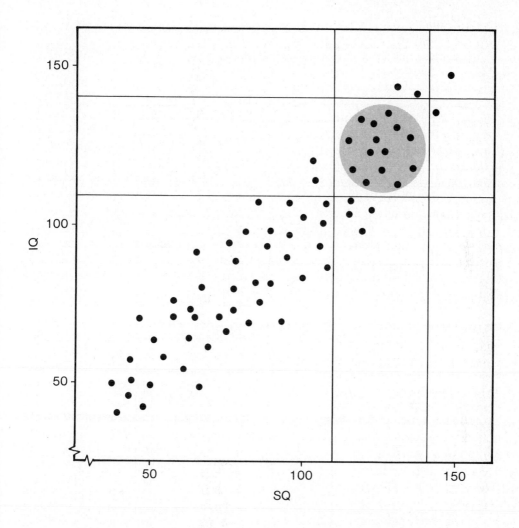

Figure 5. Scatter plot of hypothetical correlational data. Sub-plot, indicated by shaded circle, illustrates how the use of a restricted range of scores can produce a spuriously low correlation coefficient.

whose scores ranged from 50 to 150, a sample was used (such as would be found in a typical college psychology class) with a restricted range of scores in the two tests, say 110 to 140. The employment of only these subjects produces an array of scatter plot points which is much less linear in nature (see shaded area in Fig. 5) and yields a correlation coefficient very close to zero. This finding is of course quite accurate for the subsample but grossly unrepresentative of the overall picture.

Causality

In correlational research it is quite usual for the researcher to designate one of the variables in question as "independent" and the other as "dependent." For example, one might be interested in explaining the relationship between test-anxiety and academic grades on the assumption that test-anxiety disrupts efficient test-taking behavior. In this framework test-anxiety would be defined as the independent variable and the dependent variable would be examination grades. The method would involve first obtaining an index of test-anxiety on a group of subjects, perhaps by administering an instrument such as Sarason's (1972) Test Anxiety Scale (TAS). This is a question-naire containing items such as, "I sometimes find my heart beating very fast during tests." TAS scores could then be correlated with actual examination grades obtained from the same group of subjects.

Assume that, as expected, TAS scores and grades are found to be negatively correlated, reflecting the trend to low grades on the academic exam for high-scoring, anxious TAS subjects. What kinds of inferences may be drawn from such a finding? Most important, this correlational design does not permit one to speak with confidence about causality even though the study itself emerged from a classic if-then hypothesis: *if* one is anxious, *then* one will do poorly on exams. At most, it may be submitted that the results are consistent with, or do not disconfirm, the causal relationship thought to exist between anxiety and grades. The causal hypothesis would, of course, have been disconfirmed had no relationship, or a positive one, been found between TAS scores and examination grades. Thus, one important use of correlational designs is to expose a causal hypothesis to an opportunity for disconfirmation. If this does not occur, the hypothesis remains one which is viable and worthy of further test.

When it is said that the results of a correlational design are consistent with some notion of causality, it does not rule out the possibility that they are also consistent with an opposite causal hypothesis. Specifically, the negative relationship between TAS scores and grades can also be pointed to as evidence for the hypothesis: *if* one does poorly on exams, *then* one will be test-anxious. Notice that the direction of causality described in this hypothesis is the reverse of what was first presented. In effect, TAS scores, once the independent variable, are now seen as a dependent variable and poor academic grades are the independent variable.

Too frequently researchers are unwilling to interpret correlational findings by reversing independent variables in their thinking. Campbell and Stanley point out that in educational research which correlates indices of teacher and student behaviors we "almost never consider the possibility of the student's behavior causing the teacher's" (1963, p. 65). Thus one may confirm the prediction that teachers who offer frequent verbal praise produce well-behaved school children by finding a negative correlation between the number of instances of teacher-expressed praise and the number of student-initiated classroom disruptions. The hypothesis that non-disruptive children induce frequent expressions of praise from their teachers has rarely been entertained. It seems as if we are blinded by the cultural stereotype of effects being produced in children by teachers, and not the plausible rival hypothesis that students affect teacher behaviors.

Assets of Correlational Research

If correlational research inevitably leads to some confusion regarding the issue of causality it may be reasonably asked why one would substitute this approach for experimental designs, which more clearly test the validity of the hypothesis concerning the effect of an independent variable upon a dependent variable.

Inexpensive. One reason is that correlational research tends to be less expensive to conduct than experimentation. Consequently, during the early stages of a research program, when the potential worth of various hypotheses have not been determined, easily-implemented correlational designs may prove to be a most economical starting point. If, using this strategy, hypotheses are disconfirmed at least one has not invested too much in conducting more difficult and costly experiments. As an example of this general approach we will present some research of Middlemist, Knowles, and Matter (1976) concerned with personal space, defined by Sommer as the "area with invisible boundaries surrounding a person's body into which intruders may not come" (1969, p. 26). It has been found that people show evidence of stress when others invade their personal space and engage in behaviors which serve to reestablish its integrity, such as moving away from the invader. We seem to attempt to maintain a comfortable psychological distance between ourselves and others in our environment.

Evans and Howard (1973) have suggested that the characteristic behaviors which are observed when personal space is invaded occur because they serve to reduce emotional arousal brought on by the invasion. Previous efforts to directly assess arousal level as a function of other's proximity have either yielded inconsistent findings or have employed highly reactive methodologies. For instance, McBride, King, and James (1965) did find decreases in skin resistance (heightened emotional arousal) when subjects were approached by others, especially from the front and by the opposite sex. However, Knowles and Johnson (1974) point out that the subjects were knowingly participating in an experiment; they were hooked up to instrumentation and cognizant of the independent variable being manipulated by the experimenters. Under these circumstances, the findings may have little external validity.

Middlemist and his colleagues (1976) sought to circumvent these criticisms by assessing the relationship between personal space and arousal in a non-reactive way. To accomplish this they built upon research which demonstrates that the micturition, or urination, process is affected by emotional arousal and can, therefore, serve as an index of it. Specifically, it has been reported that social stress increases muscle tension, causing the detrusor muscles of the bladder to contract more strongly. This increases bladder pressure, thereby forcing urine out of the bladder. In addition, there is increased difficulty in relaxing the external sphincter of the urethra. Middlemist reasoned that the net effect of these changes should be that, if one were inclined to micturate under stress, there would be a delay of onset due to a non-relaxed external sphincter and total flow time would be reduced. These changes in micturition should be related to interpersonal distance if invasion of personal space in fact produces heightened arousal.

As an initial test of their "novel" (p. 543) hypothesis, Middlemist and his co-authors conducted a natural process correlational research at a university men's restroom containing two rows of five urinals each. An observer, apparently grooming himself at the sink, kept track of 48 different men who made use of the facilities. Of the 48 subjects, none selected a urinal adjacent to one already in use; 23 selected a receptacle once removed from the nearest user; 16 separated themselves from others by two urinals and 9 were separated by three or more urinals. These data themselves are consistent with the notion that, at least while micturating, men tend to avoid the most proximal interpersonal distance. Beyond this, and more relevant to the arousal hypothesis, it was discovered that the three levels of interpersonal distance (one, two, or three urinal separation) were negatively correlated with micturition delay ($r = -.315$), defined as the time between the unzippering of a fly and the onset of urination. Micturition persistence, as expected, was positively correlated with interpersonal distance ($r = +.562$). Incidentally, onset and offset of urination was revealed via auditory cues and calibrated with a wrist chronometer.

 While these results suggest that Middlemist's hypothesis is valid, it remains an uncontrolled study incapable of proving causality. Consequently, an unobtrusive experiment was subsequently conducted using 60 male subjects. An observer, apparently urinating, was planted in a washroom containing three receptacles. His location was systematically manipulated. He was placed at the center urinal for some subjects; for others, at the urinal to the right; and for still others, he absented himself from the washroom. The subjects always had to use the urinal to the left, either because the others were occupied by the observer or closed by a sign reading "Don't use, washing urinal" (p. 544). Thus, subjects were randomly assigned to one of three interpersonal space conditions: observer using adjacent urinal, observer using once removed urinal, or observer absent.

The results of the experiment are consistent with those of the correlational research and serve to validate more strongly the hypothesis of arousal as a consequence of personal space invasion. Specifically, micturition delay increased from a mean of 4.9 seconds when the subject was alone at the stand of urinals to 8.4 seconds when the observer was most proximal. This means difference was found to be significant at the $p < .001$ level — an extremely reliable effect. A highly significant effect was also found for the micturition persistence dependent measure. The mean flow time ranged from 24.8 seconds in the alone condition to only 17.4 seconds in the most proximal condition ($p < .01$).

These studies, therefore, serve to strengthen confidence in the hypothesis that interpersonal closeness induces an arousal increment, and the arousal can be unobtrusively assessed by recording micturition processes. The correlational design quickly established that data consistent with the hypothesis could be generated, and the experiment provided evidence for the causal relationship between personal space invasion and arousal level.

Non-reactivity. In addition to serving as an economical way to commence a new research program, the Middlemist effort illustrates a second reason why researchers may opt for correlational designs. Specifically, they lend themselves nicely to conducting non-reactive research. It is not always possible to manipulate an independent variable in the laboratory without so sensitizing the subject that his behavior becomes unrepresentative of what occurs in the real world. As mentioned, this criticism was raised against the experimental effort by McBride, King, and James (1965) in which skin resistance was assessed as a function of personal space invasion.

We also previously mentioned a hypothetical correlational research involving the variables of Test Anxiety Scale (TAS) scores and examination performance. It was suggested that high levels of test-anxiety, as assessed by TAS, is predictive of poor examination performance. It would not be difficult for a researcher to obtain TAS scores from subjects prior to obtaining measures of examination performance. Thus, at the time the dependent measurement is made, subjects are not thinking in terms of their performance being related to a level of test-anxiety. Consistent with this, it is quite common for university psychology departments to schedule a pre-testing session at the start of an academic semester. At that time Introductory Psychology students, the typical captive subject pool, can be asked to complete the TAS. Only later, when recollection of the TAS has become little more than a blur, the students' performance on examinations can be assessed.

Such an approach is much less reactive than one involving the assignment of subjects to control and experimental groups. This employs a treatment in which subjects are rendered test-anxious just prior to completing an examination. This kind of manipulation may easily sensitize subjects to the fact that the researcher is interested in the variable of test anxiety. Subjects who perceive the artificiality of the situation may perhaps consciously resist becoming anxious; or, if they choose to be good subjects, they may cooperate by performing as if they were as test-anxious as the experimenter obviously wants them to be. In any case, the external validity of the findings will inevitably suffer.

Viability. A third strength of correlational designs is that they may represent the only viable means of studying certain broad personality characteristics in any meaningful way. Specifically, many variables of interest, such as social isolation, depression, or other psychopathological behavior patterns simply cannot be induced via the laboratory manipulation of independent variables. There is no way to randomly assign subjects to a treatment group which involves inducing schizophrenia and then assessing group differences between them and control subjects on a dependent measure, such as activity level. One could, however, correlate subjects' scores on a schizophrenia scale with an index of activity level. The point is that there is often no alternative but to start with subjects who naturally manifest differences on the independent variable of interest, in this instance severity of schizophrenia.

Ethics. A fourth case in which researchers may prefer to employ correlational procedures over an experimental design is when there are ethical reservations regarding direct manipulation of an independent variable. A psychologist may be very interested in the nature of the home environment which provokes suicide. He would not however intervene in such a way as to randomly assign subjects to a treatment condition which drives them to kill themselves. He might however, quite properly, correlate the already-existing tendency in suicidal adolescents with a wide range of family characteristics.

Appropriateness. Shontz points out that "experimental manipulation is often a very poor substitute for the real thing. Experimental controls may add some precision but "when the investigator is interested in the study of whole people, as they exist in their everyday lives . . . he need not apologize for his use of (the) correlational approach" (1965, p. 156).

There are other situations in which correlational research is in no way a substitute for an experimental design. Researchers may often phrase their hypotheses in correlational terms, not to avoid being specific with respect to causality but because the relationship between variables per se is the matter of interest.

Correlational Research Variations

So far we have discussed correlational research in which scores on an independent variable are simply correlated with the dependent measure(s). However, much research which is conceptually correlational in nature does not depend upon the correlation coefficient as the basic statistical tool. Instead, whole groups are compared on a dependent variable, much the same as in experimental research. The fundamental difference is that the experiment establishes groups via the random assignment of subjects to different treatments; the correlational study defines comparison groups on the basis of measuring naturally-occurring levels of a personality dimension. For example, rather than correlate the TAS scores of all available subjects with examination performance, it is quite possible to divide the subjects into high and low TAS scoring groups and then compare the mean examination performance of the high-anxious with that of the low-anxious subjects.

There are two common ways in which subjects are divided into groups. One is the *median split* in which the total subject pool is rank ordered on the independent variable, in this case TAS scores, and simply divided at the midpoint.

Frequently, the measuring instrument used as the independent variable is relatively poor. The result is that some people who score in the upper half of a distribution of scores in fact should have been assigned to the low side of the median split. Similarly, several subjects who are really high on the personality dimension being assessed may score at the low side of the median split due to imperfect measurement by the assessment tool. In order to avoid misclassifying subjects as high on some trait when they really are low, and vice versa, the researcher may choose to establish groups using only the extreme scoring subjects, the top and bottom 25%. This *extreme group* approach is especially useful during the early stages of a research program. It is at this time that the relevance of the independent variable to the dependent variable may still be questionable. If any relationship does exist, it will most obviously stand out when the mean score on the dependent variable earned by subjects highest on the independent variable is contrasted with that of the subjects lowest on the independent variable.

The following data may be used to illustrate the above points.

SUBJECT	IQ	GRADE AVERAGE	
1	140	95	$\overline{X} = 85$
2	137	80	
3	130	80	
		$\overline{X} = 77.5$	
4	124	65	
5	116	70	
6	111	75	
7	100	90	
8	94	85	
9	90	90	
		$\overline{X} = 76.7$	
10	83	70	$\overline{X} = 65.0$
11	80	60	
12	76	65	

Suppose we hypothesize that there is a relationship between IQ and school grade average. If we conduct a median split on the twelve subjects being studied, it is apparent that high IQ students have only a slightly higher grade average (77.5) than low IQ students (76.7). This difference does not even approach the magnitude necessary to achieve statistical significance. On the other hand, the use of only the top and bottom quartiles reveals that there is a much larger grade difference between the high IQ subjects (85) and those in the bottom quarter of the IQ rankings (65). This 20 point mean grade average difference is in fact statistically significant at the $p < .05$ level. Thus, the very real relationship between IQ and grade average may have been overlooked had the researcher restricted himself to the use of a median split approach.

In addition to splitting subjects into groups on the basis of differential scores on some independent variable, contrasting groups, defined by other criteria, may also be used in research which remains conceptually correlational in nature. For example, instead of establishing schizophrenic and non-schizophrenic groups on the basis of psychopathology scale scores, a researcher interested in the relationship between schizophrenia and activity level may simply compare the mean activity levels of groups of diagnosed schizophrenics with non-schizophrenics, such as depressed patients.

This use of naturally existing groups is very similar to a procedure referred to in the previous chapter as a "pre-experimental design." Recall that the pre-experimental design is one in which an independent variable to which subjects are naturally exposed, rather than one to which they are randomly assigned, is studied. We used as an example research in which the reading readiness of children having a history of nursery school experience was compared with that of children who did not go to nursery school; nursery school experience was the independent variable and reading readiness was the dependent variable. Whether we are talking about comparing one naturally occurring group of children who attended nursery school with another who didn't attend school, or one diagnostic group which is schizophrenic with another which is depressive, the overall design takes the following form:

existing group A ——————————→post-measurement
existing group B ——————————→post-measurement

There is no treatment imposed by the researcher; rather the groups are already different in some way. The question asked in such a design is whether that difference is related to outcome on some dependent variable, reading readiness or activity level, respectively.

Whether we choose to call this a pre-experimental design or a between-group correlational design, the fact remains that causal inferences cannot be safely drawn from the results. If a relationship is found between nursery school attendance and reading readiness, is it that nursery school improves reading readiness or do parents of children with potentially high levels of reading readiness send them to nursery school? Similarly, if schizophrenics are found to have a lower activity level, does the schizophrenic process produce this or is low activity level a precursor to the development of schizophrenia? Another possibility is that both the disordered thought processes and low activity level characteristic of schizophrenia are the product of some third variable — perhaps a biochemical or metabolic imbalance.

Significance of correlational research findings

When correlational research employs a between-group contrast, the statistical analyses are quite similar to those used when evaluating the reliability of an experimental effect. That is, the mean group difference on the dependent variable is evaluated in terms of its magnitude, the within group variability, and the number of subjects within each group. If the analysis reveals that the difference on the dependent variable between subjects who scored high and low on the independent variable would occur on the basis of chance five times or fewer out of one hundred, the difference is deemed to be statistically significant. It would, however, not be proper to speak of this significant between-group differences as being a reliable experimental effect because it did not emerge from a truly experimental design in which subjects were randomly assigned to treatment groups.

When the correlational research maintains a simple correlational format, it is still possible to establish the significance of the revealed relationship. A significant correlation coefficient is one which is so large, either + or −, that it would occur on a chance basis five times or fewer out of one hundred. Thus, chance is again the hypothesis which must be ruled out. This is because whenever two variables are correlated, even if they are really unrelated, by chance the correlation coefficient will depart somewhat from zero. For example, one might correlate IQ scores and shoe sizes, using a classroom of high school students as subjects. It just may happen that a couple of the brightest students have small feet; this is sufficient to yield a negative coefficient of, say, $-.26$. The question then is, would a correlation coefficient of $-.26$ occur so rarely on a purely chance basis that we must accept it as reflecting a real or reliable relationship between IQ and shoe size; is the coefficient of $-.26$ statistically significant?

The statistical procedures used to answer this question take into account the number of scores upon which the coefficient is based. It turns out that if the classroom contains only 10 students, the coefficient is not statistically significant; if it contains 50 students, the $-.26$ value is significant at the .05 level; if the correlation is based upon 100 students, it is significant at the $p < .01$ level. Thus, the general rule is that a given correlation coefficient attains higher levels of significance the more scores it is based upon. The logical extension of this is that if very large subject samples are employed, even a very low level of relationship between two variables will be statistically significant. The researcher is then faced with separating statistical significance from psychological significance. It may be that IQ and shoe size do, in fact, correlate to some minimal degree; if thousands of subjects were employed we might even be able to say that the obtained coefficient, say $+.02$, is statistically significant. The point is that the relationship, while probably real, is so minimal that it may have little theoretical importance and no practical utility.

SUMMARY

This chapter focussed upon correlational research. The logic of the correlation coefficient was carefully examined in that the statistic is frequently used to conveniently express the results of correlational research. The meaning of positive, negative, and zero correlation coefficients was explained as was the impact of score range upon the magnitude of the coefficient. Interpreters of correlational research were cautioned against drawing conclusions regarding causality, even from those investigations in which the design superficially resembles an experiment. This resemblance occurs when two naturally-occurring groups are contrasted on some dependent measures or when groupings are established using a variation of a high-low split, e.g. a median split. We discussed the strengths of correlational research, pointing out why the method is not to be necessarily construed as inferior to experimentation. Lastly, methods in which the statistical significance of correlations are established.

TERMS TO KNOW

CHAPTER 6
Single Subject Research

A number of arguments have been raised against the use of between-group research strategies, whether they be of a correlational or experimental nature. Sidman's (1960) primary concern is that between-group research focuses upon group averages and neglects the individual case. As a consequence, a researcher may arrive at a highly statistically significant difference between two comparison groups on some dependent measure and never attend to the fact that, even in the treatment which is most generally efficacious, some subjects are less responsive than others to the experimental manipulation. The researcher is thus flushed with the success of having produced a reliable effect, rather than being sobered by the fact that the treatment was only selectively effective. Important questions concerning the kinds of subjects for whom the treatment is most and least potent, and for what reasons, then tend to be ignored.

Sidman also points out that group data can be blatantly misleading. Consider what happens when a group of 100 subjects is asked to predict whether the left or right button on a panel is correct. A correct choice produces a bit of candy when the button is pressed, with the correct button being systematically shifted from left to right and back again on successive trials. This is a relatively simple problem which tends to produce a group acquisition function similar to that in Figure 6.

It appears as if the subjects start out being correct 50% of the time, by chance, on the first block of five trials. They then seem to gradually gain insight into the left-right alternation pattern. This is based upon the smoothly ascending curve which finally levels off as perfection is reached. In fact, if the data from individual subjects are recorded, it is clearly seen that the resolution of this problem does not occur in any sort of smooth way. Instead, the performance pattern tends to be discontinuous (Fig. 7).

Subjects operate at a chance level until they suddenly gain insight into the nature of the correct left-right pattern, at which point performance immediately approximates perfection. For a few subjects the discontinuity in performance occurs very early in the sequence; for others the shift from 50% to 100% correct comes very late. Most subjects manifest this sudden ability to select the correct button during some intermediate trial

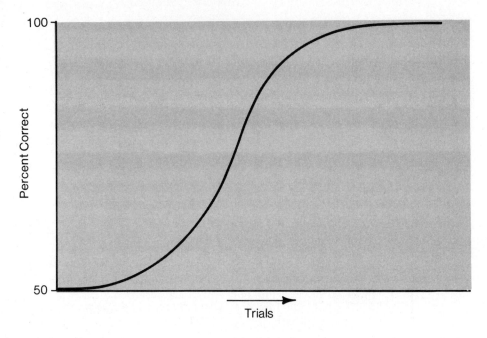

Figure 6. Stylized group acquisition on a discrimination learning problem.

block. The aforementioned smooth group function is produced when all of the discontinuous individual data are averaged. Thus, the actual nature of the learning process remains hidden because the group data misrepresent the performance of the individual subject.

SINGLE SUBJECT EXPERIMENTAL DESIGNS

While there has always been an interest in learning about individual cases, controlled procedures geared toward the discovery of causal relationships within a given individual are of relatively recent origin. *Single case experimental methodology* has been primarily an outgrowth of work in the area of operant conditioning, with its emphasis upon discovering ways to modify and manage discrete behaviors via the manipulation of rewarding and punishing behavioral consequences. Leitenberg in a review of research designs employed in single case experimental methodology says that "the major thrust of this research has been to verify experimentally in individual cases that observed changes in behavior are really a function of the therapeutic procedures applied to produce these changes" (1973, p. 88). In other words, the strategy is to demonstrate that behavioral changes are under the control of a therapy procedure.

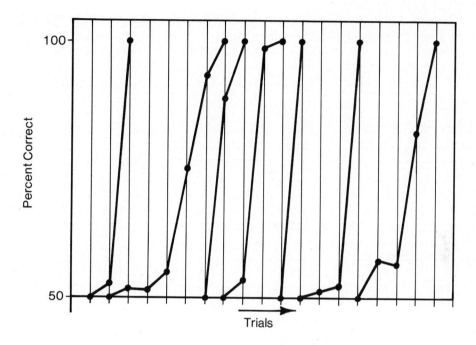

Figure 7. Stylized individual acquisition curves on a discrimination learning problem.

The simplest approach would be to impose a treatment and then observe the occurrence or non-occurrence of the expected behavioral outcome. This may be diagrammed as follows:

$$X \longrightarrow O,$$

where X represents the time of treatment, and O the time of observation. For example, a hyperactive child might be given a drug such as Ritalin. Then a record of subsequent quiet periods exceeding one minute duration could be maintained. At best, the researcher could report his actual data, but would be unable to say whether the frequency or length of quiet periods represent an improvement over the pre-treatment period. This problem is easily circumvented by adding a period of behavioral observation prior to the administration of Ritalin:

$$O_1 \longrightarrow X \longrightarrow O_2.$$

If the researcher finds that the rate of quiet periods is only two per hour prior to treatment and 10 per hour subsequent to the administration of Ritalin, he might well be tempted to construe Ritalin as the effective behavior-change agent. This conclusion, however, is open to a variety of competing explanations. The research has little internal validity due to the fact that there was no control exerted over potentially confounding variables. For example, it is possible that Ritalin was administered at a point in the child's development where he was naturally becoming less hyperactive. Thus, maturational factors may be causing the changes in behavior rather than Ritalin. Alternatively, any number of events, such as a cold or other medical conditions, may be responsible for the child's decreased activity level. It is also possible that the activity level recorded prior to the administration of Ritalin happened to be unusually high, even for the hyperactive child. Thus, the post-treatment activity decrease may only reflect the child regressing to his unusual high rate, with the Ritalin being of no consequence.

Because of these threats to the internal validity of this single subject research, a variety of more complex variations have been proposed. Each design, in its own way, serves to reduce the plausability of rival sources of influence as factors which are responsible for the observed behavior change.

Time Series

One design involves increasing the time span over which multiple pre- and post-treatment behavioral observations are made. This time series approach may be diagrammed as follows:

$$O_1 \longrightarrow O_2 \longrightarrow O_3 \longrightarrow X \longrightarrow O_4 \longrightarrow O_5 \longrightarrow O_6,$$

where O_1—O_6 represent six sequential observations of a subject's behavior, and X the time at which treatment is offered. Some possible outcomes of a time series experiment are depicted in Fig. 8.

Evidence that X is responsible for behavior changes is weakest in outcomes A, B, and C. In each case, the O_3 — O_4 shift fits in with the overall shift pattern manifest in the time series which is the product of factors other than X. Consequently, it makes little sense to single out the O_3 — O_4 shift as being uniquely the product of X. Some minimal evidence for the efficacy of X is offered in outcome D, in which an ascending trend is slightly modified concurrent with the imposition of X. The most compelling data emerge from outcomes E, F, and G. In both E and F a stable behavior pattern is rendered discontinuous, and in G there is a reversal of trend — these modifications being temporally contiguous with receipt of treatment X. However, even with these last three outcomes the researcher must be in a position to defend the assertion that the O_3 — O_4 shift is caused by X and not by some other event occurring simultaneously. To the degree that it is possible to hold constant all factors relevant to the behavior under observation, except X, it becomes more plausible to attribute the O_3 — O_4 shift to X. This kind of control over other factors is least likely when the subject is permitted to become freely involved in whatever environmental events he may naturally encounter. If the time series experiment is conducted under more predictably stable conditions, such as in a hospital or, even better, in a laboratory, outcomes E, F, and G become more powerful testimony in support of treatment X being the cause of the observed behavioral shift.

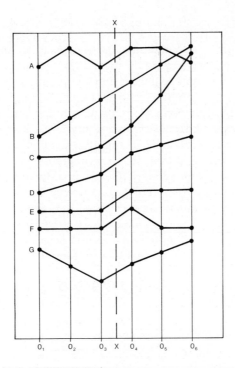

Figure 8. Some possible outcome patterns from the introduction of an experimental variable at point X into a Time Series of Measurements O1 — O6 (adapted from Campbell, D.T. and Stanley, J.C. *Experimental and Quasi-Experimental Designs for Research.* Chicago: Rand McNally, 1963, Figure 3, p. 38. Copyright© 1963, American Educational Research Association, Washington, D.C.).

It has been traditional for time series data to be published in graphic form, with the trend lines offered as evidence for the power of X. The difficulty with relying upon this sort of presentation is that no standards exist regarding the minimal degree of evidence required to deem an effect significant. For example, how great must the O3 — O4 shift be in outcome E before we are willing to see it as a reliable effect of X? There are no clear answers to this question, although Gottman (1973) has offered some proposals for the statistical analyses of time series data. There seems to be consensus on the impropriety of simply relying upon the magnitude of the behavioral shift surrounding the imposition of treatment. In our examples the O3 — O4 shift happened to be identical for all depicted outcomes. There is also argument regarding the uselessness of routinely comparing average behavior levels prior to and subsequent to treatment. It can be seen, for example, in Fig. 8 that the average of O1, O2, and O3 performance might be significantly different from the average performance noted at O4 , O5, and O6 for outcomes B and C; yet neither outcome really offers any evidence in support of treatment X. Alternatively, while outcome G is a powerful one, the mean pre- v. post-treatment levels of behavior are not likely to be found different.

ABAB Designs

A second single subject experimental approach is to alternate systematically the conditions to which a subject is exposed. If there is concommitant variation of behavior it becomes reasonable to assume that the behavior is being controlled or caused by the imposed conditions. In most of these designs the researcher begins by recording the frequency or rate at which a behavior is being emitted under naturally prevailing conditions, the *base rate* of the behavior in question. This is a no-treatment or control phase, and is designated by the letter A. In the subsequent phase, B, some treatment is offered while the behavior rate during this experimental period is still being recorded. There follows a return to the conditions of phase A in order to determine if the behavior returns to its pre-experimental base rate. If the research is terminated at this point it is known as an ABA design. More often there will be a reinstitution of phase B as a vehicle for demonstrating that the behavioral change associated with the first shift from A to B reoccurs when such a shift is attempted on a second occasion. Thus, the ABAB design is somewhat more powerful than the ABA since it involves replicating the treatment effect.

Leitenberg (1973) refers to the above ABAB design as a *"withdrawal"* design because the second A phase is simply the discontinuance of the procedures instituted in phase B. The focus is thus upon a *single* clinically important behavior and what happens to it when an experimental treatment is imposed, withdrawn, and reimposed. A straightforward example of this ABAB withdrawal design would be to first obtain the base rate of quiet periods of one minute or longer in duration exhibited by a hyperactive child. Following this control phase A, phase B might consist of administering Ritalin while the frequency of quiet periods continues to be monitored. Ritalin would then be withdrawn during the second phase A, only to be readministered during a subsequent B phase. If the frequency of quiet periods is relatively high during both B phases, and is low during the two A phases, one has obtained convincing evidence that Ritalin is an effective behavior change agent for the child.

It is not unusual for the withdrawal design to be shortened so that the initial establishment of a base rate is neglected. This results in what may be designated as a BAB design. Another variation of withdrawal ABAB methodology is to apply its principles to a group of subjects who are involved simultaneously in the same experimental procedures. Both of these modifications are illustrated in research by Ayllon and Azrin (1965) in which they sought to demonstrate the efficacy of contigent token reinforcement as a controller of work behavior among 44 chronic backward psychiatric patients. They began by providing tokens to patients who engaged in small amounts of self-selected work assignments. The tokens were exchangeable for the opportunity to become involved in preferred activities, such as attending religious services, recreation, social interaction with staff, and tangible commissary items. It should be noted that by not first establishing the base rate of work activity, Ayllon and Azrin conducted a shortened design, which, in terms of our letter designations, would be a BAB. This is a common practice, although one which is less recommended than the complete ABAB design. During the first 20 day B phase, the total number of ward hours per day spent by the 44 patients in work activities averaged between 40 and 50. The withdrawal phase consisted of providing each patient with the average number of tokens he had earned per day during the first B phase, whether or not they had participated in the work activities. Thus, receipt of tokens was kept at a constant rate even though they no longer had to be earned. During this 20 day phase, the number of work hours per day dropped precipitously. By the tenth day the 44 patients totalled less than 10 work hours; when the 20 day withdrawal period concluded they were totalling only one or two work hours. However, when phase B conditions were reinstated there was an immediate increase in the amount of total work time to between 40 and 50 hours per day. Work performance by these patients was clearly under the control of contingent token reinforcement.

Reversal Design

A more complex variant of the ABAB design involves focusing on more than one behavior and using more than one treatment. The *reversal design* begins with establishing the base rate of one target behavior (A) and a second behavior (B) incompatible with the first. After a suitable base rate phase, experimental procedures are introduced which are designed to increase behavior A while at the same time decreasing behavior B. Assuming that this is accomplished, the efficacy of the treatment is tested by reversing the procedure during the next phase so that it is now geared toward decreasing A while increasing B. The final phase required that the procedures of the second phase be readministered.

Leitenberg refers to the above reversal procedures as a "base line ABA" design (1973, p.89). He cites a study conducted by Allen, Hart, Buell, Harris, and Wolf (1964) as providing an example of the reversal design. The research focused on a four year old nursery school girl who, after six weeks, persisted in seldom interacting with her peers. In fact, a five day base rate phase indicated that she spent only 10% of the time with children, as compared with 45% of the time interacting with adults in the nursery school. Allen and his associates believed that the staff was inadvertently supporting this peer-isolate behavior pattern by providing sympathetic attention whenever the girl was alone. Adult social contact, their expressions of concern, were apparently being offered contingent upon the child being by herself.

In order to experimentally test this hypothesis, the six day A phase of the research consisted of redirecting adult attention and praise so that it was offered contingent upon her interacting with peers. Coupled with this, every effort was made to ignore the girl when she was by herself or when she attempted to engage the attention of adults. Her behavior shifted dramatically. She was found now to spend only 15% of the time with adults and about 60% of the time with other children. To confirm that attention and ignoring were the behavior-controlling factors, the contingencies were reversed during the 5 day B phase of this experiment. Specifically, peer-isolate behavior by the young girl was met with attention by adults while any peer-oriented activities were ignored by the adult staff. As anticipated, the frequencies of the respective behaviors altered in accordance with the procedure reversal; peer interaction declined and isolate behavior increased, both returning to levels which approximated that of the base rate. As a final step in this base rate, ABA design, the procedure in effect during the initial A phase was again implemented and isolate/interactive behavior pattern previously induced reemerged.

Some attempts to conduct clear cut reversal designs may be impractical. These include treatments in which once the subject experiences phase B it is impossible to reinstate the psychological conditions existent during initial phase A. A phase B procedure involving the learning of new material could easily preclude the subject from returning to his pre-phase B naivete. Psychotherapeutic interventions frequently don't permit reversal designs on ethical grounds. For example, a behavior therapist might be able to reduce severe self-mutilating behavior by an autistic child while at the same time increasing the child's interpersonal responsiveness. It would be unethical for the therapist to reverse his procedures in an attempt to decrease social responsivity and increase self-mutilation.

Multiple Baseline Design

When an alternative to the powerful single subject reversal design is needed, the researcher may use a multiple baseline design in which the treatment whose efficacy is being evaluated is directed at several different target behaviors, one at a time, in the same situation.

The intent is to demonstrate that change occurs in that particular behavior to which the treatment is directed, and not in the other behaviors until the treatment is focused on them, in turn. This design was applied in an investigation of a retardate's mealtime habits conducted by Barton, Guess, Garcia, and Baer (1970). The goal was to determine whether removing the patient from the dining hall, a punishment, immediately subsequent to his manifesting a problem behavior, would serve to decrease the frequency of that behavior. This punishment procedure was employed for behaviors such as stealing food from others' dishes, pushing food off the dish, and eating food directly from a plate without using silverware. The results clearly indicated that each behavior remained at its baseline level until removal from the dining hall was contingently imposed with respect to it. Then, and only then, was there a decline in its frequency. Thus, the technique was shown to be a powerful inhibitor of unwanted behavior when used with the child in question. The possibility that factors other than the experimental treatment caused the results is extremely remote. Any confounding variable that might serve to reduce the frequency of inappropriate eating behavior would seemingly never have an impact in the same sequential manner as the experimental treatment.

Evaluation of single subject experimentation

There is no doubt that the strength of single subject designs lies in their usefulness for systematically exploring the effect of discrete variables upon specific subject behaviors. They therefore permit causal conclusions to be drawn without involving the labor of large sample, between-group experimental designs. However, the lack of random subject assignment to different comparison groups always leaves open the possibility that confounding factors are operating. This possibility is reduced in some of the more intricate designs, to be sure, but perhaps not to the degree that it is in a well-controlled traditional experimental design. It is because of these control limitations that Campbell and Stanley refer to such single subject experimental designs as the time series as "quasi-experimental." They remind us that threats to the internal validity of single subject experimental designs are minimized to the degree its operations can be conducted in "isolation," and under "constant conditions" (1963, p. 42). Of course, total isloation of real subjects from all relevant non-experimental influences represents an ideal which can be rarely achieved.

We have already mentioned that reversal and withdrawal procedures frequently preclude the conduct of single subject research with respect to certain variables. It is, for example, impossible to withdraw or reverse the effects of an obviously permanent therapeutic intervention such as a leucotomy, a surgical brain procedure. Similarly, if one tries to assess the impact of a parent-training program whch covers principles of behavior modification using the offspring's behavior as the criterion, it is quite impossible to withdraw the treatment by suggesting to the parent that she forget what she has been taught and revert to her previous manner of child rearing.

Single subject designs also seem to have been particularly targeted for criticism on ethical grounds. Complaints are heard that it is improper to withhold an effective treatment, or to try to reinstate earlier maladaptive behavior. There are also concerns expressed over whether the discontinuance of an effective treatment tends to make it more difficult to re-establish therapeutic progress. Leitenberg addressed this last point: "The rule seems to be that if a given therapeutic procedure had a beneficial effect once, when reinstated it will have this same effect again" (1973, p. 98). In general, there appears to be no well-grounded reason to fault single subject designs on these counts any more than to criticize traditional between-group experimentation. There is nothing intrinsic to single subject experimentation which renders it more or less ethical than any other form of treatment. It may be, however, that ethical concerns become more salient when researchers provide fictitious names for their subjects and report intimate case details. This might well tend to portray the subject of research in more human terms than is typical when results are reported in terms of groups, where the members have lost all individual identity.

In his own evaluations of single subject experimentation, Leitenberg feels that there are two criteria by which these designs must be judged. "Is the procedure replicable? Are the results replicable?" (1973, p. 99). It is replication which is so crucial to the scientific enterprise. In terms of procedural replication, single subject experimentation typically fares well. The experimental intervention or therapeutic procedure is almost invariably reported with meticulous detail. The use of vague terms and generalities is eschewed in favor of operational definitions and descriptions of change and outcome in terms of specific behavioral referents. In other words, the changes in frequency of a target behavior is greatly favored over impressionistic communications about patient improvement.

Replication of results is, of course, another matter. Single subject designs are in no way intrinsically less capable in this regard. Confidence in the accuracy of any experimental effect is always heightened when it is found to re-occur after using a new subject or a new group. The question of how many replications are necessary is quite unanswerable, but certainly, the more the better; few people are interested in an experimental effect which is valid for only one patient.

As a final note, Leitenberg asserts that single case experimentation can be extremely useful in studying the within-treatment changes and outcome aspects of most psychotherapies. He cautions that its usefulness is dependent upon elimination of confounding variables operating over the several experimental phases and reliance upon reliable, objective measurement of specific patient behaviors.

THE CASE STUDY

In our discussion of research designs we mentioned Campbell and Stanley's pre-experimental "one shot case study" (1963). In this completely uncontrolled design, observations are made of a single individual or a group who has previously been exposed to some treatment, either a naturally-occurring event or an imposed manipulation. Inferences regarding the relevance of the treatment are drawn, based upon intuitive notions about what would have been had the individual or group not been exposed to the treatment. The thrust of this design may appear to be one which rather sloppily attempts to explore whether a causal relationship exists between an independent and a dependent variable. In practice, the case study more often consists of a very detailed, total description of an individual patient's history and current status. It is common for psychiatry, clinical psychology, social work, and medicine to report in their professional journals accounts of unique or important case instances. The disciplines of anthropology and sociology also use case study material to further understanding of their respective academic domains. However, group behavior and social organization become the focus of exploration rather than the individual.

With respect to the study of personality, there are several purposes for which case study material may be particularly valuable, as outlined by Shontz (1965).

The remarkable case. Any practitioner's clientele is limited, mostly filled with routine cases and rarely includes that special individual who is remarkable either with respect to the clarity with which he manifests a diagnostic category or in terms of a personality structure which is exceedingly uncommon. The reporting of such cases, including all manner of clinical detail, serves to broaden the experimental base of those working in the field.

A number of years ago Thigpen and Cleckley (1954) reported a case in which the client, Eve White, had a multiple personality. Books and film popularized *The Three Faces of Eve*; but from a more scientific perspective, the case served to illustrate several aspects of personality functioning. More recently, Osgood, Luria, Jeans, and Smith (1976) wrote a series of articles describing the "Three Faces of Evelyn," another case of multiple personality which was discovered by Robert Jeans in the course of his clinical practice.

In December 1965, Gina, a 31 year old, single, professional writer was referred to the therapist by some of her friends because she behaved at times in ways which were "out of keeping with her usual business-like, efficient, and productive self" (p. 250). Somnambulism (sleepwalking) was reported by her roommate, as well as episodic periods of amnesia. The therapist's initial diagnosis was that of a mild *dissociative reaction*, a psychological condition in which aspects of personality unacceptable to the individual are dissociated, or kept apart, from the rest of the personality.

During the course of treatment, there emerged suggestions that Gina had a more feminine counterpart, Mary Sunshine. In contrast to Gina, Mary Sunshine was much "warmer, nicer, and more accepting. . ." (p. 252). The initial evidence for the existence of Mary Sunshine, about whom Gina could, at first, relate nothing, came from extra-therapy experiences. Specifically, even though neither Gina nor her roommate liked hot chocolate, frequently cups containing the residue of hot chocolate were found in the morning. Also, Gina's bank account was repeatedly but inexplicably depleted at month's end, even though she was earning a high income. In June, 1966 Gina brought her boyfriend to the therapist's office for an interview. Smith reports that a transformation from Gina to Mary Sunshine occurred directly in his presence. The client began the session "being her usual tough self and handing out insults liberally" (p. 252). As her boyfriend, T.C., began to talk, Gina's posture, facial expression, tone of voice, and comments underwent a dramatic alteration. The client now became warm and passive, responding "Of course. I know you do," with apparent conviction when T.C. expressed a deep caring for Gina (p. 252). This contrasted sharply with previous expressions in which she referred to her boyfriend with scorn, derision, and disgust for being involved in "frantic and possibly illegal business activities," (p. 252) and for not fulfilling promises to divorce his wife so he would be free to marry her.

Late in therapy Gina was able to communicate with Mary Sunshine through a method she called "inner conversations" (p. 254). This involved asking herself questions and accepting the answers which came to mind as being from Mary.

Through the reporting of such conversations, as well as dreams, to her therapist, it became evident that Mary was preparing for marriage to T.C. and Gina was becoming progressively exhausted and weak. In December 1966, an attempt at inner conversations resulted in the revelation of a third aspect of personality, Evelyn. Gina reported:

> I was lying in bed trying to go to sleep. Someone started to cry about T.C. I was sure that it was Mary. I started to talk to her. The person told me that she didn't have a name. Later she said that Mary called her Evelyn but that she didn't like that name. I asked her what she preferred to be called. She replied that she will decide later.

> I was suspicious at first that it was Mary pretending to be Evelyn. I changed my mind, however, because the person I talked to had too much sense to be Mary. She said that she realized that T.C. was unreliable but she still loved

him and was very lonely. She agreed that it would be best to find a reliable man.

She told me that she comes out once a day for a very short time to get used to the world. She promised that she will come out to see you sometime when she is stronger.

I asked her where Mary was. She said that Mary was so exhausted from designing her home that she had fallen asleep (pp. 254-255).

Robert Jeans reports that at about this time the client began to manifest rapid improvement. This was associated with Evelyn gaining information from Gina and Mary Sunshine and from her own accumulation of daily experiences. Jeans reports that Evelyn abandoned the striving, masculine orientation of Gina and the feminine, dependent character of Mary. Instead, she "adopted more mature ways of evaluating her situation and more flexible and adaptive ways of behaving in relation to it" (p. 255). Evelyn then began to date a more marriageable prospect and eventually terminated psychotherapy in May of 1967. She ultimately married a physician and, as of 1975, has manifested no recurrence of her symptoms.

Osgood and his co-authors (1976) remind us that we all have somewhat different personalities in different situations; we behave differently with friends than with family, for example. However, there is usually no dissociation as there was in the case of Evelyn; we are not amnesic about what occurs with our friends when we are with family. The authors go on to speculate that clinical cases of multiple personality may be exaggerated forms of role playing, with each role dissociated from the other(s) because they are so emotionally incongruent. However, it is suggested that there remains a real personality, aware of all its roles — in this case probably Evelyn. It is thought that the inner conversations which occurred had probably always been mediated by Evelyn. If Gina and Mary had been in direct communication, they would, by definition, not have been dissociated from each other as they evidently were.

This very brief outline does little justice to the wealth of material presented on the three faces of Evelyn. In its entirety, the case material provides a fund of information about the workings of a particular, quite remarkable personality that could hardly have been gleaned from tightly-controlled laboratory investigations of somnambulism, amnesia, and dissociation, assuming that such investigations are even possible to conduct.

Exemplifying or illustrating a point. It is not infrequent that the ideas and terms we encounter in psychology are so abstract or unfamiliar to us that the educational enterprise is served well by illustrating them via the provision of examples. Shontz believes that the case study is especially suited for this function. Many textbooks on psychopathology spend long paragraphs describing the defining characteristics of diagnostic categories such as manic-depression, schizophrenia, and infantile autism. In many cases, however, it is not until the author provides a case illustration of the diagnostic entity in question that the reader gains a deep appreciation of what is involved.

Salzinger, quoting an early case from Woods (1938, p. 303) offered the following material replete with neologisms (new words) to exemplify the speech patterns of some schizophrenics:

Patient: "I have seen you but your words alworthern."
Examiner: "What does *alworthern* mean?"
Patient: "Ashens. Guiding the circumfrax."
Examiner: "What does alworthern mean?"
Patient: "Alworthern? Al - " (seems to be thinking).
Examiner: "Can you tell me what love is?"
Patient: "Love? Gians . . . vitrous of the vein and rhenebal
                of wehlein."

                                                        (1973, p. 66)

There can be no doubt that students of dissociative reactions will be more enlightened regarding the quality of multiple personality by reading the case material presented by Osgood (1976) on the three faces of Evelyn than they would by simply going over a purely didactic presentation of the concepts involved.

Demonstration of a technique. In order to effectively communicate the nature of a personality assessment or psychotherapeutic procedure it is frequently best to describe its operations within the context of real case material. Books on Rorschach inkblot administration and interpretation are filled with case material illustrating various practical and theoretical points. Similarly, the manuals of standardized individual intelligence tests, while spelling out the principles involved in the assignment of 0, 1, or 2 points for answers to particular test questions or items, invariably illustrate the principles by providing actual subject responses.

Carl Rogers was probably the first clinical psychologist to employ audiotapes of his psychotherapy sessions for the purpose of training others in the use of his "client-centered" procedures. Today, it is common practice for case material to be used in the training of psychotherapists. Frequently, the therapy sessions conducted by the trainees, under the supervision of a qualified professional, are either audio or videotaped. Their playback then serves as a vehicle for improving the interpersonal sensitivity and technical sophistication of the trainee.

Surveys. Public opinion polls and television rating services essentially collect case study material from large samples of subjects in order to discern general trends. Clearly, in these cases the data collected focuses upon a particular, very narrow aspect of personality, such as attitudes toward a defined event, rather than upon the fully-functioning individual. When surveys become very detailed they begin to approximate case study material. As an illustration of this, consider the work of Cumming and Cumming (1965). They explored the stigma of mental illness by surveying 22 consecutively discharged psychiatric patients and their families. The authors discovered two kinds of evidence suggesting that those with a history of mental illness are stigmatized. First, there are expressions of inferiority and shame over the hospitalization. A wife was reported to have said, "My children think he is just lazy. Of course, because of the kind of hospital he was in, the union probably didn't think it was a proper thing to help him financially." This was followed by the former patient's daughter saying, "It was hard when he came home because there was all those stories in the paper about crimes and they always turned out to be done by former mental patients." (p. 138).

The second evidence for stigmatization came from stated expectations for discrimination and inferior treatment from others. These concerns were couched in remarks such as "I didn't want anyone to know that I was in a mental hospital and call me crazy" (p. 138).

Of the twenty-two patients, nine, or 41%, were found to experience their psychiatric history as stigmatizing; four expressed some form of shame and nine revealed an expectation of discrimination.

Establishing a data pool. Sometimes a researcher may be interested in the investigation of a phenomenon but is not able to definitively specify the particular variables of concern. In these situations a strategy may be adopted in which masses of case data are collected for possible later use.

As an example of this, Mednick and his co-workers began a project in the late 1960s whose general focus was on discovering the factors which may be used to predict future development of schizophrenia. They used as subjects the children of schizophrenic mothers, these offspring being statistically at high-risk levels for schizophrenia. The investigation started by gaining detailed case material from the high-risk offspring through the use of a wide array of assessment devices. In addition, equivalent material was obtained from a sample of control children who had normal mothers.

As members of the high-risk group become deviant, their performance on the previously-administered tests is compared with that of non-deviant control subjects. In this way it is hoped that differences between normal subjects and children who are not yet, but who will become, sick can be discovered.

To date, there have been two important findings (Garmezy, 1974). First, it appears that the deviant subjects, well prior to becoming manifestly ill, exhibited atypical galvanic skin response (GSR) patterns. Specifically, their GSRs returned unusually quickly to basal level; they showed a faster response subsequent to the presentation of an eliciting stimulus by having very brief latencies; and, with repeated exposure to an eliciting stimulus, they did not manifest increased latency of responding, habituation. The second major discovery has been the unusually high rate of pregnancy and birth complications (PBCs) experienced by the high-risk children who ultimately became psychiatrically sick. In fact, 70% of these subjects went through some sort of PBC, including anoxia (lack of oxygen), prematurity, prolonged labor, placental difficulty, umbilical cord complications, multiple birth, maternal illness during pregnancy, and breech delivery; only 15% of the high-risk children who have not become psychiatrically ill and 33% of the control children were exposed to such circumstances. Theoretical interpretations of these data are currently being discussed in the literature (Kessler & Neale, 1974).

Challenging current theory. Shontz (1965) points out that a case study may be used as a *negative instance*, one which discredits a theory because it either contradicts its tenets or falls outside its realm of explanation.

Classical psychoanalytic theory views the symptoms of psychopathology as being the products of unconscious conflicts. From this perspective, the symptom which usually brings the patient in for psychotherapy is merely the outward sign of a deeper maladjustment. In this tradition, Hutt and Gibby (1957) write:

> Often we may remove symptoms very readily without at all correcting the underlying personality disturbances. To remove the symptom in this manner does not necessarily help the person, as he may often develop different sets of symptoms to enable him to deal with his particular problem. . . .
> (p. 78)

According to an hypothesis logically derived from Freud's theories, if a therapist focuses merely on symptom removal, the purpose served by that symptom will be met by the development of a new maladaptive expression. This alleged phenomenon has been referred to as *symptom substitution*.

Over the past twenty years numerous case studies of symptom removal through the use of behavior therapeutic techniques have been reported, with little or no evidence of these symptomatic successes being marred by the subsequent development of substitute pathology. Investigations have reported the rate of anything resembling substitution as being from zero to, at most, 5%. It appears then that when therapy is aimed at, and succeeds in, eliminating specific, target symptoms, "symptom substitution is the exception and not the rule," to quote Ullman and Krasner (1969, p. 158). On this basis, some behavior therapists chide psychoanalytic theory as being inadequate, asserting that in those few instances in which patients do manifest a succession of maladaptive behaviors explanations in terms of learned habits are more reasonable and parsimonious than those deduced from psychoanalytic theory.

Confirming current theory. Freud commonly resorted to the case study in order to establish the validity of his developing personality theory. One of his best known cases, that of Little Hans (1955b) which was first published in 1909, was used as the vehicle for popularizing the notion of childhood sexuality, a core principle in psychoanalytic theory.

Shontz reminds us that no single case study by itself can ever serve to establish a theory. However, the repeated disclosure of cases consistent with what is theoretically proposed can increase one's confidence in the message. Strict cautions must always be observed, for sheer quantity of report can never substitute for quality.

The Malleus Maleficarum, a document written in the late 15th century, stands as a marked warning against the imprudence of relying exclusively on case study material. This treatise, written by Henry Kramer and James Sprenger, detailed how to discover,

interrogate, torture, and punish witches. It included an appraisal of the nature, behavior, and influence of witches. The authors accumulated a mass of case study data in
support of their propositions, which semed to be irrefutable to those already predisposed to believe in the presence of witches. The religious motives and scholarly
abilities of Kramer and Sprenger resulted in the deaths of thousands of innocents,
weeded out and dealt with in accordance with their authoritative publication.

Internal and External Validity of Case Studies

The merit of case study material, as with any research method, rests in its internal
and external validity. The criteria for judging these kinds of validity must necessarily be
somewhat different from those used to evaluate experimental research. Nevertheless,
the basic issues are the same.

With respect to internal validity, it is incumbent upon the writer of a case study to
provide evidence that as little bias as possible was operating during the accumulation,
condensation, and interpretation of data. In this regard, Freud has been heavily
criticized. He saw his clients throughout the day and it was not until evening that he
typically found time to reflect upon the day's events and to record what seemed to be
the important particulars. Such a retrospective procedure can easily fall prey to
selective forgetting and recall, resulting in distortions of content which seems to fulfill
the prophesies of theoretical speculation.

In order to reduce bias, Shontz suggests that the reporting of case material be as
explicit as possible. There should be heavy reliance upon the collection and con-
veyance of information in a standardized and objective way. One way to accomplish
this is to simply record all that happens; the raw data is then part of the public record.
The obvious difficulty with this approach is that the communication of the case takes as
long as the case itself did, a highly inefficient system. Short of this, writing significant
therapeutic events immediately subsequent to a session, using trained observers to
record or rate the occurrence of clearly defined behavioral phenomena, and reporting
objectively arrived at scores through the use of standardized personality tests have
been some of the methods employed in recent decades to improve the internal validity
of case study material.

In the previously discussed "Three Faces of Evelyn," reported by Osgood and his
colleagues (1976), the explicitness of the case was greatly enhanced by having the
client complete a personality test at a time, late in therapy, when there was access to all
three major personalities — Gina, Mary Sunshine, and Evelyn. The test format used
was a *semantic differential*. This consisted of presenting each of the three personalities
with a number of concepts, such as my mother, me, sex, confusion and my spouse as
well as with the names of certain significant people in the client's life. Each concept was
then rated on ten scales of seven points each, defined by the following polar opposites:
valuable — worthless, clean — dirty, tasty — tasteless, large — small, strong — weak,
deep — shallow, fast — slow, active — passive, hot — cold, and relaxed — tense. For

example, Gina, Mary Sunshine, and Evelyn all had to rate "my father" with a check somewhere on the seven point scale of clean — dirty. Osgood reports that the intrapersonality test — retest correlations were always above +.95, while the interpersonality correlations ranged from +.23 to +.31. These data attest to the differential way in which the three personalities responded to the test material and thereby provide independent evidence for the existence of a multiple personality. In addition, they suggest that each personality was in itself a stable aspect of personality.

By further analyzing the correlational data, Osgood, Luria, and Smith were able to construct a very detailed personality analysis of the case in question. They did this blindly, that is without ever obtaining any information about the client beyond her actual responses to the semantic differential administered by her therapist, Robert Jeans. In reacting to this blind analysis, Jeans comments that it was "remarkably accurate in most instances. For example, the predictions about ethnic, economic, and family structure were strikingly close" (p. 271). Jeans also writes that, "I am glad the blind analysis reveals Evelyn to be a fusion of Gina and Mary. This confirms my view of what happens in the successful treatment of a case of multiple personality. The prejudice of each ego against the other is made weaker and weaker until the barriers between them disappear and the individual becomes psychologically whole again" (p. 274). Such an interpretation by Jeans concerning the outcome of his successful treatment could easily have been included in a report based solely upon his own observations. He undoubtedly could have provided considerable anecdotal evidence in support of his view. The fact that the same judgment was independently arrived at through utilization of a semantic differential analysis by objective personnel makes the assertion one which, in Shontz's terms, is much more explicit and, therefore, more scientifically acceptable.

In so far as the external validity of case study material is concerned, the issue of representativeness is crucial. Frequently a case study is published because it serves to validate a point of view held by the particular author. There is no telling how many cases are discarded for failing to substantiate the position being held before one is selected for presentation because it is consistent with the author's point of view. If the position is one which is alleged to have general applicability, defending its validity through the use of an atypical case report is grossly misleading.

SUMMARY

Single subject investigations were divided into those which are designed with control procedures in mind, single subject experimental designs, and those in which very careful and complete explorations of a given personality are conducted, case studies. The former category includes time series variations of the ABAB designs, and multiple base line designs. The various applications of case study research were presented. Issues pertaining to the validity of single subject investigations were raised.

TERMS TO KNOW

CHAPTER 7
Ethics of Research

Psychologists, like all scientists, have the obligation to further knowledge by carrying "forward their research as well as they know how" (APA, 1973, p. 7). Obviously, progress is facilitated by research which has immediate application. However, rarely does one investigation in itself have any meaningful scientific impact. The final outcome usually is unclear. Consequently, it is quite legitimate for most scientists to invest themselves in research enterprises which have no obvious relevance for great theoretical or practical advancement.

Psychologists who are involved in research employing human subjects are in a rather special position; one which does not permit them to cast aside the issue of potential gain from their investigatory pursuits. From a purely scientific perspective, the best research frequently is one which in a variety of ways compromises ethical obligation to the human participants; the researcher must decide whether it is justifiable to proceed. The judgment is based upon weighing the cost to the individual human subjects against the benefit to society which the research may be expected to yield. It is an extremely difficult decision to reach in many cases because, as indicated, one cannot usually anticipate with any degree of accuracy what sort of gain might be reasonable to expect from a given research effort. Furthermore, the cost to the subject is not easily ascertained. It may range from nothing, in cases where subjects leave an experiment happy, better informed, and willing to participate again, to severe in instances where subjects are psychologically or physically abused and depart from the laboratory after having been inflicted with a permanent change for the worse.

APA ETHICAL PRINCIPLES

In December, 1972, in order to provide some framework from which to deliberate on these very important matters, the Council of Representatives of the American Psychological Association (APA) adopted ten ethical principles as a guide to those choosing to conduct human psychological research. These points were incorporated into *Ethical Principles in the Conduct of Research with Human Participants,* published by the APA in 1973. If there is an overriding theme to these principles it is that "psychologists may carry out their investigations with respect for the people who participate and with concern for their dignity and welfare" (APA, 1973, p.1). This chapter is devoted primarily to presenting and discussing the ten principles.

Accountability

The first two principles serve as a strong reminder to any investigator that he is held accountable if complaints are raised against his research practice.

> Principle 1. In planning a study the investigator has the personal responsibility to make a careful evaluation of its ethical acceptability, taking into account these Principles for research with human beings. To the extent that this appraisal, weighing scientific and humane values, suggests a deviation from any principle, the investigator incurs an increasingly serious obligation to seek ethical advice and to observe more stringent safeguards to protect the rights of the human research participant (APA, 1973, p.1).

> Principle 2. Responsibility for the establishment and maintenance of acceptable ethical practice in research always remains with the individual investigator. The investigator is also responsible for the ethical treatment of research participants by collaborators, assistants, students, and employees, all of whom, however, incur parallel obligations (APA, 1973, p.1).

The decision to proceed with or abandon any research rests squarely on the shoulders of the principle investigator. Assistance in making this decision can come from any legitimate source. In particular, the Council suggests that preliminary, *pilot* studies may be valuable. The goal of pilot work is to carefully assess the impact, both positive and negative, of the research procedures upon a small number of participants. Such an effort may go a long way toward either laying to rest or confirming one's worst suspicions. Where pilot work does expose aspects of the procedure to be inductive of anxiety, dehumanization, or pain, the researcher is at least forewarned and in a position to modify his practices so that these consequences can be avoided.

Because some of the benefits of research have less to do with advancement of knowledge or practical application than with enhancing the investigator's own professional career and financial situation, the Council realized that researchers should not rely on their own possibly biased reasoning in these matters, especially in questionable cases. They strongly recommend that the advice of others be sought, including that of colleagues, clergymen or lawyers when appropriate, and of individuals who are representatives of the group who will be asked to serve as subjects, such as Introductory Psychology students, psychiatric patients, etc.

Informed Consent

The next two principles have to do with the frequently encountered ethical issues of informed consent and deception.

> Principle 3. Ethical practice requires the investigator to inform the participant of all features of the research that reasonably might be expected to influence willingness to participate, and explain all other aspects of the search about which the participant inquires. Failure to make full disclosure gives added emphasis to the investigators responsibility to protect the welfare and dignity of the research participant (APA, 1973, p.1).

It is quite clear that the ideal situation is one in which the subjects are fully appraised of all relevant details and can, therefore, give or withhold consent on an informed basis. Unfortunately, strict compliance with this ethical ideal may be impossible because of the limited ability of subjects to comprehend the technical nuances of what is being done. In addition, uncompromising adherence to full disclosure would render much research data valueless. For example, if a subject knows which aspects of his behavior are being monitored for use as a dependent variable, the data collection process becomes prone to sources of error which are introduced by subject reactivity.

We have previously discussed research designs employing non-reactive observational techniques. Frequently, such projects are conducted so that subjects never become aware of their participation in a scientific endeavor. For example, an investigator may engage in unobtrusively observing public behavior, perhaps relating age, sex, or race to the probability of crossing a street in the face of a "Don't Walk" sign. While this procedure violates the principle of informed consent, it may not abuse the subjects.

Covert observation becomes more questionable when the researcher invades the private domain of unknowing subjects. As the Council notes, "The boundary between drawing on one's everyday experience and spying is a narrow one" (1973, p. 32). For example, a student researcher interested in the behavior of faculty toward students of different races may quietly keep track of the frequency, length, and quality of in-class communications from the teacher to both black and white classmates. A more extreme example of covert observation in private situations was reported by Humphreys (1970) who sought to investigate the behavior of male homosexuals in public washrooms. In order to do this, Humphreys elected to serve as a "lookout" for homosexuals engaging in consenting relationships. The subjects of this study were not privy to the true identity or purposes of the investigator, nor did they realize that records were kept of their automobile license plates so that they might later be identified in order to gain background information. Critics of this research were vigorous in their opposition to such practices; others felt that the importance of the material being researched and the impossibility of obtaining valid data in any less devious manner legitimized Humphreys' research design.

Lack of informed consent from subjects also becomes more questionable when the naturally ongoing process under study — whatever it might be — is interfered with. This occurs typically in the conduct of disguised field experimentation where the investigator arranges or manipulates events to which naive subjects react. Doob and Gross (1968) reported one such experiment where one of two automobiles was driven up to an intersection controlled by a traffic signal. The driver prepared to delay starting his vehicle after the light had turned green for 15 seconds, or until the driver behind had honked twice. The subjects consisted of 26 men and 56 women drivers whose progress was slowed by the experimental car. The independent variable in this research was the status of the car, either a late model, black, highly-polished Chrysler Imperial or a grey, older Rambler. The dependent measures included number, length, and latency of the honks from the delayed driver. The sex and estimated age of the subject driver was also noted. The results clearly showed that car status had an inhibitory effect on honking. Specifically, in the low status condition 84% of the subjects honked at least once, whereas only 50% of the drivers honked at the Imperial. This difference was significant at the $p < .01$ level. The inhibitory impact of a high status automobile was also reflected in the latency measures; it took subjects an average of 7.2 and 9.7 seconds to honk when behind the Rambler and Chrysler, respectively. Sex of the driver was also a significant predictor of honking behavior, with men tending to honk faster than women in both status conditions.

It might be argued that this experiment does not involve high ethical cost, even though informed consent was not obtained. "Neither the anonymity nor the personal dignity of the participant is violated, and patience is only trivially imposed upon" (1973, p. 33). Even so, it would have been ethically sounder, as well as easier, for the experimenters to have obtained their data by simply asking a group of consenting subjects how they would react under the circumstances staged. In fact, Doob and Gross decided to do just that. Fifty-seven Introductory Psychology students received a questionnaire: "You are stopped at a traffic light behind a black, 1966 Chrysler (or a gray, 1961 Rambler). The light turns green and for no apparent reason the driver does not go on. Would you honk at him?" Those subjects who decided that they actually would honk in the depicted situation were also asked to indicate how long they thought they would wait before doing so, from one to fourteen seconds.

Unlike the field experiment, the questionnaire data revealed no tendency for the high status automobile to have a generally inhibiting effect on honking behavior. Eleven of the 57 subjects indicated they would not honk, six in the low status and five in the high status condition. However, all six of the subjects who claimed they would not honk when delayed by a Rambler were males; the five who said they would not honk when behind a Chrysler were all females. With respect to latency scores, males claimed they would honk sooner at the Chrysler (Mean = 5.5 seconds) than at the Rambler (Mean = 5.5 seconds); this significant trend was slightly reversed for females.

Doob and Gross are forced to conclude that "the behavior reported in the questionnaire is different from the behavior actually observed in the field" (p. 217). It might be argued that the questionnaire data is a valid representation of what would have been directly observed had the students actually participated in the field experiment. That is, the difference found between the two parts of this research may not be due to the differences in the method of data collection but to disparate samples. One test of this notion was conducted by analyzing the field experiment data obtained from the younger drivers (about 16 to 30 years old) who most closely approximated the questionnaire subjects in age. Unlike the allegations contained in the student responses, it was found that this young sub-group of drivers took significantly longer to honk at the high status Chrysler than at the Rambler. Findings such as these cause researchers to defend using non-consenting subjects in unobtrusive field experiments. Their claim is that reactive laboratory data obtained in "as-if" settings are too often distortions of reality.

Deception

So far illustrations of the informed consent point have focused upon the withholding of information pertinent to the research, including information to the subject regarding his status as an object of scientific scrutiny. More serious are situations in which informed consent becomes impossible because the nature of an experiment is misrepresented to subjects. On this matter, the Council writes:

> Principle 4. Openness and honesty are essential characteristics of the relationship between investigator and research participant. When the methodological requirements of a study necessitate concealment or deception, the investigator is required to ensure the participant's understanding of the reasons for this action and to restore the quality of the relationship with the investigator (APA, 1973, p.1).

There are some circumstances in which such use of deliberate lying may be acceptable. These include situations where the research is exploring an area of great importance; the goals of the research may not be realized unless deception is incorporated into its design; the reason for deception is so compelling that a subject, upon learning of the deceit, would find it reasonable and experience no loss of confidence in the investigator; the participants experience free license to withdraw at any time and to withhold their data subsequent to learning of the deception; and the investigator takes steps to detect and remove negative after-effects.

The Council was unable to offer clear guidelines, acceptable to all, regarding the use of deception. However, it is clear that when deception is used as an integral part of research design it may present fewer problems than when it is employed to obtain agreement from subjects to participate. A field experiment by Farina, Hagelaver, and Holzberg (1976) investigating whether physicians treat former psychiatric patients systematically differently from normal patients used deception to gain subject involvement. A 23 year old college student, complaining of stomach pains, arranged for appointments with 32 different medical practitioners. In half of his medical examinations the pseudo-patient claimed that the onset of symptoms had occurred nine months earlier while he was traveling; the remaining 16 physicians were led to believe that the symptoms first appeared nine months earlier when the patient was alleged to have been in a psychiatric hospital. In general physicians were found to deal with the patient in a similar fashion regardless of the reported psychiatric history.

It is clear that this research involves a deception which may be the ingredient responsible for active participation by many of the subject physicians. One can only guess how many would have refused to participate in a survey bearing on differential medical treatment they might offer a patient having a psychiatric history. In addition, it is reasonable to judge that the physicians were more than trivially imposed upon. True, they received routine monetary compensation for their effort; but in the process they were being deprived of the opportunity to treat legitimate patients with more sincerely felt medical needs. Thus, the negative impact of this design might have spread to individuals not even directly involved in the research.

Arguments supporting the conduct of the Farina experiment are not difficult to present. Every year about 2,000,000 people receive treatment in our psychiatric facilities. The evidence is clear in showing that these ex-patients are looked upon with disfavor by the general public in a variety of ways. Nunnally (1961, pp. 90-106) revealed that physicians hold unfavorable opinions and beliefs about former psychiatric patients which are not at variance with those of the larger society. The question of whether such a negative position translates into inferior medical care is undoubtedly an important one and worthy of careful examination.

Aside from ethical considerations, deceptions have been criticized as a research procedure on the grounds that one cannot be certain who is being deceived. It is rarely possible to ascertain which subjects have seen through the facade. Ring (1967) warns those who routinely use deceptive research strategies that the price "may be the creation of extremely mistrustful and hostile subject pools" (p. 118). The problem may be particularly acute on college campuses where it becomes common knowledge that "all experiments are put-ons." Attempts by researchers to keep the lid on what's happening by asking subjects not to tell their friends after debriefing them are probably futile gestures at best.

Ring, and others (Kelman, 1967; Schultz, 1969) have contended that a viable alternative to deceptions is role playing. This would involve revealing the experimental manipulations, asking the subjects to adopt appropriate roles, and requesting that they carry out whatever tasks are assigned to them within the context of those roles. Thus, if a researcher were interested in the effect of failure on responses to a mood check list, the subject would be told to complete the check list as if he had just been given feedback that he had done extremely poorly in an achievement test. It is felt that by requesting subjects to become active participants in a joint venture in data collection they will be responsive to the directives, not behaving as they think the experimenter may want but as they really would had they actually experienced failure. In essence, the approach is summarized by Farber's (1963) statement, "The best way of investigating the nature of man is to ask him" (p. 227).

Aronson & Carlsmith (1968) are in opposition to the use of role playing on the grounds that it simply lacks realism. It can, therefore, not serve as a substitute for spontaneous behavior provoked by actually experienced perceptions and feelings, even if these perceptions and feelings are based upon non-veridical stimuli.

There have been a few empirical tests of role playing as a substitute for deception. In one such investigation, Horowitz and Rothschild (1970) compared two levels of role playing with deception, using as their paradigm an Asch-type conformity experiment. Some years earlier Asch (1952) had taken a real subject and placed him within a small group of other subjects, who were really confederates of the investigator. The confederates had been pre-instructed to unanimously express incorrect judgments at pre-planned points during a series of visual judgment tasks concerning which of three different length lines was equal in length to a standard line. The goal was to see if the genuine subject, who was always last in expressing a judgment, would yield to the group by answering in a way which his senses revealed to be incorrect or whether he would remain a non-conformist by calling them as they were seen. Asch found that if the group consisted of only the real subject and one confederate, no conformity behavior was manifested. When two confederates expressed incorrect judgments there was an appreciable degree of conformity displayed subsequently by the subject. When three or more confederates were employed the real subject agreed with the incorrect group consensus a high percentage of the time. They selected lines as being equal to the standard which were so discrepant that any subject not burdened by group pressure would never have chosen them.

Horowitz and Rothschild replicated this deception design but added two additional conditions. In one, the real subject was advised that the experiment was fake and that he was to play the role of a naive subject (the *forewarned* role playing group). The second role play condition consisted of telling the real subject virtually everything about the experiment (the *pre-briefed* role playing group). It was found that the forewarned variant produced results quite similar to the standard deception procedure. There was a high level of conformity in both conditions. The problem is that one has little idea as to why the forewarned subjects conformed as they did. Miller suggests that any of three factors could be operating: despite the forewarning they remained naive to the nature of the deception and so were no more impervious to group pressure than subjects in the deception group; they consciously tried to avoid penetrating the deception and "bent over backward" in an effort to remain naive; or "they penetrated the deception of the Asch paradigm, but because of their positive (cooperative) attitude toward the experimenter, they gave him the conformity behavior they knew he had hypothesized" (1972, p. 629). The real subjects in the pre-briefed condition, unlike deceived subjects, showed very little conformity. In addition, their level of conformity did not increase with group size as it did with the deceived subjects.

Thus, one role play group produced results similar to deceived subjects, but for reasons which are not entirely clear; the second, completely informed, role play group did not yield data comparable with that of subjects who are deceived. This is particularly important because Horowitz and Rothschild's pre-briefed subjects, who were actively and openly made privy to the design and purposes of the study, were most like the hypothetical subjects discussed by Ring and others who advocate role playing as an alternative to deception. In summary, on the basis of this and other empirical evidence, Miller comes to the conclusion that "the prospects for role playing as an alternative to deception are poor . . . deception . . . remains as the methodology of choice for a considerable proportion of psychological research. Whether or not this proves viable in the long run is the question — one that should be asked continuously" (1972, p. 634).

Menges (1973) surveyed all the research articles published in five widely read American Psychological Association journals: the *Journal of Personality and Social Psychology,* the *Journal of Abnormal Psychology,* the *Journal of Educational Psychology,* the *Journal of Counseling Psychology,* and the *Journal of Experimental Psychology.* He found that in 17% of the studies the subjects received inaccurate information about the independent variable, and in 80% of the studies the information given was incomplete. Subjects were fully informed as to the major independent variables in only 3% of the investigations surveyed. There was somewhat less deception surrounding dependent variables, with complete information being provided in 21% of the cases. However, there was still only incomplete information about the dependent variable provided in 75% of the studies and in 4% of the research reported inaccurate information was given to subjects. Thus, in terms of what psychological researchers are actually doing, it appears that deception of one sort or another is routine.

Right to non-participation

The fifth principle for ethical research has to do with the right of subjects to refuse to participate.

> Principle 5. Ethical research practice requires the investigator to respect the individual's freedom to decline to participate in research or to discontinue participation at any time. The obligation to protect this freedom requires special vigilance when the investigator is in a position of power over the participant. The decision to limit this freedom increases the investigator's responsibility to protect the participant's dignity and welfare. (APA, 1973, p. 2)

There are a variety of circumstances in which the subject's freedom to "back out" is ostensibly unhindered but, in practice, is actually quite imposed upon. For example, many universities employ subject pools consisting of all Introductory Psychology students. It takes a special student to resist the pressures imposed, perhaps by his own instructor, for full cooperation. In order to avoid appearing too coercive, some departments permit students to engage in other prescribed activity as a substitute for research participation. Unfortunately, the options available, usually the production of a term paper, are often more aversive than that of being a subject. Thus, for most students, the choices offered are more apparent than real.

Equally important to the issue of freedom to refuse is the right of subjects to change their minds after first agreeing to participate. In an experiment designed to study human obedience to authority, Milgrim solicited subjects by newspaper advertising and direct mail. Potential subjects were told they would receive $4.50 for showing up at the laboratory, and "that the money was theirs no matter what happened after they arrived" (1963, p. 372). It can be argued that once a subject agrees to accept monetary compensation he may feel a moral obligation to fulfill whatever demands are then imposed. It is as if subjects sell their soul to the investigator and while, strictly speaking, they retain license to renege on the bargain, they rarely rise to the occasion no matter how unpleasant the experimental circumstances. In fact, Milgrim required his subjects to inflict what they believed to be painful levels of shock upon other individuals. When a subject expressed unwillingness to continue, the experimenter responded with a sequence of prods, using as many as necessary to induce the subject to continue administering shocks.

>Prod 1:   Please continue or Please go on.
>Prod 2:   The experiment requires that you continue.
>Prod 3:   It is absolutely essential that you continue.
>Prod 4:   You have no choice, you *must* go on.
>(p. 374)

Despite the nature of their task, 26 of Milgrim's 40 subjects persisted, as per instructions, to continually raise the intensity with each successive administration of shock. They gradually went through 30 lever switches on a shock generator, labeled from "Slight Shock" (15 volts) through "Very Strong Shock" (195 volts), past "Danger: Severe Shock" (375 volts) to "XXX" (450 volts).

Milgrim's research demonstrates that a scientific investigator, housed in a laboratory, and under the auspices of a prestigious university, can impose an almost incredible degree of control over the will of otherwise normally assertive subjects. At the very least, his findings should sensitize researchers to the necessity of "going overboard" in communicating the legitimacy of dropping out any time to their captive subjects. This experiment on obedience by Milgrim was one which provoked considerable debate over ethical issues in psychological research. We will come back to it several times in discussing other ethical issues.

Exploitation

The sixth ethical principle overlaps some of the previously mentioned points. It is concerned with the establishment of a fair relationship between experimenter and subjects, one that is free from exploitation of the subject by the investigator.

>Principle 6. Ethically acceptable research begins with the establishment of a clear and fair agreement between the investigator and the research participant that clarifies the responsibilities of each. The investigator has the obligation to honor all promises and commitments included in that agreement. (APA, 1973, p. 2)

The Council acknowledges that there are difficulties in trying to establish what is a fair bargain from the subject's perspective. On the one hand they are asked to give up time and, often, freedom to endure boredom, physical and/or mental stress, or a loss of privacy. This may be counter-balanced by financial compensation, increased self-knowledge, an understanding of the problem being investigated and the procedures being used, and satisfaction in the belief that science is being advanced and/or social problems are being solved. Obviously, in order to judge whether the contract being offered by the experimenter is a fair one, a subject must be completely informed regarding the nature and intent of the research and be free from coercive forces.

The common practice of using Introductory Psychology subject pools on college campuses is once again relevant. Frequently, students are heard to complain that their participation in research is irrelevant to the course material. The Council expressed the opinion that, for most psychology students, a well prepared post-experimental explanation can serve as a reasonable educational experience. This would be consistent with the students' general interest in psychology, even if it did not coincide exactly with the content of their classes. When non-psychology classes become part of a subject pool, greater effort has to be exerted by the experimenter in order to guarantee that the importance of his research legitimizes the use of possibly disinterested subjects.

Another critical problem area covered by this principle has to do with the enlistment of subject services through the exploitation of unusual needs. For example, destitute psychiatric patients or prisoners may be tempted to participate in a stressful experiment by the promise of a paltry sum, or even for a pack of cigarettes. While there is nothing inherently improper in offering money to such groups in exchange for research participation, the investigator should be cognizant that an expression of agreement does not necessarily suggest free consent (APA, p. 56). In these instances, the bargain may not truly be a fair one.

Stress

The Council's seventh ethical principle addresses the issue of subjects being placed under either physical or mental stress. Obviously, "responsible investigators would not expose research participants to actual or potential physical or mental harm if there were not a serious reason for doing so" (1973, p. 58).

> Principle 7. The ethical investigator protects participants from physical and mental discomfort, harm and danger. If the risk of such consequences exists, the investigator is required to inform the participant of that fact, secure consent before proceeding, and take all possible measures to minimize stress. A research procedure may not be used if it is likely to cause serious and lasting harm to participants. (APA, 1973, p. 2)

Physical Stress. A variety of research programs involve the infliction of considerable physical discomfort to subjects. These studies may be directly investigating the consequences of painful circumstances such as food deprivation, shock, or loud noise.

Other research employs discomforting procedures only incidentally, possibly requiring a subject to submit a blood sample, an experience which while tolerable to most can be extremely stressful to a few. In any case, under these circumstances the previously discussed principles regarding informed consent and freedom to end participation at any point are especially important to maintain rigorously.

In recent years there has been considerable psychotherapy research concerned with evaluating the utility of aversive stimulation for the relief of severe maladaptive behavior. The general paradigm is to make an aversive consequence, typically shock, contingent upon the subject eliciting the maladaptive response. Romanczyk and Goren reported a case study in which a boy, Peter, age 6½, was referred to the psychological clinic at Rutgers University. His behavior was characterized by extreme social isolation, retardation, and lack of speech. However, Peter's most severe symptom was extreme self-injurious behavior which had "worsened to the point where total restraint was required" (1975, p. 731). He had inflicted single blows to himself of magnitudes requiring immediate hospitalization. The situation was discussed with Peter's parents, who consented to the use of response-contingent electric shock as a possible vehicle to quickly suppress this self-injurious pattern.

The procedure involved the use of a hand-held inductorium which delivered an "extremely painful electric shock (average output 15mA at 500V) that was localized at the point of contact" (p. 732). Only two one minute baseline sessions were held in which one of Peter's hands was left unrestrained. "The initial rate of self-injurious behavior was approximately 5,400 hits per hour, or 1-2/sec. The intensity of these blows . . . was sufficient that redness was apparent on the face after two or three blows, and bleeding was seen after 10-15 sec" (p. 732). There was a dramatic decrease in their frequency almost immediately after shock began to be delivered subsequent to each blow. However, the rate remained at about 300 blows per hour over the six 20 minute treatment sessions.

Because this frequency was still dangerous, alterations in the manner of shock delivery were made. In the initial phase of treatment, the therapist had to reach over and make contact in order to shock Peter. There was, therefore, a time interval between Peter's self-destructive responses and his receipt of aversive stimulation. In order to minimize this interval, electrodes were attached directly to the wrist of the free hand. At first Peter was permitted to make only one self-injurious response, for which he received immediate shock followed by complete restraint for five minutes. He had 12 such sessions, each consisting of seven trials (self-destructive response — receipt of shock) per session. During these sessions there was a noticeable increase in the latency of hits from the time he was released from restraint. Also, the intensity of blows decreased. The therapist then reverted to the use of contingencies similar to those employed in the initial phase. Response was no longer prevented and each time Peter began to raise his hand shock was administered, so that its delivery actually preceded the blow making contact. There were no self-injurious responses during the first of these 20 minute sessions, with low rates of responding over the next 12 sessions — the rate not exceeding 11 blows per hour. The strategy was then again modified so that electric shock was delivered only for hits making physical contact; that is, the terminal response was punished instead of the initial components of the response as had been done in the preceding sessions. Peter's rate of self-destructive responses showed a decline under these conditions, gradually reaching and staying at zero.

This study clearly demonstrates that severe self-destructive behavior can be minimized, and even temporarily eliminated, under well-controlled conditions. "However, when treatment was continued beyond initial suppression and attempts were made to gradually expand Peter's environment, increase his pro-social skills, and at the same time maintain suppression of self-injurious behavior, the difficulty of extending the laboratory evidence to the natural environment becomes evident" (p. 738). In Peter's case, institutional care remained a necessity. Even though there had been a dramatic decrease in self-destructive behavior, one year after the termination of the formal treatment program, he persisted in self-inflicting 5 to 15 blows per hour while on a children's ward and during brief home visits.

Romanczyk and Goren state that all the research to date suggests that, at best, moderate and severe self-destructive behavior can be completely suppressed for only brief periods of time by using strong aversive techniques. They believe that reducing self-destructive behavior to low levels, as in Peter's case, is not clinically sufficient, only complete suppression for extended periods is deemed acceptable. Because of this, they recognize the ethical concern which must be faced by any clinician employing such methods; the treatment, although extremely painful to the patient, is unlikely to prove totally effective. However, they conclude that "the consequences of *not* employing such a treatment strategy, even given its limitations, are unacceptable" (p. 738).

As a final point concerning the use of physical pain, the Council recognizes that one must distinguish between situations exposing subjects to painful or dangerous conditions for pure research purposes and situations in which such treatments comprise part of a diagnostic or therapeutic activity geared toward the direct benefit of the subject. This, of course, was the nature of the situation in the case of Peter. Romanczyk and Goren sought to alleviate the symptoms of a highly self-destructive child who, to their knowledge, was more severe in terms of intensity, frequency, multiplicity, and chronicity of self-injury than any other reported case. To this end they established a treatment program which exceeded 1000 hours. This program was carefully designed so that it could also fulfill the tenets of good case study research; the treatment was carefully defined in terms of replicable therapist-patient interactions, and progress and outcome were objectively monitored.

In addition to illustrating research in which the ethics of inflicting pain upon a subject is at issue, this particular case study exemplifies those instances in which the research subjects are minors, and/or are disturbed patients, or mentally retarded. Consistent with the preceding principles, informed consent and freedom to withdraw are still important, as is the provision of a fair contract between researcher and subject. However, the explicit agreement must be reached "with a responsible person who can base his decision on an appraisal of the prospective participant's best interests" (p. 58). In the case of Peter, the researchers consulted with the boy's parents in order to fulfill these ethical requirements.

However, even when this is done, researchers are still obliged to relate to the participant himself with respect.

Mental Stress. When a researcher fails to have respect for his subjects, when he is inconsiderate, crude, thoughtless, or demeaning, the subjects are vulnerable to being psychologically upset. There is no excuse for such treatment when done out of thoughtlessness. On other occasions participants are exposed to psychological stresses as an integral part of the investigation, either because they serve as experimental variables or because they are an unavoidable byproduct of other manipulations. When this is the case, the rigor with which the principle of informed consent is upheld becomes especially important.

Milgrim's (1963) research, in which he asked participants to inflict apparently severe levels of pain upon other persons via the administration of shock, is one which clearly upset many of the subjects.

One observer of Milgrim's experiment related:

> I observed a mature and initially poised businessman enter the laboratory smiling and confident. Within 20 minutes he was reduced to a twitching, sluttering wreck, who was rapidly approaching a point of nervous collapse. He instantly pulled at his ear lobe, and twisted his hands. At one point he pushed his fist into his forehead and muttered, "Oh God, let's stop it."
>
> (p. 377)

This reaction was not unique among Milgrim's subjects. The investigator himself reported that many "showed signs of nervousness in the experimental situation, and especially upon administering more powerful shocks" (p. 375).

One of the special problems associated with Milgrim's research on obedience is that participation per se reveals to the subject certain self-weaknesses. Specifically, Milgrim's subjects may have come away with a new awareness about their capacity to act brutally toward others when told to do so by an authority figure. This realization may be unaffected by the knowledge imparted to them after the experiment that no shock was in fact delivered. Consequently, Milgrim's research may have had irreversible after-effects of a stressful nature on an unspecifiable number of his subjects.

Disabuse

In situations such as these, the researcher has a serious responsibility to his subjects following completion of their actual research participation. These obligations are spelled out in the Council's next two principles:

> Principle 8. After the data are collected, ethical practice requires the investigator to provide the participant with a full clarification of the nature of the study and to remove any misconceptions that have arisen. Where scientific

or humane values justify delaying or withholding information, the investigator acquires a special responsibility to assure that there are no damaging
consequences for the participant. (APA, 1973, p. 2)

It is not unusual for experimentally deceived subjects to disbelieve the post-
investigation clarification presented to them. They may properly feel that since they
were misled once there is no particular reason not to expect the same during the
debriefing session. In fact, this skepticism has, on a few occasions, been validated by
researchers who employ *double deception*, a procedure which the Council refers to as
"particularly reprehensible" (1973, p. 80). This practice involves the use of a debriefing procedure which is in fact just a second deception. The subject's reactions during
this stage of the study are then covertly assessed. It is felt that any confidence in the
trustworthiness of the psychologist which a subject may have after being imposed
upon by a deception design would be shattered when finally advised that he had been
misled twice.

A full clarification of experimental procedures may not be suitable in certain cases.
These may involve children, retarded, or emotionally disturbed people who might be
more confused or upset by hearing of the experiment's true nature than they were by
the experimental manipulation. For example, the Council believes that the primary
objective should be for children to leave an experiment in a positive frame of mind.
This takes precedence over honesty; children should not be told that they did not really
do as well as they had been led to believe during the experiment. On the other hand,
those children who believe that their experimental performance was poor should be
convinced of the acceptability of their performance. This may involve telling them they
did better than they in fact did, or arranging the sequence of events so that their final
efforts are programmed to experience success.

Removing Negative After-Effects

A researcher should always be vigilant to the possibility of his procedures having
an adverse psychological effect upon those participating. When negative developments do emerge, every effort must be made to remove them.

Principle 9. Where research procedures may result in undesirable consequences for the participant, the investigator has the responsibility to detect
and remove or correct these consequences, including, where relevant,
long-term after effects. (APA, 1973, p. 2)

There have been occasions when research has involved false feedback to subjects,
personal feedback of a very important nature. Ring and Farina (1969) report that in
one investigation the subjects were given personality tests and, at a second session,
told that the results indicated that they were poorly adjusted. Another experiment by
Bramel (1962) involved providing subjects with deceptive feedback regarding their
emotional reactions to photographs of men. The manipulation was designed so that

the subjects would believe their responses had homosexual overtones. Procedures such as these may have highly adverse effects upon the individual who is not firm in his level of adjustment or sexual orientation, but who nevertheless has been functioning in an adequate way. Previously unrecognized fears or concerns can be made highly salient and difficult to put out of mind once the experiment is over.

In Milgrim's (1963) study of obedience several steps were taken to lessen an unanticipated level of stress in subjects. In addition to being told that real shock had not been administered, the subjects had an opportunity to meet individually with the confederate against whom the ostensible shock had been directed and to have a lengthy discussion about the research with the experimenter. The experiment was explained to each subject in a way which supported his individual decision to have been obedient or deviant, whichever the case may have been.

One year after Milgrim (1964) completed his experimental program on obedience, 40 subjects were contacted and examined by a psychiatrist skilled in out-patient treatment. He concluded that while several subjects did undergo extreme stress during the experiment, "None was found by this interviewer to show signs of having been harmed by his experience" (p. 850).

Confidentiality

The Council's final principle emphasizes the importance of respecting the anonymity of the individual who serves as a subject and of treating his data in a confidential manner.

Principle 10. Information obtained about the research participants during the course of an investigation is confidential. When the possibility exists that others may obtain access to such information, ethical research practice requires that this possibility, together with the plans for protecting confidentiality, be explained to the participants as a part of the procedure for obtaining informed consent. (APA, 1973, p. 2)

In a clarifying series of articles, Shah (1969, 1970a, 1970b) distinguished between confidentiality and two other related, but different, concepts, *privileged communication* and *privacy*. Confidentiality is most related to professional ethics. Psychologists have an obligation not to divulge any information learned about someone with whom they have a professional relationship, except with the full consent and authorization of that person. The professional relationship referred to may be either that which exists between a clinical psychologist and a client, or a research psychologist and a subject. One exception to this rule of confidentiality would be when there is a clear and imminent danger to the individual or to society by not revealing certain information, although gained in confidence, to appropriate professionals or authorities. For example, a research psychologist working in a psychiatric hospital may learn of the suicidal inclinations of a patient. Breaking confidence in this instance would be consistent with ethical principles which have wider application than those specifically directed at the conduct of scientific research.

Privileged communication refers to the legal right of the clients of many professional groups, including doctors, lawyers, and clinical psychologists. Where the privilege exists, it protects the client from having his confidences revealed as testimony in a court of law. Where statutes exist creating privileged communication, the general intent usually is to facilitate the conduct of the professional enterprise. It would, for example, be very difficult for a clinical psychologist and a patient, or a lawyer and his client, to function in a meaningful way if the client's revelations would later be revealed and used against him.

It is important to know that research data, even if obtained under strictly confidential conditions, are generally not accorded the legal status of privileged communications. Thus, the courts or police may legally gain access to information about subjects when there is due cause. This risk is particularly great when a researcher is investigating human behaviors which are illegal such as drug use, sexual perversions, and participation in civil disobedience. The Council expressed the opinion that when personal information is being collected which may conceivably be of interest to the courts, the legal status of the data should be clearly identified to all participants in advance. One way to circumvent this problem is for investigators to record and store their data in a way which makes the identification of participants impossible; code numbers instead of names can be used. In fact, this practice is recommended for all research, where practical, because it is often difficult to predict who might become privy to data at some later date and to anticipate the ways in which the information might be used against the subjects.

The third concept discussed by Shah is "privacy," a term which is not as yet well defined. Nevertheless, in essence, privacy refers to the individual's rights "to pick and choose for himself the time, circumstances, and particularly the extent to which he wishes to share with or withhold from others his attitudes, beliefs, behavior and opinions" (1969, p. 57). Privacy, then, affirms the freedom of the individual to be protected from unreasonable intrusion by others. This right is violated when a researcher procures data through deception, or when research does not allow the subject to engage in a consent process based upon full disclosure of relevant information.

SUBJECT REACTIONS

It is easy for professionals who are well-versed in the standards for ethical research to criticize the work of others. A number of attempts have been made to obtain opinions from subjects themselves regarding the appropriateness of certain questionable research practices. One such effort was that of Milgrim (1964). As part of the followup procedure of his obedience research, Milgrim sent a questionnaire to all of his subjects. Subject replies clearly were in the positive direction; 84% said they were glad to have participated; 15% had neutral feelings; and only about 1% said they were either "sorry" or "very sorry" to have been in the experiment. In addition, about 80% believed that more research of the kind conducted by Milgrim should be carried out.

There is no doubt that at the time of their participation many of Milgrim's subjects were under considerable strain. Yet, at the same time, 75% of them found the experience a meaningful one in which they learned something of personal importance. One subject wrote: "This experiment has strengthened my belief that man should avoid harm to his fellow man even at the risk of violating authority" (1964, p. 850). It is quite possible that this person may never have come to such a righteous position had he himself not learned first-hand what it is like to be asked by another to inflict severe pain upon another human being. Another subject stated: "To me, the experiment pointed up . . . the extent to which each individual should have or discover firm ground on which to base his decisions, no matter how trivial they appear to be. I think people should think more deeply about themselves and their relation to their world and to other people. If this experiment serves to jar people out of complacency, it has served its end" (p. 850).

Milgrim contends that these comments are representative of a broad array of appreciative and insightful opinions offered by those who participated in the obedience research. Yet there were many who were prepared to discount them as an attempt to justify an ethically unacceptable study by the author himself.

Ring, Wallston, and Corey (1970) believed that the circumstances warranted an independent evaluation of the immediate and long-term consequences of participation in a "Milgrim-type" experiment. It is ironic that in order to accomplish this goal, they had to do exactly what they had expressed deep concern over; they conducted an experiment in which subjects were led to believe they were inflicting great distress on another person. To worsen matters, their attempt to discover what happens to the subjects of an obedience study also resulted in the use of a double-deception procedure with the post-experimental debriefing session a disguised experimental manipulation.

They used 57 volunteer female undergraduates who were enrolled in psychology courses, and whose "pay" was two points toward their final grade. While the general procedure duplicated much of what Milgrim did, Ring's subjects were requested to administer harsh levels of noise, instead of shock, to another person. This was ostensibly done via a noise generator with a volume control knob ranging in intensity from 0 to 10. The latter was described as "pretty painful indeed." Each subject was allowed to hear two sample noises. The first was not painful to listen to and was said to be a level two noise; the second, allegedly a level five noise, was shrill and piercing, causing most subjects to become startled and to wince. The experimenter nonchalantly remarked that the person to whom the subject would be administering the noise would be fitted with special headphones which magnify the sound by a factor of three or four!

Subjects were required to administer an ever-increasing intensity of noise each time the other person, a confederate of the experimenter, gave an incorrect response on a verbal-learning task. During the phase of the research in which the confederate was performing the verbal-learning task and the subject was administering noise for incorrect answers, the two were placed in separate rooms. The subject heard over a loudspeaker a prepared audio tape of the confederate apparently trying to come up with the solution but being correct only about one time in four over the series of 32 trials. After being administered noise subsequent to an incorrect answer on trial 19, the confederate said "Ouch." On all following noise administrations the confederate expressed stronger discomfort. After trial 24 she asked, "Do I have to continue?" After trial 26 she exclaimed, "Please, I can't stand the pain!" At trial 29 the confederate gave an agonizing scream and broke into sobs which heightened to a "piteous wail" after the final administration of noise on trial 32.

Through all of this, it was planned that the experimenter act perplexed at the confederate's reactions but always remain in control. If the subject became defiant, the experimenter went through the first three of Milgrim's (1963) prods: "Please continue; the experiment requires that you continue; it is absolutely essential that you continue."

After the verbal-learning/noise phase of the research was over, two-thirds of the subjects were put through a first debriefing session in which they were advised that the learner in the experiment was really an accomplice who did not receive any auditory stimulation. The use of the tape recording was also explained. The experimenter then proceeded to give a false, but plausible, account of what the experiment was about. The remaining one-third of the subjects were led to believe that the experiment was just as it appeared to be. These subjects continued to hold the impression that they had inflicted painful levels of noise upon someone who was apparently another subject.

As the final step, all subjects were given a questionnaire designed to elicit reactions to what they had just been through. It was presented as part of the Psychology Department's policy to monitor all research activities through participant evaluations. The subjects were told that the experimenter would not view their responses and that they (the subjects) would personally deliver the form to the secretary of the Chairman of the Psychological Experiment Evaluation Committee. As further encouragement for subjects to freely express their opinions on this questionnaire, they were not required to place their names on it. The delivery of this questionnaire was followed immediately by a second debriefing session in which all aspects of the research were meticulously explained and every effort was made to calm any subjects still manifesting sings of emotional upset.

To their surprise, Ring and his colleagues found an even higher rate of complete obedience, 91%, than had Milgrim (1963). Prods were necessary for less than half of the participants. It is reported that, in general, the subjects' reactions to the obedience experiment support Milgrim's descriptions, except that their psychological distress was apparently not as great. There was less bizarre behavior, although three subjects did cry and one who was defiant was unable to continue because she was so shaken by the experimental demands. The subjects' responses on the post-questionnaire affirm these observations. While many reported being upset at the time they had to inflict auditory punishment, those who received the first debriefing were quite calm by the time they filled out the questionnaire and reported highly positive evaluations of the experiment. Virtually none of these subjects resented the deception, regretted being in the experiment, thought that it involved unethical practices or believed it should be discontinued. In contrast to this, control subjects, those filling out the post-questionnaire while still under the misconceptions instilled by the experimental manipulations, were consistently more negative. Thus, it appears that even a cursory debriefing serves to induce a dramatic discrepancy between how a subject experiences an experiment and how it is later evaluated. At a followup interview one month after the experiment, the subjects typically retained positive remembrances.

Ring and his co-workers caution that, while there was no evidence of any serious short or long term negative after-effects, a number of the criticisms leveled at Milgrim by Baumrind (1964) proved to have some validity. About half of the subjects did say that in the future they would be more suspicious of psychological experiments and more wary of being deceived; one-third reported a residual feeling of anger or disappointment with themselves for their experimental behavior, even after the second debriefing session. A few, perhaps defensively, said that they were unaffected, but could see how other people would not be able to take the stress.

In summary, Ring and his colleagues went into their experiments as skeptics, not quite believing that subjects would be as obedient and as unaffected as reported by Milgrim. They came away having to accept the validity of both points. Still, they believe that their own data contain a sufficient basis to argue against the future conduct of this kind of research. First, about half the subjects report themselves as being very upset during the experiment. This in itself should give one pause, even if there are few who experience negative after-effects. Second, the small number who do report lingering negative feelings about themselves and the experiment is sufficient to render the research ethically unacceptable. Third, this experiment probably alters the way in which its subjects will respond to future experimental participation because of its effects on their level of trust in the researcher's communication. Fourth, whether subjects themselves entertain ethical concerns regarding this research, they have been induced to behave in a way which is degrading.

Ring's evaluation of his experimental results suggest that it may not be easy to impressionistically evaluate just how physically or mentally discomforting an experimental procedure might be to subjects. In order to obtain some empirical data on this issue, Farr and Seaver (1975) gave 86 Introductory Psychology students, representing the group whose services are probably most often enlisted in psychological research, a questionnaire listing 71 different hypothetical procedures adapted from ethical guidelines. Thirty procedures described threats to physical discomfort such as, "Bear a continuous 2-minute blast from an air horn located in the same room" (p. 771). Fifteen items described threats to psychological comfort such as, "Give a five minute speech on a current topic to a group of other subjects" (p. 772). Thirty six items described possible invasions of privacy, such as having to complete and sign one's name to an "attitude scale about racial integration in residential areas" (p. 772).

The first two groups of items were rated on a five point scale with one indicating no physical or psychological discomfort and five representing an unbearable amount of discomfort. The items relevant to privacy invasion were also rated on a five point scale, ranging from the procedure not being an invasion of privacy, with the subjects having no reluctance to provide the information requested — scale point 1 — to the procedure being an excessive invasion of privacy, with the subjects not willing to provide the information.

While it is true that subjects in this research were not reacting to their actual participation in the procedure (as was the case with the subjects of Milgrim and of Ring), the obtained scale values may provide investigators with some useful guidelines. With respect to physical discomfort, Farr and Seaver found that the following items had ratings below 2.0. "Run up and down steps for one minute;" "Eat no food for six hours prior to study;" and "Blood sample is taken by pricking a finger." The receipt of a single electric shock of painful but not harmful intensity received a mean rating of 2.99. The only two physical items rated above four concerned a "band tightened around the head to see how much pain could be tolerated" (rated 4.07), and repeated "electric shocks of the maximum tolerable intensity" (rated 4.19).

In general, psychological stresses tended to be rated as somewhat more tolerable than physical stresses. At the low end were items such as the following: "Judge the more attractive person in each of 50 pairs of photographs of college students" (rated 1.49); and "Move a handle to keep a pointer aligned with a fast moving target" (rated 1.66). Two items were rated above 3.5 in terms of their psychological discomfort: "When recalling a long list of words, you were to learn another subject received a painful shock for each mistake you made" (rated 3.51); and "Sit in a small room for 10 minutes with the thing you are most afraid of" (rated 4.09).

The most surprising results pertained to the low degree to which subjects perceived data-gathering procedures as invading their privacy. All 36 items were rated below a scale value of three. The most acceptable, according to the undergraduates, are questionnaires about "home town, family size, and family mobility," and "Occupational interest test" (both rated 1.16). The three least acceptable kinds of information gathering had to do with sexual matters: "Personality inventory measuring heterosexual/homosexual orientation — sign name" (rated 2.13); "Wear non-painful electrodes measuring physiological reactions to pictures of nude men and women" (rated 2.19); and "Questionnaire about past sexual experiences — sign name" (rated 2.93). Farr and Seaver make a point of noting that highly-invasive techniques such as wire tapping, opening mail, or screening trash for data were not included in their inventory because they are so clearly unethical and/or illegal.

Using a somewhat different strategy, Sullivan and Decker (1973) also gained reactions to ethically-questionable research. They, however, were able to directly compare the opinions of potential subjects with those of professionals. Their subjects were a sample of 357 undergraduate students of psychology and 285 psychologists, who had research experiences ranging from none to over 100 published reports. Each student and psychologist was given one of four hypothetical experiments with controversial design characteristics. These four experiments involved procedures which either induced experimental stress in subjects, induced experimental physical pain, lowered the subjects' level of self-esteem, or experimentally induced the subjects to engage in unethical behavior by administration of painful levels of shock to another person. Five questions on relevant ethical issues followed. The major finding was that in 18 of the 20 (5 questions x 4 hypothetical studies) response categories the "psychologists gave a significantly stricter interpretation of the ethical issues than did the student subjects" (p. 589). This empirical finding confirms Ring's more subjective appraisal of student subjects; while one might want and expect them to maintain ethical standards for research which are as high as those conducting psychological investigations, the evidence suggests that they do not. While students as a group have a history of being leaders of dissent in the face of a variety of society's less enviable practices, unethical psychological research appears not to be an issue which has marshalled their active concern. Perhaps it is this complacency on the part of subjects which has permitted psychologists to continue to use non-volunteer subjects and to conduct deceptive research in an almost routine fashion, despite the fact that these practices are patently inconsistent with the Council's guidelines.

In reviewing about 1000 studies published in selected APA journals, Menges (1973) found that subjects participated under an external requirement, usually the fulfillment of a college course requirement, or without knowledge of their involvement in 60% of the reports. About 20% of the reported research utilized a deception condition and, in only about 50% of these were the subjects debriefed. In one publication, the *Journal of Personality and Social Psychology*, 117 out of 248 articles appearing during 1971 involved deception; that is, the subjects were given inaccurate information about either the independent or dependent variable. There is little doubt that every investigator of every one of these deceptions could present arguments in support of his procedures. On balance, however, one does begin to question whether the "openness and honesty" spoken of by the APA Council are, in practice, "essential characteristics of the relationship between investigator and research participant" (p. 1).

SUMMARY

In the final chapter of Part I we carefully presented the principles of ethical research conduct spelled out by the American Psychological Association. In addition, investigations bearing on subject reactions to ethically questionable research were discussed. Our intention was both to provide the student with information pertinent to the important issue of research ethics and, hopefully, to induce our readers to become the most responsible subjects and researchers possible.

TERMS TO KNOW

	Page No.		Page No.
accountability	84	exploitation of subjects	91
confidentiality	97	informed consent	85
deception	87	pilot study	84
disabuse	95	privacy	98
double deception	96	privileged communication	98

PART II
Individual Personality Assessment

CHAPTER 8
Personality Assessment: An Overview

EARLY ROOTS

In an excellent summarization of the history of personality assessment, upon which this chapter draws heavily, Lanyon and Goodstein (1971) trace the beginnings of personality assessment to around 3000 B.C. At that time, 50 centuries ago, the Chinese are reported to have employed palmistry. Hand lines and the intervening swellings, called *monticuli,* were used as the basis of complete personality descriptions. Today, belief in palmistry is generally regarded as superstitious. Nevertheless, current palmist practitioners may generate surprisingly accurate personality descriptions. A careful analysis, however, will probably reveal that they are producing "Aunt Fanny" assessments, a phrase coined by Tallent (1958), in which the personality descriptions involve either very trivial or very general statements that would probably be true of anybody's Aunt Fanny.

Meehl (1956), in referring to these kinds of personality evaluations, used the term "Barnum Effect" to describe the apparent correspondence between any assessee's characteristics and those listed in a personality report filled with both trivialities and widely-applicable generalities. Several researchers, among them Forer (1949), have demonstrated that a "Barnum" personality report containing statements such as, "You have a tendency to worry at times, but not to excess," is almost always endorsed by individuals as an accurate assessment of themselves.

Another form of personality assessment having questionable validity is that of astrology, a procedure dating back 25 centuries, in which earthly events are forecast from celestial phenomena. Mesopotamians believed that individual personality structure and the course of important life events were the products of the configuration of stars at the time of one's birth. This configuration is of course known as a horoscope and its alleged predictive worth is rooted in the ancient belief that the stars are really powerful deities.

More recently, in the early 19th century, complete personality descriptions based upon the protrusions and contours of the skull became common. The system was known as phrenology and was popularized by Franz Gall, a German physician and anatomist. Gall, representing the then current state of anatomical knowledge, believed in the localization of brain function. Because each function was reputedly centered in a circumscribed cortical region, the functions could be indirectly evaluated by noting the protrusions produced on the surface of the skull. A well-developed function, such as honesty, would produce a visible bulge that could be objectively measured. Unfortunately, phrenology fell into public disfavor because it was implicitly atheistic and fatalistic, and it relieved people of moral responsibility. Less instrumental in bringing about the downfall of phrenology, but probably of more scientific import, is the fact that the assumptions of phrenology have proven themselves incorrect; that is, current understanding of brain function does not support the notion that skull protrusions are produced by the unusual development of local cortical functions.

The Study of Individual Differences

In 1796, Kinnebrook was relieved of his responsibilities as a Greenwich astronomer's assistant because he consistently recorded stellar events as occurring one second later than did his supervisor. This kind of "constant error" we now attribute to individual differences in reaction times between the astronomers. During the last century, concern over the measurement of individual differences was spurred on by Darwinian ideas regarding natural selection and evolution.

Late in the 19th century Sir Francis Galton, a British scholar, became interested in the inheritance and measurement of both intellectual and non-intellectual faculties, such as emotion. In fact, he first advocated a currently popular approach of assessing emotional arousal by recording accompanying physiological changes, such as heart rate. In the early 20th century Alfred Binet attempted to study the behavioral and physiological characteristics of uniquely bright and talented people. He also developed instruments designed to identify intellectually limited children who would not profit from receipt of formal schooling. These have proven to be the forerunners of contemporary intelligence tests.

The growing scientific interest in intellectual deficiency specifically, and in psychopathology in general, prompted others, at about the same time, to develop procedures for the assessment of psychological abnormality. Galton had used a word association technique to measure individual differences. This procedure was also adopted by Emil Kraeplin, a German psychiatrist who developed a psychiatric diagnostic scheme which, with modifications, is still being used today. One of Freud's students, Carl Jung (1910), used a standard list of 100 stimulus words to discover areas of emotional conflict in his patients. After each stimulus word was presented Jung asked his patients to "Answer as quickly as possible the first word that occurs to your mind. . ." Areas of conflict were identified on the basis of long reaction times, emotional responses (such as flushing) to certain stimulus words, blocking, and the content of the subject's associations. In an illustrative example, Jung pointed to the multiple responses of a subject, called "supplements," to each stimulus word. He commented that the characteristic use of supplements reveals the need of the patient to qualify or correct what has been said and to give the experimenter more than is called for. In this Jung sees reflected a basic quality of those diagnosed as "hysterics," namely, the tendency to become carried away, to be overly enthusiastic, and to promise much while rendering little. Using a more empirical approach, Kent and Rosanoff (1910) administered a standard list of stimulus words to over 1000 normal persons. Having established the normative associations to their word list in this manner, Kent and Rosanoff were able to demonstrate that psychotic subjects tended to differ from normal ones in the word associations they generated. Most importantly, psychotics gave far fewer common associations. This difference enabled Kent and Rosanoff to use their word association test for the identification of psychopathology in individual cases. The word association technique is still employed with enthusiasm in many clinical settings.

MODERN TRENDS

During World War I there was a need to identify soldiers whose emotional state would make them unfit for the stress of military life. A committee, headed by Robert Woodworth, developed a questionnaire for this purpose. Their test was essentially a symptom check list and a subject's score was simply the number of times he answered in what was considered to be a psychopathological direction. Woodworth tried to deceive subjects regarding the true purpose of the test by labeling it, in neutral fashion, "Personal Data Sheet." Nevertheless, the content of the items was clear in its implications for personal adjustment; "Do you make friends easily?" and "Are you frightened in the middle of the night?" It would have been easy for subjects to fake either good or poor levels of adjustment had they been suitably motivated. Despite this weakness, Woodworth's (1920) test is regarded as the precursor to current paper and pencil personality inventories. In general, the use of these instruments is predicated on a belief in the stability of the personality characteristics they presume to assess and on the need to measure these characteristics economically in large numbers of people. Frequently used personality questionnaires, such as the Minnesota Multiphasic Personality Inventory (MMPI) and the Sixteen Personality Factor Questionnaire (16 PF), represent efforts to evaluate the total personality in as scientifically sophisticated a manner as possible.

At about the time that Woodworth was advancing the ease with which large groups of individuals could be economically evaluated, another front in the testing movement was forming. Hermann Rorschach, a Swiss psychiatrist, came to realize that people's perceptions of inkblots had diagnostic significance. What was especially unique about Rorschach's work was that the formal aspects of a subject's perceptual process were considered to be important, not just the content of the perception. Thus, if a subject said a particular blot looked like a "bear," it was important to know whether the "bear" was seen to be moving, and whether the perception "bear" was based on the color, shading, or shape of the inkblot. Rorschach's intent was to relate perceptual styles, as revealed by the patient's responses, to diagnostic categories. That is, his goal was to construct a method of diagnosing conditions such as psychosis, epilepsy, and feeblemindedness through an analysis of the patient's perception of inkblots.

Rorschach's inkblot technique was immediately picked up by more psychoanalytically-oriented clinicians, whose goal went beyond mere diagnosis. They believed that subjects' perceptions of inkblots revealed the content and workings of the unconscious mind and that complete personality assessments could be constructed on the basis of such perceptions. Today, the Thematic Apperception Test and sentence completion procedures are also commonly used to provide global evaluations of the total personality. Along with the Rorschach inkblot test, they share the common technique of presenting a stimulus to a subject for the purpose of noting perceptual, behavioral, or emotional reactions. As a group, they were designated as *projective tests* by Frank (1939) because the subject "projects" or reveals his way of viewing and reacting to the world, and his manner of organizing experiences, as he responds to the test stimuli, whether they be inkblots, pictures, or sentence stems.

Most recently, dissatisfaction with what may now be called traditional questionnaire and projective assessment procedures has been expressed by some psychologists. Kanfer and Saslow (1965) discuss this at length. The new behavioral approach to assessment rejects the older emphasis on diagnosis according to the Kraeplinean diagnostic entities of schizophrenia, manic-depressive psychoses, and so on. In addition, personality assessment which is aimed at discovering hypothetical intrapsychic processes and conflicts of clients is deemed to be unproductive. Instead, a functional analysis of behavior is emphasized. This involves careful, real world fact-gathering and direct observation so that the problem, or target, behavior is clearly described and is related to both the specific situations within which it occurs and to their consequences. The objective specification of the situation and consequences sets the stage for the alteration of these behavior-controlling factors so that the client's behavior itself will be modified. The great emphasis on the situation as an important consideration of personality assessment is what sets this approach apart from Rorschach and MMPI-type assessment formats.

CLASSIFICATION OF ASSESSMENT METHODS

As with any group of events, there is an uncountable number of different ways to view personality assessment procedures. For example, they can be studied in terms of how long they take to administer, or in terms of their interest value for the subjects. While these particular considerations may be important under specific testing situations, especially when the subjects are children, their centrality to the understanding of personality assessment is questionable. There are, however, a relatively small number of conceptual dimensions which, to a large degree, can be used to define most of the important characteristics of any particular assessment process. For the present purposes, concealment of purpose, kind of subject response, and freedom of subject response will be considered.

Concealment of Purpose

Cronbach (1970) points out that some assessment approaches focus on ascertaining the individual's maximum performance quality in some general or circumscribed area. As a group, these tests tend to be measures of ability. Problems are presented to a subject who is expected to do as well as possible. Of course, knowing the demands of a situation facilitates doing well. Therefore, ability tests usually contain straight-forward instructions which sensitize subjects to the particular test requirement, usually to be "correct." Thus, they are non-disguised assessment methods. Examples of ability tests include scales of general intelligence, such as the Stanford Binet or Wechsler Intelligence Scales, aptitude tests which are used to predict gain from some experience or course of instruction, and achievement tests, designed to assess actual gain subsequent to a learning experience. While in most cases people readily comply with ability test instructions to do "as well as you can," the same cannot be said when they are asked to describe themselves, or to reveal information not about maximum ability but about their "typical self." The basic instructions of personality tests are something which people very frequently *cannot* follow or *choose not* to follow, with accuracy. Consequently, measurement of personality has frequently depended upon procedures whose purpose is hidden or disguised.

The first issue concerning the inability to reveal important personality characteristics directly is best understood from a psychoanalytic perspective. Freud's psychoanalytic personality theory suggested that the manner in which we organize experience, as well as many of our most significant behavior patterns, are determined by motives which are unconscious. That is, even though out of awareness, such motives channelize and direct conscious experience and overt behavior. An indirect assessment approach was developed in an attempt to gain information about these underlying motives as they influence an individual's behavior. The personality tests which are best representative of this indirect approach are called projective tests. They are based upon what Frank (1939) called the *projective hypothesis*. The projective hypothesis asserts that central personality characteristics, such as the above-mentioned unconscious motives, are projected, or revealed, by a subject in the process of interpreting or bringing order and reacting emotionally to an ambiguous stimulus, such as an inkblot, which has little normative meaning. The subject's actual responses are called *projections*.

In theory, projections are supposed to reflect the inner self and to reveal the subject's unconscious. For example, a particular subject may be asked what each of a series of essentially meaningless ink blots looks like. Imagine that the responses or projections repeatedly refer to human beings fighting and tearing at each other. The assumption might then be made that this subject is a basically hostile individual with a predisposition to interpret the experiences of his interpersonal world as involving high levels of aggression. Presumably, these projections are being primarily instigated by unconscious aggressive impulses and not by the outward appearance of the inkblots themselves. Because projections allegedly reveal aspects of personality unknown even to the subject himself, and since the subject is unaware of the implications of his test behavior, projective assessment tools are said to have a disguised or concealed purpose.

Probably the earliest formal example of a projective approach to personality assessment is that of word association. As mentioned earlier, Jung (1910) employed a standardized list of stimulus words to which patients reacted by expressing the first word that they brought to mind. If, for example, the responses to neutral stimulus words consistently had sexual connotations, or if the subject had difficulty coming up with responses to sex-related stimulus words, one might tentatively conclude that the subject was preoccupied with, or conflicted over, sexual matters, respectively.

In the 1930s Frank's projective interpretation of such procedures led to their popularization. Tests like the Rorschach, a series of inkblots on which subjects must impose meaning, and the Thematic Apperception Test (TAT), consisting of illustrations which serve as the stimuli for subjects' stories, were considered equivalent to X-rays by which the private fantasies and wishes of subjects would be easily revealed.

Unfortunately, the weight of empirical data has been sufficient to break this naive bubble of optimism. In general, two early assumptions about projective testing have failed to hold up. The first is that projections are relatively pure reflections of personality. In fact, there is convincing evidence that the stumulus itself is a major determinant of projections. Thus a sad story may be due more to a depressing TAT picture than to a depressed personality.

Recognition of stimulus importance does not necessarily rule out projective techniques. It does mean, however, that stimulus considerations must be taken into account when interpreting projections. In fact, by according importance to the stimulus, a basis exists for current users of projective techniques to generate normative evaluations of subjects which would not otherwise be possible. Consequently, what is *not* said may be as important as what is. Specifically, the subject who fails to produce a sexual TAT theme when referring to a picture having reasonably explicit sexual content may be saying a lot about himself through this omission.

Second, it has been realized that many subjects do not passively allow their private world to be revealed via their projections. Some are quite capable of constructing "lead shields" over those aspects of the self which they choose not to have the projective "x-ray" probe. The efficacy with which these subjects were able to maintain a secretive posture while taking projective tests came somewhat as an unpleasant surprise to psychologists. However, the matter of defensive or otherwise misleading test-taking behavior was all too familiar to psychologists using the then more traditional pencil and paper personality questionnaire.

The items on questionnaires such as these, to which subjects usually responded with a "true" or "false," were typically chosen because they had face validity; it appeared that they could evaluate the trait in question. For example, a test of adjustment would contain a number of self-referent statements whose content had obvious psychopathological implications. Consequently, if a subject wished to deliberately create a particular impression, his goal was easily attained due to the test's transparent purpose. That is, if the test was designed to measure a trait which was either particularly desirable or undesirable to possess, subjects could, without difficulty, simply claim the former or deny the latter. This, of course, made the meaningfulness of test scores questionable. Consequently, many current paper and pencil inventories have attempted to get around this problem of questionnaires by purposely disguising the intent of the test. This can often be done by including so-called "filler items" whose contents mislead the subject about the trait being evaluated. In a sense, the strategy is to hide the real test items among a confusing array of irrelevant items.

It is very important to realize that, even though projective techniques and some questionnaires may both be disguised, the reasons for the deception are based upon different considerations. In the case of projective techniques, disguised procedures came about because of theoretical preferences. It was believed that psychologically-meaningful material, inaccessible to even a willing and open subject, could only be indirectly assessed through an interpretation of projections. The users of disguised questionnaires are typically less concerned with unconscious material than they are with that of which the subject is aware. Because subjects may attempt to distort their responses in order to gain approval or to come across in a particular way, disguise is introduced to throw the subject off; it is made more difficult for him to keep from revealing straightforwardly what the questionnaire is seeking to discover.

Kind of response

Personality tests usually require the responder to express impressions or beliefs about either external stimuli or the self. These subjective appraisals may be seen as being either the projection of inner-personality characteristics or the direct expression of the subject's conscious opinions. In either case, there are no right or wrong answers, and the responses themselves are seen as a vehicle to understanding what the subject is typically like. In contrast, ability tests usually require objective responses in the sense that they are deemed correct or incorrect in terms of some accepted fact or standard. Thus, the accuracy of a guess as to the population of the United States is verifiable. Similarly, if one is asked to duplicate a geometric pattern using blocks, the objective correspondence between the subject's production and the design standard can be used as the basis for judging the response as correct.

Freedom of Response

This third test dimension has to do with the latitude of possible responses which subjects are permitted to make. At one extreme would be a questionnaire approach on which subjects are permitted only one of two responses, such as true or false. The popular Minnesota Multiphasic Personality Inventory (MMPI) consists of 550 self-referent statements of this sort. Only slightly less restrictive are achievement tests which follow the familiar four or five choice format. These kinds of assessment approaches are said to be *structured*. At the opposite pole are assessment tools which permit unlimited response variability. These would include interviews or essays. They are open-ended as to how the subject may respond. Other open-ended tests include the already-mentioned Rorschach, TAT, and word association techniques.

Figure 9 depicts the three-way classificatory scheme presented above. For illustrative purposes, some assessment approaches which characterize these most common categories are included. Most group ability tests follow a multiple choice format for ease of scoring. Also, the subjects are usually made well-aware of why they are being tested and are appropriately instructed to answer as correctly as possible. Therefore, these approaches may be understood as structured, non-disguised, objective tests. The major difference between group and individually-administered intelligence tests is that the latter, rather than being multiple choice, may have an open-ended format. Questions or problems are presented to which the subject is free to respond in any way at all. The great benefit over group testing is that the style with which the subject attacks problems can be noted in addition to the hard fact of whether or not the responses are correct.

The Mood Check List is a test which reflects moment-to-moment mood states. In our present scheme, it can be seen that the Mood Check List is deemed to be a limited-response test, since subjects either check or do not check adjectives which they believe to be currently self-descriptive. This test is also non-disguised because it is made explicit that what is wanted is an expression of how the subject currently feels. The responses are subjective because there is no objective criterion against which to judge the validity of a self-evaluation of mood. Interview assessments are usually similar, except that the subjects, of course, are not restricted as to the content or style of responding. It should be mentioned that it would not be difficult to arrange for interviews whose purpose was somewhat disguised. To the extent that a subject's answers are not taken at face value but have far reaching clinical interpretations attached to them, the interview may be seen as disguised. For example, a psychiatrist will ask a patient, "How are things?" not necessarily to obtain a patient's honest, subjective appraisal of hospital life, but to determine if a system of delusional ideas

	Non-disguised		Disguised
	Objective		Subjective
Structured (limited-response)	Multiple-choice group ability tests, e.g. Scholastic Aptitude Test (SAT)	Mood check list	MMPI
Unstructured (open-ended)	Individual ability tests, e.g. Stanford Binet and Wechsler Intelligence Scale	Interviews: clinical and employment	Projective tools, e.g. Rorschach, TAT, word-association

Figure 9. Illustrative assessment approaches categorized in terms of three dimensions: Limited response-open-ended, disguised-non-disguised, objective-subjective.

centering on, for example, food being poisoned or communications from Martians, is still active.

The MMPI's true-false response format makes it an example of a structured test. It is subjective because the task is to express an opinion regarding the self-descriptiveness of each of the 550 items. While some of the items on the MMPI have clear pathological implications, many do not have face validity as indices of adjustment. Nevertheless, they have been shown to be predictive of psychiatric diagnosis. Therefore, this instrument is considered to be disguised, in that in most cases the diagnostic meaning or importance of individual true or false responses is not obvious. This characterization of the MMPI must be tempered by the knowledge that subjects have been shown to be relatively capable of faking various kinds of personalities on this instrument. Thus, as with the TAT, subjects appear to be at least partially capable of seeing through the MMPI and monitoring what it is that they are revealing. Therefore, the categorization of the MMPI as disguised may be disputed.

Lastly, we come to the projective methods which, although categorized as disguised, also suffer from having an imperfect concealment of purpose. The projective tests, because of their open-ended format, do provide a rich body of clinical data based upon the subject's subjective reactions to inkblots, pictures, or words.

It is not always easy to neatly categorize personality tests on the three dimensions of disguised-non-disguised, objective-subjective, and limited response-open-ended. Already mentioned is the problem of construing the MMPI and projective tests as disguised instruments. The fact that some subjects have been shown to be capable of concealing aspects of personality or otherwise faking on these instruments suggests that they are at least minimally privy to their purpose. On another note, the 550 true-false items of the MMPI *collectively* offer subjects an incredible variety of response patterns. This is inconsistent with the notion of the MMPI being a limited response test. Finally, it can reasonably be argued that any response on an objective test, at least in part, reflects the person's subjective experience and evaluation of matters. This is especially true if the style of responding and not just the content is monitored. The manner in which a person expresses an objectively correct response on an IQ test may reveal something about his self-confidence; or, the content of an incorrect answer can be reflective of a person's subjective frame of reference. For example, if someone is asked, "Why do children go to school?" "Because they have to," an insubstantive answer, is qualitatively very different from the equally incorrect response, "so that their parents can get rid of them."

Purposes of tests

A conceptualization which cuts across categories based upon kind of response, freedom of response, and the concealment of purpose is that which considers the purpose of assessment per se. In general, assessment is done either to evaluate change, diagnose current status, or predict future behavior. Of course, the purpose of an assessment procedure is not a property of the procedure itself. Rather, it has to do with what is done with the test data after it is collected and scored. Consequently, the same assessment data may be used for multiple purposes. This is the case when the same ability test responses are employed both for the purpose of assessing academic achievement and for predicting scholastic aptitude. For example, final course exams are designed to assess profit from having been exposed to a particular area of instruction. As such, they are clearly achievement tests. However, the same exam grades may also be used as an index of aptitude, as a predictor of gain from exposure to future courses of study. This is done when the class professor suggests to a high-achieving student that he register for a more advanced section during the upcoming academic semester. Similarly, graduate schools indirectly use college achievement tests, final exams which determine college grades, as predictors of a student's aptitude for professional-level training.

One problem with using tests which were designed with one purpose in mind for another purpose is that their validity may suffer. That is, whereas the final exam may be a highly valid index of a student's course achievement, it may be a rather poor predictor of aptitude for graduate-level work. At best, inferences can be generated about the student's general ability to handle graduate academic material or his level of motivation for scholarship. The validity of such inferences is open to more serious doubt than is the judgment concerned with how much the student knows about the course subject itself.

The Wechsler Intelligence Scales provide a second example of assessment procedures being used for dual purposes. These scales were constructed as measures of general intelligence. They are able to discriminate between the levels of intellectual functioning associated with different chronological ages. However, over the last quarter of a century, there has been a trend to evaluate Wechsler Intelligence Scale performance in terms of the largely age-irrelevant dimension of personality. In fact, it can be argued that the Wechsler Intelligent Scales may be better than projective techniques for evaluating certain aspects of personality, such as problem solving strategies and reactions to failure. For these reasons an individually administered intelligence scale is often included by psychologists in the battery of tests they administer in order to arrive at a psychiatric diagnosis. Similarly, some of the more traditional personality evaluative instruments, such as the Rorschach test, are also used to estimate a subject's intelligence level.

While it is certainly true that all interpersonal encounters will contain information relevant to matters of both personality and intelligence, not all sources of information should be deemed equally valid for assessing these two issues. Thus, well-constructed personality tests are, in general, probably more accurate indices of a person's typical mode of functioning than are intelligence and other ability tests, which are basically designed to evaluate the maximum level or quality of performance.

Another aspect of a test's purpose has to do with the population of people for whom it is intended. The wording and format of some assessment tools are geared for specific populations. For example, Rotter's Locus of Control Scale is intended for adults only. This has prompted several efforts to develop a Locus of Control Scale which would be suitable for use with children. Battle and Rotter (1963) and Nowicki and Strickland (1973) have constructed such scales. While the children's forms may be comprehensible to all ages of subjects, adults may find them demeaning, and their reaction to the test itself may interfere with the assessment of whatever it is that the test is designed to measure.

As already indicated in other contexts, some assessment procedures are specifically designed either for individual or for group administration. Individually-administered tests are most expensive, at least time-wise, to administer. They tend to be used when an in-depth understanding of a given personality is desired. Group tests are more often used when there is an interest in screening selected individuals out of large groups, or when there is a desire to find out what people in general tend to be like along some particular personality dimension.

While group tests can, of course, be used for the individual case, the opposite may not be possible. That is, many individually-administered tests have designated examination procedures or questions which depend upon the nature of previous responses. For example, a particular subtest of an individually-administered intelligence test may have to be stopped after a specified number of incorrect answers. This close monitoring of a subject's progress is out of the question in group settings. Similarly, many personality tests, including most projective instruments, require a degree of verbal interaction between the examiner and subject which precludes group administration. Nevertheless, for research purposes, Rorschach inkblots and TAT pictures have been presented on screens visible to large groups at one time. The subjects have, in some cases, simply been asked to write their response, or even to select a projection from a multiple choice format. While these variations are interesting, the departure from usual test administration procedures is so great that the relevancy of experimental findings to more typical clinical work with the Rorschach and TAT is doubtful.

IDIOGRAPHIC-NOMOTHETIC DISTINCTION

In Chapter 1 we discussed two general approaches to the investigation of personality. The idiographic stresses careful, in-depth, analysis of individual cases in the service of gaining understanding of personality in general. Nomotheticists prefer to focus on more narrow aspects of personality, investigating large groups at a time, in order to discern overall trends.

It should be apparent that personality assessment procedures differ in the degree to which they are consistent with the nomothetic and the idiographic points of view. For the most part, individually-administered assessment techniques are intended to explore in depth the nature and characteristics of the personality in question. For example, the Rorschach and TAT permit the construction of very detailed descriptions covering multiple facets of a given personality. There is an attempt through their use to obtain a complete understanding of the person's uniqueness. This in-depth approach, of course, is consistent with an idiographic approach to personality investigation. In contrast to this, most group-administered tests have a rather narrow focus. They are typically designed to assess particular traits or characteristics. As such, they are well-suited to the nomothetic approach. There are, however, notable exceptions. The

MMPI and Cattell's 16 Personality Factor Inventory, while being questionnaires quite suitable to group administration, have as their goal a relatively broad evaluation of personality.

SUMMARY

In this overview chapter we sketched briefly the historical antecedents of contemporary interview, questionnaire, projective, and behavioral assessment procedures. (Each of these will be discussed in some detail in Chapters 12, 13, 14, and 15.) We then provided a classificatory scheme from which the major dimensions of personality assessment procedures might be understood. Disguise, nature of subject response, and freedom of response were singled out as important in this regard. In addition, personality assessment was discussed in terms of its purposes.

TERMS TO KNOW

	Page No.		Page No.
astrology	107	objective response	113
Aunt Fanny assessment report	107	palmistry	107
Barnum effect	107	Personal Data Sheet	109
Binet, Alfred	108	phrenology	108
Darwin, Charles	108	projection	111
disguise	111	projective hypotheses	111
freedom of response	113	projective techniques	110
Gall, Franz	108	Rorschach, Hermann	109
Galton, Francis	108	sentence completion test	110
horoscope	107	structured test	113
individual differences	108	subjective responses	113
inkblot technique	109	target behavior	110
Jung, Carl	108	unstructured test	113
Kraeplin, Emil	108	Woodworth, Robert	109
monticuli	107	word association techniques	108

CHAPTER 9
Personality Assessment: Some Pitfalls to Accuracy

An Informal Process

Assessing personality is an activity which is not restricted to the professional domain of psychologists. At one time or another we all try to evaluate the personalities of other individuals. This may be done, for example, in an effort to determine if another person might be an enjoyable date or is one whom we could tolerate as a potential employer. Typically, we observe the other person's behavior in one or more situations and then arrive at some predictions about such things as the nature of a potential relationship with the individual, his vocational capacities, his problem-solving skills, and so on. These predictions may emerge from noting the intensity of specific behaviors, their duration, and the environmental context within which they occur.

OBSERVER CHARACTERISTICS

It is clear that people differ in the accuracy of their interpersonal predictions and evaluations. Some people appear to have a great deal of what Gage (1953) has called *social perception*. Such individuals have been shown to be, in general, intelligent and socially well-adjusted. Of course, it is difficult to determine if brightness and adjustment lead one to acquire social perceptiveness, or whether good social perception contributes to the development of intellectual skills and social adjustment. In any case, intelligence and adjustment do not stand alone as important observer characteristics which are related to the accuracy of the interpersonal assessment process.

Cognitive complexity

Bieri (1955) has empirically demonstrated that the people who most accurately predict behavior tend to have a highly differentiated or cognitively complex way of understanding their social world. Cognitively complex individuals are able to recognize the large number of ways in which people differ from each other as well as the ways in which others differ from themselves. They, therefore, appreciate the fact that others might not experience the world or behave as they do, and they are able to be most accurate in their interpersonal perceptions and predictions. Alternatively, cognitively simple people are prone to errors of overgeneralization, such as falsely assuming the existence of similar motives, viewpoints, and behaviors in others as in themselves. The potentially misleading tendency to perceive others routinely as similar to oneself is called *assimilative projection*. This tendency is illustrated by the fact that individuals who both see themselves as hostile and who are described as hostile by others, tend to attribute hostility to others. Of course, it is possible that such hostile people are not totally incorrect in projecting their own inclinations. Their nastiness may induce a hostility in others which then makes their perception accurate.

Assessor-Assessee Similarity

The concept of assimilative projection may explain the repeated finding that personality assessment is most accurate when the evaluators are similar in age, sex, and background to those being judged. Under such circumstances, even if evaluators are cognitively simple, global in approach, and prone to engage in considerable assimilative projection, substantially correct interpersonal predictions may still emerge, simply because the individuals under scrutiny are, in fact, similar to the evaluators. The opposite condition, that is one in which the evaluator's characteristics and background are highly discrepant with those of the person being judged, typically results in relatively poor predictive accuracy. In effect, the evaluator fails to correctly assess or understand the subject. This is deplorable in settings which require understanding of others as a necessary condition for effective communication. In particular, it can be anticipated that the ''middle American'' school teacher, social worker, psychologist, or physician will be least effective in dealing with lower-class students and clients who stem from a different background. Recently, such popular books as *Up The Down Staircase* and *To Sir, With Love* have illustrated dramatically some of the problems in public education which derive from this lack of understanding.

Murray (1938) has demonstrated that even highly-trained clinical judges tend to use themselves as the standard against which to judge others and, in many cases, do not rise above the problems which the lay individual encounters when trying to understand someone unlike himself. Goldberg (1968) also reported that inaccurate personality assessments are not necessarily reduced either through exposure to extensive clinical training or through experience on the part of the psychologist. Cognizant of these issues, Goldstein (1973) has spearheaded the development of a psychotherapy, *Structured Learning*, which enables middle-class therapists to effectively treat lower-class patients. Not surprisingly, the approach moves away from a traditional talking format, which is prone to all the error inherent in any middle class-lower class communication encounter. Rather, there is an action orientation which focuses on the modeling of adaptive and pro-social behavior, behavioral rehearsal and practice on the part of the client, and social reinforcement (praise) from the therapist as the client begins to approximate the modeled behavioral display. This kind of psychotherapy tends to circumvent many of the problems which may arise from a therapist incorrectly evaluating from "where his client is coming." The focus is on the enhancement of specific social skills rather than on the understanding of possibly vague verbal and non-verbal communications between therapist and client.

Acceptance vs. Non Acceptance

There are some individuals who seem to routinely hold a favorable attitude toward others and perceive others in a generally positive manner. Janis, Mahl, Kagan, and Holt (1969) refer to this as a *leniency effect*. Those of us who have the good fortune to read large numbers of letters of recommendation probably all become familiar with certain writers who, in a non-discriminating fashion, describe all their proteges in a uniformly glowing manner. Such assessments tend to be less of a commentary on the person being sponsored than on the sponsor himself. Whatever the motive underlying this behavior, the product is one which tends to be valueless. Not too different are the people who naively have faith in and trust all comers until proven wrong. Unfortunately, proof of malice may arrive only after they have been duped in some way.

At the opposite extreme are people who are suspicious of motives, non-trusting, and always ready to discover the worst in other people. It is as if everyone must first prove himself or herself before unacceptance can become, at best, a wary acceptance. Shapiro (1965), when discussing the neurotic "paranoid style" of thinking, illustrates how these kinds of people can easily misevaluate others. Shapiro suggests that the paranoid person looks beyond mere appearance and searches for hidden malevolent intent in the behavior of others; invariably, through biased and selective attention, he discovers confirmation of his suspicions. An illustration of this could be the individual who interprets the failure of his preoccupied employer to say "Good morning" as a personal rejection having hostile intent.

Attitudes

The attitudes we hold can greatly influence the impressions we form of others. One way in which this may occur is through the operation of *stereotypes*. These are clusters of characteristics which allegedly go along with membership in ethnic, religious, or any number of other so-called "groups." One of the more benign examples is the belief that fat people are jolly. While many stereotypes do seem to have a kernel of truth to them, more often than not they lead to prejudicial assessments. The otherwise open-minded assessment process may be short-circuited by stereotyping, in that the evaluator, once having categorized the subject, is content to assume that the subject has all of the characteristics which folklore has ascribed to the category.

One stereotype which psychologists frequently deal with is that which surrounds mental illness. Nunnally (1961) has shown that the popular conception of the mentally ill is that they are, among other unpleasant things, unpredictable, dirty, and dangerous.

These kinds of beliefs render the label "mentally ill" as one of the most stigmatizing. When people are thought to be, or to have once been, mentally ill, all sorts of non-existent shortcomings are perceived. Farina, Holland, and Ring (1966) demonstrated that when college students evaluated the performance of someone who they were led to believe had a history of psychiatric hospitalization, they tended to evaluate his performance as significantly inferior to that of an allegedly normal person, even though the two performances were, objectively, identical in quality. In addition, those same college students expressed the least desire for continued contact with another person who was presented as having a psychiatric history.

Information

Closely related to the problem of stereotypes is discovering information about another individual which has the effect of inducing prejudicial assessments. In some cases the information is obtained first hand, and at other times it is the result of hearsay. Hersh (1971) experimentally demonstrated the impact which referral information might have on the outcome of an ostensibly objective clinical assessment. Examiners were given fictitious teacher referral reports prior to administering the Stanford-Binet IQ Scale to Head Start children. Each of the 28 examiners tested two children; one had a referral report stressing high intellectual and social abilities and the other was reported to be of limited academic and social abilities. In fact, there was no systematic relationship between the child's actual abilities and his referral report. Nevertheless, testers obtained generally higher IQ scores and were more favorably impressed with the children who had a good referral than with the more negatively referred children. Hersh suggests that there might be an "unconscious conspiracy" between referring and assessing agents, which he appropriately believes "raises serious ethical questions about even the most innocuous-appearing referral process" (p. 120).

Regardless of whether the information one receives induces more positive or negative assessments, it is generally believed that the initial evaluation has the capacity to influence the course of subsequent ones. This phenomenon is known as the "halo effect." In fact, the results of the Hersh (1971) study might well be described in such terms. Specifically, it is possible that the examiners formed either a negative or positive prejudgment about their Head Start clients which pushed them in the direction of either being ready to doubt the correctness of specific answers or to give the benefit of doubt. The "halo effect" leads to an artificially consistent picture of people, with any given assessment being uniformly good or uniformly bad.

Transient Emotional Conditions

The experience of feelings such as sadness, happiness, fear, or anger is instrumental in biasing our assessment of others. In some cases we may simply project these emotions, or attribute them to others, perhaps inaccurately. At other times we may misinterpret the behavior of others in a direction which further legitimizes our own current emotional state. For example, the frightened sentry, alone on guard duty in a hostile environment, is ready to have a first impression of all comers as having belligerent intent. Similarly, Murray (1933) noted that his daughter's friends rated pictures of male faces as more "mean" after having played a frightening game of Murder than when they were not so emotionally aroused.

Conflicts

Of a more stable nature than transient mood states are enduring concerns people have regarding such matters as aggression and sexuality. For whatever reasons, when people have difficulty confronting these issues themselves, they may be prone to either deny the existence of similar motives in others or, at the other extreme, to see them everywhere. In the first instance, even the casual recognition of sexual or aggressive overtones in another person's behavior may make salient these "unacceptable" impulses in the individual himself, causing him to defensively overlook what might be otherwise apparent. Alternatively, as in the case of the psychoanalytic defense mechanism of *projection*, the person may falsely attribute sexual or aggressive impulses to others. By doing this, the individual can often engage people in sexual or aggressive relationships with impunity because the aggression or sexual intent is perceived as being imposed from external sources rather than as stemming from within.

Assessor-Assessee Interaction

Sometimes errors of assessment may involve more than just the biased filtering of information on the part of the assessor. In any face-to-face confrontation the assessor becomes a *participant observer*, interacting with the subject in a way that may directly affect the very behavior which is being evaluated. The potential importance of this kind of interaction was dramatically pointed out by Greenspoon (1955), who found that those verbal expressions of subjects which are systematically and immediately followed by the responses of "mmm-hmm" and "uh-huh" by an interviewer tend to increase in frequency. In this way, the rate with which subjects use plural nouns, for example, may be increased considerably. This so-called "Greenspoon effect" takes place unbeknownst to the subject. While it is true that Greenspoon set out consciously to do what he did, it is not unreasonable to suspect that interviewers may in various subtle ways unintentionally reinforce particular interviewee behaviors and verbal expressions. Truax (1966), through a careful content analysis of psychotherapy sessions, demonstrated that this indeed happens. Most startling in this regard was the fact that the Rogerian psychotherapy which Truax studied is one in which the therapist explicitly tries *not* to direct the course and frequency of verbal behavior on the client's part.

SUBJECT CHARACTERISTICS

Probably most crucial as a contributor to assessment error is the fact that very often the person being judged is just not motivated to reveal himself openly. There is an intent on the part of the assessee to come across in a particular manner, whether it be very bright, aggressive, as "Joe Cool on Campus," or any number of other ways. Goffman (1959) calls such manipulative tactics "impression management." This involves the selective disclosure and concealment of personally-relevant information so that an intended definition of oneself can be conveyed to others. Impression management is frequently engaged in for the purpose of obtaining some goal over which the assessor has control. Such interpersonal deception may be unconsciously motivated or it can be a well-thought-out "put on."

Best foot forward

The most typical goal underlying the construction of a misleading personal facade is that of trying to appear unrealistically attractive. People are aware that first impressions count heavily and move to capitalize on the "halo effect" by becoming what they believe the assessor would like them to be. This phenomenon is all too familiar to the employer who, as he reviews his slovenly, unproductive work force, longs for the return of all those clean-cut, enthusiastic job applicants he hired.

Worst foot forward

There are circumstances in which a person's goal is to deceive the assessor into thinking that he is someone who is quite undesirable. Until recently, varieties of carefully-planned, often creative, ways to convince draft boards of one's unfitness for military duty were commonplace. A good deal of research has been conducted which reveals that many psychiatric patients are motivated to avoid discharge and that they engage in the practice of impression management for the purpose of convincing staff of their unworthiness for hospital discharge. Braginsky, Braginsky, and Ring (1969) reported an experiment in which open ward, chronic patients who had attained a reasonably comfortable in-hospital existence were given a 30 item true-false questionnaire. Prior to completing the form some patients were erroneously led to believe that many "true" answers was indicative of mental illness, while other patients were advised that "true" answers were a sign of self-insight and prognostic of early discharge. As expected, the patients tended to respond with many more "true" responses after hearing the mental illness induction. In other words, the patients in each case tried to convey the impression that they should not be considered candidates for discharge.

SUMMARY

We reviewed some of the sources of error to which both informal and formal assessment procedures fall prey. On the part of the assessor, variables such as social perception, cognitive complexity, similarity to assessee, styles of interpersonal perception, attitudes, information, emotions, and conflicts were all shown to be important. In addition, the person who is being evaluated may have some strong ideas of his own about the kind of picture he would like to convey. These motives may result in best or worst foot forward phenomena.

TERMS TO KNOW

CHAPTER 10
Reliability

If a metal ruler is used to measure the length of a wooden board and the results are noted, it would be found that subsequent measurings of that same board by that same ruler would yield extremely similar results. Any very slight variation may perhaps be attributable to temperature variation causing expansion or contraction of the metal ruler. However, for all practical purposes, the metal ruler is a highly consistent assessment tool. Repeated measurement of the same object, even if conducted by different people, would yield essentially identical results. Because of this, the ruler is said to be reliable. *Reliability* refers to the degree that an assessment tool will be consistent in its findings when repeated measurements are made of the same event.

When an assessment tool is very reliable, any variation or inconsistency in measurement of a given event over time would mean that the event itself has undergone some change. For example, a significantly smaller board length determination arrived at today in comparison to yesterday, using the same metal ruler, probably means that someone sawed off the end of the board. Unfortunately, personality assessment approaches, even the most sophisticated, cannot be compared to the metal ruler in terms of reliability. Differences in personality evaluations or test scores obtained through repeated administration using the same assessment tool may not necessarily be attributed to changes in the subject's personality. Such test-retest shifts in scores could be due to *measurement error* inherent in the assessment tool itself. It is as if the metal ruler was composed of an elastic material which easily stretched and deformed. A ruler made from a rubber band would be unreliable, and would provide readings whose accuracy would be suspect. In a sense, personality evaluation depends upon ''rubber band'' assessment approaches.

Measurement error or unreliability could be due to a variety of factors which have the capacity to influence scores or evaluations independently of the stable aspects of the personality being assessed. These factors overlap with the sources of assessment error discussed in the preceding section. They include moment-to-moment changes in subjects' moods, as well as variations in hunger, fatigue, etc. To the extent that evaluations derived from a personality test are influenced by such irrelevant, error-producing variables, the test will be unreliable. For example, a test of intelligence presumably measures a stable personality characteristic, but intelligence test scores can be highly susceptible to momentary influences of fatigue, boredom, hunger, and so on. A second major source of unreliability is inconsistent behavior, scoring, or interpretation practice among examiners. The effect of these examiner inconsistencies is that two examiners, each with his own idiosyncratic style, may arrive at different evaluations, even though they both use the same assessment tool to evaluate the same person. Examiner-based factors which can produce this kind of unreliability include mood states, prejudices, and "halo effects."

To help ease the problem of measurement unreliability somewhat, it is possible to determine approximately how reliable (or unreliable, for the pessimists) each assessment tool is. Such a determination then permits the assessor to arrive at a good estimation of the meaningfulness of a given score or of a change in scores over time. For example, if a test has been demonstrated to be very reliable, then there would be high confidence in the accuracy of a given reading or in the meaningfulness of even a small shift in scores from one testing to the next. Such shifts would then be attributable to real changes in the personality structure of the individual being assessed. However, if the assessment tool is notoriously unreliable, the assessor would have less confidence in any given reading because there would be too much chance that the score largely reflects sources of error instead of the specific trait intended as the object of assessment. In addition, the assessor would be willing to attribute test-retest discrepancies to real personality changes only if the score shifts were relatively large and therefore not reasonably due to the error inherent in a highly elastic assessment tool.

CORRELATION COEFFICIENT

There are several ways in which a test's reliability may be determined. However, all methods mathematically express reliability in the form of a *correlation coefficient*. Correlation coefficient is a descriptive statistic which summarizes the degree of consistency, or correspondence, which exists between paired sets of scores. Consequently, the correlation coefficient is ideally suited as an index of reliability, since reliability also involves demonstrating consistency between pairs of scores. In the case of reliability, pairs of scores may be obtained by administering the same test twice to a number of subjects. When a correlation coefficient is computed from such paired data and it is used as an index of reliability it is called a *reliability coefficient*.

KINDS OF RELIABILITY

As mentioned, there are a number of different procedures used to establish the reliability of an assessment tool. Each procedure deals with different sources of potential error.

Test-retest

When there is a desire to determine a test's measurement consistency over time, its test-retest reliability must be established. In this case, a set of test scores is obtained once and then again at a later time from the same subjects. The degree of correspondence between the two sets of scores is computed using one of the correlation formulas. A high positive coefficient indicates that the test has temporal stability. That is, its scores tend not to be affected by personal factors which change over time, such as hunger and mood, or by fluctuations in environmental variables, such as heat.

One of the problems in using test-retest procedures to establish the reliability of an assessment tool is that one must decide on a proper between test interval. If the interval is too brief, the reliability coefficient may turn out to be spuriously high. This is because examinees may remember during the second administration what their responses were the first time around. If they choose to say the same thing, their scores would be identical. This would produce very high consistency from one test administration to the next, but the high coefficient would reflect the reliability of the subject's memory more than the temporal stability of the test as a measuring device. At the other extreme would be a between-test interval of several months. Now the test-retest reliability may be deceptively low, because over the lengthy time span between tests there could have been real changes in the subjects which would affect their scores. A rather silly but illustrative example would be to try to determine the test-retest reliability of a tape measure by measuring groups of children at three year intervals. Not only is each child's height increasing greatly over such a period, but at different rates as well. In this case, the absence of test-retest reliability should certainly not be attributed to the tape measure lacking temporal stability. Anastasi (1968) points out that very often long test-retest intervals are used in research in studies which try to determine the accuracy of predicting IQ at an older age from IQ at a young age. However, in such studies the focus is on the stability of what the IQ test is measuring, intelligence, and not upon the test-retest reliability of the IQ test itself.

Another factor which may depress the magnitude of a reliability coefficient based on test-retest is improvement due to practice. Frequently, a test taken the second time is easier because the format and requirements are familiar. If all subjects improved to the same degree, the effect would be the addition of a constant to everyone's score. This would not affect the reliability coefficient. However, it is more likely that there will be varied score increments due to differential profit from having experienced the first test. This will serve to lower the test-retest reliability coefficient below what it would otherwise be.

Because of the problems associated with test-retest reliability such as remembering items or real subject changes, it is often deemed most suitable to establish a test's reliability at one testing session. This may be done in three ways, all of which essentially express the degree to which scores obtained from one part of a test are consistent with those obtained from a second part.

Split-half reliability

Split-half reliability, as the name indicates, involves dividing the test into halves. The particular method used to divide the test is selected because it affords maximum equivalence or congruence between the halves. For example, if a test is a *power test,* composed of a series of questions which ascend in difficulty, it would be appropriate to employ an odd numbered item-even numbered item split in order to form two equivalent half tests. Each half would then contain items at all difficulty levels. It would not be proper to use a first half-second half split because, on a power test, the second half of the items are designed to be more difficult than the earlier questions. Anastasi (1968) points out that even when one is not dealing with a power test, first half-second half-splits tend not to yield equivalent halves because of warm-up effects, practice, fatigue, and boredom.

Once two halves, as equivalent as possible, are formed, they are treated as separate tests. One set of scores based on, for example, the odd numbered items is correlated with the other set based on even items to yield a reliability coefficient. From this split-half reliability coefficient, an estimate of the overall test reliability can be determined by using a correction known as the *Spearman-Brown formula.* This is necessary because a long test usually has greater reliability than a short one. Since the split-half reliability procedure uses a correlation coefficient based upon two sets of items, each being half the length of the original whole test, the overall test reliability would be underestimated without this correction.

It is important to remember that the split-half procedure for determining reliability is not concerned with temporal stability. Since all of the items in the test are given at once, variables which affect scores over time have little opportunity to have an impact. However, split-half reliability does focus on consistency within the test itself, *internal consistency.* In effect, the split-half reliability coefficient describes the degree to which scores from one half of the test are consistent with those obtained from the other half. A high positive split-half reliability coefficient is taken to mean that both halves are measuring the same aspect(s) of personality; or, one half is doing a job which is consistent with that of the other half of the test.

The notion of *content sampling* is important here. This means that only a finite number of items comprise any test. The particular items used will invariably affect test scores to some degree. The more homogeneous are a test's items with regard to such things as content area and difficulty, the greater the split-half reliability will tend to be.

Kuder-Richardson reliability

Kuder-Richardson reliability also focuses on the consistency of scores within a single test. However, instead of noting consistency from one half to the next, consistency is evaluated across all of the test's items. Kuder and Richardson (1937) derived the computational formula used to establish this kind of reliability. Later, Cronbach

(1951) demonstrated the Kuder-Richardson reliability coefficient as being, in fact, the mean (average) of all possible split-half reliabilities that can conceivably be produced by a test with a given number of items. Anastasi (1968) points out that because a split-half reliability coefficient is usually based on a single split designed to yield the two most equivalent halves, split half reliability tends to be somewhat higher than Kuder-Richardson reliability. The discrepancy tends to be greatest when a test is composed of heterogeneous or varied items.

This observation is perhaps best explained in terms of a test which is comprised of relatively similar or homogeneous items. In this situation, any split of the items would produce a comparable reliability coefficient. Because all the items are relatively the same, the manner in which they are divided into halves does not produce critical differences in reliability results. Thus, the Kuder-Richardson reliability value, which is based on the average of all possible (in this case, comparable) splits, would also not be expected to differ significantly from any single split-half value.

Many schools and universities now take advantage of computer scoring facilities for multiple choice examinations. Frequently, the computer print-out will state the Kuder-Richardson reliability for the test. It is one way for students to evaluate the quality of an exam after it has evaluated them.

Alternate-form reliability

Alternate-form reliability is a variation of the split-half method of establishing reliability and is used when a test constructor develops two equivalent forms of the same test. The availability of alternate forms is useful in clinical and research settings where repeated test administration is considered necessary. By correlating a set of Form A scores with a set of Form B scores obtained from the same subjects, it is possible to establish the equivalence of the two forms. The higher the alternate-form reliability, the greater will be the consistency of measurement from one form to the other. In addition, if some period of time separates the administration of Forms A and B, the alternate-form reliability coefficient also reflects the temporal stability of the forms without the confounding element of subjects recalling items and answers, a problem which plagues simple test-retest reliability methods.

Examiner reliability

A final source of error which can serve to lower the reliability of a test stems from inconsistency among examiners. Some tests, such as the Rorschach or individually-administered IQ tests, require the establishment of a certain kind of relationship between examiner and subjects, skill in the administration of a complex array of test materials, and extensive training in the subtle rules of scoring. Consequently the reliability of examiners cannot always be separated from that of the test. In effect, the examiner is part of the test. Developers of complex personality and intelligence tests have, therefore, typically gone to the trouble of preparing detailed administration and scoring manuals in an effort to keep the test behavior of different examiners as consistent as possible.

The establishment of a reliability coefficient which takes into account the scoring aspect of examiners' behavior is relatively easy. All that needs to be done is to obtain a single set of subject responses and have the set scored by different examiners. If a test's scoring manual is clear and complete and the examiners are familiar with its contents, there should be a high degree of inter-scorer consistency. That is, two examiners scoring the same responses should arrive at the same scores. If this is the case, then the correlation coefficient based on the two examiners' sets of assigned scores will be positive and high.

It is more difficult to arrange for the establishment of reliability when one wants to take into account error that may be introduced by inconsistent test administrations across examiners. One way would be for a set of subjects to be given one half, or one form, of a test by one examiner and the second equivalent half, or form, by a second examiner. If there is significantly lower split-half or equivalent-form reliability using two examiners than has been found with the more usual single examiner method, it can be concluded that examiners are administering the test in ways which affect the assessment process and lower reliability. Of course, if the two examiners are allowed to both administer and score their respective halves of the test, then the reliability coefficient would reflect error due to test administration *and* scoring inconsistency.

MEANINGFULNESS OF INDIVIDUAL TEST SCORES

This last topic under the heading of reliability has to do with the confidence that can be placed in a given score obtained on a particular test. The level of confidence necessarily varies with the reliability of a test. If a test has been shown to be very unreliable, yielding inconsistent scores over time, between halves or between examiners, one must necessarily be suspicious of any given score because it may very well be based as much upon sources of error as it is upon the trait or personality being assessed.

Happily, things are somewhat less confusing than they might be because, in addition to a reliability coefficient, the reliability of a test may be expressed in terms of a statistic called the *standard error* of a single score, or the *standard error of measurement.* Through the application of a rather simple formula which takes into account the test's reliability coefficient and the overall distribution of scores on the test (the percentage of people taking the test who obtain each of the possible scores), it is possible to compute the standard error. Because of the special statistical properties of the standard error, it can be asserted with 68% certainty that a person's real or true score lies within + or − 1 standard error of the obtained score. This assertion will be correct 68% of the time. Thus, if the standard error of a test is computed to be 8, and a person obtains an actual score of 50, one can be 68% sure that the person's real score lies between 42 and 58. This 16 point spread is called the *confidence interval* and is bounded by values, here 42 and 58, called *confidence limits.* Again, because of the properties of the standard error, if one chose as a confidence interval + or − 2 standard errors from the obtained score, the assertion that the true score fell within the confidence limits could be made with about 95% certainty. In our example, therefore, one could be 95% sure that the person's real score fell between 39 and 66. Finally, by selecting a confidence interval which is + or − 3 standard error units from the obtained score, it can be said with 99% certainty that the real score lies somewhere between 26 and 74, given a standard error of 8 and an obtained score of 50.

Intuitively, it should be realized that the more reliable a test, the smaller will be its standard error of measurement. In order to be 95% certain as to the range within which a true score lies, one would have to consider a confidence interval spanning more points for a test with low reliability than for a test which has a high degree of reliability.

SUMMARY

In this chapter we dealt with one of the two major issues relevant to personality test construction and evaluation, that of reliability. In essence, reliability means consistency: consistency over time in the case of test-retest reliability; consistency across items with respect to split-half, Kuder Richardson, and alternate form reliability; and consistency between assessors when we evaluate examiner reliability. We mentioned the standard error of measurement as a statistic which permits one to make probability statements about the range within which a given subject's *actual* score lies after having been given his obtained score.

In the next chapter we will present the second fundamental issue relevant to personality assessment: validity.

TERMS TO KNOW

CHAPTER 11
Validity

Reliability has to do with consistency of measurement. Sometimes, even if a test has good reliability, producing consistent scores, it still may not be measuring what we think. That is, the test may be doing a consistently bad job. In order to exemplify this, imagine that someone believes intelligence is related to brain size and, therefore, develops an intelligence test which involves measurement of head circumference. There is little doubt that this test will prove to be reliable. That is, if groups of people come in for head measurement, there will surely be consistency demonstrated upon retest; different examiners will arrive at the same scores when measuring the same heads, and if one chose to evaluate split-half reliability, a high degree of left-right consistency would probably also be found. However, these strong reliability data say nothing about whether anything resembling intelligence is being assessed.

If the test is not measuring what it is supposed to measure, it is said to be invalid. In this case, the test is invalid as a measure of intelligence but not, obviously, as a measure of head size. This last point is important because we can't speak of a test's validity in general but only with respect to particular purposes. A penny scale which promises to tell your weight and fortune probably validly assesses the former but not the latter. In summary, the validity of a test is the degree to which it measures what it alleges to measure. From a somewhat different perspective, the problem of validating a test has to do with demonstrating what may be inferred from its results.

FACE VALIDITY

Very often a test simply has the appearance of being an adequate measure. Thus, an achievement test covering the academic area of Personality would look valid if it asked questions having to do with personality theory, research, and assessment. This kind of validity is called *face validity* and has very limited usefulness because it in no way establishes empirically that a test is doing its measurement job.

Face validity is based upon an informal judgment of overt appearance. When the measurement process is reasonably direct this may not present a problem. However, many personality tests try to assess unconscious motives or predict future behavior patterns. In these cases, the indirectness of the assessment process makes face validity particularly difficult to establish. For example, a test of overt aggression might simply ask subjects about the frequency with which they emit specific aggressive behaviors and so appear to be valid. It would have face validity. However, a test of unconscious aggressive impulses can't be so straightforward. If the impulses being assessed are indeed unconscious, one cannot openly pose direct questions which are answered on the conscious level. The assessment process would have to be much more inferential. Many assessment approaches are designed to disguise their purpose. Among these are the projective techniques exemplified by the Rorschach or "ink-blot" test, which will be discussed later. For these tests the issue of face validity is irrelevant because, by definition, a face valid test would be one whose purpose was apparent.

Anastasi discusses face validity from a "public relations" perspective (1968, p. 104). She suggests that under certain testing conditions, in order to establish proper rapport between examiner and subject and to put the subject in a reasonable frame of mind, face validity is important. That is, if a test appears childish or irrelevant to the subject, it may provoke a lack of cooperation which would affect the actual validity of the test. Anastasi presents the example of a computational test for machinists worded in terms of machine operations rather than in terms of the oranges and apples so familiar to primary school children.

The American Psychological Association's Standards for Educational and Psychological Tests (1974) lists three additional kinds of validity: content, criterion, and construct validity, all of which may be simultaneously relevant to a particular test.

CONTENT VALIDITY

We have already discussed the idea of content sampling and how the particular items selected for a test can influence reliability. Content sampling may also be relevant to the demonstration of test validity.

When one wishes to assess the quality or quantity of responding in a universe of situations, a test may be constructed whose finite number of items sample from the total universe of possible situations. Wolpe and Lang (1964) developed a Fear Survey Schedule in this manner. They wanted to construct a questionnaire which would allow them to gain information about the total array of specific events and situations to which an individual exhibits fear. The items on the Fear Survey Schedule were therefore intentionally selected so that they sample broadly from a great variety of potentially fear-provoking stimuli, including interpersonal, animal, and location stimuli. Because of this range of items, the Fear Survey Schedule is reasonably *content valid* as an assessor of people's fears. In other words, the content validity of the Fear Survey Schedule rests on the fact that it seems to include a sample of potentially fear-inducing stimuli which are representative of the total universe of stimuli that can conceivably provoke fear. Wolpe and Lang's test would clearly not be content valid for the general purpose of assessing people's fears if it only sampled interpersonal situations and neglected other content areas.

Content validity is typically relevant for achievement tests and other performance evaluations. One of the most frequently heard complaints from students is that an exam was unfair because it asked "the wrong questions." More specifically, "You didn't have any questions on Chapter Six and you asked us to read Chapters One through Six!" Such students are complaining essentially about the content validity of the exam. They are assuming that the exam is a way of assessing knowledge covering six text chapters. If one of these chapters is not represented on the exam, its item content cannot therefore be representative. Consequently, the test can be faulted as not being a content valid assessment tool for knowledge of Chapters One through Six.

It should be clear that any achievement test can only be said to be, or not be, content valid with respect to a particular domain. It is, therefore, imperative for the test developer who wishes to address himself to the issue of content validity to articulate precisely the domain which the test is designed to assess. In the case of assessing gain from an academic course, this means that the instructional objectives must be specified in terms of the specific skills and facts with which students are expected to be familiar. This kind of analysis of course content is the basis upon which the content validity of a test assessing course gain can be claimed. Such operations go far beyond merely suggesting that "This looks like a good final exam for the course," which is the case in face validity.

Another group of assessment situations in which content validity is important is that which involves behavioral evaluations of job performance or aptitude. In these cases, the job must first be analyzed in order to determine the fundamental and most frequently called-upon performance requirements. These, then, should be adequately represented in any assessment procedure, such as one which involves on-the-job behavioral observations. Frequently, job placements or graduate school acceptances are based largely on an interview which taps many skills, such as social poise and speech fluency, which have nothing to do with the actual personal qualities and strengths needed for success in the vocation. Thus, these interviews may have extremely poor content validity, with respect to what should in fact be assessed. Interestingly, both an interviewer and an applicant may feel satisfied with such interview procedures because, if the questioning covers appropriate topics, the interview appears to have face validity.

CRITERION VALIDITY

The next two kinds of validity to be discussed, *predictive* and *concurrent,* are both subsumed under the category of *criterion validity* and are similar to each other in many respects. Most importantly, both involve the use of a correlation coefficient which, because it is now being used to express validity, is called a *validity coefficient.* A validity coefficient must be conceptually differentiated from a reliability coefficient. They each require the correlation of two sets of scores obtained from the same group of subjects. In the case of reliability, these two sets come from the repeated use of the same test. When working toward a validity coefficient, the two sets of scores are obtained by using what may be substantially different operations. One of the operations is always the administration of the test whose validity is to be determined. The second operation yields a set of scores which represents either what the test is supposed to directly assess or predict, or the best index of that which the test is designed to assess. In either case, the second set of scores is called the *criterion*. To the extent test scores are highly correlated with, and, therefore, able to predict, the criterion variable, a test has criterion validity.

When there is a substantial span of time between the test administration and the obtaining of criterion data, *predictive validity* is at stake. The demonstration of a high validity coefficient, based upon the correlation between test scores and a subsequently obtained criterion measure, is at the core of assessment procedures utilized for personnel selection, whether for vocational or academic purposes. Scholastic Aptitude Tests (SAT) and Graduate Record Exams (GRE), familiar to most students, are assessment devices whose goal is to predict later academic success. The obvious criteria against which to correlate SAT performance and GRE scores, in order to establish the predictive validity of these instruments, are grade point averages in college and graduate school, respectively. In these instances, predictive validity is usually important when one is anticipating outcome of a training program or other experiences.

When the interest is not on demonstrating that a test is valid as an outcome predictor but as an evaluator of the status quo at a point in time, it may be appropriate to establish *concurrent validity*. This second kind of criterion validity is one in which the criterion data may be obtained at the same time, concurrent with, the test data. For example, it is often used to establish the diagnostic ability of a personality test. Thus, subjects' scores on a new test designed to assess depression should correlate with clinical diagnoses. People scoring high on the depression test should be diagnosed as more clinically depressed than those scoring low. It is frequently important to establish the concurrent validity of a new test, using the old, standard, assessment method as the criterion. If scores from the two tests are highly correlated, the new test may be preferred if it is more economical as a diagnostic tool in terms of time or money.

While the establishment of criterion validity seems relatively straightforward, there are complications with criteria that may cloud matters considerably. Anastasi (1968) refers to one such problem as *criterion contamination*. This occurs when the test administration has an impact on the criterion measure in some way. Criterion contamination may occur any time people who are associated with the criterion are also privy to the initial test scores of subjects. Under these circumstances, "halo effects" or prejudices based upon a knowledge of subjects' test scores are all free to operate during the process of criterion data collection. The objective or real correlation between the test and its criterion would then be obscured. It is, therefore, essential to the process of establishing criterion validity that the test scores, once they are obtained, be put aside and forgotten or hidden until the criterion measures are in hand. One common practice is not to score the test until after obtaining criterion data.

A second major problem with criterion validity is that it is often not clear just what constitutes an adequate criterion for a test. This is not the case when the test is designed to predict something very specific, such as high school grades. However, more often than not, a personality test is intended to assess relatively general characteristics. A criterion against which to correlate the test scores may be selected because it appears to be the best available index of what the test is trying to measure. In this case, the validity of the criterion, as a best index, may itself be in question. For example, test developers who use school grades as a concurrent criterion for an intelligence test may be criticized on the grounds that school grades are a less than perfect index of intelligence since they are subject to matters of health or motivation. For tests of psychopathology a commonly used criterion is that of psychiatric diagnosis; too often diagnostic labels are attached to psychiatric patients on the basis of a cursory and unreliable intake interview. To employ diagnosis as a concurrent criterion for a new test of psychopathology would be foolhardy, since the brief diagnostic interview is probably less valid than the test for which it is the ill-chosen criterion.

In summary, establishing the criterion validity of a test, either predictive or concurrent, requires one to correlate test scores with a criterion. Bechtoldt (1951, p. 1245) says, a criterion "involves the acceptance of a set of operations, or of indices which are available for use as a criterion." The availability of an acceptable criterion is least likely in the case of personality tests which attempt to assess traits, characteristics, or qualities in people. It is in these situations that one must resort to the fourth kind of validity discussed in the Standards for Educational and Psychological Tests (1974).

CONSTRUCT VALIDITY

Words such as "happiness," "warmth," "dependency," and "aggressiveness" are descriptive in a short hand way of broad classes of human behaviors. Such abstract, personality descriptive terms are called *constructs*. Each construct refers to a large number of real world events. For example, the construct "dependent" may refer to the overt behaviors of hugging another person, waiting for assistance, asking for help, and so on. Logically then, personality tests which attempt to assess "dependency" or other constructs do not have any single referent which may be used as the acceptable criterion against which they may be correlated in order to establish criterion validity. It is in these circumstances that the researcher must try to establish the *construct validity* of a test, the validity of the test as a measure of an abstract personality construct.

Cronbach and Meehl (1955), in their now classic article on construct validity, point out that construct validation does not involve any new procedures. It is simply an orientation which a researcher must take when trying to validate a test which measures a personality trait or quality for which there is no single defining criterion index or operation. It is an orientation which requires the researcher to generate varieties of predictions based on his theoretical understanding of the construct being assessed, and to employ his assessment device of that construct as a vehicle for researching the accuracy of his predictions. The predictions emerge from the general personality theory within which the construct is embedded.

An example at this point will clarify matters. Assume that a test for altruism, the tendency for people to help others without any net gain for themselves, is developed. Criterion validity cannot be established because there is no single variable which can be measured as the defining index of altruism. However, the hypothetical personality theory within which the construct altruism finds itself suggests that altruistic people give money to charity, help people in trouble, and are psychologically very healthy. It can, therefore, be predicted that people who score high on the altruism scale, if it is a valid measure of that construct, should give more money to charity, be more likely to provide help to others, and be better adjusted than people who score low. Briefly, the first prediction may be tested by correlating people's altruism scores with dollar amounts listed on their tax returns under charitable deductions. If the correlation coefficient is positive and reasonably high, the first prediction is confirmed. Similarly, the second prediction can be tested by arranging a contrived situation in which people, pretested on the altruism test, are put in a position of having to choose between helping or not helping another person in difficulty. If high scoring, high altruism subjects offer significantly more aid than do low scoring subjects, the second prediction will find confirmation. Lastly, the third prediction can be tested by correlating the altruism scores with scores from the same subjects on a test of general adjustment. Again, if high altruism scores go hand in hand with high adjustment scores, the final prediction will be supported.

The construct validity of the test is then established to the degree that such theoretical predictions concerned with altruism are empirically upheld. Notice that no single correlational research, experiment, or demonstration, in and of itself will suffice. It is a question of continually gathering information about what the test will and will not predict. Gradually the range of situations to which the test can validly be applied will be defined.

Construct validation research methods

There are no research limits set on what may be done by a test constructor interested in establishing construct validity. Nevertheless, in order to offer some idea of the more commonly used approaches, several validation designs will be summarized. They are presented in a sequence which generally moves from the relatively crude to the more highly refined validity demonstrations. This ordering should not be seen as rigid, in that it would be difficult to rate firmly the relative reference of closely-listed methods. Factors such as the kind of test being validated and the quality with which a particular validation procedure is implemented are important considerations in the individual case.

Blind analysis. This involves calling in people trained in the use of the test whose validity is in question, and having them generate personality descriptions on the basis of reviewing only the test responses. That is, they never actually see the subjects themselves; they are *blind* to them. With this method, the validity of the test rests upon the degree to which blind assessments are consistent with those based upon all available data, including personal knowledge of the subjects.

One difficulty with this approach is that the clinical skills of the assessor may be as important to the results as the validity of the test itself. This point is especially relevant, since blind analysis methodology has been most frequently used with projective techniques, such as the Rorschach whose interpretation, for assessment purposes, requires highly specialized training.

The quality of blind analyses using only the test can be compared to a condition in which the clinicians make up personality descriptions without seeing either the subjects or their responses. It may well be that with or without the test data certain expert clinicians can describe people in global terms which would apply to almost all people. In a demonstration of this expertise, Forer (1949) returned fictitious personality assessments to college undergraduates who thought they were based upon their responses to a previously administered personality test. All of the assessments were identical and included phrases which are applicable to almost anyone: "Your sexual adjustment has presented problems for you"; "Some of your aspirations tend to be pretty unrealistic." When the students were asked if the test evaluations were accurate, Forer reports that virtually every hand rose in agreement. The present writer replicated Forer's demonstration on a group of clinical psychology graduate students enrolled in an assessment seminar. Their response also was one of total acceptance; this was accompanied by surprise, since the assessments were allegedly based upon analyses of the students' handwriting samples which had been collected during the first class meeting. Thus, these findings suggest that the method of blind analysis can yield inappropriately high confidence in the validity of a personality test, especially if personal acceptance of the assessments is used as the criterion.

Forer also concludes that the procedure of blind analysis may be less fallacious if the accuracy of specific statements are evaluated rather than depending upon the "validity" of the global impression received from the overall assessment report. Along this line, the blind analysis procedure can be refined if the assessor is asked to generate specific personality evaluations or to assign subjects to psychiatric diagnostic categories. In the second instance, caution must be observed since the diagnostic classification of psychiatric patients has been shown repeatedly to have far less than optimal reliability, especially when any but the broadest categories, such as "schizophrenic", are employed. Ash (1949), Schmidt and Fonda (1956) and Zigler and Phillips (1961) discuss this point at length.

Matching. Vernon (1936) describes a second research procedure which is sometimes employed in the validation of global personality tests — matching. In matching, a clinician is provided with a number of completed test forms, or protocols, and a number of subject descriptions independently obtained from sources such as case histories. The task is to correctly pair protocols with subject descriptions.

Again, the problem of individual differences in clinical skills obscuring the actual validity of the test itself is relevant to this method. Also, the accuracy of the procedure depends upon the specific nature of what is asked for. If the clinician is given protocol-personality description pairings and simply guesses whether they go together, a chance accuracy rate of 50% would have to be improved upon in order to demonstrate test validity. It is much more difficult to sort out matches, especially if there are more personality descriptions than protocols.

Making things easier for the clinician and, therefore, tending to inflate one's confidence in the test's validity is *contamination*. This refers to information contained jointly in the protocol and in the personality description which gives away the correct matches. An example of contamination would be when a person says a Rorschach inkblot "looks like my older brother," and that subject is the only one whose personality description contains information about an older brother. An accurate match may thus be made, but on a basis irrelevant to establishing the real validity of the test in question. The most important variable influencing the outcome of matching studies is the heterogeneity of the subjects. If they differ widely in personality characteristics it will be relatively easy to derive accurate matches out of a group of protocols and personality descriptions. However, if the subjects are similar to each other in terms of age, sex, social background, and diagnosis, the teasing out of correct matches between protocol and personality descriptions will be far more difficult.

Ratings. This procedure requires clinicians to rate subjects on a number of personality variables based upon the administration of a global personality test. Ratings on the same variables are made by different clinicians using alternative sources of information. To the degree that the two sets of ratings correspond, the construct validity of the test as a measure of personality is enhanced. Familiar problems which arise from the differential skills of the clinicians involved, and from the questionable validity of the sources upon which the criterion set of ratings are based cloud the meaningfulness of this procedure. A variation of this method has one clinician administer the test and generate specific personality assessments while other clinicians rate, based on different data, the accuracy of the test assessments.

The next six validation methods are more applicable to either personality tests which purport to measure specific traits, or to particular scores from global personality tests which are claimed to be signs of certain personality characteristics.

Known groups. A personality test is administered to *known groups* of subjects who, theoretically, should tend to score one way or the other on the test whose validity is in question. If the groups in fact do score differently and as predicted, then the validity of the test is supported. For example, Rotter (1966) developed an *internal versus external control scale* (I-E) Scale. This questionnaire measures the degree to which a person believes himself to be personally influential in bringing about the rewards and punishments he accrues as opposed to these being the result of luck or chance. It is predicted that people who have an internal locus of control will be more active in trying to control and manage themselves and their environments. The externally-oriented person would be more prone to sit back and let things happen because of an expectation that events are out of his control. In comparing black Civil Rights activists and non-activists, both Gore and Rotter (1963) and Strickland (1965) found the former to manifest a greater internal locus of control than the latter. Of a more tentative nature were the findings of James, Woodruff, and Werner (1965) that smokers who permanently quit smoking after the Surgeon General's report were more internally oriented than those who did not quit, and that of MacDonald (1970) who reported that people who most frequently practice birth control tend to have a more internal locus of control.

These results clearly lend support to the validity of the I-E scale as a measure of locus of control. However, Rotter (1954) points to the fact that known group research is prone to the "error of assumed essence." This is an error in which people are selected for inclusion in a group because they share a common characteristic or label, perhaps schizophrenia. This commonality is the basis for wrongly concluding that they are all essentially similar. An older study by Snyder and Cohen (1944) illustrates how the "error of assumed essence" can lead to erroneous conclusions.

Snyder and Cohen tried to replicate a finding by Cohen (1938) which held the promise of being a powerful tool for the diagnosis of schizophrenia. Cohen had reported that, by using a time-consuming and elaborate scoring approach, it was possible to show that the imagery provoked by stimulus phrases was predominantly visual and auditory among normal subjects whereas the imagery reported by schizophrenics was largely kinesthetic, tactual, olfactory, or gustatory in type. Using a new sample of schizophrenics, Snyder and Cohen found no schizophrenic-normal differences. It was concluded that the discrepant results were due to the use of only severely disturbed patients in the Cohen (1938) experiment whereas Snyder and Cohen (1944) employed a schizophrenic sample which was more completely representative of the schizophrenic diagnostic category. Under such conditions the test lost its significance as a diagnostic tool. It failed to differentiate from normal subjects all but the most confused schizophrenics and, therefore, contributed nothing to diagnostic efficiency and little to the understanding of schizophrenia in general; one doesn't need an elaborate test to discriminate highly-confused schizophrenics from normals. Consequently, imagery-testing has taken its rightful place on the spider-spun shelves of assessment memorabilia, driven there by the recognition that "all schizophrenics are not alike."

Correlational designs. Using correlational designs, a test's validity is sought in terms of high correlations between it and other tests with which it should strongly relate, and low correlations with tests that measure theoretically unrelated variables. For example, if someone developed a test of math skills and found that it correlated +.91 with a well-established reading test, the validity of the former would be in question. That is, the high magnitude of correspondence between scores obtained from the two tests would suggest they were measuring the same skill. It is possible that the developer of the math test would later discover that the scores one obtains on his instrument are determined more by a subject's ability to read and understand the complicated printed instructions than they are by the subject's knowledge of math.

The demonstration that a test does not correlate too strongly with other, theoretically unrelated variables, is called *discriminant validity*. *Convergent validity* involves the demonstration that a test does correlate highly with other, theoretically related variables.

An important contributionn to test validation methodology was proposed by Campbell and Fiske (1959). They called for an intricate correlational research design which would, in the context of a single overall study employing one set of subjects, speak to the issues of convergent validation, discriminant validation, and reliability. This research design is referred to as a *multitrait-multimethod matrix* and requires that at least two personality traits be measured by at least two different assessment methods. All possible correlations are computed and represented in a format similar to that illustrated in Fig. 10, in which three traits — trustworthiness, altruism, and intelligence — are each hypothetically assessed using three methods — true-false questionnaire, self-rating questionnaire, and an interview. The meaning of the array of correlation coefficients becomes clearer when they are labeled in one of four ways.

First, there are reliability coefficients; these are printed in bold type in the so-called reliability diagonal. They are generated by correlating a given test with itself (mono trait-monomethod) as would be done in establishing test-retest reliability. For example, the correlation coefficient of +.93, found at the top of Fig. 10, involves two measurements of the trait "trustworthiness" through the use of a true-false test. On the assumption that the traits being measured are theoretically stable ones, test-retest stability, as reflected in high reliability coefficients, would lend support to the construct validity of the tests in question. It can be seen in Fig. 10 that, while all of the reliability coefficients are acceptable, there is a tendency for the three reliabilities based on interviewing to be slightly lower than those using the other two methods.

Second, consider the two diagonals which contain italicized correlation coefficients. In each case, these correlations were computed from scores obtained from two different methods of measuring the same trait (monotrait-heteromethod). To the degree that such correlations between independent and different methods of assessing a trait are high, Campbell and Fiske (1959) would claim that *convergent validity* had been established for the two measures. That is, our confidence in each as a valid index of the trait in question is strengthened. The correlations are, therefore, really validity coefficients, and the two italicized diagonals in Fig. 10 are called validity diagonals. As an example, it can be seen that the true-false and self-rating methods of assessing "trustworthiness" yield a validity coefficient of +.71. In addition, all of the coefficients in the validity diagonals are reasonably high. However, none are as high as the reliability coefficients. Thus, these particular data show there is greater consistency of measurement in assessing a given trait if the same method is used twice (monotrait-monomethod) than if different methods are used (monotrait-heteromethod). This discrepancy should not be surprising since some variation in personality test scores is always due to the particular test procedure used. The assessed intelligence of a person

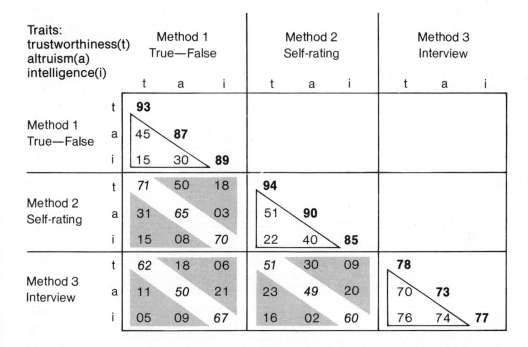

Traits: trustworthiness(t) altruism(a) intelligence(i)		Method 1 True—False			Method 2 Self-rating			Method 3 Interview		
		t	a	i	t	a	i	t	a	i
Method 1 True—False	t	**93**								
	a	45	**87**							
	i	15	30	**89**						
Method 2 Self-rating	t	71	50	18	**94**					
	a	31	65	03	51	**90**				
	i	15	08	70	22	40	**85**			
Method 3 Interview	t	62	18	06	51	30	09	**78**		
	a	11	50	21	23	49	20	70	**73**	
	i	05	09	67	16	02	60	76	74	**77**

Figure 10. Bold figures represent *reliability* coefficients bases on the correlation of a given test with itself (monotrait-monomethod). Italicized figures represent validity coefficients based on the correlations of one test method measuring a given trait with a second test method measuring the same trait (monotrait-heteromethod). The shaded (heterotrait-heteromethod) triangles contain correlations between different measurement methods assessing different traits. The line enclosed (heterotrait-monomethod) triangles contain correlations between tests using the same measurement method assessing different traits.

may be somewhat different if based on an interview than if based upon a self-report method. The data presented in Fig. 10 also suggest that validity coefficients which do not involve the use of interview methodology, such as correlations between true-false and self-report methods of assessing trustworthiness, altruism, and intelligence, have a slight tendency to be the most substantial (.71, .65, and .70, respectively).

In order for construct validity to be satisfactory, one method of measuring two different traits (heterotrait-monomethod) should yield a lower correlation than does the use of two methods to measure the same trait (monotrait-heteromethod). In other words, consistency of measurement should depend more upon the assessment of the same trait than upon the application of similar assessment methods. When a single method of assessing two different traits produces appropriately low correlations, *discriminant validity* is demonstrated.

As Fig. 10 illustrates, this standard is *not* met in the lower right, solid-outlined heterotrait-monomethod triangle whose coefficient tends to be at least as high as corresponding monotrait-heteromethod validity coefficients. For example, it can be seen that the correlation computed from assessments of intelligence and trustworthiness using only interview methodology (+.76) is improperly higher than the validity coefficient based on measuring just intelligence using an interview and a self-rating format (+.60). In fact, all three of the coefficients in the lower right heterotrait-monomethod triangle are unsatisfactorily high. This suggests that regardless of the trait being assessd, whether it be trustworthiness, altruism, or intelligence, subjects score in a consistently high or low fashion when evaluated via an interview. It is possible that some subjects just come across as generally positive or negative in an interview. Their interview behavior then yields high heterotrait-monomethod correlations, even though the interview behavior itself is irrelevant to their real level of trustworthiness, altruism, and intelligence. This, of course, would lead one to lose confidence in the validity of interview methodology as a way of evaluating trustworthiness, altruism, and intelligence.

A second way in which the multitrait-multimethod design speaks to the issue of discriminant validity is through a comparison of monotrait-heteromethod validity coefficients and those coefficients based on two different traits, each being assessed by a different method. These latter heterotrait-heteromethod correlations may be found in the shaded triangles in Fig. 10. To the degree that the heterotrait-heteromethod triangles contain correlation coefficients which are lower than validity coefficients, discriminant validity is again demonstrated. For example, the validity coefficient computed from self-rating and interview methods of assessing intelligence (+.60) is shown to be larger than the correlation coefficient computed from the self-rating of intelligence and the interview assessment of altruism (+.20). It should be obvious that heterotrait-heteromethod correlation coefficients would always tend to be lowest since the two sets of scores upon which the coefficient is based have neither a single trait nor a single method in common.

Some final words about the multitrait-multimethod design are in order. While the ideas of convergent and discriminant validity are important, these qualities are not so easily evaluated as might be suggested by the use of real numbers in the form of correlation coefficients. For instance, the degree of discriminant validity one would like to see established depends upon a rational judgment of how unrelated two traits are to each other. If they are theoretically completely unrelated to each other, then heterotrait-heteromethod and heterotrait-monomethod correlation coefficients should ideally approximate zero. However, if two traits are theoretically related, such as perhaps math reasoning and computational skills, a correlation which was too low would be as damaging to the validity of tests measuring these characteristics as would a hetero-trait correlation coefficient of +.99.

Another important point is that when Campbell and Fiske (1959) say that validity coefficients should be "higher" than heterotrait-heteromethod and heterotrait-monomethod correlation coefficients, they can't prescribe by how much. Again, the judgment of how much is enough would depend upon a rational understanding of the degree to which the various traits being assessed should theoretically intercorrelate. For two theoretically related traits, a heterotrait correlation coefficient may only have to be minimally lower than the validity, monotrait-heteromethod, coefficients of either trait.

Lastly, if one does not obtain desired magnitudes of convergent and discriminant validity, it is not always easy to tell where the problem lies. For example, if a monotrait-heteromethod correlation coefficient is too low, which method of assessment is invalid, or are they both possibly weak? These kinds of issues render the multitrait-multimethod validation designs complex to implement and to interpret.

Sociometric. Sociometric is a useful construct validation procedure which requires subjects to take a personality test, while others who are familiar with the subjects, usually their peers, rate or rank them on the same traits as those assessed by the test. The strength in this design lies in the fact that peer ratings are based upon a broad familiarity with the subjects and that each subject may be judged by a number of peers. This format would obviously be most applicable in classroom, fraternity, camp, or job settings.

A number of rules, if followed, tend to further strengthen this approach. First, the selection of subject groups should be based on their members having a long-standing and situationally varied familiarity with each other. Second, the personality test should be administered prior to the sociometric. In this way the test is administered under usual testing conditions, without the pre-test sensitization to the trait that a previously administered sociometric would arouse. This sensitization may take the form of atypical honesty while completing the test because each subject would be aware that the "goods" on him have already been delivered by his peers. Third, the sociometric itself should ask peers to rate each other on a personality dimension, or to nominate others who fulfill a certain description, which is couched in explicit behavioral terms and not just referred to by a trait name. Trait names are too often open to individual interpretation. An "honest person" may imply different things to different raters. By describing the kinds of behaviors that the ratings should be based upon, everyone starts from a more common perspective. This last suggestion also helps to get around the problem of "halo effects" and other biases.

Once the sociometric data are obtained, the average trait-rating assigned to each subject by his peers is correlated with each subject's score on the personality test measuring that same trait. If the sociometric procedure employs nominations, such as naming the three people who are most and least like the behavioral description, a variety of scoring procedures may be used. One simple method is to assign each subject $+1$ for every nomination he receives as being similar to the behavioral description and -1 for every time he is nominated as being unlike the behavioral description. The algebraic sum of points is then the sociometric score to be correlated with personality test scores. Obviously, strong positive correlations between a test and a sociometric designed to assess the same trait is evidence in favor of the test's construct validity.

The sociometric validation procedure is illustrated by Rotter (1967) in his description of the construction and validation of an Interpersonal Trust scale. This scale is intended to assess the degree to which subjects hold an expectancy "that the word, promise, or written statement of another individual or group can be relied upon." The Trust scale itself consists of 25 items which subjects self-rate from "agree" to "disagree." One sample item is: "Most elected public officials are really sincere in their campaign promises." One of the ways in which Rotter established the validity of his scale as a measure of the construct "interpersonal trust" was to arrange for the members of two fraternities and two sororities to complete the Interpersonal Trust Scale and to participate in a sociometric procedure. House members each nominated three people who matched the first behavioral description and three who matched the second:

> This person expects others to be honest. She is not suspicious of other people's intentions, she expects others to be open and that they can be relied upon to do what they say they will do.

> This person is cynical. She thinks others are out to get as much as they can for themselves. She has little faith in human nature and in the promises or statements of other people.

Every time a subject was nominated as being like the first description he earned a $+1$. A nomination as similar to the second description earned a -1. Rotter reports that the Interpersonal Trust Scale was significantly related to the sociometric trust score, with the validity coefficients from the four Houses ranging from $+.23$ to $+.55$. In addition, discriminant validity for the Trust Scale was provided by the $-.03$ correlation between it and sociometric ratings of "gullibility," defined as naive and easily fooled as opposed to sophisticated and experienced.

Behavior. A behavioral assessment can often make it possible to get around many of the inferential problems inherent in rating because the test is validated against some directly observed behavior which is theoretically related to high or low trait possession. In situations where one can conduct mass pre-testing of a captive audience, such as Introductory Psychology students, it is possible to later expose those students to an experimental situation and record if they behave as theoretically expected. The main difficulty with using the criterion of behavior is that of situational specificity. That is, the specific behavior sample observed may not be representative of the trait in general. This is especially likely if the behavior is based upon some artificial experimental or laboratory situation. Consequently, it is frequently best to try to observe naturally occurring behavior.

Condition induced change scores. Subjects are pre-tested on a personality test and then exposed to some situation or experience which should theoretically produce an alteration in test scores. Evidence of such change in scores constitutes support for the construct validity of the test. One report by Gorman (1968) illustrates the method of condition induced changes in scores as a vehicle for establishing the construct validity of the previously mentioned Rotter I-E Scale. Gorman was studying a group of active supporters of Eugene McCarthy, Democratic presidential aspirant at the 1968 National Convention. As most will recall, McCarthy failed to attain the nomination. Gorman administered the I-E scale to the McCarthyists on the day following the voting and found that their mean score was much more in the external direction than was to be expected on the basis of Rotter's normative college data. Gorman concluded that his subjects, having been exposed to a personally important experience in which their efforts to effect events proved fruitless held a stronger general belief that rewards and punishments were beyond their control. Of course, the weakness in this study is that no pre-test I-E scale measures were obtained. However, the assumption that the McCarthy supporters probably had, if anything, an internal "locus of control" prior to the Democratic Convention is consistent with other findings, in which political activists were shown to generally have an internal orientation.

In concluding this section on methods of establishing the construct validity of tests it should be said that the eight general designs which were discussed are neither exhaustive nor mutually exclusive. Any single validation project might well incorporate a number of the above proceedings in almost an unlimited variety of combinations. In addition, no single research design, no matter how complex, ever completes the job of establishing a test's construct validity. Rather, construct validation is a continuing process of experimentation and demonstration. Each finding says something new about areas in which the test might be usefully applied and where it can be expected to fail. Each finding, therefore, defines more precisely the nature of the construct for which the test is a valid measure. For example, subsequent to a large number of validational studies, it may turn out that what was once billed as a general measure of "aggression" is more precisely, an index of the level of "aggression among college students toward authority figures."

Marlowe-Crowne Social Desirability Scale: An Example of Construct Validation

When people fill out personality tests they often do not accurately report what they really are like, as we will see more precisely in Chapter 13. An example of this is when people respond in a manner which we have called the "best foot forward". It is said that such people are responding to test items in a "socially desirable" way by presenting an image which they feel is a favorable one. Most psychologists in the 1940s and 1950s viewed this kind of social desirability test-taking strategy as a troublesome source of error, contributing to the invalidity of personality tests. Crowne and Marlowe (1964), however, sought to measure this test situation behavior as a valuable index of personality in itself. They believed that when an individual completes a personality test with the goal of appearing socially desirable overriding the goal of honesty, he probably has a *need for approval*. Consequently, Crowne and Marlowe proceeded to develop a social desirability questionnaire which was intended to be a measure of the personality construct "need for approval".

The scale they constructed consists of 33 self-referent statements to which subjects respond either "true" or "false." None of the items contained content that was indicative of abnormality or psychopathology. About half were judged to be highly socially desirable to endorse, but were also quite unlikely to be actually true: "I'm always willing to admit it when I make a mistake." If a person tended to check "true" on these items, he would be saying some very socially desirable things about himself, but would probably also, for the most part, be lying. The second category of items consists of statements which would tend to meet cultural disapproval if admitted, but which are nevertheless generally true of most people: "I sometimes feel resentful if I don't get my way." Subjects who check "false" on these items would also tend to be lying, in the service of coming across as socially desirable. A person's social desirability (S-D) score is simply the number of times he responds "true" to the first kind and "false" to the second kind of item.

In order to establish validity of the Marlowe-Crowne S-D scale, a construct validation approach was necessitated. This approach was called for because there was no single criterion with which the scale might be correlated that could serve as a defining index of a "need for approval." Some of the steps taken in this construct validation process are presented here.

Because a need for approval was thought to be a relatively stable personality characteristic, it was important to demonstrate that the Marlowe-Crowne S-D scale reflected this in the form of test-retest reliability. The testing of 57 subjects on two occasions, separated by a one month interval, revealed this reliability coefficient to be a highly acceptable +.88. Also, because the scale was composed of items which were all designed to measure the same personality characteristic, its construct validity would depend partly upon showing that subjects tend to respond in a consistent manner across items. This was done by calculating an index of internal consistency, the Kuder-Richardson reliability coefficient, which also yielded a value of +.88.

As mentioned, the statements which comprise the Marlowe-Crowne S-D scale were written so that the test would not be a measure of psychopathology. Discriminant validity would therefore depend upon Marlowe-Crowne S-D scores having a low correlation with measures of psychopathology. In fact, correlations with the pathology subscales of the Minnesota Multiphasic Personality Inventory (MMPI) tended to be low to moderate, and generally negative in direction. That is, there was only a slight tendency for low S-D subjects to score high, toward the pathological, on the MMPI subscales.

If the tendency to respond in a socially desirable way reflects a need for approval, then the Marlowe-Crowne S-D scale, if it is valid, should be able to predict the behavior of high and low need-for-approval people in a variety of situations. Therefore, research was conducted with this in mind.

In one study conducted by Marlowe and Crowne (1961), it was reasoned that people with a high need for approval might be most likely to express views which conformed to what they thought an authoritative, prestigious person might wish to hear. In order to test this notion, 57 subjects were given the Marlowe-Crowne S-D scale. They were divided at the mean, yielding one high and one low need-for-approval group. All subjects were later requested by a psychologist to engage in what was intended to be a boring task. They were asked to repeatedly place 12 spools, one at a time, in a box, empty the box, and again replace the spools, one at a time. This went on for 25 minutes, at which point the psychologist interrupted by saying that he hoped the subject enjoyed the task; and he would now like to obtain personal reactions to the experiment. Subjects then rated how much they enjoyed the task, how much they learned, the scientific importance of the experiment, and their willingness to participate in a similar experiment in the future. On all four of these questions, the high need-for-approval subjects expressed significantly more positive opinions than did low need-for-approval subjects.

These results provide validation for the Marlowe-Crowne S-D scale as measuring a general need for approval. The results were interpreted by Marlowe and Crowne to suggest that high-scoring subjects perceived the psychologist as someone whose favor was worth courting. They, therefore, were motivated to tell him that his experiment was interesting, important, informative, and worth participating in again. The subjects scoring lower on the S-D scale, because they presumably have a low need-for-approval, were better able to resist the temptation to say what the psychologist would like to hear and expressed more realistic opinions of his experiment.

A second experiment conducted by Marlowe (1962) was based on the assumption that social praise, or expression of approval, is experienced as most valuable and rewarding to high need-for-approval people. It was, therefore, predicted that subjects scoring high on the Marlowe-Crowne S-D scale would most rapidly acquire a new behavior if social praise were the reward for such behavior change. Subjects having a lower need for approval would not find social praise as gratifying and would acquire the behaviors less rapidly. The behavior to be acquired in this study was the expression of positive self-referent statements such as "I get good grades" or "I was elected as an officer of my fraternity."

The Marlowe-Crowne S-D scale was administered to 76 subjects who were then immediately given a 15 minute individual interview. This was presented to the subjects as part of a research designed to find out what college students think and feel about themselves. On a random basis, half of the subjects were assigned to a treatment in which the interviewer provided social praise by saying "Mm-hmm" subsequent to each of the subject's positive self-references. The remaining subjects were not given this reward after expressing positive self-referent statements. The data which were analyzed consisted of the ratio of positive self-referent statements to total statements made, the PSR ratio.

During the first five minutes of the interview, whether experiencing the social praise or non-praise treatments, and regardless of whether they scored high or low on the Marlowe-Crowne S-D scale, all subjects tended to have about the same PSR ratios. However, when the PSR ratios for the entire interview were compared, the high need-for-approval subjects who were receiving the social praise treatment were found to have a significantly higher PSR ratio than any other group of subjects. It is especially noteworthy that the high need-for-approval subjects in the non-praise treatment obtained lower overall PSR ratios than their counterparts in the praise condition. This indicates that high need-for-approval subjects in general do not have a strong predisposition to emit positive self-references, but only begin to do so when a reward relevant to the gratification of the approval need, social praise, is provided for such expressions.

The last experiment to be considered was reported by Crowne and Marlowe in their book *The Approval Motive* (1964). It tested the hypothesis that people with a high need for approval will conform more to group pressure in the hope of "fitting in" and earning group support than will low need-for-approval people. In the case of this research, conformity was defined as a public "statement of a judgment or opinion coincident with that of an incorrect majority in the absence of logical justification for that judgment" (p. 74).

The experimental task consisted of having to identify the larger of two clusters of dots. Each pair of clusters was projected on a screen for one second. Earlier work had established that the two clusters comprising each of the twenty pairs could be easily distinguished from each other.

Twenty-six female undergraduates volunteered to participate in an experiment on "perceptual discrimination." When each arrived she found four other ostensible volunteers also present, two males and two females. In fact, these four "subjects" were experimental accomplices who had arranged to play out a prepared script. First the subject and the accomplices filled out the S-D form. Then, on four of the 20 perceptual discrimination trials, the accomplices were scheduled to give the correct response. On 16 trials they unanimously gave the wrong answer on cue.

The data for this experiment were simply the number of times, out of a possible 16, each subject yielded in judgment to the incorrect majority. Analysis showed that when the subjects were divided at the mean of the S-D scores into high need vs. low need-for-approval groups, the former had significantly more conforming responses (mean = 9.46) than did the latter (mean = 5.46). It, therefore, appears that high need-for-approval people, as defined by their Marlowe-Crowne S-D scale scores, are most likely to conform under pressure of perceived social influence.

In conclusion, it must be pointed out that each of the three experiments cited can be individually faulted as a validation study for the Crowne-Marlowe S-D scale. For example, the first spool-packing experiment, as well as the third conformity study, might both be interpreted to mean that high S-D scoring subjects don't have a need for approval, only a ready disposition to lie. As Crowne and Marlowe (1964) point out, choosing between these alternatives would be a matter of preference were it not for the evidence provided by many other experiments. That is, the conception of the Marlowe-Crowne S-D scale as a lying index does not allow one to account easily for the findings of the second experiment in verbal behavior. There is no theoretical reason to expect liars to be more influenced in verbal behavior by subtle social reinforcement than non-liars. Therefore, when all the studies are taken into account, the competing "liar" hypothesis seems to account less well for the findings than does a "need for approval" interpretation. Consequently, on balance, the validity of the Marlowe-Crowne S-D scale as a measure of the construct "need for approval" is established.

The process that has been illustrated is one which is repeated over and over as personality tests undergo the process of construct validation. In general, confidence in a test's construct validity increases to the extent that findings from research using the test are most easily accounted for by assuming that the test is measuring what it purports to.

RELATION BETWEEN RELIABILITY AND VALIDITY

Can a test be reliable but not valid; valid but not reliable? Neither? Both? Of course all of these combinations are possible. In general, reliability is a prerequisite for validity. If a test is like a rubber band, measuring whatever it is measuring very inconsistently, it is quite unlikely to be a valid index of the trait in question. There is an important exception to this rule. Some personality tests are not designed to assess stable personality characteristics. Rather, they are intended to evaluate momentary states. An example of such a test format is a "mood check list," which is simply a list of personality descriptive adjectives such as happy, angry, etc. Subjects are asked to check those adjectives which describe their state at the moment. Obviously, the particular adjectives endorsed will vary drastically over time, depending upon the subject's emotional condition. Consequently, a high degree of test-retest reliability, especially if the two administrations occur under maximally different testing conditions, would suggest that the mood check list is invalid as a state measure. Validity for this kind of test would depend in part upon demonstrating relatively low test-retest reliability. Earlier, we discussed other situations in which a test might be reliable, but invalid because it is simply not measuring what was expected.

SUMMARY

This chapter was devoted to the issue of validity: is a personality assessment procedure measuring what it is supposed to be measuring? We first discussed face and content validity. Establishment of the two kinds of criterion validity, predictive and concurrent, were shown to depend upon correlational research. Research was also at the heart of the process known as construct validation. The validity of a test as the measure of a construct must be established, using the approach of construct validation, when there is no acceptable criterion of the construct in question. Several research designs commonly used to establish the construct validity of a test were described. The multitrait-multimethod matrix correlational design was particularly stressed as a sophisticated solution to a difficult problem. Finally, some illustrative research designed to establish the construct validity of the Marlowe-Crowne social desirability scale was reviewed.

TERMS TO KNOW

CHAPTER 12
Interviewing

Probably the oldest and most frequently used vehicle for obtaining information about another person is the interview. There are as many types of interviews as there are reasons for conducting them. Employment interviews assist in evaluating the qualifications of job applicants; poll type interviews hope to uncover the pulse of public opinion; and stress interviews are geared to provide information about how the individual conducts himself under duress rather than to obtain content. Stress interviews may be used to establish the grit of a person being considered for a position of authority. They assess the interpersonal inflappability of a candidate for training in a public service-delivery field, and the emotional sturdiness of a candidate for a dangerous assignment. In general, stress interviews involve the intrusion of some potentially disruptive surprise. This writer was subject to what was in retrospect a mildly stressful interview when applying to graduate school. The interviewer repeatedly asked, "How do you think this interview is going for you?" To this day I wonder whether it would have been better to stay "cool," or become hostile; I did neither.

When we meet someone for the first time it is not unusual for interview-type questions to form the basis of initial small talk. "Where do you go to school?" "What kind of work do you do?" "Are you married?" This kind of personal background data is often at the core of interviewing processes, regardless of whether the formal setting is that of government, business, or industry.

Case History

In the mental health field, background data is commonly obtained in interviews upon *intake*, when the patient is first presented, by himself or his family, to the psychotherapist or the admitting personnel of a psychiatric hospital. Despite the seemingly objective nature of some of the data procured in intake interviews with the patient or close family members, extreme caution must be observed in taking the information at face value. Lazarus (1961) reports that mothers incorrectly relate factual information about their children, including birth data, about 11% of the time. In addition, 25% of the mothers studied inaccurately reported important matters such as the incidence of mental illness in the family.

McGraw and Molloy (1941) and Pyles, Stolz and Macfarlane (1935) sought to establish the validity of mothers' retrospective reports on their children's developmental history by using as a validity criterion the observations that had been made of the children by experts. Both sets of researchers found frequent discrepancies. However, Robbins (1963) points out that in such research it is difficult to determine whether the mothers are truly inaccurate or whether they are simply reporting matters from a frame of reference which differs considerably from that of the experts.

In an attempt to correct this ambiguity, Robbins (1963) conducted a study which examined the recall accuracy of mothers by contrasting their retrospective accounts with what they had previously said in the course of a longitudinal research that had begun with the birth of the then three year old children. A total of 47 families were studied. Robbins found that certain items were well-remembered by both fathers and mothers. These included the child's birth weight and whether he had been breast or bottle fed. In general, recall of whether or not certain events had occurred was far superior to recall of the time dimensions surrounding events. For example, onset of bowel and bladder training was not too well remembered. With regard to the former, mothers were found to err an average of +14.2 weeks, and fathers +22.7 weeks. For bladder training the discrepancies were +22.3 and 25.5 weeks, almost a half year, respectively.

Much of the distortion uncovered by Robbins seems to have been partly associated with a need to create favorable impressions. It is reported that most of the children had not been fully toilet-trained at the time of the retrospective interview. However, in those families where the training had been completed, the "parents tended to describe its accomplishment as taking place virtually overnight, and to gloss over the lengthy process of acquisition" (p. 266). In addition, there was a noted trend for parental retrospective distortion to shift in the direction of suggested expert advice. Mothers erroneously reported that they had engaged in demand feeding of their children and that weaning and toilet training had been accomplished earlier and later, respectively, than had been the case.

In all these instances, the retrospective reports corresponded more highly with the recommendation of Dr. Spock (1957) than did the original reports given during the early months of the longitudinal study. Seven mothers whose children sucked their thumbs up to a year, and who even expressed concern over the habit, retrospectively reported that their child had not sucked the thumb. In addition, four of the five mothers who incorrectly recalled their use of a pacifier did so in the direction of saying one was used when it had not been. It seems more than coincidental that Dr. Spock favors the use of a pacifier to discourage what he feels is the undesirable habit of thumbsucking.

The magnitude of these distortions are rendered even more disturbing when it is recalled that these child-rearing events were occurring much after birth and, in the case of toilet training, no more than two years prior to the retrospective report. In addition, the parents had better than average educations, a variable known to be related to parental accuracy in recalling child-rearing practices. Finally, the parents knew that their current recollections could be checked against their earlier statements. It was hoped that this "knowledge might serve both as a deterrent to distortion and as an intellectual challenge for demonstrating their acuity to the personnel of the study" (p. 269). Evidently this did not happen.

How much less validity exists when the anguished parents of a newly-admitted adolescent patient are asked by an admitting psychiatrist to reconstruct parenting practices and important early experiences of their child? There is as yet no evidence bearing on this very critical question. However, the concern is deepened by the discovery that few traumatic events turn up in the case histories of schizophrenics, as they do in over 25% of the case histories of normal individuals (Schofield and Balian, 1959). If one subscribes to the popular, but not universally accepted, hypothesis that early trauma is an antecedent of later psychological maladjustment, the reasonable inference to draw is that the case history data of the schizophrenics was not accurate.

The importance of case history data, despite its questionable validity, was dramatized by Kostlan (1954). Kostlan asked experienced clinical psychologists to produce psychological evaluations of patients using varying amounts of provided information. The validity of these evaluations was judged against the criteria of judgments made by the patients' psychotherapists and by other experts having access to all available test and background information. Kostlan found that when the clinical psychologists used the output from a battery of tests, including the MMPI, Rorschach, and a sentence completion test, but did not have access to a social case history, they did rather poorly. A social case history is prepared by social workers during an intake interview which contains family, work and military history, current social status, and presenting complaints. In fact, without the social case history, the psychologists' judgments were no more accurate than when the only data available were patient file face sheets, which reported little more than name, age, and date of admission. Kostlan concludes that the social case history is crucial as a source of cues, as well as background against which to interpret other test results, and that "diagnosis made from test results without regard for the patients' background seems to be ineffective" (p. 87).

Mental Status Interview

A second kind of interview which may accompany the case history intake interview is the *mental status interview*. This interaction is geared toward assessing the current depth of a patient's psychological impairment. Kleinmuntz (1967) lists six dimensions to which the mental status interview is addressed. First, the general impression that the patient projects, in terms of characteristic behavior and appearance, is noted. Second, mental content is explored by probing for evidence of delusions and hallucinations, obsessional preoccupations and fears. Third, emotional tone is evaluated. The possibility of depression is especially explored because of the ever-present concern over potential suicide. An effort is also made to judge the appropriateness of the patient's affect by noting whether there are spells of laughter or crying, for example, which are incongruent with the situations in which they occur. An assessment of intellectual functioning derives from questioning the patient about person, place, and time. Cognitive confusion over these fundamental facts, usually taken as one sign of psychosis, is exemplified by the patient who believes himself to be Frederick Chopin living in Paris in the 1840s. In addition, simple arithmetic problems may be administered, such as asking the patient to count backward by threes from 100. The fifth goal of an intake interview is to evaluate a patient's stream of speech; illogical utterances, nonsense words, and a general lack of coherence are considered particularly important. Last, the insight of the patient into the nature, cause, and severity of his psychological problem is assessed.

The mental status interview, when conducted upon intake, is especially prone to error because of the situational torment to which the patient is subject. The patient is usually acting on a very recent self or imposed decision to seek hospital confinement. The stigma associated with the decision to become a "mental patient," uncertainty over what the course of events and outcome will be, and the unfamiliarity with the probing intake personnel all summate to make the client behave in a rather atypical manner. Added to this is Kleinmuntz' (1967, p. 247) *hello effect*, which refers to the tendency of incoming patients to "fake bad," perhaps unintentionally, in order to legitimize their presence in the hospital. These situational aspects of the patient's experience may preclude an accurate intake assessment.

Psychotherapeutic Interviews

Apart from the content areas covered, the major difference between interview techniques has to do with the degree of structure. At one end of this dimension are completely *unstructured* interviews. Here the interviewer may only have a general idea about the areas to be covered. There is open opportunity for new topics to be pursued and for important ones to be dealt with in depth. Traditional psychotherapies, with their emphasis on communication and the interpersonal encounter between client and therapist, are rooted in this kind of unstructured interview on a long term basis.

Psychoanalytic Interviews. Psychoanalysis is one very good example of a psychotherapy based on a variation of unstructured interviewing. Early in Freud's career he learned that a patient's "forgotten" experiences, which were still the cause of inner turmoil, may be discovered if the patient is encouraged to talk openly. This openness of expression came to be adopted by Freud in the form of *free association*, the "fundamental rule of psychoanalysis." Free association requires patients to tell everything that is on their minds, no matter how trivial, embarrassing, or illogical the expressions may be. Relaxing on a couch, the patient is free to go where he may after receiving the initial instruction in the process of free association:

> Act as though, for instance, you were a traveler sitting next to the window of
> a railway carriage and describing to someone inside the carriage the chang-
> ing views which you see outside (1963, p. 147).

The analyst retreats from supplying input and the conversation becomes largely unidirectional — from client to analyst. The therapist's low profile is behaviorally expressed by remaining silently behind and out of the visual field of the client. This ritualistic aspect of orthodox psychoanalytic interviewing, the chair behind the couch, is claimed by Fromm (1959) to have been initiated because Freud "did not want to be stared at for eight hours a day" (p. 107). Only later were more theoretically-based justifications added, such as it being best for the client not to see the therapist's reactions in order to help maintain relaxation and to remain as uninhibited as possible. Freud maintained that favorable therapeutic progress could be effected if such interviews were conducted one hour a day, six days a week for as many as two to six years. Through this intensive effort the most inaccessible regions of psychological life would eventually come under the conscious scrutiny of the patient.

Sullivanian interviews. Sullivan, who developed an important theory of both personality development (1953) and psychopathology (1956) probably was as explicit as any practitioner regarding the conduct of psychotherapeutic interviewing (1954). He said that the psychiatric interview involves four stages, with the start of each dependent upon the attainment of the goals appropriate to the preceding stage. In the *inception*, the interviewer attempts to tentatively arrive at a formulation of the interpersonal problems from which the client is suffering. The *reconnaissance* has as its goal fact-gathering. It roughly corresponds to what was described earlier as a case history interview. Hopefully, a full background understanding of the problem will be acquired and a statement summarizing the conclusions of the interviewer will be presented to the patient. The point is to check the validity of the therapist's understanding against that of the client, and to come to a decision regarding the appropriateness of the problem for psychotherapeutic intervention. The third interview stage is really the core of Sullivanian psychotherapy. During this detailed *inquiry* a most painstaking examination is conducted of the patient's interpersonal difficulties, with special attention being given to the elucidation of symptomatic behaviors such as apathy, depression, anxiety, distorted thinking, and atypical mannerisms. The final stage is aptly called *termination,* where the interviewer discusses his findings and offers a plan of action which is expected to be of lasting value to the patient.

In contrast to Freudian psychoanalysis, the Sullivanian interviewing procedure is much more open. The patient is continually privy to both the interviewer's discoveries and goals, short and long range. In addition, it is more planned and less instructional than the free association interviewing process of psychoanalysis.

Rogerian interviews. A third psychotherapeutic interviewing technique, even more unstructured than free association, is that of Carl Rogers. Rogers' therapy (1951) is called "client centered" and the interviewing process itself can be characterized as being "non-directive." Rogers says that the interviewer must first create a "warm and permissive atmosphere in which the client is free to bring out any attitudes and feelings which he may have (1946, p. 416). Once the client starts to become expressive, the interviewer must be completely accepting of what is said. This is done by abstaining from pointed questioning, offering advice, or being critical. The therapist engages in "a sensitive reflection and clarification of the client's attitudes" (p. 416) and feelings.

Rogers believes that this type of highly unstructured interviewing can serve to release constructive forces within the patient which will move him in the direction of maturity, social adjustment, independence, and productivity. The theoretical rationale for this can be found in Chapter 18 on phenomenological theory.

Problems with Unstructured Interviews. One of the major difficulties with unstructured interviews is that they are extremely susceptible to all of the sources of interpersonal assessment error noted in Chapter 9. Even when the therapist fades into the background, as in the free association method, it is difficult to establish how much of the subject's interview behavior is a product of himself and how much is due to the interviewer as a "participant observer." In coining this term, Sullivan meant that the interviewer can never really stand completely apart from the person being interviewed. Unavoidably, the interviewer's own behavior, no matter how minimal, is both a stimulus for and a consequence of the subject's behavior. The importance of this was exemplified by research conducted on the interviewing style of Rogers himself. Truax (1966) analyzed the audiotapes of Rogers and found that this staunch advocate of non-directive interviewing was actually selectively reinforcing certain categories of patient statements, such as those expressive of insight. The reinforcement consisted of the very simplest verbal expressions such as "uh huh," an ostensibly non-directive statement which implicitly communicates approval. It was found that, for the most part, the patient's verbal expressions which were greeted with such verbal consequences from the therapist increased in frequency. Thus, even the most skilled and well-intentioned interviewers fall prey to the "participant observer" trap.

Structured Interviews

One of the ways in which psychologists have attempted to limit the amount of sloppiness which may permeate an interview, is to move these interpersonal encounters onto a much more structured footing. The *structured interview* follows a reasonably standard format for all subjects and is characterized by much more directiveness than we see in Freudian and Rogerian interviews. At the same time, this greater active participation by the interviewer is limited by guidelines which can range anywhere from a list of topics to be covered to a schedule of specific questions which must be posed without deviation from form.

The great advantage of the structured interview over its unstructured counterpart is that the former process is more or less standardized, the interview format remains constant across interviews. Cross-subject comparisons, thus, become more meaningful. The great disadvantage of the structured interview is that the rapport and the level of communication possible in the unstructured format may be lost. Granted, skilled interviewers can follow a rigid schedule of questions while maintaining a rather informal posture. However, the danger is always present that the interviewee will become turned off by what is perceived to be an interminable list of insensitively and impersonally presented questions.

Vineland Social Maturity Scale. One popular example of an interview which does not appear to interfere with rapport while maintaining structure is the Vineland Social Maturity Scale (Doll, 1965). This is a developmental schedule which has 117 questions covering eight content areas:

1. general self-help (sits unsupported, avoids simple hazards),
2. self-help in eating (does not drool, eats with a fork),
3. self-help in dressing (buttons coat, combs or brushes hair),
4. locomotion (walks upstairs unassisted, goes to school unattended),
5. occupation (cuts with scissors, performs routine chores, directs or manages affairs of others),
6. communication (imitates sounds, reads on own initiative, follows current events),
7. self-direction (makes minor purchases, looks after own health),
8. socialization (plays with other children, assumes responsibilities beyond own needs).

Within each content category a range of age levels is spanned. The questions bearing on eating cover the years from birth to 10, whereas those bearing on self-direction cover the years from five to 25+. The age at which subjects in a standardization group were reported capable of manifesting the behavior referred to in a particular item determined the age level at which the item was placed on the schedule. Unfortunately, only 620 subjects were in this standardization sample, with 10 males and 10 females at each year from birth to 30. Thus, the representativeness of the social maturity norms derived from this relatively small standardization sample is in question. Nevertheless, the test has been a valuable assessment tool at the younger ages, and for mental retardates in particular. The Vineland is useful in this regard because the question with profoundly and moderately retarded individuals is not so much what their IQ might be as it is what they are capable of doing. It is this degree of adaptiveness that the Vineland is geared to assess.

The schedule itself is usually administered to an informant who is familiar with the subject, such as the teacher, parent, or ward aide if the child is institutionalized. In a conversational manner, the informant is encouraged to discuss the child in terms of the eight content areas of the schedule, each being considered in turn. The interviewer must be skilled in steering the discussion so that scores for each schedule item can be assigned. This interviewing procedure is, therefore, much more difficult than simply reading the 117 items asking whether the subject is capable of doing a certain thing. The conversational tone achieved has two advantageous effects. First, it circumvents the problems encountered when the informant experiences the verbal exchange as being little more than a string of cold questions seeking quick answers. Second, the informant is more likely to provide valid data. Specifically, it is too easy for a mother to reply in the affirmative to any item which her child occasionally fulfills, even though the intent is to discover what the child routinely does. The impartial interviewer will be less biased than the mother in ascertaining the usual level of a child's behavior, if information relevant to such a determination is imparted in a conversational context.

The Vineland permits the interviewer to arrive at a Social Age for the subject. If a child earns a Social Age (SA) of six years, it does not necessarily suggest that the self-help and responsibility level is characteristic of the average six year old; this is because an SA of six years may be attained, when many items are failed which most six year-olds can pass, if the deficits are compensated for by the passing of an equal number of items which rest at an age level higher than six. This kind of uneven pattern is very characteristic of institutionalized retarded youngsters who may receive special training in some areas of self-help, such as feeding and toileting, but have less opportunity to progress in other areas, such as communication.

The test-retest reliability of the Vineland appears to be quite good. It has been reported at .92 for 123 cases in which the interval between testing ranged from one day to nine months. In addition, the test-retest reliability does not suffer too much if different examiners are used, an observation which provides evidence of the consistency of measurement which can be attained if an interview schedule meets reasonable levels of structure. Further, reliability holds up well when different informants are queried, so long as they are all familiar with the subjects' behavior patterns. As a final positive note, the Vineland scores do not correlate highly with Stanford-Binet test scores, indicating that, as intended, something other than general intelligence, social maturity, is being assessed by the schedule.

The structure of the Vineland makes salient one caution that must be observed when interpreting the scores obtained from any structured interview, as well as scores based on any intelligence or personality test. Specifically, the appropriateness of the content for the subject must be considered in drawing general conclusions. For example, there may be a depression of some scores which can be better accounted for by atypical experience than by personal deficit. It is unlikely that a rural child can earn credit on the Vineland for being "capable of making small purchases on his own." The opportunity never presents itself. While it is true that the child does not, in fact, manifest this behavior, the incorporation of this failure into the overall Social Maturity Age may misrepresent what the child is like characteristically. Thus, no amount of sophistication in the construction of structured interviews can diminish the need for good sense on the part of the interpreter of such data.

Structured Clinical Interview. A second example of the structured interview is provided by Burdock and Hardesty, whose purpose was to develop a "standardized psychological method of evaluation of psychopathology . . . designed to serve as an individual test of social and psychological adjustments" (1968, p. 62). The Structured Clinical Interview (SCI) involves the use of an interview schedule which the examiner follows fairly consistently. Questions are open-ended and tend not to be answered by just a "yes" or "no" response. "What happens when you close your eyes?" "How does your head feel?" "Tell me about your imagination." The interview explores questions such as these.

The purpose of these questions is to provoke verbal statements and behavior from the subject which enable the interviewer to score as "true" or "not true" on 179 inventory items. These items depict pathological verbalizations, attitudes, and behaviors. Thus, the SCI, via a structural interview format, provides the opportunity for subjects to manifest pathology in both verbal and stylistic or behavioral terms. In order to make the scoring of inventory items somewhat easier, they are printed juxtaposed to the interview questions which are most likely to elicit the relevant behavior. However, the examiner must be prepared to score inventory items if the relevant behavior manifests itself prior or subsequent to the stimulus question. For example, the question, "How is your sense of smell?" may inspire the verbal complaint of, "I don't know what's the matter with me! I always smell food, day and night." This expression would then result in the interviewer scoring the following inventory item "true": "Indicates that he notices smells in the absence of an adequate or appropriate stimulus."

The reliability of the SCI is quite good so long as the interviewers are well-trained. By simultaneously using two or more independent observers during an interview, the interscorer reliability has been close to .90 for the full test and in the .70s and .80s for each of the 10 subscales. These figures are probably a function of the emphasis of the SCI on the scoring of objectively-observed behavior or verbal statements, rather than less specific impressions. However, there is no question that this interview schedule, like any other, is subject to error variance from a variety of sources under certain conditions. Sherman, Trief, and Sprafkin (1975) used a modified and somewhat shortened form of the SCI in an experiment designed to assess the degree and manner in which psychiatric patients could fake various degrees of psychopathology in the course of this interview. Specifically, day-treatment patients were asked to participate in two sequential interviews, the general instruction being to behave as mentally ill as possible in one and as mentally healthy as possible in the other. The results indicated that patients were able to significantly alter their interview scores in a manner consistent with the instructions which they had received. Observers, who did not know the purpose of the experiment or that any special instructions had been given to the patients, rated the behavior and content of the patients' communications as more pathological in the "fake-sick" than in the "fake-healthy" interview condition. What was most interesting was that patients were selective in the way they chose to create the impression of heightened pathology. Specifically, an inventory item analysis revealed that patients primarily altered the content of their self-referent statements, with special emphasis on neurosis-relevant complaints pertaining to anxiety and depression. The only behavioral inventory item which was significantly influenced by the patients' manipulative intention was "impassive face". In addition, it was apparent that patients did not spontaneously express greater pathology, rather, they relied on the interview questions for cues as to what they should say. For example, the greater confession of worry in the "fake-sick" than in the "fake health" interviews routinely came about only after the question, "What do you worry about?" This kind of dissimulation can drastically affect the validity of the SCI. It is unclear whether the interview is measuring true psychopathology as intended, or the impression of pathology or health which a patient may wish to create.

SUMMARY

A survey of interview procedures was presented. Three kinds of interviews relevant to clinical psychology were described: the intake, or case history, interview, the mental status interview, and the psychotherapeutic interview. This last category exemplifies unstructured interview procedures. In contrast, structured clinical interviews are represented by interview schedules like the Vineland Social Maturity Scale and the SCI. Issues bearing on the validity of interview procedures were raised.

TERMS TO KNOW

CHAPTER 13
Self-Report Questionnaires

Allport (1937) states simply what a number of very prominent psychologists believe: "If we want to know how people feel, what they experience and what they remember, what their emotions and motives are like, and the reasons for acting as they do, why not ask them?" This assumes that a correspondence exists between what a person says about himself and what is, in fact, the case. Even more basically, the idea is predicated on the principle that people understand themselves, are able to share the information, and will do so if requested. This kind of reasoning is really at the heart of interview-based assessment, which requests people to talk about themselves.

Self-report questionnaires are similar in that subjects are asked to communicate information about themselves. The obvious difference is that the medium of personal interaction is lacking. Rather, questions are presented on a printed form, allowing for the epitome of standardization. In fact, one might construe the self-report questionnaire as a logical extension of the most structured of interview schedules.

Very often, the items of a self-report questionnaire or inventory are a series of self-referent statements such as, "I am happy," to which the subject responds by recording either "true" or "false." Thus, in terms of the classificatory schema presented in Chapter 8 self-report questionnaires usually afford a limited response format for the subject.

During World War I Woodworth developed the Personal Data Sheet (1920), and thus initiated the questionnaire approach to personality assessment. Since Woodworth's effort innumerable self-report questionnaires have been developed. The following section will sample a few of these, categorizing them in terms of the procedures used in their development.

Of the many ways in which a questionnaire can be developed, there are four approaches which stand out as having been most popular. These are not mutually exclusive and many test constructors have utilized more than one procedure in the development of their instruments. The procedures used have been content validation, rational-theoretical, empirical, and factor analytic.

CONTENT VALIDATION

It will be recalled that a test is content valid to the degree that it samples, in a representative way, the universe of possible items that might be asked in an effort to assess a skill, area of knowledge, or personality characteristic. The issue of content validation is a relevant one for many tests. However, sometimes a test is constructed with content validation as a primary goal. This might be true for a final exam, or achievement test, in a college course. It was also one of Woodworth's major goals, a fact which naturally influenced his manner of approach as he constructed the Personal Data Sheets.

Woodworth Personal Data Sheet.

Because of the prevalence of mental disorder among military personnel during World War I, a call went out for improved psychiatric assessment of draftees. A procedure was needed which could circumvent the very expensive and time-consuming task of psychiatrically interviewing all potential inductees. Woodworth's solution was a self-report inventory designed to screen out draftees who were probably emotionally unfit for military duty. It was thought that such a device could provide a service which would otherwise require innumerable man hours from a psychiatric staff.

If the Personal Data Sheet was to replace effectively an initial psychiatric interview, Woodworth had to be certain that his items adequately sampled the domain of symptoms that a psychiatrist might uncover during the course of a face-to-face encounter. Accordingly, Woodworth conducted an extensive survey of the psychiatric literature and interviewed many psychiatrists. From this information-gathering effort he gleaned his final list of 116 pre-neurotic and neurotic symptoms which served as the inventory items. The items themselves were self-referent statements covering everything from fears to obsessions, from somatic complaints to cognitive confusion. A subject's score consisted of the number of times he admitted to possessing the symptoms listed, "Do you ever feel an awful pressure in or about your head?" "Are you troubled by shyness?" "Are you frightened in the middle of the night?"

It does seem that, given the array of items employed, Woodworth's screening instrument was, at the very least, content valid. In general, people who used the Personal Data Sheet were impressed with its efficacy, despite some obvious difficulties, such as the ease with which the test could be faked. Anticipating this weakness, Woodworth intentionally gave his inventory the neutral name it still bears in an effort to lead subjects away from the idea that their mental status was being assessed. However, the transparency of the items allowed for little disguise. In fact, Woodworth chose many of the items because they had face validity; they looked as if they were relevant to emotional adjustment. Unfortunately, this look was probably quite as evident to recruits filling out the forms as it was to the test's constructor. The issue of deception on questionnaires will be discussed in some detail later on.

Mooney Problem Check List.

A second example of a questionnaire which was constructed with content validation in mind is the Problem Check List developed by Mooney and Gordon (1950). Like
Woodworth, Mooney selected items for his inventory on an *a priori* basis. Specifically,
the items emerged from records of counseling interviews and the direct expression of
problems solicited from over 4000 high school students. The problems which may be
found on the checklist include "having too few dates," "wanting to leave home," and
"being slow in getting acquainted with people." In general terms, the items cover the
areas of physical development, health, employment, financial problems, social relations, sex and marriage, morals and religion, and vocational future.

In practice, the subject is simply asked to indicate which problems are personally
troubling by underlining them. While it is conceivable that an adjustment score could
be derived from this procedure, it is not routinely done. Rather, the purpose is to use
the information obtained from Mooney's checklist as a starting point for further group
discussion or counseling. Since the information obtained from the check list is in terms
of self-perceived problems, the value of this instrument depends upon the willingness
of subjects to be open and cooperative, and the content validity of the instrument. That
is, if the check list systematically omitted important adolescent problem areas it could
not effectively operate as intended. Anastasi (1968) reports that students tend to
underline 20 to 30 problems and feels that published reports suggest that "the checklist
provides good coverage of problems that students are willing to report" (p. 439).

Fear Survey Schedule.

More recently, Wolpe and Lang (1964) reported the development of a Fear
Survey Schedule, also to be used in clinical practice. Both Wolpe and Lang are
behavior therapists who employ psychotherapeutic techniques based upon learning
theory to alleviate neurotic symptoms. Most frequently these symptoms are seen as
maladaptive habits excercised in the service of avoiding or reducing anxiety. Consequently, this perspective considers it important to discover those environmental situations and events in which patients have anxiety reactions. The Fear Survey Schedule
was constructed in order to facilitate this kind of information gathering. It is simply a list
of 72 items to which the patient responds by indicating the degree of his disturbance,
fear, or other unpleasant feelings. These are arranged on a five point scale, from "not
at all" to "very much." Wolpe and Lang report that the items are a compendium of
"the most frequent neurotic anxiety stimuli that have been encountered in patients in
the course of fifteen years of the practice of behavior therapy" (p. 27). The items fall
into six broad categories: animals; tissue damage, which includes illness and death;
social stimuli, such as ugly people; noises, a siren for example; classical phobias, such
as airplanes; and, finally, miscellaneous items represented by events such as failure
and strange places. Wolpe and Lang provided absolutely no reliability or criterion

validity data in their original article on this schedule. It seems clear that their goal was restricted to covering the field of possible fear-provoking stimuli, and, therefore, to attain mainly content validity.

Geer (1964) also published a Fear Survey Schedule which had 51 items and which was primarily intended for use as a research tool. While statistical data bearing on this schedule's reliability and validity were presented, the construction procedure again seems to have been primarily geared toward the attainment of content validity. One hundred and twenty four Introductory Psychology students at the State University of New York at Buffalo were asked, on an open-ended questionnaire, to "list their fears on a three point scale (Mild, Moderate, Severe)" (p. 46). The students were instructed to include only those stimuli that involved no realistic danger or pain, thereby making their fears of a neurotic nature. Of the 111 different fears reported, 51 were listed by two or more students. These comprise the items for Geer's Fear Survey Schedule.

It must be recalled that a test is never content valid in an unrestricted way. It is only valid for specific purposes. This important point is clearly illustrated by the fact that the Wolpe and Lang Fear Survey Schedule has only 20 items in common with the one developed by Geer. Thus, a schedule which appears to sample very adequately the domain of fears expressed by behavior therapy patients has only moderate overlap with that group of fears which has content validity for a college population. It would not be considered a wise practice, therefore, to use Geer's schedule in a clinical setting because the fear stimuli included therein would probably not be relevant for clinical patients.

It can be seen from the above examples of the content validation approach to personality test construction that the primary concern is to cover adequately a domain of possible items, neurotic fears in the case of the Fear Survey Schedule. However, in pursuing this goal it can be reasonably argued that the test constructors were operating on the basis of some assumptions about the nature of test-taking behavior. Specifically, as Lanyon and Goodstein (1971) point out, the Woodworth Personal Data Sheet is a test whose items were selected because they were thought to "act as stimuli for directly eliciting the information in which we are interested" Similarly, the responses to the items were expected to be "valid indices of the level of adjustment of the respondent" (p. 41). Consequently it can be seen that the construction of these personality tests is based, in part, upon theoretical considerations.

THE RATIONAL-THEORETICAL APPROACH

The items which comprise a rationally or theoretically derived questionnaire are selected because, in the view of the test developer, they seem capable of eliciting responses which reveal either a particular characteristic or the general structure of personality. If one were to develop a test of depression using this approach, one might ask questions about feelings and behaviors which are theoretically specific correlates of depression. Self-referent statements such as, "I cry frequently" and "I am often in a sad mood," to which subjects would respond "true" or "false," are the kind which might be included.

The items on such a rationally derived test may be chosen on the basis of common sense or knowledge obtained directly from experience with depressed individuals. Often the items are selected for more involved reasons. The test developer may have a well-organized theory concerning depression. If the theory addresses itself to childhood antecedents of adult depression, the rationally derived test may then include historically-oriented questions, items concerned with parental and early sibling relationships.

The rational test construction process may go well beyond even the most sophisticated of armchair theorizing. Given a theoretical understanding of depression, the test constructor will often enlist the opinions of other experts in the field rather than rely solely on his own judgment regarding the relevancy of items. Professionals who are familiar with the theory in question may be asked to rate the relevancy of large numbers of potential items. Only those items which receive close to unanimous acceptance from this pool of experts will be selected for the final form of the test.

Goal Preference Inventory.

A variation of this strategy was employed by Liverant (1958) in the construction of the Goal Preference Inventory (GPI). Liverant started from a knowledge of Rotter's (1954) Social Learning Theory (SLT), which states that an important determinant of behavior is the relative value placed by an individual on the fulfillment of various needs. In SLT, a need is defined by the existence of a class of observable behaviors which lead to the same or similar goals. For example, the behaviors of giving someone instructions, arguing with another person, and physically beating someone all allow the individual to dominate others and might collectively comprise a class of behavior which defines the "need to dominate." According to SLT, one can measure the relative strength of needs by asking people to indicate preferences for the behavioral indices of needs. That is, the person is asked whether he would prefer to do behavior A or B if he had equal chance to do either, each of these two behaviors being a manifestation of different needs.

Liverant attempted to measure the relative strengths of four needs which he felt were important to college students:

1. Need to be considered good or competent in academic situations (academic recognition)
2. Need to be considered competent in social situations (social recognition)
3. Need for acceptance from classmates in academic situations (academic affection)
4. Need for acceptance by others in social situations (social affection)

Liverant first defined these four needs in somewhat greater detail, including six illustrative behavioral referents for each of the four needs. He then sought out experts familiar with student life who would be able to provide additional behaviors in which college students might engage if they were trying to satisfy these needs. Not surprisingly, Liverant chose students and faculty in the psychology department of a large university. They were each asked to list at least 10 additional behaviors "which they thought the majority of college students use to satisfy each need" (p. 6). Those behaviors submitted were edited for clarity and duplicates were eliminated; the most appropriate of the remaining 239 behaviors were then given to a new panel of four judges who were familiar with the four need definitions. Their job was to eliminate behaviors which "seemed to overlap more than one need category or for any other reason did not seem well-suited to any one of the four needs" (p. 6).

The behavioral referents for each need which received the seal of approval from at least three of the four judges were considered for inclusion in the GPI. The GPI itself combines 20 behavioral referents for each need, producing the following 6 sub-tests, each composed of twenty item pairings:

Subtest	Contrasted Needs
1	academic recognition vs. social recognition
2	academic recognition vs. academic affection
3	academic recognition vs. social affection
4	social recognition vs. academic affection
5	social recognition vs. social affection
6	academic affection vs. social affection

The score on any subtest is simply the number of behavioral referents to the first-named need for which the subject indicated a preference. If, for example, the subject prefers the behavioral referent for academic recognition over that for social recognition on 12 of the 20 items in sub-test 1 the obtained score would be 12. The overall score for any need is the total number of times its referents are selected as preferred when paired with the other 60 behavioral referents (20 from each of the other three areas). The overall need scores may thus range from 0 to 60.

Liverant used a known group approach to establish the construct validity of this rational-theoretical measure of need value. In one study it was hypothesized that fraternity and sorority members would have a higher need for social recognition than non-affiliated students. The validation groups consisted of 174 Greeks and 172 independents. As predicted, in the case of both males and females, the Greeks scored significantly higher (mean about 30.5) than independents (mean about 27.5) on the need for social recognition as assessed by the GPI. A correlational procedure was employed in the second construct validation study. It was reasoned that grade point average should be associated with the strength of the students' need for academic recognition. A low, but significant positive correlation between grade point average and need for academic recognition (+.35) was found among men. The corresponding correlation among women was zero, which suggests, as Liverant admits, that the theoretical understanding of the construct "need for academic recognition" was improperly conceptualized on the GPI, at least for women.

In summary, the GPI may be considered a rational-theoretical test in view of the fact that it constitutes a logical extension of Rotter's Social Learning Theory of personality. That is, the constructs which it attempts to measure are embedded in, and derive from this theoretical network.

Edward's Personal Preference Schedule

Another theory which has generated more than one personality questionnaire is Murray's *Personology* (1938). Murray felt that the study of personality necessitated an examination of person-environment interactions. He believed that this interaction was characterized by an interplay of forces. Some of these forces stem from within the person and are called *needs*. The other forces derive from the environment and are called *press*.

Murray more specifically defined need (n) as a "readiness to respond in a certain way under given conditions . . . it is a noun which stands for the fact that a certain trend is apt to recur" (1962, p. 61). Murray defined 12 needs which reflect biological underpinnings as *primary* or *viscerogenic,* and 27 needs reflecting mental or emotional satisfactions as *secondary* or *psychogenic* (see Tables, 3, 4).

Murray further describes the characteristic operation of needs by noting that behavior is frequently the product of more than one need, a situation referred to as "fusion of needs." To put it another way, a single behavior can serve to bring about more than one kind of mental or emotional satisfaction. In addition, the presence of needs may not necessarily result in the overt actions noted in Table 4. If they do, they are referred to as *manifest* needs; if not, they are said to be *latent.* When a need is latent its expression is limited to the non-objectively-observable world of fantasy. It is in this mode, for example, that n Achievement may be satisfied by thinking about accomplishments rather than by attempting to gain them in the real world. A final important point is that needs, whether manifest or latent, influence behavior in conjunction with different types of press, or "directional tendencies in an object or situation." Press may stem from objective environmental events, *alpha press,* such as the requirement that a total score of 1200 on the Scholastic Aptitude Test (SAT) be attained for admission to the college of one's choice. *Beta press* refers to subjectively experienced environmental influences, such as the belief that people will be rejecting if one doesn't gain admittance into college. Murray says that "everything that can supposedly harm or benefit the well-being of an organism" may be considered *pressive; everything else is inert. Pressive perception* is that process which recognizes environmental events as being "good" or "bad." Importantly, Murray acknowledges that expectations of environmental events, in addition to the events per se, can be pressive. He refers to this as *pressive apperception.* Some examples of press are: p Affiliation, a friendly companion; p Dominance, an imprisoning or prohibiting object or person; and p Nurturance, a protective or sympathetic person.

Out of this theoretical framework, Edwards (1953b) developed his Personal Preference Schedule (EPPS) in an effort to measure the strength of manifest secondary needs in subjects. Edwards selected 15 needs from Murray's list and authored self-referent statements which he felt were representative of the need categories. In his manual, Edwards says that the EPPS was designed for research and counseling situations in which a quick and convenient measure of a number of relatively independent normal personality variables is needed.

Edwards employed a forced choice format. He developed 210 pairs of items in which self-descriptive statements representing one of each of the 15 needs, such as "I

TABLE 3 Viscerogenic Needs

1. *n* Air	7. *n* Defecation
2. *n* Water	8. *n* Harmavoidance
3. *n* Food	9. *n* Noxavoidance
4. *n* Sex	10. *n* Heatavoidance
5. *n* Lactation	11. *n* Coldavoidance
6. *n* Urination	12. *n* Sentience

Note. *n* Noxavoidance refers to the tendency to avoid noxious stimuli and *n* Sentience to consciousness. Murray added a need for Passivity reflected in relaxation, rest, and sleeping behavior.

TABLE 4 Psychogenic Needs

NEED	BEHAVIORAL REFERENTS
n Acquisition	Gaining possessions, stealing, gambling
n Conservance	Collecting, repairing, protecting
n Order	Organizing, cleaning
n Retention	Hoarding, miserliness
n Construction	Building
n Achievement	Overcoming obstacles, striving
n Recognition	Seeking prestige, honor
n Exhibition	Attracting attention, amusing others
n Inviolacy	Avoiding self-deprecation
n Infavoidance	Avoiding shame or ridicule
n Counteraction	Overcoming defeat through rededication
n Dominance	Controlling, influencing others
n Defendance	Justifying actions, offering excuses
n Deference	Serving or cooperating with others
n Similance	Being suggestive or agreeable
n Autonomy	Resisting influence or authority
n Contrariance	Being unique or unconventional
n Aggression	Assaulting, accusing, punishing others
n Abasement	Compliance, self-deprecation, surrendering
n Blamavoidance	Inihibition of asocial, unconventional behavior
n Affiliation	Friendliness, sociableness
n Rejection	Snubbing or ignoring others
n Nurturance	Aiding or "mothering" others
n Succorance	Seeking aid or "mothering" from others
n Play	Having fun, avoiding seriousness
n Cognizance	Exploring, seeking knowledge
n Exposition	Demonstrating, explaining

enjoy being with other people," were paired with representative statements of the other 14 needs. For each item the subject indicates which of the two statements is most self-characteristic. Thus, the strength of needs is not measured on an absolute basis. Rather, the strength of each need is assessed in terms of the frequency with which statements reflecting it are endorsed as being more self-descriptive than statements reflecting the other needs. In other words, as on the aforementioned GPI, need strength on the EPPS is assessed in relation to the strength of other needs experienced by the individual. This kind of scoring is called *ipsative;* it does not allow one to assert that person A has stronger n Autonomy than person B, only that A's n Autonomy is quite strong relative to his other needs. At most, interindividual comparisons may involve pattern analyses. For example, one could say that person A is preoccupied with n Autonomy whereas B is not.

In summary, it can be seen that Edwards' scale is a logical derivative of Murray's *Personology,* and its acceptability is largely a function of one's belief in this theory. Given that a psychologist believes it is important to study personality by assessing manifest needs, the procurement of consciously-expressed opinions as to which need-related statements best characterize the self appears to be an appropriate way to accomplish this goal.

Edwards built two important checks on the consistency of subjects' responses into the scoring of the EPPS. The first involves the identical repetition of 15 paired items. If a subject contradicts his first response when the pairings are repeated, the examiner must assume respondent error elsewhere on the test, perhaps due to random respond- ing brought on by fatigue or uncooperativeness. The second check for consistency involves an odd-even split. Specifically, the need profile obtained on the odd items is compared with that obtained from the even-numbered items. If the two, odd and even, profiles systematically differ from one another, the examiner can, again, assume that respondent error has played a significant role in determining a subject's performance on the schedule. Figure 11 presents a need profile which may emerge from the EPPS. It can be seen in the depicted example that the subject has a relatively dominant n Nurturance. In addition, the subject responded in an identical fashion on 14 of the 15 consistency score (repeated) items; this was more consistent than 97% of the subjects who comprised the normative sample, made up of 749 college males and 760 college females.

In general, the split-half and test-retest reliability coefficients reported for the EPPS have been about .75 and .80, respectively. Validity data on the EPPS are difficult to obtain because of the ipsative nature of the scores. For example, one cannot clearly predict that someone with a high n Affiliation score will seek to have more friends than persons with a low n Affiliation score. This is because the first person's n Affiliation, while stronger than his other needs, may still be weaker in an absolute sense than the level of n Affiliation in the second person. Consequently, research attempts which have sought to establish the validity of the EPPS have tended to produce conflicting results.

Assets of Rational-Theoretical Questionnaires.

There are a number of strengths in approaching test construction from a rational perspective, not the least of which is the fact that the included items, the test as a whole, and the subject's responses are all systematically understood within a theoretical framework. In other words, the assessment process is closely tied to a theory of personality. The importance or psychological meaningfulness of the test is thus based upon the theoretical centrality of the personality constructs being measured.

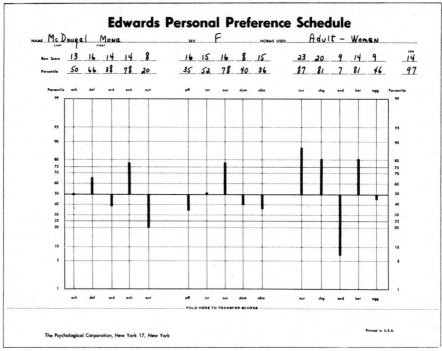

Note.—For convenience in transferring raw scores, a horizontal arrangement has been used. If chart is rotated 90°, it may be compared with the chart on the regular answer sheet.

Figure 11. Sample profile chart from the Edwards Personal Preference Schedule. (Edwards, A.L. *Manual for the Edwards Personal Preference Schedule.* (revised) N.Y.: The Psychological Corporation, 1959. Reproduced by permission. Copyright© 1959 by The Psychological Corporation, New York N.Y. All rights reserved.

A further advantage of this approach lies in the fact that any validity data which are established for the test apply simultaneously to the personality theory from which it was derived. That is, a theory might predict that people who differ from one another in terms of the degree to which they manifest a trait, anxiety, for example, will behave differently in a given situation. A rationally derived test may then be developed to assess anxiety as defined by the theory. Such an instrument can then be used to separate people into two groups, high anxious and low anxious. If these two groups are found to behave differently from each other in a way predicted by the theory, then the validity of the test as a measure of the construct "anxiety" will be established. In addtion, the validity of the theory will also be enhanced since predictions derived from it have been confirmed.

Many of the most popular personality tests which have been developed out of a rational theoretical orientation are not questionnaires. Rather, they fall into the projective test category and careful consideration of them will be reserved for Chapter 14.

EMPIRICAL TEST CONSTRUCTION.

In the rational-theoretical approach a basic reason for item selection is a theoretical rationale. In empirical test construction items are based on an empirical demonstration that responses to them relate to some criterion. For example, in the previously discussed Woodworth Personal Data Sheet the primary emphasis was on content validation, but empirical considerations were also taken into account. Thus, even though a potential item seemed to tap a symptom frequently mentioned in psychiatric literature, the item was rejected if more than 25% of a psychologically normal subject group answered in a psychopathological direction. The rationale was that if many normal people admitted to having a particular symptom, that symptom should not be taken as a sign of psychological abnormality.

Empirical test construction usually involves the use of two groups of people who are known to differ in some important way. An effort is then made to discover test items to which the two groups tend to respond differently. Those items are then used to assess the personality characteristic in new subjects.

As a hypothetical example, consider a situation in which a medical school is interested in determining what kinds of personalities succeed and fail in this demanding course of study. Such a determination would be highly useful for selection purposes, especially since most medical programs have more than enough academically-qualified applicants. In an effort to make more accurate selections they could give a large battery of personality tests to an incoming class. The next step would be to simply wait and note which students complete the programs successfully and which ones terminate prematurely. Having thus established two groups, success and failure, all personality test items are reviewed in order to discover those which the successful students had answered differently than the unsuccessful. Such items are said to *discriminate, or differentiate,* between the success and failure groups. Perhaps the success group tended to respond "false" to the question, "I find it easy to get to sleep at night," whereas the dropouts, as a group, tended to respond "true" to the same self-referent statement. All such discriminating items would then collectively comprise what might be called a "Medical School Orientation Inventory." The worth of the inventory would be established by administering it to succeeding classes of incoming medical students. The test would be deemed useful if students who respond to the items in the same manner as the previous success group also succeed, and if students who answer much like the previous failure group also tend to drop out. If the Medical School Orientation Inventory is thus found to have predictive utility, it might then be adopted by the school as a valuable selection procedure capable of helping to screen out those academically-qualified applicants who have personalities which hinder medical school success.

Minnesota Multiphasic Personality Inventory

Probably the most popular and best example of an actual test constructed from this purely empirical perspective is the Minnesota Multiphasic Personality Inventory

(MMPI). This true-false self-descriptive questionnaire was designed to assess psychological abnormality conveniently. The test now contains 10 clinical scales in its regular administration. Table 5 lists these 10 scales.

TABLE 5 MMPI Clinical Scales

NUMBER	NAME	ABBREVIATION
1	Hypochondriasis	Hs
2	Depression	D
3	Hysteria	Hy
4	Psychopathic Deviate	Pd
5	Masculinity-Femininity	Mf
6	Paranoia	Pa
7	Psychasthenia	Pt
8	Schizophrenia	Sc
9	Hypomania	Ma
10	Social Introversion	Si

These scales were constructed by reviewing text books on medical, neurologic, and psychiatric examinations, and by surveying questionnaires on social and personal attitudes. These procedures, along with the clinical experience of the test constructors themselves, Hathaway and McKinley (1943), led to the selection of 550 self-referent statements as being of probable psychiatric significance.

To this point the procedure is one that appears aimed simply at the attainment of content validity. However, Hathaway and McKinley fully intended to go well beyond a representative listing of psychiatrically relevant self-referent statements.

Each statement was printed on a separate card and it was the subject's job to sort them into "true," "false," or "cannot say" categories. As a first step, the normal sorting of the 550 cards was obtained by soliciting responses from over 1500 normal subjects, including 724 visitors to the Minnesota University Hospital who claimed to be in good health.

MMPI Pathology Scales. As an example of how the pathology scales were developed, the Hypochondriasis (Hs) scale will be discussed. A group of 50 patients were diagnosed as being hypochondriacal on the basis of careful clinical observations. In general, they were characterized by over-concern with body processes and matters of physical health. These 50 hypochondriacs were then administered all 550 items. The 33 items which were found to differentiate the hypochondriacs from the normal subjects were declared fit for inclusion on the Hs scale. These items were ones to which the two groups responded in typically different ways. If most of the hypochondriacs say "false" to an item such as "I wake up fresh and rested most mornings," and most normal subjects respond "true", then the item differentiates or discriminates well. It does not matter what the content of the item happens to be, or even which group answers in a characteristically "true" or "false" direction, only that the groups generally respond in opposite directions.

To the degree that a contemporary subject answers these 33 Hs scale items in the same "true" or "false" direction as did the hypochondriacs in Hathaway and McKinley's original patient sample, a high hypochondriasis score is earned. Since the person has shown that on this test he behaves like a hypochondriac, it is assumed that he is in some essential ways similar to the hypochondriacs.

The other MMPI clinical scales were developed in essentially the same manner. For example, the Psychasthenia scale construction involved the use of 20 carefully selected psychasthenia patients, a diagnostic category no longer typically used, who manifested the symptoms of excessive self-doubt, compulsive behavior, obsessive thinking, phobias, and anxiety. Forty eight of the 550 items were selected for inclusion on this (Pt) scale because of their power to discriminate between the psychasthenia groups and the normal subjects. One example of the items selected is, "I am inclined to take things hard." Psychasthenics generally respond "true" to this statement.

Forty six items discriminated between normal subjects and 24 patients manifesting elated but unstable mood, psychomotor excitement, and flight of ideas. These items comprise the Hypomania scale. A sample Ma scale item is, "At times my thoughts have raced ahead faster than I could speak them."

The remaining clinical scales used as criterion groups patients who manifested the symptom clusters described below and are exemplified by the sample items in parentheses.

Depression — 50 patients who were generally sad in mood, had feelings of worthlessness, entertained suicidal thoughts, and frequently exhibited slowness of thought and action ("I usually feel that life is worthwhile," responding "false" indicative of depression, 60 items).

Hysteria — 50 patients described as having alleged somatic problems such as loss of ability to talk or hear, numbness or tingling, none of these having any physical basis ("I frequently notice my hand shakes when I try to do something," "true" indicative of hysteria, 60 items).

Paranoid — an unspecified number of legalistic, suspicious, defensive patients ("I am sure that I am being talked about," "true" indicative of paranoia, 40 items).

Psychopathic deviate — 78 diagnosed psychopaths, sociopaths and an additional 100 prisoners with a history of robbery, promiscuousness in sexual behavior, untrustworthiness, truancy, and violence ("I liked school," "false" indicative of psychopathy, 50 items).

Schizophrenia — 50 diagnosed schizophrenics manifesting distorted thinking, loss of reality orientation, social withdrawal, and inappropriate emotional responses ("I believe I am a condemned person," "true" indicative of schizophrenia, 78 items).

The exceptions to this standard scale construction methodology are the Masculinity-femininity scale and the more recent Social introversion scale. The former (Mf) scale used as a criterion group 13 male sexual inverts. However, an additional empirical basis for inclusion on the Mf scale was the item's power to discriminate between males and females. Most of the items pertain to interests such as, "I would like to be a florist." This was "true" for men. There are 60 items on this pathology scale, which is keyed oppositely for males and females, so that a high score always indicates responding in a way typical of the other sex. A high score is much less likely to be indicative of sexual-orientation problems among women than among men, probably because it is more acceptable in our culture for a woman to be "masculine" than for a man to be "feminine." However, even within sub-groups of men, high scores may have nothing to do with pathology. For example, college males tend to score high on the Mf scale probably because they have interest in areas such as literature which, in the larger culture, are more typically feminine. Healthy but high Mf scoring males tend to be sensitive, unaggressive, and aesthetically oriented. Black (1953) describes high scoring college females as behaving in a somewhat unrealistic and rebellious fashion.

The last clinical scale, Social introversion, did not involve the use of a distinct clinical population in its development. Rather, the 70 items were selected on the basis of their ability to discriminate between students who scored at the extremes of a separate test for introversion-extraversion. "Whenever possible I avoid being in a crowd," is a sample item. Hathaway and Meehl (1951) report that high Si scoring subjects are modest, shy, and sensitive. Black (1953) characterizes subjects who earn low scores on the Si scale as being sociable, enthusiastic, and enterprising.

MMPI Validity Scales. In addition to the above 10 scales there are four so-called "validity" scales. These do not assess validity in the conventional sense of whether or not the test is a good measure of psychopathology in general. Instead, the validity scales permit the examiner to judge the credibility of a particular MMPI protocol as completed by a given subject.

The first validity scale is the Question Scale (?). The scores on it are simply the number of times that the subject responds "Cannot say" to items. More than 30? responses is usually taken as a sign that the subject has answered in an evasive manner, or that his motives on the remaining items are questionable. If the number exceeds 100 the entire test is deemed non-interpretable along usual lines.

The *Lie Scale* (L) consists of 15 items originally selected on the basis of their face validity. They are scattered throughout the test and have content which was believed to be very socially desirable but generally unlikely to be true; "I read all the editorials in the newspapers everyday." While it is certain that for some very conscientious people a few L scale items are true, it is extremely implausible for this number to exceed between six and eight; the average is about four. Meehl and Hathaway (1946) originally asserted that the L scale is a subtle trap for those who would pass themselves off as being better than they really are. More recent evidence suggests that the items are rather transparent, and even the person who is trying to fake may not be tricked into endorsing them in the socially desirable direction. Thus, while a high L score may indeed indicate that the test taker is being dishonest, a low L score doesn't rule out this motive for the sophisticated subject.

The MMPI F Scale consists of 64 items which were answered by the normal sample in a very uneven way; the individual items were responded to by almost everyone in the same direction, either "true" or "false." A person earns an F scale point for each response that is opposite to that of the great majority. Few normal people obtain an F scale score above seven and only about two to three percent of all respondents have an F score exceeding 12. A high score may mean a number of things. It can be brought about by an extremely disorganized personality, in which case it is a sign of pathology. It may also come about from test-taking behavior which invalidates a given protocol, such as failure to follow instructions by responding "true" when one meant to respond "false," random responding, or a wish to appear in a bad light. The last possibility mentioned becomes apparent when one considers the very atypical nature of the endorsed items' content: "Everything tastes the same," or, "I see things, animals, or people around me that others do not see."

The K Scale, also known as the *Correction scale,* is the last validity scale. The intent was to detect favorably distorted self-representations by sophisticated subjects. The construction strategy employed was similar to that used in arriving at the clinical scales; that is, the items selected were those which discriminated between normal subjects and a clinical criterion group. In this case the clinical criterion group consisted of psychiatric patients who obtained apparently normal MMPI records with an elevated L score; these patients are presumably reluctant to admit that they have symptomatic difficulties. The 30 items which comprise the K scale are, therefore, held to measure, in a subtle way, defensiveness or guardedness in one's test-taking attitude. People who adopt such a posture, as indicated by a high K score, probably deny the existence of much pathology in their responses to the clinical scales; their scores on these consequently under-represent the severity of their symptoms and abnormalities. To correct these too low clinical scale scores, a predetermined proportion of the K score is added to the Hs, Pd, Pt, Sc, and Ma scale scores. For example, whatever a subject's score is on the Hs scale, it is elevated by an amount equaling one half of the obtained K score.

Administration and Scoring. Because of the intentionally simple language used on the MMPI items, as well as the straightforward instructions, it does not require a highly trained examiner to administer it. In fact, the test easily lends itself to group administration. Further, it is not uncommon for patients to complete the lengthy questionnaire at their leisure, usually taking from one to two hours in an unsupervised atmosphere.

Scoring the subject's responses is a relatively easy matter as well, requiring only 15 to 20 minutes of clerical time. Because a booklet has replaced the original card format, a template can be used to obtain a subject's raw score on the scales quickly. The raw scores are then transferred to an MMPI profile form, illustrated in Figure 12, which allows one to convert them easily into T scores. T scores are set to have a mean of 50. That is, a person whose score on a pathology scale is at the mean of those obtained by the normal population earns a T score of 50. If a person earns a T score of 70 on a clinical scale, it means that his raw score was higher than about 98% of the normal population. T scores in excess of 70 are typically taken as a possible sign of psychological abnormality. The T scores are standardized separately for males and females.

The Minnesota Multiphasic Personality Inventory

Starke R. Hathaway and J. Charnley McKinley

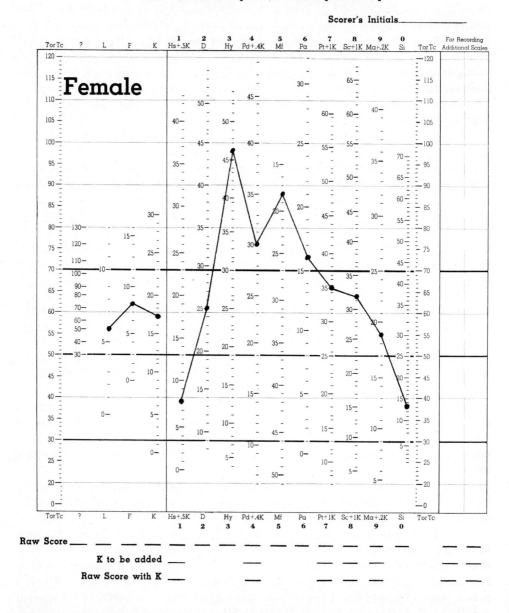

Figure 12. Sample profile chart from the Minnesota Multiphasic Personality Inventory having the code: 3546′7829-10. Reproduced by permission. Copyright© 1948, 1966 by The Psychological Corporation, New York. All rights reserved.

MMPI Interpretation. It quickly became evident that the MMPI was capable of much more than simply allowing a psychologist to assign a subject to the diagnostic category represented by the scale(s) on which a T score over 70 was obtained. In fact, the original diagnostic intention was found to be in error when it was discovered how many clinically normal people obtained "pathological" MMPI T scores. In order to mitigate the pathological significance of an elevated T score, it became common practice to refer to the scales by their abbreviated titles, D instead of Depression, for example. Eventually, even this tactic was discarded in favor of using the more neutral scale numbers — in the case of the Depression scale, the number 2.

These nominal changes occurred along with a shift in emphasis toward the interpretation of MMPI score patterns. These "profile analyses," as they came to be called, were based on noting not just the elevation of a given T score, but its elevation relative to other T scores. The combination of profile analyses, along with the exclusive use of scale numbers as a replacement for scale names, led to the development of a rather elaborate coding procedure (Hathaway, 1947). According to this method, described by Hathaway, the scale numbers are first rank-ordered in terms of the magnitude of their T score elevations from highest, on the left, to lowest. The sequence which represents the profile depicted in Fig. 12 is 3,5,4,6,7,8,2,9,1,0. A second bit of information is coded with the insertion of a prime (') after the code number furthest to the right which is associated with a T score above 70. In the case of the example presented in Fig. 12, this prime sign occurs to the right of the digit 6. A dash (-) is used to separate scale numbers having T scores above 54 from those below that figure. The digits of the lowest scales are written in descending order after the dash if they have T scores lower than 46. Finally, any scales which have T scores within one point of each other are tied together by a common underline. Thus, the profile in Fig. 12 is coded as follows: 3546'7829-10. Common MMPI profiles are often referred to by just listing the first, or highest, two or three digits of what would otherwise have been a complete code.

One frequently referred to pattern of scores is known as the "neurotic triad." It consists of elevations on the Hs, D, and Hy scales, with D being relatively lower than the other two. Because this profile has scales one and three higher than two, the left end of the graphic representation of the profile adopts a v-shaped form sometimes known as the "conversion v." The pattern is relatively frequent among conversion hysterics. Non-hospitalized women who manifest the MMPI 13 or 31 code were found by Black (1953) to be rated as being dependent, selfish, and likely to express somatic complaints.

Another frequently encountered code is the 68 or 86 pattern with scales seven and nine being relatively lower. This pattern, involving the four psychotic scales, Pa, Pt, Sc, and Ma, has been designated as the "paranoid valley" by Dahlstrom and Welsh (1960) because of the v-shaped profile formed by scales 6, 7, and 8, and the frequency of the profile among paranoid schizophrenics. These people typically manifest persecutory delusions and may be withdrawn and apathetic.

An incredible amount of research has been conducted in an effort to discover the behavioral correlates of the more commonly found MMPI profiles. A psychiatrist or psychologist familiar with these findings can produce a rather extensive personality description in almost no more time than it takes to actually write it. In order to facilitate this personality description process, a number of voluminous manuals have been developed. Dahlstrom, Welsh, and Dahlstrom (1972), Dahlstrom and Welsh (1960), and Hathaway and Meehl (1951) provide clinical descriptions of the most common MMPI profiles, and some not so frequently encountered. This enterprise has been extended to profiles obtained exclusively from college populations by Drake and Oetting (1958), and from high school students by Hathaway and Monachesi (1961).

Meehl (1956), in an article entitled ''Wanted — A Good Cookbook,'' argued that even with the availability of interpretive manuals, too much time was unnecessarily being spent ''concocting clever and flowery personality sketches from test data . . .'' He felt that, with an objectively scored test like the MMPI, it would not be difficult to associate certain test profiles with trait descriptions in an automatic or ''cookbook'' like way. It took about 10 years for the ''cookbooks'' to actually appear in print. For example, Gilberstadt and Duker (1965) published a small edition in which they associate 19 very common MMPI profile types with what are the probable patient complaints, traits, symptoms, and diagnoses. These probable patient characteristics emerged from the very careful clinical study of at least 9 or 10 of the most typical cases representing each profile type. As an example of what can be done, one of the profile types listed is the 4-9. In order for a profile to qualify as being of this type, five criteria must be met: Pd and Ma T scores must be over 70; no other T score can be over 70; the L scale must have a T score less than 60; the Ma T score must be at least 15 points higher than the Sc T score; and the Pd T score must be at least 7 points higher than the Mf T score. The ''cookbook'' interpretation, based upon 10 typical 4-9 cases is that the individual has a sociopathic personality disturbance, antisocial reaction. The individual is characterized by having poor financial status, drinking problems, hostility, and irritability, with a likelihood of marital conflict and poor work adjustment. These people are poorly socialized, tending toward immorality and impulsivity. While they are superficially friendly and outgoing, they tend to be quite self-centered, grandiose, and haughty. In their discussion, Gilberstadt and Duker even go into the probable childhood experiences of the 4-9 type, including early heterosexual relationships and characteristics of their mothers and fathers.

Since their first appearance, ''cookbooks'' have not proven themselves to function as well as hoped. They have two serious shortcomings. The less serious one is that the MMPI profile types for which clinical ''recipes'' are provided seem to repeatedly account for far more cases in the derivation sample than they do in other clinical settings where the ''cookbooks'' are applied. This means that relatively few profiles fit the types discussed in the ''cookbooks.'' The result is that as many as 80% of the new MMPI protocols have to be subjected to old-fashioned clinical interpretation. The second more serious weakness of ''cookbooks'' is that the personality characteristics which are shown to be valid correlates of types in the derivation sample do not necessarily hold up in other settings. Thus, it may ultimately be necessary for each psychiatric facility to develop its own MMPI ''cookbook,'' valid for the particular patient population which it serves. A task of this magnitude removes much of the attractiveness of the "cookbook" method, which presumably is based upon concern over efficiency.

The "cookbook" approach to MMPI interpretation appears to have reached the limits of speed and convenience with the application of computer technology to the problem. For a rather small fee, a variety of laboratories make this service available to qualified professionals. The specially adapted MMPI answer forms are fed into a computer which, following programmed decision rules, coughs out a narrative report with a delay reported to be less than three seconds. Butcher (1971) points out that the computer generated output can be remarkably similar to a report which might be produced by a highly-practiced clinical psychologist.

In one experiment conducted by Lachar (1974), the computer generated personality analyses of 1410 patients were then judged by their clinical psychologists. A total of 107 different paragraphs appeared 7555 times in these computer reports. They were rated by the clinical psychologists as being inaccurate only 10% of the time and over 90% of the computer reports were appraised by the clinical psychologists as being "favorable" reports of their patients.

One implication of computer-generated MMPI reports is that clinicians who are relatively inexperienced with the complexities and limitations of the MMPI may become enchanted with the magic of automated reports, perhaps putting naive faith in what should be taken in only the most tentative way.

Short Forms. One additional major MMPI innovation of recent origin has been the development of short forms which attempt to circumvent the tests' sometimes objectionable length. Kincannon's Mini-Mult (1968) has generated the most interest, it consists of only 71 items. Other efforts include a 166 item short form by Faschinghauer (1973), and a 168 item form by Overall and Gomez-Mont (1974). In general, the scales on these abbreviated MMPI tests seem to correlate quite well with full MMPI scales, with coefficients ranging from .74 to .96, as reported by Hoffman and Butcher (1975). However, their utility seems to recede when it comes to the issue of profiles or codes, the visual basis of MMPI analysis. Specifically, Hoffman and Butcher (1975), using the records of over 1,000 patients, found that the short forms had only fair accuracy in predicting 58 different full scale code types. The Mini-Mult hit rate was 36.7%, with rates of 40.4% established for the MMPI 168, and 49.4% for the 166 item form. Code-type hit rates of a similar magnitude were found by Hedlund, Cho, and Powell (1975) on patient samples numbering in excess of 3300. These findings cast "serious doubt on the ability of a significantly abbreviated MMPI short form to duplicate adequately the full MMPI profile so as to provide a basis for clinical interpretation in the way the MMPI is now used", to quote Hoffman and Butcher (1975, p. 37). Thus, the short forms ought not to be construed as full MMPI substitutes but, rather, as new instruments whose clinical validity remains to be established.

Reliability and Validity. Anastasi (1968) has objected to heavy reliance on MMPI profile analyses, contending that several of the clinical scales have poor split-half (as low as —.05 being reported) and test-retest (generally around .60) reliabilities. If the individual scales which go into a profile are themselves unstable, the profiles cannot be expected to be better. In defense of MMPI reliability, McKinley and Hathaway (1944) contend that because the MMPI assesses personality characteristics which themselves tend to fluctuate, especially within psychiatric populations, traditional standards of reliability should not be imposed. While his argument is reasonable insofar as test-retest reliability is concerned, it does not help to justify the low split-half reliabilities found for the MMPI scale.

A second internal weakness of the MMPI which Anastasi points to is that the clinical scales are not independent of one another. That is, they tend to be statistically correlated. This may be partly accounted for by the fact that many items are scored for more than one clinical scale because they were found to discriminate between more than one criterion group and the normal sample. Thus a person who answers a question which earns a point on scale 1 may at the same time be earning a point on scale 3. In fact, 20 of the 33 scale 1 items also appear on scale 3. This kind of item overlap between scales probably accounts for the inability of the MMPI to make fine diagnostic distinctions effectively. Some clinicians, Adcock (1965), for example, claim that this is the MMPI's greatest weakness. The test is much better used as an instrument to broadly differentiate normal from abnormal populations. It is not surprising that this should be the greatest power of the MMPI since it was constructed to discriminate between normal and abnormal groups, *not* between different subgroups of abnormal samples. Other psychologists, Anastasi (1968) for one, suggest that if a test construction procedure relevant to the latter goal had been followed, the ability of the MMPI to effect differential diagnosis would have been enhanced.

The third criticism Anastasi levels against the MMPI is that the normative sample just mentioned is grossly inadequate. She highlights the point that of all assessment procedures, personality tests are most subject to the impact of previous life experiences, one's culture. It is argued that the normal people of Minnesota who, in fact, were generally rural in background, with less than a high school education, are in no way representative of the more general population from which subjects are drawn in clinical and research settings. To attribute psychopathology to a person from New York City who has elevated scores in comparison with the Minnesota normative group is an injustice if such relative elevations are characteristic of the subculture from which the person comes. While it may be true that the New York City subculture is by some global standards more maladjusted than that of Minnesota, it is equally likely that the New Yorkers are merely interpreting some items slightly differently or perhaps have a somewhat different set of standards.

Relevant to this, Rodgers (1972) points out that if a person checks "false" on the statement, "I believe in the second coming of Christ," one point is earned on the Depression scale. It is suggested that pessimism over this eventuality "may indeed have been associated with depression in rural Minnesota a few decades ago, but is not likely to be differentially associated with depression in, for example, a Los Angeles suburb or a college community at the present time" (p. 249).

Validity for Blacks. The problem of an unrepresentative normative sample has been shown to be especially serious when it comes to the interpretation of profiles obtained from black subjects. It has been repeatedly reported that their T scores are, on the average, somewhat elevated. Gynther (1972) contends that this makes blacks appear sicker than they, in fact, are. Harrison and Kass (1967) analyzed the 213 MMPI items in which blacks differed significantly from whites, and attributed this difference to the underlying dimensions of estrangement, cynicism, and religiousness. Some writers have gone so far as to suggest that the current MMPI norms are completely inapplicable to black populations.

More recent evidence suggests that this blanket rejection of the MMPI for blacks is naively simplistic. For example, Davis and Jones (1974) provide evidence that, if the generally lower education of blacks is taken into account, the black-white MMPI differences on some scales largely disappear. Thus, on the Schizophrenic scale, poorly-educated Caucasians and well-educated Negroes and Caucasians are scored similarly; only the poorly educated Negroes had significantly more elevated scores. Davis and Jones suggest that higher levels of conventional education among blacks are associated with Caucasian-like MMPI performance. They speculate that this may be due to a selection process in which the more sensitive and suspicious blacks drop out of school at the earliest legal age. In addition, those blacks who do remain in school longer than the law demands become even more inculcated with Caucasian attitudes, opinions, and values.

Elion and Megargee (1975) claim that it is less important to study the MMPI differences between blacks and whites than it is to determine the validity of MMPI scales among blacks. In their experiment they focused on the Psychopathic deviate scale because of its special relevance in criminal justice settings. It had been established earlier that the Pd scale has both predictive and concurrent validity in white populations when the criterion is level of anti-social behavior. Among blacks, Elion and Megargee found that the Pd scale effectively discriminated between black prison inmates and culturally-deprived black college students. In addition, black prison recidivists had higher Pd scores than black first offenders. Also, among the college students, Pd scores were highest among those who were self-admitted delinquents. Thus, the Pd scale was shown to have as much validity for blacks as whites. However, these results are not generalizable beyond youthful black males. Additionally, the fact that Elion and Megargee found higher Pd scale scores among black college students and prison inmates than among comparable white samples still suggests that the traditional MMPI Pd norms are not appropriate for these particular black groups.

It seems clear that the best course of action would be to conduct validational research on all of the MMPI scales for use with blacks as well as other minority groups. In addition, periodic restandardization of the MMPI might also be warranted. Evidence for this comes from a study by Schubert and Wagner (1975), who found that college students in a large northeastern state university had significantly higher D, Pa, Pt, Sc, Ma, Si, and F scale scores and lower K scale scores in 1968 than did similar male and female students a decade earlier. The authors contend that this general shift in the direction of "MMPI pathology" can be attributed to the "glamorization of an alienated personality style" (p. 406) among college students in the 1960s; anecdotal observation seems to indicate this trend is reversing itself in the 70s. Schubert and Wagner believe that "alienation" is just one aspect of "adolescent role confusion" (p. 406). In this context they find support for their belief that the higher MMPI's of the 60s is due to alienation. Specifically, within the 1958 and 1968 student samples studied, vocationally uncommitted subjects, those who hadn't expressed an occupational choice as freshmen, had higher MMPI clinical scale scores than those who were vocationally committed. Schubert and Wagner conclude their report by asserting that if it was greater alienation and role confusion which led to elevated MMPI profiles in the 1968 sample, it does not necessarily imply greater psychopathology. By implication, this suggests that the 1968 college sample scored higher on the MMPI clinical scales for reasons which may be similar to those responsible for the elevation of scores frequently found among blacks. This again brings into question the applicability of the original MMPI normative data.

Inadequate Criterion Groups. The accusation of unrepresentative sampling has been leveled at more than the MMPI normative group. The structure of the patient criterion groups used have also come under attack. A number of the clinical samples used were exceedingly small; for example, the development of the Pa scale employed only 20 paranoid patients. In addition, the reliance upon the diagnostic procedures of a single hospital to define clinical groups is unjustifiable, given the extreme degree of variability which exists between hospitals regarding diagnostic practices. A patient who receives a diagnostic label in one psychiatric facility might easily be categorized differently in another setting. The establishment of clinical criterion groups which were more generally representative would have been a welcome improvement in this instrument.

There are additional problems with the MMPI but discussion of these will wait until the end of this section, when some limitations which are relevant to most personality questionnaires will be aired.

Strengths. On the positive side, it has to be emphasized that the MMPI might well be the most extensively used personality test, and that at least as much has come to be known about the meaning of MMPI scores as the scores from any other test. As indicated, the scales' particular strengths have proven to be the separation of normal from pathological groups. Thus, it has served well as a screening instrument in the service of selecting out emotionally unstable personalities in a variety of settings, including public schools, the military, and industry. In addition, a number of studies have demonstrated the usefulness of the MMPI for psychologists who seek to generate personality descriptions.

In one experiment, Little and Shneidman (1954) employed 11 psychologists who had extensive experience in the use and interpretation of the MMPI. They were each given the same MMPI profile and then asked to sort 150 personality descriptive statements along the dimension of "most true" to "least true" with respect to the person who had completed the MMPI, identified only as a 25 year old, single, male. When pair-wise comparisons were made among the 11 MMPI interpreters, the intercorrelations of their item sort ranged from +.42 to +.73. Thus, the inter-interpreter reliabilities were of moderate magnitude.

The criterion selected to establish the validity of the MMPI interpretation-sort was the consensus-sort obtained from 29 clinical psychologists who had access to all material on the subject, including medical reports, lab data, social history, treatment, and therapy rates *except* psychological test reports. The results indicated substantial agreement between the descriptions generated about an individual based upon an MMPI profile and those which emerged from extensive clinical data and history. Specifically, the validity coefficients for the interpreters, in the form of correlations between interpreter and criterion sorts, ranged from +.52 to +.74.

Little and Shneidman caution against interpreting their findings over-optimistically. They remind us that their data reveal what *"can* be done by competent clinicians with a specific (MMPI) protocol and not what might occur with different interpreters or with the same interpreters and different protocols" (p. 428). The last point is important because the MMPI profile selected was particularly clear-cut, having certain well-defined elevations. A more ambiguous MMPI picture might well have yielded far less impressive results.

California Psychological Inventory

It is remarkable that the MMPI has become the most popular vehicle for assessing personality, especially among non-psychiatric groups, since this function does not follow at all from the conceptual basis of the test. Between 1956 and 1960 Gough and his associates constructed a test, the California Psychological Inventory (CPI), that was specifically designed to do what was already being asked of the MMPI; its purpose is to assess the normal personality.

Gough, who did early MMPI research, fashioned the CPI after the MMPI in many respects. However, because of his intimate familiarity with some of the MMPI's weaknesses, he was able to improve upon the parent test in a variety of ways.

In terms of similarities which exist between the two inventories, the CPI consists of 480 items to which respondents answer "true" or "false;" almost half of these items come directly from the MMPI. The CPI, like the MMPI, yields a number of scale scores, 18 to be exact. Fifteen of the scales measure the personality dimensions of dominance, capacity for status, sociability, social presence, self-acceptance, responsibility, socialization, self control, tolerance, achievement via conformance, achievement via independence, intellectual efficiency, psychological mindedness, flexibility, and femininity. Of these, 11 were constructed using the empirical keying method employed in constructing the MMPI. That is, items which discriminated between contrasted groups were included in the scale. For example, the socialization scale is based upon the responses of juvenile delinquents and high school disciplinary problems, in contrast to a normal group of high school students. One significant improvement in CPI construction methodology over that used for the MMPI is the use of peer nominations to define the criterion groups. For example, the responses of the five most and least dominant fraternity and sorority members, as nominated by their "brothers" and "sisters," served as the basis of the Dominance scale. The personality trait judgments of subjects made by their familiar peers has repeatedly been shown to be among the most reliable and valid vehicles for obtaining evaluations.

The CPI, like the MMPI, also contains scales which enable the assessor to evaluate the validity of individual protocols. The "well-being scale" is used to identify subjects who are trying to generate an unrealistically poor impression. It was constructed by contrasting responses by real psychiatric patients with those of normal subjects who were asked to simulate a conflicted personality. The "good impression" scale is the second one intended for validity purposes and is based upon the responses of normal subjects who were asked to intentionally "fake good." The third validity scale, the Commonality scale, is simply a frequency count of highly common responses found among normal subjects.

One significant improvement in the CPI when compared with its parent test, the MMPI, is its use of a normative sample numbering 13,000. These men and women were selected to be a representative cross-section of the United States' population and include a wide range of ages, socioeconomic levels, and geographic regions.

Evaluation. The reviews of the CPI have been extremely mixed. Kleinmuntz (1967) says, "The CPI is already well on its way to becoming one of the best personality measuring instruments of its kind" (p. 239). This sort of positive regard for the test is primarily based upon the care and sophistication of its construction methodology. The CPI reliabilities have been carefully determined using the test-retest approach and have been reported in the range of .90. In addition, the CPI, like the MMPI, has generated a large body of research which enables practitioners who are familiar with these reports to evaluate the test's utility in a variety of settings, be they school, hospital, or industry.

Criticisms of the CPI have been directed at the large number of scales it contains. It is said that the test affords too much data for a clinician to integrate in a meaningful way. This difficulty is not helped by the paucity of guidelines in the CPI manual directed at understanding the "interaction among scales" or at determining "profile interpretation." The clinician is more or less on his own as he tries to make sense of CPI profiles. What is offered in the way of directives tends to be simplistic: "When the behaviors suggested by two or more extreme scores seem similar, they may well reinforce each other; if they seem opposing or contradictory, they may seem to counteract or ameliorate each other." Gough, as cited in Walsh (1972, p. 96), comments that "such interpretation amounts to no more than post hoc rationalization and should not be condoned."

A final criticism of the CPI was leveled by Thorndike (1959) who says that the 18 CPI scales are redundant and do not make for parsimonious personality description. The notion of scale redundancy lies in the fact that they tend to be rather highly intercorrelated; CPI Dominance and Sociability scales correlate about .65, and 14 of the 18 scales correlate with at least one other scale at the .50 level or higher. In defense of this weakness, Goldberg (1972) argued that it is not unreasonable to expect the traits of dominance and sociability to be correlated in a group of people. Therefore, it should not come as a surprise that measures of these traits are also correlated. Thus, Goldberg is saying that the intercorrelations found among CPI scales simply reflect the realities of personality structure.

A General Criticism of Empirical Test Construction

Walsh (1972) says, "The CPI is an almost comically typical product of criterion-oriented test construction" (p. 96). Essentially, Walsh is criticizing empirically keyed tests in general, suggesting that this way of developing a test "severely limits its generality and psychological meaningfulness" (p. 97) because we really have no idea *why* the test works or discriminates, only that it does. With such instruments there is no basis for predicting new fields of application. Their worth can only be judged by empirical investigation, due to the lack of a theoretical rationale for the test and its items.

FACTOR ANALYTIC CONSTRUCTION

The last general approach to the construction of personality inventories is one which has both empirical and rational-theoretical features. The empirical aspect involves the statistical process of factor-analyzing data, and is quite complex. However, the logic which underlies the method is within the grasp of anyone familiar with the meaning of a correlation coefficient.

Factor Analysis

Suppose a psychologist gave eight different ability tests, A through H, to a large number of subjects. It would be quite easy to find the degree to which scores on every one of the eight tests were related to the remaining seven by computing a correlation coefficient for each of the 28 possible test pairs. Illustrative data is presented in Fig. 13.

As a second step the psychologist could, by inspection of the resulting correlation matrix, discover which tests tended to co-vary, or be mutually intercorrelated. This means that within the cluster of tests so identified, people who score high on one test score systematically high on the others. Strong positive correlations would then exist. Similarly, if people who score high on one test tend to score low on another yielding a strong negative coefficient, the two tests are still related to each other, although in an inverse manner. Thus, a cluster of interrelated tests may involve both positive and negative correlation coefficients. It can be easily seen in Fig. 13 that there are two readily identifiable test clusters: A, B, C, D, and E, F, G, H. These clusters of intercorrelated tests are fenced in by triangles for clarity. Notice that the correlation coefficients are high within a triangle, indicating that all of the tests are mutually interrelated. Also, the correlations between tests coming from different clusters are low, suggesting a very minimal degree of relationship, if any.

Hypothetical Matrix of Intercorrelations

Measure	B	C	D	E	F	G	H
A	-90	-85	-79	01	21	00	-13
B		83	76	14	-20	07	16
C			71	19	-06	28	22
D				05	07	11	02
E					73	86	91
F						75	81
G							94

Figure 13. Hypothetical matrix of intercorrelations depicting two factors; one is composed of variables A, B, C, and D, the second of E, F, G, and H.

A *factor* is represented by a subset, such as A, B, C, D, of highly intercorrelated measures which tend to have low correlations with measures reflecting the remaining factor(s), in this case, E, F, G, H. The factor itself is the homogeneous dimension which is presumably being measured by the cluster of interrelated measures. The identification and labeling or naming of this underlying personality dimension constitutes that part of the factor analytic process which depends upon theory and judgment. For example, assume that test A measures piano playing, B drawing skill, C carpentry, and D dancing. It is possible that the factor represented by the four tests is creative expression. Alternatively, it is also possible that the underlying dimension being measured by A, B, C, and D is muscular coordination. The decision as to what to name the factor would probably depend upon a careful study of what is involved in the several tests and may, nevertheless, remain rather tentative. Notice that through the process of factor analysis one is able to summarize a large amount of data, eight tests, in terms of a small number of dimensions, two factors.

The same procedure can be applied to the items within a test rather than, as in the above example, to a number of different tests. When dealing with individual items the scores which subjects can earn on each are intercorrelated so that a correlational matrix is again produced. The data in Fig. 13 is perfectly suitable for representing the hypothetical product of this kind of effort based on a test composed of eight items. The four items which comprise each of the two factors in the example could then be dealt with as subtests of the larger eight item scale. Each subtest would be thought to measure some homogeneous dimension whose identification would rest upon an inspection of the item's content. Suppose the test asked subjects to rate the degree to which each of the eight items applied to self: item A was, "I laugh frequently"; B, "I am often sad''; C, "I hate life''; and D, "I have a sense of hopelessness." In this case the factor or underlying personality dimension might be labeled "elation-depression," and these four items would constitute a "depression" scale.

The hypothetical correlation matrix in Fig. 13 is rather small and for illustrative purposes the measures which intercorrelate were intentionally placed adjacent to each other in the matrix. It would have been quite possible for a factor to have been represented by measures A, D, and F, assuming they were shown to be mutually related. The point is that when the number of measures or items go into the hundreds, factors do not jump out at the casual observer of the huge correlational matrix.

In practice, sophisticated statistical procedures are made manageable through the use of computer technology which identifies the factors found within a matrix of intercorrelations. However, once the computer tells the psychologist which items form clusters, the naming of the factor still remains an inferential process of some magnitude. More than one researcher has dolefully admitted that the underlying dimension represented by a statistically intercorrelated cluster of items is anyone's guess. That is, it is often not apparent what the items which form a cluster have in common. An additional complication arises from the statistical procedure employed. While the reliance on empirical data is often associated with objectivity, the unhappy fact is that there are many statistical ways in which a factor analysis might be conducted. Each statistical methodology results in a somewhat different factorial solution. Thus, the same set of data may yield different clusters, presumably measuring slightly different underlying dimensions, depending upon the particular statistical procedures employed.

Cattell's Sixteen Personality Factor Test

As an example of the factor analytic test construction procedure, Cattell's Sixteen Personality Factor Test (16 PF) will be discussed. Cattell first put together a list of over 18,000 trait names by consulting textbooks on psychology and psychiatry, and by adopting the massive list of personality descriptive adjectives compiled by Allport and Odbert (1936). By eliminating essentially synonymous words, the compendium of traits and characteristics was reduced to a scanty 171.

To this point Cattell might easily be seen as trying to develop a content valid questionnaire of personality in general. However, as did Hathaway and McKinley who developed the MMPI, Cattell intended to do more than compile lists. Unlike the MMPI construction procedure which went on to identify scale items on the basis of their power to discriminate between a clinical and normal group, Cattell proceeded to get ratings of 100 subjects on his 171 trait items. The ratings were done by close friends of the subjects. After the ratings on the 171 trait items were intercorrelated, a factor analysis reduced the matrix to just 12 factors. Subsequently, factor analysis incorporating additional items brought the total factors to 16. The items which comprise each of these factors, between 10 and 13 items, form the 16 scales of the 16 PF which are claimed to assess the following personality dimensions, as compiled by Cattell, Eber and Tatsuoka (1970): reserved-outgoing, intelligence (concrete-abstract thinking), affected by feelings-emotionally stable, humble-assertive, sober-happy-go-lucky, expedient-conscientous, shy-venturesome, tough-minded-tender-minded, trusting-suspicious, practical-imaginative, forthright-shrewd, placid-apprehensive, conservative-experimenting, group dependent-self sufficient, undisciplined-controlled, and relaxed-tense.

There are four regular forms of the 16 PF which are supposed to be equivalent. However, the 1967-68 form A and B revisions involve wording changes on between 12 and 75% of the items comprising the individual scales which made up the 1961-62 Forms A and B. Bouchard (1972) feels that these are sufficient changes to make all of the research data collected on the early forms obsolete.

The job of the subject is to indicate whether the items apply to the self, being limited to the answer choices of "yes," "occasionally," and "no." Like the MMPI, the 16 PF can be quickly scored by key or computer. What emerges are scores for each of the factor analytically-derived scales. These scores can then be transferred to a profile sheet which allows for the easy conversion of raw scores into scales which range from one to 10, with a mean of 5.5.

Becker (1961) and Levonian (1961) have both expressed reservations about the apparent degree of relatedness among the 16 PF scales. If the scales do, in fact, correlate with each other, Cattell's assumption that they are measuring independent personality dimensions would be ill-founded. Other criticisms of the 16 PF have focused on the sometimes unimpressive split-half reliabilities of the scales, reported to be as low as .54. There is no test-retest reliability reported on the grounds that the personality dimensions assessed by the 16 PF are themselves subject to change over time. Lastly, while an accompanying manual describes the clinical significance of the various scales, there has been a paucity of research validating the behavioral correlates of individual scores as well as of profiles. No matter how carefully constructed the 16 PF may be, its worth can only be documented by conducting this kind of validational research.

LIMITATIONS OF QUESTIONNAIRES

As previously mentioned, early builders of self-report personality measures seemed motivated to reduce the time needed to obtain information gathered in an interview. There was a feeling that a subject's test response could be taken as a reasonable, if not perfect, reflection of reality. It became obvious that even though the test items served as a kind of standard set of interview questions, subjects did not perceive them in any standard sort of way. That is, the meaning of a given item could vary greatly over subjects. Consequently, so could the meaning of a response. Even the scaling metric used on a self-rating scale, one so simple as "true" or "false" may be given various interpretations. The subject who selects the "false" response to an item may be conveying anything from "not too often" to a completely unqualified "never". Because there is no opportunity for face-to-face clarification of meaning, these sources of individual differences just add error to the clinical interpretive process based on questionnaire data.

A second problem with questionnaires is that, despite the best efforts on the part of developers to have subjects attend only to the content of the item, the psychological situation within which the test is administered can greatly affect results. These contextual considerations can provoke motives on the part of subjects which conflict with the one intended, namely to be truthful.

Impression Management

Goffman (1959) used the term "impression management" to describe the tendency for people to present themselves in ways which they believe will facilitate the attainment of personally valued goals. For a psychiatric patient, this goal might be either remaining in or leaving the psychiatric facility. Braginsky, Grosse, and Ring (1966) have shown that patients who are motivated to remain hospitalized, perhaps because life on the outside is a constant unpleasant struggle, will act on this motive while filling out an MMPI type questionnaire. That is, they tend to answer the items in a direction which creates the strongest impression of psychopathology. Related to this, Hathaway (1957) brings attention to a "hello-goodbye" effect, which refers to the fact that upon entering a hospital, patients may effectively "fake sick" on questionnaires in order to legitimize their presence there. Alternatively, when ready to leave, the patient may thank his psychiatrist by denying all symptomatic problems contained on a questionnaire.

Whether or not such intentions are conscious, it is this behavior which prompted Meehl and Hathaway (1946) to construct the K scale as a means of correcting the problem on the MMPI. Research, including that of Cofer, Chance, and Judson (1949), has shown that at least the tendency to fake good health can be identified in some test-takers by noting elevations of the K scale in relation to the MMPI L scale, while negative malingering can be detected by the F scale. Kroger and Turnbull (1975) criticize the importance of findings such as these because they are based upon giving subjects general instructional sets to either answer normally, fake a good impression, or fake an emotionally disturbed presentation. Kroger and Turnbull instead requested college students to fake a specific social role; "complete this test (MMPI) as if you were an air force officer, that is, a regular commissioned officer of the air force" (p. 49). Another group of subjects were asked to answer the MMPI as "someone who spends his working time creating works of art, whether it be in the area of dance, theatre, painting, sculpture, or music; someone who is making his living as a professional artist" (p. 49).

It is clear from Fig. 14 that the students were able to effect MMPI profiles that are strikingly similar to those generated by actual air force officers. Importantly, the clinical profile cannot be detected on the basis of validity scale data which, in some respects, makes the simulated profile appear more valid than the actual officer profiles. The students were less able to simulate accurately the MMPI profile obtained from actual artists at the Ontario College of Art. Kroger and Turnbull reasoned that the problem in faking artistic profiles may have stemmed from misconceptions about what artists are really like. It was felt that most students believed artists to have deviant personalities. This erroneous conception resulted in simulated profiles with elevated F and clinical

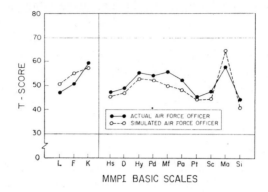

Figure 14. Simulated and actual MMPI scores for air force officers. (Kroger, R.O. & Turnbull, W. Invalidity of Validity Scales: The Case of the MMPI. *Journal of Consulting and Clinical Psychology,* 1975, *43,* 48-55. Copyright© 1975 by the American Psychological Association. Reprinted by permission.)

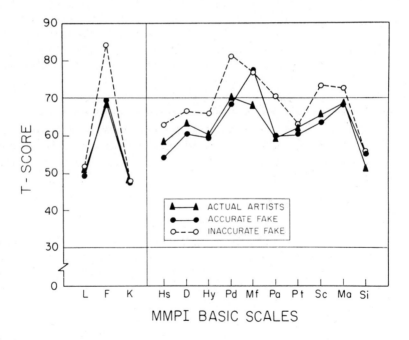

Figure 15. Comparison of MMPI scores of actual artists with simulated MMPI scores under two conditions of accuracy of role expectations. (Kroger, R.O. & Turnbull, W. Invalidity of Validity Scales: The Case of the MMPI. *Journal of Consulting and Clinical Psychology,* 1975, *43,* 48-55. Copyright© 1975 by The American Psychological Association. Reprinted by permission.)

scales as illustrated in Fig. 15. When an additional group of students was provided with an accurate and detailed personality description of the typical artist in order to counter the common misconceptions regarding this population, the students were able to very effectively simulate the real artists' profiles as can be seen in Fig. 15. The only significant scale difference was on the Mf; evidently, the receipt of accurate personality data did not dispel the students' notion that artists are deviant in terms of sexual orientation. Kroger and Turnbull conclude that it is easy to fake MMPI profiles without this deception being detected by validity scales, so long as subjects instructed to fake are able to adapt a social role of which they have an accurate conception. What remains to be determined is whether subjects who spontaneously attempt to fake on the MMPI adopt a strategy of simply "faking good" or "faking bad," or whether they complete the test by stepping into a well-conceived social role different from the one they routinely fill.

Cattell, Eber, and Tatsuoka's (1970) 16 PF 1971 handbook claims that this personality test is not easily faked because the poles of each factor represented on the scale are presumably equal in their social desirability value. Consequently subjects would have a difficult time systematically trying to appear more or less socially desirable. Unfortunately, this expectation was not upheld by research. Irvine and Gendreau (1974) found that both prisoners and college students, when instructed to either make themselves look better than they actually were or to give a bad impression of themselves, were able to do so, both with about equal ease. Specifically, depending upon the subject group and instructions, 11 or 12 of the 16 PF scales showed significant score shifts. However, the 16 PF dissimulation indices generally were able to detect in excess of 80% of the faked protocols. This finding is consistent with the impression that MMPI validity scales are also effective detectors of dissimulation when subjects are under "fake good" and "fake bad" instructions. One wonders whether the detection rate would diminish if the subjects in Irvine and Gendreau's 16 PF study had been asked to fake by adopting a well-conceived social role, as had Kroger and Turnbull's (1975) subjects in their MMPI dissimulation experiment.

Response sets and style.

Gynther (1972) says that the MMPI has survived two serious attacks in its history. One of these is relevant to most self-report personality questionnaires and has to do with the problem of *response sets*, also referred to as *response styles* or *response biases*. Most simply, a response set is the tendency to respond in a manner for reasons which are independent of whether the content of the items is true or false for the individual. For example, a person may check a statement as "true", not because it is objectively true, or even because it is erroneously perceived to be true, but because there is an intention to create a particular impression. The material just discussed on test-taking dissimulation may, therefore, be construed as the result of a response set.

In the literature, the term "response set" has been associated with the tendency to create a socially favorable or unfavorable impression—the *social desirability* (SD) response set, the tendency to agree with items regardless of item content—the *Acquiescent* response set, and the tendency to select the atypical response which goes contrary to the general trend—the *deviant* response set.

Anastasi (1968) distinguishes between response sets and styles, reserving the latter term for the broad, enduring personality characteristic which may be the basis for a test-taking response set. For example, the predisposition to check "true" on true-false questionnaires is the acquiescent response set that may be just one manifestation of a pervasive personality style where the person typically acquiesces or agrees in social situations. The early work on response biases was concerned almost exclusively with the issue as a source of test error and focused on the study of response sets as Anastasi defines them. Later, people became interested in these sets as manifestations of personality which were worthwhile studying in their own right. This latter emphasis focused on what Anastasi refers to as response style.

Rorer (1965) suggests a different distinction between response sets and styles. He uses the term "set" for situations in which the testee dissimulates, is defensive, or responds in a socially desirable manner. The commonality across all of these cases is that item content must be evaluated. If the subject's goal is defensive in nature, he must read the item and, on the basis of its content, decide how to respond in order not to reveal his psychopathology. Similarly, subjects who wish to fake particular impressions or to present themselves in a socially desirable manner must also attend to the content of each test item. Rorer reserves the term "response style" for ways of responding which can be exercised independently of the item content. The tendency to select certain response categories, such as "true" or "false", falls within the bounds of this definition. That response styles occur in non-test situations is indicated by Goodfellow (1940) who cites the fact that 80% of subjects will call "heads" on the first coin toss, even though the objective probablity is 50-50. Berg (1957) notes that three times as many patrons use the right hand stairway to a theatre balcony, even though the left hand stairway is equally accessible. Berg and Rapaport (1954) note further that people who are asked to choose one number or letter from the series 1-2-3-4 or A-B-C-D select 3 and B 60% of the time for no apparent reason. This last observation has implications for the importance of varying the position of the correct answer on multiple choice achievement exams. If a professor draws up a final exam which has too many of the correct answers in the B position, a student who knows very little might do quite well by capitalizing on his stylistic tendency to choose the B alternative when in doubt.

Acquiescence. Acquiescence was the first response style to be extensively studied. It was first identified by Lentz (1938) who thought that this tendency to agree might greatly distort the measurement of any characteristic which depends upon positive and negative reactions, "true" and "false" responses, to statements. The concern over acquiscence reached its peak in the early 60's after Jackson and Messick statistically evaluated the relative contribution of acquiescence, social desirability, and item content to MMPI scale scores. They came to the conclusion that "in light of accumulating evidence it seems likely that the major common factors in personality inventories of the true-false or agree-disagree type, such as the MMPI and the California Psychological Inventory, are interpretable primarily in terms of style rather than specific item content" (1958, p. 247). The fact that the MMPI psychotic scales are weighted with items keyed "true" while the neurotic scales have most of their items keyed "false" raised serious doubts as to whether the test was assessing psychoticism and neuroticism or simply the tendency for subjects to manifest differentially acquiescent response styles.

Much of the research on acquiescence uses an item reversal procedure which involves the presentation of MMPI-type items and their opposites within the same test form. For example, "I am usually happy," and "I am usually sad," would both be presented at some point in the test; if a subject was responding in an honest, content-relevant manner rather than according to response styles, one item would be answered "true," and the other "false." If an individual were to respond "true" or "false" to both items it would be concluded that an acquiescent response style was operating.

Most of these studies came to the conclusion that both item content and acquiescence were important determinants of test-responding. Rorer (1965) criticized the bulk of this research by pointing out flaws in the item reversal procedure. For example, he questioned whether the reversal of loving is hating or just non-loving. Similarly, a person attending to content who says "false" to the item "I like magazines," may also say "false" to "I do not like magazines," if the individual has no particular preferences regarding magazines. Thus, two "false" responses to apparently reversed items does not necessarily imply the operation of a response style.

Rorer and Goldberg carefully constructed their own form of a reversed MMPI so that "if a respondent were to be presented with the original and the reversed items simultaneously he would have to answer them in opposite directions if he were to avoid contradicting himself" (1965, p. 802). About 200 male and female college students were employed, half of each sex were control subjects who received the regular MMPI twice, two weeks apart; the other half were experimental subjects who received the original MMPI on one occasion and the reversed form on the other testing session. Among the experimental subjects it was found that, on the average, they reversed their responses on the reversed items 83% of the time. This comes very close to the 87% average test-retest consistency on individual items for the control group. This similarity between the experimental and control groups was deemed remarkable, given the problems in arriving at acceptable item reversals in the first place. Rorer and Goldberg concluded that the influence of the acquiescent response set on MMPI scores is "trivially small" (p. 815).

Interest in this particular problem seemed to dissipate subsequent to Rorer's critiques and research on the acquiescent response style. More recently, Bentler, Jackson, and Messick (1971) have managed to create a small revival of activity in the area by reconceptualizing the notion of acquiescence. In effect, these researchers suggested that there are two types of acquiescence. One type is called *agreement acquiescence* and is defined as the tendency to agree. On a true-false test, individual differences in agreement acquiescence would simply relate to the predisposition to say "true" or "false," regardless of content. It is this kind of acquiescence which had been of long-standing interest and which Rorer's item-reversal studies showed to be of minimal importance. The second type of acquiescence is called *acceptance acquiescence* and is defined as "individual differences in the tendency to consider characteristics as descriptive" (p. 190). An extreme accepter would tend to say "true" to all items which assert the existence of a personality characteristic, such as "I am happy," and "I am sad"; and the same person would say "false" to any items which deny the existence of personality characteristics, such as "I am not happy," and "I am not sad." If a person is operating under an acceptance acquiescent response set, his test behavior may at times be indistinguishable from one who is solely attending to content. For example, if an item reversal procedure is used, one might come up with a reversal pair such as "I am happy," and "I am not happy." A subject who says "true" to one and "false" to the other may be seen as attending to content. Alternatively, the person may be an extreme accepter, saying "true" to the first item and "false" to its negative reversal. Thus, Bentler and his colleagues (1971) contend that much of the findings which were construed as consistent with the idea that subjects attend to questionnaire content may be reinterpretable as supportive of their acceptance acquiescence hypotheses.

In a reply to the Bentler article, Block (1971) dismisses the arguments as little more than an abortive attempt to breathe life into a dying issue. Block points to the fact that many item reversals used in the research were not of the negation-reversal type which Bentler used as examples. On items such as "I am usually sad," and "I am usually happy," subjects did tend to answer oppositely. The acceptance acquiescence hypotheses would predict identical responses to both items of this reversal. On a more subjective note, Block expresses disbelief that subjects pay more attention to whether a statement is phrased in a positive or negative manner than they do to the content of the statement.

The revival of acquiescence as an issue by Bentler did not generate extensive interest on the topic. Possibly this was because most psychologists follow Block's (1971) suggestion that, rather than become preoccupied with agreement and acceptance acquiescences, it would be easier to minimize the possibility of their influence by appropriate test construction methodologies. In the case of agreement acquiescence, this means continuing the already routine practice of having an equal number of questionnaire responses keyed "true" and "false;" control of acceptance acquiescence requires the test constructor to employ an equal number of positively and negatively phrased items.

A somewhat different approach to the study of acquiescence was taken by Couch and Keniston (1960) who focused on this response style as a personality variable. They chose to refer colorfully to the dimension of acquiescence as "Yeasaying - Naysaying," and sought to establish that the test behaviors involved are manifestations of a "deep-seated personality syndrome — whose underlying determinants serve to explain the pheno-typical phenomenon of 'acquiescence' or 'agreement' " (151-152). Couch and Keniston found that "yeasayers," those who tend to agree or say "true" regardless of content, are generally passive and receptive people who frequently give in to their impulses. "Naysayers" were characterized as generally exhibiting greater responsibility; they were more prone to inhibit impulses and were more in control of themselves. Their personality analyses on subjects who were divided in terms of their tendency to agree to questionnaire items, led them to understand the underlying personality dimension associated with agree-disagree response styles as "stimulus acceptance vs. stimulus rejection" (p. 173), respectively. It is interesting that Couch and Keniston saw acceptance-rejection as being the personality underpinning to the test behavior of agreeing-disagreeing. A decade later Bentler, Jackson and Messick, as we saw, also focused on these two related dimensions, but as two subtypes of acquiescent test taking behavior, agreement and acceptance acquiescence.

Social Desirability. Social desirability is a response set according to Rorer (1965) because the content of questionnaire items must be attended to in order for a subject to present himself in a socially desirable or undesirable manner. Since this tendency was first powerfully brought to the attention of psychologists by Edwards (1953a), it has become the most studied of any response-distorting tendency. Edwards (1953a) did research on the probability that an MMPI type item will be said to be self-descriptive, endorsed, as a function of the social desirability (SD) of the item. A set of 140 personality statements were rated for their SD value by a group of 152 male and female judges of various ages. These rated statements were then given to subjects with the standard instructions of describing themselves by responding "true" or "false" to each item. It was found that the percentage of individuals who endorsed each item was positively correlated with the SD rating of the item. "I like to be loyal to my friends" (Edwards, 1957, p. 18) had an extremely high SD rating and 98% of the subjects responded "true" to this item. "I like to avoid responsibilities and obligations," (p. 18) of course had a low SD rating and was endorsed by only 6% of the subjects. The overall correlation between the items' SD rating and the probability of its endorsement was +.87. This magnitude of correlation has since been replicated many times and, therefore, appears to be a reliable finding.

Once one knows the SD rating of personality-descriptive statements, it is possible to define a socially desirable response as "true" to an item which has a high SD rating and "false" to one with a socially undesirable rating. Edwards (1957) then developed a scale to measure subjects' tendencies to give socially desirable responses. Edward's Social Desirability (SD) Scale consists of 39 statements selected from the MMPI. Thirty of them were rated 4.5 or lower on a 9 point scale and comprise the socially undesirable end of the scale. All these items are keyed "false." Nine items, keyed true, received SD ratings of 5.5 or higher. A subject taking the SD scale receives a point for every socially desirable response made; high scores are naturally associated with a stronger social desirability response set.

Edwards expected that "if the SD scale does provide a measure of the tendency of subjects to give socially desirable responses to statements in self-description, then the correlations of scores on this scale with other personality scales given under standard instructions, should indicate something of the extent to which the social desirability variable is operating at the time" (p. 31, 33). Using this strategy, Edwards (1964) was able to show that the MMPI Psychasthenia (Pt) scale, containing 48 items, 47 of which are rated as being socially undesirable, correlated $-.84$ with the Edwards SD scale.

This means that a person who has a social desirability response set tends to score low on the Pt scale and high on the SD scale. Another MMPI scale, the masculinity-feminity scale has about an equal number of its 60 items rated socially desirable and undesirable. As expected, since the keying on the Mf scale is balanced for social desirability value, it manifests a low correlation with the SD scale ($r=.16$). Continuing this strategy with 43 original and more recently derived MMPI scales, Edwards (1961) demonstrated that the correlation between these MMPI scales and the SD scale was very strongly related to the proportion of items on the MMPI scales rated as being socially desirable. That is, the MMPI scales having the highest percentage of their items keyed in the socially desirable direction manifested the highest correlations with the SD scale.

It might be asked whether the MMPI measures psychopathology or social desirability, and the answer would not be an easy one to arrive at since the dimension of psychopathology-mental health itself is heavily loaded with SD. One cannot present himself as psychopathological without admitting to socially undesirable personality characteristics. Heilbrun (1964) notes that the person who checks as "false" to the statement, "I loved my mother," whether accurately or not, is saying something which is of low social desirability as well as being indicative of psychopathology.

The fact that an MMPI scale is strongly associated with social desirability or undesirability does not necessarily render it invalid. In fact, Heilbrun (1963) found that the MMPI scales which are best able to distinguish between psychologically disturbed and normal subjects are the ones whose keyed responses are the most socially undesirable. Heilbrun concludes that "the dimensions of psychological health and social desirability are in large measure one and the same" (p. 386). This implies that if one tried to assess a psychopathology which is inherently undesirable, independent of the social desirability response style, the power of the measurement process may suffer. Nevertheless, there are suggested ways for controlling the influence of social desirability in personality inventories.

The first (Hanley, 1956) involves the exclusive use of items which fall at a midpoint value on a social desirability rating form. This approach would be difficult to follow if one were trying to assess a personality dimension whose behavioral correlates were deemed, in the real world, to be very socially desirable, such as altruism, or undesirable, such as psychopathology.

The second approach to controlling the influence of SD is exemplified by the MMPI. It involves allowing the person to adopt an SD response set but corrects for it afterward by including an SD scale along with the test. This procedure is followed when the clinical MMPI scales are made higher on the basis of subjects' K scale scores, the K scale being essentially an SD scale.

The third procedure was adopted by Edwards (1953) in his construction of the EPPS which has been discussed previously. The structure of this test shifts from a true-false to a forced choice format. The subject is asked to choose that member of a pair of statements which is more self-descriptive, with the two statements comprising the pair having been equated in terms of their SD ratings. There is some difficulty with effectively employing the forced choice procedure. It frequently happens that two items may receive very nearly identical SD ratings. This suggests that one would not appear more socially attractive in endorsing one than the other. However, when the two are joined to form a forced choice pair, the endorsement rate may become very imbalanced. When they are juxtaposed in the same paired item, one comes to appear much more socially desirable than the other. This effect is strongest when the items comprising the pair receive individual SD ratings which are far from neutral. Thus, the problem is particularly acute when trying to develop a forced choice method of assessing a personality variable high or low in social desirability, such as psychopathology.

The final vehicle for controlling the influence of SD on structured questionnaires is to emphasize honesty to the responder, stressing that there are no "right" or "wrong" answers. This approach may allow the examiner to feel comfortable, for at least "something" was done to control the problem. However, it probably has little impact on most subjects. As Edwards (1957) has pointed out, there is no reason to believe that the SD response set is consciously adopted, a fact which in turn suggests that it may be minimally reduced by conscious input designed to attenuate its impact.

Just as Couch and Keniston (1960) chose to study acquiescence as a personality variable rather than as a source of testing error, so did Crowne and Marlowe (1964) shift the attention of SD research to the exploration of this response set as a manifestation of a pervasive personality characteristic. This has been discussed in Chapter 11.

Crowne and Marlowe (1964) found that people who scored high on their SD scale were conforming, cautious, persuadable and, typically non-deviant.

Deviation. The third source of response bias which has received some significant attention is that of deviant responding. This may be either content irrelevant, in which case it would be a style; or it may be the result of a careful reading of item content, thereby qualifying as a set according to Rorer. Berg has extensively studied people whose test responses go counter to the general trend and has emphasized the independence of test deviance from item content. Berg defines a deviant response as "one which differs from the modal response. . ." (1955, p. 63) to a significant degree. He feels that an individual whose test behavior is characterized by deviant responses is revealing a test-taking pattern which is associated with a more general personality deviation. Berg refers to this notion as the "deviation hypothesis" (p. 62). In order to test the deviation hypothesis experimentally Berg and Hunt (1949) developed a test consisting of 60 meaningless abstract designs which subjects were asked to rank on a four point rating scale ranging from "like much" to "dislike much." Because clear preferences for some of the designs were found in the general population, it was possible to define deviancy as a response which was counter to the popular trend. As expected, groups differing in adjustment showed significant differences in the degree to which they manifested response deviation. Barnes (1954) found that many more deviant responses were given by various diagnostic patient groups than by normal subjects. Berg (1955) finally suggested that by employing well-defined criterion groups, deviant responding to almost any set of stimuli for which norms have been established could be used as the basis for constructing empirically-derived personality scales.

For many practical purposes, the entire issue of test bias is a moot point. If one is interested solely in the predictive utility of an instrument, as were the developers of the MMPI, empirical keying is employed and it matters little whether responses are due to item content, acquiescence, SD, or deviance so long as the item discriminates between criterion groups. If, on the other hand, one's interests are more theoretical in nature and tests are valued as being measures of particular personality traits or characteristics, it does make a difference whether the Sc scale is assessing schizophrenia or some associated, but nevertheless conceptually different, dimension like SD.

INVASION OF PRIVACY

The second major attack against personality questionnaires did not come from within the field of psychology, as did the response bias issue, but was perpetrated, according to Gynther, by "journalists in the muck-raking tradition and wooly-minded editorial writers who said the MMPI was a dastardly invasion of privacy" (1972, p. 240). Critics argued that the MMPI asked "Communist-inspired" (p. 240) questions regarding sex, religion, and mother love and should not be used as a condition of employment, as was often the case in the early 1960's. Gynther agrees with this judgment regarding the proper, or improper, use of the MMPI, but bases his complaint on the fact that the MMPI was never intended to function as a screening device for jobs in government and industry. Nevertheless, it was not scientific concern over the predictive utility of the MMPI in new areas of application so much as arguments allegedly inspired by high morality which gained prominence. The events culminated in the spring of 1965 when both the Senate, under the leadership of Sam Ervin, more recently of Watergate prominence, and the House, led by Representative Gallagher, investigated personality inventories and the related invasion of privacy issues. The November 1965 issue of *American Psychologist* was devoted entirely to "Testing and Public Policy." It presented reasoned critical evaluations of the matter, as well as transcripts from the Congressional hearings. In an article in that issue Senator Ervin explained the reason for Senate hearings on psychological tests as a prerequisite for government employment. He said that "numerous complaints" had been received "that some of the questions contained in the personality inventories relating to sex, religion, family relationships, and many personal aspects of the employee's life constitute an unjustified invasion of privacy" (p. 880).

Conrad, (1967) studying the objectionability of questionnaires used in federally-funded projects, proposed eight criteria for evaluating questionnaire items. He suggested that test constructors should avoid including items which 1) deal with highly personal matters, 2) might have an adverse psychological effect on some respondents, 3) request self-incriminating or demeaning confessions, 4) emphasize extremely abnormal behavior, feelings, or impulses, 5) seem to accept or condone generally immoral or reprehensible behavior, feelings, or impulses, 6) request confidential or personal information about another without their permission, 7) are interpretable as propaganda for or against an emotionally charged issue, and 8) deal with a politically sensitive domain.

Over a five week period Conrad reviewed the item content of 109 data-gathering questionnaires submitted to the United States Office of Education for use in 50 funded projects. These included personality, intelligence, achievement, vocational interest, and curriculum questionnaires, as well as questionnaires on the professional background and training of the educational staff. Of the 109 instruments studied with the above criteria in mind, objections were raised against only five questionnaires. More specifically, concern was expressed over only 10 of more than 5300 items reviewed. Conrad's subjective impression was that the number of objectionable items which passed through the Office of Education was minimal.

Using Conrad's criteria on a test like the MMPI would undoubtedly result in many more objections. The research on MMPI offensiveness was not conducted until after the Congressional hearings. In general, the findings paint a benign picture in comparison to what one might have expected based on the testimony given during the hearings. It must first be remembered that a subject who objects to an MMPI item's content is free to omit his response. However, Rankin (1966) found that most females omit only one item and most males complete all items. Butcher and Tellogen (1966) have reported modal rejection rates of 10 items. While the Congressional hearings focused on the objectionable nature of sex and religion-oriented items, the research documented that only 15% of these items were objected to by respondents, who found the most offensive items were those pertaining to body elimination functions. Of interest was the report that items tend to be judged as more objectionable if the subject believes the test will be used for personnel selection. This, of course, was the very use which generated so much concern.

It is of course incumbent upon psychologists to avoid prying any further than is absolutely necessary. Nevertheless, it is quite likely that some amount of probing into areas which most people consider private is necessary if psychologists are to render the best assessments possible. Hathaway, writing on this point, notes that if a psychologist cannot inquire into personal matters "he suffers as did the Victorian physician who had to examine his female patients by feeling the pulse in the delicate hand thrust from behind a screen" (1964, p. 206).

What was possibly a more important concern of both Senator Ervin and Representative Gallagher was that the use of personality tests violate "due process" (Ervin, 1965, p. 880). On this point, Representative Gallagher (1965, p. 881) writes, "There is little or no effective appeal procedures for our citizens who choose to challenge personality testing as an invasion of privacy, or contest interpretations of the findings in the event they do take the tests." Senator Ervin (1965, p. 880) suggests "that the employee and his attorney and private physician be allowed to examine the psychological reports and data which may adversely affect his employment. Otherwise, the employee is unable to confront the evidence against him, and is therefore unable effectively to present contradictory evidence on his own behalf." These are certainly serious concerns which can only be reduced if testing practitioners employ questionnaires which have been validated as predictive instruments for job success, and the employee is fully appraised of the reasons for having to complete the forms. It is undoubtedly true that the government-sponsored administrations of the MMPI frequently fell outside the bounds of these guidelines.

In summarizing the outcome of the Congressional hearings, Amrine (1965) points out that the general public might well have received the impression "that some sinister things called personality tests were being used on Government applicants by the thousands or perhaps millions" (p. 867). In fact, the MMPI was being used at the time for Peace Corps screening and by the State Department, usually to evaluate prospective overseas personnel in whom emotional stability was of high concern. The hearings found no evidence of widespread MMPI misuse. The clarity of this simple fact in the public's mind was easily overshadowed by the media's exploitation of what was then a headline subject. A variety of popular magazines published negatively biased perspectives on the reliability and validity of the MMPI. In addition, humorist Art Buchwald wrote a Washington *Post* column with the emotionally appealing title, "Psyching Out: You can't flunk this test but it tattles on your id" (June 20, 1965). Buchwald also proposed his own substitute for the MMPI, employing items such as "My eyes are always cold," "A wide necktie is a sign of disease," and "I use shoe polish to excess."

One other major question about personality questionnaires which frequently echoed through the halls of Congress concerned whether the tests were scientifically valid. It has already been mentioned that the data bearing on the validity of the MMPI for employment purposes is meager. Whenever any instrument is intended for use as a predictor of job success there can be no substitute for empirical verification of its worth. This verification must be obtained with respect to the particular employment situation because generalization of validity data is always a questionable procedure. A test may have considerable predictive validity for one occupational position and absolutely none for another. Because psychologists are in a position to judge the merit of assessment procedures by bringing to bear their sophisticated awareness of the issues involved, it is incumbent upon the field to be its own harshest critic.

Brayfield (1965) wrote that the Congressional hearings "show how citizens, through government officials and through their representatives, are asking psychologists some large questions: How much power do you really claim? How can you prove it? How do you propose we should be protected from false claims or from abuse of real powers? . . . Society . . . accords us (psychologists) special privilege and expects from us special responsibility" (p. 857).

SUMMARY

In this chapter we presented a sampling of self-report questionnaire approaches to personality assessment. Material was organized in terms of the test construction procedure employed in the development of the questionnaire.

The content validation test construction procedures were exemplified by Woodworth's Personal Data Sheet, the Mooney Problem Check List, and the Fear Survey Schedules. Rational-theoretically derived questionnaires emerge systematically from the test constructor's preference for a particular theory of personality. Liverant's Goal Preference Inventory was shown to be a logical extension of Rotter's Social Learning Theory. Similarly, Murray's personality theory, called Personology, has given rise to the Edwards Personal Preference Schedule. The third questionnaire development procedure discussed was the empirical approach. The most popular questionnaire, the MMPI, is an example of a test developed from a purely empirical perspective. The use of "cookbooks" and computerized MMPI profile interpretations represents the empirical approach at its highest level of sophistication. The CPI was presented as a second example of empirical questionnaire construction methods. The final questionnaire construction procedure considered was factor-analytic. It was shown that this approach has both rational-theoretical and empirical elements. The logic of factor analysis was described and Cattell's 16 PF was used as an illustration.

This chapter concluded with a discussion of the limitations associated with questionnaires. The focus here was primarily upon response distortion by subjects due to response sets and style. In addition, the issue of invasion of privacy through the administration of questionnaires was presented.

TERMS TO KNOW

CHAPTER 14
Projective Techniques

Like personality questionnaires, projective techniques provide the subject with stimuli to use as the basis for responding. As we have seen, personality questionnaire items are worded and presented in a manner which renders their meaning as unambiguous as possible. In addition, the subject is made aware of the nature of the expected responses, "Answer either 'True' or 'False' to each self-descriptive statement."

In contrast, projective personality assessment techniques are intentionally ambiguous on the point of the subject's task. He may be asked to say what an inkblot looks like or to make up a story about a picture but, beyond that, instructions are kept vague. The subject is simply encouraged to say whatever he wants within very broadly-defined guidelines. Projective responses are thus open-ended. In addition to task ambiguity, projective techniques frequently employ ambiguous stimuli. In this context, "ambiguous" means that the stimulus item to which the subject must respond is open to a wide array of reasonable interpretations. Thus, an inkblot certainly has objective dimensions, but what it looks like or what it should suggest to the viewer is not at all clear-cut.

The rationale for projective assessment was clearly presented by Frank (1939). In essence, he described the projective technique as a kind of "X-ray" into those aspects of personality which subjects either cannot or will not openly reveal. Presumably the test format allows the subject to expose core ways of "organizing experience and structuring life" inadvertently as meanings are imposed on and reactions made to a stimulus having "relatively less structure and cultural patterning." Because subjects do not realize the interpretive implications of their responses, called *projections,* the projective instruments fall into the disguised category of personality assessment tools.

The disguised aspect of projective techniques allegedly facilitates gaining access to aspects of personality which the subject may not openly acknowledge. For example, a subject might interpret a picture of two interacting people as depicting a violent argument which will lead to one physically assaulting the other. According to the theoretical rationale of projective testing, the aggressive content of this projection may be instigated more by unconscious aggressive impulses than by the outward appearance of the picture itself. It might then be hypothesized, given additional confirming assessment data, that this subject is an angry individual with a predisposition to experience his world as peopled by hostile individuals.

RORSCHACH INKBLOT TECHNIQUE

The use of inkblots for the study of personality was first suggested in 1895 by Binet, the founder of modern intelligence testing. His was concerned with exploring the processes underlying imagination. It was not until 1921 that Rorschach published *Psychodiagnostik*, in which he advocated the use of inkblots for diagnostic purposes.

Rorschach's early work was of an experimental nature. He sought to develop a way of scoring perceptual responses to inkblots which would allow the examiner to discriminate between subjects having different psychiatric diagnoses. In this sense, his interests were very much like those of Hathaway and McKinley, who developed the MMPI for similar diagnostic purposes. As would later be the case with the MMPI, the inkblot technique provided rich clinical data. Its use was, therefore, quickly extended beyond mere diagnostic assessment. It is currently a major vehicle for achieving an in-depth understanding of the complete personality.

The Rorschach test consists of ten cards (8 x 10 ¾ inches), each having a picture of a bilaterally symmetrical inkblot which was formed by dropping ink on paper which was then folded in half. The development of the final set of blots culminated ten years of work, and represents those blots which Rorschach found to be the most diagnostically useful. Five Rorschach cards are achromatic, having only black and shades of grey on them. Two additional cards have small areas of bright red added to the predominantly black and gray format. The remaining three chromatic cards utilize a spectrum of pastel colors. All the blots appear against a white background.

Administration and Scoring

There exists today some variation in Rorschach administration and scoring. One of the most popular methods is described by Klopfer, Ainsworth, Klopfer, and Holt (1954) and by Klopfer and Davidson (1962).

The method of Rorschach administration consists of four phases; the first two are required, and the last two are optional. During the *performance proper*, or "free association" phase, the examiner adopts a highly "permissive and unstructured" posture (Klopfer et al., 1954, p. 6). Neither subtle direction nor limitations are imposed permitting the subject to follow his "spontaneous inclinations" (p. 6). The subject is asked to respond to each card by saying what it looks like or might represent. The subject might ask, "May I turn the card?" or "Should I tell you what comes to my mind immediately or think it through?" (p. 7). These queries are met with a non-directive answer from the examiner; "You may do it any way you like" (p. 7). Klopfer feels that these factors result in "throwing the responsibility for making decisions right back upon the subject" (p. 7). This, coupled with the generally low profile maintained by the

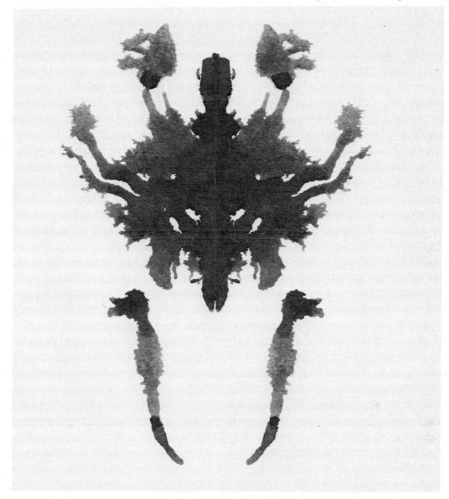

Figure 16. Illustration of inkblot similar to those on the Rorschach.

examiner during the performance proper, makes it most likely that the responses are spontaneous and, in as much as possible, the production of the subject alone.

The examiner's main task at this point is that of record keeper. A verbatim written account of the subject's responses is made for each of the 10 cards as they are presented in order. In addition, recording forms allow the examiner to keep track more easily of which cards led to which responses, the order of responses, the time elapsed initial presentation of the card to the expression of the first response, and the total response time spent on each card.

The second testing phase is the *inquiry*, during which the examiner obtains information required for scoring the protocol. Because there is, necessarily, more verbal exchange between the examiner and subject during the inquiry than during the performance proper, the examiner must be especially careful not to lead the subject in any particular direction.

Inquiry specifically seeks to explore two aspects of the subject's responses, *location* and *determinants*. Inquiry for location involves going back over each card and asking the subject exactly what parts of the blot led to each response. In order to facilitate this, the responses are read back to the subject and he indicates the source of his perceptions on each card in turn.

There are five main location categories and scores

1. W (Whole response): All or nearly all of the blot is used.
2. D (Large usual detail): A large sub-area of the blot is used, marked off by space, form, shading, or color.
3. d (Small usual detail): The subject uses a small sub-area or detail marked off by space, form, shading, or color.
4. Dd (Unusual detail): A detail of an unusual nature is used, one not naturally marked off on the blot as are D and d locations.
5. S (White space): The subject uses the white areas of the card; the blot itself may serve as mere background for the projection.

As these locations are being scored, the determinants of each percept are found by inquiring into what made the blot look as it did to the subject. There are four major determinants, some with important subcategories.

1. Form: The percept is determined by the shape of the blot. Form is scored F.
2. Movement: The subject imparts action onto the card and reports humans moving (M), animal activity (FM), or inanimate movement (m).
3. Shading: The subtleties of dark and light areas on the blot determine the perception by suggesting a sense of surface or texture (C), or by producing the impression of three dimensions of depth (K).
4. Color: The response is due to the chromatic aspects of the blot (C) or to the achromatic grey and black areas which may be used as color, a "black cat" or "grey hair" (C').

Many Rorschach projections are the product of more than one determinant, in which case the response is scored with the primary determinant appearing first. For example, FC would depict a percept based mainly on form and, in a secondary way, on color.

The third and fourth exam phases are optional. The *analogy* period may be used to clarify ambiguities in scoring which remain after the inquiry. The examiner probes into the possible use of additional determinants for some responses by asking about determinants admitted to for other purposes. For example, the examiner may recall for the subject that color was used for another response and then wonders out loud whether color might have been a determinant of the response in question as well.

The last administrative procedure, also optional, is that of *testing the limits.* It is here that the examiner may become much more directive. For example, he may rather pointedly probe into whether the subject sees any human form in the blots if none had been spontaneously reported; or the examiner might suggest that a particular blot is frequently seen in some way and openly ask the subject if he can perceive that projection. While the intention of testing the limits is to explore the perceptual experience of subjects beyond what was possible during the inquiry, some Rorschachers claim that the procedure is too affected by subjects' suggestibility and openness to new ideas. A subject who is receptive rather than close-minded, for whatever reasons, is thought likely to simply accept as perceptually valid whatever the examiner suggests.

Three dimensions of the subjects' protocol are scored in addition to location and determinant already discussed. First, the responses are scored for *content*. There are a moderate number of different content categories, some of which are human figures (H), parts of humans (Hd), animals (A), nature concepts (N), food (F), plants (Pl), abstract concepts such as "power" or "force," (Abs), and responses pertaining to sexual organs and activity (Sex). These content scores do not weigh too heavily in the traditional interpretive hypotheses which are used in the formation of a personality description. However, as we will see, content has recently become relatively more important to some interpreters of Rorschach protocols.

Second, the projections are scored for *popularity-originality*. If the percept is one of the 10 which Klopfer lists as being extremely common to particular cards, the score of P is assigned. The score 0, for original, is one which beginning Rorschachers can't use because it is reserved for responses which occur less than once in a hundred records. Therefore, the examiner must have some degree of experience before he can determine whether a projection is sufficiently uncommon to be scored 0.

The last scoring dimension is that of *form level rating*. A rating of -2.0 to $+5.0$ may be assigned to each response. The score value depends upon the accuracy or fit of the perception to the form of the blot. Attempts by the subject to organize different areas of the blot into a meaningful integrated concept are acknowledged with a raising of the form level rating.

Interpretation

The interpretive process begins with the examiner constructing a psychogram, which is simply a bar graph indicating the frequency with which the several determinants were used.

Each determinant is alleged to have potential interpretive significance. For example, M implies "imagination" because the subject has enlivened the blot with "movement" which is not objectively present. M is also suggestive of the ability to experience the world as "peopled" and implies that the subject is capable of feeling "empathy with others" (Klopfer et al. 1954, p. 254). The determinant m, if used more than a couple of times, may indicate that the subject experiences forces which are out of control. It may therefore reflect threat from external sources, or tension and conflict from within.

The frequent use of K as a determinant suggests anxiety of a diffuse and free-floating nature, reflecting a frustration of affectional satisfactions. In general, the use of shading determinants is related to the way in which the subject deals with affectional needs. This notion is based on a hypothesis which relates tactile interest, focusing on the textured appearing aspects of the blot, to affectional needs.

The manner in which color is used is held to provide insight into the subject's "mode of reacting to an emotional challenge from his environment" (p. 276). For example, a subject whose responses are determined solely by color is said to reveal "a pathological lack of emotional control, emotionality of an explosive, hair-trigger variety'' (p. 285).

This kind of quantitative analysis goes beyond attaching significance to the frequency count of different determinants. A series of ratios between the frequencies of various determinants may also be computed, the values of these ratios having interpretive significance in themselves. For example, the use of form as a determinant, coupled with a neglect of both color and shading, can be taken to mean that the person's life is impoverished by a lack of emotional and affectional aspects.

Location scores are also analysed in terms of ratios and frequencies. When the subject is able to use the entire blot for his percepts (W), he may be said to manifest ''organizational interest and ability'' (p. 299). A sub-category of the W response is the cut off (W̵). These are scored when the subject uses essentially the entire blot for a percept but makes a point of spontaneously excluding some area. For example, ''It looks like two bears climbing a tree except for these blotches at the bottom.'' In moderation the W̵ response ''indicates an interest in organizing experience, tempered with a critical intellectual attitude which prompts the subject to omit from a generalization (W response) those aspects of experience (minor parts of the blot) that do not fit'' (p. 301). While this might seem to be a desirable characteristic, ''an over emphasis on it would indicate an over-critical and perfectionistic approach which tends to inhibit the processes of generalization and integration'' (p. 301).

The most common location scores are D, insomuch as they ''are obtained by breaking the blot up into its most obvious subdivisions'' (p. 304). Over 55% D responses, in conjunction with good form level ratings, indicates a practical and common sense orientation to experience, with only minor interest in integration or organization. If the subject tends to focus more on smaller, but still obvious, blot areas, building up a high count of d responses, it is taken to indicate a differentiated interest in his experience of the world. One sub-category of the d location response is scored de for edge detail. This is scored when the subject bases his perceptions on minor configurations along the perimeter of the blot. A significant number of de scores ''indicates a fear to go into anything too deeply, a fear of becoming involved if one does, and a tendency to skirt the fringe of a situation without coming to grips with it'' (p. 308). The use of white areas of the blot (S) ''relates to an oppositional tendency . . .; it is the reflection of the competitive or self-assertive aspect of intellectuality'' (p. 309). This hypothesis rests upon the fact that subjects are specifically asked to respond to the inkblot and an S response is a reaction to a non-blot area.

There are many other aspects of the Rorschach record which may be taken into account as the examiner tries to make clinical sense of a particular record. For example, a low total number of responses is held to be suggestive of an underproductive personality, while an excessive number may reflect a ''compulsive need for completion or quantity'' (p. 311). An average response latency to the cards which is lower than 30 seconds indicates a hurried quality of functioning which, if associated with poor form level, can suggest that the subject is being subversively uncooperative. Finally, a popular (P) count much lower than the average of five may imply that the person is not viewing his world in conventional ways; if P is over eight, it might indicate that the subject is motivated to experience life with an emphasis on what is obvious or agreed upon. In contrast, the intellectually superior person may have twice as many original as popular responses, but an excess of Os which have a bizarre quality may show "a serious weakening of ties with reality" (p. 313).

As far as content is concerned, over-emphasis on any content category is revealing of a narrow perspective of the world. Frequent use of any content area, such as sex may reflect an underlying preoccupation with that area. Often, however, the excessive use of a content area is not so much a sign of pathology as it is a reflection of the person's vocation or station in life. Thus, a physician may produce many anatomical responses (At). The most common content category centers around animals because they are easiest to see. However, if the percentage of A responses goes much above 50% it may indicate immaturity, low intelligence, or disturbed adjustment.

The reader should be cautioned against coming away with an impression that Rorschach interpretation simply involves noting the occurrence of various signs as they occur, e.g., "more than 50%A responses = immaturity," and then writing a personality description. In fact, the interpretive process is highly complex. The experienced Rorschacher synthesizes all of the Rorschach results and typically arrives at a personality formulation which is something more than a mere sum of the signs. Exner describes as "pure non-sense" (1974, p. 230) the notion that Rorschach interpretation can be approached in "cookbook" fashion. He asserts it is crucial that the totality of the test be considered, for the importance and meaning of a given sign can be dramatically modified by the presence of other protocol features. Often, these important moderating features emerge from the free associations of the subject as he responds to the test. For instance, a singularly bizarre projection may lose its pathognomic import if the patient spontaneously reports it to have been provoked by a science-fiction movie seen the previous evening. According to Exner, effective Rorschach interpretation is neither "cookbookish" nor magic, but depends upon "a thorough knowledge of the test plus a thorough knowledge of people and their peculiar kinds of maladjustments" (p. 229).

Reliability

One of the basic problems which has to be surmounted when trying to evaluate the Rorschach empirically as a global measure of personality is the confounding impact of R, the total number of responses. When a person is generally productive in terms of R, the frequencies of other individual scores will also tend to be high. The problem associated with this can be exemplified by the following sample question: Are five M responses in a protocol of 15 total responses relatively more or less psychologically important than 10 M responses in a total R of 50? There is no easy answer. Anastasi (1968) points out that the use of proportions doesn't help the matter because certain scores, such as the location W, seem to have an upper limit which doesn't fluctuate too greatly regardless of how lengthy the total record becomes. More disturbing is Anastasi's report that R, a major determinant of other Rorschach scores which are used for personality interpretive purposes, may itself be related to "factors quite extraneous to the basic personality variables allegedly measured by Rorschach" (p. 497-498).

These factors include the subject's age, education, and even the examiner; (some examiners seem to routinely pull greater R from their subjects than others).

The answers to specific questions pertaining to the Rorschach's reliability are no less confusing. The use of test-retest reliability appears to be quite inappropriate in the case of the Rorschach since the first test administration will invariably have a strong impact on the second. Some subjects may try to recall past performances, tending to inflate the reliability coefficient. This can occur when the subject interprets the second administration as a memory test. If an attempt is made to dispel this erroneous idea, the subject may make a concerted effort to be creative and not repeat anything. This has the effect of undermining test-retest reliability. In addition, because the total frequency of many Rorschach scores is low and typically has a limited range, small shifts greatly change certain numerical proportions used for clinical interpretations.

When test-retest reliability becomes a problem, split-half reliability can usually be resorted to as an estimate of a test's consistency of measurement. However, even this form of reliability is of very limited worth when applied to the Rorschach. Again, because of the small number of responses and low magnitude of individual scores, which is made half again as small when the protocol is split, very slight variation will produce drastic reductions on the computed split-half reliability coefficient. There is just not enough data in one record with which to work in a statistically meaningful way. Overriding this is the fact that there is no way to split the Rorschach into equivalent halves. Different kinds of scores as well as different numbers of responses tend to be associated with particular cards. For example, one can't have a C determinant for an achromatic card and card X, which is chromatic, elicits more responses than any other. On a more theoretical level, several cards are alleged to have unique interpretive implications which render them inequivalent. For example, card VII is referred to as the "mother card" and IV as the "father card." Presumably responses to these inkblots have special significance for the way in which the subject experiences his mother and father. However, empirical justification for this distinction between cards VII and IV is lacking.

Because of the extensive judgmental factor which is involved in the scoring of a Rorschach protocol, inter-scorer reliability is especially important to demonstrate. McArthur (1972) reports that at least this crucial aspect of Rorschach reliability has received favorable reports. It seems that when Rorschach examiners are well trained, they consistently attain 95% scoring agreement. McArthur suggests that reports of low inter-scorer reliability are often due to the crippling impact on effective scoring of experimental methodologies which do not permit the scorers to conduct reasonable inquiries.

Inter-interpreter reliability is as important as scorer reliability. The issue here is the degree to which two Rorschach examiners viewing the same record arrive at similar clinical interpretations. Datel and Gengerelli (1955) approached this reliability problem by using a matching technique. They had 27 clinical psychologists score and blindly write clinical interpretive reports on one of three sets of six Rorschach protocols. These psychologists were then asked to match the clinical reports of other psychologists (who had scored and interpreted the same six protocols) with the proper test protocol. One set of six protocols came from a homogeneous group of bright paranoid schizophrenic patients. The other two sets of six protocols employed were obtained from heterogeneous groups of patients who had been assigned an array of diagnostic labels.

The results of this study at first seem reasonably positive in that the overall matching rate was higher than it would have been on the basis of chance alone. However, only 14 of the 27 clinical psychologists were able to attain better than chance matches, and, of the 324 separate matches attempted, only 148 were correct. It can be mentioned in this context that the experience levels of the 27 psychologists varied from trainees to Ph.Ds with up to 15 years of experience in covering many hundreds of Rorschach administrations. Despite this range, the matching performance of the examiners was not related to experience; and only one of the three most prominent Rorschachers was able to exceed a chance level of matches. Datel and Gengerelli (1955) suggest that any individual differences in the ability of the psychologists was overshadowed by the particular Rorschach material being matched. Specifically, the ability to match interpretive reports correctly with original protocols dropped precipitously in the homogeneous sample as compared to the heterogeneous sample. In fact, 9 of the 14 judges who matched at an above-chance level had been assigned to work with the data from the heterogeneous group of patients.

What appears to be an unimpressive matching performance may be explained in one of two ways, the first being far more optimistic. It is possible that mismatches were attributable to clinical formulations which were all legitimate, yet were based on different aspects of the Rorschach protocol. This hypothesis rests on the belief that there is such a tremendous amount of data in a Rorschach protocol that it is unlikely that two interpreters would focus on the same aspect of the material. An alternative explanation for mismatches is that the Rorschach provides too little information for interpreters using different protocols to come up with discriminably different clinical interpretations.

Validity

The establishment of Rorschach validity is similar to that of Rorschach reliability in that it, too, is a highly complex matter. It is difficult to determine predictive validity for the Rorschach because, as a "wide band" instrument which assesses the whole personality, assertions based upon it tend to be conceptualized in relatively global terms such as "The patient is impulsive." Consequently, it is hard to find clear-cut criteria against which to test the validity of such a conclusion. Concurrent validity studies have frequently involved the use of the Rorschach to differentiate between diagnostic categories. The results of these efforts are not easy to interpret because of the unreliability of the criterion. The psychiatric assignment of psychopathological diagnoses to patients is not done with any high degree of consistency, as Zigler and Phillips (1961) mention. Therefore, if a concurrent validity coefficient is low, one doesn't know whether to attribute it to the Rorschach, to the diagnostic enterprise, or to both. This kind of research reached its low point when Wittenborn and Holzberg

(1951) reported a zero correlation between 36 different Rorschach scores and the clinical diagnoses of almost 200 patients.

The method of blind analysis, has been a common validational approach. In this procedure, interpreters are asked to draw conclusions about patients working only from Rorschach data; they are blind to all other sources of clinical information. To the degree that blind Rorschach formulations coincide with criterion personality descriptions rendered from more complete sources of data, the Rorschach interpretations are deemed to be valid. Unfortunately, blind analysis reveals nothing about what is being attended to and what kinds of decision rules are being used when formulating the personality description. Unless the interpretive processes can be made public and explicit, blind analysis research, even if supportive of Rorschach validity, is worth little because of its lack of generality. Specifically, one Rorschacher may be skilled with the test on the basis of strong clinical perceptions which are independent of the Rorschach per se, while other clinical psychologists may not be so skilled. This speaks more to the validity of the clinician than to the validity of the test.

When the matching procedure is added to that of blind analysis, no additional light is shed on the rules of clinical interpretation which are being covertly employed. In addition, it is now well known that the matching procedure is methodologically weak. A report derived from Rorschach protocols may be correctly matched with clinical interpretations stemming from other sources, but for reasons which are essentially irrelevant to the validity of Rorschach. For example, the language level of Rorschach responses may allow for the easy matching of a protocol with other personality descriptive data containing information on IQ or the number of school years completed. Because one never can be sure of the basis for correct matches, the possibility always exists that "validating" matching data is really attributable to the skill of the matchers in picking up trivial clues common to the two sets of data. Because of these problems, matching should be regarded as providing equivocal data as far as Rorschach validity is concerned.

Probably the greatest number of Rorschach validity studies have adopted a "sign" approach, in which the predictive efficacy of a particular Rorschach index is evaluated. One Rorschach sign is "eyes." This response is taken to be typical of subjects who manifest paranoid personality trends. Presumably these people believe others are watching and there is a projection of these beliefs onto the inkblot in the form of eyes. DuBrin (1962) investigated this hypothesis empirically, employing as subjects 24 paranoid schizophrenics, 24 non-paranoid schizophrenics, and 24 subjects having character and behavior disorders. A paranoid content response was defined as a perception of eyes, face, or mask given during the performance proper phase of test. Paranoid content was evaluated in terms of the percentage of paranoid responses. This was found to be 17.8% for paranoid schizophrenics, and only 3.5% and 1.7% for the non-paranoid schizophrenic and character-behavior disorder groups, respectively.

In a more ambitious experiment, Ives, Grant and Ranzoni (1953) evaluated the validity of Rorschach characteristics that are frequently taken as neurotic signs or as signs of adjustment. More specifically, these researchers were interested in testing the validity of the following statement: "The neurotic signs occur so infrequently or the adjustment ones so frequently in a normal adolescent population that present diagnostic uses are warrented'' (p. 31). The subjects in the study were 145 well-adjusted adolescents from families above the national mean in education and occupational status. They were each tested three times over the span from 11 to 18 years of age. All records were scored by two or three workers whose scoring agreement reached about .84%. Thus, the interscorer reliability was more than acceptable.

Ives, Grant and Ranzoni report that the frequency of 14 neurotic signs occurred at a rate above what would be expected if they were truly indicative of neuroses. The incidence of adjustment on the other hand, was quite variable. For example, the absence of pure C responses is taken as an index of adjustment, and the No C sign indeed occurred in 90% of the records. However, just two adjustment signs, No C, and Dd and S being less than 10% of total R, occurred consistently in 60% of the records over all ages and for both sexes. The researchers concluded ''that it seems justifiable to state that they (adjustment signs) occur with less frequency than would be anticipated if they were validly representative of the normal or 'adjusted' Rorschach'' (p. 45). They advise against using a sign approach to discriminate neurotic from non-neurotic Rorschach records.

This warning is thought to be an attack upon a ''straw man'' by many Rorschach advocates. In actual practice Rorschach neurosis and adjustment signs are not used in any sort of mechanical or additive way. Rather, the clinician adopts a global approach to Rorschach analysis and takes into account the overall content and configuration of the record. In fact, in many settings it is common practice for Rorschach protocols to be subject to no more than impressionistic reactions which are devoid of any systematic effort to score the record quantitatively or note the presence and absence of particular signs. When scoring is done, it may be limited to content and form level with no attention paid to the traditional formal response dimensions of location and determinant.

The Projective Hypothesis

It must be recalled that the Rorschach procedure was conceived within the context of a perceptual experiment. The focus gradually shifted so that the effort became one of refining ink blot methodology as an empirically-based diagnostic tool. As clinical psychology adopted the technique for diagnostic and general personality assessment purposes, Frank's (1939) projective hypothesis became the theoretical underpinning. It was then assumed that subjects' projections were primarily a function of their unique personality, with special emphasis placed on the importance of unconscious trends as a projective response determinant. Once the Rorschach procedure became subject to empirical investigation, the projective hypothesis came under attack from several fronts.

Subject Expectancies. A number of experiments have studied the effect on Rorschach protocols of the subject's specific expectations and perceptions regarding the nature of the Rorschach and the interpersonal assessment situation. In terms of pre-test information, Coffin (1941) provided students with the content of one of two especially prepared "journal articles." The information contained in these allegedly created the impression that a high status group produced either many W locations and A content responses, or many D locations and inanimate content responses. When the students later completed the Rorschach, their protocols showed inflation of those scores which had been emphasized in the fictional information previously received. These results point to the importance of suggestion, perhaps transmitted to subjects via the mass media or by the examiner, as a source of influence on Rorschach protocols.

Henry and Rotter (1956) manipulated subjects' understanding of the purpose of the Rorschach by varying instructional sets. Thirty female college students received the standard Klopfer instructions which ask subjects to report what the inkblots could be, look like, or are remindful of, in conjunction with the communication that there are no "right" or "wrong" answers. Another sample of 30 female students also received these instructions but, in addition, were told, "For many years the test has been used in mental hospitals to study emotional disturbance and to discover how seriously disturbed patients were. We are now making a college survey with it" (p. 458). All subjects then were administered the Rorschach under standard procedures. The general results were that the experimental group, those given the impression that their emotional stability was under investigation, produced more cautious and conforming records. These subjects gave fewer total responses, emphasized more form determinants and animal content, had better form level ratings, and had a tendency to emit fewer aggressive content responses than those receiving only standard instructions. These findings should encourage the interpreter to take into account the subjects' beliefs and general perceptions regarding the nature of the testing experience in order to interpret protocols validly.

In a less research-oriented paper, Schactel (1950) also discusses how the subject's personal definition of the Rorschach situation may influence performance. As an illustration, Schactel points out that subjects are primed in the performance proper to respond as if any response were acceptable. Given this set, they might easily be surprised by the more probing behavior of the examiner during the inquiry phase and feel under pressure to justify what they had reported seeing (p. 446). This may result in a subject "failing to see" during the inquiry his more creative or fantasy ridden perceptions previously reported during the performance proper. In addition, he may try to improve the quality of other responses by generating new determinants which cause the projection to fit better with the blot. Thus, what was an amorphous W location response may become a cut off W in the service of attaining greater accuracy.

Other aspects of Rorschach performance are also thought to be susceptible to the influence of the subjects' testing beliefs or attitudes. People who take the assessment process seriously may be contemplative and have rather long reaction times to each card. Those who wish to remain uninvolved, who minimize the importance of the Rorschach, or who are moved by passive-aggressive feelings toward the examiner frequently manifest very short response latencies.

Schactel points out that in our western culture experience in evaluation situations tends to be associated with competitive achievement. When in such situations people may habitually strive to attain superior status and demonstrate high competence. This competitive set may be manifested in the Rorschach situation in more than one way. The subject who interprets the test as one of imagination may come up with only one masterpiece of a response per card, or else may relate over 100 responses in an effort to demonstrate that his imaginative resources are inexhaustible.

In a similar vein, Schactel suggests that subjects who are superficially acquainted with psychoanalytic free association may feel obliged to produce as many sexual responses as possible during the performance proper; few people are unfamiliar with the story about the patient who accused the psychiatrist of showing him "dirty ink-blots". On the other hand, if the subject sees the examiner as an intimidating authority figure, there is likely to be a conscious effort to suppress sexual content. In an experimental context Rabin, Nelson and Clark (1954) have shown that such inhibition operated when male subjects are administered the Rorschach by a female examiner.

Examiner Influence. The examiner as an important situational influence has been explored by many Rorschach studies. Lord (1950) had 36 subjects take the Rorschach from three different examiners who were instructed to adopt either warm and appreciating, neutral, or harsh and rejecting tones, respectively. Her results showed that the experimental manipulation had an effect but more important was the discovery that the particular examiner tended to be a greater determinant of Rorschach responses than was the affective tone he intentionally adopted. This strongly suggests that a Rorschach examiner may not be able to be neutral after all; the examiner's characteristic personality may have an impact regardless of any role which is attempted.

The relationship between specific examiner personality variables and subjects' Rorschach scores was studied by Sanders and Cleveland (1953). Nine psychology graduate students completed the Rorschach before receiving extensive training in its administration. Each newly-trained graduate student examiner then went on to administer Rorschachs to 30 different undergraduates. The examiners' personalities were evaluated for covert and overt anxiety and hostility. The covert measures of anxiety and hostility were based on a content analysis of the examiners' own pre-training Rorschachs. Sanders and Cleveland assumed that "this criterion measures the anxiety and hostility present in the examiner's perceptual and fantasy living and hence is covert" (p. 39). Ratings of overt examiner anxiety and hostility were obtained from the 30 undergraduates which each examiner tested. These subjects indicated whether or not 15 adjectives and phrases applied to their examiner. Five of these were indicative of examiner anxiety — "under some strain, uneasy, apprehensive, nervous, worried"; five were signs of hostility — "critical, expecting too much, somewhat prying, irritating, disdainful"; and five suggested low levels of both anxiety and hostility — "easy-going, unruffled, nonchalant, undisturbed, self-assured" (p. 38). There was a strong tendency for examiners to be perceived consistently as either overtly high or low on anxiety and hostility throughout the experiment.

The main concern of the study was to determine if a relationship existed between the examiners' personalities and the Rorschach protocols they elicited. The protocols from the three examiners ranked highest and lowest on each of the four personality variables, overt and covert hostility and anxiety were contrasted. It was found that the subjects who rated their examiners as being overtly anxious had been generally more responsive on the Rorschach. Sanders and Cleveland suggested that these subjects may have produced more responses in an effort to help their examiner and smooth over uncomfortable periods of silence. The importance of covert anxiety seemed to be a less important influence on Rorschach responding.

Subjects who experienced their examiners as being the most overtly hostile produced records which revealed passivity, low hostility content, and stereotypy. It seems clear that an overtly hostile examiner elicits a constricted record from an inhibited subject. This finding is consistent with the research of Henry and Rotter (1956) and Eichler (1951) which indicates that subjects under stress produce standard, uncreative, and generally constricted protocols. Higher levels of hostility are found in the records of subjects whose examiners were high as opposed to low in covert hostility.

Once again this study demonstrates the fallibility of the projective hypothesis. Rorschach responses were clearly and significantly influenced by more than the subjects' own personalities. Sanders and Cleveland reassure us, however, that the amount of error introduced by examiner personalities does not render Rorschach protocols totally unreliable as personality indices. In fact, they were able to demonstrate statistically that only 3 to 7% of what goes into the Rorschach scores can be attributed to the influence of the examiner's personality. Most of the remaining 93 to 97% is a function of the subject's own personality.

One weakness of the Sanders and Cleveland experiment is that relatively inexperienced examiners were employed. They suggest that experienced examiners may effectively minimize the impact of their personalities on Rorschach responses by restraining even subtle expressions of their own conflicts and needs. An experiment relevant to this hypthesis was conducted by Gibby, Miller, and Walker (1953). Twelve examiners with at least two years of Rorschach experience administered the Rorschach under standard conditions to equated groups of psychiatric patients. The records were then coded and scored blindly by one of the authors. The frequency of form, color and shading determinants was found to be significantly related to the particular examining psychologist. In this experimental design, unlike that of Sanders and Cleveland, no attempt was made to ascertain the source of this influence.

The sex of the examiner has evoked some interest as a focus of Rorschach research. Harris and Masling (1970) investigated the number of Rorschach responses offered by male and female subjects to male and female examiners. The authors found that males produced about the same number of responses for both male and female examiners, but that females were more likely to have a higher R count when the examiner was male than when female.

The procedure used in the Harris and Masling (1970) study involved looking at the first Rorschach administration of male and female graduate students in clinical psychology to both a male and female subject. The female examiners did not note any trend, whereas 12 of the 16 male examiners had their first female Rorschach subject produce more responses than their first male subject.

Thus, there is clear evidence that female subjects are most productive for male Rorschach examiners. No other examiner-subject sex combination produces as high R scores. The data point to this effect as being a two-way affair; unverified hypotheses invoked to explain this phenomenon include the notion, "Women like to be looked at, just as men like to look" (p. 62). In other words, perhaps both sides covertly conspire to lengthen the duration of interaction. The male examiner may subtly encourage the female subject to keep the card longer or may directly reward multiple responding on each card. The female subject may inadvertently comply with the male examiner's voyeuristic motives by excercising her own motive to please or to be submissive.

One major limitation of the Harris and Masling study is that the examiners were graduate clinical students and the subjects were university clinic clients. Because all concerned were young, the cross-sex effect may have been greater than if old, more experienced examiners had been employed. It should, however, be noted that male examiner influence on female subjects has been demonstrated for other personality tests by Masling and Harris (1969) and occurs in research as well (Rosenthal, 1966, 1967). Harris and Masling conclude that even psychologists "remain quite clearly men and women" (p. 62).

Two lines of research have studied the effects of examiner variables on Rorschach performance, but from viewpoints other than the personal characteristics of the administrator. One focus has been on studying the effect of reinforcement provided by the examiner for certain classes of Rorschach responses. Wickes (1956) and Gross (1959) have shown that verbal statements made by the examiner, such as "Fine" or "All right," if expressed selectively after M and H responses, respectively, significantly increase their incidence. Magnussen (1960) demonstrated that non-verbal reinforcement (a nod of the head) was as effective as a simple verbal "uh-huh" in producing significant increases in the number of popular responses. The mean number of popular responses rose from seven to about ten or eleven in the two reinforcement conditions.

A second track of research has been concerned with examiner expectancies. The issue here is whether subjects produce the kind of protocols which the examiners anticipate. Is there a self-fulfilling prophecy on the examiner's part with regard to the type of protocol generated by his subject? It is not unreasonable to predict that subtle types of verbal and non-verbal reinforcement might bring about this state of affairs, and, in fact, such a phenomenon has been empirically identified.

Masling (1965) trained 14 graduate students on Rorschach techniques. Seven of these trainees were advised that experienced Rorschachers always elicit more human than animal content responses; the remainder were led to believe that the opposite was true. Each graduate student then administered the Rorschach to two undergraduates. As anticipated, the ratio of animal to human responses was significantly different between the two groups of examiners. Surprisingly, audiotape recordings of the sessions revealed no discernible evidence of verbal conditioning by the examiner. In addition, neither the examiners nor their subjects expressed any awareness of examiner coercion in the direction of the induced expectancies.

Examiner expectancies have also been shown to have an effect on the interpretations assigned to Rorschach records. For example, Haase (1964) demonstrated that when information about a respondent's low socioeconomic status is provided along with his protocol, the interpretation generated by an examiner indicates greater pathology and poorer prognosis than if the examiner believed the subject to be of middle class background. In a later study by Koscherak and Masling (1972), the opposite results were obtained using a similar experimental design. This time, the Rorschachers interpreted the lower class Rorschach record as less pathological than an identical set of responses allegedly coming from someone of better education, residence, salary, and occupation. Koscherak and Masling suggested that the reversal of findings reflects the greater awareness and sensitivity to lower class culture by clinicians in the 1970s as compared to a decade earlier. Traditional middle class norms are presumably no longer applied in blanket fashion to people from different social backgrounds. Rather, it is suggested that Rorschachers ask, "What does this event (Rorschach response) mean for *this patient*?" (p. 418).

Other Situational Influences. Henry and Rotter (1956) point to the tendency of subjects to be less open, less creative, and more constricted in their Rorschach performance when under a stressful informational set. This would be the case if they were aware they were being assessed for mental disturbance. This is highly relevant to the nature of clincal settings within which patients may have to complete the Rorschach. Often this testing is done soon after admission to a psychiatric facility when stress is augmented by the anxiety-producing unfamiliarity of the hospital setting and personnel, and when the patient is, in fact, being evaluated in terms of severity of mental disturbance.

Eichler (1951) directly studied the effect of induced stress on 15 indices of anxiety on the Rorschach. Before being administered the Rorschach, 60 male college students were asked to compute a series of relatively simple subtraction problems in their heads. The 30 subjects assigned to the experimental stressed group, were, in addition, told that they would receive three electric shocks of increasing intensity at varying intervals during their computations. They were seated in an "electric chair" and each had two electrodes attached to his cheek and wrist. These 30 subjects actually experienced shocks of 25, 30 and 35 volts during this phase of the procedure. When then asked to complete the Rorschach, experimental subjects were told to expect additional shocks at varying intervals. "The longer the time interval that elapses without the receipt of shock, the more intense will the next shock be" (p. 347). In actuality, these subjects received no additional shocks.

All identifying data were removed from the Rorschach protocols, which were then coded and blindly scored by a skilled Rorschach interpreter. Of the 15 alleged Rorschach anxiety signs, seven were affected by the induction of stress, four of these to a significant degree. Consistent with the results of Henry and Rotter (1956), Eichler found that stress induces a constricted Rorschach record. Thus, his results, too, are in conflict with the position that the Rorschach taps basic personality structure, independent of external influence. Rather, situational factors were found to be quite relevant to the kinds of protocols which subjects produce.

The effective Rorschacher then must be one who makes an effort to include the test-taking situation and the subjects' beliefs about that situation as variables important to the process of data interpretation.

Current Status of the Rorschach Technique

Over the years, many innovations in application and interpretation of the Rorschach have been introduced. There have been dozens of scoring systems devised for the detection of anxiety, hostility, homosexuality, schizophrenia, neuroses, suicide-proneness, brain damage, and therapy prognosis.

One of the more recent of the major innovations is the scoring of Rorschach records for *body-image boundary.* Fisher and Cleveland (1958) devised this scoring system to evaluate whether subjects experience the boundary between their bodies and the external world as firm and substantial or weak and penetrable. A person with firm body boundaries is said to feel secure in his dealings with outside agents. He acts on the basis of a substantial self-image, while a person with poor body boundaries is said to have a weaker self-concept. It is theorized that the former kind of personality produces Rorschach responses which have rather definite structural or surface features; for example, people with secure self-images are believed to project many humans wearing unusual articles of clothing, such as hoods, chaps, and fancy costumes; animals with distinctive skins, such as alligators, porcupines, and zebras; shelled animals; protective articles, such as umbrellas; armored things, such as tanks and knights, and covered things, such as a man behind a tree. The total number of such responses comprise what has been called a *Barrier score.*

There has been a fair amount of construct validity established for Barrier scores. For example, high-scoring subjects have been shown to be better able to adapt to stress and illness and to be more resistant to outside influence. One problem with the research in this area is that some studies have used Rorschach inkblots, while others have employed Holtzman inkblots. The Holtzman inkblot technique is more suitable for research purposes since subjects are restricted to one response per card. This eliminates the confounding problem of different R scores between subjects, which plagues Rorschach research. However, matters tend to become complicated when studies are done using non-comparable methodologies. As a last point, it remains doubtful whether Barrier scoring will be of use in individual clinical cases. Even if significant Barrier score differences emerge when research is done on contrasted groups, there remains a considerable overlap of scores between the groups. The median score tends to range from three to six, depending upon the subject sample and whether the Rorschach or Holtzman inkblots are employed. Thus, unless the Barrier score were quite deviant, it would probably not be wise to use it for assessment purposes in the individual case.

Unlike Fisher and Cleveland's Barrier scores, which are content-based, Friedman (1952, 1953) developed a scoring system to assess perceptual-cognitive maturity. This focuses only on the organizational aspects of Rorschach perceptions. Friedman's *Developmental scoring system* is based on Werner's (1948) theory of cognitive development, which stresses that development "proceeds from a state of relative globality and lack of differentiation to a state of increasing differentiation, articulation, and hierarchic integration" (1957, p. 126). The child's initial state of cognitive globality and diffuseness is in part determined by lack of a clear differentiation between self and environment. Certain forms of psychopathology are seen as regressions to developmentally early cognitive levels. This regression is not viewed as total; the schizophrenic can be expected to have maintained areas of mature functioning despite regressive tendencies in other areas. Thus schizophrenic behavior is not seen as identical to a child-like state.

In the Developmental scoring system high scores are earned for perceptually clear and integrated responses; for example, if sub-areas of the blot are perceived with good form level, and are then combined into a well-articulated perception, the subject receives a high score. More diffuse impressions yield low Developmental scores. These latter responses are not clearly tied to the blot form, and could quite easily be given on one card as another; examples would include responses citing maps, clouds, and human body interiors.

Most research which has tested the cognitive regression theory of schizophrenia mentioned above has used cross-sectional data. This means that schizophrenics and non-schizophrenics were compared on single occasions. Such data leaves open the possibility that the schizophrenics were developmentally immature even in their pre-morbid days. In order to determine if cognitive maturity declines with onset of schizophrenia, and rises with symptom remission, longitudinal research must be conducted in which schizophrenics are assessed over the course of time. This longitudinal strategy was adopted by Glatt and Karon (1974). Over a twenty month span, schizophrenics were assessed with a psychiatric interview in order to determine their clinical status. In addition, subjects were given the Rorschach which was scored in terms of Friedman's Developmental system. Changes in eight of Friedman's (1952) Developmental scoring categories were then correlated with changes in clinical status.

The findings indicated that four developmental indices changed systematically with clinical status. "Thus when subjects got better . . . thought processes became more flexible, realistic, available, and communicable. Conversely, when a subject got worse, cognitive processes became more rigid and autistic as well as less available and communicable" (p. 574). Additional developmental indices were shown to correlate with changes in clinical status when only non-medicated subjects were studied. Apparently when subjects receive medication, changes in clinical status are related to less consistent shifts on Rorschach Developmental scores. This study serves to further establish the validity of Friedman's Developmental scoring of Rorschach records as well as the cognitive regression notions of schizophrenia.

Despite recent favorable results in Rorschach research such as those just described, the impressionistic interpretation of Rorschach protocols in a clinical setting has come to be the mode. Under these circumstances the Rorschach technique becomes little more than a clinical interview revolving around the examiners' presentation of, and subjects' reactions to, a standard set of visual stimuli. This in itself does not qualify the Rorschach as a test. In fact, McArthur (1972) has strongly asserted that because the Rorschach is not a test with norms and standardization data, it should not be subject to appraisal in terms of standards which are more applicable to psychometric personality measures, such as reliability. Rather, McArthur sees the Rorschach as a vehicle for procuring a unique sample of behaviors not obtained by standardized personality tests. Although tests of the latter type may provide important measures of personality, the Rorschach technique "lets us get to know the man, live and functioning . . . to make his acquaintance . . . to see him operate . . ." (p. 443). McArthur further asserts, in a manner representative of Rorschach advocates, that "a Rorschach is a slice of total behavior . . . (which) allows us to watch another person in full flight" (p. 443).

Not all reviewers of the Rorschach are equally enchanted with the instrument. Almost all reports in Buros *7th Mental Measurement Yearbook* (1972) indicate that the Rorschach is in a state of decline. This may be due largely to the growing disinterest among clinical psychologists for their traditional testing role. For those practitioners who are now more interested in psychotherapy and community mental health efforts, the Rorschach represents an unwanted reminder of the days of clinical psychology's servitude to medical psychiatry. Those psychologists who remain interested in personality assessment tend to gravitate toward the psychometrically rigorous tests in an effort to rest their enterprise on a more sound scientific footing. The newest directions in assessment have been adjuncts to the learning theory-behavior therapy movement. The Rorschach is obviously ill-fitted to the philosophy of this newer movement which neglects the operation of unconscious factors.

Jensen (1965) seemed to sum up the most extreme negative position regarding the Rorschach when he wrote, "The rate of scientific progress in clinical psychology might well be measured by the speed and thoroughness with which it gets over the Rorschach" (p. 238). At the opposite end of the continuum, McArthur (1972) says, "The rich sample of patterned interactions among a man's perceptual, cognitive, emotional, and social sides that appears in even one Rorschach response is neither matched nor approximated by any other psychological tool" (p. 443).

Evidence that the Rorschach is far from dead comes from Exner (1974). He introduced a modernized scoring system based upon the "best" of commonly-used systems. To a greater extent than previous workers, Exner seems to have attended to the research literature when deciding upon what should be retained from times past. Exner hopes that his contribution will make the Rorschach "better prepared to stand the tests of reliability and validation, and hopefully provide the greatest amount of descriptive information from which understanding can be gleaned" (p. 16). It is too early to tell if Exner's goals will be realized.

THEMATIC APPERCEPTION TEST (TAT)

The Thematic Apperception Test (TAT) is a projective instrument which was developed from Murray's Personology. Unlike the Edwards Personal Preference Schedule which was derived from a similar theoretical framework, the TAT is designed to assess latent rather than manifest needs. A latent need was defined by Murray as "the amount of need tension that exhibits itself in thought and make-believe action" (1962, 257). Murray went on to reason that some of the imagery-reflecting latent needs will be projected onto objects as they are perceived or "apperceived." Apperception is the process of perceiving against the background of the personal experiences one brings into a situation. An example of the kind of projection Murray speaks of occurs when a hungry person mistakes the smell of factory smoke for a delicious roast beef.

It was a short step from this rationale to the provision of pictures to subjects about which they were to make up stories. It was believed that latent needs would influence the apperception process and that the content of the stories produced by the subjects would reveal unconscious desires, inner tendencies, attitudes, and conflicts.

Psychologists who adopted the TAT in clinical and research work frequently added two additional theoretical assumptions. First, the personal material revealed in TAT stories could not be obtained except via a projective format. Second, the main character in the stories, called the "hero," was considered the best reflection of the subject's inner self.

The TAT consists of 20 cards. These are selected by the psychologist from an array of 31, with only those most relevant to the age and sex of the subjects actually being used. For example, there may be two similar pictorial depictions, one of males in conversation and one of females, the former is typically used for a male subject and the latter for female subjects. The actual content of the pictures is quite varied — thoughtful-looking solitary figures, people in various sorts of social interactions, an apparent boudoir scene, and even a totally white, blank card.

Administration and Scoring

In the TAT manual (1943) Murray suggests that the test be given over two sessions, with no more than 10 cards administered at each sitting. The examiner asks the subject to generate a story which addresses itself to what is happening in the picture, what led up to the situation depicted, what the characters are thinking and feeling, and what the outcome will be. The examiner may probe, encouraging the subject to round out these various story aspects. It is also necessary for the examiner to keep a verbatim account of the subject's verbal projections, either by writing quickly or by enlisting the aid of a tape recorder.

In current practice, it is the rare diagnostician who administers the entire 20 card set. Usually in the interest of time, the psychologist will select anywhere from 7 to 12 cards which he feels are most likely to provoke especially revealing themes from a particular subject. For example, if there is any concern over the sexual orientation of the subject, cards which depict interactions between both the same and the opposite sex may prove especially useful.

Although there have been many proposals for the scoring of TAT protocols, none has attained a degree of acceptance that one might expect considering the widespread use of the TAT. This problem was precipitated by Murray's superficially-described

Figure 17. Illustration similar to those on the Thematic Apperception Test.

scoring procedure in his 1943 manual. Murstein (1963) claims the dilemma was compounded by the apparent simplicity of the instrument, which seemed to encourage every third clinician and researcher to invent his own system. In general, researchers have tended to adopt variations of quantitative systems, whereas clinicians have remained more satisfied with a wholistic content analysis. The non-quantitative procedures suggested by Murray have been at least as influential as any others proposed and will now be briefly described.

Consistent with his theory, Murray suggests that the focus of TAT analyses should be on a qualitative appreciation of the interplay of needs and press as these are represented and experienced by the hero of the story. Consequently, the first step is always to ascertain who the thematic hero is. Theoretically it is the character in whom the subject is most interested. This may be fairly obvious in some stories; at other times the hero role may shift from one character to another, or even be completely absent. If a hero is identified, Murray says it is useful to make judgments about his characteristics in terms of such dimensions as intelligence, leadership, belongingness, and quarrelsomeness.

The second step in story analysis is to discover what specific primary and psychogenic needs are important to the hero, such as n-Food, n-Dominance, and n-Aggression. Along with this, the press perceived to be operative in the hero's world should be noted. This might be p-Aggression — with others destroying the hero or the hero's belongings p-Dominance — with the hero being pressured by the will of others, or p-Rejection — with the hero being rejected or ignored by others.

As a last step, the relative strengths of needs and press are weighed, their importance judged, and their resolutions noted. This leads finally to abstract representations, called *themas,* of the interplay of needs, press, and outcome. A review of the themas should permit the examiner to judge the actual psychological issues and concerns of the particular subject.

Reliability

As is the case with the Rorschach, study of the reliability of the TAT has produced unimpressive evidence. The issues which preclude clear-cut judgments on this matter again have to do with the inapplicability of traditional procedures for estimating reliability. Tompkin (1947), using Murray's need-press scoring system, found the test-retest reliabilities to be about .80 when the between-test interval was two months; this dropped gradually, reaching about .45 with a one year interval. While these figures are not overwhelming, Tompkin correctly points out that the fantasy life of a person does change over time, and the TAT test-retest reliability coefficients probably reflect these psychological changes as much as they do the temporal stability or instability of the instrument in question.

The establishment of split-half reliability is as completely inappropriate for the TAT as it is for the Rorschach. There is no reasonable way to divide the set of cards into equivalent halves so that this kind of reliability coefficient would be meaningful.

The most favorable reliability data comes from the research area and is based on quantitative scoring systems for needs such as n-achievement. It has repeatedly been demonstrated that the interscorer reliability can regularly exceed .90 when a well-worded manual is available to describe scoring criteria, and when the scorers themselves are provided with carefully supervised training in manual use.

Validity

With regard to matters of validity, the question must be reformulated as, "How valid for what?" In general, the TAT is even less effective than the Rorschach for diagnosing patients into psychiatric categories. Eron (1950) obtained TAT records, using all 20 cards, from 150 World War II veterans. Fifty of these subjects were college students at the time. The remaining 100 subjects came equally from non-hospitalized neurotics, hospitalized neurotics, hospitalized schizophrenics, and a heterogeneous group of hospitalized psychiatric patients. By Eron's admission, the most "outstand-ing" finding was the great similarity in story content among the five groups of subjects. Where differences emerged, they seemed more often related to whether or not the subjects were hospitalized than to their psychiatric diagnoses. It was thought that perhaps the routine of the hospital milieu was an important environmental determinant of TAT responses.

Eron suggests that his results do not speak of the validity of the TAT as a measure of the narrator's personality. It is quite possible that normal subjects, neurotics, and schizophrenics all share common needs, goals, conflicts and misconceptions; the differences between these groups may be only a matter of degree or emphasis. Thus, the TAT may be quite adequate as a means of uncovering the dynamics of the individual personality, even if it is a poor instrument for categorizing people into diagnostic groups.

In another diagnostic study by Cox and Sargent (1950) a difference was found between the TAT records of well-adjusted adolescent school children and a second group of children from the same school who had received psychological or psychiatric counseling. In general, the emotionally-disturbed youngsters produced more con-stricted stories; that is, their stories were shorter and had more superficial content. They frequently were lacking in expressions of feelings, needs, story action, and outcome. As a second part of their study, Cox and Sargent gave the TAT records of the adjusted adolescents to eight experienced clinical psychologists. Each psychologist received only two of the records along with information regarding age, sex, race, and intellectual level — normal or above. They were told that the pair of records submitted to them came either from two adjusted or maladjusted students or from one adjusted and one maladjusted student. The clinician's job was simply to categorize each of their two records as being from an adjusted or maladjusted subject. The surprising discovery was that all but 4 of the 15 records from adjusted adolescents were categorized as malad-justed.

Cox and Sargent believe that the experienced clinicians may have operated under the erroneous belief that a normal TAT protocol is the opposite of one which is indicative of psychopathology. In fact, expressions of hate, frustration, aggression, anxiety, and depression are contained in the records of normal subjects as well as disturbed individuals. Thus, they concluded, as did Eron that TAT responses may not be the best vehicle for arriving at judgments of normality or diagnoses.

A considerable amount of TAT research has focussed on the validity of personality descriptive statements found in TAT interpretive reports. Horowitz (1962) demon-strated that when the criterion is therapists' personality descriptions of their patients, experienced clinicians did no better predicting the personalities from the TAT, plus the Rorschach and demographic data, than they did using only the demographic data of age, sex, marital status, occupation and education. Even more demoralizing for the clinicians in this study was the finding that their demographic-based personality predic-tions correlated with the therapists' criterion personality descriptions $(r = .32)$ at only a slightly higher level than did those descriptions produced by naive Introductory Psychology undergraduates ($r = .21$).

In a study of similar design, but with more favorable results, Little and Shneidman (1955) evaluated the validity of specific inferences generated by 17 psychologists working individually from the TAT of a single patient. The criterion was the consensus evaluation of 29 clinicians who had access to the complete clinical record of the patient. The mean validity coefficient was .60 but considerable variation was observed between clinicians, the range being from .21 to .76.

Needs and Behavior. The methodological strategy illustrated above has been criticized by McClelland (1972) because one set of opinions is being validated against other opinions which are of questionable validity. It is thought that a more appropriate criterion against which to test the validity of TAT interpretations is the actual behavior of subjects. Relevant to this, numerous studies have reported on the behavioral correlates of various needs as assessed by the TAT. For example, the TAT index of n-Achievement has been shown to predict speed of performance and rate of learning by deCharms, Morrison, Reitman, and McClelland (1955). Risk-taking behavior, task persistence, and exam performance were also predictable, as shown in a study by Atkinson and Litwin (1960). However, the relationship between thematic imagery and overt behavior has proven to be one of the knottiest problems confronted by users of the TAT. The matter becomes particularly complex when the TAT is used to assess behavior which is associated with guilt feelings, or behavior which may be culturally taboo, such as sexual and aggressive behavior. An appreciation of what is involved must take into account the subject's background, the nature of the testing situation, and even the particular TAT cards employed.

One very popular hypothesis is that while latent needs for sex and aggression can be active and strongly reflected in TAT themes, conflict frequently prevents the overt expression of behaviors relevant to these needs. It is reasoned that when a need is expressed both in fantasy and overtly, it is because the culture encourages, or at least accepts, the overt behaviors in question. In support of this thesis, Murray (1943) reports little relationship between overt and fantasy aggression among middle-class subject populations. Presumably, within this social class, aggression is a form of expression which is frequently punished and which, therefore, tends to be inhibited. Using a lower-class group of disorderly juveniles, Mussen and Naylor (1954) found that the most overt aggression, the number of aggressive behaviors reported by the boys' teachers, was manifested by those having the highest levels of fantasy aggression. The explanation offered was that lower-class children are not punished as much as other children for outwardly expressing aggression. Consequently, the discovery of a direct relationship between overt and fantasy aggression among lower-class children is to be expected. In this same study, a direct test was made of Mussen and Naylor's idea that the relationship breaks down when subjects anticipate punishment for their behavior. This was made possible by scoring the children's TAT stories for aggression, as well as for fear of punishment. A fear of punishment score was obtained by cumulating the number of times the story hero was subject to such press as assault, killing, hate, deprivation of privilege, and scorn. As expected, high fantasy aggression was related to the highest levels of overt aggression when fear of punishment was low; the lowest levels of overt aggression were found among boys having both low levels of fantasy aggression and great fear of punishment.

Lesser (1957) assessed the fantasy aggression of 10 to 13 year old school boys using a modified set of TAT pictures. The boys' overt aggression was determined via a "Guess Who" sociometric approach. In this procedure the boys received a booklet which contained a series of written behavioral descriptions, such as, "Here is someone who is always looking for a fight" (p. 219). A number of different aggression behaviors were included. Overt aggression scores were assigned to subjects according to the number of times their classmates nominated them as the "Someone" who engaged in the aggressive acts depicted. A structured interview with the boys' mothers was the third measure used by Lesser. The mothers were asked questions which pertained to their support or prohibition of aggressive behavior in their children. Lesser found a correlation of + .43 between the measures of overt and fantasy aggression in the 23 boys whose mothers were most supportive of aggression. The relationship between these variables for boys whose mothers discouraged aggression was − .41; among this sub-group high levels of fantasy aggression were related to low levels of overt aggression. These findings are clearly consistent with those of Mussen and Naylor (1954). In each case, overt aggressive behavior could be predicted directly from fantasy levels of aggression only for those who appear to have a social learning history which did not prohibit the expression of aggressive behavior. Purcell (1953) referred to this phenomenon as the *impulse control balance*. Overt behavior can best be predicted for TAT stories if the thematic content is scored for both the intensity of drive or need to respond in some way, aggressively or sexually, and the strength of the inhibition against such behavioral expressions.

Purcell assessed the role of inhibitory tendencies in the impulse-control equation in terms of two dimensions, internal and external punishment. A TAT external punishment score was obtained by summing the frequency of themes of assault, injury, threat, and domination. The internal punishment score was based on the frequency of themes of suicide, self-depreciation, guilt, shame, and remorse. Using 57 male army trainees, Purcell was able to show that overt aggression, as rated from the trainees social history data, was directly related to the level of fantasy aggression and inversely related to the level of thematic internal punishment. Trainees with high levels of fantasy aggression, accompanied by low levels of fantasy expectation of internal punishment, obtained the highest overt aggression ratings. The anticipation in fantasy of external punishment as a consequence of aggression was not found to be related to whether or not the trainees had an anti-social case history. In fact, rather than being associated with behavioral inhibition of aggression, Purcell reports that fantasies of external aggression seemed to be employed frequently as a kind of externalization for other aggression fantasies. Specifically, there was a tendency for the anti-social trainees to develop themes in which aggression is a justified retaliation against a harshly punitive world.

A series of related studies by Clark (1952) illustrates that Purcell's (1956) impulse-control balance concept is also relevant to understanding the way in which the TAT assesses sexual needs. In each of three experiments, Clark had college males complete the TAT after half of them had been aroused by presumably sexually provocative stimuli. In the first experiment the "aroused" group was presented with photographic slides of nude females, while an equivalent group of men in the control treatment viewed slides of trees and architecture. This was done in the context of a research allegedly having to do with "factors affecting aesthetic judgment." Immediately afterward, all subjects were asked to participate in what was billed as a separate research project for the "standardization of a test of creative imagination." It was at this point that a separate experimenter had the subjects complete the TAT.

The second experiment called for the administration of the TAT to college males, either by a male or by a very attractive female who was dressed in an alluring fashion and who related in a warmly receptive, if not openly inviting, fashion.

Clark's third experiment was designed with the work of Conger (1951) in mind. Conger had shown that alcohol clearly reduces fear in rats and Clark believed that alcohol probably has a similar effect on humans. He felt that anxiety over the expression of sexual thematic content should, therefore, be reduced via the ingestion of an alcoholic beverage. Consequently, Clark went to fraternity beer parties under the guise of studying the effect of an informal environment on a test of creative imagination. In this study the groups had been drinking for over an hour by the time the TAT was administered. In addition, the "aroused" group had also been viewing a set of nude female slides under the belief that this was simply a routine, fraternity-sponsored activity.

The results of Clark's research are quite impressive. The "aroused" groups in the first two experiments manifested significantly *less* sexual imagery than the control subjects. Either the slides of nude females and the sexually provocative female TAT administrator were far less arousing than Clark had anticipated or, more likely, the subjects were aroused but inhibited expression of sexual fantasy because of anxiety or guilt over doing so. This alternative was supported in the third experiment which found reliably more sexual imagery in the slightly drunk, aroused group than in the control group.

Clark concluded that a person's manifestation of sexual imagery depends upon the strength of n-Sex, as well as the strength of opposing forces which arise from guilt and anxiety. It was only when the opposing forces were reduced by alcohol that Clark was able to find evidence in the TAT themes of n-Sex. These notions are quite consistent with Purcell's impulse control balance hypothesis.

In an experiment similar to Clark's research, Mussen and Scodel (1955) also administered the TAT to college males after they had been presented with photographs of nude females. This "arousal" occurred in the context of a research purportedly concerned with Sheldon's body-type theories. One group of subjects rated the attractiveness of the photographs in the presence of a "formal, professorial, and somewhat stern man in his sixties." A second group undertook the same task under the supervision of a "young looking, informal, permissive graduate student" (p. 90). After the photographs had been rated, both groups then saw the experimenter depart and a new researcher arrived asking for help in the development of a test of "creative imagination." The TAT was then administered.

Scoring of the TAT protocols for sexual content revealed significantly lower levels in the "formal experimenter" group than in the "informal, graduate student experimenter" group. Mussen and Scodel echo Purcell and Clark in their thinking that the presence of an authoritiy figure results in the subsequent inhibition of expression of socially disapproved needs on the TAT.

Importance of the Stimulus. There is strong evidence to the effect that behavior prediction procedures which take the impulse-control balance into account can be further improved if the nature of the particular TAT stimulus card is also considered. Kagan (1956) found that thematic stimuli which unambiguously depicted fight scenes actually elicit fight themes from 75% of six to ten year old middle-class boys, whereas very ambiguous pictures provoke such themes from only 33% of the boys. This "pull" of stimuli for fight themes was shown to be highly-related to whether the boys were overtly aggressive, as based on teacher ratings. That is, between 20% and 30% of both the most and the least overtly aggressive boys produced fight themes to highly-ambiguous thematic stimuli. This percentage rose to 57% among the least aggressive boys and to a significantly higher 95% among the most aggressive boys when they responded to unambiguous pictorial depictions of fight scenes. Kagan explains this last finding as being symptomatic of higher anxiety among the boys with low overt aggression. Specifically, he suggests that an unambiguous fight scene almost always elicits a fight story from boys who are not fearful over their own aggressive inclinations. Those boys who experience anxiety over such tendencies both inhibit their overt expression and their fantasy expression when the thematic stimulus makes aggression a salient issue. Consistent with these results, Epstein (1966) speculates that thematic cards which have strong relevance for a particular personality dimension, such as aggression, may be most suitable for measuring inhibitory tendencies. It may be most psychologically meaningful when subjects fail to elicit a theme which is consistent with the strong "pull" of the card.

The utility of thematic cards with strong "pull" for particular story content has been demonstrated in the area of sexual motivation as well. Eisler (1968) enlisted the services of 24 "high sex conflict" and 24 "low sex conflict" male college students. These were volunteers from a large pool of male students whose conflict over sex had been assessed using a 24 item self-report questionnaire containing statements such as, "When I have sexual thoughts or daydreams, I feel ashamed of myself," and, "Sex is a fine and full part of life" (p. 217). The subjects were then administered four thematic stimuli which had been previously rated as high in sexual relevance and four which were low in sexual relevance. Only one picture actually came from the standard set of TAT cards; the remaining stimuli were selected from magazines such as *Playboy*.

Eisler found that the "high" and "low conflict over sex" subjects differed in the way they responded to the high sex relevance cards but not to the low relevance cards. Specifically, those cards which had salient sexual depictions tended to elicit significantly fewer themes with sexual content from "high conflict" than from "low conflict subjects." In addition, subjects who had self-reported conflict over sex produced projective themes involving significantly more negative affect — guilt, hostility, conflict, and anxiety — than did the subjects with low levels of sex conflict, with both groups responding to the same set of cards. Thus, stimuli which are structured to be highly relevant to a need area were shown to be most effective in producing differential responding between groups differing in their levels of conflict over the expression and satisfaction of that need.

These findings are important to the future development of projective instruments. Traditionally, it has been felt that the most useful projective stimuli are those with the most ambiguous meaning. Frank (1939) and others who advocated the "projective hypothesis" believed that greater stimulus ambiguity produced more information about respondents' personalities. The studies by Kagan (1956) and Eisler (1968) suggest that conflict areas may be more readily identified with structured stimuli which unambiguously depict the expression of needs such as aggression and sex. Epstein (1966) believes that thematic assessment can be improved if separate card sets are developed for the assessment of each personality dimension. Epstein proposes that each set contain high and low ambiguity cards. In addition, the interpersonal situation which might be associated with the personality dimension in question should be systematically sampled.

Figure 18, taken from Epstein (1966, p. 186), illustrates how these suggestions can be implemented. The nine pictures are designed to assess the personality dimension of nurturance-rejection. The left column of pictures is structured to be high nurturance-relevant while the right column is high rejection-relevant; the middle column is neutral. In addition, nurturance-rejection is depicted with respect to mother, father, and peer figures. Such an array of thematic stimuli would provide a much more systematic-thematic assessment of the nurturance-rejection personality dimension than is now possible with the TAT, which contains clear illustrations of both a rejecting and a nurturant mother but no corresponding father stimuli.

TAT Evaluation

There is a growing body of research, some of it abstracted above, which illustrates the severe limitations of the projective hypotheses as an explanation of TAT responses. Recent studies have indicated that there may be more worth in using explicit thematic stimuli for assessing inhibitory personality trends than in employing the more generally ambiguous TAT illustrations and photographs. These findings are inconsistent with Frank's (1939) assertion that the interpretive significance of a projection is greater when the stimuli which provoke it are most ambiguous.

Murstein (1965) reviewed a substantial body of TAT research pertaining to the stimulus properties of the TAT cards. He, too, recommends that the most productive use of thematic apperceptive techniques must involve the analysis of stories in relation to the stimulus value of the pictures. Like Epstein (1966), he suggests that thematic stimuli should be scaled for all important personality dimensions. It is only by knowing the "pull" of a card for aggressive themes that one can appreciate the significance of aggressive, or non-aggressive, thematic projections.

Holmes (1974a) offered more recent evidence against the validity of the projective hypothesis as it applies to the TAT. Sixty subjects were each administered three TAT

Figure 18. An example of parallel stimulus dimensions arranged according to a 3 X 3 design for source and degree of nurturance-rejection. Epstein, S. Some Theoretical Considerations on the Nature of Ambiguity and the Use of Stimulus Dimensions in Projective techniques *Journal of Consulting Psychology,* 1966, *30,* 183-192. Copyright© 1966 by The American Psychological Association. Reprinted by permission.

cards. Half of the subjects were instructed to be honest; the other half were told to "write stories which will lead the person scoring your stories to believe that you have a high level of motivation or a high need to achieve . . . We want to know if you can fake this test without being caught" (p. 325). Three weeks later the subjects were called back. On this second occasion they were again asked to respond to the three TAT pictures. Subjects who had been asked to be honest during their first TAT session were now asked to fake n-Achievement; subjects previously asked to fake were requested to respond as honestly as possible. The results of this manipulation on n-Achievement scores are presented in Table 6. Both groups of subjects showed highly significant changes in their TAT n-Achievement scores across the two testings. In addition, the subjects who were instructed to fake high n-Achievement at each session scored significantly higher on this personality dimension than did the subjects responding honestly. Thus, it is clear that TAT responses are prone to effective intentional influence. That is, subjects can "consciously introduce false projections, indicating that they possess a trait that in fact they do not possess" (p. 328). In addition, an experienced clinical psychologist, who was not involved in the experiment, attempted to categorize the TAT records into those written by honest and those written by faking subjects. He was unable to do this at a better than chance rate.

TABLE 6
Mean Need Achievement Scores for Honest-Fake and Fake-Honest Conditions

CONDITION	SESSION I	SESSION II
Honest-Fake (29 subjects)	12.47	17.93
Fake-Honest (31 subjects)	20.20	12.45

From Holmes, D.S. The conscious control of thematic projection. Journal of Consulting and Clinical Psychology, 1974, 42, 323-329(a). Copyright 1974 by the American Psychological Association. Reprinted by permission.

As a second experiment in the same report, Holmes asked another group of undergraduates to respond to three TAT cards under "be honest" instructions. Three weeks later they were again administered the same three cards. On this occasion, half the subjects were again given "be honest" instructions. It was acknowledged that they might remember their previous stories, and they were instructed to tell whatever story seemed most appropriate. The remaining subjects were instructed to "tell stories that would conceal their personalities as much as possible" (p. 327). An experienced clinician scored each story for what was thought to be the primary trait, need, or conflict revealed. A second scorer was found to have over 93% agreement with the first, indicating that the detection of the major personality characteristics in the stories were occurring with a very high degree of reliability. Table 7 shows the proportion of subjects in the honest-honest condition and the honest-fake condition whose stories were thought to reflect the same major personality characteristic in both testing sessions. It can be seen that for all three cards this proportion was lower in the honest-fake than in the honest-honest condition. The difference was only statistically significant for card one. Failure to attain a significant difference on the other two cards might well be due to the very low rate of consistency in the honest-honest condition. That is, there may have been a "floor effect" such that the test-retest consistency in the honest-honest condition was so low that it could not go much lower, even under honest-fake instructions. In any case, the evidence still strongly suggests that "persons have the ability to consciously withhold projections that would be revealing of traits which, judging from their previous responses, the persons actually possess (p. 328). As in the first phase of this research project, judges were not able to detect effectively which TAT projections were the product of honest or of false instructions. All in all, Holmes' findings resoundingly contradict the optimism Murray expressed when he said that the TAT has a "capacity to reveal things that the patient is unwilling to tell or is unable to tell because he is unconscious of them" (1951, p. 577).

In an earlier comprehensive review of studies relating to the nature of projective responding, Holmes (1968) reported that conceptions of projection have differed. Some writers have focused on studying the projection of traits of which the subject is aware, while others have explored the projection of traits unknown to the responder himself. Holmes concluded that there is "no evidence of any type of projection resulting from a trait which S (the respondent) is not aware that he possesses" (p. 248). This directly contradicts Murray and may lead one to conclude that the TAT is a rather elaborate scheme to gain personal information about a subject which the subject already knows and which he seems no more likely to reveal via TAT projection than by simple, direct questioning. On the other hand, our review of literature bearing on the impulse-control balance suggests that TAT-like stimuli may be used quite effectively for personality assessment. Consideration should be given to what the subject both says and does *not* say in response to stimuli having well-established "pull."

TABLE 7
Proportion of Subjects Whose Stories Reflected the Same Major Personality Characteristics in Both Testing Sessions

| | CONDITION | |
TAT CARD	HONEST-HONEST	HONEST-FAKE
1	48.1%	22.6%
3BM	29.6%	9.7%
7BM	25.9%	16.1%

From data of Holmes, D.S. The conscious control of thematic projection. Journal of Consulting and Clinical Psychology, 1974, 42, 323-329(a).

SUMMARY

We reviewed the characteristics of the two most commonly employed projective techniques, the Rorschach and the TAT. In each case the instrument was described and its administration, scoring, and interpretation briefly explained. A major part of this chapter was devoted to a review of the literature bearing on the reliability and validity of the Rorschach and the TAT. It seemed fair to conclude that the original assumption underlying projective approaches to personality assessment, Frank's projective hypothesis, must now be considered inadequate. Nevertheless, recent developments in Rorschach and TAT theory and practice indicate that these clinical tools are not yet ready for the wastebasket. On the contrary, a heightened sophistication regarding their use now holds the promise of improved future utility.

TERMS TO KNOW

CHAPTER 15
Behavioral Assessment

TRADITIONAL VS. BEHAVIORAL ASSESSMENT

Traditional theories of personality emphasize underlying, *non-observable* personality characteristics as important causes of behavior. These underlying causes have been conceptualized as needs, traits, conflicts, and instincts. The assessment goal which has emerged from this traditional position involves measuring these underlying characteristics in an attempt to understand the personality. The responses of subjects to questionnaires and projective instruments were viewed as signs or reflections of these behavior determining factors. Thus, a large proportion of cF, or shading-form, determinants on the Rorschach may be taken as a sign of an underlying need for affection. The measured strength of this assumed need is then used to explain overt interpersonal behavior, such as an infantile search for physical contact with others.

The most recent developments in personality assessment are associated with learning theory. Very generally, this position views behavior as largely due to certain situational events, stimuli, which provoke particular responses, and rewarding and/or punishing consequences of the responses. Notice that these theoretically important factors are potentially observable; the situation and the response, as well as the response consequences can be observed. In addition, the advocates of this position, *behaviorists,* have a strong interest in predicting overt behavior. They do this on the basis of assessing currently operating stimuli and response consequences. This contrasts with the aim of much traditional assessment in which in-depth understanding of the subject's personality is of primary interest. This understanding may then be employed for predictive purposes.

Behaviorists argue that there are a number of weaknesses in predicting behavior from the traditional assessment approaches. First, Goldfried and Kent (1972) emphasize that a series of possibly unwarranted assumptions are employed. Probably the most crucial assumptions are that the traditional test adequately samples the number of possible signs which are thought to indicate underlying personality characteristics, and that the underlying characteristics are related to the set of criterion behaviors we are interested in predicting.

237

Goldfried and Kent pointed out that underlying personality characteristics may be viable theoretical inferences for some purposes; however, when relied upon solely, they may be inefficient predictors of overt behavior. The limitations of the "underlying characteristic" position for behavior prediction purposes was probably first made salient by the results of an investigation by Hartshorne and May (1928). In what is now considered to be a classic research effort, they observed the honesty of children in several different contexts. More specifically, 10 to 13 year-olds were exposed to situations in which they could conceivably accrue some gain via cheating on exams, keeping money which wasn't theirs, or by falsifying records. The main conclusion from the Hartshorne and May studies which has withstood the ravages of almost a half century of critical evaluation, is that one cannot speak of a person as being honest or truthful independently of the situation in which he is found. This is based on their discovery that exceedingly few children were honest in all of the observed settings; most cheated in some and none cheated in all situations. The conclusion cannot be made that there is no generality or consistency in one's moral behavior, only that if there is an underlying disposition, such as honesty, trying to measure it alone will fail to yield predictive power if the situation is neglected.

In contrast to traditional orientations which stress consistent underlying predispositions, behavioral assessment tends to focus upon direct observation of the criterion behavior one is interested in predicting. Wernimont and Campbell (1968) stress that "it will be much more fruitful to focus on meaningful samples of behavior, rather than signs of predispositions of later performances . . . The best predictor of future performance is past performance" (p. 372).

These writers introduced the notion of *behavioral consistency* (p. 373) to describe their assessment recommendations and, to exemplify this, examined employment procedures. They suggested that the process begin with a thorough job analysis. This would result in a listing of the specific behaviors required for adequate on-the-job performance and the relative importance of the various behaviors to job success and failure. Care must be taken not to state the behavior requirements in terms of their inferred underlying characteristics, such as loyalty or initiative. Applicants' credentials could then be scrutinized to discover past evidence of having exhibited the requisite behaviors. In addition, various applicant work samples or simulations could be directly observed in order to detect the presence of the important behaviors at the time.

This procedure has multiple benefits according to Wernimont and Campbell. Because *sample* is given preference to *sign* assessment, one does not have to depend upon inferences of dubious worth regarding hypothetical underlying characteristics. Rather, specific observable behaviors are employed to predict the future occurence of those same behaviors. If the criterion behaviors are noted in the sample observed the behavioral assessor can be sure that they exist in the individual's repertoire of behaviors. This certainty is non-existent when affectional responses are predicted from cF determinants of Rorschach projections. Certainty is established only through the direct observation of affectional behavior.

Assessing behavioral consistency has the additional advantage of minimizing some very troublesome assessment issues which have plagued the traditional approaches. First, the claim is made that response sets and intentional faking would be less of a problem. It is easier for subjects to manipulate the expression of attitudes and beliefs on questionnaires than to alter their overt behaviors. Second, because behavior is used to predict behavior, there is unlikely to be concern over the appropriateness of the assessment procedures and the fairness of test content for minority groups, an issue in traditional assessment. Third, since no attempt is made to pry into the unconscious motives and underlying predispositions of subjects, the invasion of privacy controversy is effectively squelched.

One particular advantage of observation for assessment purposes is the extremely high degree of reliability which can be attained. As an example, Mariotto and Paul (1974) describe a behavioral observation procedure for use with psychiatric patients. The Time Sample Behavioral Checklist (TSBC) requires observers to code and record, once every waking hour, patient behaviors which occur over a two second span. The relative frequency of behaviors such as cursing, injuring oneself, hurting others, and destroying property yield a Hostile-Belligerence score. Cognitive Distortion is assessed in terms of the relative frequency of verbalized delusions, incoherent speech, and unprovoked smiling, and other seemingly uncalled-for reactions. The score for Schizophrenic Disorganization is based on the relative frequency of behaviors such as stereotypic and repetitive movements, blank staring, and pacing. The combined relative frequency of all of the above comprise an Inappropriate Behavior score. The Appropriate Behavior score is a function of playing games, social conversation, reading, and other appropriate pursuits. The inter-rater reliability using the TSBC was found to range from .97 to a perfect 1.00.

Redfield and Paul (1976) asked trained observers to assess video-taped samples of familiar patients' behavior using the TSBC. When the videotaped behavior samples were intentionally biased so that the familiar patients were seen to be manifesting atypical responses, inter-rater reliability was still found to be .97. This finding is consistent with the claim that direct behavioral observation can provide a highly reliable source of clinical data which is not easily tainted by factors such as assessor expectancies and preconceptions. This is probably because the ratings follow closely from the actual observed behavior and little, if any, inference is required on the observer's part.

ROLE PLAYING: AN ALTERNATIVE TO *IN VIVO* OBSERVATION

Often it is impossible to assess behavior in the setting of interest. This might be especially true when one wants to evaluate the way in which one member of a family relates to other members. It may simply be impractical to go into a home to observe patterns of family interactions. In these cases a valuable alternative to such *in vivo* observation is the observation and rating of *role playing*. An interpersonal scene might be verbally presented to the subject who is instructed to respond as he naturally would in that setting.

Rotter and Wickens (1948) were among the first to see that role playing might be the best alternative to behavioral observation in real settings. They argued that predictions which are drawn from role plays are based on a behavior sample which is very much more similar to the criterion behavior, or what one wants to predict, than are typical test-taking responses. Consequently, only a minimal number of inferential leaps are involved in role play assessment.

The potential efficacy of role play as a behavioral assessment tool was demonstrated in an experiment by Rehm and Marston (1968). Their research was designed to test the worth of a behavior therapeutic procedure for relieving the anxiety of male college students in heterosexual social situations. The students who participated in the research came forth in response to a description of the social anxiety problem, along with an offer of help in relieving it.

As part of a pre- and post-therapy evaluation, Rehm and Marston developed a Situations Test. It consisted of 10 social situations involving females. The situations were depicted on an audio tape recording, "As you are leaving a cafeteria, a girl taps you on the back and says . . ." This was followed by the voice of a female saying, "I think you left this book." The subjects enacted their verbal response to this by talking into a second tape recorder; they engaged in a role play.

A number of different scores were derived from the Situations Test, including self-ratings of anxiety in each of the situations depicted. The subjects were also rated by undergraduate girls regarding the anxiety, adequacy, and likeability of their verbal responses. In addition, the number of words spoken in response to each situation, the latency of response, and the number of anxiety signs such as stuttering, silence, and repetitious speech were scored.

Evidence testifying to the validity of the Situations Test comes from two sources. First, males who admitted experiencing social anxiety when in the company of females were compared with those not having this interpersonal difficulty. All seven of the Situations Test scores manifested the predicted directional difference between the two groups, with only the ratings for adequacy and number of words ratings failing to attain statistical significance.

The second source of validity data was not quite so favorable. Some Situations Test scores were responsive to the therapy treatment. That is, they revealed a greater change within the therapy treatment group than among males who had the same social difficulties but who did not receive active behavior therapy. For example, the treatment group had the greatest decrease in rated anxiety, and greatest increase in rated adequacy and likeability of response. Unfortunately, none of these three effects were statistically significant. This, of course, may be due either to role play assessments which are of poor quality, to the therapy being ineffective in bringing about real change, or both. Evidence that the former possibility is at least in part responsible comes from the inter-scorer reliability data. The reliability coefficients for rated anxiety, adequacy, and likeability were only .47, .69, and .65, respectively. It seems reasonable that the rather poor inter-scorer agreement was due to the global nature of the ratings they were asked to make. For example, each response was rated on a seven point scale for anxiety and adequacy; the 10 response tape was rated on a 50 point scale for overall likeability. The procedure clearly departs from that recommended by behavioral assessors. Had a greater emphasis been placed on specifically defining the nature of a likeable response or, even better, if specific responses were targeted and counted, inter-rater reliability would have been much higher.

Another effort to establish role play as a viable assessment procedure was initiated by McFall and Marston (1970). The focus in this case was on the assessment of assertiveness. McFall and Marsten constructed a Behavioral Role-Playing Assertion Test consisting of 16 vignettes presented via audiotape recording. Each vignette depicts a situation calling for assertive behavior. Subjects are instructed to verbally respond as they would if actually in the situation. Their responses are recorded for subsequent rating. Examples of situations depicted on the test include friends interrupting studying, a waiter bringing a too rare steak, and a boss requesting overtime work when it is inconvenient.

In a series of studies, McFall and Twentyman (1973) administered the Behavioral Role Playing Assertion Test to subjects who had scored at the extremes on the Conflict Resolution Inventory of McFall and Lillisand (1971). This inventory is a paper and pencil measure of refusal behavior. It contains 82 items which describe situations in which college students have reported having difficulty refusing unreasonable requests. The subject indicates the kind of response he would offer to each item: "I would refuse and not feel uncomfortable about doing so," or "I would not refuse because it seems to be a reasonable request" (p. 314). It was found that the group of students who had been identified as highly assertive by the Conflict Resolution Inventory were rated to be significantly more assertive on the Behavioral Role Playing Assertion Test than subjects whose Conflict Resolution Inventory scores identified them as under-assertive. This particular finding helped to establish the validity of both assessment tools as indices of assertiveness.

In a second research, McFall and Twentyman (1973) reported that the Behavioral Role Playing Assertion Test ratings rise significantly when unassertive students are provided with behavioral treatment for their problem. The therapy itself consisted of various combinations of rehearsal, modeling, and coaching — all geared toward the development of a more assertive subject.

The rating of role play behavior samples is subject to all the sources of error to which *in vivo* observation is prone. Consequently, they will not be reiterated here. However, one problem which is unique to role play assessment has to do with whether the role play is really an adequate representation of the subject's typical behavior. On the one hand, role plays can be influenced by factors such as social desirability, and other motives which are aroused in the reactive context of talking into a microphone. While this may tend to produce some unrealistically favorable impressions, the opposite is equally possible. Some subjects are so self-conscious at the prospect of role playing, or so upset by the presence of a tape recorder, that their performance is disrupted. In effect, instead of assessing a subject's assertiveness with females in social situations, one may inadvertently be measuring a subject's assertiveness in the face of a threatening recording "monster." In recognition of this, it is not unusual for the assessment procedure to involve a warm-up period in which the subject can acclimate to the role play task and to the tape recorder, if one is present. In addition, various strategies have been employed in the service of encouraging the reluctant role player to become involved in the "as-if" situation.

PROBLEMS WITH BEHAVIORAL OBSERVATION.

Unreliability

We have indicated that behavioral observations can be made with high reliability. However, one should not conclude that behavioral assessment is immune to error. Romanczyk, Kent, Diament, and O'Leary (1973) found that inter-rater reliabilities tend to be higher when observers know that reliability is being checked. When they are led to believe that their ratings are not being carefully monitored, the inter-rater reliabilities decline significantly. Earlier, Reid (1970) had reported an inter-observer reliability drop from .76 to .51 under these circumstances.

Romanczyk and his colleagues (1973) also report that the highest inter-observer reliabilities are found when the observers not only know that they are being checked but also when they know the other observers against whose ratings the reliability will be calculated. In such instances it seems that observers may strive more to match what they think the other observers' ratings will be than to conform to the prescribed observational guideline. One then runs into a peculiar situation described by O'Leary and Kent (1973). Two observers, who have the opportunity to communicate with each other, maintain high inter-observer reliability but *drift* toward a mutually-agreed-upon interpretation of the observational rules which is at variance with the original intent and format of the observations. To make matters even worse, O'Leary and Kent found that, when observers were asked to compute their own reliabilities under ostensibly unsupervised conditions, there was a tendency for computational "errors" to emerge which were consistently in a direction which yielded inflated reliability coefficients.

Goldfried and Sprafkin (1974) assert that these problems are not insurmountable if care is exercised in the training of observers and covert reliability checks are routinely done. These defenses can guard against decay in the inter-observer reliability. In addition, they strongly suggest that the task of the observers be kept to reasonable limits. Specifically, the number of different scoring categories should be small enough to be kept in mind easily; each response category should be clearly defined behaviorally and distinguished from other potentially overlapping categories; and the procedures should be paced so that there is ample time for observations to be legibly coded or scored.

Reactivity

A second major problem with the observational approach is that of *reactivity*. This term means that observed subjects react to the presence of behavior-raters in a way which alters the very behavior under scrutiny. Consequently, the rater may be assessing the frequency of a particular response, but under very atypical conditions when the subject knows his responses are being counted. So long as the subject is uncertain as to the purpose of the behavioral observations, it is difficult for him to bias his responses systematically in a way which greatly influences the assessment outcome. However, once the subject is privy to either the observers' specific purposes or to the particular responses which are being rated or counted, there is a high probability that relevant behavior change will occur in reaction to the observational procedure. This may happen as soon as a behavior modification program is instituted with respect to a target response. The therapist then wouldn't know the degree to which behavior change was due to his prescribed therapy program or to the subject's reactivity to being behaviorally assessed.

Goldfried and Sprafkin (1974) suggest that these difficulties can be kept to a minimum if the observers are trained to, in effect, "fade into the woodwork." The more unobtrusive they are, the more likely it is that the observed subjects will fall back into their typical behavioral patterns. Alternatively, it may sometimes be appropriate to make subjects explicitly aware of the behaviors which are being assessed. In this way, the effect of reactivity alone can be assessed. Then, if further change occurs subsequent to a treatment program, it can reasonably be attributed to the therapy itself and not to any sudden insight into the fact that certain responses are being observed.

Other Factors Affecting Behavioral Prediction

Wallace (1967) points out that behavioral observation may be used to determine if individuals have certain specific criterion responses in their "response capability" (p. 412). Wallace expands upon the traditional definition of capacity as "ability" and takes into account such personality relevant behaviors as the capacities for aggressive, dependent, and assertive behaviors.

The fact that a person is known to be capable of responding in a particular way does not guarantee behavioral prediction; the person may not respond with this capacity in all situations. Wallace believes that appropriate incentives must exist for capacities to be acted upon. In order to most effectively predict actual behavior, he points to three specific situational issues which should be assessed once capacity has been established.

Reward Values. Consider a potential supervisory foreman whose work history and observed behavior reveal that he is capable of assigning unpleasant work details to even the most complaining of factory line workers. Whether this capacity will yield on job performance will depend, in part, on rewards which the potential foreman values. If the employer is prepared to provide verbal praise to a foreman who effectively assigns unpleasant work to linemen, and the potential foreman much prefers monetary bonuses, he may come to the conclusion that the available rewards don't warrant the effort. He may then become an ineffective foreman, despite his capacity, because valued incentives are not forthcoming. What all of this suggests is that, in addition to the assessment of response capability, a judgment must be made regarding the relative value of rewards for the particular individual.

Situation Properties. A second factor which influences the degree to which observed capability can be used to predict future behavior accurately is the formal properties of situations. Among the relevant situational properties or dimensions which might be profitably assessed is the degree to which the situation provides the incentives valued by the subject. Wallace reports that in a study he conducted in a classroom setting it was found that teachers vary greatly in terms of the ratio of rewarding to punishing statements. Some were found to emit twenty times more rewarding than punishing statements; others were extreme in the opposite direction.

Another formal situational property which affects behavior is the degree to which others are performing the criterion response. If the potential foreman finds that he is the only one in his position who assigns unpleasant work details, he may be less prone to continue this effort than if all foremen are seen to engage routinely in this practice.

Subject Expectancies. The third focus of assessment which Wallace feels is a desirable supplement to behavioral observation is the expectation held by the subject with respect to the specific situation in which he must perform. For example, if the potential foreman entertains the hypothesis that his valued monetary bonus will be forthcoming if he effectively assigns unpleasant work details, he is likely to live up to his capability to perform this behavior. If, however, he believes that a monetary bonus will be earned only if the factory director learns that his supervisees like him, the foreman may be loathe to exercise his work assigning capabilities. Wallace points out that subjectively-held expectancies are more important than objective reality. In addition, he suggests that while expectations may be assessed via self-report questionnaires and interviews, behavioral prediction will be enhanced if the questionnaire items are situation specific. By this he means that there will be more utility in asking subjects for their beliefs about the situation in which their behavior is to be predicted than their beliefs about life and the world in general.

THERAPEUTIC APPLICATIONS

Most traditional psychotherapies, like traditional assessment procedures, are predicated on the idea that there are unconscious needs, and conflicts which motivate behavior. When there is overt evidence of psychopathology, the traditional therapist asserts that one or more of these inferred characteristics is responsible. Treatment is then geared toward the rectification of the hypothesized underlying difficulty. In contrast to this, the behavior therapies are not geared to the resolution of underlying conflict or reduction of incapacitating needs. Instead the focus is on directly modifying specific target behaviors which are deemed to be the crux of the subject's difficulty.

Morris (1976) points out that the target behaviors which comprise the behavior therapeutic problem may be creating personal difficulties for any one of three general reasons. First, the behavior may not exist; the person may be having problems in living because he has not acquired certain responses or skills. For example, recent Head Start programs for culturally deprived preschoolers have repeatedly discovered children who have had no experience with crayons or other writing implements. Imagine the frustration and confusion of such a youngster who enters a kindergarten situation in which this kind of knowledge is taken for granted. An unsuspecting teacher might well construe the child's behavior as a sign of deep emotional disturbance. Certainly the child is disturbed, or upset, but for a reason which is easily corrected via new learning.

A second reason that a behavior might become the target of modification is that it exists at an intensity or frequency which is too low for the situation. The goal is then to somehow provide incentives which increase the probability and strength of the target response.

Thirdly, behaviors may be problems when they are too strong or frequent for the situation. In these instances, therapeutic efforts are usually aimed at decreasing the attractiveness of engaging in the response and/or increasing the probability of alternative, more acceptable behaviors through the provision of valued incentives.

Functional Assessment

Intimately related to these three behavior therapeutic issues is the necessity to assess the problem from a behavioristic perspective. Kanfer and Phillips (1970) refer to this as a *functional* or *behavioral-analytic* assessment. Functional assessment involves essentially three concerns. First, there is an attempt to clearly define the target behaviors. This is often not as simple as it sounds. A teacher may complain that a child is not motivated or is undisciplined. But such statements have more to do with inferred underlying characteristics than with overt behavior. Frequently it is only through direct observation that the specific maladaptive behaviors, or the lack of adaptive responses, become known.

A second goal of behavioral assessment for therapeutic purposes is the identification of situational conditions which are in some way supporting the target behavior. This involves discovering the environmental events which provoke or "set the occasion for" the target behavior, and the rewarding and punishing consequences which function to maintain the target behavior.

Once these factors are known, the psychologist is in a position to embark upon the third phase of assessment, a phase which is entwined with treatment per se. Basically, a judgment is made about which aspects of the situation should be changed and how this can be accomplished. For example, it may be decided that the environment must provide more frequent rewards for a behavior which has been occurring too infrequently, or that punishment should be imposed in order to quickly suppress a self-destructive-head-banging response in a schizophrenic child.

ADOPTION AND ADAPTATION OF TRADITIONAL APPROACHES

Behavioral assessment does not only rely on behavior counts and ratings of subjects made by trained observers. A variety of other techniques are employed, some of which are not too different from the assessment procedures employed by traditionalists.

Self-Monitoring

It is clear that behavioral assessors have continued to rely on self-report data. Some of these self-report procedures are very close to the more usual observational approaches, except that the subject acts as his own observer. This is usually done when it becomes impossible or impractical for external agents to conduct the behavioral observations. This has routinely been the case with research on the behavior therapeutic reduction of cigarette smoking. Because the smoking response may easily be made during any waking moment and in almost all settings, the only person who can easily monitor the number or rate of cigarettes consumed is the smoker himself. A variety of specific techniques have been employed to assist him, ranging from wrist counters which are essentially similar to those worn by many golfers to keep track of their strokes, to small cards with tally marks which are carried in the cigarette pack.

Two problems have been associated with self-monitoring as an assessment vehicle. First, there is no guarantee that subjects will not commit errors. McFall (1970) had students monitor the number of cigarettes consumed during a class period. The cigarette consumption of these self-monitoring smokers was also surreptitiously recorded by other class members. The smoker-observer correlations over six such pairs ranged from −.05 to 1.00, with only three being above .75. Of course, it is possible that some of the lower correlations were due to observer error rather than self-monitoring errors. In fact, on one occasion two observers rated the same smoker. McFall reports them to have attained only 75% agreement, with the observer sitting closer to the subject recording a greater number of cigarettes consumed than did the more distant observer.

A second problem with self-monitoring, whether it be used to assess the frequency of sexual, eating, or smoking behaviors, is that the process is reactive. That is, merely keeping track of one's behavior can have the effect of changing the rate of the behavior being monitored. In McFall's (1970) research on the effects of self-monitoring on smoking behavior, he employed two commonly used monitoring approaches. In one the subjects were requested to record the number of cigarettes consumed; in the second smokers were asked to count the number of times they resisted the temptation to smoke, for whatever reason. McFall found that the two monitoring procedures had different effects. Student smokers who were counting the number of cigarettes consumed increased their smoking rate while decreasing the time spent on each cigarette. Those smokers concentrating on the number of times they thought of smoking but did not indulge decreased smoking frequency but spent more time "enjoying" each cigarette.

It should be noted that the smokers in McFall's (1970) experiment were not motivated to stop their habit and were encouraged to smoke as usual during the self-monitoring period. When smokers who are motivated to quit the habit present themselves at a clinic, it has been found that self-monitoring, even the kind which focuses on the number of cigarettes consumed, has a depressing effect on smoking rate. In fact, McFall and Hammen (1971) demonstrated that the monitoring of either smoking or non-smoking behavior was as effective in reducing cigarette consumption as active behavior therapeutic interventions. Specifically, it was reported that after a three week self-monitoring period, cigarette consumption among the 38 subjects had dropped to an average of 25% of what had been the pre-treatment smoking rate. In addition, about 25% of the subjects had achieved total abstinence by the end of the three week self-monitoring period. As in other smoking-therapy research, this initial effect gradually faded over the weeks following treatment. A six week follow-up revealed consumption at about 60% of what it had been prior to self-monitoring. By the time six months had elapsed, smoking had again approached the pre-treatment rates, with only 5% of the subjects remaining abstinent.

Questionnaires

In addition to self-observation procedures such as those described above, self-report questionnaires have also been put to considerable use by behavioral assessors.

Fear Survey Schedule. Geer's (1965) Fear Survey Schedule (FSS) is frequently employed as a quick means to assess the extent of subjects' fears. Subjects simply report their degree of fear, from "None" to "Terror," over 50 objects and situations. These cover the areas of live animals, social interactions, unfavorable social evaluations, illness, death, and water. It has been noted that the FSS responses do not necessarily coincide with observed behavior. Goldfried and Sprafkin (1974) suggest that this may be because different aspects of the total fear responses are being assessed. That is, the FSS asked how frightened the person feels, whereas observation of behavior in the fear-provoking situation assesses what the person does. For example, a person who is highly afraid of dating may, nevertheless, go out on dates because he does not wish to be different from his peers. Thus, one must be cautious in the employment of the FSS if it is used as a substitute for direct behavioral observation.

S-R Inventories. A more sophisticated anxiety schedule was developed by Endler, Hunt, and Rosenstein (1962). Their S-R Inventory of Anxiousness consists of eleven pages. At the top of each page potentially anxiety-provoking situations are spelled out, "You are just about to take an important final examination." Beneath this situation descriptive statement there are 14 modes of response listed, all presumably components of a possible anxiety reaction. Included are the response modes of "heart beats faster," "perspire," "emotions disrupt action," and "get an uneasy feeling." The subject is asked to self-report his response intensity for every response mode in each of the eleven situations. This is done on the basis of a five point rating, from "not at all" to "very much." Thus, if a person tends not to perspire at all at the start of an important final examination, the self-rating would be one; if the same situation provokes rapid heart beats, the self-rating would be four or five.

Using this assessment format allows one to study anxiety in a rather complex fashion. Specifically, if large groups of subjects are administered the S-R Inventory of Anxiousness it is possible to determine the degree to which scores are due to the particular subject, the situation, and the mode. Therefore, it can be determined whether some people are more anxious generally than others, whether some situations provoke more anxiety than others, and whether some anxiety response modes are strong and others weak. If it turns out that the individual is the most important factor then it would be reasonable to deal with anxiety as a trait which people have in varying degrees. However, this was not found to be the case. In fact, the situation and the response mode were found to be at least as important as the individual as a determinant of anxiety scores. Even more impressive is the fact that Endler and Hunt (1966) found that anxiety scores were in large measure determined by the interaction of the three variables of subject, situation, and response mode. That is, it may be that anxiety can best be predicted if one takes into account the individual in particular situations, or the individual's different modes of response, or the different mode of response provoked by specific situations. Predicting on the basis of the triple interaction, then, probably yields the most accurate assessments. The greatest precision may be obtained if one predicts the strength of a response mode in a given person who is confronting a specific situation. While such a level of detail may seem overwhelming, its appropriateness is justified by Endler and Hunt's obvious but often forgotten assertion, "Human behavior is complex" (p. 344). Any attempt at behavior analysis which relies on person, situation, or response mode alone can only result in a level of predictive accuracy which is less than that of which we are capable.

A slightly revised form of the S-R Inventory of Anxiousness was developed by Endler and Okada (1975). This has been named the S-R Inventory of General Trait Anxiousness. It presents subjects with four general, as opposed to specific, situations.

1. "You are in a situation involving interactions with other people."
2. "You are in situations where you are about to or may encounter physical danger."
3. "You are in a new or strange situation."
4. "You are involved in your daily routines."

In each case the subject is asked for his general reaction to each situational category. For each of the four general situations the subjects rate the severity of nine modes of reaction on a five point scale, from "very much" to "not at all."

1. seek experiences like this
2. perspire
3. have an uneasy feeling
4. feel exhilarated and thrilled
5. get fluttering feeling in stomach
6. feel tense
7. enjoy these situations
8. heart beats faster
9. feel anxious

Endler and Okada administered this format to 286 high school students, 347 normal adults, 125 neurotic hospitalized adults, and 45 psychotic hospitalized adults. They found that the general situation greatly determined the level of reported anxiety across all subject groups. The physical danger situation provoked the most anxiety, whereas the routine situation was least prone to elicit anxious responses. New and strange situations were found to be the second most potent source of anxiety.

These findings are taken as further evidence that one cannot speak of anxiety as a general trait. This personality dimension must be assessed in terms of the relevant situation. In addition, it was also reported that different response modes do not react in identical fashion. Specifically, the physiological responses — perspiring, fluttering in stomach, and heart rate — were reported by subjects to be the least responsive anxiety modes. Of course this finding was procured at the level of conscious self-awareness. Direct physiological measurement of perspiring, gastric activity, and heart rate may yield a somewhat different picture.

Certain between-group differences of interest were also found. Among the normal adult and high school samples, females reported a greater level of anxiety to physical danger than did males. Endler and Okada speculate that this might be caused by greater confidence on the part of males in physical danger situations, or to their reluctance to admit anxiety in face of physical danger because it is socially unacceptable to do so.

Normal youths reported themselves to be less anxious in the face of physical danger than did adults. Perhaps a feeling of vigor and strength in the youths, which was lacking in adults, led the high school subjects to report being less anxious. Again, however, the adult-high school differences may be due to a social desirability effect in which it is least acceptable for high school students to report being upset by physical danger.

In general, it was found that normal subjects and psychotics are less anxious on this modified S-R inventory than neurotic subjects. It is felt that normal subjects tend to remain most unruffled by the fear situations because they have the best capacity to cope and, therefore, remain unthreatened. Psychotics report anxiety levels equivalent to normal subjects because they are out of touch with the reality of a threatening situation. Neurotics are most anxious because they try to cope with a recognized threat but are less effective than normal subjects in their efforts.

Pleasant Events Schedule. Another recently developed self-report inventory is the Pleasant Events Schedule developed by MacPhillamy and Lewinsohn (1972). Subjects respond to 320 social and non-social situations by reporting how often they have experienced the circumstances in the past month. The enjoyment level of the situation is recorded on a five point scale. Sample Pleasant Events Schedule (PES) items are: "being with happy people," "having sexual relations with a partner of the opposite sex," "taking a walk," and "reading stories or novels." In the construction of the PES, items were selected from those actually generated by college undergraduates who were asked to list events, experiences, and activities which were found to be pleasant, rewarding, or fun.

A test of the behavioral theory of depression, which claims that the depth of depressed mood correlates with encountering few rewarding experiences, was done by Lewinsohn and Libet (1972) using the PES. They first had college undergraduates fill out a partial MMPI questionnaire. On the basis of their responses, 10 depressed subjects, 10 non-depressed but otherwise neurotic subjects, and 10 normal subjects were identified. An activity schedule was then drawn up for each of the 15 males and 15 females. The items incorporated into each activity schedule consisted of the 160 PES items which the subject had judged to be most pleasant for him or her. Multiple copies of each activity schedule were produced, and the subjects were asked to keep records for 30 consecutive days. Each subject was to complete his or her own activity schedule at the end of each day. They simply had to indicate in which of the activities they had engaged. In addition, at about the same time each day every subject completed an adjective checklist especially geared to the assessments of depressed mood.

The most important finding of Lewinsohn and Libet was that the performance of all three groups of subjects indicated a strong association between the number of pleasant activities experienced on a given day and mood. Specifically, fewer pleasant experiences were related to more depressed mood. An item analysis revealed that some activities were more related to mood than others. For example, "being with happy people," "being relaxed," "having spare time," "having people show interest in what you have said," and "laughing" were the five situations in which daily experience, or non-experience was most related to mood. The correlational nature of the Lewinsohn and Libet study does not permit one to determine if pleasant experiences produce a good mood or whether the experiences are sought out when one's mood is positive. Clearly, more work must be done to evaluate this important question. In the meantime the PES might, at the very least, be considered a potentially useful assessment tool which will perhaps aid both in the understanding and treatment of depression from a behavioral perspective.

In summary, it can be seen that behaviorists have developed self-report measures which are quite similar in appearance to the questionnaires used by traditionalists. This is particularly true of the FSS and the S-R inventories which ask for self-reports about matters which are quite covert, such as levels of felt fear. If there is a major difference here between traditional and behavioral assessment, it has to do more with the goal of the assessment process than with its form.

TRADITIONAL ASSESSMENT APPROACHES AS BEHAVIOR SAMPLES

Both questionnaire and projective responses can be looked at as behavior samples in a manner which is consistent with the previously mentioned notion of "behavioral consistency" put forth by Wernimont and Campbell (1968). For example the Marlowe-Crowne Social Desirability Scale (1960) consists of self-referent statements which vary in their desirability values. It will be recalled that those items which are highly socially desirable are likely to be untrue for most people, whereas those items which are socially undesirable are typically accurate self-descriptions. To the degree a subject endorses socially desirable and denies the undesirable items he is, in effect, behaving in a way on the test which results in the presentation of an erroneously positive self-image. One can predict from this test-taking behavior that the individual will engage in behaviors which generate a falsely favorable portrait in other interpersonal-evaluative situations, such as meeting new people. Consequently, behavior in meaningful non-test situations is being predicted from the characteristics of test-taking behavior. In addition to using the S-D scale as a behavior sample, Crowne and Marlowe also construe S-D scale responses as signs of an underlying personality disposition; the Need for Approval, an idea which has gained considerable research support. However, it should be realized that the level of analysis which invokes a Need for Approval involves inferences which go beyond what is typically acceptable from a behavior analytic perspective.

Even the Rorschach technique has been systematically approached from a behavioral orientation. As an example, recall Friedman's Developmental scoring system which, in effect, scores the responses not as signs of inferred underlying needs and/or conflicts, but as samples of perceptual behavior. For example, the response, "Two figures beating up a woman," would not be interpreted as having possible aggressive or sexual implications. Rather, Friedman's system only attends to the nature of the perceptual and cognitive activities which would result in this kind of response. If the percept requires the subject to separate the whole blot into sub-units which are then integrated into a meaningful, interrelated configuration, it is taken as a sample of capacity. That is, the subject is seen as able to differentiate and reintegrate his perceptual field in a manner indicative of cognitive-developmental maturity. It has been suggested by Goldfried and Kent (1972) that Friedman's Developmental scoring system has yielded consistently favorable empirical support because it sticks "close to the data." In other words, the level of developmental maturity indicated by Rorschach responses is used to predict cognitive developmental maturity, a process involving much fewer assumptions than are required to predict personality characteristics from traditional Rorschach scoring systems.

PHYSIOLOGICAL ASSESSMENT

For those who were engrossed with the assessment of personality traits, needs, and dispositions the advent of projective techniques was considered a blessing. It will be recalled that the projective approaches were at first naively thought to be X-rays into the unconscious, not subject to the errors induced by conscious motives and situational contexts. Of course, the flood of empirical data soon forced an agonizing reappraisal.

In similar fashion, physiological indices of personality were also received as a panacea by many behaviorally-oriented psychologists. They were construed as vehicles which would circumvent the problems of other behavioral assessment approaches, such as biased self-report, observer expectancies, self-conscious role play, and reactivity. Unfortunately, this physiological road to assessment glory appears now to be almost as rocky as was the projective route.

Physiological Indices of Personality

There is no one physiological index of a personality characteristic or overt behavior pattern, much less a single physiological response indicative of personality in general. Rather, a variety of indices have been used in psychological research and clinical practice. Although the major approaches will be briefly described in this section, the interested reader is referred to Lykken (1968). This abstract is based largely upon his review.

Biochemical measures. It is clear that a number of hormonal changes accompany intense emotional states. One area of research has centered on *hydrocortisone*, a hormonal secretion of the adrenal cortex. In general, anxiety seems to be associated with elevated concentrations of hydrocortisone in the blood plasma. This has been found in acutely anxious psychiatric patients as well as in subjects who have undergone hypnotic induction of anxiety.

Some of the metabolic products of hydrocortisone, also found in blood plasma and urine samples, have been shown to be correlated with anxiety. For example, urinary excretion of these end-products is elevated in anxious patients and in students who have just completed a stressful final exam. On the other hand, low plasma levels were discovered in subjects who were relaxed via hypnotic suggestion or who had just viewed an uneventful movie.

A second focus of hormonal research has been concerned with norepinephrine (NE) and the chemically similar hormone epinephrine (E), or adrenalin. This latter hormone is secreted into the blood stream by the adrenal medulla, especially under conditions of emergency. It promotes metabolism and blood flow to the skeletal muscles, preparing the person for "fight or flight." It has been established that the absolute and relative concentrations of NE and E in the blood plasma and urine are associated with emotional arousal. A variety of studies have found high NE/E ratios among individuals who have participated in overtly aggressive activities, such as boxing. There is some evidence that characteristically aggressive personalities may be correlated with high ratios of NE to E. On the other hand, subjects rated as anxious but not especially aggressive tend to manifest low NE/E ratios.

Electroencephalogram (EEG). The EEG is a graphic record of rhythmic variations in the minute electrical potentials of the brain. These can be measured between two electrodes placed on the scalp surface or between one scalp electrode and a reference, or neutral, electrode which is often placed on the ear lobe. The electroencephalograph is capable of producing multiple channel recordings simultaneously. The graph may be recorded via an inkwriter, or stored on magnetic tape for later retrieval. At that time a permanent ink record can be made or the electrical patterns may be viewed on an oscilloscope.

There are several brain wave rhythms which can be readily identified. The slowest waves, Delta rhythms, appear at a rate of .5 to 4 cycles per second (cps) and are characteristic of sleep. Frequencies ranging from 4 to 7 cps are commonly seen in the EEG of young children and are called Theta rhythms. Alpha rhythms, those ranging from 8 or 12 cps, are most pronounced during a relaxed state of wakefulness. The fastest waves, Beta rhythms, range from 12 to 30 cps and seem to be associated with a cognitive state of alertness. The condition of excitement may produce a desynchronization of the wave patterns and a generally flattened record.

Considerable evidence has been accumulated which suggests that EEG characteristics may be different among certain diagnostic groups, such as schizophrenics and sociopaths when compared to normal individuals. However, the differences do not appear with sufficient regularity to permit their use for diagnostic purposes. Part of the difficulty lies in the great degree of differences in EEG patterns which are found within a normal population. Reitan (1976) believes these individual differences are strongly determined by genetic factors. These perhaps diagnostically irrelevant individual differences, coupled with uncontrollable electronic noise which is introduced into the recordings, tend to mask any stable EEG differences there may be between psychopathological groups and normal groups or between different psychopathological categories.

Circulatory Measures. The *Electrocardiogram* (EKG) is also a graph, over time, of electrical activity as picked up between two electrodes. However, the recording site shifts from the skull, as with EEG, to body surfaces capable of easily picking up electrical activity generated by the heart muscle. The electrocardiogram allows for a determination of heart or pulse rate. One area in which the EKG has been used with some success has been in the evaluation of systematic desensitization, a behavior therapeutic procedure used for the reduction of anxiety responses. Craig (1968) found that imagining painful or emotional events, an integral part of systematic desensitization, is correlated with as much heart-rate increase as the actual presentation of the feared stimulus. In addition, Lang, Melamed, Hart (1970) found that the subjects' reports of the vividness of fearful imagery is correlated with heart-rate. Reports of subjective anxiety level while imagining fearful scenes are also correlated with heart-rate. Thus, heart-rate seems to be a useful vehicle for monitoring subjects' emotional responses to phobic stimuli, as well as for assessing the outcome of behavioral therapy.

A more simply obtained cardiovascular measure is that of blood pressure, gauged by a sphygmomanometer. Generally elevations in blood pressure have also been noted to be a correlate of psychological duress. The difficulty with using blood pressure as an assessment tool is that it can only be read on an intermittent basis. That is, there is no effective means to continually monitor blood pressure and keep a running record of changes over time.

A third way of assessing circulatory activity is by measuring blood volume through the use of a plethysmograph. This is a device, worn over an extremity, which allows for the measurement of volume changes produced by blood engorgement. The mechanism has proven to be particularly useful in the study of human sexuality. It has been found that non-genital circulatory indices of arousal, those of blood pressure and heart-rate, do not neccessarily correlate with sexual excitement. However, direct measures of penile erection, using a plethysmograph, have provided sensitive measures of sexual arousal (Zuckerman, 1971). Freund (1963, 1965) used this device to expose male homosexuals and heterosexuals to pictures of nude males and females in five age categories, from children to adults. Using penile erection as the dependent measure, he was able to successfully diagnose 48 out of 58 homosexuals, and all 65 heterosexuals. However, a comparison of normal heterosexuals with pedophiliacs revealed little overlap in terms of the age range to which there was maximum penile volume.

Similar results have been reported using a less cumbersome strain gauge device which simply measures penile circumference. It has the advantage of not inducing as much direct penile stimulation as the plethysmograph which can promote an initial arousal reaction.

These procedures are not without drawbacks, the most important of which is the capacity of males to consciously inhibit erections. Even when conscious inhibition fails, the erection tends to have less volume and is of shorter duration. Because of this, additional research must be done to determine whether homosexuals who are unwilling to reveal their sexual preferences can successfully provide misleading plethysmograph or strain-gauge data.

Genital circulation measures on females have been less successful because of accessibility problems. A recently developed thermal flowmeter which can measure the changes in vaginal wall blood flow appears to have solved some of these difficulties. Two thermistors are mounted one centimeter apart and held against the vaginal mucosa, or lining, by a self-inserted diaphragm. Low voltage is then used to heat one of the thermistors a few degrees above body temperature. Blood flow in the vaginal wall alters the rate of thermal conductivity. Consequently, changes in the amount of current to the heated thermistor required to maintain a constant temperature difference between the two thermistors is a sign of blood flow changes in the underlying tissue. This technology appears to make possible a considerable amount of research which will be of an analogous nature to that done with males.

Pupil Size. Changes in pupil diameter are affected by smooth muscle on the iris. The size of the pupil may vary from 1.5 to over 9 millimeters in humans and can have a response latency to available light variations as low as .2 seconds. It has long been recognized that pupil diameter may vary in accordance with sources which are independent of available light. Interest in the psychological significance of these spontaneous changes was heightened by the research of Hess and Polt (1960). Their work indicated that pupil diameter increases when one is viewing a preferred or attractive stimulus. Women tend to manifest larger pupil sizes at the sight of a baby, mother and baby, or male nude; men tend to dilate more to pictures of nude females. Hess, Seltzer, and Shliew (1965) reported that they were able to discriminate between homosexuals and heterosexuals on the basis of the pupillary responses to pictures of male and female nudes. Zuckerman (1971) has found that later research efforts failed to support the degree of response specificity alleged by Hess. Specifically, it seems that nudes, regardless of sex, will elicit pupil dilation in males. Also, heterosexual males frequently demonstrate greater dilation responses to nude males than to females. Zuckerman suggests that there may be a novelty effect operating under these circumstances caused by the surprise value of seeing pictorial displays of nude males.

Evidence for cross-modal effects comes from a study by Hess (1965) in which experience with preferred tastes and music were found to be associated with pupil dilation. Goldwater (1972), in reviewing the more recent literature on pupil size, notes that there has been little support for Hess's assertion that pupil constriction is associated with aversive stimulation.

There are some difficulties encountered in trying to employ pupil size as a physiological index of preferences and affect state. The most important is that the content of a visual stimulus is confounded with its physical characteristics. Even as one scans a single visual presentation, the pupil will dilate and constrict with the passing of darker and lighter areas. A second problem is that the pupillary reflex seems to be influenced by mental activity and attention. Hess and Polt (1964) found that pupil size gradually dilates when one is presented with a problem. The dilation reaches its peak just prior to the expression of the verbal answer, and is followed by constriction. Goldwater (1972) further confounded these difficulties with his discovery that physiological arousal seems to coincide with verbalization and preparation for verbalization. Thus, pupil research, in which subjects are required to express preference while dilation is being recorded, produces findings open to various interpretations.

Electrodermal phenomena. Electrical characteristics of the skin vary along with one's psychological state. The sweat glands in the palm of the hand and sole of the foot, which appear to be particularly responsive to emotional conditions, are responsible for the electrodermal phenomena.

There are two common indicies of palmar or plantar electrical changes. If two electrodes are attached to the skin surface and a weak electric current is driven between them, one can measure the skin's resistance to current flow. As the region becomes moist, resistance goes down, or, conductance increases. Both *skin conductance* (SC) and *resistance* (SR) show diurnal wave-like changes. Conductance is lowest during sleep; it increases during the day, decreases toward evening, and falls off rapidly as one sleeps. Overriding these average, or tonic, levels are the more transient, or phasic, changes called *galvanic skin reflex* (GSR). Any high amplitude stimulus, whether it be physical, such as a loud noise, or emotional, will produce a temporary increase in conductance which lasts for 5 to 10 seconds before returning to the tonic level.

A third measure of electrodermal activity is based on *skin potential* (SP). In man, the palm tends to be 5 to 60 millivolts negative in comparison with a reference electrode placed on an inactive region. Lykken (1968) found that SP also shows diurnal waves along with phasic effects called the *skin potential reflex* (SRP). The reflex is typically biphasic, starting with an initial increase in palmar negativity, alpha wave, and followed by a beta wave when the palm becomes positive with respect to the reference electrode. A relaxed individual, or one who has adapted to the stimulus input, may only manifest alpha wave SPRs. The presence of the beta waves signifies either a stronger stimulus or a more excited subject. Highly-aroused subjects may only manifest a uniphasic beta wave SPR.

Zuckerman (1971) says that "Certainly, GSR has been the favored psychophysiological toy of psychologists" (p. 326). However, despite its relative ease of measurement, the GSR has proven to be far less reliable than direct genital indices in sex arousal research. This may be due to the fact that palmar electrodermal reflexes are not directly related to sexual behavior. The GSR has been shown to have moderate degrees of relationship with self-report measures of current anxiety states or *state anxiety;* however, this is not true among all subjects. The GSR has been shown to be an even less efficient predictor of an individual's predisposition to become anxious, *trait anxiety*. Certainly, using the GSR as the only index of arousal is risky.

There are two important sources of error in the interpretations of the GSR as a measure of arousal to specific stimulation. First, there is the fact that people emit spontaneous GSRs which are uncorrelated with the presentation of specific stimuli. The second problem is that repeated presentation of a stimulus leads to habituation. The presentation of a familiar stimulus will produce a lower amplitude response resulting in a decrease in the probability of the GSR.

Both spontaneous responses and habituation are an annoying source of error, just as the social desirability response set is in questionnaire assessment. However, like SD, spontaneous responses and habituation may be used as an assessment device in their own right. This approach has been used in the study of schizophrenia.

A number of theories of psychopathology relate schizophrenia to persistent, high levels of arousal. However, Depue and Fowles (1973) found that neither tonic nor phasic electrodermal responses seem to differentiate chronic schizophrenics from normal subjects. These two groups do seem to be characteristically different with respect to spontaneous responses and habituation. Research shows that chronic schizophrenics have higher rates of spontaneous electrodermal activity than normal subjects, the only exceptions come from those studies which employed patients medicated with the phenothiazines, a group of major tranquilizing drugs. In addition, chronic schizophrenics show a tendency to maintain the probability of a GSR over repeated stimulus presentations; they do not habituate as rapidly as normals. Both of these findings are consistent with the theory that chronic schizophrenics are in a state of high arousal. These data are quite similar to those obtained with anxiety neurotics. However, Venables and Wing (1962) presented evidence that certain sub-groups of schizophrenics, especially those on the behaviorally active end of an activity-withdrawal dimension, are physiologically under-aroused.

GENERAL ISSUES

In the course of this superficial review of psychophysiological assessment techniques, a number of measurement problems have been mentioned. Issues of fakeability and reactivity are certainly not unique to this form of behavioral assessment; it is in fact a problem associated with almost all assessment approaches.

An especially perplexing difficulty with psychophysiological assessment is that any given response measure can mean several different things. For example, in a research in which males have to express a preference for photographs of nudes, a pupillary dilation may be the result of attraction or appreciation of the visual stimulus,

stimulus novelty, intense cognitive activity, or preparation for action necessary for vocal expression. Thus, the specific psychological meaning of the physiological response may remain obscure.

A problem which is unique to psychophysiological assessment is that the various indices of autonomic arousal are not necessarily correlated with each other; one response mode, such as heart-rate, cannot be predicted from another, such as EEG. Subjects appear to have preferred modes of autonomic expression, with some people consistently responding to stress with a strong, stable GSR and others manifesting unreliable GSR but stable heart-rate reactions. If the researcher happens to tap the inactive mode, he may come away with erroneous conclusions regarding the physiological responsivity of particular subjects to stress. Goldfried and Sprafkin (1974) suggest that additional research is needed in order to determine whether an individual manifests different physiological patterns in different kinds of stimulus situations. In effect, they are calling for the kind of work with psychophysiological indices of arousal that was done by Endler and Hunt (1966) with S-R Inventory of Anxiety. The goal would be to determine the importance of the interaction of person, mode, and situation to the valid assessment of personality via psychophysiological indices.

SUMMARY

This chapter reviewed some of the major assessment approaches associated with the behavioral perspective. In many respects, the assesment tools employed differ little from traditional assessment procedures. Self-report questionnaires for example are commonly used by behaviorists. What is novel is that behavioral assessment tends to be primarily, although not exclusively, interested in overt events and the behavioral psychologist is typically more interested in prediction than is his more traditionally-oriented counterpart.

Among the assessment procedures uniquely associated with behaviorism is systematic observation of subjects, role playing and behavioral self-monitoring. In addition, a variety of physiological indices have been utilized as potentially useful sources of assessment data. Throughout, the assets and limitations of the various techniques were raised.

TERMS TO KNOW

PART III
Personality Theory

CHAPTER 16
Personality Theory: An Overview

There are a variety of ways in which we could answer a question such as, "What's Mary Like?." At one extreme, we might provide an interminable list of specific behaviors, detailing every movement and expression we have seen Mary emit and including the situational context of each observation. Such an answer would be both boring and only slightly less time-consuming for the inquisitor than if he had himself observed all that Mary had done.

CONSTRUCTS

Fortunately most personality descriptive statements are couched in terms such as "intelligent," "gentle," and "happy." Descriptive generalizations are used as a vehicle for succinctly conveying information that is based upon a possibly vast amount of discrete observations. These generalizations are called *constructs*. It is important to consider with some detail the nature of constructs; they may be thought of as the building blocks of theories. The interested reader is referred especially to Rychlak (1968) and Rotter (1954). They cover this material insightfully and this presentation borrows heavily from their ideas.

Levels of Abstraction

Because constructs are abstractions, they necessarily leave out the details of the real world events to which they refer. Johnson (1946) says that the abstracting process begins even at the non-verbal level of sensation. By this he means that our sensory contact with the world is never complete or perfect; we simply do not perceive all that is available in the stimulus. Thus, even if we are so inclined, we cannot precisely observe what is "out there." Johnson goes on to say that as soon as we apply labels or names to our experience, when we use constructs, we leave out additional details. For example, if we say, "Mary is a person who smiles a lot," we are neglecting to communicate other aspects of Mary's behavior. Even with respect to describing her as one who "smiles," we are omitting the minutiae which comprise her smiles — the way she curls the corners of her lips, flashes pearly teeth, and shows her dimples. If the responder were faced with a further question asking what "smile" meant, he could point to Mary smiling as a way of fully communicating what was meant by the construct "smile." Constructs which can be defined by a physical demonstration are called first order facts; they represent a level of abstraction which, appropriately, Johnson calles *first order*. In the words of Rychlak (1968), first order constructs describe events "as they appear to the naked eye," such as "smile" or "chair."

If all our communications were on this first order level of abstraction they would rarely be misinterpreted by others because they could be defined by pointing to objectively-observable events. However, we typically think and communicate about people and things in a much more abstract way. We leave out more and more details; that is, we abstract experience at higher and higher levels. All levels of abstraction above first order are referred to by Johnson as *inference levels*. A description of Mary at the level of inference involves saying, "She is a happy person." The construct "happy" cannot be defined directly in terms of observables. It may be defined in terms of first order abstractions, such as "smiles," which are directly related to observables. In this way, we can indirectly come to know rather well what another person means by "happy."

In psychology, we use the words "molecular" and "molar" to define descriptions characterized by low and high levels of abstraction. Molar personality descriptions are primarily at a highly inferential level. Wide ranges of behaviors are considered and these are reduced to highly abstract generalities — "She is a good person." A molecular personality description focuses upon first order facts and is exemplified by communicating the frequency with which specific responses occur in specific situations.

A first order construct, "chair," abstracts something with certain common features: legs, a back, a seat, etc. When constructs abstract personality - relevant events they are called *personality constructs*. Personality constructs, like any others, can vary in their degree of abstractness. Some may be at a first order level and refer to observable behavior such as smiling, crying, or slowness. Other personality constructs may be at the inferential level and refer to hypothetical events or conditions which are not directly observable; "anxiety" and "happiness" are examples of inferential personality constructs.

Personality constructs at this level of abstraction are frequently used to account for empirical relationships between first order facts or to explain empirical propositions. For example, behavior change as a consequence of being exposed to some training material is often explained by the construct "learning", a term which refers to a hypothetical, not directly observable, process intervening between exposure to material and subsequent performance. When different people manifest different qualities of performance after receiving the same training program, we might infer that they have different learning capacities. People who continually appear to learn easily find that their behavior is abstracted by the word "intelligence," another highly inferential personality construct.

When inferential constructs are used to explain empirical propositions, or are related to other inferential constructs, they are known as *theoretical constructs* and the assertions are called *theoretical propositions*. Thus, statements, explaining differences in learning on the basis of intelligence, or ones which relate intelligence to overt performance, are theoretical propositions.

Reductionism

Some scientists believe that it is best for our propositions to be as molecular as possible; that is, the constructs they contain should be at the lowest level of abstraction. This position is called *reductionism*. The reductionist feels that molecular constructs are somehow more real or basic than molar constructs because they approach first order facts and are more clearly tied to observables. The reductionist view has merit in that it encourages clarity of communication.

Unfortunately, in practice reductionism has come to imply a preferential ordering of descriptive perspectives. Physiological constructs are deemed to be most real or basic. They are thought to underlie biological, behavioral, psychological, and social constructs, with these latter seen as progressively more abstract. Rychlak rejects this position, calling the reasoning fallacious; he asks, "Is it really true that physiological constructs are more basic than psychological constructs?" (1968, p. 47). The answer depends upon how the theorist is reasoning at the moment. The words "gene" or "chromosome" are used very abstractly when referring to biochemical features of animals in general. They are much more abstract than the behavioral construct "run" which can be a first order fact, or the psychological constuct "fear" when used to refer to a specific individual.

It is important not to confuse the issue of abstraction levels with that of abstraction perspectives. The same event may be abstracted from many different perspectives. What we call "fear" can be understood or described in terms of hormonal and biochemical events. Fear can also be abstracted from a behavioral perspective, the idea being defined in terms of specifiable facial expressions, tremulousness, and other body movements. The psychological perspective is certainly a legitimate one from which to study fear, as is the interpersonal or social perspective. Rotter (1954, p. 42) points out that the correlations between the various constructive perspectives does not imply causality or dependency of one perspective upon another. When one is afraid, physiological, biological, behavioral, psychological, and probably social events are all happening at the same time. Which perspective to take when abstracting the event depends upon the interests and purposes of the analysis. A physician may be very concerned with a biological analysis of fear, wanting to understand it in terms of hormonal and cardiovascular processes because of their implications for physical health. Knowing about the hormonal correlate of fear is of little use to a parent who is trying to calm a hurt child or to a psychologist seeking to understand an isolate child's avoidance of peers.

Constructive Alternativism

It should be clear that even from a given perspective, such as the psychological, there are an infinite number of ways to abstract events. George Kelly (1963), a personality theorist, adopted the philosophical position known as *constructive alternativism*. According to this view, understanding experience, or "construing," consists of actively creating a personal picture of reality. According to Kelly, "Man looks at his world through transparent patterns or templates (i.e., constructs) which he creates and then attempts to fit over the realities of which the world is composed" (p. 9). Thus, each of us has a somewhat different reality because we each have constructed for ourselves a somewhat different set of constructs with which to bring meaning, order, and predictability to our experience. The core notion of constructive alternativism is that there is no single nor even necessarily best way to construe experience.

To the degree that one downplays the importance of an external reality having an existence apart and independent of the perceiver, an idealistic position is being adopted. According to *idealism,* man looks at a world of his own making, a world which he has constructed. Stress on the existence of a world having an immutable existence of its own is called *realism.* Realists say the words we use to describe the world are abstractions of reality rather than constructions of it. For the realist our constructs may neglect detail, but they, nevertheless, are intended to be a map of nature as it really is. In general, American psychology has gravitated toward realism ever since John Watson (1913) focused the attention of psychologists upon overt behavior. Even George Kelly, who Rychlak categorizes as an idealist, is careful to adopt a middle position on the idealism-realism dimension, "lest he be accused of talking about nothing more than mental apparitions" (1968, p. 20.) In this regard, Kelly presumes that the universe is really existing "but people's thoughts also really exist, though the correspondence between what people really think exists and what really does exist is a continually changing one" (1955, p. 6).

Today the extreme realist position is well represented by behaviorists such as Skinner who suggests that we stop trying to explain the world through inferential construction and stick to manipulating and discovering relationships between first order facts. Thus does Skinner reject idealism and constructive alternativism as well as theorizing in general.

Reification

As a science, psychology is always geared toward the explanation of human phenomena. It has been pointed out that inferential constructs such as "intelligence" are used for this explanatory purpose. Typically, the process of finally employing inferential constructs in this explanatory way begins at a relatively low level of abstraction. For example, the successful problem-solving behavior of an individual might be abstracted or described by the term "intelligent." This word conveniently summarizes the nature of the individuals' behavior in a variety of situations. The meaning of "intelligent behavior" may be adequately communicated to others via a detailed description of examples or by pointing to someone engaging in intelligent behavior.

It is not uncommon to go beyond describing behavior, in a general way, as intelligent and to describe the particular person exhibiting such behavior as intelligent. The word in this usage refers to an attribute of the individual which is not directly observed but is inferred from the quality of observable behavior. We should be cautious when using inferential personality constructs in this manner because often we fall into the trap of labeling people as "intelligent," or "happy," or "schizophrenic" without re-evaluating the first order facts to determine if the label remains an appropriate one. Failing to do this results in errors of over-generalization similar to those involved in racial and ethnic prejudicial attitudes and behaviors.

So far in this digression the word "intelligent" has been looked at as a term which is descriptive of the behavior of people. "Intelligent" may also be used as an explanation of behavior; "She behaves that way because she is intelligent." It should be clear that the construct "intelligent," when used with this explanatory intent, really brings no new understanding to the matter. This is because the only evidence for the explanatory attribute "intelligent" is the intelligent behavior we seek to explain. In effect, one might just as well say, "Her behavior is intelligent because she is intelligent." It is hoped that the circularity inherent in such explanatory attempts is obvious.

Attempts at explaining behavior become potentially more confused when the explanatory construct "intelligent" is *reified,* when it is implied to be real or tangible. The form of the construct then shifts from that of adjective to noun and the explanatory statement, "She is intelligent," becomes, "She has intelligence." Thus, what was once an abstract descriptive generalization has evolved into a hypothetical "thing." Of course, the reification of this construct does nothing to eliminate the aforementioned circularity or to provide further insight or understanding. To say, "Her behavior is intelligent because she has intelligence," is as circular as an explanation can be.

There are numerous instances of reification throughout psychoanalytic writings. Freud for example, in discussing the principal characteristics of ego processes says that the "ego" has the task of self preservation. "It performs that task by becoming aware of stimuli, by storing up experiences about them (in the memory), by avoiding excessively strong stimuli (through adaptation) and finally by learning to bring about expedient changes in the external world to its own advantage (through activity)" (1949, p. 2). In reading this it is easy to misunderstand the construct "ego." One may understand it not as a description of a class of psychological processes, but as a perceptive, active, problem-solving homunculus scurrying around somewhere behind and between the eyes and ears. Behaviorists, too, frequently communicate in ways which are quite at variance with their ostensible objective orientation. It may be said that a behavior therapeutic approach, such as systematic desensitization, results in the fear being extinguished. The construct "fear" is thus being reified within a context which erroneously implies that what was once tangible is now "gone."

Errors of reification are also frequently committed by psychopathologists. If a person manifests a variety of highly unusual and maladaptive activities, talks incoherently, and claims to hear and see things which are not present to the objective observer, it is likely to be said that he is exhibiting schizophrenic behavior. In this usage, "schizophrenic" is a descriptive generalization. However, to say that one manifests schizophrenic behavior because he has schizophrenia is a very different matter. This assertion implies that the person has some disease entity within him, the existence of which is a matter of conjecture and not material fact. Yet, use of this unwarranted reification persists, perhaps because it may falsely provide a sense of closure in that the schizophrenic behavior appears to be explained. Such an explanation, however, is no better than saying, ''She behaves in a happy way because she has a lot of happiness in her.'' The intention here is not to malign the ideas of Freud, behaviorists, or psychopathologists; it is simply that the use of nouns to describe psychological proces-ses is often misleading and should, therefore, be avoided.

Construct Definition

As we have seen, there are many personality constructs which are far removed from observable reality. In these cases the meaning of the constructs become vague and people may not agree on its referents. Such constructs are said to be ''subjective'' because, for all practical purposes, their meanings are private.

As an example of a subjective personality construct, consider the central motiva-tional principle of a number of related personality theories, ''self-actualization.'' Mas-low says that self-actualization refers to ''man's desire for self-fulfillment; namely, to the tendency for him to become actualized in what he is potentially. This tendency might be phrased as a desire to become more and more what one idiosyncratically is, to become everything that one is capable of becoming'' (1970, p. 46). The problem here is that it is not entirely clear what self-fulfillment means, and this difficulty in turn rests on the notion that whatever it is, it is different for each of us. While the idea of self-actualization no doubt has emotional appeal to many, its subjectivity renders the term scientifically weak. It is difficult to assess self-actualization with reliability at even the lowest level of measurement, which would be that of two people agreeing as to the presence or absence of the phenomenon in question. Even when Maslow describes the characteristics of the individual who is self-actualized, there is a deluge of additional subjective constructs employed. Specifically, self-actualized people are said, by Mas-low, to be comfortable in their relations with reality, self-accepting, relatively spon-taneous, and pursuing a mission in life. They have the quality of detachment and autonomy, while also having profound interpersonal relations with others; they are democratic, have a non-hostile sense of humor, are creative, and have a ''deep feeling of identification, sympathy, and affection'' (p. 165) for mankind.

In summary, self-actualization is a vague construct because it is defined in terms of other constructs whose meanings appear to be no less vague. At the other extremes are constructs which are themselves first order facts or are defined in terms of observables. Thus, while the meaning of intelligence can be communicated by relying upon other inferential constructs, precision in communication is obtained when intelligence is defined by a specific score on a standardized intelligence test; that is by an *operational definition*. Similarly, the construct ''hunger drive'' can be understood as a ''motive to consume food,'' but it can also be operationally defined as ''speed of running'' toward a goal box containing food or as ''some number of hours of food deprivation.''

Thus, operational definitions move us away from vagueness and subjectivity. They render constructs more objective and relate them with precision to first order facts. The use of such constructs, called *operationism,* is thought by many to be a prerequisite for the establishment of any theory having scientific utility. According to Bergmann and Spence, "No body of empirical knowledge can be built up without operational definitions of the terms we use" (1941, p. 2). There are others who claim that strict operationism is premature for psychology. It is feared that adherence to critical operational standards may serve to inhibit productive research on important theoretical topics, such as interpersonal relations, which are abstracted by constructs that we cannot easily operationalize.

Rotter (1954) proposed that some middle ground on this issue must be reached. He suggested that constructs which are not strictly operational might still be used in an acceptably reliable fashion if behavioral examples of the construct were provided. The construct "need for recognition" becomes more objective when followed by the phrase, "as evidenced by boastful statements." Another example is provided by the construct "latent homosexuality," which is a tendency toward homosexual inclinations without overt evidence of homosexual activity. In fact, many so-called "latent" homosexuals actually manifest typical or even excessive heterosexual behavior. This is explained by the concept "repression," in which personally unacceptable thoughts and impulses are actively excluded from consciousness. By relying on this process of repression, the latent homosexual is presumably protecting himself from recognizing and acknowledging his homosexual inclinations. The problem then becomes one of determining how the latent homosexual is identifiably different from the heterosexual. "Concepts employing words like *latent* or *repressed* are only meaningful and scientifically useful if they describe what behavior is actually present" (p. 53). By way of illustrating how the construct "latent homosexual" may be behaviorally clarified, Rotter suggests using referents such as, "falls in love with improbable objects (such as married women and engaged girls) whom he does not approach, believes intercourse is debasing, associates with men primarily, . . . shows excessive modesty with other men" (p. 53).

While such verbosity may appear cumbersome, it may well be a necessary price to pay until more reliable constructs are commonplace. "It is mandatory . . . that referents be stated for crucial terms in experimental and clinical reports whenever concepts are likely to mean widely different things to different people" (p. 53).

It should be realized that it is insufficient for a construct to be defined only in an operational way. That is, while hunger may be operationally defined in terms of the running speed of a rat approaching a food box, we don't usually think of running as defining hunger. Running speed is merely a convenient way to measure hunger under laboratory conditions. In order to determine if running speed is an adequate operationalization of hunger, there must also exist a definition of hunger in more conceptual terms. In fact, the conceptual definition of a construct invariably precedes the operational definition.

Rotter's (1954) Social Learning Theory contains a central construct, that of *behavior potential.* In terms of everyday language behavior potential is the probability of occurrence of a specific behavior. The definition of any construct in such common-sense terms is its *ideal definition.* Most constructs are originally conceptualized in ideal terms, making it then possible to arrive at appropriate measurement operations. In the example, it is easy to move from the ideal definition of behavior potential to the operational definition which is the relative frequency of the behavior in question in comparison with other behaviors. Thus, operationally, we are defining behavior potential in terms of a simple counting process. Those behaviors which are observed to occur with greatest frequency in a given situation are said to have a high behavior potential, and those which occur infrequently are said to have a low behavior potential.

In addition to an ideal definition and an operational definition, good theoretical constructs are also defined with a *systematic definition*, one which defines the construct in terms of other constructs within the theory. In effect, systematic definitions are the assumptions of the theory. As statements of relationships between constructs, systematic definitions are basically nothing more than what we have previously called theoretical propositions. In systematically defined terms, behavior potential is a function of "expectancy" and "reward value," two additional constructs in Social Learning Theory. Essentially, then, this systematic definition asserts that the probability that a behavior will occur is a function of the subjective expectancy held by the individual that the behavior in question will lead to reward and the value of that reward. Thus, one would theoretically anticipate that the behavior potential of a specific behavior would be very low if the individual either does not expect any reward for engaging in the behavior or does not value the available rewards. For instance, a child may not raise his hand to correctly answer a question in class if he does not anticipate reward for doing so because he expects to be incorrect or he does not value the available rewards of peer esteem or teacher recognition.

It is usually true that systematic definitions clarify the meaning of constructs much more than a simple ideal definition. They are especially important because they explicitly point out what the construct relates to and what it may, therefore, predict. For example, if a behavior has a low behavior potential, one can predict from the systematic definition of behavior potential that expectancy for reward or reward value is also low. As we will see in a later chapter, Rotter specifies operations whereby both expectancies and reward values may be measured. Systematic definitions are least productive when the related constructs are subjective. We saw this in our discussion of Maslow's self-actualization construct. The constructs used to define self-actualization systematically appear no less vague than self-actualization itself.

THEORY

We previously defined a theoretical proposition as an assertion which relates one inferential construct to another inferential construct or first order fact. Two or more theoretical propositions related to each other constitute the beginning of a theory. Naturally, a personality theory will contain abundant numbers of personality constructs which abstract the patterns of behavior, thought, and emotion characterizing what we call "personality." In addition, most theories will include constructs referring to various situations and kinds of interpersonal relationships because these are usually seen as being relevant to a total understanding of personality.

Importance of Personality Theory

There are psychologists who claim to be atheoretical in their professional conduct. Their style derives from a strict realist philosophy in which facts are collected without effort to understand why. This so-called "dust bowl empiricist" approach characterized the way in which the Minnesota Multiphase Personality Inventory (MMPI) was constructed. Recall that items were included on the MMPI subscales because they were found to discriminate empirically between diagnostic groups, such as depressive patients and a non-psychiatric sample of subjects. No interest was expressed in trying to comprehend *why* depressed persons responded oppositely from normal subjects on the discriminating items, or *why* it was that some normal subjects answered the questions as did the typical depressed patient and vice versa. Yet, in spite of disclaimers one cannot ignore the likelihood that Hathaway and McKinley were guided by what Rychlak (1968) calls an "informal personality theory" as they developed the MMPI. "Informal" here refers to a non-explicit set of assumptions, often unrecognized, about the nature of personality. For instance, among other things, the format of the MMPI is predicated upon notions of verbal self-report being a relevant expression of personality and of personality being reasonably stable over time.

Rotter believes, "It is almost impossible to carry out a professional psychological activity without some implied (i.e. informal) theoretical position" (1954, p. 8). Because of this, he feels it is best for psychologists to make their theoretical assumptions explicit so that they may be examined and made consistent both among themselves and with known facts.

Organizational Functions. Probably the most basic purpose of a personality theory is to provide a framework with which to organize and understand personality-relevant phenomena. In other words, the student of personality is not left to his own abstracting resources as he observes his subject because the theory from which he is working contains a set of potentially applicable constructs. For the clinical psychologist, a theory can be an indispensable aid in bringing order to what might otherwise be a confusing array of patient behaviors. For example, many personality theories, including that of Freud, contain constructs which permit one to make sense of inconsistent clinical data. In this regard, the Freudian construct "reaction formation" may be particularly useful.

Reaction formation refers to a hypothetical process which results in the person overtly stressing behaviors which are opposite from what is unconsciously desired. Presumably, reaction formation allows the person to defend against acknowledging his unconscious wishes which, if they were to come into awareness, would cause considerable anxiety or guilt. In theory, the unconscious wishes which are denied expression through use of reaction formation are typically of a sexual or aggressive nature. Despite the operation of reaction formation, the unconscious wishes are thought to remain potent, capable of indirectly influencing overt behavior in a variety of devious ways. To see how reaction formation can serve as an explanatory construct, consider a situation in which a mother brings her child to a clinical psychologist because the child feels and acts rejected. The mother, however, honestly expresses the belief that she loves her child greatly. If the psychologist's theoretical frame of reference includes the construct reaction formation, he will consider the possibility that the zeal with which the mother expresses her love is a cover for hostile or punitive tendencies of which she is not aware. With this in mind, careful interviewing may lead to the discovery that the child came too early in the woman's marriage, disrupting what was a peaceful and harmonious existence with her husband. The mother's frustration and anger are taken out on the child, but only in the most oblique ways. She may send her child to bed at an early hour in the evening, not out of the caring and love which she claims to be her motive but out of unconscious wishes to be rid of the little intruder. It could be the very subtly-communicated hostile overtones surrounding this bedtime routine which is the cause of the child's sense of rejection. The child has sensed the hostility of which the mother is unaware.

In addition to having utility in the psychotherapy arena, personality theory also assists the psychologist in his conceptual organization of research findings. If the empirical observations which emerge from the research enterprise can be incorporated under the umbrella of broad theoretical generalizations, their meaning, importance, and implications will be very much more apparent. The organizing function of personality theory can also be extended to evaluate the worth of personality assessment procedures. If one's personality theory considers unconscious factors to play a large role in defining the individual, any assessment procedure which does not tap unconscious motives and conflicts may be judged inadequate.

On the negative side, it is not uncommon for a psychologist to adopt an orthodox theoretical posture which can lead to a closed mind. A psychologist in a psychiatric hospital may utilize a theory which incorporates the construct "interpersonal withdrawal" to explain the generally low activity level of chronic schizophrenics. While this construction may indeed be a valuable one, if the psychologist persists in thinking only in terms of his preferred theory he may be led into making gross errors of judgment. He must be flexible enough to consider other personality theoretical alternatives as explanations of what is observed. The psychologist must also be willing to construe events from non-personality perspectives. It may be necessary to consider the possibility that patient inactivity can best be understood by abstracting their behavior with biochemical constructs; perhaps they have been administered behavior retarding psychotropic medication. Situational constructs might need to be explored also; perhaps there are no incentives for doing anything on the ward, or the 95°F ward temperature obviates wanting to engage in any vigorous activity.

Delimiting function. A second major purpose of personality theory is that of *delimitation*. By supplying abstractions which may be used to describe and explain complex human phenomena, a personality theory at the same time excludes countless other ways of abstracting. In other words, the user of a personality theory comes into a situation with a preconception of what is important as well as what is unimportant. Hall and Lindzey (1970) write that a personality theory prevents "the observer from being dazzled by the full bloom complexity of natural or concrete events. The theory is a set of blinders and it tells its wearer that it is unnecessary for him to worry about all the aspects of the event he is studying" (p. 14). The delimiting function of personality theory is, in part, determined by its general position on overriding issues like realism vs. idealism. For instance, a behaviorist might eschew abstracting events like people's thoughts. He would instead emphasize abstracting what can be objectively observed at a first order level.

The specific constructs contained within a theory serve additional delimiting functions. Thus, Skinner believes it is important to describe the situations which set the occasion for behavior and the consequences of behavior, but not the physical characteristics of the person himself. Sheldon (1940), in contrast to Skinner, has developed a *constitutional psychology* in which an individual's physique is seen as a major correlate of personality.

Generative function. Organizing what is important and indicating what should be ignored are useful functions of theory. However, these are secondary to the main purpose of personality theory, which is to lead us in the direction of postulating new relationships. Personality theory helps us to arrive at new theoretical propositions. We are talking here about the capacity of personality theory to promote novel ideas whose validity can be tested via research. The consequent accumulation of new empirical propositions will, in turn, find explanation in terms of new constructs from which new theoretical propositions will emerge. There is thus a spiraling expansion of both empirical and theoretical propositions.

Hall and Lindzey (1970, p. 13) differentiate between what they call the "systematic" and "heuristic" generation of research. The former is based on the systematic and orderly growth of a theory, with each expansion a logical derivative of all that has preceded. Rotter's Social Learning Theory began by seeing behavior as the product of subjects' expectancies for rewards and reward values. A logical extension of this theoretical proposition is to consider how the nature of situations interact with expectancies and reward values to determine behavior. For instance, it was thought that a person's expectancy for reward would be partly determined by whether receipt of the reward was seen as being under his personal control, as when one earns social praise for performing skillfully, as opposed to it being seen as a chance event, such as a payoff from a slot machine. Over the past decade dozens of experiments have been conducted in which the impact of reward upon behavior in skill and chance situations has been studied.

Heuristic influence is exerted by a theory when it prompts novel theoretical propositions and provokes new areas of research which are not an explicit, logical extension of the mother theory. Freud's psychoanalytic theory is probably the best example of a personality theory which has fulfilled this heuristic function. In the first half of this century a number of Freud's disciples adopted certain of his central constructs, such as the "*unconscious,*" and then went on to develop and popularize new theories of personality. While men like Carl Jung and Alfred Adler borrowed liberally from their mentor, their own theories were constructed in part to discredit Freud. Hall and Lindzey (1970) believe that a theory may exert an heuristic influence as much by arousing disbelief and resistance as by encouraging others to build on it. It is clear that psychoanalytic personality theory has generated far-reaching ideas through the medium of love as well as of hate.

AN EXEMPLARY MINI-PERSONALITY THEORY

As mentioned previously, a theory is a statement of interrelated empirical and theoretical propositions. It presents all relevant personality constructs and indicates how they are concurrently tied together and related to situational, biological, and other constructs. A temporal dimension is added when the personality constructs of the theory are related to constructs descriptive of antecedent events on the one side, such as an abusive parent-child relationship, and consequent events on the other, the development of psychopathology. This matrix of interrelated constructs is called a *nomological network,* a simple example of which is illustrated in Fig. 19. This mini-personality theory introduces nine constructs; the nature of their mutual relationships is indicated by a + or − sign. A + sign between two constructs means they are positively related; if evidence of one is present, so should evidence of the other. A − sign means the two constructs are negatively related; evidence of one means absence of evidence of the other.

Because the referents of constructs may exhibit themselves in degrees rather than be totally present or totally absent, the constructs of a theory are often called *variables.* For example, the construct "depression" abstracts a range of behaviors, including crying, loss of sleep and appetite, and experiences of hopelessness and self-debasement. Each of these behavioral referents may vary in their intensity and frequency. When they are intensive and frequent, we speak of deep depression; when they are weak and infrequent, the depression is said to be mild. The referents of any variable with which depression theoretically positively correlates should be present in greater number, intensity, and frequency when there is deep depression; similarly, the referents of variables which are thought to be negatively correlated with depression should be few, weak, and infrequent to the degree that depression is deep.

Descriptively, the theory in Fig. 19 says that depression is positively related with rejection on the antecedent side, and with suicide on the consequent side. If someone is depressed, this hypothetical theory asserts that it is likely there was a history of rejection and that precautions should be taken against suicide as a probable outcome. Similarly, the communication of statements indicative of self-esteem are assumed to depend upon a previously-developed sense of security. Also, to the degree the person is seen as having high self-esteem, he is predicted to attain personal fulfillment. Rejection, depression, and suicide are all negatively related to security, self-esteem, and personal fulfillment. Where evidence for the former three constructs is present, evidence for the latter three is counter-indicated. Lastly, the two constructs of intelligence and social success are thought to positively correlate; evidence of one is predictive of evidence of the other.

A Mini Personality Theory

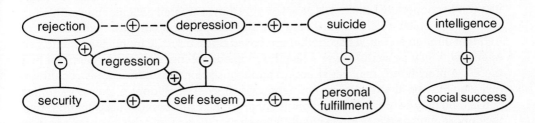

Figure 19. Represented above is a system of nine interrelated constructs (a nomological network). Positive relations between constructs are indicated by a + sign; inverse or negative relationships are indicated by a − sign.

To this point the theory is quite straightforward. The ninth construct, that of repression, greatly complicates matters. For our current purposes we can define repression as the process of keeping recollections of distressing experiences unconscious, or out of awareness. With the addition of this construct, we do not know whether a rejected person will suffer from depression or whether he will repress the experience of rejection and still develop positive self-esteem. Similarly, if a person is discovered to have positive self-esteem, it is not immediately clear whether he successfully avoided childhood experiences of rejection or whether rejection was encountered and subsequently repressed.

CRITERIA FOR A GOOD THEORY OF PERSONALITY

Expert Opinion

Many psychologists establish a professional identity associated with a particular personality theory. They call themselves Freudians, or Rogerians, or Skinnerians. How do they choose? What are the criteria by which one theory is rejected as inadequate, and another adopted? In all too many cases this very important decision is made by simply following "expert" opinion. It is not uncommon for the so-called "expert" to be a college or graduate school professor who can overpower relatively naive students with authoritative scholarliness. The professor, an orthodox " ____ian" extolls the virtue of his preferred theoretical position because he honestly thinks he's correct. By successfully converting a group of obviously bright students, his own beliefs receive confirmation. Unfortunately, the students may not have had a legitimate opportunity to exercise their brightness since their biased professor only exposed them to his own point of view. Once the student attains professional rank and begins to work with the theory adopted from his mentor, it is all too easy to find supportive evidence of its worth. For example, in clinical practice a large proportion of patients will show symptoms of remission, and the practitioner will confidently attribute his "cure" rate to the efficacy of his theory. At the other extreme, therapy failures can be easily chalked-up to an uncooperative client. It is easy to forget that untreated patients show remission rates quite similar to those receiving psychotherapy. Spontaneous remissions are frequent enough so that a psychotherapy based upon a totally ineffective theory can appear clinically powerful. After a lengthy professional investment has been put in a theory, a practitioner may resist accepting inconsistent data because his reputation now depends on the theory he has espoused. If the practitioner makes a name for himself, he may be offered an appointment at a major university. This will afford him the opportunity to seduce intellectually a new generation of students, thereby assuring perpetuation of the theory. In this way, a bright person can come to believe in, and be committed to, a bad theory.

Research Support

An excellent criterion upon which to judge the worth of a theory is its ability to generate new ideas which are confirmed by research. When theoretical predictions find such confirmation, confidence in the utility of the theory is enhanced.

One difficulty in using this as a primary criterion is that many major theoretical constructs are extremely difficult to research because they lack generally acceptable operational definitions; "repression" is one such construct. Researchers are often in disagreement among themselves regarding whether someone is, or is not, repressing. In addition, even when an operational definition of repression is utilized by a researcher, more clinically-oriented psychologists are apt to find that definition theoretically inadequate. There are some who argue that a theory which is not open to empirical verification because of too many non-operational constructs should be rejected as unscientific.

Related to this is what Ayer (1946) has called the "principle of verifiability." Ayer stresses that we must be able to spell out what observations are necessary to accept a proposition as being true, or to reject it as being false. If this cannot be done, then the proposition is beyond verification. It is claimed that such non-verifiable propositions raise pseudo-problems, which provoke interesting discussion but do not contribute to the advance of empirical knowledge. With respect to our mini-personality theory, it can be argued that the construct "repression" renders many theoretical propositions non-verifiable; they are not open to empirical confirmation or disconfirmation. For instance, if we determine that a child is currently experiencing feelings of rejection, our mini-theory cannot be disconfirmed regardless of the adult which that child becomes. If we find evidence of depression, there is consistency with the theory; if no depression emerges, we can invoke the hypothetical process of repression. Similarly, by exploring the personal history of a person with high self-esteem, the discovery of either a rejecting or a non-rejecting parent is consistent with our mini-theory; in the former case we can explain the subject's current status on the basis of the process of repression. Our mini-theory could circumvent the problem of non-verifiability by specifying ways in which a person, who has had a childhood experience and later repressed it, is identifiably different from one who has never had the childhood experience. If this were done, the construct "repression" would become potentially measurable and, therefore, open to empirical test. Lacking this subtle but extremely important addition, the construct "repression" only muddies the conceptual water.

Formal Analysis

A third general way to evaluate a theory is to expose it to a formal analysis, noting the degree to which it conforms to certain internal organizational and substantive criteria.

Systematization. Our mini-theory contains propositions which interrelate the constructs of "rejection," "depression," "repression," "security," "self-esteem," "suicide," and "personal fulfillment." If we can assess where a person stands on any one of these seven variables, we should be able to predict standing on the others. Knowing that a child is experiencing a sense of security, enables us to predict a later high sense of self-esteem which, if present, will in turn be predictive of personal fulfillment. It is but a small step to generate the proposition that childhood security is directly predictive of adult personal fulfillment. To the degree the constructs of a theory are related to each other i.e. prediction is enhanced. The most efficiently predictive theory would be one in which every part of the nomological network is systematically related to every other part. The beauty of such systematization would be that measurement of a variable at any point in the nomological network would permit one to say something about any other construct within the network. In our mini-theory no relationships are specified between the two constructs "intelligence" and "social success" and the rest of the theory. Because of this, the predictive process is effectively short-circuited between these two constructs and all others. One may know something about an individual's intelligence and, therefore, be able to predict social success, or vice versa. However, measurement of either variable says nothing about depression, personal fulfillment, security, and the other constructs.

One of the reasons for the continued popularity of psychoanalytic theory is its unusually high degree of systematization. Psychoanalytic personality theory consists of three sub-theories, each systematically related to the other two. Thus the theory is able to provide an incredibly rich source of hypotheses when trying to understand an individual case in a clinical setting. As soon as anything is known about a client, the psychoanalytic therapist has a theoretical framework which immediately provides direction in his search for the childhood antecedents, the current character of the patient, and the prognosis for psychotherapy outcome.

Operationality. A good personality theory is one whose constructs are either measurable or are systematically related to others which are measurable. By measurable, we mean at the very least, inter-rater agreement as to the presence or absence of a construct's behavioral referent(s). For example, if two people are observing the same phenomenon and independently abstract what they are viewing with the same construct, (They both say: "That is *sad* behavior.") the minimum criterion for operationality is met. Operationality reaches higher levels of precision when scaling procedures are available which permit raters to judge the strength of the construct reliably. The measurement question then is no longer whether a person is sad but, "How sad is the person?"

There is a very important relationship between the criteria of systematization and operationality. Specifically, each, without the other, is worthless. No matter how systematic a personality theory, prediction is impossible unless some of the constructs contained in its nomological network are operational. One has to have a measurable starting place in order to get a foothold from which to generate predictions. Our mini-personality theory would be nothing more than a literary exercise, completely void of predictive utility, unless one or more of its nine constructs could be measured. Alternatively, a psychologist may have at his disposal an array of operational constructs which allow him to measure a number of personality variables. However, each of these operationalized constructs must be systematically related to other variables, or there is nothing to predict.

Levels of construction. Many psychologists believe that a good theory must systematically include constructs at several levels of abstraction. Proponents of this view say that a theory should embrace first order constructs which have objective referents, as well as highly-inferential constructs having broad generality. Consistent with this, Maddi (1976) suggests that in useful personality theories the lowest level abstraction should refer to what he calls "concrete peripheral characteristics." These are personality characteristics on which people manifest individual differences. Constructs having the periphery of personality as their referents are usually easily operationalized because they are abstracting patterns of observable behaviors. These constructs are the smallest explanatory units of a theory and are labeled with terms such as "drive," "motive," "trait," "need," or "habit."

Concrete peripheral characteristics are systematically related to each other and are organized by other constructs which are at a higher level of abstraction. These middle level constructs are generally few in number and collectively comprise a statement about all the different types of personalities. The psychoanalytic constructs of "oral character," "anal character," and "phallic character" exemplify a typology which theoretically covers all personality possibilities.

At the highest level of generality are constructs which refer to assumed inherent attributes of people — the *core characteristics* of personality. Maddi points out that most theories include only one or, at most, two or three constructions regarding core characteristics. The core of personality is usually conceptualized as providing an overriding purpose or directionality to behavior. For example, psychoanalytic theory sees everyone as being governed by a striving for "instinctual gratification." It is important to realize that core personality constructs are at a level of abstraction so far removed from specific overt behaviors that they are exceedingly difficult, if not impossible, to operationalize. Their validity can, however, be assessed indirectly because they are systematically related to peripheral constructs. The empirical verification of hypotheses regarding the periphery of personality serves to establish the worth of core constructs from which the peripheral constructs are logically derived.

As the reader may suspect, some personality theories emphasize one level of abstraction to the relative neglect of other levels. A simple personality theory which stresses a single core personality trend, and claims that all behavior is a reflection of this core, is often very appealing. To anticipate an individual's behavior, one would only have to discover how much of the core trend the individual had. From this single observation, every prediction would follow; this would be a tremendously efficient system, if it worked. Unfortunately, core-emphasis personality theories, by failing to take into account individual differences in the way the core manifests itself at the peripheral level, and by neglecting situational influence on behavior, may generate far-reaching, but inaccurate, predictions when applied to the individual case.

Carl Rogers' theory of personality has a core-emphasis, which he describes as a tendency to actualize potentialities. His theory is relatively weak at the lower levels of abstraction because he does not provide categories of potentialities which might serve to establish middle level typologies. He deals with individual differences only along the single dimension of personality organization, with the most organized being a "fully functioning person" and the least organized a "maladjusted person." Thus, everyone is assumed to lie at a slightly different point along this continuum, but there are no discrete sub-classifications provided by Rogers.

In contrast to core-emphasis theories, some theories focus upon low level abstractions. These may adopt a narrow trait approach, in which almost every category of behavior is seen as being the product of a different trait, or need, or instinct. Because these explanatory units are not systematically held together by higher order abstractions at the level of types or at the core level, the potential for cross-behavioral prediction becomes minimized. At the extreme is Skinner's position, which totally excludes core level constructs and sticks exclusively to a description of discrete response patterns in relation to contemporaneous environmental events. Because Skinner remains at the first order level of abstraction, he argues that his position is not theoretical at all. It seeks only to describe behavior, not explain it with inferential, theoretical constructs.

In summarizing the importance of the three levels of abstraction, Maddi writes that our theories must attend to peripheral characteristics if we are to study seriously "the many obvious, though concrete and small differences among people. Without typology, a theory is mute concerning larger patterns of differences among people. If a theory does not include a statement of core tendencies . . . it is not possible to consider persons to share some attributes by virtue of their common species" (p. 595).

Maximum inclusiveness. In order for a theory to be optimally useful it should include enough constructs to deal adequately with the phenomena it claims to abstract.

As we have already indicated, a theory which places all of its explanatory eggs in one core basket is probably oversimplistic. Additional constructs at other levels of abstraction are usually needed.

In addition to having constructs at all levels of abstraction, a good theory should include constructs at both poles of two additional dimensions. The first of these is that of *internal-external behavioral determination*. Both Freud and Rogers look to the "why" of personality primarily in terms of internal determinants, the constructs of "instinct" and "actualization" being invoked respectively. Skinner, of course, ignores internal behavioral determinants and identifies the antecedents of behavior in terms of external environmental events. In either case, half of the factors which account for behavior are being relatively neglected.

Historically there has been a shift from internal to external causation in personality theorizing. However, even with the recent attention given to situational determinants of behavior, there is yet to be developed any well thought-out system of constructs which adequately abstracts the environment in any but the broadest of terms. Learning theoretical positions construe environmental consequences of behavior as either rewarding or punishing, and, therefore, as increasing or decreasing the frequency of behaviors. Rotter's Social Learning Theory (1954) takes a middle position on the internal-external behavioral determination continuum. On the one hand, Rotter brings attention to internal factors, such as subjectively-held probabilities for reinforcement, and subjectively-held reinforcement values. However, both reward values and expectancies are clearly seen to be a function of the situation. For example, a child may engage in help-seeking behavior, including crying and whining, with his parents because he anticipates and values the attention which will be awarded him when the parents respond. These particular responses may not be expressed when he is with the peer group, because in that situation the expectation of receiving sympathetic attention is probably less and/or sympathetic attention from a peer is far less valued than similar overtones from the parents. Thus, behavior potential is seen by Rotter as due to both internal and external determinants.

A second dimension along which a good personality theory should have constructs if it is to be maximally inclusive is that of *process-content*. *Process* constructs are those which deal with personality development and change. These constructs describe the manner in which behaviors are acquired and how they can be modified. Any personality theory which talks about childhood development or psychotherapy must include process-oriented constructs.

Learning approaches to personality are among those placing heavy emphasis upon process. However, unlike learning theory, which also stresses external determinants of behavior and personality as largely acquired through experience, other process theories or sub-theories, such as Freud's sub-theory of childhood psychosexual development, talk about personality development from the perspective of internal, biological determinants. Freud's ideas regarding the biologically-programmed unfolding of instinctual behavior patterns over the developmental years is one example of a process theory which emphasizes internal determinants.

Content-oriented constructs abstract categories of personalities, motives, and behaviors. They address themselves to the make-up of personality and to the different kinds of personalities which exist rather than to how they evolved or how they can be altered. Sheldon's (1940) "constitutional" psychology is very close to being a pure content theory. He goes into considerable detail describing the three all-inclusive types of physique and how these correlate with personality characteristics. Sheldon has extremely little to say about the development and change of personality variables and, therefore, his position is lacking in process constructs.

The most useful theories of personality not only include both process and content components, but they systematically relate the two. This combination is extremely important for those who conduct psychotherapy. The practitioner is in his best position when he knows not only what procedures are necessary in order to effect favorable personality change, but which procedure (process) might be most effective with a particular kind of patient (content). Goldstein and Stein (1976) have called the tailoring of different treatments to different patients with different problems a "prescriptive" approach to psychotherapy.

Despite Carl Rogers' emphasis upon understanding and dealing with the unique individual, he stands behind a process theory of psychotherapy which is offered as being universally appropriate for all. This non-prescriptive approach is analogous to a physician administering the same medication regardless of the pathology. Psychoanalytic psychotherapy is at a somewhat more prescriptive level. Although Freud also offers only one kind of psychotherapy to the practitioner, he relates its efficacy to content aspects of his theory. Specifically, Freud offers guidelines as to the kinds of patients which might be expected to profit most, and least, from psychoanalytic treatment. There is no doubt that Freud's attention to both process and content details of personality has helped to maintain his popularity over the years. In recent years the most prescriptively-geared psychotherapeutic proposals have come from behavior therapists. This group has popularized a substantial number of different behavior change procedures whose proper applications are linked to specific kinds of behavior problems.

Parsimony. It has been traditional for theories to be evaluated at least partially in terms of how parsimoniously they explain their domain. If two theories abstract the same domain and one relies on fewer assumptions than the other, the former is presumably superior if all else is equal. Of course, all else is never equal, and Maddi (1976), therefore, broke with the past by down-playing the relevancy of this particular criterion. He claimed that this criterion can never be effectively applied because theories rarely specify with precision the data they wish to explain, and when theories do offer such specifications there is never complete correspondence between any two. In addition, the data base of personality research is enlarging at an enormous rate. All of this makes it virtually impossible to compare theories on the dimension of parsimony, except in the most general terms.

Accepting Maddi's reasoning still permits one to maintain an efficiency standard which Rotter (1954) described as "minimum overlap" between constructs. In other words, if a theory contains two or more constructs which do not have identifiably different antecedents or consequents, they are probably referring to the same phenomenon and are, therefore, overlapping. It is simply a case of "too many words with the same behavioral referent" (p. 46). If a psychoanalyst were viewing a behavior sample of an obviously highly emotional man, he might possibly describe the person as experiencing "castration threat," or "internalized aggression," or "anxiety." All of these theoretical constructs have similar referents and it is, on an operational level, virtually impossible to distinguish between them. Rotter points out that in such circumstances, the meaning of constructs becomes vague. "Constructs that have the least overlap also provide the least ambiguity, the highest reliability of measurement, and the maximum of communication . . . it is desirable to have a minimum number of terms describing the same event from the same point of view" (p. 47).

Value judgments. No matter what aspect of a psychologist's work we may choose to look at, the question of values becomes relevant. When a researcher selects a particular area to explore he is saying that, for him, the topic is a good or important one. The clinical psychologist has no way of avoiding the influence of his own values as he goes about the business of trying to improve a patient's behavior. What is considered to constitute "improvement"? The goals of psychotherapy are nothing but value judgments on the part of the therapist, arrived at, hopefully, with the knowledge and consent of his client.

Nowhere are theories more susceptible to being value-laden than in their exposition of what they claim constitutes psychological health or illness. The issue may boil down to a very simple question with an unfortunately complex answer: Who needs treatment? Is it the non-conforming person whose behavior lies outside of some "acceptable" range of deviation? It is clear that mere deviation is not necessarily deemed maladaptive; it is the direction which seems to be an important consideration. Thus, extreme honesty, confidence, and social skills are usually thought of as less of a psychological problem than their equally extreme opposites of dishonesty, lack of confidence, and social ineptitude. In addition, many of our most socially productive people statistically deviate far from the societal norms, while large numbers of conforming individuals are not especially productive. This presents a problem because social productivity is frequently cited as a mental health criterion. Another criterion is a subjective sense of happiness. This too does not necessarily correlate with the dimension of conformity, or with productivity either. We could further illustrate the complexities involved but feel that the point has been made. A theorist, in many ways, must take a stand on issues which necessarily are dictated by his personal values. We believe that it is best when a theory is explicit as to where such subjective judgments are being rendered. In this way the user of a theory can avoid being duped into accepting as a theoretically derived law of nature what is really nothing more than the theorist's personal wishes as to what people should and should not be.

Freud has been accused of being most indulgent toward his value judgments as he developed psychoanalytic personality theory. In particular, Fromm (1959) has suggested that Freud's theoretical views mirrored his negative opinions regarding the emancipation of women. "To look at women as castrated men, with a weakly developed Super-Ego (sense of morality), vain and unreliable, all this is only a slightly rationalized version of the patriarchal prejudices of his times" (p. 22).

SUMMARY

In this overview chapter we began by describing the building blocks of theories, constructs. It was noted that constructs are descriptive generalizations which may exhibit varying degress of abstraction. The notions of reductionism, constructive alternativism, and reification were discussed as issues important to the use of theoretical constructs. The problem of arriving at adequate definitions of the constructs we employ was singled out as particularly important.

The importance of personality theory was presented in terms of organizational, delimiting, and generative functions. In order to illustrate some of the characteristics of personality theory, we went on to present a hypothetical mini-theory. Finally, three major criteria for judging the worth of a theory were described. The first two were expert opinion and research validation. The third criterion was a formal analysis of a theory which involved issues of systematization, operationality, levels of construct, maximum inclusiveness, parsimony, and value judgments.

OVERVIEW OF REMAINING CHAPTERS

Having laid the ground work for the student to evaluate critically a theory of personality and the research and assessment procedures associated with it, we will move on to a presentation of representative positions. Included in this sampling are theories reflecting four major orientations: psychodynamic, phenomenological, situationist, and cognitive learning. The intention of Chapters 17 through 21 is not to provide an exhaustive survey of all that has been accomplished in the area of personality theory during the 20th century. Rather, it is to promote an appreciation of the different vantage points from which personality has been successfully, and sometimes not so successfully, explored.

TERMS TO KNOW

CHAPTER 17
Psychoanalytic Theory

The term *psychoanalysis* has multiple referents, including, of course, the theories of Freud. However, despite the best efforts of Freud's proteges to distinguish themselves from their mentor, the theories of Adler and Jung are also routinely called "psychoanalytic." The same can be said of other theoretical positions, including that of Klein, which choose to identify themselves with Freud, but which are rejected by orthodox analysts. Even as psychoanalysis applies to the work of Freud himself, the term means several different things. First, it is the name of an exceedingly well-known psycho-therapeutic technique. Second, psychoanalysis is a research method whereby, within the psycho-therapeutic context, knowledge about the personality organization, functioning, development, and change of the individual patient is discovered. This is done both for the patient's elucidation and as a clinical data base from which to extrapolate general psychological principles applicable to all. Third, psychoanalysis is a theory of personality composed of three systematically-related sub-theories: the theory of instincts deals with motivation; the theory of psychosexuality studies personality and development; and the structural theory is concerned with the organization and processes of the mind. It is this personality theory developed by Freud which will be of primary concern to us.

BASIC ASSUMPTIONS

Freud's personality theory is built upon three basic assumptions, the first two of which are widely accepted as part of the general tenets of psychology; the third is more controversial and is rejected even by some theorists who are identified as psychoanalytic in the strictest sense of the term. All three assumptions relate to Freud's views of the core nature of personality.

Psychic determinism

During the 18th and 19th centuries, natural scientists took the position that events follow an immutable lawfulness and are completely determined. This position is known

283

as "fatalism"; Rychlak referred to it as "hard determinism" (1968, p. 123). It is the orientation which Freud was exposed to as a physiology student. His teachers held that the workings of the human body must be explained by deterministic principles borrowed from chemistry and physics. It is, therefore, consistent that Freud, in his wish to have his ideas on psychology accorded the same status and respectability in the scientific community as the disciplines of chemistry and physics, would adopt a determinist posture. The goal seemed attainable to Freud as a consequence of his discovery of unconscious mental forces. He reasoned that if these psychological forces had biological underpinnings, then it was but a small step to formulate a psychology ultimately rooted in the quantifiable laws of physical science (Jones, 1953). The construct "instinct" which he used to label these psychological forces is a term borrowed from biology.

Despite this acknowledged hard-deterministic preference, Freud was the first to admit that he was unable to predict in advance the behavior of his patients. To quote Rycroft, "All he claimed was that in retrospect it is possible to assert that such-and-such an event or situation in childhood had been the cause of the neurosis; a procedure which is more reminiscent of a historian than of a scientist" (1970, p. 327). Thus, when Freud translated the physical determinism of the natural sciences into the psychic determinism of psychoanalysis, its inexorable, strict regulative connotations were lost. Fatalism was, in practice, replaced by "soft" determinism in which "two lines of action — each itself determined completely — coincide to bring about a single, unpredictable and entirely novel result" (Rychlak, p. 123).

In an additional step away from the notions of causality held by the natural sciences, Freud implicitly accepted *final causation* as one of the aforementioned "lines of action." When an event is explained by final cause it is done so in terms of goals; for example, a tree has limbs so that the leaves will have some place to hang. The legitimacy of final causation was rejected by chemistry and physics, but teleological explanations seemed plausible for psychological phenomena. Thus, for Freud, the purposefulness of the mind, its motives and goals, were as much of a real cause as physical and biological factors (Rychlak, p. 128).

Psychic determinism, as a basic principle of personality theory, was a statement of commitment to the orderliness of personality functioning. As such, it had the effect of making the mind a proper subject for scientific inquiry. In terms of its negative impact, by adopting a deterministic position Freud ran the risk of alienating those for whom determinism implied lack of free will. Probably inadvertently, he avoided this problem by accepting final cause explanations. Rychlak explains this, "People live within a world of intentions and aspirations — beliefs, attitudes, hopes 'for the sake of which' they behave — and therefore they need some way of thinking about that world in precisely these terms" (p. 425). Freud's presentation of psychic determinism fulfilled that need.

Unconscious Motivation

With this second basic assumption Freud is asserting that many of the final psychological causes which instigate personality functioning lie outside of one's awareness. We don't, therefore, always know why we act, think, and feel as we do. The assumption of unconscious motivation emerged from Freud's studies of *post-hypnotic behaviors*. These were induced on the basis of suggestions or directives given to subjects while they were hypnotized but which could not be recollected during the post-hypnotic period. Converging evidence for unconscious psychological processes was provided when subjects were able to recall material while hypnotized that was not available to their consciousness at other times.

Freud interpreted a variety of commonplace actions as being unconsciously motivated. He saw, for example, jokes as being aimed at the satisfaction of unconscious aggressive or sexual impulses whose expressions are otherwise restricted. In particular, smutty jokes are presumably directed at a person of the opposite sex who sexually excites the narrator. The joke itself reveals the narrator's excitement which, in turn, serves to excite the listener. Freud asserted that the embarrassment which may be experienced by the listener is "only a reaction against the excitement and, in a roundabout way, is an admission of it. Smut is thus . . . equated with attempts at seduction" (1960a, p. 97). When enjoyment is experienced by listening to smut in a group of individuals of the same sex, it is because "the original situation, which owing to social inhibitions cannot be realized, is at the same time imagined. A person who laughs at smut that he hears is laughing as though he were the spectator of an act of sexual aggression" (1960a, p. 97).

A second group of behaviors which are related to unconscious motives are so-called "Freudian slips," everyday slips of the tongue, misreadings or misspellings, the temporary forgetting of names, accidents, etc. Freud wrote that "errors" such as these are "mental acts" that have meaning (1952a, p. 64). For instance, the most common slip of the tongue occurs when unconscious motives exist which are opposite to what the individual intends to overtly express: ". . . the President of our Parliament once opened the session with the words 'Gentlemen, I declare a quorum present and herewith declare the session *closed*' " (1952a, p. 38). It is also noted that similar things happen with misprints. One such stubborn error occurred in a newspaper generally critical of the monarchy. In recounting some festivity these words appeared, "Amongst those present was His Highness, the Clown Prince." In an attempted apology and correction the next day, the newspaper wrote: "The sentence should of course have read, 'the Crow-Prince.' " (1952a, p. 35). In a second example of a slip easily "attributable to a devil in the type-setting machine," Freud related a war correspondent's references to an ill-respected general as involving the phrase "this battle scared veteran," later to be corrected to "the bottle-scarred veteran" (1952a, p. 35). In *Psychopathology of Everyday Life* (1951) Freud asserted that "the temporary forgetting of a name is observed as the most frequent faulty action of our mental functions" (p. 30). These lapses presumably occur when "the name itself touches something unpleasant, or when it is brought into connection with other associations which are influenced by such effects" (p. 30).

A third area of psychological functioning in which unconscious motivation is thought to play a great role is that of dreaming. In his most famous work, *The Interpretation of Dreams* (1955a), Freud says that dreams are caused by unconscious motives, impulses, and wishes which, in our waking state, we keep from finding conscious expression by *censoring* them. By definition, whatever is censored is in a state of repression. For a number of reasons, repressed motives are able to exert a greater pressure on the direction of thought processes while we are asleep. First, "there is a relaxation of the censorship; when this happens it becomes possible for what has hitherto been repressed to make a path for itself into consciousness" (1955a, p. 94). Second, because external stimulation is minimal during periods of sleep, sources of internal stimulation, the unconscious motives, become relatively more salient. Third, during the waking state, the psychological energy which gives potency to unconscious motives can be redirected so that it innervates motor activity, thereby weakening the power with which the unconscious motives can press for conscious fulfillment. Such motor activity is, of course, precluded during sleep so that the unconscious motives retain their full energy charge.

All of these factors combine to allow the unconscious motives to gain gratification in a developmentally primitive way; that is, via the conjuring up of a visual perception. Freud has called this nocturnal hallucination or dream a "wish fulfillment" (1952a, p. 34). The word "wish" is here defined as an unconscious motive or impulse and *not* as a conscious desire of the dreamer, although Breger (1967) points out that Freud and other psychoanalysts have been inconsistent in their use of this construct.

Because the censorship is never completely eliminated, the content of the dreams are forced to become somewhat indirect depictions of the unconscious wishes clamoring for gratification. The original unconscious wishes, the *latent* content of dreams, are expressed in a disguised fashion, the *manifest* content of dreams. This is a compromise between one's wishes and what is consciously acceptable or tolerable for the dreamer. The processes which transform the latent into the manifest content Freud calls the "dream work" (1955a, p. 27).

With respect to the nature of latent content, Freud states, "No one who accepts the view that censorship is the chief reason for dream distortion will be surprised to learn that most of the dreams of adults are traced back in analysis to *erotic wishes*" (1955, p. 105). Freud goes on to explain that the sexual ideas can only be represented in the dream by indirect representation, through hints and allusions. "The modes of representation which fulfill these conditions are usually described as 'symbols' of the things they represent" (1955a, p. 107). Thus, the analysis of dreams really involves interpreting them. To give them meaning one must be familiar with the dreamer's symbolic "language" — a language which, to a large degree, we are said to all share. Among the universal symbols are "the Emperor and Empress (or the King and Queen) which stand for parents, rooms represent women and their entrances and exits the openings of the body" (1955a, p. 108). A variety of sharp weapons or stiff objects, such as tree trunks, symbolize male genitals; boxes, ovens, or other containers may represent the uterus. Sexual intercourse may be symbolized by a staircase or the action of climbing stairs.

It must be realized that when Freud interpreted dreams and other expressions of unconscious motivation he did not engage in the scientific enterprise of causal explanation. His activity was restricted to the semantic process of translating dreams and neurotic symptoms so that they made sense. In fact, Rycroft gives Freud credit for the revolutionary semantic discovery that dreams and symptoms are "disguised communications'' (1970, p. 328). It was Freud's preoccupation with scientific respectabil- ity which caused him to formulate these ideas within the framework of causality.

In *The Interpretation of Dreams*, Freud (1955a) advises that the meaning of particularly confusing dream reports may be found if the analyst requests his patient to repeat his dream description. Invariably, revisions occur in the second accounting of the dream. Presumably, these revisions are attempts by the narrator to cover up weak spots in the dream's disguise. By weak spots Freud meant those parts of the first account which failed to adequately disguise the latent content of the dream. The revisions may thus be seen as second-chance attempts to alter the most upsetting elements of the dream into a more acceptable form.

An Empirical Test of Freud's Dream Theory. In order to research these ideas, Fancher and Strahan (1971) conducted an experiment in which 15 female Introduc- tory Psychology students participated. Each subject was asked to relate a recent dream into a tape recorder while their GSR activity was continuously monitored. After a brief pause, during which information was gathered about the date of the dream, the subjects were asked to repeat their dream report into the recording microphone.

First-account dream passages, occurring over the period from three seconds before to three seconds after a GSR onset, were defined as "GSR passages." Equiva- lent "control passages" were obtained by selecting random passages of equal length as each GSR passage but which had not been accompanied by a GSR. For example, Fancher and Strahan recorded one dream account which contained three GSR pas- sages of 20, 23, and 15 words. From that same dream, three control passages of 20, 23, and 15 words were selected by entering the narration at random points. In all, 40 control passages were selected for comparison with the 40 GSR passages.

After GSR and control passages had been identified, Fancher and Strahan deter- mined the fate of each passage in the second accounting. This was accomplished by defining each major idea in every GSR and control passage, and then searching for their corresponding expression in the second account. If a major idea was completely missing in the second version, one omission was scored. Because most passages contained more than one idea, more than one omission could be scored per passage. One passage was, "I was over at the other side of the island pulling my sister along." This was considered to have two major ideas: "I was over at the other side of the island," and, "I was pulling my sister along" (p. 310). The second kind of revision scored was that of substitution. The scoring category was assigned whenever an idea in the first telling was present in the recounting, but in a way which modified its meaning. Substitution is illustrated by the subject who first said, "I was three people away from where I was going to be taken," and then reported, "I was three people away from having my turn" (p. 310).

Two sets of scores were obtained for each subject. One set was from her GSR passages and one from her control passages. The question, of course, was whether there would be a greater number of omissions and substitutions in the recounting of GSR passages than of control passages, as is predicted from Freudian theory. In fact, substitutions were few and occurred with about equal frequency in a subject's control passages (mean = .77) as in her GSR passages (mean = .85). However, contrary to expectations, there were about twice as many omissions from control passages (mean = 2.84) as from GSR passages. Fancher and Strahan, therefore, interpret their findings as inconsistent with Freud's dream theory. They reasoned that Freud would have construed material in the first account which was completely dropped in the second version as a sign that it was especially anxiety-arousing. It was assumed that Freud would have interpreted the omission as the product of the process of repression. "The data, however, indicate that most omissions were *not* examples of repression since most of the omitted ideas originated in the presumably non-arousing and emotionally 'indifferent' control passages" (p. 311).

While this research qualifies as a partial disconfirmation of Freud's dream theory, it also serves to illustrate some of the difficulties in conducting unequivocal dream research. The authors acknowledge the "uncertainties inherent in interpreting GSRs" (p. 311). GSRs cannot be blindly accepted as an adequate operational definition of emotional arousal since their occurrence is not restricted to emotional states. Second, it is obvious that the laboratory setting used by Fancher and Strahan departs markedly from the clinical setting in which Freud conducted his dream analyses. In the context of psychoanalysis, a strong relationship of trust serves as a foundation upon which the patient is encouraged to report dream content which might be especially revealing. Thus the initial dream reports of psychoanalytic patients may be less heavily censored than those of the research subjects with whom no meaningful personal relationship was established, and who were probably not particularly motivated to reveal dream material which would normally be censored. Each subject was merely instructed to "recite an account of her dream into the microphone" (p. 309). Third, because psychoanalytic patients correctly anticipate that their dream reports will be exposed to a searching scrutiny, they may experience more psychological pressure between the first and second tellings to further disguise the dream's latent content. The research subjects had no reason to entertain such expectations. In summary, the research situation of Fancher and Strahan can, at best, be considered a very rough analog of the psychoanalytic setting to which they wished to extrapolate their findings. In effect, the external validity of their investigation is questionable. Unfortunately, this is a criticism which presents itself over and over again as one reviews research literature bearing on the validity of psychoanalytic theory. It is exceedingly difficult to design a well-controlled study that does not operationalize psychoanalytic constructs in a way which seriously distorts their theoretical definitions.

On a somewhat different matter, the purpose of dreams, Freud writes: "It is commonly said that sleep is disturbed by dreams; strangely enough, we are led to a contrary view and must regard dreams as the *guardians of sleep*" (1955a, p. 97). Thus, dreams are thought to preserve sleep by protecting the dreamer from the onslaught of unacceptable unconscious motives. True, they are an expression of the unacceptable motives and, as such, partially gratify them. However, they are supposed to do this in a sufficiently disguised way so that the dreamer remains at rest. Freud acknowledges that "there are dreams which represent a repressed wish but do so with insufficient or no disguise. These . . . are invariably accompanied by anxiety" (1952b, pp. 90-91).

What empirical evidence exists bearing on Freud's hypothesis that dreams serve a sleep-protective function? Before answering this, the reader should understand that it has been known for 20 years that dreams coincide with periods during which the sleeper manifests rapid eye movements (REM). Thus, the timing and duration of dreams is easily monitored today.

There are some research findings which are consistent with the idea that, due to the latent content of dreams, REM periods should be somehow characterized by agitation. For instance, just prior to REM periods there is typically an increase in body movements which is suggestive of disturbance. Also, during REM, EEGs become similar to those obtained during wakefulness; the respiration rate increases and becomes irregular, and cardiovascular changes occur which bring about higher systolic blood pressure and a rapid, irregular pulse. However, on balance, enough evidence exists so that "the view of dream function as discharging . . . impulses in compromise form should be abandoned," according to Breger (1967, pp. 18-19). Similarly, Altshuler concludes that "if the dream's purpose is to preserve sleep it fails miserably, since more than half of all REM periods are interrupted by brief periods of wakefulness" (1966, p. 236). Altshuler also points out that the terrifying nightmares of childhood and the many frightened awakenings of adults may occur during non-REM periods. One might reasonably ask where the dream was when it was needed if its function is sleep preservation. Finally, Altshuler finds it unreasonable to accept the notion that dreams arise in response to unsettling unconscious motives; REM periods show a "regular appearance on a clock-bound schedule of ninety minutes" (p. 230). He prefers to assume that unconsciously-provoked stresses are not confined to REM periods but may occur throughout the night, as they do throughout the day; it is just that dreams permit them to be represented in a mode which is most accessible to clinical scrutiny.

Psychic energy

Freud's third basic assumption has to do with the source of power behind all mental functioning, *psychic energy*. This form of energy was seen as one form which energy in the universe might take, in addition to electrical energy, thermal energy, mechanical energy, etc. At a more specific level, Freud saw the possibility of psychic and biological energy being mutual transformations of each other. Their interdependence can be illustrated by recalling the dearth of psychological energy available for such mental functions as creative thought and caring for others when one is utilizing great amounts of biological energy to fight disease. Alternatively, Hendrick (1958) reports that individuals whose psychological processes are extremely active, such as those caught in the emotional webs of love or hate, commonly complain of physical fatigue.

While these ideas seem to smack of reductionism, Freud did not believe that mental processes were equivalent to physical processes, that a thought could be quantified in terms of amperes, watts, or volts. Once the transformation into psychic energy occurs, the phenomenon is mental and can be understood as nothing other than mental. The mechanism for this transormation is left unspecified, however. Freud can be faulted for borrowing the term ''energy'' from physics to describe psychological events. Intermixing constructs emerging from widely different perspectives and levels of abstraction, in this case the physical and the psychological, probably adds nothing except, perhaps, some semantic confusion.

THEORY OF INSTINCTS

The three assumptions of psychic determinism, unconscious motivation, and psychic energy combine to form the underpinnings of the first of Freud's three sub-theories of personality — the *theory of instincts*.

We are again presented with a semantic problem because instinct in Freud's theory, while referring to innate functioning, does not imply what we usually mean by the term. Traditionally, instinct suggests a biologically built-in, fixed-action pattern in response to specific external stimuli. The referents for instincts are the stereotypic behaviors which many species of animal manifest under well-programmed circumstances, such as a bird's nesting behavior. In psychoanalytic language an instinct is a behavioral initiator which imparts directionality to personality functioning but whose output is highly-modifiable by complex environmental influences. Several writers have, therefore, suggested that the German word used by Freud, *trieb,* would have been better translated as drive instead of instinct.

Characteristics of Instincts

A Freudian instinct may be theoretically defined as a parcel or quantum of psychic energy which arises from ''a state of excitation in the body'' (1965, p. 97). This excitation is known as the *source* of an instinct. Freud admits that he is ignorant regarding the specific nature of instinctual sources, but speculates that it is probably some sort of chemical or mechanical process (1957, p. 74) which may be thought of as a *need*. In other words, instincts are the psychological representations of a somatic need. We should be clear in pointing out that Freud is *not* simply saying that the same phenomenon can be abstracted from both a biological (need) and a psychological (instinct) perspective. Instead he is being reductionistic; he sees the biological as causing the psychological event; the source is ''that somatic process . . . from which there results a stimulus represented in mental life by an instinct'' (1957, p. 74).

Because the source of instincts is not specified, instinct, as a motivational construct, is less operational than other constructs in psychology intended to explain similar phenomena. For instance, Clark Hull's (1943) construct of *drive* is tied to observable events on both the antecedent and consequent side. A sex drive is defined on the antecedent side in terms of hours or days of sex deprivation; on the consequent side, a Hullian sex drive is observable in the form of search and copulation behavior. In contrast to this, Freudian instincts are known only by their consequences. The hypothesized somatic needs understood to be the source of instincts are not related to measurable antecedents. Thus, there is no way to determine the presence or strength of an instinct except after the fact. If a person is observed to act in a sexual way, that behavior may be assumed to be a reflection of an underlying sex instinct. However, since the sex instinct is not identifiable in any way other than through the behavior it purports to explain, we are left with a highly inferential construct which has no predictive utility.

In addition to the source of an instinct, three other characteristics were identified by Freud. First, every instinct varies in the amount of psychic energy it possesses. The greater its charge, the more it will be able to command the direction of psychological processes and influence behavior. Freud called this quantitative aspect the *impetus*. "By the impetus of an instinct we understand its motor element, the amount of force or the measure of the demand upon energy which it represents" (1957, p. 73).

It is, of course, not possible to measure directly the amount of psychic energy at the disposal of any given instinct. At best, the trained clinician can make estimates about the relative distribution of instinctual energy over the entire personality. Thus, a patient may be characterized as having more of one instinct in comparison to another; this judgment is based on the psychoanalyst's understanding of the patient's thought processes and behaviors. There is, in addition, a supposition of a fixed amount of psychic energy available to the personality. Hendrick (1958) suggests that a dramatic decline in the energy in one area probably means that the energy has been withdrawn from that area of personality functioning and has a new focus.

The third characteristic of Freudian instinct is its invariable *aim* which is "in every instance satisfaction, which can only be obtained by abolishing the condition of stimulation in the source of the instinct" (1957, p. 74). Thus, Freud equates satisfaction with the reduction in the somatic tension, or need, which gives rise to the instinct. For example, a need for nourishment provokes instinctual mentation having to do with obtaining food and eating. The mental processes involved, including perception, recollection, and planning, are all geared toward the ultimate reduction of the somatic need. It is, therefore, the case that, while the final instinctual aim is satisfaction, "an instinct may be found to have various nearer or intermediate aims" (1957, p. 74). The searching for and obtaining of food in the above example illustrates intermediate aims which necessarily come prior to actual satisfaction.

Because satisfaction is always the final instinctual aim, the theoretical law governing instinctual processes is called the *pleasure principle*. In describing this principle, Freud writes:

> It seems that our entire psychical activity is bent upon *procuring pleasure* and *avoiding pain* . . . pleasure is *in some way* connected with lessening, lowering, or extinguishing the amount of stimulation present in the mental apparatus; and pain involves a heightening of the latter. (1952a, p. 365)

The final feature of an instinct is its *object:*, "that in or through which it can achieve its aim" (1957, p. 74). The object of instinctual activity aimed at somatic tension associated with nourishment is food. Thus, the object is not inherently connected to an instinct but becomes involved because of its unique capacity to fulfill the instinctual aim. Obviously, a given instinct may attain satisfaction through commerce with a wide variety of potential objects; a slice of pizza can prove to be as satisfying as a peanut butter sandwich. Even when the object of an instinct is reasonably stable, such as a heterosexual partner, it still may undergo changes over the course of life. In summary, the object "is the most variable thing about an instinct" (1957, p. 74). This variability allows for highly-adaptive and socially-appropriate functioning, in that the person's efforts to attain satisfaction can be responsive to the nature of the current situation.

When a person thinks about or relates to the object of an instinct, there is said to be an investment of psychic energy in that object. The importance or centrality to personality functioning of the object is directly related to the amount of psychic energy channeled in its direction. Freud defines the amount of energy with which an idea regarding an object is charged as its *cathexis;* and the person is said to "cathect " the object. Of course, the object per se is not cathected; energy is not extended from the person into an external agent. More precisely, energy is invested in the idea of an object.

Different Kinds of Instincts

On the question of how many instincts exist, Freud accepted terminology in which almost every different kind of behavior or preoccupation is said to be caused by an instinct in its own name. "No objection can be made to anyone's employing the concept of an instinct of play or of destruction, or that of a social instinct, when the subject demands it and the limitations of psychological analysis allow of it" (1957, p. 75). He, nevertheless, was also moved to categorize specific instincts into broad classes which are based upon the *primal* instincts from which they derive. Freud originally proposed two groups of primal instincts, the *self-preservation,* or ego, instincts and the *sexual* instincts; these correspond to the fact that all living things act both in terms of self and species survival.

Sexual instincts come to mental representation through expenditure of that psychic energy called *libido.* The ontogeny of the sexual instincts is at the core of Freud's theory of personality development. The ego instincts are experienced in the mind as, for example, a desire to eat or a will to power. Like all instincts, they act in accordance with the aim of gaining pleasure. However, ego instincts are prone to take reality into account as they instigate behavior. They are, therefore, said to be governed by the *reality principle;* this is the capacity to renounce immediate pleasure temporarily in order to guarantee future pleasure or pain avoidance. The reality principle is not then opposed to the pleasure principle, but may be seen as a modification of it which is acquired with experience and exercises a greater degree of maturity. To delay gratification until the most appropriate time is the hallmark of pleasure-seeking behavior modified by reality considerations.

Freud later altered the dichotomous instinct theory, subsuming both sex and ego instincts under the name *Eros.* The energy libido was now seen as serving all Eros functions. Freud made this change when he decided, from his clinical experience, that ego instincts are only a special case of libido cathexis in which energy is invested in the self rather than in external objects. When the self is the object of libido, a condition of *narcissism* exists. This term is derived from the Greek hero Narcissus who, according to legend, fell in love with himself.

A second revision in Freud's instinct theory involved the introduction of *Thanatos,* the name given to destructive motives bent on undoing the organization and preservation brought about by Eros. Freud arrived at Thanatos by first recognizing that all instincts show evidence of a compulsion to return to an earlier state of quiescence; this penchant is called the *repetition compulsion.* In fact, Freud turned to biology to gather evidence for his thesis, drawing an analogy between the psychological instincts of man and the "fixed action pattern" instincts so prominent in animals.

> The spawning migrations of fishes, the migratory flights of birds, and possibly all that we describe as manifestations of instinct [Instinkt] in animals, take place under the orders of a compulsion to repeat, which expresses the *conservative nature* of the instincts [Triebe]. (1965, p. 106)

In the development of his position, Freud then rhetorically asks, "But how can this conservative characteristic of instincts help us to understand our self-destructiveness? What earlier state of things does an instinct such as this want to restore?" (1955a, p. 107). His answer is that "life once proceeded out of inorganic matter . . . an instinct must have arisen to do away with life once more and to reestablish the inorganic state" (p. 107). It is for this reason that Thanatos is also known as the *death instinct.*

Deriving from the death instinct are all destructive ideas and behaviors which are theorized to be originally aimed at the self but which may be redirected outward. The energy for hostility and aggression is thereby explained. During the course of life the process may again be reversed causing the individual to commit suicide or to entertain suicidal ideas, to experience extreme melancholia, or to be obsessed with self-deprecating thoughts. It is not uncommon for such a reversal to be precipitated by a loved one's rejection. The desire for retaliation cannot be fulfilled because, consciously or unconsciously, such action is prohibited. The destructive impulses are, therefore, again turned inward (Hendrick, 1958).

Of all Freud's theorizing, that having to do with the death instinct was least well-received. On the one hand, the death instinct was seen as inconsistent with the other instincts; Hendrick calls it, "A failure of life processes rather than a fulfillment of innate biologic tendencies" (1958, p. 127). The second counter argument rested on a preference for seeing destructive behavior as a reaction to frustrated pleasure; the thwarted lover is a good example. The Freudians, in defense, still insisted that the energy source for such frustration-produced aggression is left unexplained unless a death instinct is postulated.

The two major instinctual currents, Eros and Thanatos, are theorized to have distinctly different biological sources. However, in the course of personality development, psychoanalysis sees evidence of a fusion of the two, so that both are gratified by common personality patterns. This fusion is most prominently illustrated in two kinds of phantasy and behavior patterns: *sadism,* in which maximal erotic pleasure is contingent upon the infliction of physical pain and *masochism,* in which the receipt of pain is a prerequisite for sexual gratification. The merging of Eros and Thanatos is not at all confined to these phenomena. "Every instinctual impulse that we can examine consists of similar fusions or alloys of the two classes of instinct. These fusions, of course, would be in the most varied ratios" (1955a, pp. 104-105). Even eating can, therefore, be understood as involving destructive activity for the purpose of growth and sustenance. We are left with the idea that, in general, our personality functioning is *overdetermined;* it is always the product of a confluence of instinctual forces.

THEORY OF PSYCHOSEXUAL DEVELOPMENT

In Freud's time it was commonly believed that human sexuality involved all of the thoughts, feelings, and actions associated with bringing one's genitals into contact with those of an opposite sex member. Sexual appetite was presumed to be first aroused at puberty. In contrast to this, Freud came to believe that people are sexual at a much earlier age. For instance, Freud was struck by the interest which even very young children have in their genitals, and by the apparent pleasure they derive from them. He finally concluded that sexuality in a general sense, as distinct from that which only involves the genitals, begins soon after birth. By sexuality "in a general sense," Freud meant *pleasure* experienced through the use and manipulation of various body sites, called *erotogenic zones.* These zones include the mouth and anus, in addition to the genitals.

The second of Freud's three subtheories of personality, his *theory of psychosexual development,* focuses upon the shifting locus of erotogenic zones with development. The capacity of a zone to become prominent as a seat of pleasure, and the order with which it gains prominence, is said to be biologically predetermined and the same for all. What is variable is the length of time over which a zone is active and the amount of temporal overlap exhibited as one zone fades into relative obscurity while the next is gaining salience. So-called "psychosexual stages" are named for that erotogenic zone which is most active at the time. How quickly and completely a stage is passed through is determined by the quality of interaction between the child and his environment. This, in turn, greatly affects the character of the adult personality.

Oral stage

Even the newborn engage in activity for no other reason than the pleasure of it. Specifically, sucking behavior is a response which at first appears in the process of obtaining nourishment but which the infant soon enjoys independently of food intake. One has only to observe the persistence with which infants suck their fingers to find evidence for this. Thus, the mouth is the first erotogenic zone to gain prominence and the pleasure derived from its exercise is called sexual. To phrase it differently, it is the mouth which provides the first vehicle through which the sexual instinct can be expressed via the utilization, or expenditure, of Libido.

During this oral stage then, the mother's breast is thought to gratify the infant's two paramount needs, nourishment and sexual pleasure. In fact, Freud believed that "the point of departure from which the whole sexual life develops, the unattainable prototype of every later sexual satisfaction . . ." (1952b, p. 323) is sucking at the mother's breast. "As it [the infant] sinks asleep at the breast, utterly satisfied, it bears a look of perfect content which will come back again later in life after the experience of sexual orgasm" (1952b, p. 322).

Freud subdivided this first psychosexual stage into two sub-stages, each involving a different relationship between the child and its first love object — the breast. During the first *oral incorporative* sub-stage there exists no ambivalence toward the breast. Later in the first year of life, biting behavior testifies to the emergence of ambivalence toward the mother. This *oral sadistic* sub-stage, as we will see, is only the beginning expression of sadistic trends which will peak in the second psychosexual stage, the *anal* stage.

Fixation and regression. In Freud's earliest presentations he emphasized the manner in which each stage passed away before the next arrived. However, in *New Introductory Lectures* (1965) he wrote that "much of each earlier stage persists alongside of and behind the later configurations [stages] and obtains a permanent representation in the libidinal economy and character of the subject" (p. 100). The person, therefore, persists in seeking sexual satisfactions of a certain kind past the point in time when it is maturationally appropriate from a psychosexual perspective. This situation Freud calls *fixation*. Libido fixations may be partial, even trivial, extensive, or numerous; it is not a question of "all or none." That is to say, we are all probably fixated at the oral incorporative and, for that matter, at every other psychosexual stage to at least a minimal degree.

The construct of fixation bears a close relationship to Freud's construct of *regression,* which is "a reversion from a higher to a lower stage of development" (1952b, p. 351). When there is psychosexual regression, the libido expresses itself in a way characteristic of a more primitive stage; there is a resurgence of the first erotogenic zones and "a return to the first objects invested with libido" (p. 350). Regression occurs when the sexual impulse at a relatively mature level "meets with powerful external obstacles, which thus prevent it from attaining the goal of satisfaction" (p. 350). To what point does the libido regress? To the point(s) of earlier fixations. The stronger the fixations, the less persistent the mature expression of libido will be before it reverts. Freud illustrates these principles by drawing an analogy between the flow toward sexual maturity and the advance of migrating people who leave some of their numbers at stopping places along the way. "The foremost will naturally fall back upon these positions . . . when they meet with an enemy too strong for them. And again, the more of their number they leave behind in their progress, the sooner they will be in danger of defeat" (1952b, p. 350).

Without getting overly involved in Freud's theories of psychopathology, it is sufficient to say that libidinal fixation, with its potential for contributing to later regressions, is at the core of his understanding of neurosis. This being the case, it is obviously crucial to gain an awareness of what Freud professed to be the antecedents of fixation. The possibility of hereditary factors are entertained, but not dwelled upon because of the impossibility of exploring constitutional precursors. It is simply assumed that people differ in the degree to which their erotogenic zones are charged with libido. This quantitative issue, though understandably neglected, interacts in important ways with the following five experiential antecedents. The predictive power of these factors, the first four of which are otherwise potentially operationalizeable, is, therefore, attenuated because of the existence in the equation of an unknown constitutional quantity.

Excessive libidinal gratification can lead to fixation. It is as if the child is saying, "Things are so great I don't want to go on." When later libidinal frustrations are met, the individual is only too prepared to fall back and express himself in a manner reminiscent of the "good times."

Excessive frustration or undergratification at a psychosexual level can also lead to fixation. Here, in effect, the child is saying, "I'm not going on until I gain satisfaction." If the instinctual impulses which are frustrated become repressed, they remain behind in the unconscious while the rest of the personality matures. Unfortunately, the unconscious remains of frustrated sexual impulses continue to exert influence, continue to clamor for their infantile sorts of gratification, and continue to beckon the maturing personality back to their level when later frustrations are encountered.

Inconsistent gratification, in which both over and under gratifications are experienced, is theoretically a common precursor to fixation. Early overindulgence may, for instance, render the personality less able to tolerate later deprivations, even though these are of mild nature.

Abrupt withdrawal of gratification is clearly an especially potent fixating experience. The child who has been indulged at the breast may be considerably unsettled when the mother, carefully following the developmental schedule in a child care manual, decides that weaning will take place on the 180th day of life.

Instinctual satisfactions instrumental in anxiety reduction are viewed as the most common roots of fixations. A child becomes especially reluctant to move away from a libidinal expression if that expression serves both to satisfy the sexual instinct and to reduce anxiety. Fenichel (1945) believes that the fearful child, finding fulfillment of drive and security from upset at the mother's breast, is a high risk for fixation.

In summary, fixation is the necessary but not sufficient condition for regression. The usefulness of fixation as a scientific construct is weakened by the fact that identification of its antecedents is thwarted by their interaction with a non-operational quantity, the cathexis attached to an erotogenic zone. Without any means of assessing this quantity, there is no way to determine what is over- and what is undergratification; indulgence for one child with low libidinal demands may be deprivation for another.

Matters are not helped by Freud's inclusion on his list of fixation antecedents of almost all parent-child interaction patterns: overgratification, undergratification, inconsistent gratification, and abrupt withdrawal of gratification. By so oversystematizing the construct "fixation" on the antecedent side, one can go back into the history of *any* person and find evidence consistent with later fixation and/or regression.

The predictive utility of fixation is weakened on the consequent side because, here too, it is linked to so many possibilities. All of us, in a variety of ways, can be accused of manifesting evidence of fixations at the oral stage. The pleasure we derive from drinking, smoking, even talking, can be understood as products of oral fixation. In the derogatory remarks and "biting wit" of some stand-up comics we can see infantile oral sadism theoretically reflected. On the other hand, where antecedents of fixation are discovered but adult preoccupations derivative of that stage are not manifest, the psychoanalyst may invoke additional constructs, such as repression, to maintain the explanatory adequacy of his theory.

Oral Character. Personalities in which substantial residues of the oral stage persist are said to have an *oral character.* In these individuals the broad outlines of infantile oral satisfaction-seeking are prototypes of their current ways of relating to and experiencing the world. According to Fenichel,

> If a person remains fixated to the world of oral wishes, he will, in his general behavior, present a disinclination to take care of himself, and require others to look after him . . . this demand for care may be expressed through extreme passivity or through a highly active oral sadistic behavior . . . Persons of this [latter] type request and demand a great deal (1945, p. 489).

Fromm has described the oral character as having a "receptive orientation" (1947, p. 62); the person feels that anything good must come from others. Their interpersonal relations are, therefore, overshadowed by a dependency upon others for love, tangible goods, advice, etc. Oral personalities are consequently very sensitive to rejection or withdrawal by others. They try to guard against such eventualities by being ingratiating and overly willing to agree.

The validity of some of these hypothesized oral personality characteristics was tested in a series of studies done by Blum and Miller (1952). The first step in their research program was to identify oral characters. Their criterion measure of orality was the manifestation of non-purposive mouth movements, such as thumb sucking, lip licking, tongue rolling, and bubbling by a class of 18 third grade boys and girls. A time-sampling procedure was employed in which the children's oral activity was observed by trained personnel. This resulted in the ranking of the 18 subjects on the personality dimension of orality.

Drawing upon the psychoanalytic literature, Blum and Miller hypothesized that orality should be associated with the consumption of food beyond the dictates of simple hunger and an expression of unusual interest in food consumption. In order to gain data bearing on the first hypothesis they arranged for the children to have access to an unlimited supply of one ounce cups of ice cream soon after they had taken their fill at lunch. This occurred for 40 minutes during an arts and crafts period, and was repeated daily for three weeks. Blum and Miller were impressed with the range of ice cream consumption for individual children; on any given day this varied from zero to 39 cups. With respect to the second hypothesis, the children's teacher and five teaching assistants were asked to nominate those who appeared most impatient to eat at lunch time, or those for whom eating appeared to be particularly important. Both ice cream consumption and teacher nominations were correlated with the children's orality ranking. The results of these statistical analyses revealed that orality was, as predicted, correlated positively with both ice cream consumption ($r = .52$; $p < .05$) and eagerness at lunch time ($r = .51$; $p < .05$).

The one other hypothesis for which particularly strong support was found had to do with social isolation. Specifically, it was predicted that strongly oral children would be least well-liked by peers due to their characteristic passivity, excessive demand for attention, and hostility in the face of ungratified demands. Using a sociometric format in which the children themselves nominated their most and least well-liked classroom peers, orality ranking was found to correlate highly ($r = +.68$; $p < .01$) with rejection as measured by the sociometric.

Of the eight other psychoanalytic hypotheses tested, Blum and Miller report that three received "fair" and three "equivocal" support. They express the belief that a main contribution of their effort lay not so much in the evidence marshalled in support of psychoanalysis but in their demonstration that psychoanalytically derived hypotheses may be tested using conventional psychological research strategies such as correlational designs.

Anal stage

While anal pleasure is probably present from birth, usually during the second year libido associated with anal functions becomes most prominent and the developing child embarks upon the anal psychosexual stage. Pleasure during this period is intensely derived from the stimulation accorded the rectal membrane via the function of retention and from the tension reduction experienced during the process of excretion. This stage is also known as the *anal sadistic* because retention and excretion may have destructive overtones. That is, during the anal stage the death instinct becomes intimately involved with the expression of anal sexuality. Fenichel sees the act of "pinching off" the feces as a sadistic act of destruction (p. 66). Also, in the course of the interpersonal struggles surrounding toilet training, the child may use retention and expulsion as vehicles for expressing hostility toward the parents who are the restricting agents of socialization. Children are capable of exerting great power and control over others through a refusal to eliminate at an opportune juncture or, more often, by their excretory acts at an inopportune moment. Retention and expulsion are thus weapons deployed on a battleground containing, on the one hand, the wish to defecate or retain, instinctual cathexes, and, on the other, parental discipline and authority.

Anal Character. Interference with anal erotic gratification, most typically the product of early and severe toilet-training practices, sets the stage for fixation and the subsequent development of an *anal character*. Fenichel suggests that anally-oriented traits may be seen as a reaction for which the infantile responses of expulsion and retention are prototypic. The three main anal trends are listed as orderliness, frugality, and obstinacy.

> Frugality is a continuation of the anal habit of retention . . . Orderliness is an elaboration of the obedience to, obstinacy of the rebellion against the environmental requirements covering the regulation of excretory function . . . obstinacy may become so extreme that the person in question is compelled always to do the exact opposite of what is required of him (1945, p. 278).

The insightful reader will by now realize that in many respects the behavioral trends expected from an oral and an anal character are quite opposite when they are faced with certain social situations. For example, orality is predictive of acquiescence in the face of social pressure, while anality is predictive of a resistance. As a first step in the testing of these hypotheses, Tribich and Messer (1974) administered the Blacky pictures, designed by Blum (1950), to 107 male Introductory Psychology students. The Blacky pictures constitute a theoretically-derived projective instrument containing 12 illustrations depicting the adventures of Blacky, a dog, and Blacky's Mama, Papa, and sibling. Each drawing is designed to elicit stories relevant to a stage of psychosexual development. For example, oral sadism is made salient by the second picture in which Blacky is shaking Mama's collar in his teeth. The subjects are asked to respond to each drawing with a statement of what is happening and why. Subjects also complete multiple-choice questions about the pictures and indicate which of the pictures are most and least well-liked. These data are integrated by following complex and subtle scoring rules. If done properly, information is allegedly obtained about conflicts and preoccupations relevant to the stages of psychosexuality and to the most common instinctual objects of these stages.

In their research, Tribich and Messer chose to administer only the first three Blacky pictures because these are specifically intended to tap orality and anality. Through this procedure they were able to identify 20 oral dependents; these subjects were defined by their high oral dependency and low anal expulsive scores. Twenty anal expulsives were selected on the basis of their high anal expulsive score coupled with a low oral dependency score.

From psychoanalytic theory it was predicted that the oral dependent group would express subjective judgments which conformed more to those of another person than would the anal expulsives. Subjective judgments were obtained by having each subject experience the *autokinetic phenomenon* in the presence of a confederate of the researcher, who was falsely introduced as another undergraduate subject. The autokinetic phenomenon refers to the apparent movement of a stationary point of light when seen against a totally dark background. Tribich and Messer employed reasonably complex equipment to elicit the autokinetic phenomenon; the reader may experience it by viewing the first star to appear on a clear and moonless night. Under these naturally-occurring conditions the star, for practical purposes stationary in the sky, may at first be mistaken for a rapidly moving airplane light or space satellite. Each subject was exposed to a series of 12 autokinetic trials, each lasting for 30 seconds. They were led to believe that the pin point of light would actually move and were requested to estimate, in inches, the distance traveled over the 30 second span. On half of the trials the real subject was the first to express a judgment; on the remaining six trials, the confederate ventured a prearranged "guess" ranging from one to 23 inches.

This study incorporated two dependent measures. The first was the discrepancy between a subject's guess and that of the confederate, when the confederate was first to express an opinion. The second dependent measure was the average discrepancy between a subject's guesses on those trials where he went first, his "base level" of responding, and his guesses on those trials when he responded after the confederate. With respect to the first measure, it was found that, on the average, the responses of oral dependents were about five inches closer to those of the confederate than were those of anal expulsives. This difference was statistically significant at the $p < .01$ level. Thus, as anticipated, in a subjective situation, the oral subjects were much more prone than anally-oriented subjects to follow the lead of the confederate. The oppositional tendencies of the anal expulsives were particularly highlighted by the analysis of the second dependent measure. Here, it was found that on trials in which subjects were second to respond, orals tended to shift their guesses away from their own base level in a direction which was more consistent with that of the confederate. For example, an oral subject with a base level of 10 inches might guess 12 inches after hearing the confederate guess 13 inches. In contrast to this, anally-oriented subjects tended to shift their guesses from their base level in a direction opposite to that of the confederate. Thus, if an anal subject's base level was 10 inches, he might typically respond 8 inches after hearing the confederate's guess of 13 inches. This relationship between character type and movement from base level was highly reliable ($p < .001$).

Tribich and Messer conclude that their results serve to establish both the validity of certain psychoanalytic notions about the personality correlates of anality and orality, *and* the construct validity of the Blacky pictures as a vehicle for assessing psychosexuality.

In addition to orderliness, frugality, and obstinacy, other personality trends have been associated with the anal character. For example, a continued preoccupation with rules, first experienced during toilet-training, may cause a person to be intolerant of flexibility in himself and others. Such a person rigidly demands that things be done in the correct or proper way, even to the neglect of legitimate extenuating circumstances. Sometimes pleasure derived from retention is particularly valued in infancy, and the feces themselves become valuable possessions with which one only very reluctantly parts. This may then become the prototype of later reluctance to give up valued possessions; the person may manifest great stinginess or be overconcerned with economy. Other derivatives of infantile erotic pleasure obtained through retention are thought to be interests in collecting things, such as stamps or other valuables.

Phallic stage

Freud was quick to cite evidence consistent with the view that soon after birth the genitals function as an erogenous zone. He especially pointed to genital masturbation by infants. However, by the third or fourth year of life almost all erotic satisfaction is gained via this zone and the child is said to be in the *phallic stage*, so-called because of the psychological significance of the penis to both boys and girls at this time. Also common to all pre-phallic children is the fact that more libido is invested in representations of the mother than any other object, except for the child's own body. This is consistent with the mother's long-standing role of being instrumental in providing satisfactions at earlier psychosexual stages, those of nourishment and oral erotic pleasure via her breast. The mother is, therefore, seen as being the *primary love object*. From this point of departure, Freud describes somewhat different psychological events occurring in boys and girls.

Male phallic stage. One relatively early consequence of the main locus of psychosexuality shifting to the penis is that expectations for gratification from the mother come to strongly involve that organ. This may be based upon nothing other than the mother having been previously implicated in other sorts of infantile erotic gratifications. In addition, the child's growing intellectual sophistication may lead him to anticipate females as a source of pleasure. Perhaps this realization emerges from observing the quality of the relationship between his own mother and father. At first, such observations may only serve to facilitate the boy's growing admiration for and identification with his father, the wish to be like daddy and to do what daddy does, vis a vis mommy.

Oedipus Complex. This comfortable positive relationship toward both parents is doomed because of the great intensification of sexual wishes involving the mother. Ultimately, the father is perceived to be an obstacle in the way of phallic gratification. ''The identification with the father then takes on a hostile coloring and changes into a wish to get rid of the father in order to take his place with the mother'' (Freud, 1957, p. 221). This psychological state, in which there exists, side by side, a sexual yearning for unrivaled possesson of the mother and jealous hostility for the father, is known as the *Oedipus complex*. It is named after the mythological Greek king who was destined to slay his father and wed his mother.

With respect to the behavioral referents of the Oedipus complex, Freud writes:

> When the little boy shows the most open sexual curiosity about his mother, wants to sleep with her at night, insists on being in the room while she is dressing, or even attempts physical acts of seduction, as the mother so often observes and laughingly relates, the erotic nature of this attachment to her is established without a doubt. (1952b, p. 342)

In addition, Freud describes the little boy as ''restive'' when the father is seen to caress the mother and manifests satisfaction when the former is away (1952b, p. 341).

As it happens, the Oedipus complex turns out to be an exceedingly unpleasant experience for several reasons. First, the young boy's feelings toward his father are best labeled as ambivalent — not straight-forwardly hostile. This is because in most instances the father is, in reality, not such a bad person and the boy will at times even "display great affection for the father" (1952b, p. 341). Thus the boy's hostile posture becomes a source of conflict because its perpetuation may provoke a loss of love. However, much more important than this is the fear of retaliation from the father for the harboring of hateful and destructive passions. The form of this feared retaliation is that of castration, and it is *castration anxiety* which is mainly instrumental in bringing to a close this, the most psychologically tumultuous stage of development.

Castration is seen as a logical retaliatory act in that it is directed at "his own little member," the offending organ with which he "has phantasies of carrying out some sort of activity . . . in relation to his mother" (1949, p. 12). While the origins of castration anxiety may lie in parental prohibitions and other comments expressed upon discovering his own masturbatory activities, the "horror" of it all is made unbearably salient when the boy discovers that the world is peopled by great numbers of apparently already castrated individuals — girls!

Resolution of Oedipus Complex. While there are other factors operating as well, for example, the mother's rejection of the boy's phantasized sexual fulfillment with her, it is predominantly because of the traumatic threat of castration that the boy passes beyond the Oedipus complex and closes the phallic stage. Two psychological processes are involved in doing this. The first is that of repression. The incestuous wishes for the mother and the destructive intentions directed at the father are rendered unconscious, although not necessarily inactive. Dreams and artistic creations of normal adults and maladaptive behavior patterns of neurotics show that these wishes and intentions are present in the unconscious. Like all unconscious instincts, the Oedipal wishes retain their capacity to channelize adult psychological processes indirectly. The amount of energy invested in these repressed Oedipal strivings and the degree of influence they exert depend upon how much fixation has taken place. In the normal adult, to use Freud's own metaphor, few of the "migratory" forces are left behind at the phallic "stopping place" along the way to psychosexual maturity. Those persons who leave great numbers of forces behind, or who "retreat" back to the phallic stopping place because of later duress, will show evidence of behavior for which the Oedipal relationships were prototypic. The adult may exhibit a defiant or hostile attitude toward all male authority figures or, once true genital heterosexual encounters become possible, may be predisposed to seek out a female who is reminiscent of the mother. There is then, from the psychoanalytic perspective, more than a germ of truth to the song which idolizes the prospect of marrying someone "like dear old mom." Unfortunately the adult realization of this dream may be tainted by intense anxiety, a reflection of yet active, but unconscious, castration fears.

The second psychological process involved in a successful resolution of the Oedipus complex is that of desiring to become like the father, or *identifying* with him. It is as if the boy were adopting an "if you can't lick 'em, join 'em" philosophy.

Identification as a part solution to the Oedipus complex must be understood as a regression to oral modes of dealing with life problems. When the boy infuses his own personality with representations of the father he is *incorporating* within himself a former adversary. The act of incorporation at this time is not psychologically different from early infantile oral incorporative actions in that both have highly destructive overtones. What is taken in, consumed, and made part of the self is also what is destroyed. Because of its positive and negative overtones, it would seem that incorporation is an ideal solution to a troublesome relationship problem which was itself filled with ambivalence.

Oedipal complications. Freud calls what we have described above a "simple positive Oedipus complex in the boy" (1957, p. 219). It is thought to begin in the third year of life and to last for two or more years. In most instances, careful analysis will reveal that in addition to ambivalence toward the father and an affectionate object-relation toward the mother, the boy adopts a feminine orientation in his relationship with his father and an associated jealousy toward his mother. Thus, the complex becomes *twofold*, with both positive and negative attitudes felt toward each parent. In part this is due to the boy becoming jealously angry at his mother for not fulfilling his fantasies of sexually possessing her. He reacts by wishing her away and becoming her replacement as the father's love object. This unfortunately does nothing to alleviate castration anxiety once the boy becomes cognizant of the implication of womanhood — no penis! The twofold Oedipus complex, however, is more importantly attributed to bisexuality which Freud sees inherent in all children. ". . . the relative strength of the masculine and feminine sexual dispositions is what determines whether the outcome of the Oedipus situation shall be an identification with the father or with the mother" (1957, p. 220).

If a boy has an unusually strong feminine constitution, his Oedipus complex might be characterized by a prepotency of the wish to replace mother. The resultant strong identification with the mother will, of course, yield a personality with obvious feminine overtones. In effect, the wish to *have* the mother as an instinctual object is over-shadowed by a wish to *be* mother. In extreme cases, the grown man looks for sexual objects "on which he can bestow such love and care as he has experienced from his mother" (Freud, 1957, p. 186); homosexual relationships are pursued in which the individual plays out a maternal role.

Whether such an outcome will emerge probably depends upon the degree to which it is favored by environmental events during the phallic stage. In fact, psychoanalysts are, in Brenner's words, "as a rule ignorant of constitutional factors . . . [they] tend therefore to lose sight of their possible importance as compared to the environmental factors, which are usually more obvious and hence more impressive" (1957, pp. 123-124).

Fenichel (1945, pp. 91-98), in detailing the kinds of environmental circumstances which bear on the Oedipus complex, suggests that if the father is missing or weak, "this might create a predisposition toward femininity, because children identify more with the parent who is regarded as the source of decisive frustrations" (p. 45). In addition, the prospect of phallic stage fixations are made more likely by any circumstances which add stress to the Oedipus complex. These hypothesized circumstances are of two kinds. First, there are *traumatic* events, such as a seduction by one parent, which may arouse unmanageable levels of excitation. A similar consequence can emerge if the child views the so-called primal scene, sexual relations between his parents. Depending upon exactly what is observed and how it is interpreted, the child might construe the scene as one of aggression and sadism or might be overwhelmed by castration anxiety at the sight of adult genitals. Even the birth of a sibling can be traumatic if it means a severe reduction in Oedipus gratifications from the mother. Finally, the loss of a father, through divorce or death, may be experienced by the boy as the fulfillment of his Oedipal wishes and create an overbearing sense of guilt.

The second class of stressful circumstances which help predispose the boy to phallic fixations are of a more *chronic* sort. Fenichel (p. 93) writes about the implications of parents' own unresolved phallic wishes. If the continuance of such infantile concerns interfere with the establishment of a mutually-satisfying sexual relationship, the parents may unconsciously turn to their children as love substitutes. The father's love for his daughter and the mother's for her son may then be of a nature which repeatedly arouses sexual temptations in the children, thereby making the Oedipus complex much more intense. Often, at some level, the parents are aware of their behavior and become threatened or guilt-ridden, and then react by expressing anger or rejection. The child is thus subjected to inconsistent phallic experiences in which there are wide swings between extreme over- and undergratification. The parents' overall attitudes toward sexuality also may prove important. Children who are made to feel that sexual expressiveness is forbidden, dangerous, or dirty may experience their Oedipal cravings as particularly upsetting.

Female Phallic stage. Freud's *New Introductory Lectures* (1965), first published in 1933, addresses itself in detail to the issue of femininity and to the phallic stage as experienced by girls.

Apart from the structural genital differences between the sexes, Freud sees little girls as being constitutionally more passive; he frequently equates passivity with femininity. A girl is thought to be inherently "less aggressive, defiant and self-sufficient; she seems to have a greater need for being shown affection and on that account to be more dependent and pliant" (p. 117). On the other hand, at least during the pre-phallic stage, girls are judged to have experienced a psychosexuality essentially identical to that of boys. In fact, Freud asserts that little girls engage in clitoral masturbation in a manner analogous to boys who "have learned how to derive pleasurable sensations from their small penis and connect its excited state with their ideas of sexual intercourse" (p. 118).

In summarizing the pre-phallic psychosexual state of girls, Freud feels we are "obliged to recognize that the little girl is a little man" (p. 118). That is, sexual excitement is principally derived from her clitoris which is homologous to the male penis, and she relates to mother as the primary love object. As complicated as Freud's description of the male phallic event may appear, at least these two infantile trends are retained in adult malehood. For the female, the sexual object must shift from that of mother to father, or some male substitute. In addition, Freud asserts that females must change their principal erotogenic zone from the pre-phallic clitoris to the vagina. "The clitoris should wholly or in part hand over its sensitivity, and at the same time its importance, to the vagina" (p. 118). This, for Freud, defines the emergence of true femininity. The manner in which femininity is attained is the main theme of his writings about phallic stage girls.

What is responsible for bringing to an end the girl's powerful attachment to her mother? Freud mentions a number of possibilities, such as a sense of oral deprivation incidental to being weaned from the breast, resentment toward a faithless mother who refocuses her love upon a later-arriving sibling, and frustrations imposed by maternal prohibitions against genital masturbation. All of these, however, are dismissed as unlikely in that they are equally relevant to the psychosexual development of the boy, in whom they do not promote a turning away from the mother as the primary love object. Instead, Freud falls back upon the anatomical differences between the sexes and their physical consequences. "It was . . . a surprise to learn from analysis that girls hold their mother responsible for their lack of a penis and do not forgive her for their being put at a disadvantage" (p. 124). Freud goes on to claim that the discovery makes girls feel "wronged" and they go on to develop an "envy for the penis" (p. 125). *Penis envy* is thus seen as arising from the girl's awareness of the genitals of the opposite sex, the same awareness which provoked castration anxiety in boys. Since both of these phenomena, penis envy and castration anxiety, have common origins they are together referred to as the "castration complex" (p. 124).

The situation, then, is such that what precipitated the decline of Oedipal sexuality in the boy, the castration complex, is responsible for the onset of Oedipal wishes in the girl. Freud sees the emergence of the castration complex as a turning point in the girl's psychosexual development. This turning point has three possible outcomes. First, the girl may be "so mortified by the comparison with the boy's far superior equipment . . . [that] she renounces her masturbatory satisfaction from her clitoris, repudiates her love for her mother and at the same time not infrequently represses a good part of her sexual trends in general" (p. 126).

A critical issue here is the magnitude of repression. If it is considerable, the girl becomes sexually inhibited; if only moderate, then the second possible outcome of the castration complex becomes viable — normal femininity. For this to occur, clitoral masturbation is replaced by a wish for the penis which was denied by her mother, but which is now expected from her father. "The feminine situation is only established, however, if the wish for a penis is replaced by one for a baby, if, that is, a baby takes the place of a penis in accordance with ancient symbolic equivalence" (p. 128). Thus, at this point, the girl is in a psychosexual state quite analogous to the boy who is embroiled in his own Oedipus complex. Specifically, she is now the rival of the same sexed parent, and is in competition for the sexual favors of the parent of the opposite sex. The girl wants from her father what he has previously provided her mother, a baby. This "most powerful feminine wish" finds fulfillment in reality when, as an adult, she finally bears a child, "and quite especially so if the baby is a little boy who brings the longed-for penis with him" (p. 128).

There is one fundamental difference between the male and female Oedipus complexes. Whereas the boy is strongly motivated to resolve his Oedipus complex due to the awful threat of castration, the girl is under no such pressure. In fact, as was mentioned, for the girl it is the castration complex which drives her into an Oedipal situation for refuge. She, therefore, experiences no overwhelming force to seek its resolution. True, she may feel threatened with loss of maternal love, or have to acknowledge the impossibility of replacing her mother as her father's love object. However, in the absence of a castration threat, the female Oedipus complex lingers on for an indeterminate length of time. Girls are thought to "demolish it late and, even so, incompletely" (p. 129).

One characterological implication of an incompletely-resolved Oedipus complex is that of feminine vanity. Freud feels the women "are bound to value their charms more highly as a late compensation for their original sexual inferiority" (p. 132). In addition, jealousy is seen to play a larger role in the mental life of women than men; this is a derivative of their ever-active penis envy. Also, many women compensate for their anatomical inferiority by entertaining castration wishes with regard to men, wanting to deprive males of their prized organ. It is from this that we have acquired the notion of "castrating women" who constantly belittle or "cut down to size" their male acquaintances. In summary then, even feminine women are construed as being essentially discontented with their sex, a conclusion which is an inevitable outcome of the so-called "phallocentric" point of view which Freud regards as valid.

We have mentioned sexual inhibitions and femininity as two outcomes of the female castration complex. A third possibility is "the development of a powerful masculinity complex." By this, Freud means that the girl refuses to acknowledge her anatomical inferiority, even to the point of exaggerating her previous masculinity and clitoral masturbatory activities (p. 130). Such an outcome is seen to be primarily due to constitutional factors. Even in these cases, however, Freud reveals that his analytic experiences show that the girl, at least temporarily, enters into an Oedipus complex. Then, due to "the inevitable disappointments from her father, she is driven to regress to her early masculinity complex" (p. 130). This regression may ultimately cause the woman to choose another female as an object of sexuality, in which case she becomes a manifest homosexual.

Empirical validation. One of the obvious implications of Freud's theory regarding phallic stage psychosexuality is that boys will experience varying degrees of castration anxiety. In those cases where castration anxiety was high, the adult male may re-experience the threat not only if he should contemplate incestuous relations, but even when he tries to engage in what should be a routine heterosexual encounter. The castration anxiety per se may remain quite unconscious. However, it may be manifested in a variety of disguised ways, including conscious fears over bodily injury and even over death. It is, therefore, reasoned that males who have been victim to especially intense castration fears will most likely express a habitual fear of death. Such expressions are most likely in situations where there is sexual arousal.

Sarnoff and Corwin (1959) designed an experiment to test these very ideas. Fifty-six male undergraduates at Yale University were first requested to complete a Fear of Death Scale (FDS) consisting of five items to be rated on a seven point scale. "I am disturbed when I think of the shortness of life," was one of the items. These items were embedded within a larger 22 item rating scale to disguise their purpose. In order to evaluate the subjects' castration anxiety (CA), they were shown the so-called "castration anxiety" card from Blum's Blacky Pictures (1950). This card depicts a blindfolded dog about to have his tail chopped off by a descending knife while a second dog, Blacky, looks on. The subjects were provided with three statements describing the card and they were requested to rank them in terms of their appropriateness. One of the statements, representing a low CA description, suggested that Blacky was experiencing some tension but was viewing the imminent amputation with relative detachment. There was also a medium CA description in which Blacky was said to be afraid that he was to be next but was not overwhelmed by anxiety. The high CA description suggested that Blacky was overwhelmed with anxiety over the prospect of losing his own tail. Thirty-six of the subjects ranked the low CA description as most appropriate and the high CA description least appropriate. These subjects constituted the low CA group. The 20 subjects who said that either the medium or high CA description was most appropriate were defined as the high CA group.

About four weeks after this pre-testing, half the subjects in each group were assigned to a high sexual arousal treatment, the remaining subjects received a low arousal treatment. The former consisted of having the subjects write their aesthetic reactions to four pictures of nude women; the low arousal treatment was identical, except that the pictures were of clothed fashion models. Immediately subsequent to this experimental manipulation, all subjects were again given the FDS.

The results of this investigation indicated that there was a strong relationship between a subject's level of castration anxiety and his initial FDS score; high CA subjects expressed a significantly higher fear of death at pre-testing. In addition, when changes on the FDS were analyzed, it was found that both high and low CA subjects expressed a slightly lower fear of death after experiencing the low sexual arousal treatment than they had at pre-test. There was no difference between the two CA groups in this regard. However, as predicted, the high sexual arousal treatment increased the high CA subjects' fear of death scores significantly more than it did those of the low CA subjects. Thus, not only were high CA subjects found to have an initially higher fear of death, but, when aroused through exposure to photographs of nude females, their fear of death was raised significantly more than that of their low CA counterparts. The authors conclude that their results lend support to Freud's conceptions of castration anxiety and the impact of this anxiety upon adult males.

In another investigation, using very different methodology, Silverman, Kwawer, Wolitzky, and Coron (1973) sought experimental validation for the Freudian idea that adult male homosexuality represents a defensive flight from unconscious incestuous wishes left over from an unresolved Oedipus complex. Presumably, because of the anxieties to which such personalities are subject, they find themselves either "disinterested in or repelled by females as sexual 'objects' and instead [are] attracted to males" (p. 179). Theoretically, heterosexual behavior is, in the homosexual's unconscious mind, equated with incest and, therefore, punishable by castration. In addition, the sight of female genitals unbearably reminds the homosexual that penis-less beings inhabit the world. Male sex objects neither make salient the incest taboo nor serve as a reminder of the possibilities for castration.

Silverman and his colleagues reasoned that if the unconscious incestuous wishes could be activated in male homosexuals they would intensify their conscious homosexual orientation in an effort to reduce the threat of castration. A technique developed by Silverman (1976), the *subliminal psychodynamic activation method*, seemed to be especially suited to accomplish such unconscious wish activation. The method involves presenting a stimulus related to an unconscious wish subliminally; the stimulus is exposed for a time, four milliseconds, which is sufficient for it to register at the unconscious level but not long enough for the subject to become aware of its content consciously. To do this, an apparatus called a tachistoscope is used. Silverman (1976, p. 625) suggests that the subliminally presented stimulus makes "contact" with the relevant unconscious wish and activates it. More specifically, a subliminal incest stimulus should activate the unconscious incest wishes homosexuals are presumed to have.

The experiment itself was conducted with 36 male homosexuals who responded to advertisements in *The Village Voice*, a weekly New York City tabloid. Thirty-six heterosexual males were also included; these subjects volunteered on the basis of "word of mouth" information about the experiment or through bulletin board notices. Each subject served as his own control; he was exposed to a subliminal incest stimulus during one of two sessions, and to a subliminal neutral stimulus in the other session. The former stimulus consisted of a "picture of a nude man and woman in a sexually suggestive pose," accompanied by the printed message, "FUCK MOMMY;" the neutral stimulus consisted of the verbal message, "PERSON THINKING," accompanied by a picture of a "single bland male figure" (1973, p. 182).

In a given session, a subject first saw four subliminal tachistoscopic presentations of a base-line stimulus, a printed message such as "PERSON WALKING." The subject was then given a sexual feelings assessment. This involved showing him pictures of 10 males and 10 females taken from a college yearbook. Each picture was rated on a 20 point scale in response to the question, "How sexually attracted do you feel toward the person in the picture?" (1973, p. 182). Using the same scale, additional ratings were obtained by asking the subject how inclined he then felt for a sexual contact with a male and with a female of his own choosing. From this, the dependent measure, a sexual orientation index was derived by subtracting the total of the 11 ratings for heterosexual feelings from the total of the 11 ratings for homosexual feelings. After completing the sexual feelings assessment, each subject was tachistoscopically shown either the control or the incest stimuli four successive times at 15 second intervals. The sexual feelings assessment was then again filled out by each subject. The second session was identical to the first except that the critical stimulus, either control or incest, not used in the first session was then employed.

Because a sexual orientation index was derived from subjects' responses obtained both before and after the control and incest stimuli were presented, it was possible to analyze the experimental data in terms of sexual orientation change scores for the "control" and for the "incest" sessions.

Silverman and his colleagues (1973) found that heterosexuals changed only slightly during each of their two sessions. In fact, there was no statistical significance attached to the differences in the amount they changed when the two sessions were compared. They thus appeared to have been unaffected by subliminal exposure to incest stimuli, presumably because either they did not have active unconscious incest wishes, or, if they did, they were not particularly motivated to defend against them. The picture was, as predicted, quite different for the homosexuals. This group became much more homosexually oriented during the incest session than they did during the control session, the difference between sessions being significant at the $p < .01$ level. These findings "lend support to the psychoanalytic hypothesis that a homosexual orientation in males is linked to conflict over incestuous wishes" (1973, p. 185).

A third investigation worth considering was conducted by Hall and Van de Castle (1965). This focused on the impact of the castration complex on dreams. According to Freud, males suffer castration fear and females experience penis envy. In addition, the jealousy of females theoretically drives them to entertain castration wishes toward males. Since dreams are allegedly a veritable "royal road to the unconscious," Hall and Van de Castle anticipated that they should contain evidence pertaining to the aforementioned components of the castration complex. These researchers had 120 male and female college undergraduates keep accounts of their dreams on standard report forms. In all, 953 dreams were described by the male subjects and 956 by the females. The content of each dream was scored for *castration anxiety*, *castration wish*, and *penis envy*. Dreams involving the loss or mutilation of a body part or of an object or animal belonging to the dreamer, the inability to use the penis or an object having symbolic phallic meaning, or the changing into a woman either entirely or in part were indicative of castration anxiety. The criteria were the same for castration wish, except that the events were happening to someone other than the dreamer. Dreams of acquiring a penis or a phallic object and dreams of changing into a man or acquiring male characteristics were the criteria used to determine penis envy. Each dream could receive a maximum score of one point for each of the three content areas. The results indicated that castration anxiety was evident in 151 male dreams and in only 57 female dreams; 37 male dreams contained castration wishes, in comparison to 61 female dreams; and 16 male dreams showed penis envy content in contrast to 32 such dreams among the females. This pattern was statistically significant at a very high degree of reliability ($p < .001$) and is consistent with psychoanalytic theory. In explaining the frequency of castration anxiety content in the dreams of females, Hall and Van de Castle suggest that, while males may dream of what might happen, women may dream of what they think has happened. Also, the authors relate castration wish dream content among men to "an archaic wish in the male to castrate the father." Male penis envy dreams are thought to be a reflection of the competitive life roles in which they frequently find themselves.

Freud, in describing the female Oedipus complex, sees the little girl as changing from penis envy to a wish for a penis and then, finally, to a wish for a baby. Accordingly, Hall and Van de Castle counted the frequency of dreams in which weddings and babies were present. They found 60 wedding dreams among females and only 9 among the males; females had 85 dreams in which babies were present, in comparison with only 32 such dreams among males. While other interpretations are possible, these data are consistent with psychoanalytic theory and add validity to the construct "castration complex."

Latency

This period, extending from around the age of six or seven until puberty, is one in which there are few obvious signs of sexuality. If the child has successfully dealt with the Oedipus complex, incestuous and aggressive feelings will have been repressed and put out of awareness. Relief from the earlier turmoil is sought in a pursuit of protection and security through identification with the parent of the same sex. In effect, the child focuses attention upon becoming a man or a woman, using the parent as a model for behavior. At this time the play of children, girls with girls and boys with boys, may be seen as a vehicle for practicing and consolidating masculine and feminine roles.

Genital Sexuality

Collectively, the oral, anal and phallic stages are called the *pregenital period*. During this period, the sexual life is entirely autoerotic; the child constantly pursues body pleasure, and relationships with others are designed to mediate attainment of this goal.

After the quietude of latency, puberty brings a second wave of sexuality. New genital urges are experienced which have physiological origins, and pregenital concerns are reactivated as the personality regresses to earlier modes of functioning in the face of adolescent uncertainties. If pregenital fixations have not been too pervasive, there will be a sufficient amount of psychological resources available for the person to master the problems of this sexual rebirth. The road, however, is not a smooth one. For instance, the safety of same-sex camaraderie persists during adolescence but may take on more sexually active overtones. Therefore, a time of homosexual encounters is not unusual, nor is it pathogenic if not prolonged. Such experiences may enable the person to explore the novelty of sexuality without being overwhelmed with excitement by the presence of the opposite sex.

Freud's concept of a mature *genital character* is an ideal which most of us never fully attain. The sexual instinct, now directed at reproduction, is capable of discharging great quantities of dammed-up energy through orgasm. Libido also becomes freed from its goal of self-gratification and may now be invested in objects for whom there is a deep sense of love and caring. As much satisfaction is derived from the giving of pleasure to the love object as there is from receiving it. Some infantile libidinal cathexes remain but they —

> are taken over by the sexual function as preparatory, auxiliary acts, the satisfaction of which produces what is known as fore-pleasure . . . Other [infantile] urges are excluded from the organization, and are either suppressed altogether (repressed) or . . . undergo sublimation with a displacement of their aims. (Freud, 1949, p. 12)

In *sublimation* the energy of an instinct "is turned aside from its sexual goal and diverted toward other ends, no longer sexual and socially more valuable" (Freud, 1952b, p. 27). This is not to imply that the source and aim of the instincts undergo change; they do not. The means by which tension is reduced are primarily modified in sublimation. Thus, Freud believed that the energy consumed by da Vinci in painting madonnas was derived from a wish for his own mother from whom he had been separated at an early age. Other artistic expressions have been construed as sublimated homosexual impulses. In fact, according to psychoanalytic theory, the creativity and resourcefulness necessary for the development and maintenance of civilization itself is made available through the sublimation of infantile sexuality (Hall, 1954).

With respect to women, Freud believed that sexual maturity was associated with an abandonment of active trends and an adoption of passivity. Psychosexually, this means the female renounces clitoral sexuality and libido becomes invested in the vagina, the prime organ of sexual pleasure in truly genital females.

Contrary to Freud, Masters and Johnson (1966) have presented evidence that there is only one female orgasm, a complex reflexive response. It involves all of the pelvic sex organs and is not, therefore, restricted to either the clitoris or the vagina. These authors also point out the orgasm in women is a possible response to many different kinds of sexual stimulation, including the breasts and lips, and is not solely dependent upon clitoral or vaginal stimulation. However, the clitoris is probably the cite of greatest erotic potential and, even during the vaginal penetrations of intercourse, continues to retain this prominence (Sherfey, 1966). Given these facts, it is futile for a woman to strive for orgasmic experience which is localized in the vagina as a sign of mature femininity (Bardwick, 1971).

When a child has been massively fixated at the pregenital stage, there is difficulty in establishing mutually satisfying relationships in adulthood. Libido remains cathected to the body and the pursuit of self-satisfaction is continued. It is not so much that we might expect such a personality to literally keep seeking out mother's breast; there will be, however, a self-centered quality about the person. Clearly, if one's libido is still oriented toward derivatives of infantile sexuality, there can be little attention given to the wants and satisfactions of others.

THE STRUCTURAL THEORY

This third part of Freud's theory of personality has to do with the organization of the mind and the manner in which the energies associated with each organizational unit, or structure, interact with each other. Freud's explanation of the functioning of personality, couched as it is in terms of forces and counterforces operating on and between the structures, is called *dynamic*. As we will see, the principles presented are systematically related to the theory of instincts and to Freud's theory of psychosexual development. In fact, the three sub-theories of personality are so interwoven that the distinction we have made among them is, to a degree, artificial.

The first models of the mind

Freud's earliest conceptions about the mind emphasized the existence of distinct but interrelated neuronal systems. One was for perceptual functions; one, for memory, stored what was perceived; and one was for consciousness, which retrieved memories and brought them into awareness. This model of the psychical apparatus was presented in the last chapter of *The Interpretation of Dreams*, first published in 1900. In 1912 Freud presented a greatly modified statement in which he focused upon the psychical dimension of conscious-unconscious, approaching this topic from four perspectives: descriptive, topographic, dynamic, and systemic.

Descriptively, conscious ideas are those "of which we are aware" and an unconscious conception "is one of which we are not aware" (Freud, 1957, p. 47). Overlapping this descriptive orientation in which "conscious" and "unconscious" refer to the quality of an idea is a *topographic* one, wherein ideas are seen as being located in one of three "regions" of the mind — the unconscious, preconscious, and conscious regions. Ideas in the first region, the unconscious, "seem to be cut off from consciousness." In fact, from his clinical experiences, Freud believed that topographically unconscious ideas are met with "a distinct feeling of *repulsion*" (1957, p. 50) when an effort is made to move them into the conscious region. In other words such ideas are subject to an active repressing force which resists having them acquire the quality of consciousness. As such, topographically unconscious ideas are also said to be *dynamically* unconscious because of the forces operating to maintain their regional and qualitative status. Ideas in the preconscious region, while being descriptively unconscious since they are not in awareness, are capable of "passing into consciousness with no difficulty . . ." (1957, p. 50). An example of a preconscious idea is your phone number. While it may not, at a given moment, have the quality of consciousness, or be located in the conscious region, the idea of your phone number can, with ease, be brought to full conscious awareness.

The fourth perspective from which Freud dealt with the conscious-unconscious issue was *systemic*. Specifically, conscious and unconscious ideas were seen as being part of a "system conscious" (Cs) and a "system unconscious" (Ucs) respectively. Each of these two systems presumably features its own characteristic ideation. The system Ucs involves a sort of ideation known as *primary process* thinking. Primary process thought is primitive in nature and is evidenced by infants and psychotic personalities, as well as by normal adults during dreaming. There are some rather distinctive features of primary process thought. For example, a single idea or symbol may represent several unconscious wishes, *condensation*, or an emotionally innocuous idea may substitute for a highly charged wish, *displacement*, with the former assuming an unwarranted degree of prominence. Displacement theoretically is relevant to the psychopathological condition called "phobia." According to Freudian theory, the phobic object, perhaps a snake, is only a substitute upon which an extreme unconscious fear is displaced from an original feared object, perhaps a penis. Also characteristic of primary process thought is a preponderance of loose and illogical relations between ideas, and a neglect of temporal and spatial considerations. In *illogic,* images of people who existed at different times and/or in different places may appear together in a dream. Finally, in primary process thinking, contradictory thoughts may exist side by side, *coexistence of opposites*. Dreaming about the activities of an individual who, even in the dream, is dead (Holzman, 1970) is an example of coexistence of opposites.

In contrast to the above, the kind of thought called *secondary process* is characteristic of the system Cs, as well as the preconscious (Pcs) system. Secondary process thinking is what we usually engage in during a normal, waking state. It is essentially logical, ordered, controlled, and reality-oriented.

Gradually, it became apparent to Freud that his notions of a neat mind structure consisting of unconscious, preconscious, and conscious systems were internally inconsistent at several points. For instance, idea constellations were found to exist which have the logical features of secondary thought yet are dynamically unconscious, such as the Oedipus complex. Also, Freud envisioned the system Pcs as guarding against the entry of dynamically unconscious ideas into the conscious region, a function called "censorship." However, in the course of his psychotherapeutic activities it became evident that this system Pcs function was itself dynamically unconscious. Freud's patients were as incapable of becoming aware of their resistance to unconscious ideas as they were to the unconscious ideas themselves.

The new "structural" hypothesis

In *The Ego and the Id*, published in 1923, Freud added to his theory regarding unconscious, preconscious, and conscious functioning. He introduced a new systematic statement involving three mind structures: the *id*, the *ego*, and the *superego*. This conceptualization cross-cuts the preceding one in that ego functions include unconscious, preconscious, and conscious psychical processes.

Id. In many ways Freud's descriptions of the id ties up under one umbrella a great deal of his earlier statements about instincts and the unconscious as a system. "It contains everything that is inherited, that is present at birth, that is laid down in the constitution — above all, therefore, the instincts, which originate from the somatic organization and which find a first psychical expression here [in the id]" (1949, p. 3).

At birth, therefore, the id is the total of the psychical apparatus and contains the complete reservoir of psychic energy.

What has been previously mentioned as characteristic of instincts is now relevant to the id. In particular, id functioning is typified by immediate movement toward the reduction of tension via the discharge of energy. From a more subjective frame of reference, we can say that the id functions in accordance with the pleasure principle since, for Freud, pleasure is the mental correlate of tension reduction. In addition, the nature of id functioning is quite similar to that previously associated with the system Ucs. This is not surprising since the instincts which comprise the id are themselves unconscious; id activity is of a primary process sort.

In the very beginning, all that the id is capable of doing in the service of tension reduction is to utilize built-in reflex systems which immediately discharge energy through some motor activity, such as sneezing, coughing, eye blinking, etc. While these actions may serve to reduce tension caused by nose, throat, or eye irritation, there are many needs of the infant for which no adequate reflex system exists, hunger for one. No amount of stomach contractions will bring the food necessary for tension reduction. The child is, therefore, left either to cry from distress until the mother brings food, or to finally fall asleep from exhaustion.

It is fortunate that the infant's psychological apparatus has more than just sensory and motor systems consisting of receptors, such as eyes and ears, and muscles, respectively. The apparatus also contains a perceptual system which forms visual or other representations of the sensory input, and a memory system which preserves the perceptual representations. Through perception and memory, the infant gradually acquires the capacity to conjure up mental images of that which served to reduce tension on previous occasions; these images are called "wish fulfillments."

Because of the primitive nature of the id, it is not able to differentiate between a perceptual image based upon sensory input and a wish fulfillment based upon a memory image. In other words, objective images are indistinguishable from subjective images. For the id this means that the wish-fulfillment is as capable of holding out the promise of satisfaction as is the presentation of the real object. Of course, the promise of satisfaction is not equivalent to real tension reduction; the infant would fail to survive if it had to depend upon phantasized promises, or wish fulfillments. Because primary process thinking is incapable of reducing tension, a more mature mode of thinking emerges, which we have previously called *secondary process*.

Ego. As soon as we begin to talk about the emergence of secondary process we are also talking about the differentiation out of the id of a new mind structure, the ego, which alone is capable of reality-oriented thoughts.

> . . . the ego is that part of the id which has been modified by the direct influence of the external world . . . Moreover, the ego has the task of bringing the influence of the external world to bear upon the id and its tendencies and endeavors to substitute the reality-principle for the pleasure-principle which reigns supreme in the id. (Freud, 1960b, p. 15).

If you are under the impression that this material has been covered once before, in a sense you are correct. It will be recalled from the section on instinct theory that one of Freud's early formulations pitted sex instincts against the self-preservation instincts, which were also called ego instincts. The self-preservation instincts were then seen as utilizing secondary processes and were said to function in accordance with the reality principle. They were able to delay instinctual gratification until the object capable of satisfying the need could be found in the real world. Of course, later, Freud subsumed both sex and self-preservation instincts under the label Eros, and still later added the category of Thanatos. These so-called life and death instincts comprise the instinctual reservoir contained originally within the id.

By the time he wrote *The Ego and the Id* in 1923, Freud believed that self-preservation instincts can find satisfaction during the earliest hours of life. For instance, the mother brings food and warmth to her child in response to distress calls provoked by heightening somatic needs. Later, in infancy wish-fulfillments serve to temporarily placate these id demands for self-preservation. However, it is not until around the middle of the first year of life, with the emergence of secondary process thinking that the infant is at all capable of even beginning to deal with the issue of self-preservation on his own. The mind structure called ego is then emerging.

In describing the principal characteristics of the ego, Freud brings our attention back to the motor activity which once served the id as a primitive vehicle for discharging instinctual energy. The ego gains control over the motoric function and is capable of utilizing voluntary movement in the service of insuring self-preservation. For instance, it can avoid excessively strong external stimulation by directing flight. Similarly, while memory functions serve as the basis for primary process wish fulfillments of the id, the ego stores up a vast repertoire of experiential memories. These memories ultimately serve to guide activity, moderate it, and change it. Again, the task of self-preservation is served.

> As regards *internal* events, in relation to the id, it performs that task by gaining control over the demands of the instincts, by deciding whether they are to be allowed satisfaction, by postponing that satisfaction to times and circumstances favorable in the external world or by suppressing their excitations entirely. (Freud, 1949, pp. 2-3).

The many ways in which the ego manages to control and suppress id impulses will be discussed in a following section on anxiety and defense.

On the relationship which is theorized to exist between the ego and unconsciousness, Freud wrote: "A part of the ego, too — and heaven knows how important a part — may be Ucs, undoubtedly is Ucs" (1957, p. 212). Drawing upon his clinical experience, Freud is reminded of evidence pointing to "difficult intellectual operations" being conducted without conscious awareness.

> Instances of this are quite incontestable; they may occur, for example, during the state of sleep, as is shown when someone finds, immediately

after waking, that he knows the solution to a difficult mathematical or other problem with which he had been wrestling in vain the day before. (Freud, 1960b, p. 17)

By so stressing the unconscious aspects of ego functioning, Freud effectively does away with his earlier idea of the Ucs as a system of special importance. The dynamic aspects of personality have now been clearly taken over by the mind structures of id, ego, and the soon-to-be-discussed superego. Ucs, therefore, remains as simply descriptive of the quality of a mental process.

Once the ego has become a differentiated structure of the personality, a process which is especially important to its continued development is that of *identification*. This is the process whereby the child becomes like someone, or something, in his style of behaving or thinking. One form of identification is that of verbal imitation. Freud sees this as being central to the acquisition of speech, an important ego function, once a sufficient degree of neurophysiological maturation has been attained. Imitation of mannerisms and appearance, important during childhood, continue to exert a modifying influence on the ego in later life. Adolescents often conduct themselves in a way which reflects their personal heroes, who could be athletes, movie stars, or parents; grown men adopt working habits and dress which are characteristic of their esteemed boss, to the point of even growing a similar mustache or combing their hair in the same fashion.

In all the above cases, the tendency for identification occurs in relation to those objects in which there has been a substantial investment of libido. In addition, Freud saw a tendency for people to identify with objects which are highly cathected with aggressive energy, a process called "identification with the aggressor." Presumably, by becoming like one's feared but respected opponents, one can, in fantasy, become glorified in the power of the enemy. A third situation in which identification is especially likely to occur is when a highly cathected object is lost. When one loses a parent through death or a lover through abandonment, there seems to be a powerful but unconscious motive operating for the ego to become like the lost object.

All three bases of identification — libido cathexis, identification with the aggressor, and object loss — serve to mold the nature of ego functioning. The ego's penchant for identification also results in the emergence of the third structure of personality, the superego, toward the end of the phallic psychosexual stage.

Superego. During the anal stage, fear of punishment in the context of toilet training causes the child to accept parental admonitions as his own. That is, the child identifies with parental standards and develops a genuine dislike for fecal play and a feeling of propriety on the matter of expulsive activity. Toward the end of the phallic stage, the fear of punishment and rejection associated with the Oedipus conflict pushes this conformity to parental demands to new extremes.

The boy, shocked by castration anxiety, draws back from a position in which the opposite sex parent is sought as a love object. The frustrated child regresses to an oral solution in which there is an introjection of parental standards. The boy most typically indulges in an intensified identification with his father, although also identifying, but to a lesser degree, with his mother. Identification which is primarily influenced by object loss occurs more frequently among girls than boys. Freud asserts that it is not unusual for the girl to "bring her masculinity into prominence and identify herself with her father, that is, with the object which has been lost, instead of with her mother" (1957, p. 220).

These identifications with the mother and with the father are described by Freud as being "the broad general outcome of the sexual phase governed by the Oedipus complex" (1960b, p. 24). This "outcome" is seen as constituting a major modification within the ego which stands apart in the form of a *superego*.

The superego, therefore, as the internalization of parental authority, represents the moral branch of the personality. As a product of identification, it is epitomized by the precept "you *ought to be* like this" (1960b, p. 24). However, the superego is also partly a reaction formation against the earlier Oedipus wishes and, as such, contains prohibitions against some parental actions. Most importantly, identification with the same sex parent does not include adopting the role of that parent vis a vis the parent of the opposite sex. Quite the opposite occurs as the incestuous wishes are repressed. Freud believes the ego becomes capable of this repressive act against powerful libidinal cathexes only by identifying with and, therefore, borrowing the power of the parent. Through this process the child develops a superego which contains within itself the same psychological prohibition against incest that was once enforced by the parents (1960b, p. 24).

With the organization of superego processes, the child becomes capable of controlling his own behavior; this self-management is an indirect prolongation of parental influence (1949, p. 3). What the child once did or did not do out of an expectation for praise or a fear of punishment from the parents, he now does on the basis of believing that it is morally right or wrong. The expression of morality, religion, and a social sense, "the chief elements in the higher side of man," are all seen as being reflections of the superego. (1960b, p. 27).

That part of the superego which continues to represent all that is right and proper is known as the *ego ideal*; the internalized psychic representation of what is bad and wrong is known as the *conscience*. It should be realized that the specific imperatives which comprise the ego ideal and conscience are the product of the child's understanding of what the parents have expressed to be right and wrong through their administration of rewards and punishments. The child's understanding tends to be rather primitive, of course; he is not sophisticated to the degree that he can appreciate the nuances of motives which lie behind apparently moral or immoral behavior, nor can he take into consideration extenuating circumstances. Thus, the superego's "oughts" and "ought nots" constitute a set of relatively inflexible, uncompromising rules of conduct which are self-imposed in a harsher and more rigid fashion than were the rules of the parents themselves.

When the ego causes the person to behave in a manner which is consistent with the ego ideal, it is rewarded by the superego — which makes it feel pride, experience self-love, and perhaps encourages it to engage in some self-indulgent activity such as going out to a movie. On the other hand, transgressions of internalized moral standards bring upon the ego the punishment of *guilt*, a distinctly unpleasant feeling. One very important consideration to keep in mind is that superego processes tend to be less accessible to consciousness than are many other aspects of the ego. Thus, subjecting the ego to guilt may occur entirely out of awareness. The person may be aware of vaguely uncomfortable feelings, yet not be consciously in touch with the reasons for these. Keeping self-criticism at an unconscious level is theoretically facilitated by the ego's use of repressive forces against the conscience, a somewhat paradoxical occurrence in that repression is more usually employed by the ego against morally unacceptable id impulses. In this case, however, the weapon of repression typically wielded against the id by the ego is turned against its "harsh taskmaster," the superego (Freud, 1960b, p. 42).

Freud suggests that, like all unconscious forces, an unconscious sense of guilt may still find expression through the activation of overt behavior. Thus, the individual who becomes sick or is involved in an unfortunate "accident" may, in fact, be experiencing the painful products of unconscious motives at work, motives intent upon inflicting self-punishment.

> In many criminals, especially youthful ones, it is possible to detect a very powerful sense of guilt which existed before the crime, and is therefore not its result but its motive. It is as if it was a relief to be able to fasten this unconscious sense of guilt on to something real and immediate. (Freud, 1960b, p. 42)

Freud explains that one of the reasons why the sense of guilt so often remains unconscious is that the superego's origin lies with the Oedipus complex which is itself unconscious. Thus, whereas the unconscious id causes us to characterize man as more irrational, base, impulsive, and self-concerned than he outwardly appears, the unconscious superego must also force us to conclude that man is "far more moral than he has any idea of" (1960b, p. 42).

In a number of places we have straightforwardly or indirectly characterized the criticizing faculties of the superego as harsh, even punitive. In his own description of an excessively "strong" superego, Freud says that it "rages against the ego with merciless fury, as if it had taken possession of the whole of sadism available in the person concerned . . . we should say that the destructive component has entrenched itself in the super-ego and turned against the ego" (1960b, p. 43). The superego gets this strength and aggression from the id and from the aggressive aspects of the Oedipal phantasies. Theoretically, the destructive id instincts cathected in the parents are withdrawn from their object as the child is resolving the Oedipus conflict. This aggressive energy is then, in part, captured by the newly-formed superego. Thus, the later harshness of one's superego against the ego is less related to the severity of former parental standards which have been incorporated than it is to aggressiveness contained within the child's own Oedipal phantasies. In other words, the phallic stage child who entertained especially destructive wishes is the one who will later experience the strongest sense of guilt.

This assertion by Freud constitutes somewhat of a poetic turn of events. The superego was taken on by the ego during the phallic stage as an ally against id-instigated wishes for destruction of the parent(s) and the feared consequences of these Oedipal wishes — castration and/or loss of love. Now, the ego becomes the object of the id's aggressive instincts acting through the superego's harshly imposed categorical imperatives, which are experienced by the ego as pangs of guilt. In a sense, such an outcome has a good systematic basis in that the aggression, once directed outwardly at the parent, is now aimed at the structure within which the parental representation has been embodied through identification, the ego.

There is an additional theoretical relationship between id aggression and the capacity of the superego to inflict guilt upon the ego. Freud later asserted that "the more a man checks his aggressive tendencies toward others the more tyrannical, that is, aggressive, he becomes in his ego ideal" (1960b, p. 44). Ordinarily we would probably expect a harsh superego would cause us to become less aggressive. However, Freud points out that when we suppress aggressive impulses, they are not abolished but rather are displaced so that they may find indirect expression; they take on a new object in the ego itself and act through the pathway of superego-induced guilt. Thus, we are forced to confront the paradox in which the person who best controls his overt hostility and, by objective standards, should be most guilt free, is the very one who is most subject to the wrath of his superego.

Anxiety

Freud sees the ego as "a poor creature owing service to three harsh masters and consequently menaced by three dangers: from the external world, from the libido of the id, and from the severity of the superego" (1960b, p. 46). When there is a threat from either within or without, when there is an expectation of an increase in "unpleasure" (1949, p. 3), the ego produces and feels *anxiety*, a conscious emotional experience.

Anxiety is seen as serving the purpose of self-preservation by signaling the presence of some potential danger. Events are anticipated to be dangerous when they are reminiscent of certain prototypic situations in which the individual was overwhelmed. In these so-called "traumatic" situations the individual was incapable of tension reduction; functioning in accordance with the pleasure principle became paralyzed. The first of the traumatic situations is thought to be that of birth. The neonate is bombarded by varied and heavy doses of external stimulation with which it is totally unprepared to deal. Freud also saw the threat of being castrated as traumatic. While this event is not real as is the process of birth, "what is decisive is that the danger [of castration] is one that threatens from the outside and that the child believes in it" (1965, p. 86). Of course, castration fear is a non-issue for phallic stage girls, but in its place is a fear of loss of love which can also be traumatic. Indeed, Freud believed that loss of love or, more particularly, separation from maternal care can be traumatic for both sexes during the pre-phallic years. Young children, not being self-sufficient, are highly dependent upon a maternal presence for a variety of satisfactions. "If a mother is absent or has withdrawn her love from her child, it is no longer sure of the satisfaction of its needs and is perhaps exposed to the most distressing feelings of tension" (1965, p. 87). The child may then remain reliant upon the love, care, and respect of others, and any movement toward independence is experienced with unsettling anxiety, even as an adult.

Freud spoke of three main kinds of anxiety: *reality*, *neurotic*, and *moral*. These forms arise from the ego's relationships with the external world, with the id, and with the superego, respectively. While one may, in theory, be able to distinguish between the three kinds of anxiety, it is not always possible to do so on an experiential basis. In other words, the anxious person may be no more aware of whether the immediate source of his anxiety stems from the external world, the id, or the superego than he is of the infantile trauma from which the current anxiety derives. All three kinds of anxiety are not in any way subjectively perceived as being different from each other, as the unpleasant states arising from thirst and hunger tensions can be discriminated.

Reality anxiety. Any time a person confronts an environmental situation which is, at least in part, reminiscent of an early traumatic experience, reality anxiety may be felt. The current anxiety-provoking situation might involve the prospect of physical injury. This is especially frightening due to the earlier trauma of the castration complex; or the anxiety may be brought on by the loss of a loved one, thus also reflecting infantile traumatic circumstances. In both of these examples, the person is reacting to the outside world with anxiety because of the danger of repeating an earlier traumatic moment.

Reality anxiety is also felt as a consequence of being directly embroiled in a situation whose quality or intensity is such that new trauma threatens; a deranged person rushing at you, with axe in hand could certainly be a traumatic experience. We would commonly refer to the emotion associated with such events as straightforward "fear." In summary then, Freud cited the twofold origin of reality anxiety, "one as a direct consequence of the traumatic moment and the other as a signal threatening a repetition of such a moment" (1965, p. 94-95).

Neurotic anxiety. The source of neurotic anxiety is internal instead of external. The neurotically-anxious person is concerned over the expression of an instinctual impulse which, should it be acted upon, would serve to get the person into trouble. Notice that while the source of concern is the internal instinct, the impulse per se is not feared. It is only the anticipated consequences of its expression which provoke anxiety.

Freud suggests that our instincts become a source of neurotic anxiety because their expression has, in the past, been met with punishing consequences. As children we may be verbally threatened by our parents or spanked severely for manifesting aggressive or sexual behaviors. The instincts upon which such childhood aggressive and sexual behaviors were based later arouse neurotic anxiety in the adult as they come close to being overtly acted upon.

Neurotic anxiety manifests itself in three ways. It can be experienced as a "freely floating, general apprehensiveness" (Freud, 1965, p. 82). The person feels upset but does not have the slightest idea as to the cause of the disquietude. In such cases, the threatening id impulse is still deep enough in the unconscious so that one is not consciously aware of being troubled by sexual or aggressive inclinations. However, the ego, which has roots in the unconscious, becomes sensitized to, and anxious over, the id's thrust.

It is not unusual for the person experiencing free-floating anxiety to be as troubled by not knowing what he is anxious over as he is by the anxiety itself. There is thus a readiness on the person's part to find a reasonable explanation of the anxiety. If this search meets with success, the anxiety is firmly attached to an external event or situation which, while it may contain some reality-based elements of threat, is reacted to in a manner which is all out of proportion to the threat. In other words, the external object becomes the basis for the very strong, irrational fears we call *phobias*.

Through the development of a phobia, the neurotically-anxious person trans- forms an internal danger, the unconsciously recognized id instinct, into an external one. Thus neurotic anxiety is apparently changed into the more easily-manageable reality anxiety, which can be dealt with by simply keeping away from the external source of danger. Some common phobias include fear of heights (acrophobia), en- closed places (claustrophobia), animals (zoophobia), fires (pyrophobia), crowds (och- lophobia), being alone (monophobia), and darkness (nyctophobia).

By way of illustration, we can consider the person who experiences periods of free floating anxiety as a consequence of unconscious sexual interests. If, while riding in an elevator, the person's anxiety happens to be aroused by the close proximity of others who are sexually tempting, he may "solve" the puzzle of the free floating anxiety by concluding that the fear is one of enclosed places or, more specifically, of elevators. Thus, the fear of internal urges is transformed into an apparently more realistic fear of elevators, enabling the person to deal with his difficulty. Freud noted that, "One can save oneself from an external danger by flight; fleeing from an internal danger is a difficult enterprise" (1965, p. 84).

In addition to being in a free floating or phobic form, neurotic anxiety sometimes "emerges independently as an attack or more persistent state, but always without any visible basis in an external danger" (1965, p. 82). Here we are talking about *anxiety attacks* in which the person is in a near-panic state. The impulsive acting-out behavior associated with these extreme emotional states may serve to discharge some instinctual tensions through motor channels. In addition, the instincts may find more direct gratification if, while in the panic state, the individual can express that which has heretofore remained forbidden. We thus may see the blurting out of sexual or aggres- sive thoughts, or even the frantic expression of apparently-unprovoked hostility or sexuality. While the person may indeed temporarily experience heightened reality anxiety as his impulsive actions are punitively reacted to by others, there will still be a sense of relief in that the "explosion" has effected instinctual tension reduction and, therefore, escape from a chronic condition of neurotic anxiety.

Moral anxiety. This third kind of anxiety, otherwise known as *guilt,* is experienced by the ego if it perceives that a superego standard is in danger of being transgressed.

The source of moral anxiety is, therefore, also internal, only now the punitive conscience is implicated instead of the instincts. A second similarity between moral and neurotic anxiety is that the origins of both can be traced to real world events. In the case of neurotic anxiety, one can see that the instincts serve as a source only because their impulsive expression had been met with actual aversive consequences at earlier times. Similarly, the origins of moral anxiety can be found in the punitive actions of parents toward their children; these actions are later internalized within the child's personality as a conscience.

Another similarity between these two kinds of anxiety, neurotic and moral, is that, when extreme, both can provoke unusual behavior. We have already mentioned how the unbearable pressure of neurotic anxiety can finally be experienced in the form of a panic reaction which may serve to reduce instinctual tensions. Similarly, the conscience can often be placated and guilt expiated if the person engages in behavior which invites punishment from external agents. It is, for instance, not uncommon for the motive behind an illegal act to be getting "caught" rather than revenge or monetary gain. What the courts may impose is unconsciously welcomed as punishment for "crimes" against the superego. In this way the conscience is relieved and guilt reduced; the positive aspects outweigh the unpleasant components of penal incarceration.

Finally, moral and neurotic anxiety may be intimately entwined in that the instinctual impulse which promotes neurotic anxiety can be the same one which, when indulged, causes behaviors which fall short of the high standards contained in one's ego ideal. Thus, one instinctual consideration can be at the roots of both neurotic anxiety and guilt.

Defense

Whenever the ego becomes alert to imminent danger from the external world, from the id, or from the superego through the signal of anxiety, it can reduce the danger, and also the anxiety, through the use of operations which were called *defense mechanisms* by Anna Freud (1936), Sigmund Freud's daughter.

Repression. The first defense mechanism recognized and the one which has received the most attention is that of *repression*. When an instinctual demand is threatening and is capable of generating anxiety, the ego will resist entrance into consciousness of any idea, emotion, behavior, or fantasy associated with the instinct. The ego accomplishes this by counteracting the energy charge of these instinct derivatives with an *anti-cathexis,* a charge of energy directed at the nullification of the instinctual cathexis. This deployment by the ego of psychic energy for the purpose of keeping dangerous instincts and their derivatives in the unconscious is called repression. Fenichel describes repression as a kind of "purposeful forgetting or not becoming aware of internal impulses or external events which, as a rule, represent possible temptations or punishments for, or mere allusions to, objectionable instinctual demands" (1945, p. 148).

The process of repression itself is as unconscious as is the material against which the anti-cathexes are exerted. Just as we are not aware of the "forgetting" of ideas, so are we consciously oblivious to this more active process of repression. The conscious exclusion of ideas from our awareness of ideas is called *suppression,* an ego process which may bear some close kinship to repression. In fact, it has been suggested that the two ego defenses of repression and suppression are really extreme poles on a continuum of awareness, with the basic process being essentially the same.

What happens to an instinct which has been repressed? Freud answers, "In some cases the repressed instinctual impulse may retain its libidinal cathexis, and may persist in the id unchanged, although subject to constant pressure from the ego" (1965, p. 92).

In other words, although the instinctual energy charge is forced to remain in the unconscious because of the imposition of anti-cathexes, the charge continues to be active. Consequently, the ego must continually be vigilant and deploy anti-cathexes whenever the ideas or emotions associated with the instinctual charge threaten to force their way into consciousness.

There are some counterproductive implications of this process. First, because the ego has at its disposal only a limited reservoir of energy, a major diversion of its resources for the purpose of maintaining repression may significantly deplete the ego's capacity to deal with other life problems. Consistent with this is the frequent finding that personalities who use repression to excess in an attempt to manage pervasive anxieties often report being physically fatigued. They simply can't muster up the energy to confront even simple issues or obstacles; there is a sense of personal impoverishment.

There is a second way in which repression weakens the ego. When an id impulse is repressed, ideas and emotions which are part of the ego but associated with the id impulse are also repressed. This means that some of the energy of the ego itself is repressesd and, consequently, becomes part of the id; it is separated from consciousness and lost in so far as adaptive, reality-oriented functioning is concerned.

It should be noted that repression, as we have been describing it, is not a one-shot affair. Rather, it is a chronic condition involving intra-psychic conflict between cathexes and anti-cathexes. In addition, these opposing forces vary in their relative strengths over time and across situations so that any dynamic equilibrium reached tends not to be a stable one. For instance, it is believed that while one is asleep or under the influence of intoxicants, the ego's capacity to resist invasion by repressed instinctual impulses into the conscious realm is diminished. For this reason dreams may contain relatively undisguised wish-fulfillments, and the behavior of the intoxicated person is often unusually aggressive or sexual in nature. Also, instinctual cathexes may be strengthened if environmental stimuli act as a temptation, or if biological changes occur. This latter factor is presumably operative at the onset of puberty when sexual impulses, until then successfully contained within the unconscious since the resolution of Oedipal conflict, begin to once again find overt expression.

There is a second outcome of repression which Freud addresses, ". . . what seems to happen is that it [the impulse] is totally destroyed, while its libido is diverted along other paths" (1965, p. 92).

This describes a *fully successful* repression because the ego is not saddled with continuously having to maintain a vigilant posture against an ever-present threat of impulses clamoring to find satisfaction. Freud believed that in a well-resolved Oedipal complex, the incestuous wishes are actually destroyed in the id; their energy, therefore, is freed for any number of other functions.

One difficulty with this idea of a fully-successful repression is that there is no evidence for the existence of the process. If an analyst sees no sign of a repressed conflict or idea is it because the conflict or idea itself was destroyed? Is it that the anti-cathexes are powerful enough to maintain an active impulse deeply in the unconscious? Perhaps the impulse is active and finding expression, but in a sufficiently disguised manner so that neither the subject nor the analyst is sensitive to its existence. It is only when repression is *unsuccessful* that clinical evidence of a repressed impulse becomes clearly manifest in the form of anxiety or other behavioral byproduct.

In Freud's work, *On the History of the Psychoanalytic Movement,* he wrote, "The theory of repression is the cornerstone on which the whole structure of psychoanalysis rests" (1966, p. 16). Given the acknowledged centrality of repression to psychoanalysis, it is not surprising that there have been numerous attempts to validate empirically the operation of this hypothetical process. In general, research in this area has been slow to accumulate convincing affirmative findings, although a variety of investigatory approaches have been employed.

Zeller suggested that it is not enough to demonstrate that cognitive material associated with threat is not recalled as well as neutrally toned material, ". . . no test of repression can be considered adequate until the removal of the repression factor has resulted in the restoration to consciousness of the repressed material" (1950a, p. 46). In other words, one must demonstrate a "return of the repressed" consequent to a removal of the threat. Zeller (1950 b) conducted an experiment in which he attempted to meet this criterion. Subjects had to study a list of nonsense syllables until they had a trial in which all were correctly recalled. Three days later they were required to relearn the same list, again to the criterion of one correct trial. In that same session, the subjects performed on a psychomotor task. This task was so arranged that half of the subjects, the controls, believed they were doing quite well, whereas the remaining experimental subjects, who had been equal to the controls in their nonsense-syllable recall, were led to believe they were doing very poorly on the psychomotor task.

It was predicted that the ego threat associated with failure would spread to the nonsense syllable task. Theoretically this should result in experimental subjects repressing the nonsense syllable material. As anticipated, the experimental subjects did indeed recall fewer of the nonsense syllables immediately subsequent to their failure experience; they also required more trials to reach the criterion of one perfect recall than did the control subjects. Zeller found that this experimental-control group difference was maintained three days later, with the control subjects still manifesting superior syllable recall.

Subsequent to this post-test, all subjects were again administered the psychomotor task under success-feedback conditions. The intention was to provide a favorable experience which would serve to eliminate the ego threat associated with the nonsense syllable and act to "lift the repression." Zeller reports that this apparently occurred because, upon being retested on the syllable task, there was no difference between the two groups. The syllable task was administered for a sixth, and final, time three days later. Again, the experimental and control groups manifested virtually identical recall and relearning performance.

Zeller concluded that his investigation did demonstrate that repression of material, the nonsense syllables, associated with the ego threat of task failure does occur, and that the lost material is recovered when conditions are arranged so that the ego threat is removed and the repression lifts. Other researchers felt similarly, and several, using Zeller's basic research strategy, replicated his results. However, the groundswell of optimism was not unanimous. For example, Merrill, one of the researchers who obtained results similar to those of Zeller's wrote,

> The ease with which the task-anxiety effects were reduced raises serious questions as to the appropriateness of considering such experimentally induced threats as analogous to clinical repression. It is concluded that the appropriate design for studying clinical repression, if such a concept has meaning, has not yet been devised. (1954, p. 172).

Merrill was not alone in his belief that the kind of "threat" induced by a task-failure situation within the context of a Zeller-type psychological experiment is very superficial in comparison to an ego threat in natural circumstances, which is the theoretical basis for repression. One must question what is producing the recall and relearning deficits among task-failure subjects if it is not a process akin to psychoanalytic repression. Aborn (1953) has suggested that the failure-feedback condition might somehow interfere with attentional processes necessary for optimal performance on the syllable task. For instance, a person might be preoccupied with thinking about his past failure and so not be able to concentrate sufficiently on the syllable task. Consistent with this hypothesis, D'Zurilla (1965) found that, subsequent to a failure experience, 62% of subjects reported that they continued to think about the task, whereas only 24% of those subjects who succeeded on the same task reported thinking about it afterward. Not only do such data support the interference hypothesis, but they are inconsistent with the theory of repression. According to Freud's, theory, threatened subjects would repress the experience rather than dwell upon it.

In a recent review of investigations of repression, Holmes felt that the most central conclusion to be drawn is that

> there is no consistent research evidence to support the hypothesis derived from the theory of repression. The lack of evidence for the theory is especially notable in view of the wide variety of approaches which have been tried and the persistent effort which has been made during the last half century to find support for the theory (1974b, p. 649).

Holmes is careful to point out that the research has clearly shown less recall and poorer relearning of material which has been associated with threat. Nevertheless, these findings do not always follow from the theory of repression and often may be more parsimoniously explained by competing hypotheses, such as the "attentional" one mentioned above.

Holmes feels that an explanation in terms of *non-defensive attentional processes* can best explain even those examples of repression drawn from clinical settings. He suggests that when a psychotherapy client fails to remember aspects of experiences which are deemed by the therapist to be significant, it may not be due to the client's repression of material. Instead, the client may simply have adopted a perspective on the events which is different from that of the therapist. In other words, the client may never have been aware of certain aspects of his experience. Thus, failure to recollect what was never there should not, according to Holmes, be construed as evidence of repression. Finally, Holmes asserts that what has been called the "return of the repressed" in psychotherapy, the "recall" of material which previously had been repressed, is probably nothing more than the client learning his therapist's perspective on things and now adopting that new frame of reference as he reconsiders old events.

By way of illustrating these points, think of a musical neophyte and a learned pianist attending the same concert featuring Chopin's E minor concerto. Each will come away with very different impressions of the evening's entertainment. The neophyte will not recall certain tones and nuances of the musical offering which the pianist found most important. This does not mean that the neophyte repressed material relating to the concert. After some discussion between the two concert-goers, the neophyte may talk about Chopin's concerto in terms very similar to those used by the pianist; this doesn't mean that repression has been lifted, but that a reconceptualization has occurred with the assistance of the pianist.

In conclusion, it should be pointed out that even if Holmes is correct in his judgment that research has failed to support Freud's theory of repression, one can not conclude that repression does not exist. As Holmes himself said, "We can only conclude that there is no research evidence that repression does exist" (1974b, p. 650). Since it is impossible to prove that repression does not exist and since it has so far been impossible to find conclusive evidence that it does exist, we are left in a never-never land with respect to the construct "repression." It is probably safe to say that use of the term will continue unless a new construct emerges which can theoretically account for the phenomena presently dealt with by "repression" and which is more susceptible to empirical verification. It remains to be seen whether Holmes' "non-defensive attentional processes" will fill this role.

Anna Freud (1936) suggested that repression is our first line of defense against anxiety. She reasoned that it is only when repression must be reinforced, or when it fails to keep threatening material in the unconscious, that the other defense mechanisms are employed. As we will see, some of these defense mechanisms are more complex than repression alone. However, like repression, they all function at an unconscious level; we are not aware that we are using them.

Denial. Sometimes we consciously tell ourselves to behave as if some unpleasant reality were non-existent. A person who is nervous over the prospect of an employment interview may decide it would be best to forget that a job hinges upon the impression created. "Just act natural and don't think about how important the job interview is," the person may hear himself saying. When this process operates unconsciously and is used by the ego to defend against anxiety, we speak of the defense mechanism *denial*.

Denial has been referred to as a primitive defense mechanism since it theoretically can only operate on the condition that the ego functions are in a weak or immature state. A strong, mature ego is well able to attend to the reality of situations. This reality orientation makes denial unlikely. However, when the ego's ties to reality are weak, "wholesale falsification of reality" becomes quite possible (Fenichel, 1945, p. 144) and the perception of this reality is replaced by wish-fulfilling fantasies which ignore unpleasant truths. "The job interview will be nothing more than a pleasant conversation," is a denial of reality.

Fenichel points out that even in mature, normally-functioning adults, the use of denial may occur. For instance, we may temporarily drift off into a state of reverie not too different in many ways from the wish-fulfillments of very early childhood. However, such a lapse from reality contact is only a brief refuge of a transient nature. It is superficial in comparison to the pervasive and persistent use of denial which characterizes the individual who is so out of contact with reality that he is diagnosed as psychotic.

While the mechanism of denial is usually thought of as being directed against the recognition of threatening external reality, it has also been seen as an important mechanism whereby the person defends against acknowledging the presence of internal feelings, memories, or inclinations. Freud suggested that adults frequently operate at a midpoint between blatant denial of painful internal perceptions and full awareness of them. At such times they may negate the internal perception of explicitly telling themselves that they are not experiencing what, in fact, they are. For instance, someone who is coming down with a virus cold may say, as the first signs of disease are being felt, "It really feels good to be healthy!" Such negations may also operate with respect to external stimuli. I vividly recall an incident in which I was verbally patting myself on the back for having waged a successful campaign to keep field mice out of my house. No sooner had this thought come to mind when a mouse arrogantly ran across a kitchen counter in full view. Coincidence aside, I probably had become subconsciously aware of the mouse's presence through peripheral vision, or by a sound it made. This perception then served to provoke the statement of negation which was only momentarily satisfying. Once the mouse moved directly into my field of vision, reality was too blatant to go on denying.

Reaction formation. When an impulse is repressed, one way in which anticathexes may be buttressed is through the development of an opposite trend. When there is an accentuation of feelings, lines of thinking, and/or behaviors opposite to those which are repressed, we speak of the defense mechanism called *reaction formation*.

The tendency to use reaction formation may be either reasonably circumscribed or pervasive. In the first instance, we may think of the mother who resents the presence of her child who was born too soon, or too late, or is not of the sex she desired. The guilt experienced consequent to the harboring of negative feelings about her child may be controlled by the mother behaving in an overly-loving, caring fashion. In this instance, it is only with respect to her child that these behavior patterns emerge.

It is not always easy to discern true love and caring for a child from a reaction formation against basic feelings of ill will. However, in the latter case, the love may be expressed in a driven, overwhelming way. In fact, the mother may so smother her child with love, so restrict its activities and curtail its free expression in the name of concern or protection, that normal and healthy psychological growth is thwarted. In effect, through the excessive expression of "love," the mother may damage her child as severely as if her resentment and hostility had been openly displayed.

Reaction formations may also reveal themselves by the manner in which one responds to questions relevant to the impulses against which the reactions are directed. With regard to our exemplary mother, we can expect that an inquiry into the circumstances under which hostility toward the child is felt, will provoke an animated rejection of the idea that hostility or anger is ever felt. In contrast, most parents would be able to respond unemotionally by citing instances and behaviors which cause them to become angry at their children. They experience such anger as natural, not as a source of guilt, and not something to hide with a thick overlay of false love.

The more pervasive use of reaction formation occurs when a person quite literally modifies his personality in the service of accentuating the opposite of what causes anxiety or guilt. The individual who cannot be comfortable with anal wishes to smear, to be messy, and to be generally unorganized may struggle to develop a personality characterized by neatness and orderliness. Similarly, the person who must defend against oral-dependent wishes may self present as a highly independent, self-assured, and assertive individual.

Undoing. Undoing may in some ways appear similar to reaction formation. However, instead of emphasizing the opposite of an unacceptable impulse, the individual undoes real or imagined behavior which derives from an unacceptable impulse. The person who ritualistically washes his hands, over and over again, may be trying to cleanse away, or undo, a recurrent impure deed or thought. Once the hands are washed it is as if the impurity had never been committed.

Freud refers to undoing as

> a kind of negative magic which by means of a motor symbolism would 'blow away,' as it were, not the consequences of an event . . . but the event itself . . . the individuals second act abrogates or nullifies the first, in such a manner that it is as though neither had taken place, whereas in reality both have done so. (1936, pp. 53-54).

Like most defense mechanisms, undoing has its counterpart in conscious experience. This is exemplified by the child who intentionally says, "I'm sorry!" after committing a transgression. In the child's mind, that verbal statement effectively does away with the antecedent behavior. Of course, the actual response of parents to the child's, "I'm sorry!" may serve to foster the belief that a few well-chosen words can undo even the most ill-advised actions. In such cases, the undoing is not nearly so magical an accomplishment as it is when utilized as an unconscious defense mechanism.

Isolation. People often try to adopt an objective posture by considering an issue or event without having their emotions interfere with or color their reasoning processes. This is the normal correlate of what Freud referred to as the mechanism of *isolation*. With isolation, the person is aware of past traumatic events, the memories per se have not been repressed, but the recollections are stripped of their emotional significance. The event and the emotion, which truly belong together, are kept psychologically apart. Brenner has said that, when isolation is used to excess "the individual has hardly any awareness of emotions of any kind and seems like a caricature of that equanimity which ancient philosophers put forward as an ideal" (1957, p. 99).

Fenichel presented a case report in which isolation dominated the patient's neurosis. It was reported that a 17 year old young man who masturbated, and who routinely watched as his friends engaged in mutual masturbation, heard a sermon in which the minister warned against associating with anyone who masturbated. Taking this message "to heart," the patient at first avoided the others who masturbated, especially one boy who indulged a great deal. The patient gradually began to develop a variety of neurotic symptoms which were designed to facilitate physical as well as psychological avoidance of the other boy. In order to avoid using the boy's name he referred to him as "The Avoided One." The patient refrained from all contact with The Avoided One's friends and family. Because The Avoided One's father was a barber, the patient also stopped going to barber shops. He finally was even avoiding the "forbidden" part of the city where the barber shop of The Avoided One's father was located. Indeed, he did not associate with men who were shaved by barbers.

As the neurosis developed, the patient himself had little difficulty in giving up masturbation and in avoiding the forbidden city area. He was, however, greatly disturbed by his own family members, whom he referred to as "congenial" ones, entering the forbidden neighborhood. It was at this point that the patient's neurosis became a fully developed isolation neurosis. He exerted great effort to keep ideas of congenial family members isolated from "uncongenial persons and localities," The Avoided One and the forbidden neighborhood. Unfortunately, the patient found that whenever he thought of The Avoided One, as he frequently did, he also immediately thought of a congenial person. This circumstance was called "connecting" by the patient; he dealt with it by a procedure he referred to as "disconnecting," in which he mentally focused upon an uncongenial person or place completely isolated from all congenial people. Once this was done, everything was "set right" again and he was calmed. It was not long before the patient was almost totally consumed by his effort to effect "disconnections." Notice that the patient's disconnections are a good example of the previously-discussed mechanism of undoing. Thinking of an "uncongenial" person or place in isolation undoes a previous ideational "connection" between an "uncongenial" idea and a "congenial" one. Thus, in this case there is a blending of undoing and isolation in the same symptom complex.

This patient's neurosis progressed to the point where he continually forced himself to think of only uncongenial persons and places, hoping to disconnect or isolate these from congenial ideas. In effect, the patient became obsessed with ideation which stood for masturbation. ". . . he now was unconsciously masturbating continually. And in point of fact, when his tension was greatest and he could not make a disconnection in spite of all his effort, he would occasionally, to his great astonishment, have an ejaculation" (Fenichel, 1945, p. 159).

In this case, the patient is depicted as isolating one ideational content area from another. In more typical personalities, it is not unusual for individuals to try to isolate different aspects of their lives. Fenichel suggests that the separation of school from home, or of social life from business, is common. Usually one sphere involves "good," socialized behavior and the second sphere encompasses behavior more directly reflective of instinctual inclinations. In more extreme instances it is possible that some cases of split personality are primarily based upon this defense mechanism of isolation.

Projection. It is commonplace for young children to attribute motives to others which they experience within themselves. This may be nothing more than an overgeneralization in which the child simply sees others as being too much like the self, and fails to appreciate self-other differences. The attribution of personal motives to others takes on a more defensive flavor in the mechanism of *projection*. With projection, the ego externalizes the source of an unacceptable id impulse. Thus, sexual or aggressive inclinations are attributed to others rather than being seen as stemming from within. Projection permits the person to legitimize his involvement in sexual or aggressive encounters in that blame for these is fixed on others, while the person sees himself as merely a victim.

The basically hostile person, the one who always finds himself in fights and arguments, may fail to appreciate the way in which he instigates these exchanges. Rather, he may perceive the world as peopled by hostile characters who leave him no choice but to retaliate with force. Similarly, the girl whose superego generates guilt over any expression of genital sexuality may attribute an unbounded sexual appetite to her male dates. "I just don't know what to do; everyone I go out with is all over me, tearing at my clothes and pawing at my flesh. Men are nothing but perverted animals!" The young lady probably is oblivious to her own seductive role in these matters. Instead, the sexual tone of her relationships is seen as the result of others' sexual motives.

It should be noted that the person who projects aggressive or sexual trends is able to function in a reasonably guiltless fashion because there is no acknowledgement of these "base" impulses within the self. In addition, the person may be able to engage freely in the very behaviors against which he is defending. That is, one may engage in aggressive or sexual behavior with impunity because consciously he believes the other person is always the provoker or seducer.

Pathogenic and successful defenses. The above-discussed defense mechanisms are termed "pathogenic" by Fenichel (1945, p. 143) because their excessive use is associated with psychological dysfunction. To a considerable degree, they all work against the routine discharge of instinctual energy. Impulses which are evaded through the use of defense mechanisms remain unconsciously active, and essentially unchanged. These impulses may periodically associate themselves with other impulses which are expressed, imparting to them an intensity and an affective quality which is characteristic of neurosis. Such modified impulses are called *derivatives.*

In contrast, the mechanisms called *sublimations* were seen by Freud as an inherent part of normal ego functioning. Sublimations permit pregenital instinctual discharge through a shift in the object of an instinct. That is, pregenital instinctual energy is not impeded; instead it is rechanneled so that the original object is abandoned in favor of some other pursuit. Characteristically, the sublimated activity is desexualized. This desexualization of pregenital libido is most likely to occur if the person is otherwise capable of achieving complete sexual discharge through a mature genital orgasm, and if pregenital strivings have not been repressed and, therefore, fixed enduringly in the unconscious.

The behavioral substitutes of pregenitality which are sublimations generally conform to the constraints of reality and social standards. The child may sublimate infantile inclinations to smear feces by playing in mud; the adolescent may shift to sculpture. Another person, preoccupied in childhood with sadistic impulses, can rechannelize and desexualize this energy as an adult by entering a medical-surgical career. In these examples, the person has attained a mature level of sexual, or genital, functioning and has effected a harmony between what was once infantile sexual energy and environmental expectations.

It should be noted that some psychoanalytic writers speak of the above processes under the more general term of *displacement,* referring to the fact that the object of an instinct undergoes a shift. In this context, sublimations are seen as displacement which results in culturally-valued behavior. Many humanitarian, intellectual, or artistic behaviors may be the result of sublimation. Earlier, we mentioned that Freud believed civilization rests upon the displacement of primitive sexual inclinations into socially productive channels; sublimations exemplify his point.

PSYCHOANALYTIC THERAPY

No discussion of Freud would be complete without some mention of his therapeutic work. To a large degree his theory of personality development and structure emerged from insights gained during contact with patients. Also, it is with respect to psychoanalytic therapy that the value of Freud's theories have been most vigorously debated.

It is the job of the ego to preserve the personality in the face of impositions stemming from three sources: reality, the id, and the superego. Probably its *severest* test is in relation to the id, whose instinctual demands are kept under harness only by dint of large energy expenditures in the form of anti-cathexes. This, of course, has the effect of draining ego resources which could otherwise be earmarked to facilitate adaptive functioning in a complex world. The superego, too, can debilitate ego functioning by thrusting so many limitations and prohibitions upon it that the ego is effectively paralyzed as it endeavors to meet responsibilities. If either the id or superego, or both, become too powerful relative to the ego, the latter organization becomes loosened, weakened, and "its proper relation to reality is disturbed or even brought to an end" (1949, p. 30). Freud illustrates this circumstance by reminding us of what happens to the ego during sleep when it is in a relatively weakened position. At that time it loses its attachments with reality and becomes dominated by the internal psychic world. In a word, during sleep, the ego slips into "psychosis" (1949, p. 30).

The Therapeutic Alliance

Freud colorfully describes the intrapsychic conflict ever-present in his patients as a kind of "civil war," whose outcome will be determined by alliance with an outside force — the therapist! "The analytic physician and the patient's weakened ego, basing themselves on the real external world, have to band together into a party against the enemies, the instinctual demands of the id and the conscientious demands of the superego" (1949, p. 30). The analytic therapy itself is the acting out of a pact between the patient's ego and the psychoanalyst. The goal of this pact is for the ego to regain mastery over all aspects of mental life.

Freud offers some advice at this point about the sort of patient with whom the analyst may successfully work. He warns against treating psychotics who are unable to enter into the aforementioned pact. Both the therapist himself and the help he offers to a debilitated ego are relegated to the same external world, a world which the psychotic is incapable of dealing with in a meaningful manner. Neurotics, however, for all their pain, can at least relate symptomatic relief to the establishment of an intensive therapeutic relationship. They are, therefore, the clients of choice.

The specifics of the therapeutic alliance are simply put, ". . . complete candour on one side and strict discretion on the other" (1949, p. 31). Freud advises that he is talking about much more than the therapist adopting the role of a "secular father confessor." What the therapist must hear goes beyond what his client knows but routinely conceals from others; it must ultimately include what the patient conceals from himself.

Free association. In order to facilitate such revelation, the patient is pledged "to obey the *fundamental rule* of analysis . . ." (1949, p. 31). This is to *free-associate,* to say everything that comes to mind, no matter how disagreeable, unimportant, or nonsensical it may seem to the patient himself. Presumably, these free associations will contain ideations which are more than simply influenced by the unconscious; they will contain direct derivatives of it. With these reflections, the therapist can assist the ego of his patient to gain knowledge of, and mastery over, the unconscious.

Transference. One of the aspects of the therapeutic relationship which Freud found most important, as well as remarkable, was the patient's penchant for relating to him in ways which were unjustified by reality considerations. Of course, Freud was there as a helper, but this alone could not explain the intensity of positive feelings of which he was so often the recipient. Similarly, the therapy experience was undoubtedly often frustrating, even painful, but this was an insufficient basis for the powerful expressions of anger and hatred hurled at him. Freud concluded that such intense positive and negative utterances were due to the fact that the patient sees the therapist as the "reincarnation of some important figure out of his childhood or past, and consequently transfers on to him feelings and reactions which undoubtedly applied to this prototype" (1949, p. 31). This, then, is *transference*.

One simple illustration of transference is reported by Hendrick. It involves a patient who developed strong affection for his analyst and entertained "phantasies of doing things *with* him . . ." (1958, p. 193). It was ultimately discovered that the patient, an only child, had once longed for a sibling "with whom to share love and secrets, when the parents left him alone" (p. 193). This long forgotten need was rekindled at an unconscious level in the context of the therapeutic relationship and greatly colored the quality of it.

Transferences such as these are not unique to the analytic setting. It occurs in other psychotherapeutic relationships as well, although certain procedural features of psychoanalysis may indeed facilitate the expression of a more intense transference. In this regard, the lack of self-disclosure on the part of the therapist, his dispassionate demeanor, and his positioning of himself behind and out of view of the reclining patient work to encourage the patient to fill the blank image with emotionally-charged, but erroneous, understanding of the therapist.

The phenomenon of transference occurs in everyday life as well. It is not uncommon for men to find it particularly difficult to relate to male employers. The resentment, hostility, and competition felt toward their superiors may well have their origins in old and now unconscious negative feelings toward their fathers. In a sense, the employer has come to symbolize the father and is the recipient of all the destructive fantasies and hot emotion which, at an unconscious level, are still earmarked for the father.

We can, therefore, conclude that transference is rather common. Hendrick says that "the phenomenon is a fundamental property of human nature, and under the conditions of free association is as spontaneous and inevitable as water running down a hill to seek its lowest level" (1958, p. 194). What is unique is the way in which transference is dealt with in psychoanalysis. The therapist uses it as a major source of information in his quest to understand the unconscious world of his patient. Transference within the analytic relationship "becomes a sample of life, and a sample under special conditions which permit of closer, more exact analyses than is possible in other relationships" (Hendrick, 1958, p. 196). This kind of examination provides insight into how the client is relating to people in the outside world and the nature of the infantile relationship which now stands as the unconscious prototype of current relationships. Freud believes that the transference "produces before us with plastic clarity an important part of his life-story, of which he would otherwise have probably given us only an insufficient account. He acts it before us, as it were, instead of reporting it to us" (1949, p. 33).

Another important asset of transference lies in the power which it imparts to the therapist. Because the therapist is thrust into the parents' place, the analyst becomes capable of influencing the superego in much the same way as the real parents did in the formative years. The possibility of an "after education" (Freud, 1949, p. 32) of the patient therefore becomes viable. Freud warns the therapist against abusing this source of power. Certainly, psychologicially infantile patients will have to be dealt with as children; for most patients, however, it is deemed improper for the therapist to indulge his inclination to teach, model, or become an ideal for the patient — "to create even in his own image" (p. 32). To do so would be only to repeat the mistakes of the real parents "who crushed their child's independence by their influence, and he will only be replacing the patient's earlier dependence by a new one" (p. 32). The analyst is obligated to respect the individuality of his patient.

During the initial phase of therapy it is most common for the transference to be positive in nature. This *positive transference* is expressed in the form of tremendous enthusiasm for therapy and admiration for the analyst. At first the initial goal of therapy becomes lost for the patient and is replaced by an insatiable desire to please the therapist and earn his love. Paradoxically, this new direction frequently results in the rapid alleviation of symptoms and a general flight into health, a "transference cure" in the service of gaining applause from the analyst.

It will be recalled that the child's relationship with parents is routinely ambivalent in tone, involving both affectionate and hostile overtones. Therefore it should not come as a surprise that the transference relationship with the therapist, which is a displacement of one with the parents, also is bipolar in its emotional coloration. Inevitably, the positive transference fades, only to be replaced by a *negative transference,* which reflects the hostilities of the past.

The shift from positive to negative transference is precipitated by the patient's unavoidable frustration with the conduct of his analyst. The fantasies of love and union with the analyst which characterized the early phase of transference can never be realized. Even the more acceptable expressions of favor from the analyst, a word of affection or the offering of preference, are only infrequently heard by the patient. This feeling of rejection not only effects a reversal in the emotional tone of the therapeutic relationship but also washes away, in a tide of negative passion, all of the apparent "gain" previously observed. The original pact is largely forgotten, and the patient becomes preoccupied with his struggle against the analyst. Unresolved issues revolving around relationships with the real parents now reappear in the transference with full fury. Hendrick noted, "Petulance, irritability, defiance, a childishness in the tone of voice are frequent, even in people who are otherwise in their daily lives quite mature" (1958, p. 204).

It is the task of the therapist to interpret transference. The patient tends to experience his feelings as new ones. Positive feelings for the therapist are attributed to genuine love. Later, feeling rejected, the patient turns his hatred toward the therapist and moves toward abandoning the therapeutic enterprise altogether. Freud saw it as the analyst's task to tear the patient out of his menacing illusion and to show him again and again that what he takes to be new real life is a reflection of the past" (1949, p. 34). In this way the patient gradually comes to fully appreciate the nature of his transference and gains insight into the ways in which old, unconscious issues are maladaptively guiding current interpersonal relationships, including the one with the therapist.

Freud cautions psychoanalysts against assuming that their own insight into the patient's difficulties will be readily shared by the patient himself. It is suggested that interpretations of the transference be offered only when the patient has, on his own, almost arrived at the same conclusion. The therapist then prompts the patient into taking that final step necessary to arrive at "the decisive synthesis" (1949, p. 35).

Resistance. If the therapist tries to thrust his knowledge upon an unready patient, his remarks will be met either by indifference or, more threatening to the continuance of therapy itself, by active *resistance*.

It will be recalled that the ego is almost always vigilant to invasions of threatening material from the unconscious into the conscious. The ego's penchant for utilizing anticathexis in this regard is contrary to the initial agreement to free associate and, therefore, counterproductive to therapeutic progress. Nevertheless, with the assistance of the therapist, as more and more undesirable elements move toward conscious recognition, "The more hard pressed the ego feels, the more convulsively it clings (as though in a fright) to these anticathexes . . ." (1949, p. 35). Each new groundwork covered brings on anew this resistance, which continues throughout all of treatment.

The operation of resistance is betrayed in several ways as the patient free associates. He may suddenly pause during what had been a free-flowing soliloquy, start to stammer, abruptly change topics, ask a question, or become overly intellectual. He may also simply claim that he can't think of anything or he may dwell on banalities; he may come late to therapy or miss appointments. In essence, what all of these behaviors have in common is that, one way or another, they interrupt the process of free association; this is the behavioral definition of resistance.

As the analyst interprets for the patient the nature and meaning of his resistance, he appears to be temporarily abandoning his alliance with the patient's ego. The initial pact was between the patient's ego and the analyst; now the analyst opposes the anticathexes with which the ego is so involved. He tries to tear the resistance apart, giving freer reign to the natural "upward drive" (1949, p. 36) of the heretofore threatening unconscious material, encouraging the unconscious to become conscious and part of the ego.

Once the unconscious has been made conscious, the patient's ego is in a position to reassess its meaning and import in a way never before possible. Remember that its content became lost to the ego early in childhood, at a time when the cognitive abilities of the individual were decidedly immature. Now the person's more mature capacities, as well as those of the analyst, will be brought to bear on the problem. The ego may, at this time, choose to either accept the unconscious, now conscious, wish as something which is really not too terrible and act on it, or it may reject the whole issue as no longer relevant and dismiss the wish as currently meaningless. The analyst himself is indifferent to the particular outcome. "In either case a permanent danger has been disposed of, the compass of the ego has been extended and a wasteful expenditure of energy has been made unnecessary" (1949, p. 36).

In his analyses of resistance, Freud does not neglect that part played by the superego. In this regard he speaks of a "need to be ill or to suffer" (1949, p. 36) of which the patient is consciously oblivious. An especially harsh superego, therefore, may work against cure by embracing resistive forces because "the patient must not become well but must remain ill, for he deserves no better" (1949, p. 37). Interestingly, Freud believed that these self-punitive patients may manifest spontaneous cure if they are, paradoxically, fortunate enough to encounter misfortune. Should the patient have a severe accident, or medical illness, or personal loss, the experience may be sufficient retribution for the transgressions over which the superego has been inflicting guilt. The person becomes as unburdened as the criminal who finally earns the right to leave prison after serving his time. Neurosis is no longer a necessary punishment and, within therapy, resistive forces will dramatically fade away.

Transference and resistance reflect the components of emotional forces which gave rise to neurosis in the first instance. The unacceptable unconscious wishes are now being replayed in the context of transference. The ego's anticathexes and the superego-induced punishment fantasies are observed in the form of resistance. These are the therapeutic issues. Hendrick describes psychoanalysis as "a recurring conflict between transference and resistance, apparent as the alteration of free association by the patient and moments or days of involuntary interruptions of his effort to free associate. . . . This is a repetition of the very same sexuality-guilt conflict that originally produced the neurosis itself" (1958, p. 207).

In summary, the psychoanalyst begins by encountering a patient whose ego has lost contact with significant portions of memory, is constrained by unreasonable superego prohibitions, and is drained of resources in its struggle against id demands. The mental forces of the ego are raised to a normal level by bringing it back into touch with what was lost, and by helping it reappraise both superego prohibitions and id demands. The regaining of contact with unconscious material is brought about via the interpretation of free associations, and the evidence of transference and resistance contained therein. Additional bases upon which the analyst rests his interpretation are dream reports offered by the patient and the patient's *parapraxes*, Freudian slips, which can be highly revealing of unconscious wishes.

At the conclusion of psychoanalysis, nothing has really been gained or lost in terms of the overall resources available to the individual. The successful therapy results in a redistribution of energy. According to Hendrick, there is a "significant reduction in the amount of time devoted to unconscious infantile objects, conflict, and the maintenance of repression . . . and more is then available for mature, guiltless, less-stereotyped activities (friendship, home-making, work, art, erotic love, etc.)" (1958, p. 214).

EVALUATION

The "Movement"

Psychoanalysis was Freud's own creation, one which he protected and defended with as much zeal as any mother could possibly muster for her own child. His capacity and willingness to stand apart from others, buoyed only by faith in the accuracy of his own observations and reasoning, were challenged during much of his career. At the time of its presentation psychoanalysis was revolutionary; many considered it to be deviant. The cornerstones of psychoanalysis — unconscious motivation, infantile psychosexuality, the relationship between childhood experiences and adult personality, energic conceptions of mind functioning — resulted in a picture of humanity which, while more balanced than any previous theory, was too complex and unpalatable for general acceptance.

It took Freud more than a decade to gather a small band of advocates, and in 1908 they held the first international meeting of psychoanalysts at Salzburg. The security of a unified "movement" was short-lived, however. Two of the brightest disciples broke with Freud a few years later; Alfred Adler left in 1911, and Carl Jung in 1914. In fact, when Freud wrote his *History of the Psychoanalytic Movement* in 1914 he included a blistering polemic against both Adler and Jung:

> Of the two movements under discussion Adler's is indubitably more important; while radically false, it is marked by consistency and coherence . . . Jung's modification . . . is so obscure, unintelligible and confused as to make it difficult to take up any position upon it. (1966, p. 60).

The diatribe continues,

> Every analysis conducted in a proper manner, and in particular every analysis of a child, strengthens the convictions upon which the theory of psychoanalysis is founded, and rubuts the re-interpretations made by both Jung's and Adler's systems. (1966, p. 65).

Freud was especially protective of the purity of psychoanalysis and reacted strongly against Jung for trying to pass off his system as a "new, improved" modification of Freud's authentic product. In drawing an analogy between his own and Jung's systems and a knife, Freud wrote of Jung:

> He has changed the hilt, and he has put a new blade into it; yet because the same name is engraved on it we are expected to regard the instrument as the original one . . . I think I have made clear, on the contrary, that the new teaching which aims at replacing psychoanalysis signifies an abandonment of analysis and a secession from it. (1966, p. 66).

It is clear from Freud's own words that there were political overtones to what started out as an intellectually-based camaraderie. Fromm goes further and suggests that the psychoanalytic movement was, in fact, a kind of "secular and scientific *religion* for an elite which was to guide mankind" (1959, p. 105). Like any "religion," Fromm points out that the psychoanalytic movement had a dogma — the written and spoken word of Freud himself. Analysts who were critical of Freud, even if they were constructive and had no intention of founding their own "schools," were deemed to be out of the orthodox fold.

A second parallel noted by Fromm between psychoanalysis and religion is that both have ritualistic elements. The so-called "sacred ritual" of psychoanalytic therapy involved a trinity of elements: "the couch with the chair behind it, the four or five sessions every week, the analyst's silence, except when he gives an 'interpretation' . . ." (p. 107). While these elements were initially vehicles for reaching specified goals, they soon became ends in themselves and any analyst not conforming was not conducting a "real" psychoanalysis. Fromm reminds us that "in the beginning" Freud sat behind his reclining patients because he "did not want to be stared at for eight hours a day" (p. 107). It was only later that justification for this juxtaposition of therapist and patient became more theoretically grounded. Arguments were presented that the patient was more relaxed when not facing the analyst, and thus his capacity to free-associate was enhanced.

Finally, Fromm argues that Freud presented himself and was seen by his loyal followers as the supreme authority on matters of doctrine. Freud's students tended to idolize their mentor and were always ready to acknowledge the source of their ideas in their own lectures and writings. The phrase, "as Freud has already said," is one which was excessively invoked according to Fromm.

The consequence of this, in Fromm's opinion, is that psychoanalysis quickly lost its "enthusiasm, freshness, and spontaneity." Prestige was invested in a relatively small inner circle at the pinnacle of the psychoanalytic hierarchy. These men had the power to dictate "correct" interpretation and application of orthodox dogma and to excommunicate the faithless. "Eventually, dogma, ritual, and idolization of the leader replace creativity and spontaneity" (1959, p. 106).

While the quasi-religious aspect of psychoanalysis may well have undermined the submission of productive contributions and innovations from his immediate followers, Freud himself, in his passion for truth, was never reluctant to modify his own views. Repeatedly, in the development of psychoanalysis, major revisions were effected by him on the nature of the unconscious, the substitution of a conflict theory for trauma theory of neurosis, the introduction of id, ego, and superego mind structures, to name a few. This presents more than a little confusion because in his later writings Freud often neglected to remind his readers that the meaning of some major terms had undergone revision. It is, therefore, necessary for the student of psychoanalysis who chooses to delve into the original sources to be aware of the first publication date of the selection at hand and be able to accurately place it into the chronology of Freud's ideas. This task is made easier by books, such as that by Holtzman (1970), which very nicely organize the development of psychoanalytic theory.

Methodology

There appears to be consensus regarding Freud's powers of observation. They were unquestionably excellent. Yet, Freud has been faulted for the circumstances under which he chose to observe and the manner in which he did so. It was not until evening, after seeing eight or more patients, that Freud gave himself the opportunity to collect his thoughts on the day's events and take notes on the critical occurrences. Hall and Lindzey (1970) claim that his recollections were, therefore, both incomplete and inaccurate, and this is probably true. Too much empirical evidence has been gathered testifying to the poor quality of retrospective testimony for us to conclude otherwise. Given this, the clinical data, Freud's notes and memories, from which psychoanalytic theory was constructed may well have been subject to a kind of bias analogous to that which occurs in the context of research. We are of course referring to experimenter bias, a source of error in which the experimenter's own expectations regarding outcome have an impact upon what is found, a "self fulfilling prophecy" phenomenon. It is certainly plausible that if experimenter bias can distort research results under reasonably controlled circumstances, this factor can exert even greater effects under the free-wheeling conditions which characterize case study investigations of the sort conducted by Freud.

Even if one were willing to grant that Freud's cognitive powers were so great that his notes accurately reflected what had actually occurred in the therapy arena, the patients' behaviors themselves may still have been subject to the bias of Freud's own expectations. In other words, though Freud, for the most part, was passive, quiet, and outside of the patients' field of vision he was still a *participant observer* (Sullivan, 1953). The patient's behaviors are, therefore, not pure reflections of his own personality, but are to a degree made in reaction to the therapist's characteristics.

> . . . to even attempt to observe the "personality" free from the "distorting" effects of one's own influence upon the person's behavior is to seek after an illusion. For the person is always responding to some situation, and a silent unresponsive analyst is no less "real" a stimulus than a warm, energetic, or humorous one. (Wachtel, 1973)

In this regard, Kiesler (1966), has brought attention to the "myth of therapist homogeneity." It is simply not true that all therapists are alike in the way they affect their patients. Therapy research clearly points out that the therapist himself is a stimulus variable which has a great bearing on the process and outcome of the therapeutic encounter. Because Freud was less sensitive to these issues than we are today, he failed to consider adequately what kind of a stimulus he was for his patients, how he may have personally affected their within therapy activities, and how this, in turn, had a bearing on the conclusions which he ultimately drew.

In a more positive vein, it must be said that Freud sensitized psychologists to the value of intensively studying the individual case. With no other investigatory procedure can the full complexity of human functioning be as well-appreciated. In addition, it can be argued that conclusions about personality functioning which emerge after seeing a particular client five hours a week for several years may be more valid and meaningful than those gleaned from experimental research in which a given subject is seen usually for no more than an hour or two. By employing the former procedure, Freud was able to utilize the validation method now called *internal consistency*. This checks tentative conclusions drawn from one bit of clinical data against other aspects of the clinical data. "Everything had to fit together coherently before Freud was satisfied that he had put his finger on the correct interpretation" (Hall and Lindzey, 1970, p. 54). While the experimental procedure may reveal something about what people are like on the average, that so-called "average" may be best discovered via in-depth case study exploration.

Because Freud relied almost exclusively upon case studies, he remains open to criticism with respect to the representativeness of cases he observed. For the most part, his patients were middle and upper class neurotic Victorian women who were in no way an adequate cross section of humanity. The narrowness of this observational base is further reduced by the fact that this restricted range of patients was, of course, all seen by only one therapist, Freud himself. Thus, no matter how adequate Freud's conclusions were for this select group, one can question their external validity. In other words, how legitimate was it for Freud to extrapolate from his clinical experiences and render generalizations about personality development and functioning which were allegedly applicable to virtually all population sub-groups?

Finally, the data from Freud's case studies were exclusively drawn from the patients' verbal self-reports. It has been argued that the patients may have omitted, distorted, or even added crucial events as they free associated about their past. For example, a patient's recollections of parental over-indulgence may have greatly misrepresented the actual quality of the parent-child relationship. Why could not Freud have tried to corroborate his patient's claims by seeking validating information from others who might know, such as parents or siblings? The problem with this solution was that Freud was really less interested in the events themselves than he was in the unconscious memories of them which the patient harbored. According to psychoanalytic theory, it is only through free association and dream analysis that the unconscious can be revealed. Later, of course, projective assessment techniques, such as the Rorschach inkblots, were added to this repertoire of tools by the practicing clinician. If it is the unconscious that one is after, it does seem that no one but the person himself can be an acceptable data source.

Psychoanalysis as a theory

There is no question that psychoanalysis is comprehensive. In fact, it probably deals with more aspects of personality development and functioning than any other theory of personality. Nevertheless, there are some areas which Freud has been accused of neglecting. Specifically, Mischel (1968), among many, believes that psychoanalysis emphasizes internal determinants of behavior to the relative exclusion of external determinants. This is not to say that Freud was oblivious to the impact of situations upon personality functioning. In fact, psychoanalysis and other psychodynamic theories "are totally explicit in their recognition that 'overt' behavior varies depending upon specific conditions, but they construe diverse behavioral patterns as serving the stable, relatively generalized *underlying* dynamic (motivational) dispositions" (Mischel, 1973b, p. 336). In other words, while situational factors such as the availability of instinctual objects, yield apparent behavioral inconsistencies across situations, Freud did not see behavior as being situationally specific in any important sense. What really counted were the very general, stable, underlying intrapsychic personality structures and dynamics.

Some post-Freudian revisions of psychoanalysis have tended to remedy this condition. Like Freud, these more modern theorists do not see the stable personality organization of an individual as causing him to behave in a predetermined fashion regardless of the prevailing situation. However, they go beyond this and say that behavior is the product of the way the individual characteristically perceives and understands his world. Thus, the situation, or at least the individual's perception of it, has become a very central issue for contemporary psychodynamicists Wachtel, 1973).

Also relevant to the issue of comprehensiveness is the fact that psychoanalysis is one of the few major personality theories which strongly attends to both process and content. Specifically, it emphasizes personality processes in its theory of psychosexual development, in its description of mind dynamics, and, of course, in its statement of personality change — psychoanalytic psychotherapy. Psychoanalysis also provides a theory of personality content with its enumeration of general personality character types, such as the oral, anal, and phallic characters, and with its listing of the various defense mechanisms. Thus, we are told not only about the different kinds of personalities, content, but also about how they got to be that way and how they might be changed, process.

The attention of psychoanalysis to both process and content issues has been greatly instrumental in maintaining the theory at a high level of popularity, especially among practicing psychotherapists. This is because even though Freud provides only one psychotherapeutic process, he does relate its effectiveness to different personality types. Psychoanalytic therapy is believed to lose effectiveness according to the time in the developmental stage when primary fixations occurred; the earlier the fixation, the less effective is the therapy. The therapy is presumably most curative for neurotics who are troubled by phallic fixations. Anally-fixated personalities, such as obsessive-compulsive, are less susceptible to the treatment. Finally, psychotic individuals, who are thought to have been fixated during the oral stage, are considered very poor prospects for a successful psychoanalysis. Naturally, this kind of prognostic information is of extreme value to the therapist who can only see a limited number of clients and is concerned with the most productive allocation of his time.

One of the major criteria for an adequate theory is systematization. There is no question that psychoanalysis more than meets this standard. Not only are the individual constructs related to each other, but the main theoretical subdivisions are also highly integrated. For instance, the theory of psychosexual development is intimately rooted in the theory of instincts on the one hand and is tied to the theory of mind structures, the id, ego, and superego, on the other.

At certain points, Freud's theory is over-systematized; an event referred to in the theory is related to so many other constructs that confusion creeps in. If a large number of antecedents to an event are spelled out and/or a large number of possible consequences, precise postdiction and prediction becomes impossible. This is best illustrated by the construct "fixation." A fixation is theoretically caused by just about any parenting practice, from overindulgence to underindulgence, and can result in a great range of adult behavior patterns. Because of this, one can delve into the personal history of almost anyone suspected of being fixated at a psychosexual stage and find some supportive evidence in the form of parenting practices theoretically conducive to the development of fixation. Similarly, if one believes that the early life relationships of a person probably caused some degree of fixation at a given stage, confirming evidence can almost always be found by even a cursory examination of adult behavior patterns. For instance, oral fixation, because of the vicissitudes of instinctual expression, can theoretically manifest itself in an almost infinite variety of ways: there may be excessive eating, smoking, and talking, or there may be dependency, or there may be "no" ways if the instinct has been subject to repression. While it is always true that a theory cannot be proven invalid because of lack of evidence, a theory does not gain respect if it is so designed that even if it is invalid, supportive evidence can be furnished. The latter condition is applicable to psychoanalysis.

Probably the most serious fault with psychoanalysis as a theory, in terms of current scientific criteria, is its lack of operationality at several very key points. Most important is Freud's silence on how one can go about assessing the magnitude of instinctual cathexes and anticathexes. These central behavior determinants are not in any way measurable. The strength of an instinct can only be indirectly inferred from its behavioral consequences. Since the relationship between an instinct and the behavior it instigates is frequently very indirect, overt activity is far from an acceptable yardstick for judging the amount or strength of an instinct. Certainly no help is obtained from looking at instinctual antecedents, since the underlying need states of instincts have never been located or measured.

Just how central this deficit is to the acceptability of psychoanalytic theory is an issue open to debate and represented by rather extreme positions. Some, such as Lashley, believe that, since Freud's notions of instinctual energy and its transformations are at the very heart of the theory, we should accept the coronary failure of psychoanalysis and let a system of scientific nonsense rest in peace (Lashley & Colby, 1957). At the opposite pole, Loevinger (1966), while not denying the scientific weakness of Freud's energy concepts, argues that they are "irrelevant" to his psychological theory. She believes that all of the phenomena usually explained in terms of psychic energy can be more parsimoniously handled by other psychoanalytic principles found in Freud's original writings. This de-emphasis of psychic energy is consistent with the other modernizations of Freud's theory; these are characterized by movement away from a heavy focus upon intrapsychic functioning and toward more situationally sensitive cognitive and interpersonal processes.

There are many other psychoanalytic constructs which are too far removed from observables to be operational. As we have mentioned, there is some serious question as to whether behavioral evidence of repression has ever been empirically demonstrated in a way which has relevance to Freud's theory. Certainly, the death instinct has been a sore spot for many analytic thinkers, and has been discarded by all but the most orthodox of Freudians. As a final example, we can mention the construct "trauma." Like so many of Freud's terms, this one has a theoretical definition which is not easily translatable into an operational format. How much stimulation has to enter the mental apparatus before the person is traumatized? Because of differences among people, and within a given person over time, in their capacity to manage stimulation from internal and/or external sources, the question is unanswerable. In addition, the "birth trauma," theoretically the basis for an experience which is protypic for all later anxiety reactions, is a construct which probably will never have empirical utility.

One final area of evaluation worth considering is that of value judgments. No theorist can avoid having his opinions about "good" and "bad" remain completely apart from his theoretical assertions. However, Freud's personal preferences may have influenced the sweeping generalizations about personality which he was prone to generate. Of central concern here are Freud's ideas regarding the nature of femininity and the events surrounding the phallic state. To what degree did Freud's values, representative as they were of a patriarchal society, color his interpretations and conclusions? To what degree were ideas of penis envy, of castration anxiety, and of women having to accept passivity to be truly feminine the fulfillment of Freud's own culturally-biased expectations? No firm conclusions on this point are possible but one is tempted to say that there does appear to be evidence of bias.

Freud wrote that, "Nature has determined woman's destiny through beauty, charm and sweetness . . . in youth an adored darling, and in mature years a loved wife" (in Fromm, 1959, p. 22). On the matter of equality of the sexes, Freud said, "That is a practical impossibility. *There must be inequality* and the superiority of man is the lesser of two evils" (in Fromm, 1959, p. 23). Fromm reminds us that these opinions are quite similar to those which prevailed in Europe at the turn of the century. We are also reminded that Freud was no "average" man.

"He rebelled against some of the most deeply ingrained prejudices of his time, yet in this aspect he repeats the most conventional line on the problem of women . . . This attitude certainly shows how strong and compelling Freud's need was to put women in an inferior place" (1959, p. 22).

"His genius is unassailable; but his formulations about women reflect values that emerged during the Victorian era" (Bardwick, 1971, p. 5).

As a final word, we can say that it is always easy for sophisticated psychologists to quite properly criticize the crudity of pioneering ideas at the headwaters of personality theoretical development. Accusations of value judgments, non-operational constructs, and unscientific data gathering procedures all are valid. Yet, despite these shortcomings, Freud's theory has proven itself vital enough to survive for three quarters of a century and still be well-represented when psychologists gather to debate the merits of one approach as opposed to another. In addition, two contemporary neo-Freudian trends are serving to help keep psychoanalysis an active area of both theory and research. On the one hand, a rapprochement between psychoanalysis and general psychology has been effected by Ego Psychology, which sees many ego processes, such as memory and other cognitive functions, as having their own reservoir of energy independent of the id. As such, they are called *autonomous ego functions* and comprise the *conflict-free* sphere of psychological functioning. On the other hand, much psychoanalytic thinking has focused more extensively on interpersonal relations. Both E. Erikson and H.S. Sullivan have constructed major theories of personality development derived from Freud, but which place more emphasis upon the relevance of interpersonal phenomena to psychological growth than they do upon intrapsychic processes.

SUMMARY

In this, our first detailed odyssey through a theory of personality, we presented and evaluated Freud's psychoanalysis. Each of the three sub-theories of this most impressive creation, the theory of instincts, of psychosexual development, and of mind structure, were abstracted from the voluminous writings of Freud himself. This effort hardly does justice to the sub-issues and complexities which Freud provides in his original writings. The interested reader is encouraged to delve into these works on a first-hand basis.

It was pointed out that much of the strength in Freud's theory rests upon its highly systematized organization and the inclusion of substantive aspects concerning both process and content issues. This has provided clinical psychiatry, psychology, and social work with a highly workable structure from which to operate. On an even more general level, Freud's ideas regarding the unconscious and psychic determinism have changed not only the way in which professionals deal with their clients but the way in which we all have come to understand human behavior. We saw that the major weaknesses in Freud have to do with failing to meet some of the criteria for good scientific theory, particularly that of operationality. This we judge to be a very real deficit, yet in fairness to Freud it must be said that the imposition of such after-the-fact criteria should in no way detract from his reputation as having been at the forefront of knowledge. Few in history have had such a significant impact upon the thinking of the scientific and lay community.

TERMS TO KNOW

CHAPTER 18
Phenomenological Personality Theory

There are two basic ways to study personality. One uses an objective, external frame of reference; the other utilizes a perceptual, personal, phenomenological one. The former vantage point is the older one in psychology; it examines behavior from the point of view of an outside observer. Today, psychologists who study personality in terms of the relationships which can be found between overt responses and objective-stimulus conditions are called "behaviorists." They represent this external frame of reference.

The "phenomenological" frame of reference involves the study of personality from the point of view of the individual himself. What is held as important is not the world or the person as they appear to the psychologist, but as they are perceived by the individual. What the individual perceives in his world, including himself, is called his *phenomenal field*. Combs, an early proponent of the phenomenological frame of reference, asserted that all behavior "is completely determined by and pertinent to the phenomenal field of the behaving organism" (1949, p. 20).

Smith (1950) criticized the phenomenological orientation of Combs because he equated the phenomenal field with consciousness. Combs' psychology was, therefore, considered to be neglectful of unconscious forces as determinants of behavior. In fact, Smith cites Freud as a major source of evidence "that a psychology of experience or consciousness has distinct explanatory limits" (1950, p. 518). Reluctant to discard the phenomenological frame of reference because of this limitation, Smith suggested that a similar, but more inclusive and appropriate position could simply be referred to as "subjective." The *subjective frame of reference* includes the individual's phenomenal field. However, it adds considerations of which the individual may not be aware, but which are still subjective and uniquely his own.

Recent phenomenological theorists have tended to broaden their use of the term "phenomenal field" to make it equivalent to Smith's "subjective frame of reference". Carl Rogers, for instance, describes the phenomenal field as the private world of the

347

individual. "It includes all that is experienced by the organism, whether or not these experiences are consciously perceived" (1951, p. 483). George Kelly is also considered to be a major proponent of this broadened phenomenological perspective. While there are substantive differences between the formal propositions of Rogers and Kelly, both heavily emphasize the subjective experiences of the individual as the main determinant of personality functioning; both theorists seek to assess the individual's own perceptions and understandings of his world as a main vehicle for studying personality. In this chapter we will restrict ourselves to a thorough presentation of the personality theory of Carl Rogers. A brief statement on Kelly's main emphasis will be found in Chapter 21.

CARL ROGERS

The personality theory of Carl Rogers is one that has been labeled in a variety of ways. Sahakian (1965) is among those who refer to it as a "phenomenological theory." This follows from Rogers' belief that if we are to really understand personality, it must be done from the individual's subjective frame of reference. The person's own viewpoint and feelings about himself and his environment are deemed to be most important, not objective reality. Hall and Lindzey (1970) and others have used the term "self-theory" to describe Rogers' position because the *self* is considered to be important in personality development and functioning. For Rogers, the self is an object of subjective perception. It is that part of the phenomenal field that one experiences as "I" or "me." As we will see, the value one attaches to his or her self, whether it be positive or negative or somewhere in between, is central to Rogers' theory. Maddi (1976) spoke of Rogers' theory as a "fulfillment model" of personality. This is consistent with its emphasis upon a single motive called the *actualizing tendency*. When actualization is pursued vigorously, the individual moves toward the realization and fulfillment of his personal potentialities. This emphasis upon self-fulfillment, coupled with belief in the importance of creativity, individual uniqueness, and the basic goodness of people, characterizes the position which Maslow (1962) called *humanistic psychology*. Today, Rogers is seen as one of the more influential members of humanistic psychology (Sarason, 1966). Rogers himself simply describes it as "a theory of personality and behavior" (1951, p. 481).

Regardless of what it is called, Rogers' theory is widely accepted, and has held an important place in psychology for more than a quarter of a century. There are a number of rather clear reasons for this sustained popularity. First, some key Rogerian constructs have been operationalized, making the theory a fertile ground for scientific inquiry. Psychologists in academic and research settings have thus been drawn to investigate empirically the validity of what Rogers says, and to extend the range of application of his ideas through research.

A second reason for the attention accorded Rogerian personality theory is that it is systematically related to his psychotherapeutic method, "client centered therapy." This form of psychotherapy is widely practiced by psychologists, social workers, and other counseling practitioners, such as the clergy. Not the least important reason for the broad professional appeal of client centered therapy is that it can be conducted by a relative novice. Rogerian therapists do not require the very lengthy and intensive training which psychoanalytic therapists must undergo. Secondly, unlike psychoanalysis, client centered therapy does not demand from the practitioner great insight into the meaning of dreams, free associations, symptoms, or the historical antecedents of current pathology. What is needed is a good measure of human sensitivity, an ability to "tune into" the experiences of others, and the capacity to "accept" the patient completely. A third reason for the widespread practice of client centered therapy has to do with time. In comparison with other more dynamically-oriented approaches, client centered therapy is relatively brief and, therefore, can more easily accommodate the often heavy case loads of psychologists and social workers. For these reasons, a substantial core of professionals naturally gravitate to Rogers' personality theory as their working model of human growth and behavior.

There is one more very important basis for the popularity which Rogers' personality theory enjoys. Once a student gets beyond the deluge of new constructs and understands what is being communicated, Rogers' message is often thought to make great intuitive sense and to afford significance for self-understanding. For many, Rogers is relevant for personal reasons which transcend academics or professional concerns.

Rogers reports that he grew up in a family "where hard work and a highly conservative (almost fundamentalist) Protestant Christianity were about equally revered" (1959, p. 186). This background, coupled with later exposure to a more liberal religious viewpoint at Union Theological Seminary, left Rogers with a strong belief in the inherent potential of people to solve their own problems in their own ways — a belief which, as we will see, influenced both Rogers' personality theory and his therapeutic orientation.

Rogers' "deep and abiding respect for the scientific method as a means of solving problems and creating new advances in knowledge" (1959, p. 186) also has early roots. In adolescence he became interested in scientific agriculture and read the latest research in areas such as feeding, soil, and animal husbandry. Once in college, Rogers maintained his attraction to science and focused upon physical and biological sciences. His graduate education began at Columbia University's Teachers College after two intervening years at Union Theological Seminary. While at Teachers College, Rogers was exposed to a rigorous statistical and learning theory approach to psychology. This contrasted with the more "speculative" (p. 186) Freudian thinking which abounded at the Institute for Child Guidance, where Rogers did his internship while earning his doctorate at Columbia. This combination of "hard" and "soft" psychology led Rogers to believe that science does not have to begin in the laboratory under carefully controlled circumstances. He felt that important scientific advancements can arise in the mind of the curious, perceptive observer of natural events who is clever enough to sense significance and implication where others see trivia or confusion.

It was this belief that Rogers brought to a Rochester, New York community child guidance clinic, where he remained for 12 years. Consistent with his previous scientific training, Rogers strove to bring order out of the apparently chaotic myriad of interpersonal events to which he became privy during his therapy hours. Out of this organizing effort grew an understanding of the psychotherapeutic relationship, which was also influenced in its development by his previously-formed religious beliefs. Specifically, he evolved a system of psychotherapy which was highly non-directive. It was not for the therapist to tell the client how to conduct his life. Rather than guide, Rogers claimed only to establish the conditions necessary for favorable personality change. He believed that in an accepting, non-criticizing interpersonal atmosphere the "client," Rogers' preferred word for "patient", would become freed from past psychological constraints and inhibitions; the client would finally have the chance to act on his own natural potential for personal growth and fulfillment. In effect, the client was given the opportunity and responsibility to save himself psychologically.

When Rogers accepted an academic position at Ohio State University, he was provoked by his students to articulate more clearly his therapeutic activities and assumptions. Out of this effort, Rogers developed a theory of personality which was a logical extension of his therapy practice. Thus, as with Freud, the formal personality theory of Rogers emerged after years of clinical work had afforded him uncountable observations, hypotheses, and conclusions. An early version of his theory appeared as a final chapter in *Client-Centered Therapy* (1951).

At about this time, Sigmund Koch, who was editing a six volume work entitled *Psychology: A Study of a Science,* (1959) asked Rogers to contribute a chapter. According to Rogers, "this was the slight nudge I needed, and for the next three or four years I worked harder on this theoretical formulation than on anything I have written before or since. It is, in my estimation, the most rigorously stated theory of the process of *change* in personality and behavior which has yet been produced" (1974, p. 119). Rogers later commented that his chapter, "A Theory of Therapy, Personality, and Interpersonal Relationships as Developed on the Client-Centered Framework," was "the most thoroughly ignored of anything I have written." In a manner quite unlike what one might have expected Freud to have said under similar circumstances, Rogers wrote: "This does not particularly distress me, because I believe theories too often become dogma . . ." (1974, p. 120).

A THEORY OF PERSONALITY

Basic Assumptions

Rogers begins his theory by mentioning three essential features of personality functioning. These assumptions about the nature of people represent the theoretical core from which Rogers' other constructs follow.

Experience is reality. "Experience," as a noun, means all that is going on in and around the person at a given time which is either in awareness, consciousness, or potentially available to awareness. Thus, experience may include various external stimuli, such as sights, sounds, and smells, as well as internal events, such as the psychological aspects of hunger or currently active memories of past experiences. Excluded from experience are biological events, such as changes in blood sugar, which are never directly accessible to awareness.

The experience of every person is unique, and constitutes reality for that person. Reality is thus subjective, and is best known to the individual himself. It therefore follows that no one can presume to have the same internal frame of reference as another; no one can properly claim that his own sense of reality is necessarily better or more correct than that of someone else; no one has the right to impose his reality upon others, as so many parents and teachers do.

These ideas are basic to a theme running throughout Rogers' writings; other people's points of view should be respected and valued, no matter how different they may be from our own. This theme is important because the experience of one person is very often quite inconsistent with that of another. The teacher's experience of her lesson plan is that it will be an intellectual challenge for her pupils; the student may find it boring or incomprehensible. The child's experience of creamed spinach is that of unpalatable mush; in the parent's experience it is a delicately-seasoned gourmet's delight. Rogers' position in matters of such potential conflict is that neither of the realities represented is more valid than the other. Each experience must be accepted as valid reality for its respective beholder. By accepting the point of view of others, we are in a position to be accepting of their behavior as well.

Actualizing tendency. Rogers' second basic assumption has to do with motivation. He believes people have, from birth on, an inherent tendency to develop all "capacities which serve to maintain or enhance the organism" (1959, p. 196); he calls this an "actualizing tendency." Rogers is clear in saying that this motive is the *only* motive operative; however, it finds expression in a variety of ways. Specifically, the actualizing tendency includes what other theorists have understood in terms of deficiency needs or drives for tension reduction. The behaviors we engage in so that we may maintain satisfactory levels of air, water, food, warmth, and sexual gratification are all seen by Rogers as the product of the actualizing tendency. But the actualizing tendency extends far beyond the mere gratification of somatic cravings. The development of skills and talents, and the utilization of these in creative ways, are also expressions of the actualizing tendency. Lastly, this core motive manifests itself through movement toward conditions of greater "differentiation." At a perceptual level, differentiation is seen in the child's developing capacity to attend to ever more subtle aspects of his environment. Cognitively, our understanding of the world undergoes differentiation in that we have mental access to increasing numbers of ideas and concepts. Rogers sees the effect of differentiation even in the interpersonal sphere; the individual is thrust toward autonomy, toward becoming a person who is unencumbered by the constraints and impositions of others.

It must be understood that actualization is a motive and is, therefore, best conceptualized as an ongoing process. Actualization is not a final state of personal perfection. One never becomes actualized to the point of permanently abandoning the motive altogether. There are always more talents to develop, more skills to enhance, more efficient and pleasurable ways to satisfy biological needs. One can, however, speak of people as engaging in the actualizing process to a greater degree than others; they have moved further along than others toward functioning in a self-fulfilling, creative, autonomous manner.

Another important feature of Rogers' thinking is that this actualizing motive will always manifest itself in individually unique ways. Behaviors which are consistent with one person's actualizing tendency may be quite different from behaviors of another which are, to an equal degree, consistent with his actualization. We all have different potentials and, therefore, different avenues to follow if we are to develop them to their fullest.

A final point of emphasis with respect to the actualizing tendency is Rogers' belief that the organism, as it engages in goal-directed behavior within the context of perceived, subjective reality, does so as an organized whole. At the psychological level, sub-motives do not operate independently of each other. Rather, they interact and orchestrate functioning in the direction of actualization. The interdependence of functions is also seen at the physiological level. By way of illustration, Rogers points to animal research which shows that the water concentration of the body is usually kept at optimal levels via the operation of the pituitary gland. This gland secretes an antidiuretic hormone when body water concentrations are low, thereby retarding the elimination of body fluids. Removal of that part of the pituitary gland responsible for this regulation results in an animal consuming large quantities of water. Increased drinking behavior serves to maintain acceptable concentrations of body water.

"It is thus the total, organized, goal-directed response which appears to be basic, as evidenced by the fact that, when one avenue is blocked off, the animal organizes to utilize another avenue to the same goal" (1951, p. 487). Alteration of one body system invariably has an impact upon other systems because all function in harmony as a total organized system; they are always moving in the direction of overall self-maintenance and enhancement.

Research presented by Davis (1933) on dietary self-selection provides evidence for the capacity of even young children to naturally alter their eating habits when nutritional imbalances exist. Using an array of 30 unmixed and unseasoned foods from which they could freely select, Davis demonstrated that over a four and a half year span children maintained themselves on balanced diets. They were kept under medical supervision, and were judged to be not only healthy but remarkably free of digestive upsets. Most interesting is Davis' report that one child who had advanced rickets spontaneously chose to consume cod liver oil which, although unpalatable to most children, is high in the vitamin D necessary for symptom remission. The child's appetite for cod liver oil waned as his rachitic symptoms faded.

Other "cafeteria" research with animals tends to substantiate Davis' results. For example, Rozin (1968) presented rats with various nutrients in solution. When the protein solution was diluted, the animals showed an increase in consumption which was highly correlated with the degree of dilution; cutting the protein concentration in half resulted in the rats doubling their intake of the solution.

In his review of the research on dietary self-selection, Overmann (1976) reached the conclusion that both experimental and anecdotal evidence on animals and humans documents the ability of organisms to "select and qualitatively monitor their intake of nutrients" (p. 218). Such phenomena are clearly consistent with Rogers' notion of an actualizing tendency in which all aspects of functioning are involved.

Before we present Rogers' third basic assumption, some important constructs and research closely associated with the actualizing tendency will be discussed.

The self. One universal consequence of the actualizing tendency is the emergence of differentiated experiences from initial diffusion. Early in life some of these differentiated experiences become *symbolized;* they attain the level of consciousness or awareness. Those symbolized experiences which relate to the organism as a separate, functioning, actual agent, differentiated from the rest of the phenomenal field, are called *self-experiences.* The self-experience of sucking one's thumb is different from that of sucking on a toy block. This qualitative distinction ultimately becomes symbolized so that the thumb is perceived as part of the self, whereas the toy block is not so perceived.

Self-experiences are the bases from which a subjectively held, organized, but ever-changing notion about the self is built. This is the *self-concept.* Unlike Freud's concept of ego with which the self is often compared, the Rogerian self is not an active sub-part of the personality. Rather, it can be best understood as an object of perception. It is that part of the phenomenal field which is differentiated as "I" or "me." While the person's concept of self tends to be somewhat fluid, at any given moment it can be operationalized in terms of overtly expressed self descriptions.

Q-sorts. It has been traditional among investigators to assess the self concept using what Stephenson (1953) called Q-methodology. This is a self-rating technique in which the subject is asked to sort cards containing self-descriptive statements, such as "communicates clearly and effectively," into several piles labeled from "least" to "most" self-descriptive. In order to keep subjects from placing all of the highly socially-desirable characteristics in the "most like me" pile and all of the socially undesirable cards in the "least like me" pile, the responder must sort the cards in a manner which approximates a normal distribution. For example, Block's (1961) California Q Set contains 100 cards which are sorted into nine piles. The most extreme piles, one and nine, must each contain five cards; piles two and eight each have to contain eight cards; and the greatest number of cards, 18, have to be placed in the center pile. In this way, extreme response sets are largely circumvented.

Of course, the Q-sort is not without its difficulties. The sorting of 100 or more cards is not an easy task and one must have a highly motivated and cooperative subject in order for the results to be meaningful. In addition, many subjects complain that the forced distribution places an uncomfortable restriction on how they feel they should present themselves. For example, the subject may honestly feel that there are only two or three cards which really capture what he is like as a person; yet five cards must be placed in the "most" self-descriptive pile. Finally, Q-methodology is, in a sense, inconsistent with Roger's emphasis on the subject as the one who knows himself best, in that the self-descriptive statements are supplied by the assessor. Thus, the pool of items may not be adequate for the self-description of many personalities; there may be an over-abundance of items in some content areas, while other important traits of a particular subject may not be represented on the cards at all. Despite these limitations, Q-methodology has proven itself to be a valuable assessment strategy for Rogerian researchers. Particular investigations employing Q-methodology will be presented later in the chapter.

   Self-actualization. Several writers use the term ''self-actualization'' in a way which is virtually synonymous with Rogers' actualizing tendency. Maslow (1970) defines the need for self-actualization in terms of the individual being true to his own nature. Self-actualization is the tendency for man ''to become actualized in what he is potentially. This tendency might be phrased as the desire to become more and more what one ideosyncratically is, to become everything that one is capable of becoming'' (p. 46). In contrast, others define self-actualization in terms which do not so much imply maintenance and enhancement of the total organism, but rather in terms of maintenance and enhancement of the self-concept. In this line, Combs and Snygg (1959) say that self-actualization involves man's nature to ''build up and make more adequate the self of which he is aware. Man seeks both to maintain and enhance his perceived self'' (p. 45).
   Rogers himself draws a theoretical distinction between the actualizing tendency and self-actualization. His definition of the latter term is narrower than the former and very close to that of Combs and Snygg. Rogers says that self-actualization is that aspect of the general tendency toward actualization which is specifically relevant to ''the actualization of that portion of the experience of the organism which is symbolized in the self'' (1959, p. 196).

   The POI. In an earlier chapter we singled out the construct of self-actualization as being scientifically weak. It was said that its meaning is not precise, and it is defined in terms which are themselves vague. There nevertheless have been attempts to operationalize self-actualization. Shostrom's (1963) Personal Orientation Inventory (POI) stands out as the major effort in this cause.
   The POI is a 150 item questionnaire using paired opposites; the subject's task is to select that member of the item pair which is most self-descriptive. ''I do what others expect of me,'' or ''I feel free to not do what others expect of me;'' ''I will continue to grow only by setting my sights on a high-level, socially approved goal,'' or, ''I will continue to grow best by being myself.''
   The POI is scored twice. The first time for two ratio scales of personal orientation. The *Support Ratio* is based upon the 123 Inner Directedness (I) scale items. It measures the degree to which one is reactive to the self as opposed to others, and thus taps the variable of autonomy, a characteristic basic to self-actualization. The Support Ratio is thought to be the best overall measure of self-actualization contained on the POI. The

other ratio scale, the *Time Ratio* (TR) is based upon the 27 item Time Competence (TC) scale. It purports to measure the degree to which one is present-oriented and utilizes time effectively.

The POI is then scored a second time for the 10 subscales. These contain 9 to 32 items each, with some items appearing on more than one subscale. Subscale names and brief descriptions appear in Table 8.

TABLE 8 POI Subscales

SUBSCALE	ITEMS	DIMENSION MEASURED
Self-Actualization Value (SAV)	26	Agreement with the primary values of self-actualizing people
Existentiality (Ex)	32	Existentially or situationally determined reactions as opposed to the rigid adherence to principles
Feeling Reactivity (Fr)	23	Responsiveness to own needs and feelings
Spontaneity (S)	18	Freedom to react spontaneously, to be one's self
Self-Regard (Sr)	16	Self-affirmation based upon self perceived worth or strength
Nature of Man (Ne)	16	Belief that man is good and constructive as opposed to being basically evil
Synergy (Sy)	9	Ability to transcend dichotomies (be synergistic)
Acceptance of Aggression (A)	25	Capacity to accept one's own aggression as opposed to defending (denying, repressing) against it
Capacity for Intimate Contact (C)	28	Capacity to develop intimate and meaningful relationships free from expectations and obligations
Self-Acceptance (Sa)	26	Acceptance of self despite weaknesses or deficiencies

There is not a wealth of data concerning the reliability of the POI. Klavetter and Mogar (1967) report a study in which 48 college students served as subjects. The POI was administered twice to these subjects, with the test-retest interval being only one week. Subscale test-retest reliabilities ranged from .52 to .82; the important Inner Directedness and Time Competence scales were found to have reliability coefficients of .77 and .71, respectively. Ilardi and May (1968) used 64 entering nursing students as subjects and administered the POI twice, with a 50 week test-retest interval. Spuriously high reliabilities due to memory factors were now removed, and the coefficients ranged from .32 to .71. Those for the Inner Directedness and Time Competence scales dropped to .71 and .55, respectively. Ilardi and May point out that these levels of temporal stability are of a magnitude which is comparable to that of the Minnesota Multiphasic Personality Inventory (MMPI) and the Edwards Personal Preference Schedule (EPPS), two well-established personality inventories.

Klavetter and Mogar (1967) also investigated the degree to which the various subscales were mutually independent. Low between-scale correlations would provide justification for them as measures of discrete personality dimensions. Unfortunately, these between-scale correlations were generally moderate to high. In fact, some between-scale correlations were higher than the test-retest reliabilities of the scales themselves. For instance, while the test-retest reliability of the Inner Directedness scale was .77, it was found to correlate with the Ex, Fr, S, and C scales at levels ranging from .77 to .83. These high between-scale correlation coefficients are not surprising since most of the items on the Ex, Fr, S, and C scales are also to be found on the 123 item I scale. On the basis of such figures, it can be argued that the 12 subscales of the POI are statistically redundant. Klavetter and Mogar concluded that "performance on this test would be expressed more accurately and parsimoniously in terms of fewer dimensions" (p. 424).

The validity of the POI has been assessed in a variety of ways. Knapp (1965) tested 136 college students and obtained "high neurotic" and "low neurotic" subsamples which were based on their scores on the Neuroticism (N) dimension of the Eysenck Personality Inventory (Eysenck and Eysenck, 1963). Knapp then compared the POI subscale scores of these two groups. As expected, on every POI subscale, the low neurotic group scored in a significantly more self-actualizing direction than the high neurotic group. In another effort, Lieb and Snyder (1968) predicted that high self-actualization would be related to academic achievement. As a measure of self-actualization, the Support Ratio of the POI was used. After testing 354 college students, Lieb and Snyder were forced to conclude that no relationship exists between this measure of self-actualization and college achievement.

Culbert, Clark, and Bobele (1968) were interested in ascertaining whether POI scores would reflect personality change as a consequence of participation in sensitivity training. They had viewed participation in a sensitivity group as a "self-actualizing treatment," and, therefore, they anticipated that POI scores would increase. Two training groups were formed, each containing 10 university seniors and graduate students. The groups met for a two hour session each week for 14 weeks. Both groups were led by the same pair of trainees, who asserted that their purpose was to "promote authentic interaction and increased self awareness" (p. 54). The POI was administered prior to the first sensitivity training session, and again prior to the final meeting.

Unexpectedly, despite efforts to randomly assign the 20 subjects to the two training groups, the first group was found to contain many more high scoring POI participants than did the second group. In fact, the authors characterize members of the first group as being equivalent to "a population of self-actualizers" (p. 55). The students in the second group had POI scores "relatively similar to a population of normal adults" (p. 55). Given this start, it should not come as a surprise that the predicted rise in POI scores from pre- to post-training for the first group failed to materialize. They actually showed nonsignificant declines on 10 of the 12 POI subscale scores. On the important Inner-Directedness scale, the mean score dropped slightly from a self-actualizing high of 89.33 to 88.44 at post testing. In contrast, the members of the second group did manifest the expected changes on the POI. Their mean scores increased from pre to post-training on all twelve POI subscales. The rise was statistically significant on the four subscales of Capacity for Intimate Contact, Synergy, Spontaneity, and Inner-Directedness. On this last subscale, the mean of Group II rose from an initial level of 79.60 to 89.80 (p < .01) at post training, thus bringing the second group up to the level of the first on Inner-Directedness. The authors concluded that sensitivity training, an experience designed to facilitate self-actualization, brought "about increased POI scale means for a group initially resembling normals and did not disturb the mean scores for a group which initially appeared to be near the self-actualizing level" (p. 56).

The meaning of this empirical finding is not entirely clear. One is tempted to assume the validity of the POI and, therefore, assert that sensitivity training results in people who indulge their actualizing tendency more vigorously. However, it is also possible that the post-training POI scores are, at least in part, *not* due to high levels of self-actualization. For instance, the high scores may have been induced through experimenter bias; the researchers do not report who the administrators of the POI were, and whether they were blind to the purposes of the research. If either the experimenters or the trainees administered the POI, their own expectations regarding the outcome might have been sufficient to subtly influence the subjects.

It has been reported that POI scores can be faked under certain circumstances. Braun asked 15 college students to take the POI twice; first they were to respond as a "typical neurotic," and then as "this same hypothetical person would after two years of therapy" (1966, p. 1282). Mean differences of substantial magnitudes occurred on every POI subscale. In all cases the change was in the direction of greater self-actualization on the "after therapy" test. Of particular note is the shift on the Inner Directedness subscale, which went from 48.1 with the "typical neurotic" set to 91.7 under "after therapy" instructions.

These results are particularly relevant to the sensitivity training research done by Culbert and his colleagues (1968). The "after therapy" set induced by Braun is a good analogue of the set which may have been spontaneously adopted by Culbert's subjects at the conclusion of their own group sessions. That is, some of the subjects who underwent 14 weeks of sensitivity training may have been motivated to present themselves as the healthful products of a "therapy" experience. Such a motive might well have functioned in a way quite similar to the "after therapy" set artificially induced by Braun and which was capable of greatly raising "apparent" levels of self-actualization as measured on the POI.

An experiment by Foulds and Warehime (1971) also looked at the fakeability of the POI. This research, however, prompted the authors to come away with quite favorable evaluations of the POI. Ninety five undergraduates were first given the POI under standard instructions. This was immediately followed by a second administration in which the subjects were told to "imagine that you are applying for a job that you very much would like to have and you want to present yourself in the most favorable light possible" (p. 279). In this case, deliberate attempts to please a hypothetical employer resulted in depressed scores of 10 of the 12 subscales. The mean difference was statistically significant on 9 of these. Of the two scales which manifested an increase, only one was significant in its magnitude of change. Foulds and Warehime appropriately point out that their induction did not promote the production of profiles characteristic of the self-actualizing person. From this, they go on to conclude that college students' conceptions of the "well-adjusted person" are different from the model of the "self-actualizing person" utilized by Shostrom in the construction of the POI, and one should have "increased confidence in the results of studies using the Personal Orientation Inventory . . ." (p. 280).

We feel these assertions are tenuous, at best. It must be recalled that Foulds and Warehime did *not* ask their subjects to fake either a "well-adjusted person" or a "self-actualizing person." Thus, any conclusions about college students conceptions of either is pure speculation. The students were only asked to present themselves "in the most favorable light possible" to a prospective employer. Could it be that many subjects anticipated that a generally conservative, other-oriented person would be viewed with more favor by an employer than would one who appeared to be invested primarily in his own actualization? Such strategy on the part of subjects is one way to explain why their POI scores tended to be lower in the "fake" condition when compared with the scores obtained under standard instructions. Finally, regardless of why the scores were affected, the fact does remain that they were, and to a substantial degree. It seems that one firm conclusion which may be drawn is that POI scores are highly susceptable to situational variables salient at the time of testing. Such a conclusion directly follows from this research by Foulds and Warehime, as well as from that by Braun.

One last point about the POI should be mentioned. This has to do with whether the instrument is a theoretically adequate operationalization of the construct it purports to measure. Self-actualization is a very individual matter; the potentials which one person has available to actualize may be quite different from those of anyone else. Despite this, scoring on the POI is based upon the degree to which responses are consistent with a standard profile of the self-actualizing individual. It would seem then that the use of a limited number of items having limited response format, and the comparison of subjects' responses with a hypothetical standard are inconsistent with the theoretical definition of self-actualization. This problem is not a new one in psychology. Historically, there has been conflict between psychologists' desires to view individuals as unique, each worthy of intensive study in his own right, and the need to develop standardized personality assessment tools which depend upon normative data against which to compare individual scores.

Organismic valuing process. Rogers' third basic assumption has to do with a regulatory mechanism which serves to keep the organism "on the beam" (1959, p. 222) of actualization. This mechanism is called the *organismic valuing process*. It is the basis of the individual's awareness of what is most self-enhancing, and what behaviors are consistent, or inconsistent, with his own actualizing tendency.

Rogers asserts that subjectively-perceived experiences are constantly being evaluated. Those experiences which are consistent with actualization, either in terms of the immediate situation or in the long range, are valued positively. To put it simply, we naturally prefer what is good for us. Experiences which in some sense maintain or enhance the organism have associated emotions which are pleasant. An effort will, therefore, be made to maintain or to repeat such experiences. When experiences are inconsistent with the individual's actualizing tendency, they will be evaluated as negative and will tend to be avoided.

Thus, two points are important. First, actualization is the criterion against which experiences are evaluated. Second, the conscious evaluation of an experience may be understood as the symbolization of the affect associated with that experience; if the affect is positive, we organismically evaluate the experience favorably, and if the affect is negative, our organismic evaluation will be unfavorable.

The value placed upon a subjective experience will vary due to transient situational or biological conditions. For example, a hungry infant will positively value the receipt of food since at such a moment, eating is consistent with actualization. Within a short time, however, eating will be negatively valued and food avoided. The opportunity for sleep may then be positively valued; rest after a belly-filling meal best serves to enhance and maintain the organism.

Personality Development

Roger's theory of personality development again introduces us to an array of new constructs.

Need for positive regard. As the young child interacts with his parents, certain of his behaviors will make a positive difference in their experiential field and the parents will experience *positive regard* for their child. The experiencing of positive regard for another promotes responding in the form of expressing "warmth, liking, respect, sympathy, acceptance" (1959, p. 208). For example, a twelve month-old might babble something faintly resembling a word. This utterance effects a positive change in the parents' experiential field. They are happy to hear the "word" and respond with strong expressions of joy and attention; they manifest positive regard for the child.

From the child's perspective, the receipt of positive regard is organismically valued as favorable. The child may, therefore, try to reinvoke self-experiences which are associated with obtaining positive regard more frequently. In our example, we might observe the child engage in more frequent verbalizations, to the delight of the parents. We thus see a motive emerge, one which involves the seeking of warmth, acceptance, and approval from others. This is the *need for positive regard.* The overt expression of this need is the emission of behaviors, in this case the verbalizations, which provoke positive regard from others.

Rogers believes that the need for positive regard is universal, but he does not take a firm stand as to whether its origin is innate or learned. He acknowledges that some writers see an infant's need for love and affection as inherent. However, Rogers himself seems to lean toward a learning explanation. Specifically, he appears to be saying that certain external consequences of our behaviors, such as positive regard from others, have the effect of increasing the frequency of those behaviors. As we will see when we discuss *operant learning* in Chapter 20, any consequence which increases the frequency of preceding behaviors is a reinforcement within that conceptual framework. The behaviors which show an increase in their frequency of occurence are said to be "reinforced." Thus, Rogers' ideas about the development of a need for positive regard, operationally defined in terms of the increase of positive regard-seeking behaviors, seem to be quite similar to what operant learning theory has to say about the processes surrounding increases in behavior frequency.

In our example of the babbling infant, the child's behavior created a positive change in the parents' phenomenal field; it made them happy. Their positive response in turn created favorable affect in the child. Everyone was made to feel good! In a more general sense, Rogers says that the expression of positive regard toward another person is usually followed by receipt of the same from the other person. By being made to feel good by another through their expression of positive regard toward us, we naturally express positive regard back; the other person then experiences a positive change in his experiential field also.

This reciprocity notion is at the core of Rogers' optimistic belief that, if left to their own resources, people would naturally gravitate toward being socialized, interpersonally satisfying, and satisfied individuals. The idea is a simple one with profound implications; to express acceptance, respect, and liking for others brings forth a reciprocal expression from them ". . . when an individual discriminates himself as satisfying another's need for *positive regard,* he necessarily experiences satisfaction of his own need for *positive regard"* (1959, p. 223).

Need for self-regard. Regardless of whether the need for positive regard is learned or innate, Rogers is clear in saying that there is a learned derivative of this need called the *need for self-regard.*

The child learns that certain self-experiences are associated with satisfaction of his need for positive regard. Other self-experiences might be associated with expressions of disfavor from the parents. Through such association, the self-experiences themselves become value laden. Some come to be seen as better or are more prized than others. Consequently, the child will develop a need to reinvoke the more positively-valued self-experiences, independent of their current interpersonal impact. This is the basis of the need for self-regard.

An individual satisfies this learned need to regard himself positively to the degree that he experiences himself in ways which have previously been associated with positive regard from others. In effect, the person becomes his own provider of positive regard. Another way to view this phenomenon is to understand the person as learning to like best those self-experiences, or those aspects of the self concept, which other important people have liked.

The characteristics of the need for self-regard appear in some important ways to be similar to the psychoanalytic construct of the superego. In both theoretical systems, the child is thought to reach a point in his personality development where he begins to accept, as his own, the standards of good and bad communicated to him by others through rewards and punishments. In both systems, the child theoretically feels best about himself when he conforms to the adopted standard. For Rogers, the good feeling is explained in terms of satisfying a need for self-regard and having a positive self-concept. In Freud's terms, such conformity brings about a feeling of pride for behaving in a manner consistent with one's ego ideal. The need for self-regard is the construct used by Rogers to explain how the individual can experience positive regard, or its loss, independent of others; "He becomes in a sense his own significant social other" (1959, p. 224). Similarly, in Freud's theory, the emergence of superego processes results in an individual who is his own dispenser of pride or reward, and, guilt, or punishment.

It is always risky to try to translate one theory into the terms of another. The constructs are rarely synonymous, and adherents of each position become offended when their view is even slightly distorted in the service of illustrating between-theory parallels. Nevertheless, similarities do exist in this instance, however imperfect they may be. Such similarities are not the result of imitative theorizing. Rather, both theorists probably observe the same phenomena, which they then proceed to describe in terms of their own respective constructs. It would be unreasonable not to expect conceptual overlap between even very different theories, because they are all dealing with common subject matter — human personality development and functioning.

Summary of the reward-punishment systems. According to Rogers, behavior is influenced by two reward-punishment systems. The first is innate, the organismic valuing process. Through the conscious symbolization of affect, the individual most positively evaluates self-experiences which are consistent with his own actualizing tendency, and negatively evaluates self-experiences which do not maintain and enhance the organism. The person, therefore, knows, likes, and pursues that which is in his own best interest. The second reward system, although also internal, has an external origin based on the needs for positive regard and for self regard. Within this system, the person is made to feel good, or experiences high self-esteem, for behaving in ways which have effected positive changes in the phenomenal fields of significant others. In a manner of speaking, the person chooses to do that which others would have him do.

Unconditional positive regard. So long as the two reward systems are consistent, the child can pursue his actualizing tendency and at the same time receive a full complement of positive regard from others. For example, no problem is presented to the developing personality of a child who organismically values the self-experiences correlated with musical expression, and who also receives positive regard from others for the display of budding vocal talents. This kind of consistency between the two reward systems is likely to exist to the degree that the child's parents offer positive regard on an unconditional basis; they are willing to accept as equally worthy all of the child's feelings and motives. Such parents are said to manifest *unconditional positive regard* for their child.

Rogers considers unconditional positive regard to be one of his key theoretical constructs. "To perceive oneself as receiving unconditional positive regard is to perceive that of one's self-experiences none can be discriminated by the other individual as more or less worthy of positive regard" (1959, p. 208). The feeling of unconditional positive regard for another person is described by Rogers in simpler terms as the acceptance of the whole person. Rogers points out that the accepting parent may express dissatisfaction, establish rules, and impose sanctions without departing from a posture of unconditional positive regard for the child.

This is not as contradictory as it may appear. Rogers suggests that the accepting but limit-setting parent is one who genuinely communicates this message: "I know how angry you get at your little brother and there is nothing bad about having those feelings, but I have my feelings too. When you hurt your brother I become distressed, and so I won't permit you to hit him." In effect the parent is saying that the feelings and motives behind specific behaviors are accepted, even if the particular behaviors themselves are not sanctioned. The result of such a relationship is that the child is *not* forced to "disown feelings of satisfaction and dissatisfaction" (1959, pp. 225-226).

By being allowed to acknowledge his own organismic evaluations, while also becoming aware of those of the parent, the child is in a position to say to himself, "I enjoy hitting baby brother. It feels good. I do not enjoy mother's distress. That feels dissatisfying to me. I enjoy pleasing her" (1959, p. 225). The child is then free to choose between the joy of beating up his younger sibling and the joy to be gotten from basking in the glow of parental approval. No doubt, there will be times when each is sought.

In a similar vein, Haim Ginott draws a distinction between "acceptance and approval," relating the former term to tolerance and the latter to sanction (1969, p. 31). Ginott says that like a physician who does not reject the bleeding patient, who tolerates the unpleasant flow of blood, so does the parent "tolerate unlikable behavior without sanctioning it" (p. 32). By way of illustration, Ginott points to the father, irritated by his son's long hair, saying "I'm sorry, Son. It's your hair but it's my guts. I can stand it after breakfast, but not before it. So, please have breakfast in your own room" (p. 32). Comments such as these communicate an awareness and respect for both his own and his son's feelings. The son is free to do as he pleases. He can keep his long hair, but he must also be responsive to the feelings of father. No one is forced to lose face.

The receipt of unconditional positive regard has the effect of inducing in a child a sense of *unconditional self-regard*. To quote Rogers, "When the individual perceives himself in such a way that no self-experience can be discriminated as more or less worthy of positive regard than any other, then he is experiencing unconditional positive self-regard" (1959, p. 209). It should be obvious that any child who has learned to value equally all aspects of self would have a firmly rooted positive self-concept; the need for self-regard would be completely fulfilled.

Conditional positive regard. The less optimal situation is when parents do not equally accept all aspects of their child; that is, they express *conditional positive regard*. Such parents dispense rewards such as acceptance, love, and respect, on the condition that the child manifest particular behaviors, feelings, and attitudes; expressions which vary from these may be met with negative regard. In this case, instead of merely showing disfavor for a behavior, central features of the child's character are attacked and deemed unworthy.

It is important to realize that conditional positive regard establishes a stage upon which the child may earn rejection for pursuing his actualizing tendency, or receive positive regard from others for self-expressions which are organismically valued as unfavorable. Unlike the self-satisfied recipient of unconditional positive regard, the child who is only valued on a conditional basis is not so certain of his self-worth; there are aspects of self which are being rejected by others. It follows that this child will not have his needs for positive regard and for self-regard met adequately. In fact, because of their chronic state of under-satisfaction, these needs may well become prepotent; the child may be driven to gain whatever positive regard he can. This can be accomplished by behaving in ways which are valued positively by the parents, regardless of whether such patterns are consistent with the child's own actualizing tendency. Alternatively, the child may seek to avoid certain self-expressions, even though they maintain or enhance the organism and are organismically valued as positive, simply because the parents meet such expressions with rejection. Thus, in the service of desperately trying to gain positive regard from significant others, the child behaves in ways which are quite discrepant from those he would have pursued had he been free to follow his actualizing tendency unencumbered by the constraints of conditional positive regard.

Conditions of worth. Even more important than the behavior alterations which are encouraged by parents who express conditional positive regard, are the cognitive and affective changes. Rogers asserts that, "When *self-experiences* of the individual are discriminated by significant others as being more or less worthy of *positive regard,* then *self-regard* becomes similarly selective" (1959, p. 224). In other words, the child learns to value self-experiences as good or bad on the basis of the appraisals delivered by his parents; he comes to value his own self-experiences in a manner which reflects the parent's valuations of them. Thus, not only might the child's behavior be inconsistent with his actualizing tendency, but his learned evaluations of the behaviors may be discrepant from his organismic evaluations of them as well. For the child who receives only conditional positive regard, and whose sense of self-worth is fragile, the learned evaluations of self-experiences can become more important than the organismic evaluations of the same experiences. When a *self-experience* is avoided (or sought) solely because it is less (or more) worthy of *self-regard,* the individual is said to have acquired a *condition of worth* (1959, p. 224).

A condition of worth may be understood as a standard, first imposed by the parents and, later, adopted as one's own, which must be lived up to if feelings of self-worth are to be had. Among middle class American youth, a common condition of worth is a college degree. The positive value of the degree is repeatedly and strongly communicated by parents to offspring who, ultimately, acquire the belief that they won't be worthy unless they too carry home a diploma. Many a college career is pursued solely to establish a sense of self-worth, despite the fact that the college experience is unfavorably evaluated at an organismic level.

Again, one is tempted to draw parallels between Rogers and Freud. What Rogers calls "conditions of worth," sounds quite similar to the sub-system of the superego referred to by Freud as the "ego ideal." Hall said, "The ego ideal corresponds to the child's conceptions of what his parents consider to be morally good" (1954, p. 31). Values are transmitted to the child via rewards for behavior which is consistent with the parent's values, and punishment is administered for those behaviors inconsistent with these values. If a child is rewarded for honest behavior, then honesty will become part of his ego ideal. It is not unlikely that the kinds of parental rewards and punishments Freud thought of as instrumental in the development of a child's ego ideal are much the same as those Rogers discussed relative to conditional positive regard; they both involve the selective giving and withholding of acceptance, love, and warmth.

There is, as well, a semantic similarity between the Rogerian conditions of worth, and the psychoanalytic concept of the ego ideal. Freud sees the ego ideal as coming about via a process of identification in which, most often, the parent of the same sex is taken as the ideal and "introjected" into the ego (1957, p. 185). Rogers has chosen to employ the term "introjected value" (1959, p. 225) as a synonym for a condition of worth.

Personality Organization

Living in terms of conditions of worth, or introjected values, is typically not an all or none issue. It is the very rare person who could be said to have no conditions of worth. Even the most accepting parents probably respond on a conditional basis to at least some aspects of their children. Consequently, almost everyone feels obliged to do, or not do, certain things solely because these behaviors promote positive regard from others and/or positive self-regard.

According to Rogers, the degree to which we harbor conditions of worth is related to our level of psychological well-being; fewer conditions of worth usually imply superior mental health.

The Fully-Functioning Person. Let us first consider the optimal case, the person who has received nothing but unconditional positive regard. Rogers believes that this fortunate individual is likely to have five important characteristics.

Congruence of self and experience. Rogers describes the psychological state of the person who lacks conditions of worth as being one of *congruence.* By this he means that the self-concept is a mirror reflection of what the person, in fact, organismically experiences. If the person has hostile feelings, these are accurately symbolized and become part of the self-concept; if there are self-experiences which relate to sexuality, these too are incorporated into the self-concept. The personality is, therefore, said to be "integrated, whole, genuine" (1959, p. 206).

Openness to experience. The congruent person is open to new experiences. All experiences, whether they be perceptions of environmental stimuli, memory traces of previous events, or visceral sensations accompanying fear, pleasure, or disgust, are "completely available to the individual's awareness" (1959, p. 206).

Psychological adjustment. When the individual is completely open to all of his experiences and maintains a self-concept which is perfectly congruent with those experiences, he is said to be "psychologically adjusted." Rogers, therefore, uses the term "adjustment" in a manner which renders it synonymous with the previous two constructs.

Extensionality. Extensional behavior requires the individual to be well-anchored in the world of reality, a state to be expected from the psychologically-adjusted person. Experiences are differentiated from each other, are tied to temporal and spatial limits, and are evaluated from different perspectives. Real world events are used as the criterion against which to judge the validity of inferences and abstractions.

Maturity. Rogers uses the word "maturity" to describe, in a broad way, the characteristics and behaviors of the well-adjusted person. The mature person is congruent, open to experience, and realistic in his perception and behavior; the mature person accepts himself as being different from others and does not force himself to behave like others for the sake of gaining self-regard. The mature person acknowledges responsibility for his actions. Maturity also implies independence in evaluating experiences. These evaluations are based upon first hand sensory data, not upon the recommendations of others. This reliance upon one's own sensory data is theoretically very appropriate for the adjusted person who is fully and accurately aware of all experience.

Rogers sums up congruence, openness to experience, psychological adjustment, extensionality, and maturity with the construct of the *fully-functioning person*. The fully-functioning person shows all of these characteristics, but not in a static sense. It is not that the person has "arrived." Instead, Rogers sees the fully functioning person as a "person-in-process, a person continually changing" (1959, p. 235). He is always adapting to new situations and always further actualizing the self. Rogers' ideas regarding the fully-functioning person is a particularly positive feature of his theory. Most major theorists exert considerable effort defining the maladjusted person; few provide an explicit conception of psychological health. Even Freud is neglectful of this important issue, except to say that health entails being able to love and work.

The Maladjusted Personality. In contrast to the fully-functioning personality who was the recipient of unconditional positive regard, the maladjusted personality has been offered only conditional positive regard. He subsequently adopts many conditions of worth in an effort to satisfy needs for positive regard and for self-regard.

The major cognitive implication of this is that, instead of being open to experience, the person remains incompletely aware of his organismic evaluations. According to Rogers, this kind of individual *"perceives his experience selectively, in terms of the conditions of worth which have come to exist for him"* (1959, p. 226). Self-experiences which fulfill, or which are consistent with conditions of worth, are indeed symbolized in awareness with accuracy. For example, the college student who views the earning of a degree as a condition of worth will be cognizant of each positive step taken in the direction of fulfilling degree requirements. However, self-experiences which violate conditions of worth are subject to cognitive machinations comparable to Freudian defense mechanisms. Such self-experiences "are perceived selectively and distortedly as if in accord with the *conditions of worth*, or are in part or whole, denied to awareness" (1959, p. 226). The student with the "college graduate" conditions of worth might interpret a low exam grade not in terms of a self-failing, but in the context of the exam itself being ill-conceived and a poor test of his academic expertise, he has taken refuge in distortion. Less common is blatant denial of an experience which is too discrepant from one's introjected values. The failing student, for example, might never acknowledge that his matriculated status is in jeopardy. He simply does not consciously appreciate the tenuousness of his position.

Rogers' use of the term "defense" is probably more inclusive than that of Freud. Rogerian defense subsumes all of the traditional psychoanalytic defense mechanisms, such as rationalization and projection; and it also refers to symptomatic behaviors such as fantasies, compulsions, phobias, and even the more severe behaviors of the paranoid and catatonic psychiatric patients who are usually psychotic. At one extreme are the simple rationalizations used in order to justify mildly questionable behavior: "I didn't get my term paper done on time because of the heavy course load I'm carrying." More distorted than this are projections: "I do not have a sexual appetite; you force it upon me!" This latter ideation permits the individual to maintain a sexually pure self-concept, while at the same time indulging in sexual activity which violates conditions of worth. The sexual behavior is probably organismically valued as favorable, but the defensive person would never consciously admit to this. Finally, there can be outright denial of experience, a difficult defense to maintain because it contradicts apparent reality.

When there is widespread denial and distortion of self-experiences because they conflict with conditions of worth, the individual is obviously not in touch with himself. Defensive maneuverings keep him from becoming accurately aware of all that he is, or could be. And the self-concept, instead of being a reflection of the total configuration of self-experiences, only mirrors those which do not do violence to introjected values. Thus, the self-concept has become a distortion of the true self, a distortion in the direction of imposed values and standards which were adopted in the face of conditional positive regard.

Rogers uses the phrase "incongruence between self and experience" (1959, p. 203) to describe this state of affairs. A person fitting this description may see himself as an academician who is desirous of obtaining a university teaching appointment; but this self-conception may be a defensive deception masking self-experiences and organismic evaluations which should be telling the individual that he is an artist rather than an academician, and he aspires to be a musician rather than a university professor.

By definition, "incongruence between self and experience" means that the personality is in a state of internal confusion. One part of the personality is trying to actualize a self which is not valid for the individual; the other part of the personality is still trying to actualize the organism in terms of true organismic experiences. It is at this juncture that the fine distinction between the terms "actualizing tendency" and "self-actualization" becomes most relevant. Rogers writes, "If the self and the total experience of the organism are relatively congruent, then the actualizing tendency remains relatively unified. If the self and experience are incongruent, then the general tendency to actualize the organism may work at cross purposes with the subsystem of that motive, the tendency to actualize the self" (1959, pp. 196-197).

Incongruity between the self-concept and actual experience is seen by Rogers as the most fundamental psychological dilemma. Self-experience incongruity implies not being true to oneself. Incongruous people deny and distort experiences so that consistency is maintained with an invalid self-concept. They covet this invalid self-concept, carved by introjected values, "for the sake of preserving the positive regard from others" (1959, p. 226).

Incongruent people may behave inconsistently. At times they will act in accordance with their self-concept in an effort to enhance and maintain it, while at other times their behavior will be directed toward the enhancement and maintenance of aspects of the organism which have not been accurately symbolized in the self-concept. These latter behaviors will probably be experienced in a distorted fashion, or their existence may even be denied in order to preserve the integrity of the self. To illustrate this, let us momentarily return to the college student who spends his "spare" time playing the flute, a behavior which is quite consistent with the actualization of his natural artistic and creative potential. His musical talent, however, has been misconstrued by the individual. Its meaning has been distorted so that the "academician" self-concept would be able to accommodate it; the student understands his flute playing only as a vehicle for clearing his mind between study sessions. Thus, he construes it as serving a function which is syntonic with academics.

In order to emphasize its potential for negative outcome, Rogers uses the term "vulnerability" to describe the state of "self-experience incongruity." So long as the person successfully denies and distorts experience, he can deceive himself into believing that he is someone he is not. However, psychological defenses can carry one only so far, and an experience may be encountered which forces the person to become at least minimally aware of the incongruity. Our illustrative student who sees college graduation as a major condition of worth, and whose invalid self-concept centers around being an academician, may find that being thrown out of college for failing to meet grade requirements is an awakening experience, one which forces him to acknowledge that he is not an academician. Of course, this realization, so inconsistent with core aspects of his self-concept, would be expected to introduce psychological discomfort.

When the individual is responsive to his self-experience discrepancy, even though the discrepancy is not consciously symbolized, Rogers says the individual "subceives" the self-experience discrepancy and feels *anxiety*. Phenomenologically, anxiety is a state of tension or dread, a realization that something has gone wrong which the individual cannot pinpoint. In fact, experiences are occurring which, if symbolized, would force some major restructuring of the self-concept upon which the person has become rigidly dependent, violate conditions of worth, and frustrate the need for self-regard; the integrity or unity of the self-concept would be under siege.

From an external frame of reference, Rogers describes the condition under which such a self-experience incongruity is subceived as one of *threat.* Thus, the vulnerable person is one who is susceptible to having his condition become one of threat, and to feel the tension of anxiety, should be become at least dimly cognizant of his self-experience incongruities. Unfortunately, Rogers is guilty of generating some semantic confusion by using the word "threat" to refer also to the phenomenological sensations which accompany becoming clearly aware of self-experience descrepancies.

The general term "psychological maladjustment" refers to this collection of states and processes which are the consequence of having many conditions of worth. One who is psychologically maladjusted will, of course, deny and distort significant segments of experience so that these never become accurately symbolized, thereby creating greater self-experience incongruity.

Empirical Validation. Rogers' ideas concerning the nature of psychological maladjustment have been put to a variety of empirical tests. Suinn, Osborne, and Winfree (1962) investigated Rogers' hypothesis that material which is inconsistent with one's self-concept will be subject to psychological defense. The particular defense studied was inaccuracy of recall.

The investigators had 100 Introductory Psychology students rate 100 common, socially desirable adjectives on a six point scale. A rating of one meant "most like me"; six meant "least like me." Subsequent to obtaining these self-ratings, which were taken as an index of the self-concept, every subject was rated by two of his classmates on the same rating scale. Five days later each subject was given what was reported to be the average ratings made of him by his two classmates. In fact, the ratings given were prepared by the experimenter in such a way that each subject received feedback varying in its degree of discrepancy from his original self-ratings. Each faked composite adjective rating scale contained fifty items which were not discrepant from the subjects own self-ratings; these 50 items comprised Group 0. Twenty five items were assigned a rating which was discrepant from the subject's self-rating by one scale point; these made up Group I. The remaining 25 items were allegedly rated by the classmates as being two points discrepant from what the subject had said of himself; these were called Group II. Two days subsequent to receiving the false feedback, all subjects were asked to complete the same adjective rating scale "as they remembered the composite ratings to be" (p. 473).

The dependent measure in this research was an *accuracy score,* which was the difference between a subject's "recall rating" and the "faked rating." If recall for an item was perfect, a score of zero was assigned. If the subject's memory of the composite rating was off by one rating point, his item score was one. A maximum score of three could be attained for any single item. The average accuracy scores for Group 0, Group I, and Group II items were calculated and the means were found to be .53, .68 and 1.09, respectively. Thus, consistent with Rogers' predictions, "accuracy decreased with increase in degree of discrepancy [from the self-concept] of the adjectives to be recalled" (p. 474).

Another Rogerian hypothesis about the nature of psychological adjustment which has been put to empirical test has to do with self-acceptance. Specifically, Rogers asserts that acceptance of, and satisfaction with, one's self-concept is a prime index of the adjusted personality. The poorly-adjusted individual is not satisfied when he surveys that most important of all objects within his phenomenal field, the self. Instead of feeling self-satisfaction and acceptance, such an individual wishes to be different from what he is.

Q-methodology easily lends itself to the testing of these hypotheses, since all that is necessary in order to obtain an index of self-acceptance is to have the subject complete the Q-sort twice. One administration is completed after instructions to sort the cards as the self is currently seen, while the second is completed after instructions to sort the cards in terms of the "ideal self."

Using this basic strategy, Turner and Vanderlippe (1958) administered a 100 card Q-sort developed by Butler and Haigh (1954) to 175 upperclassmen at a private college. After the two administrations, two groups of 25 students each were selected from this sample; one group showed the highest correlation between their "self" and "ideal" sorts (r range from +.75 to +.91), and the other showed the lowest correlations (r range from −.08 to +.25). Turner and Vanderlippe then proceeded to compare the high and low groups on several indices which were thought to reflect personal adjustment.

The first index, a Q-adjustment score, was based upon the judgments of clinical psychologists regarding what the well and poorly-adjusted person would do on the Q-sort. Specifically, Dymond (1954) had determined that there are 37 items which clinical psychologists agree the well-adjusted person should place on the "self" side of the Q-sort. These include statements such as, "I am assertive," "Self control is no problem for me," and, "I am responsible for my troubles." An additional 37 items were judged by the psychologists as indicative of mental health if the subject indicated that they did not pertain to him. Examples of such items are, "I feel helpless," "I don't respect myself," and, "I put on a false front" (p. 79). The Q-adjustment score used by Turner and Vanderlippe was simply the number of these 74 items that a subject sorted on the side of the distribution representing high self-adjustment. It was found that the high group had a mean Q-adjustment score of 52.0, whereas that of the low group was only 29.7. Thus, as predicted, those subjects whose "self-ideal" sort conditions were highest also tended to have self sorts which were quite similar to what clinical psychologists predicted the healthy personality would exhibit.

The second and third adjustment indices used by Turner and Vanderlippe were behavioral in nature. Physical health was looked at in terms of the number of days per college year spent in a hospital, the frequency with which medical assistance was requested, and the number of negative health items mentioned on a pre-college entrance health-history form. There was no evidence that the high and low groups differed from each other on any of these health measures. The other behavioral index pertained to participation in extra-curricular activities. The number of years each subject spent in an extra-curricular activity was multiplied by a weight, ranging from one to 15, which reflected the amount of time the activity demanded, the status of the position held within the campus organization, and the status of the position on the campus as a whole. Thus, a time-consuming, high-status extra-curricular activity, such as the presidency of a prestigious club, might receive a weight of 15; and, if the student had been president for two years, his activity score would be 30, 15 multiplied by two. Extra-curricular activities were summed for every subject, and this sum was then divided by the number of years the student had been on campus to yield an average yearly participation index for each student. Turner and Vanderlippe report that the high group had a mean participation index of 20.2, while the index for the low group was 13.8. This difference was statistically significant at the $p < .05$ level of confidence. It can, therefore, be concluded that there is a higher degree of extra-curricular activity among subjects manifesting high "self-ideal" sort correspondence than among those students whose "self" and "ideal" sorts are discrepant.

The students in the high and low groups were also ranked by their peers through a sociometric procedure. The nine dormitory students living closest to each subject, plus the subject himself, were asked to rank each other on various questions. "With which person do you spend the most time when you are in a mood to relax?" "Which person do you feel has had the most favorable influence upon you?" There were 11 questions in all. Turner and Vanderlippe reported that, when the rankings on the 11 questions were averaged, subjects in the high group received significantly more favorable rankings than those in the low group ($p < .03$). The directional difference was as predicted on all 11 individual items.

Finally, it was found that subjects whose "self" sort and "ideal" sort were similar had a higher cumulative academic grade than did subjects whose two sorts were minimally correlated.

In summary, most of the predictions derived from Rogers' theory relating self-acceptance with indices of personal adjustment were confirmed. Turner and Vanderlippe found that high self-accepting subjects engaged in more extra-curricular activity, were more favorably rated by their peers on several dimensions, had better academic grade averages, and completed their "self" sort in a manner most consistent with what clinical experts believe a well-adjusted person would do on such a test.

An earlier research program conducted by Rogers and his associates at the University of Chicago Counseling Center consisted of several investigations which were similarly concerned with the relationship between Q-sorts and adjustment. However, in these studies the subjects were university and non-university clients who had completed six or more psychotherapy sessions at the Center. For purposes of comparison, a control group was constituted of people volunteering to serve as subjects in personality research. These subjects were matched with members of the therapy treatment group on the variables of sex, student vs. non-student status, age, and socio-economic level.

In one of the studies, conducted by Butler and Haigh (1954), the treatment and control groups were given a "self" sort and an "ideal" sort to complete. Considerable variability in the degree of correspondence between the two sorts was found within each group. Specifically, the range of "self-ideal" sort correlations for the 25 subjects in the treatment group was from −.47 to +.59. The range within the no treatment control group was similarly great, from −.01 to +.89. Thus, on an individual basis one would not want to predict that someone maladjusted enough to seek psychotherapy will have a very low correspondence between the "self" and "ideal" sorts. Alternatively, not being in therapy does not guarantee a high positive "self-ideal" sort; note the one subject in the control group with a −.01 correlation between the two sorts.

Despite this large within-group variability, there were considerable average differences between the groups. The average "self-ideal" correlation among treatment group members prior to entering psychotherapy was −.01, virtually zero; that correlation for the control group was +.59, revealing considerable "self-ideal" sort correspondence. In terms of group means then, that group which was presumably less well-adjusted, the treatment group, showed a lower "self-ideal" sort correlation than did the group which was probably better adjusted, the control group.

Further evidence that "self-ideal" sort correspondence relates to adjustment comes from the finding that the average "self-ideal" sort correlation rises from −.01 at pre-therapy to +.34 at a post-counseling time. This increase in the correlation from pre to post-therapy is significant at the $p < .01$ level of confidence. It should be noted, however, that while the treatment group as a whole manifested this significant effect, there was even greater variability at the completion of therapy when individual correlations were studied; these ranged from −.56 to +.78. Thus, there are very strong individual differences in the degree of "self-ideal" sort correspondence which a researcher might discover after his subjects have completed a series of counseling sessions.

This variability was even apparent among a subgroup of counselees who were rated at least five on a nine point scale of improvement. Among these 17 therapy successes, the "self-ideal" correlations ranged from −.20 to +.78. The mean correlation of this improved group was +.44 at follow-up, which was significantly higher than that of the eight subjects judged by their therapists as not having improved from counseling.

It seems clear from this collection of results that the "self-ideal" sort correlation is associated with adjustment, but at a level which is too crude for the index to be used by itself as an index of adjustment. Further, it would probably be inappropriate to use the "self-ideal" sort correlation as an index of improvement over therapy in individual cases. While it is true that 15 of the 17 clients rated as improved by their therapists did show more highly positive self-ideal sort correlations at post-therapy than at the pre-therapy assessment time, so did five of the eight clients who were rated below five on the nine point improvement scale filled out by each client's therapist. Butler and Haigh themselves conclude that their results validate the "self-ideal" sort correlation as a measure of adjustment based upon one's self-esteem.

Another research in this series conducted by Dymond (1954) examined the same treatment and control subjects as did Butler and Haigh. However, instead of looking at "self-ideal" sort correlations, she investigated the Q-sort adjustment scores of the subjects. This adjustment index has already been described in the context of presenting Turner and Vanderlippe's investigation. It will be recalled that in that study college students with high "self-ideal" sort correlations had a mean Q-adjustment score of 52.0; the mean of those exhibiting low correlations was only 29.7. Dymond came up with surprisingly similar figures when she compared her two groups, who also were assumed to differ on adjustment level. The control group was found to have a mean Q-adjustment score of 45.0, and the presumably less well-adjusted treatment group had a mean of 28.8 just prior to their therapy experience. Dymond also found that the Q-adjustment scores of a sub-sample of treatment subjects remained quite stable over a 60 day waiting period prior to receiving therapy. However, all of the treatment subjects combined showed significant ($p < .01$) increases in Q-adjustment scores over the course of therapy. At the time of termination, their mean of 39.8 was not reliably different from that of control subjects tested at a corresponding point in time whose mean was 45.1.

We thus have seen that two adjustment indices derived from Q-sort data, the "self-ideal" sort correlation and the Q-adjustment score, are valuable research tools. Predictions derived from Rogers' personality theory which used these measures are, for the most part, confirmed. This speaks to the validity of both the measures themselves and Rogers' theoretical assertions regarding the relationship between the self-concept and adjustment. The research also illustrates that one of Rogers' central constructs, the self, can be operationalized in a way which renders it accessible to scientific inquiry.

Breakdown and Disorganization. The ideas surrounding psychological maladjustment are theoretically applicable to most people. Rogers noted that almost everyone has some degree of personality incongruity.

An extreme case of such incongruity is evidenced in the development of acute psychotic behavior which occurs when some of the aforementioned conditions persist to an excessive degree. Specifically, a condition of major incongruence between self and experience must be present. With this as a backdrop, some significant experience revealing the incongruity suddenly occurs. The person's defenses are incapable of denying and distorting the experience, so that extreme anxiety is felt; central conditions of worth are known by the person to be blatantly violated; the inconsistency between what one really is and the self-concept is rudely thrust into awareness; the personality becomes *disorganized.*

The person who is in such a state of disorganization exhibits behaviors which appear grossly inconsistent. At one moment the person will be functioning in accord with his conditions of worth. In the next instant behavior will conform to what would have been the case had not major segments of experience been denied and distorted; the person is responding to his organismic evaluations and actualizing tendencies. Rogers believes that the supposedly irrational behavior of the individual who is undergoing an acute psychotic episode is of this latter type. "Thus, the person who kept sexual impulses rigidly under control, denying them as an aspect of self, may now make open sexual overtures to those with whom he is in contact" (1959, p. 230). Imagine how such behavior would appear, coming from a person who never before gave the slightest sign of being lascivious, to close family members, especially to parents who might well have been instrumental in imposing asexual values on the individual in the first place.

Psychotherapy

The theoretical relationship between the sudden awareness of previously denied or distorted experience and personality disorganization is one which is relevant to the conduct of psychotherapy. In particular it speaks against the therapist offering his own interpretations about what the client is "really" like. Rogers believes that such interpretations are never justified. It will be recalled that Freud, while sympathetic to the view that the patient's defenses have to be respected and not put under attack, was somewhat less extreme. He merely advised analysts not to thrust too much too soon upon the patient but to wait until the patient himself was at the threshold of the interpretation. At this critical point, the analyst's comment amounts to little more than a gentle nudge.

In his discussion of this important issue, Rogers mentions the early use of sodium pentathal, a drug which was used to facilitate patients in contacting unconscious material. It was not unusual for patients receiving this treatment to become quite disturbed subsequent to its use. Rogers' interpretation of this phenomenon is that "under the drug the individual revealed many of the experiences which hitherto he had denied to himself, and which accounted for the incomprehensible elements in his behavior . . . The patient, no longer being able to successfully deny and distort the experiences became disorganized and a psychotic break occurred" (1959, p. 229).

On a more positive note, Rogers offers some clear guidelines on the necessary and sufficient conditions for a successful client-centered psychotherapy (1959, p. 213). "Success" is defined in terms of the client becoming more like the "fully-functioning" person. The following six conditions are listed as being requisites for therapeutic progress.

1. *The client is in a state of incongruence.* If the client subceives or perceives this incongruence, he will be anxious. Most clients who present themselves for therapy are probably of this type. They are feeling anxious and are motivated to find relief. Some number of clients will be merely vulnerable; it is common for them to enter therapy upon the recommendation of someone else. Perhaps their excessive use of psychological defenses causes them to behave and think in ways which raise concerns among friends or relatives.

2. *The client and the therapist are in contact.* By "contact" Rogers means that, at the very least, the relationship between the two is such that each is making a difference in the experiential field of the other. It is not unusual for the relationship to be characterized by little more than "contact" for many sessions before the processes basic to therapeutic gain begin to have some impact.

3. *The therapist is congruent.* By being congruent, the therapist can remain open to all experiences within the therapy relationship. If the therapist is incongruent, certain within-therapy experiences will be denied and distorted by him to the degree they violate his own conditions of worth. Of course, it is the rare person, therapist or not, who is completely congruent. Thus, the "congruent therapist" is an ideal. The closer the real therapist comes to this ideal, the more potentially effective he can be.

4. *The therapist "empathically" understands the client.* Empathy is defined as the accurate perception of another's internal frame of reference, his sensations, perceptions, meanings, and memories. The therapist has "tuned into" the world of another human being *without* losing the "as - if" quality of the experience. When the observer actually feels the pain, happiness, or sadness of another, Rogers speaks of "identification." With empathy, the therapist knows his client but does not lose his objectivity, as would be the case if he were to identify with the client.

5. *The therapist experiences unconditional positive regard for his client.* This is a crucial condition! It permits a relationship which the client has perhaps never before experienced.

6. *The client is at least minimally aware of the therapist's communications of empathic understanding and unconditional positive regard.* The perception of conditions four and five by the client tells him that the therapist genuinely knows him and, despite this, still values all aspects of his being. The importance of such a message cannot be over-estimated for the client who has learned to be so uncertain of his own worth.

Therapeutic process and outcome. When the above six conditions are met or, more likely, approximated, the client finds himself in a safe situation. Since he is not faced with the prospect of conditional positive regard, more and more experiences become accurately symbolized. That is, defenses are used less frequently, and the client becomes more open to experiences which had previously been denied or distorted.

With this as a start, the client can move toward a reorganization of his self-concept. Specifically, as the previously-denied and distorted experiences become accurately symbolized, the notions of self held by the client will undergo changes. No longer will the self-concept be a fraud, maintained in the service of fulfilling conditions of worth. Instead, it will increasingly become a reflection of actual experience. In other words, the client gradually becomes more congruent.

The final aspects of this therapeutic process are two-fold. First, the client increasingly feels unconditional positive self regard. This is due to the continued receipt of unconditional positive regard from the therapist throughout the uncovering of all previously-denied and distorted experience. Imagine how it is from the client's perspective. He anxiously symbolizes and talks about some experience which he had always construed as a basis for rejection by others, and yet the therapist persists in maintaining a posture of total acceptance! Ultimately, the client arrives at the realization that the experiences he previously defended against are not so bad; "*I* am not so unworthy after all!" The second dimension of this process is that the client's locus of evaluation becomes more self-centered. In other words, the client no longer evaluates experiences in terms of the conditions of worth imposed by others. Instead, evaluations are based upon the individual's own organismic valuing process. Finally, an important corollary of the above is that the individual, now more congruent, open to experience, and responsive to his organismic valuing process, is free to proceed with the business of actualization.

Psychotherapy Research. Rogers was the first major figure to conduct rigorous investigations on both the process and outcome of psychotherapy — in this case, client-centered therapy. His research was made possible by technical advancements in audio recording, which permitted him to obtain verbatim transcripts of therapy sessions.

After listening to many recorded client-centered therapy interviews, Rogers (1958) felt that client changes within psychotherapy followed a predictable pattern. In the beginning, the clients tended to be rigid and inflexible; toward the end of a successful therapy, the client was much more open, fluid, and changeable. This shift was thought to occur in stages over the course of psychotherapy. Each stage was conceptualized as falling along the dimension of *stasis-process*.

In 1960, Walker, Rablen, and Rogers reported on the development of a Process Scale to measure the stages that clients are at on the stasis-process dimension. Seven stages are conceptualized. Stages I and II are called "Low" and involve behavior and thought which is primarily fixed or rigid. "Medium" stages are III, IV, and V. Stages VI and VII are called "High"; it is during these last two therapy stages that the client becomes most open and fluid. In addition to the seven stages, the overall process of change is broken down into seven sub-dimensions called *strands*.

1. *Feelings and personal meanings.* This strand has to do with the degree to which the client is in touch with his emotional experiences. At the low end, the client neither expresses nor recognizes his true feelings. Toward the middle stages of therapy, there will be some acknowledgment of feelings. During the last two stages, the client fully experiences his emotions and is aware of constantly changing feelings.

2. *Manner of experiencing.* The client who is unaware of his own experiences in general, and who distances himself from the personal meanings of his experiences, is judged to be at Stage I or II on this second strand. In contrast, clients who are high on this strand fully utilize all experiences in trying to understand and bring meaning to their phenomenal world.

3. *Incongruence.* This strand refers to the degree to which clients are able to resolve incongruity. At the low end is the beginning client who is aware of a self-representation which is quite discrepant from his experience, although at this stage he

is not aware of the incongruity. Gradually, the client becomes more aware of incongruities, until he finally reaches a point in the high stages where any incongruity which emerges is fleeting. The client is no longer defending against the recognition of experiences which might previously have been threatening.

4. *Communication of Self.* This strand is one of "openness." At the low end, the client does not reveal any experience to others. Stages VI and VII are characterized by willing self-disclosure of all aspects of experiencing.

5. *Construing of experience.* During the low stages, the client's understanding of the world is rigid and dealt with as facts. There is no recognition that this understanding is the product of a personal process of bringing meaning to bear on events, the process of construing. The client doesn't appreciate that his understandings, constructions, are subjective, not objective. Toward the end of a client-centered therapy, meanings are always dealt with as tentative, subject to alteration on the basis of future experience. For example, the construction of someone as "hostile" is readily changeable should some new experience warrant the modification.

6. *Relationship to problems.* Problems tend either to be unrecognized or, if recognized, are seen as having an external source during Stages I and II. During the middle stages, some desire for change is felt, but this is associated with fear over the prospect of change. During the high stages a clearer recognition of self-responsibility for problems emerges. The locus of blame becomes more appropriately internal and desire for change is stronger.

7. *Manner of relating.* This final strand refers to the degree to which the client can tolerate close relationships. In the beginning the client views intimacy as dangerous and to be avoided. Later, the client is able to relate openly and freely with others.

In order to empirically test the merit of this dimensional conceptualization of therapy, Walker and his colleagues (1960) selected six fully-transcribed client-centered therapy cases from the University of Chicago Counseling Center. These cases showed varying outcomes, from dramatic to minimal improvement. For each of the six cases, two transcribed pages from the second or third interview and two pages from the interview just preceding termination were extracted, with all identifying material removed. Thus, a total of 24 transcribed pages of interviews were chosen.

Two clinical psychologists trained in making the discriminations called for by the Process Scale, were asked to make a *global* stage rating for each of the unidentified 24 transcribed pages that were used in this study. Each page was rated on its own merits and independently by these two "judges." However, instead of just using the seven points of the Process Scale, the judges decided to add decimals, thereby effectively transforming the instrument into a 70 point scale. In addition to the assignment of a rating to every page, each judge rank-ordered the pages in terms of the process stages. Finally, the judges divided the 24 pages into three equal groups labeled "Low," "Medium," and "High" on the dimension of stasis-process.

The two judges were found to have better than acceptable levels of reliability as they went about their tasks. Specifically, their independent ratings of each page on the 70 point scale correlated (Pearson r) .83, and on the ranking task the correlation (rho) was found to be .84. Lastly, judgments regarding which pages represented the eight High, Middle, and Low segments showed 75% exact agreement. In no case did one judge place the same page in the Low group.

Validity information on the Process Scale was gathered in two ways. First, Rogers himself ranked the six cases for improvement on the basis of all information available. Rogers' ranking was not known to the judges at the time they were working on the 24 pages of transcript. From the judges' ratings, an improvement index was derived by subtracting the sum of the ratings each assigned to the two early pages of transcript from the sum of the ratings assigned to the two pages which had been extracted from therapy interviews just prior to termination. For example, let us suppose that the first judge assigns ratings of 1.5 and 2.0 to the transcribed pages coming from sessions two and three of case X. In addition, the first judge assigns ratings of 3.0 and 3.2 to the transcriptions coming from the late interviews. In this instance, the improvement index for case X derived from the first judge's ratings is: $(3.0 + 3.2) — (1.5 + 2.0) = 2.7$. A change index of this magnitude would reflect perceived improvement in the judge's part.

Using this improvement index as a basis for ranking the six cases for improvement over the course of therapy, it was found that the two judges arrived at identical improvement rankings. In addition, the improvement rankings obtained from the judges differed only slightly from that of Rogers; the rank order correlation (rho) comparing Rogers' and the judges' rankings was .89.

A second validity check involved noting the improvement indices for the three cases which Rogers felt had shown marked improvement, as compared with the improvement indices for cases Rogers judged to have minimally improved. In order to do this, the improvement indices obtained from the two judges' rankings of a given case were averaged. Using this method, Walker found that the improvement indices were 2.3, 2.0, and 1.5 for the three cases which Rogers judged to have improved markedly. For those three cases which Rogers thought showed minimal improvement, the indices were 1.2, 0.3, and −.6. Thus, the overall improvement index means for the two groups was 1.93 and 0.30, respectively.

It would seem from this research that it is possible to extract reliable ratings of where a client stands on the dimension stasis-process by using brief extracts from therapy transcripts as behavior samples. In addition, such ratings can be made without knowing anything about the client's personality, background, or length of time in therapy.

In their discussion of the Process Scale, Walker and his colleagues report that considerably more difficulty was encountered rating the seven strands at the end of therapy than at the beginning. "The strands seem more separable and distinct at the fixity end of the process continuum, where they can be more independently evaluated and rated" (p. 83). It appears that the seven strands become fused to "form a unified stream of change in which the contribution of the separate tributaries [strands] can no longer be accurately distinguished . . .'' (p. 83). In other words, at the start of therapy a client may at one moment reveal that he wants to avoid a close relationship with the therapist, then express no desire for personality change, then manifest incongruence, and at all times he is oblivious to his disorganized condition. Evidence for the various strands seems to stand out. However, late in a successful therapy, the client will be intimate, problem-oriented, and "tuned into" momentary incongruities, all at the same time. Instead of seven strands, the client who is close to becoming a fully-functioning person "is one who is a [single] stream of process himself . . .'' (p. 84).

In another research, Truax (1966) examined some of Rogers' own behaviors vis a vis a client. One of the transcribed cases used in the development of the Process Scale was utilized in this project. The specific purpose of this study was to explore the degree to which Rogers himself expresses empathy and warmth, or positive regard, in a manner which is non-contingent upon patient behaviors. This determination is quite important, since Rogers claims that he merely establishes the necessary relationship conditions within which the client may improve. In contrast, learning theorists, such as Skinner, assert that where patient behaviors change due to therapy, it is because the therapist selectively reinforces or punishes specific behaviors in a systematic manner; and in so doing, he increases and decreases their observed frequencies.

Truax extracted a random sample of 40 therapist-patient-therapist (TPT) interactions from one of Rogers' successful, long-term cases. Each TPT interaction was transcribed, coded, and given in random order to five raters who were clinical psychologists. The raters had to analyze each TPT unit in terms of Rogers' behaviors. Specifically, the raters focused upon three behavior categories: empathic understanding, acceptance or positive regard, and directiveness. The first two categories are, of course, endorsed by Rogers as being enhancing to therapeutic gain. They might also be viewed as reinforcers, from a learning theory perspective, if used on a conditional basis. According to Rogers, the category of directiveness is one which should be avoided by client-centered therapists. Directiveness may be construed as a punishment which is likely to inhibit preceding behaviors if it is expressed contingently upon specific client behaviors.

In addition to the three categories of therapist behaviors, Truax rated nine categories of client behaviors. These included, "(a) degree of discrimination learnings by the patient, (b) ambiguity of patient's statements, (c) degree of insight development by the patient, (d) degree of similarity of patient's style of expression to that of the therapist, (e) problem orientation of patient, (f) degree of patient catharsis, (g) degree of patient blocking, (h) degree of patient anxiety, and (i) degree of patient negative versus positive feeling expression" (1966, p. 2).

Each time one of the therapist or patient behaviors was to be rated, the rater was given the TPT units in a new random sequence so that maximum independence of ratings would be procured. The ratings themselves were obtained by using graphic rating scales, each of which consisted of a 170 millimeter horizontal line, labeled "most" at one end and "least" at the other. The rater simply had to place "X" at the point along the line which he thought best reflected the therapist, or patient, behavior dimensionalized by the graphic scale.

After all ratings had been made, the TPT units were decoded; and the degree of relationship between each of the three therapist behaviors with each of the nine patient behaviors was assessed statistically. Significant correlations would mean that a given category of therapist behavior, say directiveness, was systematically related to a category of patient behaviors, such as patients' expressions of insight. For example, a significant negative correlation in this instance would indicate that Rogers tended to be directive when his client was non-insightful.

Inter-rater reliability estimates were obtained from the five raters. The reliability coefficients were .48, .59, and .68 for the ratings of the therapist behaviors of empathy, acceptance, and directiveness, respectively. The reliability coefficients for the nine patient behavior ratings ranged from .26 to .64. These relatively low reliabilities work against uncovering systematic relationships between therapist and patient behaviors unless these relationships are particularly strong.

Despite this, a number of significant correlations were found which were contrary to what would be predicted if Rogers was responding to his client in a completely unconditional way. Specifically, patient expressions of discrimination learning were positively associated with therapist empathy ($r = +.47$) and therapist acceptance ($r = +.37$). Patient insight was similarly related to these two therapist behaviors ($r = +.46$ and $+.37$, respectively). Therapist acceptance alone was related to the patient's adoption of a problem orientation ($r = +.35$). All three therapist behaviors of empathy, acceptance, and directiveness were discovered to be significantly related to patient ambiguity ($r = -.35$, $-.38$ and $+.33$, respectively), as well as to similarity of patients' style of expression with that of the therapist ($r = +.48$, $+.32$, and $-.31$, respectively).

There thus can be little doubt that Rogers himself selectively responds with different classes of behaviors to different kinds of patient behaviors. The next important question is whether these differential response tendencies on Rogers' part have the effect of selectively increasing and decreasing patient behaviors, as they should if they are functioning as rewards and punishments. In order to assess this, the difference in the rating between early and later sessions was statistically evaluated for each of the nine patient behaviors. Of the five classes of patient behaviors to which Rogers selectively responded, four showed significant changes in the expected directions. For example, "insightful expressions" was associated with empathic and accepting statements, rewards, from Rogers, and showed a highly significant increase during the later therapy sessions in comparison with early sessions. Only one of the four patient behaviors to which Rogers did not selectively respond manifested any significant change over the sessions.

It is clear then that "important reinforcement effects do indeed occur even in client-centered therapy" (p. 6), and even when the therapist is Rogers himself. Consciously or unconsciously, Rogers is altering the behavior of his clients through the systematic use of empathy, acceptance, and directiveness in a way which is predictable from the standpoint of learning theory. It does not seem that Rogers engages in positive, accepting behaviors which are independent of patient behavior, as he prescribes.

This evidence should not be taken to mean that Rogers' "necessary and sufficient conditions" for successful therapy are patently incorrect. Relationship variables might be quite central to therapy progress, even if the "ideal" is difficult, if not impossible to achieve. In this regard, Morris and Suckerman (1974) recently investigated the impact of a relationship variable, "therapist warmth" on the outcome of a learning theory approach to the treatment of snake phobias. They found that there were significantly higher levels of approach behavior to a snake subsequent to treatment delivered by a warm therapist than there were to treatment received from the same therapist when he intentionally behaved in a more formal, matter-of-fact fashion.

Evaluation

In our earlier discussion of personality theory, it was mentioned that one criterion frequently used as an index of the worth of a theory is "expert opinion." If this was the only yardstick used, Rogers' theory would have to be counted among the top three. His notions about parenting, interpersonal relations, and psychotherapy have had significant impacts on a broad array of professional disciplines. Not only psychiatrists and psychologists, but educators, clergy, physicians, businessmen, and management personnel include themselves among Rogers' followers.

In the beginning of this chapter we stressed that much of Rogers' attractiveness has little to do with the validity of his theory. Many of his ideas have intuitive appeal and deep personal meaning, once they are fully understood. Client-centered therapy is "picked up" quickly because it is much simpler to conduct than other relationship-oriented therapies, such as psychoanalysis. The practitioner does not have to have great knowledge of psychology to be effective, and he can anticipate a relatively small number of contact hours with a given client, an important consideration when caseloads become burdensome. Finally, as Hall and Lindzey (1957) pointed out, people gravitate to Rogers because he presents a pleasant alternative to Freud's pessimism regarding human nature, and to the impersonal objectivity which characterizes so many of the learning theorists.

A second major criterion by which personality theories may be judged is the degree to which their theoretical propositions find empirical confirmation. Rogers is committed to the gathering of such "hard" data. Consequently, he is one of the best models of the combined clinical practitioner-researcher to be found. His recording of therapy interviews established a starting point from which all substantive therapy research derives. Through such recordings he rendered open and objective what had been private and creative. Areas which others felt were too complex to be scientifically dealt with were made manageable and subject to systematic scrutiny. A fine example of this is Rogers' work on the development of the Process Scale, which evaluates psychotherapy progress and outcome within the client-centered framework. This effort is testimony to Rogers' belief in the lawfulness of psychotherapy, and to his commitment to the scientific method.

It must also be said that, as any good empiricist, Rogers believes that conclusions are always tentative, and are subject to revision under the weight of new evidence. With respect to his theoretical ideas on psychological defenses, he writes, "It is hoped that this portion of the theory may be further elaborated and refined and made more testable in the future" (1959, p. 231).

On the other hand, despite this open-minded stance, Rogers has not affected any major revisions of his formal personality theory since 1959. He has continued to write and has expanded his ideas to the treatment of schizophrenic patients (Rogers, Kiesler, Gendlin & Truax, 1965). He has also been in the forefront of the Sensitivity Group movement (1970). However, after almost two decades of research, he has not gone back to his monumental beginning and taken a second look.

There are many formal criteria for a good personality theory which can serve to measure what Rogers has produced. One of the most important of these criteria is that of systematization. On this dimension, Rogers' theory easily holds its own. Probably more than any other theorist, he has endeavored to lay forth his constructs and their interrelationships in an explicit fashion. In his 1959 statement for example, there is a unit entitled "Specification of Functional Relationships in the Theory of Personality" (p. 231) which spells out nine systematic relationships theorized to exist between constructs. Included are functional relationships such as "The more numerous or extensive the conditions of worth, the greater the proportion of experience which is potentially threatening"; and, "The more congruence between self and experience, the more accurate will be the symbolizations in awareness" (pp. 231-232).

Systematization, as exemplified by Rogers' theory, is the prerequisite for the making of theoretical predictions. However, a systematic theory is not sufficient. The constructs contained therein must be operational, so that a measurement base can be established from which to make the predictions. In this regard, the theory does not fare uniformly well. For instance, "congruence between self and experience" and "accurate symbolization" are both subjective in nature. By tying two subjective constructs together, neither of which is operational, scientific prediction is short-circuited. Related to this particular example is the fact that research on Rogers' theory has virtually neglected self-experience congruity/incongruity as an index of psychopathology; the self-experience component is not susceptible to measurement. Instead, there has been an exaggerated emphasis upon exploring the implications of "self-ideal self" discrepancies; undoubtedly this is because both components have been operationalized through the use of Stephenson's Q-methodology.

The use of the "self-ideal self" discrepancy measure as an index of psychopathology has been criticized on several grounds. From a theoretical perspective, Pervin (1975) rightly points out that the notion of "self-ideal self" incongruity is not a central Rogerian construct; what is central to Rogers' notions regarding psychopathology is self-experience incongruity. Unfortunately this has been abandoned by researchers due to measurement problems. Thus, there emerges an "incongruity" between what is stressed as being theoretically important to psychopathology and what is viable for scientific investigation. Also criticized is the Q-methodology used to assess "self-ideal self" incongruity. Q-sorts are probably highly susceptible to response sets, such as social desirability, as are most self-report measures. To date there is insufficient evidence to support a claim that the forced sort-distribution effectively minimizes these sources of assessment error. In addition, Q-sorts are maligned for possibly lacking adequate levels of content validity. Specifically, it is argued that inadequate data exists to support the belief that the array of self-referent statements contained on a Q-sort are a good representative sampling of self-concept ideation.

Operationally, Rogers' theory is most noticeably weak with regard to two of his most important constructs — the actualizing tendency and the organismic valuing process. As we discussed earlier, Shostrom's Personal Orientation Inventory (POI) which is used as a measure of self-actualization, has several limitations, including its susceptibility to faking. Also mentioned was a theoretical limitation. Rogers' notion of self-actualization has inherent within it the idea of uniqueness, yet the POI assesses self-actualization in terms of an ideal standard; it is one person's conception of what the self-actualized person should be.

At this juncture a second theoretical failing of the POI as a measure of self-actualization may be raised. This concerns the appropriateness of the POI for people who, in Rogers' terms, are actualizing a "self" which is discrepant with experience. When there is a schism within the personality between the organismic actualizing tendency and self-actualization, is the POI measuring the former or the latter? It would seem that the POI, which is scored on the basis of conscious choices made by subjects, is prone to all of the defensive maneuverings in which the disorganized personality might be expected to engage. Thus, for these people, POI responses would reflect denials and distortions more so than the "true" strength of the actualizing tendency. Clearly, more investigation of the POI's validity is in order.

With respect to the organismic valuing process, there has been virtually no empirical work conducted. It is, unfortunately, an example of a crucial construct which cannot be measured. Ford and Urban (1963) also fault this construct in light of empirical findings reported from sources outside of the client-centered framework. It has been shown that emotional responses may be acquired in response to virtually any stimulus. People routinely become anxious, or happy, or relaxed as a function of various sorts of learning processes. This being so, Ford and Urban question whether the affective experiences from which organismic evaluations emerge are "natural," as Rogers would have us believe, or whether they are learned. If at least some aspects of these affective experiences are acquired, then the theoretical distinction between the organismic valuing process and conditions of worth becomes tenuous.

There can be little doubt that Rogers' 1959 presentation is impressive in its comprehensiveness. He offers us a theory of personality, a method of psychotherapy, a description of mental health, and an analysis of interpersonal relationships. Yet, enough is omitted so that the formal criterion of maximal inclusion does not appear to have been attained. Pervin (1975) is critical of Rogers' neglect of certain motives which occupy our thoughts much of the time — sex and aggression, and their consequences which so frequently are of concern to us — anxiety, guilt, and/or depression. Also, Rogers pays insufficient attention to the antecedents of personality. It is true that attention is given to parenting styles, but there is no mention of either biological or societal and sub-cultural determinants.

Rogers' emphasis upon subjective phenomena placed him in the center of controversy for a long time. Recently, the greater emphasis on cognition among learning theorists and psychologists offered some measure of vindication. However, some reviewers, among them Ford and Urban (1963), believe that Rogers' phenomenological emphasis precluded his consideration of more objective response and situational variables. A more balanced approach would have included references to all three classes of events.

Two other rather surprising omissions in Rogers' theory are his failure to emphasize unconscious motivation and his evasion of learning theory. The former weakness is salient because Rogers is well-versed and trained in psychoanalytic theory. In fact, many of his ideas appear to be rather direct derivatives of Freudian conceptions. Yet, the unconscious as an important operative force is missing, even though it is not in the least inconsistent with Rogers' subjective frame of reference. On the matter of learning theory, Rogers, like Freud, implicitly includes many ideas which are easily translatable into the language of modern learning theory. While Freud preceded the explicit statement of many of these learning principles, Rogers was contemporaneous with them and, from his public debates with Skinner, we know that he was fully cognizant of them. We might also note that learning theory and Rogers' theory share an emphasis on process as opposed to content. Consequently, the two would seem to constitute an easy marriage; but they never do meet. In our view, no personality theory can be judged inclusive unless it attends to modern principles of behavior acquisition and change through learning.

Relevant to the matter of inclusiveness, it was just mentioned that Rogers' theory is mainly concerned with process, not content; he speaks of core functions, such as the actualizing tendency and the organismic valuing process. What desperately needs to be added, however, is a good amount of content theory. Rogers provides some content in the form of a self-concept and an organism, but no categories or typologies are suggested; perhaps these were omitted in the service of emphasizing individual uniqueness. Nevertheless, taxonomic systems are basic to all sciences and Rogers is remiss in not at least venturing a first gesture in this direction.

The same criticism can be raised against the self-concept and Rogers' notions regarding psychopathology; no sub-categories or differential diagnoses are listed. This latter deficit, the omission of diagnostic nomenclature, is not an oversight on the part of Rogers. In presenting client centered therapy, he wrote: "The same conditions are regarded as sufficient for therapy, regardless of the particular characteristics of the client . . . It is not necessary nor helpful to manipulate the relationship in specific ways for specific kinds of clients" (1959, pp. 213-214). It is this sort of over-generalization which weakens Rogers' position. Goldstein and Stein (1976), reporting on the differential effectiveness of various therapies as a function of the patients' characteristics, argued against the continued advocacy of such simplistic ideas. This is but one of several places in Rogers' theory where he could update his position so that it would be more consistent with current knowledge.

Rogers is relatively guiltless as far as imposing value judgments upon an unsuspecting audience is concerned. He does, of course, stress the idea that people are basically good and resourceful. Psychotherapy presumably releases an innate capacity for growth and adjustment in a potentially competent human being. All of these human characteristics are theoretically subsumed by the overriding force, the tendency toward actualization. In a footnote, Rogers takes care to point out that this actualizing tendency "was not an assumption or bias with which we started our therapeutic endeavors." Instead, the idea of this "human capacity grew out of continuing work with clients in therapy" (1959, p. 221). Thus, Rogers' understanding of the actualizing tendency emerged from first-hand experience. Rogers claims that those therapists whose client contacts do not likewise provide insights into the reservoir of strength contained within each patient simply do not believe in their clients' innate capacities. The therapist who has faith in the innate potential of his client will find it; if the potential is not found, it can only mean a lack of faith. These are peculiar assertions from a man who outwardly rejects dogma and who is an advocate of empiricism.

As a last word on Rogers, we must be reminded once again that while criticism is healthy, it is also easy to become "carried away" by it. There is, no doubt, much that could be done to improve Rogers' theory. However, for all its current weakness, it remains the third force in psychology, along with psychoanalysis and modern learning theory (Buhler, 1971).

SUMMARY

This chapter reviewed the most important phenomenological personality theory, that of Carl Rogers. It was shown how Rogers' theory was a natural outgrowth of not only his clinical practice but of his earlier religious and academic training. Perhaps more than any other personality theorist, Rogers consciously intended to put forth an important systematic statement. In the minds of many, he succeeded. We presented Rogers' basic assumptions about the nature of personality: personal experience is reality, the actualizing tendency, and the organismic valuing process. This was followed by a detailed presentation of the "working" constructs provided by Rogers. These constructs dealt primarily with the self, the need for positive regard, and adjustment. To his credit, Rogers details not only his conceptions of psychological disorganization but of the fully-functioning person as well. Throughout this chapter, illustrative examples of assessment procedures relevant to Rogers' theory and validational research were presented.

TERMS TO KNOW

CHAPTER 19
Behaviorism/Situationism: Classical Conditioning

An intervening variable is a hypothetical process which is invoked to account for relationships between observables. "Learning" is the intervening variable in psychology which has probably received the most attention. The observable events between which learning is thought to occur, or intervene, are, on the antecedent side, experiences such as training or observation of events, and, on the consequent side, relatively permanent behavior changes:

Experience ⟶ Learning ⟶ Relatively Permanent Behavior Change.

Thus, we might say that the behavior changes which may be observed to occur subsequent to certain experiences are mediated by the intervening variable "learning."

Learning is not thought to intervene in all situations where systematic alterations of behavior are observed. Specifically, it is not involved when the frequency of a response temporarily decreases due to muscle fatigue, or when responses show transient increases in their frequency or intensity due to heightened states of motivation. In addition, even some permanent behavior changes do not fall within the range of phenomena explained by learning; included in this category are changes which are attributable to organic modifications such as disease, drug stimulation, or brain injury.

A number of different learning processes have been theorized to account for behavior change. No single explanation can be pointed to as the definitive statement on the matter. Nevertheless, most approaches to the study of personality which explicitly emphasize some learning process, regardless of its nature, do share some common features. The most fundamental of these is a commitment to the study of personality from an objective perspective. This translates into the development of theories, descriptive statements, and research investigations which accentuate public and verifiable events. Private psychological phenomena, such as the "self-concept,"

386

are ignored for the most part because they are beyond the scope of direct measurement.

The general orientation to psychological study which excludes all but observables as subject matter is known as *behaviorism* after an article by Watson (1913) in which he stressed that psychology would be best off if it restricted itself to the study of overt behavior and got over its preoccupation with inaccessible mental phenomena.

A second related commonality among learning approaches is that they underplay internal determinants of behavior. Emphasis upon constructs which refer to covert states or events, such as "instinct" and "actualizing tendency," is the exception. Instead, as Harré and Secord have stated, the trend is "either to ignore organismic factors, or to regard them as . . . subsidiary to the primary impact of the external stimulus" (1972, p. 27). In other words, situational factors are looked to as the antecedents of behavior which can be most profitably studied. One corollary of this viewpoint is that behavior is best understood as primarily learned or acquired on the basis of experience vis a vis the environment. Conceptions having to do with so-called natural or innate response potentiators, such as Freudian "instincts" and the Rogerian "actualizing tendency," are rejected as not worthy of investigation. A second corollary of conceptualizing behavior as determined by situational variables is that behavioral stereotypy is attributed to situational constancy, not to the functioning of stable, underlying motives, instincts, or needs. While one might argue against the idea that behavior is completely situationally specific, the power of the situation as an elicitor and controller of behavior cannot be denied. The next time you are in a classroom notice the incredible degree of inter-individual stereotypy; everyone is sitting reasonably quietly and generally oriented toward the speaker, even those who are asleep! In other words, the inter-individual behavioral stereotypy within the same situation is very marked, much more so than the intra-individual stereotypy observed across different situations. Thus, different people in the same setting tend to behave more alike than does a single person in varied settings.

Because of this emphasis upon the situation as the cause of behavior, behaviorists have recently come to be called *situationists* by Bowers (1973), and their orientation has been referred to as *situationism*. Regardless of whether a psychologist is referred to as a strict "behaviorist" or as a "situationist," the belief is held that a scientific psychology can rest upon the accumulation of theory and data pertaining to relationships among overt variables, primarily responses and situations.

As a point of clarification, note that subjective verbal reports are legitimate data from the perspective of behaviorism. However, to quote Brody and Oppenheim (1967), "The behaviorists take as the data the statements themselves, that is, the *fact* that the statements are made, and not the experiences described in the statements." There can be inter-rater agreement on the point that someone said, "I am happy;" but whether or not the person actually is experiencing the emotion of happiness lies outside of the behaviorist's range of immediate concern because happiness is not directly observable.

Just as psychoanalysts differ on the degree to which they follow Freud's orthodox model, so too do behaviorists differ in their adherence to strict Watsonian behaviorism. In this and the following chapter we present two orientations to the study of learning which have assumed enormous significance, not just for the understanding of personality but for psychology in general; these two orientations are classical conditioning and operant conditioning. Both approaches deal mainly with observable environmental events, or stimuli, and responses. Consequently, they fall within *conservative* behaviorist traditions. It should be pointed out that the principles of neither classical nor operant conditioning are to be construed as a theory of personality. In fact, their focus is not even explicitly on personality; these two systems are concerned with *behaviors,* their acquisition and their change. However, because behavior acquisition and change are processes which are clearly of primary interest to personologists, they warrant very careful study.

In Chapter 21 we deal with some learning orientations which can perhaps best be described as *liberal* behaviorism. Psychologists representing this trend are frequently called "social learning theorists." As a group, they are much more open to the consideration of intra-organismic variables as significant determinants of overt behavior. Their ideas tend to approximate more closely those of "traditional" theorists of personality, such as Freud and Rogers.

CLASSICAL CONDITIONING

Behavior can be categorized into that which is emitted by the organism, and that which is elicited by some known stimulus. Behaviors in the former class are called *operants;* they operate upon the environment, effecting some change in it to which the responder becomes, in turn, responsive. Operants are usually voluntary in nature, and are discussed in the next chapter.

Elicited behaviors are called *respondents.* Much respondent behavior is unlearned; it is exemplified at the animal level by instincts, which naturally occur consequent to the presentation of an elicitor, called a stimulus. In this context, instinctual behavior refers to the complex chains of responses which are involved in nest-building, mating, migration, etc. These response chains show a very high degree of stereotypy among members of species and are, therefore, called "fixed-action patterns."

At the human level, there is no evidence for the existence of complex fixed-action patterns set off by specific releasing stimuli. Nevertheless, there is a variety of respondent behavior to be seen, particularly at the level of reflex activity; reflexive behaviors include sneezes, knee jerks, and eye blinks. They, like fixed-action patterns among animals, are naturally elicited by particular stimuli; one does not have to learn to blink when the eye is invaded by a dust particle or by a puff of air.

Acquisition of Conditioned Response

At the beginning of this century, a Russian physiologist, Ivan Pavlov, was researching animal reflexive behaviors, including salivation, as part of a larger investigation on digestive processes. One serendipitous observation made by him was that his animals eventually exhibited the reflexive response, salivation, to stimuli other than the natural eliciting stimulus, food. After conducting a series of investigations bearing on this phenomenon, Pavlov was able to explicate the elements involved. He termed the elicitor of a reflexive response an *unconditioned stimulus* (US), and the response provoked by it an *unconditioned response* (UR). Other stimuli which are not capable of eliciting the reflexive behavior acquired the capacity to do so when paired with the US. These stimuli were referred to by Pavlov as *conditioned stimuli* (CS), and the reflexive behavior ultimately elicited by them as *conditioned responses* (CR).

In his actual experiments, Pavlov harnessed a canine subject in a chamber. Implanted in the dog's cheek was a glass tube which collected the saliva secreted by the animal, thus permitting careful monitoring of salivation. Food was used as the US and a tone served as a CS. At first, the following occurred:

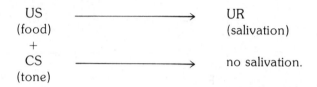

Through the repeated pairing of the tone with food presentation, the dog finally acquired a conditioned salivation response to the tone. This was demonstrated by following a series of *acquisition trials,* in which the US and CS occurred together, with a *test trial,* in which only the CS was presented. A conditioned response was believed to have occurred if the dog salivated to the CS, a tone in this case:

CS   ⟶   CR
(tone)   (salivation).

Because this behavior change was reasonably stable and experientially-based, Pavlov and others believed it was legitimate to say that the animal had "learned" to salivate to the sound of a tone.

In his research, Pavlov varied the temporal relationship between the US and CS, documenting the effects upon the reliability with which the CR was acquired. The most efficient way to establish a CR is to present the CS prior to and during the presentation of the US:

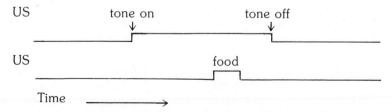

Using this paradigm, it can be observed that a conditioned salivation response will commence soon after the tone comes on and continue until the food is actually presented. At this point salivation intensifies, signalling the start of the unconditioned salivation response. A slightly less reliable method for establishing a CR is by *delayed* conditioning, which may be diagrammed as follows:

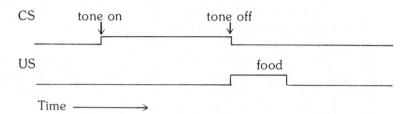

Notice that in delayed conditioning the tone terminates just as the food is presented; there is no temporal overlap of the CS and the US. Delayed conditioning results in the CR manifesting itself relatively late in the sequence, long after the onset of the CS, in this case the tone, and just prior to the presentation of the US, food. It is even more difficult to establish a conditioned response using *trace conditioning,* a variation of delayed conditioning, in which there is a time lapse between the offset of the CS and the onset of the US:

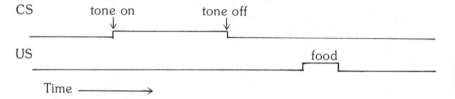

Using trace conditioning procedures, the establishment of a CR depends upon the capability of the animal to bridge, or mediate, the time interval between the CS and the US. During acquisition trials the animal must "remember" at the time of the US that the CS has just occurred, thus paving the way for an "association" between the two.

A fourth procedure employed by Pavlov is *temporal conditioning* and involves only the repeated presentation of a US at regular intervals:

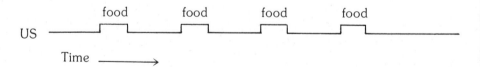

Using this procedure, salivation will eventually occur prior to the onset of each food presentation. Thus salivation is a CR, but what is the CS? While none is explicit, it is probably true that time serves this function. That is, the animal learns that a certain interval must pass before the receipt of food. The approaching termination of such a stable interval signals the impending presentation of food in a manner quite analogous to that of a more obvious CS, such as a tone.

Measurement of Classical Conditioning. There are two common methods of measuring classical conditioning. One way to evaluate the conditioning process is in terms of the percentage of trials on which the CR occurs. Of course, prior to the start of training the CS will not elicit any behavior, except perhaps certain orienting responses such as turning the head. After some number of pairings with the US, the organism will respond to the CS with a CR a small percentage of the time. This percentage will increase with further acquisition trials until it gradually approaches 100%. A second way in which conditioning is measured is in terms of response amplitude. The amplitude of the CR gradually increases over acquisition trials. In Pavolv's early studies, the amplitude of the CR was assessed by counting the number of saliva drops secreted by the dogs. Generally speaking, a CR will show the following acquisition curve:

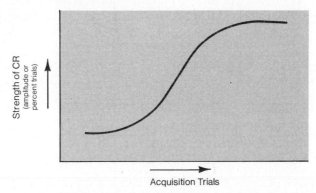

Acquisition Trials

Because the two indices of CR strength, amplitude and percent trials are not highly correlated, they frequently produce somewhat different results. It is not uncommon for a researcher to employ both in the same investigation.

Latency of the CR, a third index of CR acquisition, is used less frequently. It is based on the time between the onset of the CS and the start of the CR. Results using latency vary from study to study as a function of the particular conditioning procedures used. When conditioning involves some temporal overlap of the CS and US, it is usual for latency to become shorter with increasing numbers of trials. However, when delayed or trace conditioning is used, one frequently finds that latency increases as learning progresses. Instead of emitting the CR immediately subsequent to the onset of the CS, the animal learns to wait until just before the presentation of the US. Thus, a well-trained animal might not salivate until immediately prior to receiving food, and well after the tone has come on.

Generalization. A phenomenon which is basic to classical conditioning and related to that of CR acquisition is that of *generalization*. When an animal learns to make a response to a stimulus, the CS, which was formerly neutral with respect to the behavior, it is at the same time learning that same CR to other stimuli which are similar to the CS, even though these similar stimuli have never been experienced. This increase in response potential to stimuli which are in some respect similar to the CS is known as *stimulus generalization*.

By way of illustration, imagine that in Pavlov's classic experiments the frequency of the tone used as the CS was 1000 cps. If a trial subsequent to the establishment of a stable CR to the 1000 cps tone introduced a 900 cps tone instead, the animal would still emit a conditioned response. Similarly, if the novel tone was slightly higher than the one used in acquisition training, perhaps 1100 cps, a CR would again be observed. In general, the more similar to the acquisition tone are the novel tones, the more similar in strength will be the CR. As the novel tones become more dissimilar from the acquisition tone, the strength of the CR, perhaps measured by response amplitude, will diminish. This generalization effect may be illustrated as follows:

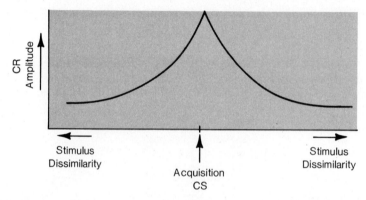

The importance of generalization has to do with efficiency. Because we acquire CRs to classes of stimuli and not just to the particular CS which happens to be present during acquisition, we do not have to experience extensive retraining every time there is a slight alteration in the quality or quantity of the CS. It is not difficult to see how the efficiency brought about by generalization facilitates adapting to the environment. For example, the emotional responses of distress, fear, or avoidant movements are automatic consequences of pain, a powerful US. These responses are initially neutral with respect to animals. In fact, it is usual to see children approach all sorts of animals, apparently in delight. However, if bitten, the child will quickly acquire conditioned emotional and avoidant responses to the animal, a CS, because of its association with pain, a US. The child attaches these conditioned responses not just to the single animal which provoked pain; similar animals, even those of different species, may elicit fear and avoidance when they are brought into the child's presence.

Fear. In what is now considered to be a classic study, Watson and Raynor (1920) conditioned a fear response in an infant using techniques very similar to those abstracted above. Specifically, these researchers first determined that 11-month-old Albert manifested approach behavior to a variety of small animals, including rabbits, rats, dogs and cats. Therefore, Watson chose as a CS a white rat, because of its neutrality with respect to the responses of fear and avoidance. As the US for fear, Watson used a sudden loud noise which was produced by striking an iron bar with a hammer just to the rear of Albert's head. On the first acquisition trial the white rat was presented to Albert. Just as he made contact with the tame animal, the bar was vigorously struck and a strong startle response was provoked in the infant; Albert fell forward, his face landing in the mattress upon which he had been sitting. The second trial prompted Albert to jump, fall, and cry. A conditioned fear response, as evidenced by crying, was established to the white rat alone after only seven acquisition trials. In addition, the fearful behavior was elicited by a variety of other stimuli which had not been present during acquisition of the CR, but which were, in some ways, physically similar in appearance to a furry white rat. Specifically, Albert had generalized his fear to a rabbit, a dog, a fur coat, and a Santa Claus mask.

This discovery led Watson to conclude that many of the very intense fears which we experience, phobias, might well be nothing more than generalized conditioned responses. The original conditioning may occur at such an early point in life that neither it nor the US responsible for it are recalled.

In the case of Albert, it was unfortunate that an illness in the infant forced termination of experimental work, giving Watson no opportunity to develop a technique for removal of the conditioned fears which had been developed through classical conditioning. Watson imagined that the fears would persist; perhaps one day Albert would seek help from psychoanalysis, a form of therapy Watson looked at with skepticism.

> The Freudians twenty years from now, unless their hypotheses change, when they come to analyze Albert's fear of a seal skin coat . . . will probably tease from him the recital of a dream which their analysis will show that Albert at three years of age attempted to play with the pubic hair of his mother and was scoldeld violently for it . . . If the analyst had sufficiently prepared Albert to accept such a dream when found as an explanation of his avoiding tendencies, and if the analyst had the authority and personality to put it over, Albert may be fully convinced that the dream was a true revealer of the factors which brought about the fear. (Watson and Raynor, 1920, p. 14)

One focus of continuing debate between psychoanalysts and learning theorists is Freud's (1955b) phobia case study *Little Hans,* first published in 1909. Freud himself only saw the youngster on one occasion. Most of his information about Hans was communicated by the father, who regularly corresponded with Freud regarding the little boy's illness. Despite his indirect knowledge of the situation, Freud believed that this case was important because it served to illustrate the operation of several psychoanalytic constructs, including infantile sexuality, the Oedipus complex, castration anxiety, and the manner in which these relate to the development of symptom formation. In this instance, Hans developed a fear of being bitten by horses.

Freud's theoretical analysis revolves primarily around Hans' desire to possess his mother and his rivalry with his father. With respect to the former aspect of the Oedipal conflict, several incidents are cited as being revealing. For example, Hans' seductiveness was thought to have been expressed one day while he was being dried and powdered after having been given a bath. Apparently Hans' mother was being careful not to touch his penis during these ministrations. Suddenly the three-year-old Hans asked, "Why don't you put your finger there?"

Mother:	"Because that'd be piggish."
Hans:	"What's that? Piggish? Why?"
Mother:	"Because it's not proper."
Hans (laughing):	"But it's great fun."

(Freud, 1955b, p. 19)

The basis for castration anxiety is found in several places. Freud reports that Hans, at the age of three and a half, took special delight in playing with his "widdler." Being discovered at such play, Hans was told by his mother: "If you do that, I shall send you to Dr. A. to cut off your widdler. And then what will you widdle with?" (1955b, pp. 7-8). In addition, Hans is reported by his father to have denied the anatomical differences between the sexes until he was about four and a half. This insight apparently came about while Hans observed his younger sister being bathed.

However, Hans' curiosity regarding genitals predated this insight considerably. When he was only three his mother asked Hans what he was staring at while he watched her disrobe. Hans replied, "I was only looking to see if you'd got a widdler too . . . I thought you were so big you'd have a widdler like a horse" (1955b, pp. 9-10). This remark is tied by Freud to other comments made by Hans regarding the size of "widdlers" to be found on horses. Freud interprets Hans' preoccupation with large penises to a basic dissatisfaction with the puniness of his own organ. It is for this reason that large animals were offensive to Hans from a very early age.

With the intensification of the Oedipal conflict, offensiveness turned to fear, and horses became the symbolic representation of the father. Freud's one interview with Hans revealed that the boy was particularly troubled by the blinders worn by horses and by "black," the muzzle around their mouths. These were interpreted to represent the father's eyeglasses and mustache.

Thus, the fear of horses was held to be a symbolic fear of retaliation from the father "who was going to punish him for the evil wishes he was nourishing against him." The phobia itself served to keep Hans at home and generally close to his mother, thereby partially fulfilling a central component of his Oedipal wishes. According to Freud, Hans really was a little Oedipus who wanted to have his father "out of the way," to get rid of him, so that he might be alone with his beautiful mother and sleep with her.

As a source of scientific data, the case of Little Hans is prone to all of the limitations inherent in the use of clinical material. Problems are compounded because of the second-hand nature of much of the information. Beyond these drawbacks, Wolpe and Rachman (1960) have offered their own, more specific criticisms of Freud's psychodynamic explanation of the case. They assert that many of Freud's conclusions rest upon very questionable reasoning, at best. For instance, at one point in the case presentation Freud describes how Hans knocked over a toy horse. This action is taken as evidence of Hans' destructive fantasies for his father, who he was talking with at the time. Wolpe and Rachman point out that the correctness of this interpretation depends upon three assumptions whose validity is debatable. The first assumption is that the horse symbolizes the father in Hans' mind; the second is that the act was intentional and not accidental; and the third is that knocking over the toy horse is an action which reveals destructive urges.

Wolpe and Rachman also are critical of Freud for his presumption that an event which immediately preceded the outbreak of Hans' illness, the viewing of "a bus-horse fall down and kick with its feet," was merely the "precipitating cause" of the phobia. They instead believe that this incident "was in fact the cause of the entire disorder" (p. 145).

In their view, it is more parsimonious to understand the case of Little Hans in terms of his "illness" being a conditioned emotional reaction. Just as Albert developed a fear of white rats on the basis of respondent conditioning, so too, they claim, did Hans develop his fear of horses on the basis of having an experience in which horses were associated with extreme distress. It will be recalled that Albert's conditioned fear generalized to an array of other stimuli, such as furry objects. Wolpe and Rachman contend that many of the behaviors which constituted Hans' "illness" also can be best construed as conditioned fear responses which generalized to other related stimuli. For instance, Hans was fearful of a broader array of stimuli than merely horses; he was also intimidated by stimuli related to horses which were present at the time of the initial acquisition trial, horse blinkers and muzzles. It is also pointed out that Hans expressed considerable fear of large carts and buses similar in size to the one drawn by the horse when it fell in such a frightening manner. Smaller carts were not nearly so upsetting to Hans. This pattern appears to approximate closely what would be expected on the basis of a simple generalization effect, in which stimuli most similar to those present during the acquisition of a conditioned response elicit relatively strong conditioned responses, those dissimilar only elicit weak conditional responses.

Eysenck and Rachman (1965) have summarized what they consider to be the core elements of phobia development from the perspective of classical conditioning. Basically, phobias are considered to be learned responses to stimuli which are either sporadically or temporarily associated with a frightening or painful situation. Based upon experimental and clinical data, Eysenck and Rachman also suggest that neutral stimuli which are most likely to acquire the capacity to provoke phobic behavior are those which are related to the frightening situation in some meaningful way. Stimuli which happen to be present at the time of the fright, but which are quite irrelevant to it, are much less likely to become phobic objects. With respect to the strength of the learned phobia, two dimensions are considered important. First, repeated association between the phobic object and fright or pain will increase the magnitude of the phobia. In other words, a dog phobia is likely to be more extreme if a person has the experience of being bitten twice instead of only once. Second, it is believed that the probability of acquiring a phobic reaction to a formerly neutral stimulus is related to the magnitude of the US; the more fearful it is, the more likely one is to develop a strong phobic response to associated stimuli. It is to be expected that generalization will occur to other objects which are related, or in some ways similar, to the phobic object.

Sexual Deviancy. The acquisition of deviant behaviors other than phobias has been experimentally demonstrated using classical conditioning procedures. In a frequently cited research, Rachman (1966) sought to demonstrate that classical conditioning is relevant to the etiology of a sexual fetish. Three unmarried male volunteers viewed color slides of attractive nude females for thirty seconds, the US. The UR studied was penis volume changes as measured by a plethysmograph. For the fifteen seconds immediately prior to every presentation of the US, Rachman had his three subjects view a colored slide of black, knee length women's boots. For the subjects involved in the experiment, this stimulus was initially neutral with respect to sexual arousal; it was selected because women's boots are not infrequently found to be fetishistic objects when this behavior disorder occurs outside of the laboratory.

The subjects were given 18 acquisition trials per day divided into blocks of six trials separated by five minute rest periods. One subject needed only 24 acquisition trials, another as many as 65 trials, before reaching the acquisition criterion for a conditioned response. This criterion was set at five successive penis engorgements to the previously innocuous image of black boots. Finally, each subject showed evidence of a conditioned arousal response to at least one generalization stimulus consisting of boots which differed in style and color from the CS. It was concluded from these findings that behavior which is generally considered to be sexually deviant can be induced through classical conditioning procedures in much the same way that Watson had earlier conditioned fear responses in Albert.

Adaptive Classical Conditioning. We certainly do not want to impart the impression that classical conditioning is only relevant to the development of abnormal behavior. In fact, this process is implicated in the acquisition of all sorts of stimulus-response associations. For instance, to a small child, money is a reasonably neutral stimulus. However, because it is so often paired with experiences to which we naturally react with favor, these little green slips of paper gradually become very powerful conditioned stimuli which are quite capable of eliciting favorable reactions on their own.

A number of investigations have shown that expressed attitudes can be manipulated via classical conditioning procedures. One general format of these research designs, used by Insko and Oakes (1966) and others, is to associate neutral nonsense syllables with words already having positive or negative connotations, such as "beautiful" and "ugly." Through repeated, temporally contiguous, paired presentations, affective evaluations of the syllables gradually become similar to those of the associated word.

Higher Order Classical Conditioning. At this juncture it is important to note that the US employed in these attitudinal investigations are quite dissimilar to those once used by Pavlov. Originally, the US was invariably some object or event, such as food or shock, to which the animal evoked a "built in" response. That is, the US-UR bond for Pavlov was unlearned. In contrast, Insko and Oakes used words as "unconditioned stimuli." The subjects do not emit an innate response to "Beautiful" and "ugly"; they have an already-learned emotional response to the words when they arrive at the laboratory. This previously-acquired stimulus-response bond is then dealt with *as if* it were a US-UR bond of the innate kind used by Pavlov.

Stimuli to which responses have already been acquired routinely function as unconditioned stimuli outside of the laboratory. If other neutral stimuli become somehow paired with the acquired US, they, too, will gain the power to provoke conditioned responses. Money was mentioned as a stimulus to which we acquire positive emotional reactions. It is common for money, which is originally a CS, to ultimately function as a US. For example, an originally neutral person who regularly gives us money will gradually come to evoke positive conditioned emotional reactions because of his repeated association with money. Bandura calls this general phenomenon *higher order* classical conditioning, "in which a stimulus that has acquired eliciting power through its direct association with primary experiences serves as the basis for further conditioning" (1969, p. 22).

Extinction of conditioned responses

Pavlov (1927) was the first to use the word "reinforcement" when referring to the US. In his original experiments, after salivation was conditioned to the bell, the bell had to be occasionally re-paired with food, the reinforcement, in order for the bond between bell and salivation to be maintained. It is proper to describe such a trial, in which the CS and US are again presented together subsequent to the development of a CR, as a *reinforcement trial*, because it "reinforces" the strength of the CR.

Trials in which the CS is presented alone may serve as test trials which demonstrate the existence of the CR. Generally, however, when the US is not presented along with the CS, we are referring to an *extinction trial*, because the repeated use of this operation serves to gradually weaken or extinguish the conditioned response. Of course, the unconditioned response remains unaffected. Pavlov was able to extinguish salivation at the sound of the bell by repeatedly ringing it but not following this with the food. After a series of such extinction trials, salivation gradually diminished and finally no longer occurred.

Fear. Watson, in his book, *Behaviorism*, commented on the aforementioned case of Albert: "Finding that emotional responses could be built in with great readiness, we were all the more eager to see whether they could be broken down, and if so, by what methods" (1924, p. 132). Watson himself was not destined to make this discovery. His academic career was prematurely terminated when Johns Hopkins University disapproved of a divorce suit in which he was involved. A good friend of his second wife, Mary Jones, who had had the opportunity to study with Watson, took up the gauntlet. In 1924 she used extinction procedures in what is believed to be the first practical application of conditioning methods to the treatment of a behavior disorder. The case involved Peter, a three year old who had a well-established fear of animals when he was brought to Jones' attention. She effected the extinction of the conditioned fear response by repeatedly presenting the CS, a rabbit, in the absence of any US capable of innately provoking a fear or avoidant response. Jones at first presented the rabbit at a distance, and while Peter was eating. With each new presentation, the rabbit was brought closer and closer. Finally Peter was able to tolerate being close to the animal without any outward display of fear.

The extinction process was temporarily set back when, on one of the later trials, the rabbit actually scratched Peter. This, therefore, constituted an unwanted reinforced trial in which the CS, rabbit, was unfortunately followed by a US, pain. Many years later, Jones wrote, "It has always been of the greatest satisfaction to me that I could be associated with the *removal* of a fear . . ." (1974, p. 581).

Lundin (1969) attempted to construe Freud's therapeutic approach to the treatment of phobias in terms of classical conditioning. In psychoanalysis, the patient is at first typically unable to recall the frightening or overwhelming circumstances surrounding the original trauma which has caused the phobic symptoms. He is, therefore, encouraged, through free association and perhaps hypnosis, to reconstruct gradually and consciously what has been repressed. A point will finally be reached where the person experiences a curative "abreaction," a reliving of the original trauma which is accompanied by all the emotional behavior that occurred when the trauma first was experienced. From a classical conditioning perspective, if this treatment is effective, it is because the patient is producing conditioned responses without additional exposure to unconditioned stimuli which are naturally capable of provoking negative emotional responses. In essence, this constitutes the essentials of an extinction procedure.

It is unlikely that conditioned responses will fade through simple non-use. This is particularly true of conditioned fear or avoidant responses which seem to be especially persistent. Therefore, the elimination of CR depends upon exposure to repeated extinction trials. Intuitively, many people seem to be aware of this principle even if they do not articulate it in the language of classical conditioning. It is not unusual for a parent to encourage a child to return quickly to the water after a frightening swimming or boating experience, or for a person to be pressured to drive again very soon after an automobile accident, to prevent the fear from becoming set or firmly established. In each case, the frightened person is being forced back into a situation in which the one trial conditioning of fear responses took place. These responses can now be extinguished once they are no longer associated with the unconditioned stimulus which first provoked the fright. Of course, just as Peter's progress was thwarted when he was scratched by the rabbit, a second water or automobile incident of painful proportions would work against the hoped-for extinction process.

COGNITIVE MEDIATION OF CLASSICAL CONDITIONING

A casual look at Pavlov's conditioning procedures gives the distinct impression that he is dealing with an automatic process. If a CS is paired with an US, it will acquire the capacity to provoke a CR; if the CS continues to be presented in the absence of the US, the CR undergoes extinction. While it is certainly true that this generally describes what takes place, there is no question that cognitive variables are greatly involved in the course of both the acquisition and extinction of conditioned responses.

Cognitively Mediated Acquisition

It has been shown that conditioned autonomic responses to a CS can be accomplished without the CS ever actually being paired with a US, such as shock. Instead, the subjects are advised that shock will, on some trials, accompany the CS. This induced anticipation of pain is sufficient to condition emotional responding to the CS. Grings (1965) suggests that conditioning effects produced through instructional sets, sometimes called *pseudo-conditioning,* should be distinguished from real conditioning in which there is an actual pairing of the CS and US. Bandura, in a plea for parsimony, suggests that the phenomenon probably does not involve any basically new principles and doubts that pseudo-conditioning takes place independent of a US being paired with the CS. He suggests that the imagination of aversive events is quite capable of evoking emotional responding and, consequently, can serve as unconditioned stimuli. In other words, simply being told that the CS will sometimes be paired with shock is theoretically insufficient to produce conditioning; the subject himself must have fear-producing thoughts temporally proximal to the CS. According to this conceptualization of pseudo-conditioning, "autonomic responses are cognitively induced rather than directly elicited by aversive stimuli under the experimenter's control" (1969, p. 580).

The potential for subjects to undergo physiological reactions as a consequence of visualizing fearful stimuli was empirically demonstrated by Grossberg and Wilson (1968). Subjects were requested to imagine stimuli checked on Wolpe and Lang's (1964) Fear Survey Schedule as being either "not at all disturbing" or "very much disturbing." These neutral (N) and fearful (F) stimuli were to be imagined four times each in counter-balanced order: N F F N N F F N. As the subjects imagined each scene for a 25 second interval, automatic indices were being continuously recorded.

It was found that both heart rate and skin conductance showed similar increases while the experimenter read the scenes to be imagined. Heart rate and skin conductance showed further increases once the subjects began to imagine their fearful scene. These indices declined from the reading to the imagination phase of the procedure when the neutral scenes were being imagined. This differential effect of fear vs. neutral scene imagination upon heart rate and skin conductance was statistically significant at the $p < .01$ level. Grossberg and Wilson believe "that self-produced stimulation such as that involved in following instructions to imagine fear scenes produced more tension or arousal than the externally presented [read] stimulation . . ." (p. 131).

This, and other investigations, provide a basis for believing that classical conditioning may routinely take place without the immediate presence of an external US. If thoughts are capable of functioning as a US, then the potential of classical conditioning is virtually unlimited.

Cognitively Mediated Extinction

Grings and Lockhart (1963) demonstrated the role of cognition with respect to the extinction of classically conditioned responses. Typically, the extinction process expresses itself in the form of a gradual decline of CR strength. This decline can be made precipitous if the subject is advised just prior to the onset of extinction trials what to expect. Specifically, if someone has acquired a conditioned autonomic response to the color green because green has been paired with receipt of shock, the green CS will very quickly lose its response-provoking capability if the person is told that shock will no longer be forthcoming.

Bridger and Mandel (1965) have further demonstrated that the effect is much more dramatic among subjects who trust the verbal message received from the experimenter. Those who remain suspicious, believing that perhaps more shock will accompany the presentation of the green CS, manifest extinction rates similar to subjects who are not told anything prior to the inception of extinction trials. Thus, believability of cognitive input interacts with actual experience in predictable ways.

The question of how much control symbolic mediators have over extinction seems to be in part related to the nature of the CR acquisition procedure. If the CR was acquired through primarily cognitive channels, its extinction appears to be highly susceptible to cognitive factors. For example, an autonomic CR to a green stimulus, acquired under the verbal threat of green being paired with shock, will quickly extinguish if the threat is verbally withdrawn. In contrast, a conditioned autonomic response to green, when this stimulus is actually paired with receipt of shock, will be far less susceptible to the influence of verbal mediation once extinction trials begin. On the basis of this evidence, Bridger and Mandel suggest that conditioned responses contain dual components. One is mediated via self-arousal mechanisms and is highly susceptible to the influence of cognitions. The second component is independent of cognitive mediation, and its acquisition or alteration is a function of direct experience with the presentation and withdrawal of actual stimuli.

A Cognitive Explanation of Extinction. Pavlov explained extinction with the term "inhibition." He felt that extinction involved more than a passive wiping away of the CR; active inhibition of the CR was presumed to operate. Evidence for this emerged from a demonstration in which a dog who had undergone extinction of a salivation response suddenly salivated if the tone (CS) was presented along with an unexpected, loud noise. It was reasoned that the noise disrupted an active inhibitory process, thereby freeing the old CR. In other words, the loud noise produced "disinhibition." Of course, if a dog had never acquired a conditioned salivation response to a tone, the pairing of the same sudden, loud noise with the tone would not produce salivation.

Pavlov's reasoning would suggest that once a response has undergone extinction, it is more difficult to recondition the subject to the old CS than to a new CS; through extinction, the old CS has become evocative of response inhibition instead of response excitation. However, contrary to expectations, Pavlov (1927) discovered that an extinguished CR reconditioned quite quickly to the old CS. Other researchers, including Rescorla (1969), have firmly established "that a formally conditioned stimulus, no matter how much extinction intervenes, will recondition faster than a novel stimulus condition."

More recent explanations of extinction have become increasingly cognitive. In particular, the *discrimination theory* of extinction falls within this general framework.

This position holds that a CR continues to be emitted on the early extinction trials because the organism has not yet recognized that the situation has been altered, and that the CS should no longer be construed as a signal indicating a forthcoming US. Support for this view comes from research in which rates of extinction were noted as a function of the previous schedule of reinforced trials. When there is a long series of trials, all consisting of a CS-US pairing, the introduction of an extinction series results in a relatively rapid decline in the strength of the CR. Presumably this is because the shift from reinforced to non-reinforced trials is quite distinct. However, extinction proceeds much more slowly if it follows a series of CS presentations where only a percentage have been paired with the US. The lower the percentage, the less obvious is the shift to a full extinction schedule, and the longer the CR tends to be maintained. In general, from this point of view, the speed with which extinction proceeds depends upon the degree to which the extinction trials are discriminable from the preceding series of trials.

THERAPEUTIC APPLICATIONS OF CLASSICAL CONDITIONING

Several different behavior therapeutic procedures have directly emerged from research with classical conditioning, or are readily explainable in terms of the principles of classical conditioning. To a large degree, these procedures seem to depend upon higher order and cognitively-mediated conditioning.

Maladaptive approach and avoidant behavior

There are no limits to the ways in which deviant behavior can be categorized. Certainly the diagnostic nomenclature of the American Psychiatric Association is the system which is most frequently used. A more general system simply differentiates maladaptive behavior on the basis of whether it involves approach or avoidant components.

If a person is unhappy, gets into social or legal difficulties, or upsets others because of the way he interacts with people, objects, or events, he is said to be exhibiting *maladaptive approach* behavior. Over-assertiveness, obesity, fetishism, and drug dependencies are examples of maladaptive approach behaviors. *Maladaptive avoidant* behaviors are characterized by the tendency to dodge people and shun situations, causing personal unhappiness to the self or to others. As a generalization, we can say that maladaptive avoidant behaviors are associated with high levels of anxiety, characterized by unassertiveness and phobias. Behavior therapists have encouraged the use of different therapeutic interventions, depending upon whether the problem is understood to be mainly approach or avoidant in nature. If the behavioral difficulty involves both possibilities, then the therapeutic treatment will be appropriately tailored to the complexities of the case.

Treatment of Maladaptive Approach Behavior

Aversive classical conditioning. When a CS is paired with an aversive US, such as painful shock, the organism quickly learns responses to the CS which suggest that it, too, has acquired aversive characteristics. Of particular importance to the treatment of maladaptive approach behavior is the well-established finding that stimuli which have a positive valence lose their attractiveness after being paired repeatedly with an aversive US.

Many of the early efforts to utilize aversive conditioning for therapeutic gain employed nausea-inducing drugs, such as apomorphine, as the US. Lavin, Thorpe, Boucker, Blakemore, and Conway (1961) employed this particular drug in a case study which dealt with a transvestite. The patient was a young, married truckdriver who, although he had satisfactory sexual relations with his wife, experienced sexual pleasure from dressing in female clothing. By the time he was seen for treatment, the condition had existed for seven years. As a preparatory step, Lavin and his co-workers produced photographic slides of the patient in several stages of female dress and made an audio recording of the patient describing the process of getting into several erotically stimulating garments.

The aversive conditioning consisted of first inducing nausea via an injection of apomorphine. As the drug began to bring on a wave of sickness, the US, the slides and audio tapes, the CS, were presented until the patient began to vomit. Lavin reports that both the patient and his wife considered the therapy completely successful; there was no recurrence of transvestion or emergence of other sexual deviations over the course of a six month follow-up.

Bandura (1969) notes that a number of methodological difficulties exist when an intramuscular injection of an emetic is used as an US. The temporal arrangement of the CS and US are not easy to control. Typically, the CS, a fetish object, is presented after the onset of nauseous reactions in order to preclude the possibility of a long interval between the CS and the US. The gradual onset of the nausea also works against its effectiveness, since it is known that objectionable stimulation of sudden onset is most aversive (Fromer and Berkowitz, 1964). In addition, the therapist cannot readily control the magnitude or the duration of the UR. As Bandura (1969) points out, many patients who undergo this form of therapy experience needlessly long sessions of discomfort; and seeing a client become sick is not a pleasant experience for the therapist.

For these reasons, electrical stimulation, which is easily controlled, has come to be preferred as an aversive US. It is common for shock to be administered to the arms or to the feet temporally contiguous with the presentation of stimulus material to which the subject maladaptively approaches.

McGuire and Vallance (1964) report that this form of aversive conditioning was used successfully in the treatment of a 25-year-old graduate student who masturbated to fetishistic fantasies on an average of three times per day. What was novel about the case was that the therapists supplied the client with a portable shock generator so that aversive conditioning trials could be self-administered whenever there was an urge to masturbate. This was supplemented by in-office treatment which consisted of pairing shock with fantasies of the fetishistic clothing and, when imagery was weak, with pictures of people dressed in the sexually-stimulating clothing. The outcome of this treatment program was the total elimination of fetishistic fantasies. In addition, the frequency of masturbation declined considerably, and, when practiced, was for the first time accompanied by heterosexual fantasies.

Counterconditioning. The examples of aversive classical conditioning described above are considered to be instances of a more general class of conditioning procedures called *counterconditioning.* What distinguishes counterconditioning is the fact that the CS is one which, while it is neutral with respect to the CR, already has acquired the capacity to provoke certain unwanted behavior. For example, in the treatment of fetishistic behavior by McGuire and Vallance (1964), the US was shock and the UR was avoidant behavior; the CS was fetishistic fantasies, neutral with respect to avoidance. The aversive conditioning procedure resulted in the substitution of avoidant behavior for sexual arousal responses in the presence of the CS. O'Leary and Wilson (1975) define counterconditioning as "the displacement of a particular conditioned response [e.g. sexual arousal to fetishistic objects] by the establishment of an incompatible response [e.g. avoidance] to the same stimulus."

Using the McGuire and Vallance design for illustrative purposes, we can diagram the situation at the start of treatment as follows:

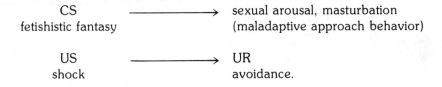

After repeated pairing of the CS and the US, the following occurred:

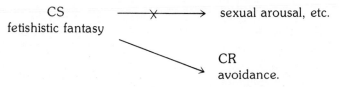

Thus, an avoidant response displaces a maladaptive approach response.

Covert sensitization. An aversive counterconditioning procedure popularized by Cautela (1966) moves "behavioral" treatment to a point quite different in many ways from what Watson had once envisioned. In this method, both the US and the CS are cognitively self-induced and, therefore, completely removed from direct therapist control or observation. Covert sensitization requires the patient to visualize the stimulus to which he has learned to become inappropriately attracted; this imagery functions as the CS. The patient then continues to fantasize about the CS in relation to another imagined aversive scene, the US.

This form of aversive cognitive counterconditioning has been effectively used to treat a variety of maladaptive approach behaviors, including cigarette smoking, alcoholism, and sexual deviance. In an attempt to treat obesity by using covert sensitization, Janda and Rimm (1972) worked with 18 undergraduates who had presented themselves to the university health service for assistance in losing weight. They ranged from being two to 149 pounds overweight, with a mean excess of 41.4 pounds. The 18 subjects were divided into triplets, with each member having approximately equal amounts of excess weight. Members of each triplet were then randomly assigned to one of three groups. One received no active treatment, although weight was monitored on a weekly basis; another, an attention-control group, was trained in deep muscle relaxation and discussed situations which the subjects claimed gave rise to anxiety; and the third was a covert sensitization group.

Cautela (1966) suggests that the vivid imagery necessary for a successful treatment is facilitated if the subject can relax. Therefore, subjects in the covert sensitization group also received muscle relaxation training. Following this, they were required to imagine that they were approaching a fattening food, the CS, and then to imagine feeling extremely sick, the US, just at the point of placing the taboo food in their mouths. The following is a representative scene as presented by Janda and Rimm.

> Imagine yourself sitting in your room late in the evening studying. All of a sudden you notice a craving to have something sweet to eat. You decide to go the snack room (in the dormitory) and buy a candy bar. As you walk into the room and toward the machine, you notice kind of a sick feeling in the pit of your stomach. You walk over to the machine anyway, and as you are standing in front of it, you *really* start to feel sick! You have that unpleasant, queasy feeling in your stomach. But you decide you want the candy anyway so you drop your money into the machine. As you pick up the candy, you are really feeling sick! You can now feel the vomit start to come up your throat but you manage to choke it back down. You unwrap the candy and lift it to your mouth. Just as you're ready to put it in your mouth your stomach *violently* rebels. You can feel the vomit in your throat. You try to choke it back down but you can't! You finally vomit all over yourself, all over the candy bar, and all over the person standing next to you. The taste of vomit in your mouth and the smell of it make you so sick you vomit *again* and *again*. Finally you decide to leave, and as soon as you start to walk away from the candy bar and the candy machine, you begin to feel better. You go to your room, take a shower, put on clean clothes, and now you feel much better. Your stomach now feels completely calm, and you feel good about yourself for not eating that candy bar. (1972, p. 39)

Thus, when this study began, the following situation existed:

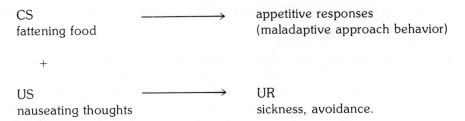

CS   → appetitive responses
fattening food   (maladaptive approach behavior)

   +

US   → UR
nauseating thoughts   sickness, avoidance.

The plan was to effect the following change in stimulus-response bonds through the process of covert sensitization:

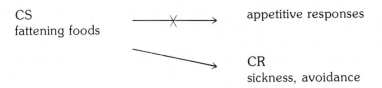

CS   ⤬→ appetitive responses
fattening foods

                                      CR
                                      sickness, avoidance

When treatment was started the mean weight for the control, attention-control, and covert sensitization groups was 164.7, 182.0, and 178.5, respectively. After six weekly sessions of 40 minutes, the control group had lost an average of 4.5 pounds; the attention-control subjects averaged a gain of .7 pound; and the subjects who had undergone covert sensitization showed a mean decrement of 9.5 pounds. Five of the six subjects in this latter treatment group manifested a weight loss. These mean group differences, while in the expected directions, were not large enough to attain statistical significance.

As part of the covert sensitization procedure, the subjects were asked to rate, among other things, their subjective distress while visualizing the aversive scenes. As might have been anticipated, there was a high correlation ($r = +.53$) found between these ratings and weight loss. The more subjectively aversive were the scenes for a subject, the more weight the subject tended to shed. The data were then reanalyzed using only the three subjects from the covert sensitization treatment who had the highest distress ratings. Their mean weight loss was 17.3 pounds, and the overall between-group treatment effect was now found to be statistically significant at the $p <$ .01 level.

These findings show covert sensitization to be an effective treatment for the management of maladaptive overeating. It resulted in rapid weight loss for those subjects whose visualizations of the aversive scenes produced high levels of subjective distress. Among this sub-group, weight loss continued over a six week follow-up period, reaching a mean of 21.0 pounds. The strong relationship between subjective distress and weight loss clearly points to the necessity of monitoring the effect of visualization upon subjects throughout treatment. Low distress levels might be remedied through additional visualization practice or by raising the "volume" on the scenes depicted. It is also possible that some subjects would be most susceptible to aversive visualization not having to do with nausea and vomiting. In any case, it is clear that maximum effectiveness can be achieved only if the specifics of a covert sensitization therapy are tailored to the needs and reactions of a particular patient.

One other favorable finding from this investigation is worth mentioning. Concern has been frequently expressed that aversive conditioning, including covert sensitization, might result in unwanted stimulus generalization. This does not appear to occur; subjects seem to establish appropriate discriminations between the conditional stimuli used in their treatment and other similar or related events. In the Janda and Rimm study, the covert sensitization group gave no evidence of negative responses to the therapist, treatment room, and the general surroundings. In fact, the therapist was rated as warm, interested, and competent. The covert sensitization subjects were also the most motivated, missing only 6% of their sessions; in comparison, the attention-control group missed over 30% of their appointments.

Cautela suggests that, to a large degree, the success of covert sensitization can be attributed to the aversive conditioning it produces. The study by Janda and Rimm was not concerned primarily with investigating the merits of Cautela's interpretation, or with trying to uncover any other possible effective ingredients in the covert sensitization program. They were, however, able to rule out therapist attention as an important factor, since this variable was controlled by the inclusion of the attention-control group.

An effort was made by Foreyt and Hagen (1973) to determine if the effects of a covert sensitization treatment can be attributed to aversive conditioning as Cautela asserts, or to some other factor, perhaps simple suggestion. Their general design was similar to that of Janda and Rimm, except that the attention-control treatment was replaced by a "covert sensitization placebo" condition. This placebo treatment was designed to match covert sensitization in all respects but one; pleasant scenes replaced scenes of nausea and vomiting. Both treatments used visualizations involving the same situations and foods. Patient expectations for success in the placebo group were equated with those of the covert sensitization group members through a lengthy rationale describing how imagining fattening foods in the context of other pleasant images would weaken the desire for such foods. On the basis of classical conditioning, one would expect the opposite; specifically, the pairing of the two sets of images, fattening foods and pleasant scenes, would seem to heighten the positive valence of the foods.

Pre- and post-treatment rating of food palatability revealed that the attractiveness of favorite foods which were included in the imagery of both covert sensitization and placebo subjects declined equally, and to a significant (p < .01) degree. Palatability ratings of two other groups of foods, fruits and vegetables, which were not included in the imagery showed no systematic shifts from pre- to post-treatment assessments. In addition, the control subjects who participated in no active treatment at all showed, as expected, no change over time in their ratings of the favorite foods.

Because palatability ratings were equally affected by covert sensitization and placebo treatments, Foreyt and Hagen feel that aversive conditioning could not have been the effective ingredient in bringing about this shift. "If, as the data indicate, suggestion rather than conditioning was operating for the covert sensitization placebo group, it is reasonable to assume that suggestion was also a critical independent variable for the covert sensitization group" (p. 22). While this conclusion may be tenable for this particular study, the external validity of such an assertion is to be questioned; the subjects in neither treatment group manifested significant actual weight loss over the nine week program of 18 sessions. In fact, the placebo group lost slightly more pounds (mean = 8.5) than did the covert sensitization group (mean = 4.1). It is quite possible that in the absence of an effective treatment, or even with it, suggestion is an important determinant of food palatability ratings. This, however, says nothing about the role of aversive conditioning in a covert sensitization treatment program which successfully brings about the desired behavior change. One can only speculate as to why covert sensitization failed in this study. The findings cited earlier by Janda and Rimm suggest that the quality and intensity of the imagery produced by the subjects themselves may have been inadequate.

Treatment of Maladaptive Avoidant Behavior

Counterconditioning procedures have also been employed for the treatment of maladaptive avoidant behaviors. When so used, the procedure involves the enlistment of a positively-valenced stimulus as the US; this is then paired with the negative stimulus, CS, whose avoidant-provoking capacity we wish to alter.

By way of illustration, return to the first behavior therapeutic demonstration conducted by Jones (1924). Recall that our earlier interpretation of her method was in terms of extinction. Specifically, Peter made conditioned emotional fear responses in the presence of the rabbit, CS, without the rabbit being re-paired with a US, pain. Gradually, the conditioned fear responses weakened; they underwent extinction. That same case study can also be understood to at least partially involve counterconditioning, because more was going on than a simple extinction process. In particular, Peter was being encouraged to eat a preferred food, in the company of a supportive therapist, while the rabbit was present. In terms of a counterconditioning paradigm, we can diagram the beginning situation as follows:

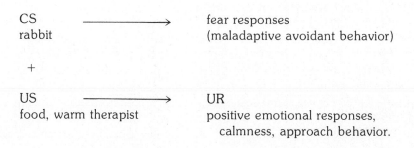

CS   ⟶   fear responses
rabbit   (maladaptive avoidant behavior)

    +

US   ⟶   UR
food, warm therapist   positive emotional responses,
                                        calmness, approach behavior.

The treatment consisted of effecting the following modification:

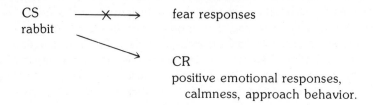

CS
rabbit
                          ✕ ⟶   fear responses

                                     CR
                                     positive emotional responses,
                                       calmness, approach behavior.

Bandura points out that counterconditioning may in fact be an integral part of all extinction procedures. Repeated non-reinforced presentations of a CS invariably result not just in a loss of the CR but in the evocation of other responses which compete with the fading CR. "According to this interpretation of the process, conventional extinction procedures often involve a form of unguided counterconditioning" (1969, p. 429-430). Therefore, the great advantage of an explicit counterconditioning treatment is that the competing behavior is built in and not left unmanaged. For example, in the case of Peter, calmness was intentionally induced by Jones as a logical response to compete with fear, since the two behaviors are mutually incompatible.

Systematic Desensitization. The most popular counterconditioning procedure for the treatment of maladaptive avoidant behavior is Wolpe's *systematic desensitization.* In this behavior therapy, deep muscle relaxation is typically used as the response intended to compete with that of anxiety. "The autonomic effects that accompany deep [muscle] relaxation are diametrically opposed to those characteristic of anxiety" (1969, p. 96).

When a patient has a maladaptive conditioned fear response to a stimulus, such as snakes, this stimulus will be dealt with in a manner analogous to the CS in a counterconditioning paradigm. That is, the snake will be paired with another stimulus, the US, which already has the power to provoke the competing response, relaxation. Unfortunately, most patients do not enter therapy possessing such a US-UR bond involving relaxation. Consequently, it is incumbent upon the therapist to have his patient acquire such a US-UR bond before treatment can begin.

Notice how far we have come from Pavlov's original conceptualization of the US-UR bond being one which is "built in," typically at the level of reflexive behavior. In our earlier discussions of covert sensitization, the US-UR bond involved a previously learned association between the US and UR. For example, nauseating thoughts (US) brought forth avoidant responses (UR) which the patient already possessed when he came for treatment. Now, with systematic desensitization we are presenting a model of counterconditioning in which the stimulus-response bond employed as the US and the UR must first be acquired as part of the treatment process.

Despite the fact that systematic desensitization primarily involves imagery of both the CS and the US, Wolpe himself interprets the counterconditioning involved as not being verbally mediated. He writes that "since anxiety involves a primitive (subcortical) level of neural organization, its unlearning can be procured only through processes that involve this primitive level. Neurotic anxiety cannot be overcome purely by intellectual action — logical argument, rational insight . . ." (1969, p. 14).

Wolpe goes on to say that anxiety responses are eliminated if they are inhibited by a competing response. This notion is captured by his *principle of reciprocal inhibition:* "If a response inhibitory of anxiety can be made to occur in the presence of anxiety-evoking stimuli it will weaken the bond between these stimuli and the anxiety" (p. 15). It follows from this principle that, in order for reciprocal inhibition to work in the desired manner, the anxiety response must be weak enough to be inhibited by the competing behavor; if the opposite is true, then the competing behavior would be inhibited by the anxiety.

In terms of the actual technique used, systematic desensitization involves a set of three operations. First, there must be training in deep muscle relaxation so that a sufficiently strong response will be available to inhibit the anxiety. Jacobson (1938) developed a method for deep muscle relaxation in which different muscle groups of the body are first tensed and then relaxed. This experience helps the patient become aware of the different body sensations which accompany tension and relaxation. Once the discrimination is acquired, deep states of relaxation can often be easily self-induced.

The second operation involves the construction of an *anxiety hierarchy*. As described by Wolpe and Lang (1964), this is a list of stimuli which share a common anxiety-provoking theme, such as heights, and which are ranked in order of their power to provoke tension. The data for the construction of this hierarchy come from case history material, interviews with the patient, and questionnaires, such as the Fear Survey Schedule.

The identification of all the fearful stimuli is not always an easy matter and may require a level of clinical exploration which is usually only associated with insight-oriented therapies such as psychoanalysis. Many of the fears may not involve external events but instead may relate to internal, response-produced stimuli. In addition, the final product may encompass not one but several hierarchies, each one relevant to a separate anxiety theme. Finally, the rank ordering of hierarchy items is frequently less than obvious. For instance, some test phobic students find themselves in a greater state of distress on the way to an examination than while actually writing it.

Wolpe tries to facilitate the ranking of hierarchy items through the use of a *subjective anxiety scale*. The patient is told: "Think of the worst anxiety you have ever experienced or can imagine experiencing, and assign to this the number 100. Now think of the state of being absolutely calm and call this zero. Now you have a scale" (1969, p. 116). Each unit on this 100 point scale is called a "sud," subjective unit of disturbance. Many patients find it much easier to express the anxiety-provoking capacity of stimuli in terms of "suds" than through open-ended verbal description.

"The stage is now set for the conventional desensitization procedure, the patient having attained a capacity to calm himself by relaxation, and the therapist having established appropriate hierarchies" (p. 121). First the subject brings on a deep state of relaxation, hopefully to the point of "a positive feeling of calm, i.e. a negative of anxiety; but it is *not* mandatory and one is always well-satisfied with zero subjective units of disturbance" (p. 122). Wolpe feels that desensitization is rarely possible if anxiety levels remain above 25 "suds." If this problem is encountered, medication, such as chlorpromazine, or hypnosis may be used to bring on a lowered condition of tension. Also, the visualization of "relaxing" scenes may be encouraged. "Imagine that on a calm summer's day you lie on your back on a soft lawn and watch the clouds move slowly overhead. Notice especially the brilliant edges of the clouds" (p. 125).

Once a satisfactory level of relaxation is achieved, a neutral first scene is presented to see how well the patient can visualize material. If the patient is successful, the therapist continues, "I am now going to ask you to imagine a number of scenes. You will imagine them clearly and they will generally interfere little, if at all, with your state of relaxation" (p. 126). The subject is instructed to raise an index finger as soon as a scene is clearly visualized. The scene is terminated at the instruction of the therapist, usually after about five to seven seconds. The patient then states how disturbed he was in terms of "suds." The interval between scenes usually lasts about 10 to 20 seconds, and is a period during which the patient tries to reestablish a deep relaxation before embarking upon his next visualization.

It is common for scenes to be presented three or four times before appropriately low "suds" levels are reached. A total of from 10 to 50 scenes may be presented during a 30 minute session. The number of sessions in a treatment varies considerably; one snake phobic was reported to have completely overcome his fear after one 90 minute session while a patient with a death phobia required more than 100 sessions and 2000 scene presentations before the problem was alleviated.

Research on Systematic Desensitization. There has been some research on the course of fear reduction over a series of desensitization sessions. Wolpe reports that with conditions in which anxiety goes up with increasing proximity to the feared object, the rate of progress positively accelerates as the treatment moves toward 100% recovery; this would apply to a snake phobic, for example. In contrast, when anxiety depends upon the number of objects present there is a negatively accelerated function; progress slows down the closer to 100% recovery the patient moves. Someone who feared crowds would have this reaction. This conclusion is based upon the proportion of scenes, relative to the total, required for progress at each stage of recovery.

In a somewhat more sophisticated design, Schroeder and Rich (1976) investigated the course of fear reduction over the systematic desensitization of 15 female snake phobics. Fear was defined in a multidimensional way. The behavioral measure involved a "14 performance task behavioral avoidance test" in which the subjects had to engage in a graded range of activities, from being in the same room as a four foot boa constrictor to holding the snake. The physiological measures employed included indices of skin conductance and heart rate. Several cognitive self-report scales were also used. These included a "fear thermometer," which is a 10 point rating scale of fear; a semantic differential questionnaire which rated the fear on four bi-polar adjective scales of good-bad, awful-nice, pleasant-unpleasant, and beautiful-ugly; and the S-R Inventory of Anxiousness, on which subjects describe their level of activity on 14 different autonomic response dimensions.

Significant changes were reported on all measures except amplitude of skin conductance. More importantly, there was considerable inter-subject variability, contrary to the implications of Wolpe's earlier report using a single dependent measure. Schroeder and Rich reported,

> Some subjects initially showed more cognitive changes, others more behavioral change, and still others more autonomic changes. It is clear that changes in one system could not be considered primary in initiating changes in the other fear systems. Cognitive and behavioral changes were not the simple consequence of reductions in autonomic levels, nor were behavioral and autonomic changes the simple result of changes in cognitive sets. Instead, the process of fear change appeared to involve complex interactions among the components of the fear response. (1976, p. 198)

In 1966, Gordon Paul conducted what is today considered to be an exemplary research on the comparative effectiveness of the psychotherapies of systematic desensitization and insight-oriented therapy. The subjects were college students who had debilitating levels of public speaking anxiety. A thorough pre-treatment evaluation was made, during which personality questionnaires were administered; these asked gen-

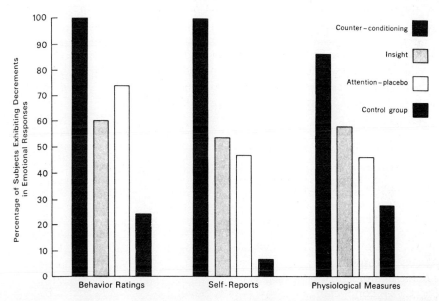

Figure 20. Percent of subjects in each of the four conditions who displayed decreases in anxiety as measured by behavior ratings, self-reports of emotional disturbance, and indices of physiological arousal. (Paul, G.L. *Insight vs. Desensitization in Psychotherapy.* Stanford: Stanford University Press, 1966. Reprinted by permission).

eral questions, as well as ones specific to the anxiety. Also, physiological measures were taken and the subjects' behavior was reliably rated while they were presenting a brief speech before an audience. Using a matching procedure to equate the groups on symptom severity, the subjects were assigned to one of four conditions: systematic desensitization, insight-oriented psychotherapy, attention placebo, and no treatment control.

All the treatments were conducted by psychotherapists who were well-practiced in insight therapy. They conducted interviews with the clients, and tried to bring about self-understanding of the psychological nature of subjects' problems. Because the therapists were engaging in their preferred therapeutic activity, insight therapy, and they were confident about its efficacy, this insight therapy treatment served as a control for therapist biases and expectations. If anything, they were less predisposed toward the systematic desensitization therapy which was relatively unfamiliar to them.

Attention-placebo subjects received what was considered to be a treatment having no active ingredients going for it other than the subject's own high hope for success. They were given an alleged tranquilizer and were then required to work on tasks defined for them as being "stressful." These placebo treatment subjects were led to believe that this procedure would innoculate them against becoming disrupted in the face of stress outside of therapy. This condition was designed to control for subject expectations and relationship variables upon the outcome of treatment. The no-treatment control group only filled out the pre- and post-measures and received no therapeutic contact at all.

The results of this research are depicted in Fig. 20. It can be seen that regardless of the dependent measure, systematic desensitization was the most efficacious treatment. This pattern was consistent across all therapists and generally maintained itself at a two year follow up. In commenting upon the research, Paul (1969) wrote,

> The findings were overwhelmingly positive, and for the first time in the history of psychological treatments, a specific treatment package reliably produced measurable benefits for clients across a broad range of distressing problems in which anxiety was of fundamental importance. (p. 159)

While there seems to be little dispute over the utility of systematic desensitization, controversy continues over the nature of its effective ingredients. For instance, despite the clear superiority of systematic desensitization over the attention placebo treatment in Paul's (1966) research, a decade later questions are still being raised regarding the importance of client expectations to successful outcome. In a comprehensive survey of the research to date, Kazdin and Wilcoxin (1976) say that so-called non-specific treatment effects, such as client expectations, cannot be ruled out as crucial to the success of systematic desensitization. There is no firm evidence that effective systematic desensitization depends upon a specific active ingredient, such as reciprocal inhibition or counterconditioning.

Desensitization Variations. A number of variations on the basic systematic desensitization theme have also been utilized with apparent success. One of these is group desensitization, in which several subjects with the same maladaptive avoidant problem undergo treatment. In these situations an anxiety heirarchy common to the entire treatment group is utilized. Progress may be geared to the group members slowest in showing improvement.

The second major variation is *in vivo* desensitization, in which actual stimuli are presented to the patient in graded amounts. This approach is particularly useful for the 10% to 15% of patients who find themselves unable to generate sufficiently clear imagery in the more traditional format. It may also be used as a supplement to imaginal desensitization in order to facilitate transfer of therapeutic gain to the real world. There are, of course, serious limitations to the viability of *in vivo* desensitization when the patient's anxiety involves cumbersome objects or interpersonal situations which are not easy to arrange, such as fear of humiliation.

The value free behavior therapist?

We will conclude this section with a discussion of a recent case study with highly controversial overtones. Kohlenberg (1974) treated a 34-year-old male homosexual, Mr. M., whose most pressing concern was pedophiliac inclinations. The patient had a long standing sexual attraction to male children. In his childhood he enjoyed sexual contacts with both an older and a younger brother. He had twice been arrested for child-molesting, and was troubled by his desire to go "prowling" for six to twelve year-old males. These escapades rarely resulted in actual sexual relations, but were a source of erotic excitation in their own right. "Mr. M. stated that his desire for children was immoral and had ruined his life" (p. 193). A second issue for the patient was that he did not find male adults sexually attractive and became "apprehensive and tense whenever a sexual encounter with an adult was imminent" (p. 193).

Before treatment began there was a four week baseline period, during which the rates of prowling, thoughts of children, and male adult contacts, were obtained. The actual treatment consisted of two phases. The first phase was designed to reduce attraction to male children, an *approach* behavior. A classical conditioning procedure was employed using shock as an aversive US paired with "imagined scenes of prowling and thoughts of children" (p. 193). As can be seen in Fig. 21, this aversive conditioning treatment was ineffectual.

Rather than increase the intensity of shock at this point, it was decided to implement the second treatment phase, one designed to deal with the avoidant component of Mr. M.'s sexual difficulties. The second phase, therefore, had as its goal the production of arousal and orgasm with adult male partners. The therapeutic vehicle for attaining this end was Masters and Johnson's (1970) modification of Wolpe's (1958) *in vivo* systematic desensitization procedure. Basically, it consisted of a series of graded experiences with an adult male partner which the patient had procured. These began with sessions in which the two were nude in a bed. Once Mr. M. was able to tolerate this level of interaction without anxiety, the intensity of sexual activity between the two men was gradually increased in a systematic fashion. The final step in the 13 weekly sessions placed no restrictions on the sexual activity and orgasm was permitted.

A follow-up interview was conducted six months after the termination of treatment. At that time, Mr. M. submitted reports which detailed his previous six months' sexual behavior. Figure 21 illustrates that the second phase resulted in a decline in the frequency of thoughts about children, and in the elimination of prowling behavior. These gains were maintained during the follow-up period. In addition, the frequency of adult contacts, which had been zero during baseline, stabilized during the follow-up period to a rate of between one and three per week.

There are two major ethical issues raised by this case report. First, there is the matter of the use of aversive conditioning for potential therapeutic gain. Davison and Wilson (1974) suggest that when a behavior problem involves both approach and avoidant components, as did that of Mr. M., the therapist may not have to subject the patient to unpleasant aversion therapy in order for there to be a favorable outcome:

> . . . given that the client's problems included anxiety in approaching male adults . . . It does not seem necessary to interrupt a prepotent pattern of sexual behavior before attempting more positively to instate another set of feelings and responses . . . (p. 196)

In fact, this proposal is consistent with Kohlenberg's own *post hoc* analysis of the case. Kohlenberg explains the decrease in prowling and thoughts of children in terms of response incompatibility. That is, as more time was spent searching out adult male partners, less time could be devoted to prowling. In addition, adult males and thoughts of adults presumably became conditioned stimuli for sexual arousal, replacing those of children and thoughts of children.

On the basis of Kohlenberg's analysis and the suggestions of Davison and Wilson, it might be concluded that behavior therapists should never use aversive conditioning as an initial step in treatment unless more "humane," positive, approaches are first tried, or at least given very careful consideration. The use of shock to suppress maladaptive approach behavior should be earmarked for cases in which there is a severe threat to property, life, or general well-being. Of course, one might reasonably argue that Mr. M.'s prowling for male children falls within this domain and that a severe form of treatment was warranted in the first phase of treatment.

The second ethical issue raised by this case involves the unusual therapeutic decision to prescribe a treatment aimed at producing a "well-adjusted" homosexual instead of one which stressed heterosexual orientation. Davison and Wilson support this decision, claiming there is no justification for assuming that "heterosexuality is a biological-psychological norm and that homosexual attachments are the result of some pathological deviation from the normal psychosexual developmental process" (1974, p. 196). It is further asserted that the entire question of psychological normalcy is one which simply reflects prevailing cultural value judgments. For instance, the dropping of "homosexuality" as a diagnostic entity by the American Psychiatric Association "illustrates how the psychiatric nosology is more a product of socio-historical pressures than of scientifically justified generalizations" (pp. 196-197). Finally, Davison and Wilson argue that behavior therapy involves the application of value-free principles for be-

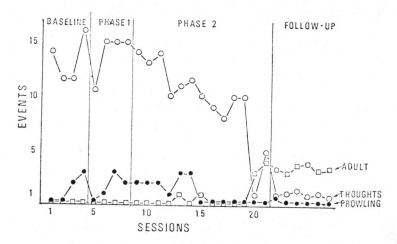

Figure 21. The number of "thoughts" and "prowling" incidents concerning children and "adult contacts" for the three treatment phases and follow-up. The follow-up data are means for each of the six months following treatment. (Kohlenberg, R.J. Treatment of a Homosexual Pedophiliac Using *in vivo* Desensitization: A Case Study. *Journal of Abnormal Psychology,* 1974, *83,* 192-195. Copyright© 1974 by The American Psychological Association. Reprinted by permission.

havior change to a behavioral problem; it does not, according to these authors, involve a system of ethics.

The notion of "value-free" psychotherapy is questioned by Strupp, who considers Kohlenberg's efforts to have encompassed more than the mere treatment of a sexual response. At least implicitly, Kohlenberg is thought to have made the value judgment that adult male homosexuality is *"in keeping with his own, as well as society's values* . . . Would a value-free therapist have instituted a program of assertive training . . . [to improve the effectiveness of Mr. M.'s prowling behavior]" (1974, p. 200). Garfield asks, "What if the client instead had asked for therapy which removed the concerns he had about his pedophiliac behavior? Does the client alone select the goals of therapy and does this then remove any ethical responsibility from the therapist?" (1974, p. 202).

There are no clear answers to the questions which may be raised by this case in terms of what is "right" or "wrong." Garfield concludes, "The discussion, however, does indicate that the neutral or value-free therapist is a myth. Values not only reflect the culture and time in which events transpire, but also the variation among individual therapists" (1974, pp. 202-203).

EVALUATION

The evaluative issues relevant to classical conditioning greatly overlap with those pertaining to operant conditioning. Consequently, we will reserve critical judgment until the conclusion of the next chapter. At that time, the assets and liabilities of situationism in general will be discussed.

SUMMARY

In this first chapter on situationism we dealt with Pavlovian, or classical, conditioning. This is a form of learning in which neutral stimuli acquire the capacity to provoke behavior through being paired with other stimuli already capable of exerting this effect. The acquisition of conditioned responses was discussed, and the relevancy of classical conditioning to the development of both adaptive and maladaptive behavior exemplified. In the latter case, we discussed fear and sexual deviation. The process of extinction was also described, and its usefulness in the treatment of behavior disorder illustrated. It was pointed out that, far from being "automatic," both the acquisition and extinction of a classically conditioned response is subject to influence by cognitive factors, such as expectancies. We completed this unit by surveying some of the most popular behavior therapeutic approaches based upon classical conditioning principles. In this context, aversive conditioning and covert sensitization were judged useful in the treatment of maladaptive approach behaviors; systematic desensitization was shown to be particularly appropriate for maladaptive avoidant behavior problems, such as phobias.

TERMS TO KNOW

CHAPTER 20
Behaviorism/Situationism: Operant Conditioning

In the previous section on classical conditioning emphasis was placed upon the way in which stimuli lead to responses. Learning was seen to involve the building of associations between stimuli, a CS and a US, with the resulting formation of new stimulus-response (S-R) bonds. In contrast, operant conditioning is more concerned with what happens after a response is made than with the stimuli which provoke it. Of special interest is the way in which the *consequences* of a response affect the future occurrence of that response.

This distinction may be highlighted by recourse to a model for behavioral analysis presented by Kanfer and Phillips (1970, p. 54):

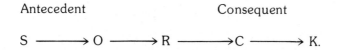

S stands for prior stimulation and, in terms of classical conditioning, would be represented by the US or the CS. The biological state of the organism upon which the stimulus impinger is indicated by O. In combination, S and O may be construed as the immediate antecedent of the response, R. This S-O-R chain of events lies firmly in the domain of classical conditioning. As previously indicated, however, operant conditioning focuses upon the events which follow the response. In particular, there are consequences (C) which may be either "good," such as getting a cookie or verbal praise, or "bad," such as a shock or a spanking. In addition, consideration is given to the response-consequence contingency relationship (K). In other words, the future probability of response occurrence depends upon the nature of the consequences which follow (C), and upon the conditional probability of those consequences when the response in question was emitted in the past (K). Did the consequences always follow the response or did they occur only some percentage of the times that R was emitted?

Operant conditioning deals mostly with manipulations of C and K, although S and O are not totally neglected.

Before we embark upon a detailed discussion of the ideas put forth by B. F. Skinner, the chief spokesman for operant conditioning, we will report on some of the early developments in psychology which gave rise to this important contemporary movement.

INSTRUMENTAL CONDITIONING

Edward Thorndike is credited with conducting the first laboratory experiments which demonstrated a kind of learning then called "instrumental" to distinguish it from Pavlov's classical conditioning. This research typically involved placing an animal in a "puzzle box." The puzzle box was essentially a cage with a door which could be opened by the animal if it emitted the necessary response, such as stepping on a lever or pulling on a cord. This action was considered "instrumental" in that it effected release from the cage. Of course, when an animal was first placed in the puzzle box it did not have the slightest notion about how to escape. It would try to claw or push its head through small openings in the walls, or walk around, even jump, in an agitated fashion. Eventually, by chance it would seem, the necessary action was emitted and the door would open. Because a fully-satiated animal tends to just lie around and wallow in its state of satisfaction, Thorndike routinely deprived an animal of food before putting it in the box; he would then place some food just outside of the puzzle box door. This procedure produced an agitated animal, one prone to be active and, therefore, more likely to make the correct movement upon which release and the receipt of food were contingent.

The dependent measure in this research was the time required for successful release. Thorndike found that there was generally a systematic decline in correct response latency as the number of successful trials increased. In other words, the animal was able to obtain its release ever more quickly, finally reaching a point where the correct movement was efficiently enacted almost as soon as the hungry animal was placed in the puzzle box.

This inverse relationship between latency and number of correct trials was explained by Thorndike in terms of the Law of Effect,

> Of the several responses made to the same situation, those which are accompanied or closely followed by satisfaction to the animal, other things being equal, will be more firmly connected with the situation, so that when it recurs, they will be more likely to recur; those which are accompanied or closely followed by discomfort to the animal will, other things being equal, have their connections with the situation weakened so that, when it recurs, they will be less likely to recur. The greater the satisfaction or discomfort, the greater the strengthening or weakening of the bond. (1911, p. 244).

In less turbid style, the Law of Effect states that behaviors which result in satisfaction will tend to be repeated if we are back in the same situation; those which result in dissatisfaction will tend not to be repeated. Notice that this law is an expression of the future probability of response occurrence as a function of prior response consequences; the emphasis is on the C in Kanfer and Phillip's (1970) behavioral model.

The satisfying consequence which Thorndike says will stamp-in a response is called a *reinforcement*. Theoretically, for instrumental learning to take place, a response must be followed by reinforcement. However, the notion of "satisfaction" was far too subjective to be scientifically productive. It remained for Clark Hull (1943), who developed a complex theory of instrumental conditioning, to explicate the nature of reinforcement in more rigorous fashion.

According to Hull, activity is based upon the existence of *drives*. These are internal conditions which are innately brought about by the experience of pain, or by deficiency states relevant to food, water, sex, etc. The labels for these exemplary drives are fear, hunger, thirst, and sex. The greater the pain or the deficiency, the stronger the drive and the more active will be the organism.

Although the notion of drive is not itself directly observable, it is tied to measurable antecedents and consequences. On the antecedent side, hunger drive, for example, can be defined in terms of number of hours of food deprivation. In theory, an animal which has not eaten for 10 hours will be more driven than one which has experienced only five hours of deprivation. One which was recently fed and is fully satiated will have no appreciable hunger drive.

On the consequent side, hunger drive can be operationalized in terms of activity level. High drive should be reflected in high activity rates, while low drive produces a quiescent organism. The just-fed animal is usually found asleep! Thorndike was appreciative of these issues, even if he did not articulate them with the precision found in Hull's writings. Recall that Thorndike purposely used hungry cats in his puzzle box so that he would not have to wait around for the animal to start behaving.

For Hull, reinforcement is involved in the learning process when the consequence of a response is *drive reduction*. In other words, outcomes which Thorndike termed reinforcing because they provided "satisfaction" Hull saw as reinforcing because they served to reduce drive. As a specific example of this, the food obtained by Thorndike's hungry cat when it successfully escaped from the puzzle box reduced its hunger drive. Therefore, the response instrumental in effecting release from the box, stepping on a lever, was immediately followed by reinforcement. As one would expect from Hull's learning model, lever-stepping then becomes a high probability response every time that cat is returned to the puzzle box in a hungry state.

Hull's explanations of behavior acquisition and change, broadly rooted in the ideas of Pavlov and Thorndike, temporarily made a major impact upon psychology. Guttman (1977) found that in 1940, only 4% of the articles appearing in the *Journal of Experimental Psychology* referred to either Hull or to his closest collaborator, Kenneth Spence. By 1950, just seven years after Hull had published his *Principles of Behavior* (1943), a remarkable 39% of the published papers made reference to his works.

Also in that year, Dollard and Miller (1950) applied Hullian learning theory to a broad array of phenomena relevant to personality and psychopathology. In part, this was accomplished by introducing an important revision with respect to the nature of drive. For Dollard and Miller, any internal or external stimulus, if sufficiently intense, will function as a drive and impel behavior. Hull's drive reduction notion of reinforcement was thus translated into one of *drive stimulus intensity reduction.* Included in the range of stimuli which drive behavior are those attended to by Hull: pain, thirst, sex, cold, etc. These they called *primary* drives because they are innately capable of provoking activity. Dollard and Miller also included responses as drive stimuli; strong responses, such as that of fear, are construed as capable of driving other behaviors. In fact, Dollard and Miller attempted to develop a theory of psychopathology centering on the idea that maladaptive avoidant behavior persists because it serves to reduce the drive stimulus of fear and is, therefore, reinforced. This is most obvious with phobic behavior in which the symptom physically removes the person from the proximity of fearful stimuli, thereby effecting a decrease in the level of fear. Intrusive obsessional ideas are similarly seen as habits which serve to keep the patient's mind off of other very frightening thoughts. To the degree that the obsessional ideas accomplish this each time they are conjured up, they are reinforced by the reduction of fear and so will occur with ever more regularity.

In addition to these varied drive stimuli, any other stimulus may acquire the capacity to function as a drive through association with primary drives via classical conditioning. As such, these so-called *secondary* or learned drives are considered to represent elaborations of primary drives. Most of our important social behaviors are understood by Dollard and Miller to be products of secondary drives, although the precise conditions under which these drives are acquired may not always be evident. In theory, a drive for affection might emerge from making a close association between the receipt of food and maternal expressions of affection. However, attempts to test this hypothesis experimentally have not always produced supportive evidence. The well-known study by Harlow (1958), for example, demonstrated that infant monkeys do not prefer to cling affectionately to a wire surrogate mother which is their source of food. Instead, "love" is exhibited toward a non-nutritive, soft, terry cloth mother surrogate. It is clear that the infant monkeys have a drive for contact comfort, but it is also clear that this drive is not a simple elaboration of the hunger drive.

Hull's theory as an explanation of instrumental conditioning, and Dollard and Miller's application of it to personality and psychotherapy represent high points of sophistication. However, the initial enthusiasm for these positions has been diminished by a wave of apathy. This decline of interest is exemplified by the fact that by 1970 the rate at which articles in the *Journal of Experimental Psychology* were referring to Hull was back to the 4% level of 1940, according to Guttman (1977).

It would be erroneous to conclude from this that the notion of reinforcement, as originally outlined by Thorndike, has faded from the psychological scene. Quite the contrary, reinforcement is alive and thriving in B. F. Skinner's adaptation of instrumental conditioning, today popularly known as *operant conditioning.*

Why has Hull become a memory and Skinner a giant? Guttman speaks of Skinner's success,

> [It] comes down to the reiterated application of a single, graspable, eminently teachable idea, an evidently true and general formula: There is a situation, and the organism does something, and the situation changes, and lo and behold, the state of the organism changes, toward greater or less activity of a certain kind. The formula goes by many names: reinforcement, operant conditioning . . . contingency stimulus upon response, reward and punishment, law-of-effect, feedback. There are far too many to list, but what is described is exactly the same in essence and basic form . . .

> One is reminded here of Isaiah Berlin's famous observation about hedgehogs and foxes: The fox knows many things, while the hedgehog knows only one thing, but he knows it exceedingly well. The Skinnerians are like the hedgehogs of psychology, and reinforcement is the thing they know exceedingly well.

> Clark Hull knew about the reinforcement principle, but for him it was buried amidst a multitude of other ideas and themes. He was unable to give it emphatic expression . . . He wanted explanations as well as descriptions. (1977, p. 325)

Skinner is content to merely describe the relationships between responses and other stimuli. He tells us nothing about what goes on within the responder's head, and cautions us not to waste our time looking. Consequently, his position is atheoretical.

BASIC OPERANT PROCEDURES

Only four categories of consequence exist with respect to the emission of a response, an operant. An operant may be followed by:
  1. onset of a reinforcing event (*positive reinforcement*)
  2. offset of a punishing event (*negative reinforcement*)
  3. onset of a punishing event (*positive punishment*)
  4. offset of a reinforcing event (*negative punishment*)

The word *positive* always refers to a consequence in which something starts after an operant; *negative* refers to the withdrawal or stopping of an ongoing event contingent upon the elicitation of a response. *Reinforcement* procedures, regardless of whether they are positive or negative, result in the strengthening of the preceding operant. Thus, if by pressing a bar an animal receives food, positive reinforcement, or terminates shock, negative reinforcement, the outcome should always be an increase in the rate of response emission; bar pressing becomes more frequent. In contrast, punishment procedures, whether positive or negative in nature, tend to decrease the future frequency of operants upon which they are contingent. Thus, the rate of bar pressing declines if it is followed by receipt of shock, positive punishment, or by the cessation of food availability, negative punishment.

In addition to referring to procedures which have defining behavioral outcomes (increasing or decreasing operant rates) the words "reinforcement" and "punishment" refer to the stimuli themselves. According to Skinner, a "reinforcing stimulus" is one whose presentation increases the emission rate of the preceding operant. Once a stimulus has been empirically demonstrated to have this capacity, it may then be employed in the operant procedure called "positive reinforcement" or in that called "negative punishment." If the onset of a stimulus is empirically shown to decrease the rate of a preceding operant, that stimulus qualifies to be called an "aversive" or "punishing" stimulus. It may then be used in the procedures of "positive punishment" or "negative reinforcement." By defining stimuli as reinforcing or punishing in this empirical way, Skinner completely circumvents the subjective issues raised when one tries to define them as a function of the degree of "pleasantness" or "unpleasantness."

The importance of avoiding subjective determinations of reinforcing and punishing stimuli becomes apparent as soon as one tries to actually modify behavior using operant procedures. It is quite common for an event to be subjectively construed as punishing by one person, and to be experienced as reinforcing by another. For example, a parent might inflict "punishment" upon a bed-wetting (enuretic) child by screaming at him in the middle of the night right after the accident occurs. From the child's frame of reference, the verbal tirade might be a reinforcing event if the parent is generally a neglecting one, and the nocturnal attention is the best that may be obtained by the child. The outcome of these encounters would be opposite from that hoped for by the parent; instead of there being a resulting decline in the frequency of bed-wetting, the behavior may remain quite stable, or even increase, because the procedure being used is not positive punishment but, inadvertently and unknown to the angry parent, positive reinforcement.

Unfortunately, the terms "positive reinforcement" and "negative reinforcement" were used in a slightly different way by Thorndike with respect to his law of effect. For Thorndike, any procedure which involves a subjective change for the better as a behavioral consequence qualifies as positive reinforcement. This, then, is probably equivalent to *both* positive and negative reinforcement in Skinner's model. Also, Thorndike defined any procedure which results in a subjective change for the worse as negative reinforcement. It therefore follows that this interpretation of negative reinforcement probably encompasses what Skinnerians refer to both as positive punishment and negative punishment. Thus, for Thorndike, "negative reinforcement" decreases the future rate of the operant upon which it is contingent, and is roughly equivalent to Skinnerian punishments; Skinner's term "negative reinforcement" is a sub-type of what Thorndike refers to as "positive reinforcement."

Henceforth in this chapter we will follow Skinner's use of the terminology. However, not all books do so and it is, therefore, incumbent upon the reader to be aware of the particular operations which are being referred to by the terms employed. For example, does "negative reinforcement" mean the administration of shock contingent upon a bar press, as Thorndike would have it; or does it mean the withdrawal of shock contingent upon the same response, as Skinner would have it?

REINFORCEMENT

The operant conditioning procedure known as positive reinforcement will be first illustrated by animal research using the *operant conditioning chamber,* widely known as the "Skinner Box." This apparatus may vary, but it generally consists of a well-lit and ventilated room, perhaps the size of a picnic basket if the animal is a pigeon or a rat. It is typical for the chamber to be constructed of sound-deadening material so that extraneous noise will be filtered out, leaving the animal undistracted. Two elements, at the very least, must be present in the chamber. First, there must be an *operandum,* frequently called a *manipulandum,* which is utilized by the animal every time the operant in question is emitted. If a pigeon is used, the operandum might be a target disc on the inside wall of the chamber which can be pecked; if a rat, the operandum is frequently a lever which can be depressed. Second, near the operandum there should be a dispenser out of which the reinforcement, usually food, emerges contingent upon the emission of the "correct" response.

A third frequently incorporated design feature of an operant conditioning chamber is a light. Typically, reinforcement can only be obtained when the light is on. It, therefore, "tells" the animal when response contingent reinforcement is possible. Skinner refers to the light, or another similar stimulus, as a *discriminative stimulus* (S^D). Unlike the CS or US in classical conditioning which is construed as provoking behavior, an S^D is described as "setting the stage" for operant behavior to be emitted. A real world example of an S^D might be a soft-hearted mother who sets the occasion for the verbal response, "Gimmie a cookie!" The child's past history tells him that, if this verbal response is made in her presence, the obtaining of a cookie will be the happy consequence. In contrast, the stern father may function as an antecedent stimulus which sets the occasion for non-responding; the child has come to expect no cookies from the father if the aforementioned verbal response is made. A discriminative stimulus which signals that an operant response will not be followed by consequences is coded S^Δ. The father, in the above example, is an S^Δ, as is an "Out of Order" sign on a candy machine. For the rat in a conditioning chamber, the unlit bulb may function as an S^Δ. Once behavior is guided by discriminative stimuli, it is said to be under *stimulus control;* some operants will be emitted in the presence of an S^D, and others emitted when S^D is absent, or when an S^Δ is present. The presence of "Smokey" on an Interstate is usually an S^D for "light foot on the gas"; his apparent absence may set the occasion for speeding.

In summary, discriminative stimuli reveal the nature of the contingencies currently operative. In themselves, they do not provoke behavior but set the occasion for the emission of operant behaving. Finally, discriminative stimuli, in contrast to the CS and US of classical conditioning, are not in themselves thought to be either reinforcing or punishing.

Almost invariably, the conditioning chamber is designed to graph automatically the number of responses per unit time. This graph is called a *cumulative record* or a *cumulative response curve,* and is produced by having a pen trace a continuous line as a role of paper travels under it. Every time the operant response is made, such as a bar press, the pen is deflected one unit upward. Consequently, the more responses per unit time, the greater the number of upward deflections and the steeper will be the overall slope of the graph. In contrast, an absence of responding will produce no upward deflections. The graph will then be just a horizontal line. Figure 22 schemati-

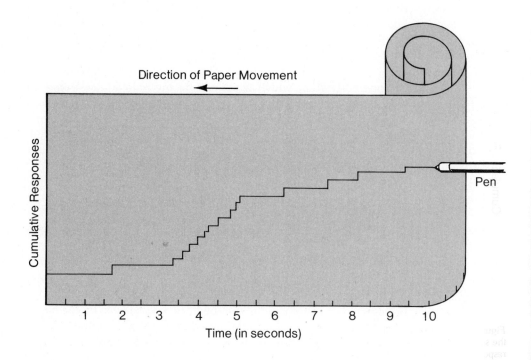

Figure 22. Stylized illustration of cumulative record being produced.

cally depicts a cumulative record being produced. It can be seen that one operant response was made between the first and second second; there is a burst of responses between the third and sixth second of the record, and few responses thereafter. Note the steepness of the graph during the three seconds of rapid responding, and the much flatter graph which reflects a low response rate after second six. The six slant marks on the graph indicate operant responses which were followed by the provision of reinforcement. After the pen has worked its way across the width of paper it drops back to the starting level and once again begins a step-wise track to the opposite side. If the pen deflections are programmed to be small and the number of responses great, relative to the rate at which the paper moves, a cumulative record loses its step-wise appearance and takes on a much smoother look. On such records, the slope of the graph is the only feature in which the researcher is interested. Because graph slope is so important, most published cumulative records appear with a slope key having some number of operant responses on its vertical coordinate, an amount of time on its horizontal coordinate, and several reference slopes illustrating different response rates (see Fig. 23).

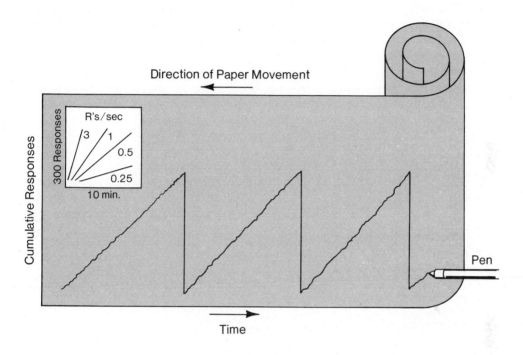

Figure 23. Stylized cumulative response curve. The record reflects a constant rate of responding. Reference to the slope key indicates that this rate is slightly higher than 0.5 per second. At this rate, the animal emits 300 responses in less than a ten-minute period.

In Skinner's early work in the 1930s, an animal was first simply placed in the chamber for a certain period each day over a span of perhaps two weeks. This seemed to acclimate the animal to its new surroundings. On subsequent sessions, food was presented in the receptacle, a tray, thereby making proximity to the tray and the adjacent bar a relatively high-probability behavior. Once training actually began, food was presented contingent upon the response of pressing the bar, and this operant was, sooner or later, emitted. After the food was consumed, it was common for the second bar-press response to follow shortly; and in a remarkably short time the animal was responding at a maximum rate (see Fig. 24). It is not unusual for the preconditioning rate of bar presses for a rat to be about five times per hour. This may rise to five times per second after conditioning. The rate of disc pecking for a pigeon may reach 15 times per second after operant conditioning. In one research, conducted by Ferster and

Skinner (1957), the simple experimental arrangement of reinforcing contingencies resulted in a pigeon pecking at a disc 70,000 times during one four and a half hour session.

Other researchers have modified the standard operant conditioning chamber in a variety of ways, tailoring its design to suit the particular response and reinforcement which is being studied. One particularly novel change, introduced by Olds and Milner (1954), is that of making electrical stimulation to the rat's brain contingent upon a bar press response. Depending upon where the electrode is permanently implanted, a rat will either press once and never go back, presumably because the electrical stimulation is aversive, or expend considerable energy to maintain a constant flow of electrical brain stimulation. Hypothalamic and mid-brain nuclei stimulation produced rates of

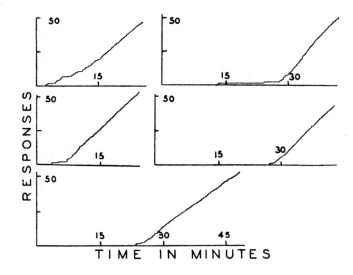

Figure 24. Cumulative response curves generated by five rats undergoing original conditioning. All bar press responses were reinforced. (Skinner, B.F. *The Behavior of Organisms,* © Renewed 1966, p. 68. Reprinted by permission of Prentice-Hall, Inc., Englewood Cliffs, New Jersey.)

responding which, in some rats, resulted in about 50,000 bar presses over a 24 hour span. When other brain centers served as the site of electrical stimulation contingent upon a bar press, rates of from 200 to 5000 bar presses per hour were demonstrated. Olds (1956) interpreted his results to mean that these are discrete centers in the brain which, when stimulated, evoke sensations analogous to pleasure or punishment. Olds (1958) found that, unlike the pleasure associated with other positive reinforcers, rats do not appear to satiate on electrical stimulation of the brain. That is, a hungry or thirsty rat will only press a bar so long to obtain food or water; once it has had its fill the response rate declines dramatically. The rat receiving reinforcing brain stimulation will work at pressing the bar to the point of physical exhaustion; some animals maintain high, stable response rates for two days.

The control of behavior via reinforcing consequences need not be limited to biologically relevant outcomes such as food, water, or sex. An event which has, through classical conditioning, become associated with a primary reinforcer may acquire the capacity to function as a secondary, or conditioned, reinforcer within operant procedures. Once again, money can be pointed to as an extremely common, and powerful, secondary reinforcer. People will work for long hours over many days in order to receive a sum of money at the conclusion of their labor. The money, presumably, derives its reinforcing value from the fact that it may be exchanged at a later time for primary reinforcers. As Lundin said, "The expression 'money talks' is more true than many of us would like to believe. Few people, other things being equal, will turn down a job that pays more or will refuse an increase in salary when it is offered" (1969, p. 66).

Schedules of reinforcement: (K)

The number (n) of operant responses which must occur for there to be reinforcement and/or the amount of time (t) which must elapse between reinforced responses are the two dimensions which define K in the S-O-R-C-K model of behavioral analysis. K, therefore, refers to the nature of the contingency which exists between R and C. Sometimes C, a reinforcement, is contingent upon the making of just one response; that is, every response is reinforced. At other times reinforcement may be contingent upon the making of a few or even many responses, in which case the proportion of reinforced responses becomes rather small; or, a reinforcement may be contingent upon a response coming after a prescribed amount of time subsequent to the previous reinforced response. When a time-based contingency exists, no matter how many responses are made, none will be followed by reinforcement until the necessary delay has elapsed.

When one is interested in producing a rapid increase in the rate of an operant, it is usual to reinforce the response every time it is emitted by the organism. This is known as a *continuous reinforcement schedule* (CRF). The CRF schedule has two main drawbacks. First, it is very expensive; there is no need to keep "paying" the animal, or person, for every response made in order to maintain high operant rates. In fact, as we will see, some schedules which only provide reinforcement on a "sometimes" basis tend to provoke greater response rates than the CRF schedule. The second problem has to do with extinction; specifically, an organism trained on a CRF schedule will show a very rapid decline in response rate if the reinforcement is suddenly withheld. The withholding of reinforcement in this way defines the operant procedure of *extinction*. In the real world there are some responses which are maintained on CRF schedules — such as putting a quarter in the soda machine. Every response is followed by a refreshing payoff. But think how quickly the response fades when there are non-reinforced trials. How many people will make the response a second time after not getting a drink for their quarter? Is there anyone who will insert a third quarter after

undergoing two extinction trials? Not many. We can see in our own lives how susceptible to extinction are responses maintained on a CRF schedule.

Responses which have a history of resulting in only an occasional payoff are much
more resistant to extinction. In fact, most of our behaviors are reinforced in this *partial*
or *intermittent* way, and so tend to persist despite long periods of nonreinforcement.
This phenomenon may account for the temporal stability of behavior which we
observe in both animals and in people; it helps to explain why personality patterns
remain unchanged for so long, even though the reinforcements originally responsible
for the development of particular habits have long since faded from the scene.

Four major partial schedules of reinforcement have been studied extensively.
Their characteristics and the unique impact each has upon behavior will now be
examined.

Fixed Ratio Schedules. Fixed ratio (FR) schedules are defined by having every
nth response yield a reinforcement. Thus, the CRF schedule is really a special case of
FR schedules in which $n = 1$.

Regardless of whether $n = 1$ or some substantially higher number, one feature of
FR schedules is that the rate at which reinforcement is earned, reinforcements per unit
time, is entirely contingent upon the rate of responding. The higher the response rate,
the sooner the number required for reinforcement will be reached. This characteristic
of FR schedules tends to produce very rapid rates of operant responding. However, the
rate is not uniform; there is typically a brief period of non-responding immediately
subsequent to the receipt of reinforcement. This is because responses on a FR schedule
which come right after reinforcement are never themselves reinforced (except on a
CRF schedule). Thus, reinforcement comes to function as an S^Δ, signaling "no reinforcement for responding." The higher the ratio of responses to reinforcement, the
longer this "break" in responding will be. Figure 25 illustrates a typical cumulative
response curve generated by an animal on an FR schedule of reinforcement. In this
case, the record is from a pigeon on FR 200. Each pause lasts from a few seconds to a
minute or two. This is followed by the abrupt starting of pecking at a rate of about three
responses per second.

In our daily lives, FR schedules are best illustrated by work arrangements in which
payment is on the basis of piecework. The money earned depends purely upon the
number of items assembled or the number of units sold, in which case we speak of
commission. FR payment schedules provide strong incentive for the worker to maintain high rates of production or sales because income is so clearly contingent upon
these factors. In fact, in order to protect laborers from "working themselves to death,"
it is not uncommon for unions to set upper limits upon the amount of time or effort one
is permitted to put into a piecework job.

As a counter-strategy, management may introduce some improvement, such as
better lighting or more efficient tools, and bargain for a higher ratio of responses per
reinforcement; whereas ten assembled knives could once be turned in for one dollar of
pay, management may push for the assembly of twelve units per dollar payoff after
"improving" work conditions. Labor is constantly wary of such maneuvers, and well
they should be. Research shows that it is very easy to gradually thin out the rate at

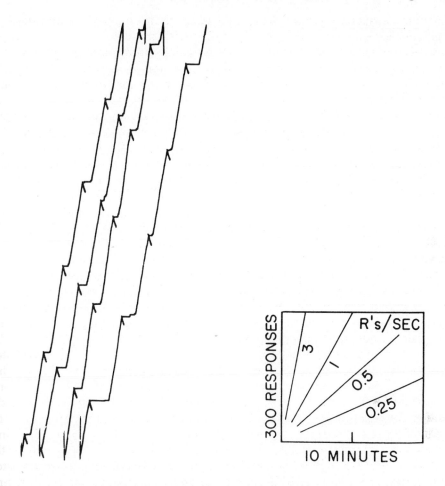

Figure 25. Example of stable performance on FR 200 after a history of almost 4000 reinforcements on Fixed Ratios from 50 to 180. (Ferster, C.B. & Skinner, B.F. *Schedules of Reinforcement,* Copyright© 1957, p. 52. Reprinted by permission of Prentice-Hall, Inc., Englewood Cliffs, New Jersey.)

which reinforcements are dispensed on FR schedules, so that one might finally end up with an incredibly large work output per reinforcement. For example, Findley and Brady (1965) trained a chimpanzee to emit 120,000 responses in order to obtain food, a primary reinforcer. This was accomplished by providing secondary reinforcement every 4000 responses; a green light which had previously been paired with food served this function. Similarly, it is not unusual for management to try to make "monkeys" out of labor by offering higher order conditioned reinforcers prior to the giving of money. Specifically, pieceworkers are frequently required to trade in assembled units for paper receipts, analogous to the green light in Findley and Brady's experiment, which are, in turn, redeemable for paychecks. The receipts serve to provide at least some reinforcements on a denser schedule than would otherwise be the case, and behavior is maintained at a high rate.

We see evidence of the post-reinforcement pause at the human level, just as we do with animals, on FR schedules. The worker, after vigorously assembling twelve knives and getting his receipt, may stop at the water cooler or chat with a friend before picking up work again.

Responses which have been maintained on FR schedules are not especially resistant to extinction. High rates of responding will continue for a time, primarily because the animal's history is such that high response rates have been followed by reinforcement; finally, if for no other reason than exhaustion, there will be a pause, which will end abruptly with the onset of another rapid response run. Gradually, the runs become shorter and the pauses longer; but when there is a response run, the rate remains high, producing a step-like extinction curve. Figure 26 is an illustration of this.

It is not unusual for human behavior to undergo similar extinction patterns. An artist who formerly worked very hard may find his efforts are no longer marketable and "give up." Perhaps he decides to indulge in one more shot at it, in which case there will be a response run of high rate. If he still cannot sell his paintings, the artist may trade in his palette and brushes permanently and become a real estate broker. Since he would still be on a ratio schedule of reinforcement with commissions, the same pattern may be repeated. What this person may need for job stability is a comfortable civil service slot where salary is relatively independent of output.

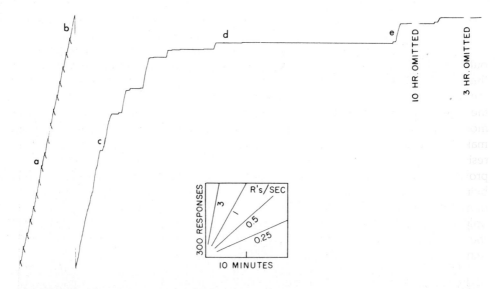

Figure 26. Extinction after a short history of FR 60 during which the bird earned 360 reinforcements (curve sections a and b). Extinction begins at b but more than 150 responses continue to be emitted at a high rate until c where there is a short break. Shorter response runs and longer breaks become the rule. Extinction is virtually complete by d. (Ferster, C.B. and Skinner, B.F. *Schedules of Reinforcement,* Copyright© 1957, p. 60. Reprinted by permission of Prentice-Hall, Inc., Englewood Cliffs, New Jersey.)

Variable Ratio Schedules. The Variable Ratio (VR) schedules provide reinforcement after a predetermined number of responses. Instead of this number (n) being fixed and, therefore, predictable, it varies in chance fashion around some average number. Thus, a VR 10 schedule may sometimes produce two consecutive reinforcements, and at other times the animal might have to emit 20 responses. On the average, the number of responses per reinforcement on a VR 10 schedule will be, of course, 10.

Like the FR schedule, the VR schedule differentially reinforces rapid rates of responding, and so high levels of output are to be expected. In fact, by starting off with relatively low ratios, extremely high response rates will occur. Unlike FR schedules, VR schedules do not promote post-reinforcement pauses. Due to the variable nature of the schedule, receipt of reinforcement is not discriminated as a signal for the onset of a predictably long series of non-reinforced responses. Thus, the cumulative response curve is smooth, and not characterized by small scallops subsequent to each reinforcement.

Games involving gambling are probably the best examples of VR schedules outside of the laboratory. The well-known "one-armed bandit," or slot machine, is a device programmed to provide a "jackpot" on a very sparse VR schedule. This mode of payoff serves to keep people feeding coins and pulling levers at a steady, high rate over long periods. The phenomenon of gambling also illustrates another feature of the VR schedule, its tendency to promote responding which is highly resistant to extinction. Suppose someone at a slot machine has been on a VR 100 schedule and suddenly, unknown to him, the machine jams. The gambler will probably persist and, as the number of non-reinforced responses grow, he will become convinced that his "pot of gold" must surely be no more than a few responses away.

In some child-rearing situations the inadvertent use of a VR schedule promotes outcomes which are unwanted, and unexpected, by the parent. For instance, imagine that a resolution has been made to no longer give in to an unreasonable demand from the child. If the demand is made enough times and is not followed by reinforcement, then that verbal behavior will finally extinguish. However, if the parents give in at a moment of weakness, a VR schedule has been immediately established which will maintain the demands at a steady rate and will render demanding behavior highly resistant to extinction. The particular demand which is followed by reinforcement is probably expressed in an especially assertive way; thus, not only is a VR schedule being unintentionally employed, but it is selectively reinforcing the most extreme demanding behaviors. Ultimately, this will make for a very unhappy parent who can only legitimately blame himself. From the perspective of operant learning, it is not that the parent is saddled with a child of flawed character, rather, it is that the parent has reinforced extreme demanding behavior on a VR schedule.

On a more positive note, parents can very effectively employ a VR schedule, in combination with CRF, for specific child-rearing purposes. For instance, the establishment of appropriate toileting behavior is quickly accomplished if the parents reinforce *every* successful attempt in the early stages of training. Then, it is good practice to shift from a CRF to a VR schedule with a gradual build-up of the average number of correct toilet responses necessary for reinforcement. This keeps the desired behavior going at a steady rate and, because of the variable nature of the schedule, maintains the behavior in the face of an unusually long series of correct but unreinforced toileting responses; that is, the toilet behavior is resistant to extinction.

These general principles were implemented by Foxx and Azrin (1973) in a program of toilet-training for 34 normal children, who ranged in age from 20 to 36 months. The children were left for the day and were exposed to an intensive learning experience. After becoming friendly with the therapist the children were encouraged to drink liquids and to "feed" liquids to a large doll, which then "urinated" through a hole between the legs. The children were instructed to place the doll on the "potty," and to reward the doll with potato chips and candy for "using" the "potty." The children were then urged to sit on toilets; when one finally urinated, he or she was given enthusiastic verbal and food reinforcers, much as the child had given the doll. In addition, when not on the "potty" the children's pants were checked every few minutes. If they were dry, lavish reinforcement was given, if not, reinforcement was withheld. This phase of treatment involved only one half hour to 14 hours of a happy child's time. The parents continued this program at home by inspecting their child's pants several times per day, offering enthusiastic praise if they were not wet or soiled.

Foxx and Azrin report that dramatic results were obtained by this method. On the average, the number of accidents dropped to 0.2 per day after one week of at-home training, down from a pre-training rate of more than six per day. This trend is depicted in Fig. 27, which also reveals the stability of the therapy gains over a four month follow-up period. In summary, toilet training need not be an unpleasant experience. Through the arrangement of many continuously reinforced trials, plus some instruction and prompting in a distraction-free setting, impressive changes can be brought about in just one day. A gradual fading out of these factors then serves to maintain appropriate toileting behavior.

Fixed Interval Schedules. The defining characteristic of a Fixed Interval (FI) schedule is that a designated period of time (t) *must* elapse before a response will meet with reinforcement. Usually the timing of the fixed interval commences at the last reinforcement. Unlike an FR schedule which rewards high rates of responding, there is absolutely nothing to be gained from high response rates on FI schedules. In fact, it is most efficient not to respond until the interval has passed and then to make only one response in order to obtain reinforcement. Even more so than FR schedules, FI schedules promote scalloped response curves. Figure 28 illustrates this pattern. The curve was generated by a bird after being on a FI schedule for 66 hours of training; the interval was 5 minutes.

Many reinforcements in our lives follow some variation of the FI schedule. Certainly the weekly pay check is one common example; payment is not tied clearly to the number of responses or to output, but to certain responses being made late in the interval, such as showing up for work on payday. Responses made on an FI schedule immediately after reinforcement never result in a payoff. This is also true on FR schedules, but at least the early responses help to bring on the reinforcement; on the FI schedule, such responses serve no purpose at all with respect to receipt of reinforce-

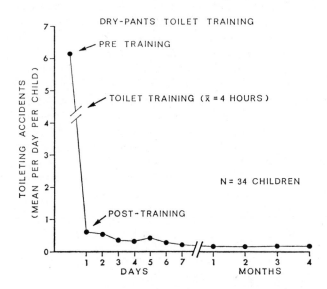

Figure 27. Effects of the "Dry Pants" toilet training procedure on the frequency of toileting accidents, both bladder and bowel, of 34 normal children. The toilet training period is shown as an interruption in the curve and required an average of four hours per child. The "Pre-Training" data point represents the children's accident rate per day during the week prior to training. Data points are given for the first seven days after training and monthly thereafter. Each datum point is the average number of accidents per day per child. (Fox, R.M. & Azrin, N.H. Dry Pants: A Rapid Method of Toilet Training Children. *Behavior Research and Therapy,* 1973, *11,* 435-442. Copyright© 1973 by Pergamon Press, Inc., Elmsford, New York. Reprinted by permission.)

ment. It is for this reason that absenteeism in industry is so high on Monday; management has tried, with some success, to accommodate to this phenomenon by eliminating "Mondays" through the introduction of the four-day work week.

The amount of work produced by students also tends to follow a well-defined scalloped function when they are on a Fixed Interval schedule. Reading and studying simply does not occur just subsequent to an exam; they build to a frantic crescendo the night before the next exam. In my own lecture classes I have observed that only about 50% of the enrolled students come to the first class after an exam; however, everyone is there for the class immediately prior to an exam.

There is no question that both people and animals on FI schedules acquire a temporal discrimination based on the fact that responses early in the interval are not reinforced and those which come later are more closely followed by reinforcement. The better one is able to time the interval, the more pronounced should be the difference in response rates between early and late phases. In order to enhance the timing ability of pigeons, Ferster and Skinner (1957) provided the birds with an external "clock," consisting of a spot of light projected on a translucent screen. As the interval progresses, the spot grows in size and the bird is provided with a visual stimulus which is perfectly correlated with the passage of time and which resets itself after a reinforcement has been obtained.

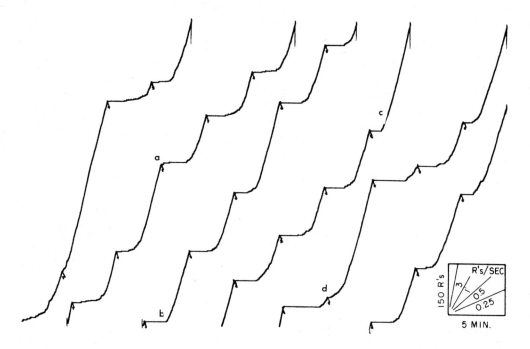

Figure 28. Cumulative response curve of bird on FI schedule (four-minute intervals) 66 hours after CFR. Note marked pauses after each reinforcement, lasting one to three minutes. (Ferster, C.B. and Skinner, B.F. *Schedules of Reinforcement,* Copyright© 1957, P. 159. Reprinted by permission of Prentice-Hall, Inc., Englewood Cliffs, New Jersey.)

Figure 29 illustrates the very pronounced effect which the addition of a clock can have on behavior. This curve was generated by a pigeon after 25 hours of FI training with the clock; the interval was 10 minutes. It can be seen that there was virtually no response for the first 7 to 8.5 minutes of every interval. This was followed by a rapidly increasing response rate, and then by a very high, stable rate of about 10 responses per second.

In order to maintain at least a moderate rate of responding early in the interval of FI schedules, it is usually necessary to provide supplementary reinforcers. In industry and education, this could involve social approval for interim work efforts. The foreman or the teacher may offer a word of praise for some quality output or for the expression of an insightful idea. Without the addition of these supplementary reinforcements, the twice-monthly paycheck or the final exam may be insufficient to keep people responding throughout the fixed interval.

Variable Interval Schedules. Variable Interval schedules bear the same relationship to the FI schedule as the VR does to the FR schedule. Ferster and Skinner describe the Variable Interval (VI) schedule as "one in which the intervals between reinforcements vary in a random or nearly random order" (1957, p. 326). Like the VR schedule,

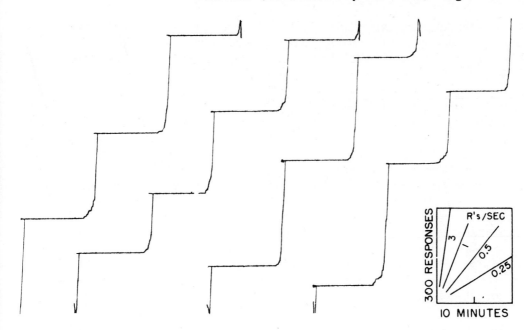

Figure 29. Cumulative response curve of bird on FI schedule (10-minute intervals) after 25 hours of exposure to the clock. The performance is uniform from segment to segment, with a pause from 7 to 8.5 minutes, followed by a short period during which the rate accelerates to a terminal rate well above 10 responses per second (Ferster, C.B. & Skinner, B.F. *Schedules of Reinforcement,* Copyright© 1957, p. 269. Reprinted by permission of Prentice-Hall, Inc., Englewood Cliffs, New Jersey.)

the VI schedule promotes stable rates of responding, because receipt of reinforcement does not become a discriminative stimulus signaling a period of non-reinforcement; another reinforcement *may* be immediately forthcoming if a response is emitted. In fact, to guarantee that no scalloping will emerge on the cumulative response curve, the shortest interval used on a VI schedule is frequently either zero or very close to zero time.

In general, the rate of responding on a VI schedule is slower than on ratio schedules. The overall slope of the cumulative record produced by an animal on a VI schedule is steeper than one on a FI schedule; although, with the latter schedule, it will be recalled that rates of responding may become very high for a brief period at the end of every fixed interval.

Because the VI schedule is the most conducive of all schedules to yield stable rates of behavior, it should be employed whenever behavioral constancy is a desired outcome. As a college professor, I can virtually guarantee a steady rate of work from students by replacing three scheduled exams, an FI schedule, with a relatively large number of surprise quizzes, a VI schedule. And just to keep the students from enjoying any post-reinforcement pause, quizzes should be given in consecutive classes at least once or twice a semester. This may sound inhumane, but it does permit one to control student behavior in a very predictable fashion.

Another common example of a VI schedule involves fishing. When the fisherman drops his line overboard and waits for a bite, he doesn't know how long it will be before a fish will swim by and take his bait; it is the fish who will determine the duration of the variable interval. It is not unusual to see fishermen behave as if they were on a ratio schedule, retrieving and casting out their lines repeatedly. Presumably, the many responses they make are instrumental in bringing on the reinforcement. Of course, if bait falling through water is more likely to entice a fish than bait which hangs out at a constant depth, then perhaps some sort of VR schedule is indeed involved. That is, reinforcement may be contingent upon both the frequency of casts, VR schedule, and the availability of hungry fish in the area, VI schedule.

Such a complex schedule of reinforcement, involving both ratio and interval components, is not uncommon in our social encounters. Words of praise, a cookie, an affectionate hug are all reinforcements which are probably dispensed on the basis of naturally-occurring complex schedules, in which both the frequency of the recipient's response and the timing of the response combine to yield payoffs.

The four schedules of reinforcement we have discussed, FR, VR, FI, and VI, have been shown to produce characteristic response patterns. These are diagrammed, in a stylized way, in Fig. 30. In summary, the most striking features of these schedules are: the generally higher response rates produced by ratio, in comparison with interval, schedules; the smooth cumulative curves generated under variable schedules, in contrast to the scalloping which is produced with fixed schedules; not illustrated, but very important, the greater resistance to extinction of variable schedules, in comparison with fixed schedules; and the greater resistance to extinction of any intermittent schedule of reinforcement over a CRF schedule.

Shaping

So far, we have talked only about changing the frequency with which a response occurs by providing reinforcement on some prescribed schedule. It is also possible to use operant techniques for the development of new responses which, while they may not naturally exist in the organism's repertoire of behaviors, are still behaviors of which the organism is potentially capable.

In general, *shaping* involves the reinforcement of successive approximations. In effect, the trainer plays a "hot-cold" game with the animal, providing reinforcement for a "hot" response and withholding it for a "cold" one. Specifically, shaping begins by reinforcing any response which vaguely resembles the one we ultimately wish to condition. Once that first reinforced response is emitted at a stable rate, reinforcement is withheld unless a variant of the response occurs which is slightly more similar to the "goal" behavior. For example, in order to shape a clockwise 360° body rotation in a pigeon, we would first provide reinforcement contingent upon the pigeon turning its head to the right, a naturally-occurring, high-probability response. In a few trials, the pigeon will be vigorously emitting the repeatedly-reinforced head turn to the right. Then, instead of reinforcing just any head turn, we dispense reinforcement contingent upon a head rotation of at least 30°; then we require 45° for a reinforcement, and then

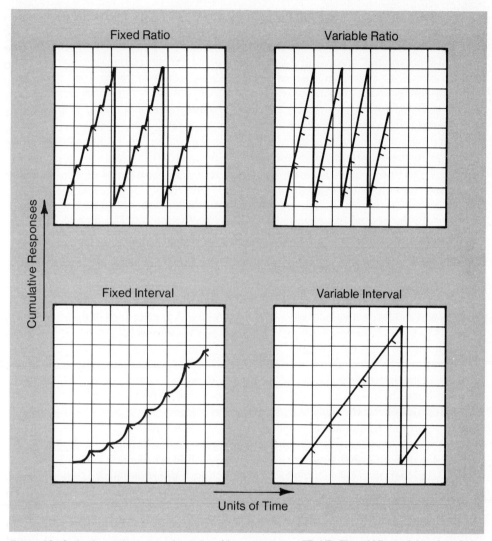

Figure 30. Stylized cumulative records produced by organisms on FR, VR, FI, and VI schedules of reinforcement.

90°, and so on. Before long, the pigeon will not only be turning its head widely to the right but its entire body will follow suit; the result is a pigeon doing what may appear to be a well-executed dance.

Using such shaping procedures, pigeons have been operantly conditioned to play tunes on a xylophone, chickens to play baseball, and pigs to operate a vacuum cleaner. Virtually any complex behavior of which an animal is physically capable may be brought about by implementing a shaping program. With humans, too complex tasks are often best learned through this method of successive approximations. A young child is initially quite incapable of properly dressing himself or engaging in well-mannered eating habits. Frequently, parents will reward a child's "good try" which, although it does not meet an ideal standard, is a step in the right direction. On subsequent occasions, more and more is required of the child before reinforcement is offered; but, since each step is a small one, the new response upon which reinforcement is contingent has a high probability of occurring.

In shaping it is is particularly crucial for reinforcement to occur immediately subsequent to the response upon which it is contingent. If there is a delay, some incidental behavior may occur in the interval and it will be reinforced instead, even though such behavior was not instrumental in bringing forth reinforcement. Consequently, if you intend to shape a response in your dog, Skinner suggests that the usual means of reinforcing the dog with food will be inefficient. "The best way to reinforce the behavior with the necessary speed is to use a 'conditioned' reinforcer. This is a signal which the animal has observed in association with food. The animal is always given food immediately after the signal, and the signal itself then becomes a reinforcer" (1959, p. 413).

Those of you who keep pets have probably already noticed the development of conditioned reinforcers via classical conditioning in the very way that Skinner describes. For example, it is not unusual for the sound of a can opener to become a conditioned reinforcer because of its association with the receipt of canned food. The behavioral effect of this conditioning is that the dog will come running when the opener is heard.

Because of its portability and ease of operation, Skinner suggests that a toy hand "cricket," which makes a clearly-heard sound, is an ideal conditioned reinforcer. In order to build up its reinforcing power, take your dog to a place which is free from distractions. Begin by tossing small bits of food to the dog, one at a time, about once a minute. After the animal has become accustomed to this game, precede each toss of food with a cricket sound. Do this repeatedly, but never when the dog is begging, facing you, or close to you; wait until the animal is a short distance away and not oriented toward you, then sound the cricket and toss the food. Before long, the dog will jump toward the spot where he usually receives food as soon as the cricket is sounded; the cricket has become a classical conditioned reinforcer.

The actual shaping of the dog's behavior may now proceed quickly. Suppose you wish to train the dog to walk over to a handle on a low cupboard door and touch it with his nose. As soon as the dog begins to orient in the correct direction, sound the cricket and then give food. The dog's movement should be followed by the cricket sound as closely as possible; quick reflexes on the trainer's part helps here. Thereafter, reinforce only when the dog approaches the cupboard. "If you withhold reinforcement too long at this stage, you may lose the facing response. If so, go back and pick it up" (p. 414). It will not take more than a couple of minutes, if all goes well, before the dog is standing close to the cupboard. Now, "reinforce any movement which brings the nose close to the handle . . . Presently the dog will touch the handle with its nose, and after reinforcement [cricket sound, then food] it will repeat this behavior so long as it remains hungry" (p. 415).

Superstitious behavior. We mentioned earlier that shaping procedures most often fail when the delay between reinforcements and the responses upon which reinforcements are contingent is too long. Instead of the target behavior being reinforced, some other, incidental behavior may be strengthened instead. The occurrence of incidental conditioning is not restricted to sloppily-conducted shaping programs. Anytime a response "happens" to be followed by a reinforcement, it will be strengthened. Skinner (1959) writes, "To say that a reinforcement is contingent upon a response may mean nothing more than it follows the response . . . conditioning takes place even though we have paid no attention to the behavior of the organism in making the presentation" (p. 404). For example, if a reinforcement is programmed to be presented to a pigeon at regular, short intervals regardless of what the bird is doing, it will necessarily follow the emission of *some* response, whether it be standing still, turning, pecking, or walking. That response, whatever it might be, then tends to be repeated once or, perhaps, twice. If the interval between programmed reinforcements is not too long, it is quite probable that the second or third emission of the reinforced response will again be followed by reinforcement. In no time, the animal has conditioned itself to behave as if reinforcement were contingent upon the behavior. Since no "real" contingency is involved, the behavior is called superstitious. However, that does not make the conditioning any less real or the behavior any less stable; the pigeon is not privy to "reality," only to apparent contingencies.

In this way, Skinner (1959) observed the development of a variety of superstitious behaviors, including head bobbing, counter-clockwise turns, and pecking movements. Similarly, many people behave in ways which suggest that they believe in a causal relationship between a response and an outcome, even though, objectively, no such contingency exists. The student who happens to do well on a test while wearing a particular shirt might wear his "exam shirt" during every subsequent test. The remark made by a baseball pitcher who was on a winning streak, "I won't change my socks until I lose," and the body contortions exhibited by the bowler after he releases the ball are other examples of superstitious behaviors.

Reinforcement Applications

The use of reinforcing contingencies to modify rates of operant responses is widespread. In this section a few exemplary applications will be presented for purposes of illustrating the range of possibilities.

As a first simple example, we have selected a reinforcement program which has been tried with considerable success by a great number of students. The program consists of reinforcing a teacher response with a nod. To begin with, the student obtains a base rate by noting the percentage of time a lecturer is looking at him. During the reinforcement phase, every time the lecturer looks at the student he is met with an affirmative head nod. What could be more reinforcing than to believe that someone is agreeing with you? It will invariably follow that the lecturer will increase the amount of time spent oriented toward the nodding student. If a greater degree of sophistication is desired, the lecturer might be gradually shifted to an intermittent schedule of reinforcement and the effect noted; or the original student can be programmed to cease nodding at a prescribed time and some other student, located elsewhere in the room, can begin to dispense the same reinforcement. The variations are endless.

Marriage therapy. A more serious, and somewhat recent application of operant reinforcement principles is in the area of reviving troubled marriages. Stuart called it an *operant interpersonal* approach to marital treatment, because it is based on the assumption that the kind and level of interaction existing between the spouses is present because that interpersonal pattern is the most reinforcing of available alternatives. Thus, the husband who spends long hours at a job, or with the "boys," is doing so because these activities are more reinforcing to him than time spent with his wife. From this viewpoint, a successful marriage depends upon each spouse being a dispenser of reinforcement for the other. "When disordered marriages are evaluated . . . it is seen that each partner reinforces the other at a low rate and each is therefore relatively unattractive to and unreinforced by the other" (1969, p. 675). It follows that a marriage might be saved by encouraging each partner to provide reinforcement for the other more frequently.

Two kinds of contractual arrangements between spouses have been used. The most common is the *quid pro quo* agreement, in which each spouse agrees to increase a behavior which is reinforcing to the other; but change in one is contingent upon prior change in the other. For example, a wife might agree to manage and balance the family checking account if the husband agrees to assume dishwashing responsibilities. The roadblock which may be encountered is that, in a marriage lacking in trust, neither partner is willing to "go first"; unilateral change is impossible. In addition, since the failure of one partner to change relieves the other partner of any responsibility for change, the *quid pro quo* agreement may never be implemented.

A second contractual form is known as the *good faith contract.* Here, each partner commits himself to increase the frequency of a particular target behavior in exchange for a reinforcement, with the implementation of either change not dependent upon the other. A husband may agree to talk to his wife more, his targeted change, in return for any number of reinforcements, such as a goodbye kiss in the morning or a neatly-pressed shirt. At the same time the wife might agree not to work overtime, her targeted change, for which she would earn reinforcements, such as dining out more frequently with her husband. Tokens have been used as reinforcement to encourage increases in the targeted behaviors. The tokens are earned when the target behavior is emitted, and they may later be redeemed for other reinforcers at an agreed-upon rate. For instance, Stuart (1969) arranged for husbands to earn tokens by talking to their wives. "The tokens were redeemable at the husband's request from a menu stressing physical affection . . . husbands were charged three tokens for kissing and 'light petting' with their wives, five tokens for 'heavy petting,' and 15 tokens for intercourse" (p. 679).

Stuart described the use of good-faith contracting with tokens as successful; there were reported behavior changes in his four client couples, and these changes were the very ones sought by the spouses involved. In addition, all four couples expressed increased satisfaction with their marriages at the conclusion of 10 weeks of therapy. The level of satisfaction continued to increase at six and 12 month follow-ups.

Stuart's conclusions have been deemed promising, but his non-experimental approach has been criticized. Jacobson and Martin (1976) brand his report as essentially a case study involving no control group and totally relying upon self report data. A more rigorous investigation was conducted by Jacobson (1977). His clients were 10 unhappily married couples. At a pretest session, each couple generated a list of "major" and "minor" problem areas in their relationships. They were then given between 5 and 10 minutes to reach some agreement on one of their major and one of their minor problems; these discussions were videotaped. Each spouse also completed the Marital Adjustment Scale (MAS), a self-report index of marital satisfaction. Five couples were then randomly selected for a treatment which consisted of eight sessions in which good-faith contracting, to be carried out at home, was explained; the sessions also included instruction and practice on how to engage in positive problem-solving behavior. The remaining couples were asked to wait before beginning treatment and, therefore, served as a control group. At the conclusion of the treatment period, both experimental and control couples were again asked to solve one major and one minor problem while being videotaped; and each spouse filled out the MAS.

Jacobson's results revealed significant gains for the couples who had been given practice in good-faith contracting and problem solving. Specifically, the videotaped discussions revealed significant decreases in negative interactions, such as commands, criticisms, complaints, put-downs, and interruptions, from pre- to post-test; and there were significant increases in positive interactions, such as compromises, requests for change, and acceptances of responsibility. In addition, the active treatment spouses revealed highly significant changes, in the direction of greater marriage satisfaction, on the MAS. The reported increased level of satisfaction at post-test was even greater, but not significantly so, at a one year follow-up. In contrast, these behavioral and self-report measures remained virtually unchanged over the time span of the investigation for the control couples.

The Token Economy. When we discussed shaping the behavior of your pet, the utility of a cricket sound as a conditioned reinforcer was stressed. The cricket sound served to provide immediate reinforcement and was, therefore, able to bridge the temporal gap between the target behavior and the primary reinforcer, food. Similarly, you will recall that Stuart (1969) used tokens as conditioned reinforcers in marriage therapy to bridge the time span between talking to a wife and obtaining physical affection from her. The reinforcing value of the tokens was drawn from the fact that they could be cashed in for other reinforcements at a later time; in the case of Stuart's husbands, they were redeemed for sexual activity.

In 1965 Ayllon and Azrin made the first attempt to apply operant reinforcement principles in a psychiatric hospital ward. Many reinforcers were used to strengthen a variety of necessary and/or useful patient behaviors. Again, in order to bridge the delay between behavior and reinforcement, the procedure employed was the immediate dispensing of conditioned reinforcers contingent upon the emission of target behaviors. The conditioned reinforcers in this case were special metal tokens which could later be exchanged for other reinforcements.

This ward-wide program, and others like it, are now known as "token economies.'' In many ways the token economy functions much like a monetary economy in which people work at jobs, earn conditioned reinforcers, money, and later exchange the conditioned reinforcers for more primary reinforcers.

In order to facilitate the operation of their ward's token economy, Ayllon and Azrin (1965) chose behaviors and reinforcers which were as objective and observable as possible. Behaviors included washing dishes, mopping floors, and serving meals. Accurate record-keeping was thus possible because, in each case, the target behavior resulted in a "fairly permanent, physically-identifiable change in the environment." Similarly, the reinforcers used had to be clear-cut. A friendly smile or a warm comment from an aide, while possibly reinforcing, are too transient and subjective. However, the privilege of going to the coffee bar qualified.

In the selection of reinforcers, the primary consideration still had to be their effectiveness for a given patient. There were no pre-judgments made on this important matter:

> Instead, patients' behavior was used to discover reinforcers. What the patients did, or tried to do, was observed throughout the day . . . For example, patients might continuously hoard various items under their mattresses, stay at the exit to the ward and try to leave, frequently request special interviews with the social worker or ward psychologist, or push their way into the cafeteria in order to eat before others.

The assumption here is that any preferred activity may function as a reinforcer. This general principle was expressed by Premack (1959) and has gained considerable empirical confirmation. Accordingly, Ayllon and Azrin report that "behaviors of high natural frequency were arranged as reinforcers by allowing the patients to engage in them at a scheduled time."

After a year and a half of preliminary development, Ayllon and Azrin conducted a series of experiments to determine the effectiveness of the token economy as a vehicle for maintaining patient behaviors. All of their experiments followed the A-B-A design, in which each patient serves as his own control. For example, phase A provides reinforcement for one patient activity, while phase B may involve the withdrawal of reinforcement; in the third (A) phase, reinforcement is again available for patient activity.

In their first experiment, the reinforced activity was off-ward work assignments, either dietary, clerical, laboratory, or laundry. Each job required six hours of work, five days per week, and paid 70 tokens. These tokens could be exchanged for preferred activities or commissary items: the use of a room divider cost one token; leaving the ward for a 20 minute walk cost two tokens; a trip to town with escort cost 100 tokens; a private audience with a psychologist cost 20 tokens; extra religious serves off-ward cost 10 tokens; choice of a TV program cost three tokens; the purchase of toilet articles cost between one and five tokens; reading materials cost between two and five tokens.

The patients were five schizophrenics and three mentally retarded adults, all living on the same ward and having a mean length of continuous hospitalization of nine years. Prior to the experiment, all had the opportunity to work at the four available jobs and to participate in the token economy. With the start of the experiment, each was given the chance to work at her *preferred* job and earn the regular rate of 70 tokens. After 10 days, the patients were told individually that they could continue on their preferred jobs, but would no longer earn tokens. However, tokens could be earned at one of the less-preferred jobs. The choice of staying or changing jobs was left entirely up to the patients. Ten days later, each patient was told that her current, non-preferred, job would no longer pay but that her original, preferred, job was available for token reinforcement.

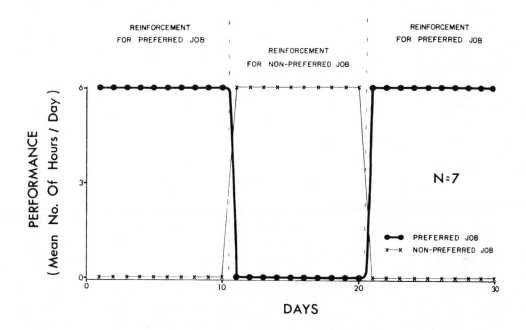

Figure 31. Mean number of hours of performance by seven of eight patients (Ayllon, T. & Azrin, N.H. The measurement and reinforcement of behavior of psychotics. *Journal of Experimental Analysis of Behavior,* 1965, *8,* 357-383. Copyright© 1965 by the Society for the Experimental Analysis of Behavior, Inc.)

Figure 31 illustrates that the behavior of seven of the eight patients was perfectly controlled by the opportunity to earn tokens. The shift from preferred to non-preferred jobs was immediate, as was the return to the preferred job when it once again paid. One patient chose to stay at her original job for an additional 11 days, without token pay. She told her attendant, "Doctor _____ needs me and I told him I'd do his typing next week, so I'll keep my work. I can live without tokens." On the 21st day, the patient switched to a reinforced job assignment, stating to an attendant, "I have finished the work that I promised to do for Doctor _____ . . . when I make a promise, I keep it." This was the only instance in which uncontrolled reinforcement contingencies overrode the token economy.

In another experiment, Ayllon and Azrin started out by making tokens contingent upon on-ward activities. After 20 days, and for a 20 day span, tokens were still dispensed and could be exchanged for reinforcers, but they were not given contingent upon ward performance. In the third 20 day phase, tokens were again dispensed on a contingent basis. The very dramatic effect of these manipulations upon patient behavior is illustrated in Fig. 32.

Overall, the work of Ayllon and Azrin (1965) demonstrates that "uninvolved," "apathetic" patients are highly responsive to reinforcement, and that a token economy is a suitable vehicle for encouraging high rates of desired patient behaviors. In each of their experiments, performance was maintained when tokens were offered on a contingent basis; performance deteriorated, falling to near zero, when the response-reinforcement contingency was in some way disrupted.

Since this pioneering attempt by Ayllon and Azrin, token reinforcement programs have been utilized in a large number of different institutional settings, including schools. A review of classroom token programs by O'Leary and Drabman (1971) was generally optimistic in its evaluation of what could be accomplished. More specifically, the effectiveness of the programs has been documented with respect to decreasing disruptive behavior, increasing study time, raising academic achievement, and modifying the frequency of a variety of other behaviors, including class attendance.

One of the main questions raised concerning the use of token economies and other extrinsic reinforcement programs has to do with the issue of generalization. To what degree should one expect similar but non-reinforced behaviors to change in their rates? Will reinforced behaviors be maintained after the token program has been terminated? The answers to these questions seem to be negative. Recall that in Ayllon and Azrin's original investigations it was found that work activity by patients dropped to zero when behavior reinforcement contingencies were removed; the work had apparently not become, in and of itself, a reinforcing activity. In a recent article, Levine and Fasnacht warned that "token rewards may lead to token learning" (1974, p. 816). This concern is based upon research which shows that one's preference for an activity which has earned reinforcements is lower when the reinforcements are withdrawn than it would have been had no reinforcements ever been earned. An attributional explanation is frequently invoked for this phenomenon: "If one is doing activity X without reward, then activity X must be worth doing. If one is getting a reward for activity X, it must not be worth doing without the reward" (p. 818). In other words, Levine and Fasnacht, while not questioning the efficacy of extrinsic reinforcement with respect to increasing the rates of behavior, do claim that rates may be expected to fall below the pre-reinforcement rate once reinforcement is discontinued.

In an empirical test of this hypothesis, Lepper and Greene (1975) had 80 preschool children complete some puzzles. Half the children were told that they could earn the opportunity to play with a variety of highly attractive toys if they worked hard and solved the puzzles quickly. The remaining children were encouraged to solve the puzzles, but were not told that a special play opportunity was contingent upon their work. After completing the puzzles, these children were simply given an opportunity to play with the attractive toys, and this activity was in no way tied to the previously-worked puzzles.

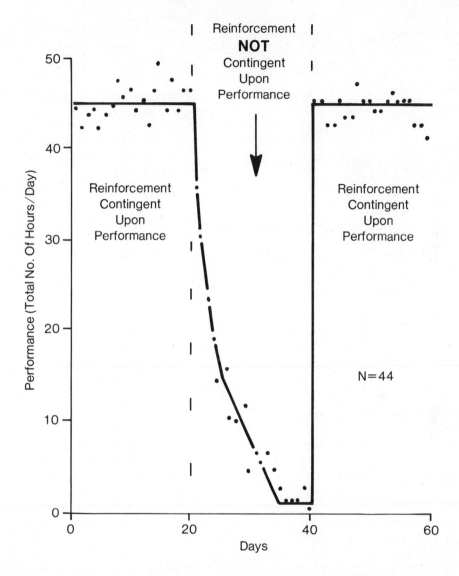

Figure 32. The total number of hours of the on-ward performance by a group of 44 patients (Ayllon, T. & Azrin, N.H. The Measurement and Reinforcement of Behavior of Psychotics. *Journal of Experimental Analysis of Behavior*, 1965, *8*, 357-383. Copyright© 1965 by the Society for the Experimental Analysis of Behavior, Inc.)

One to three weeks after the completion of this phase of the procedure, the dependent measure was obtained; the puzzles were made available to preschoolers during play periods and the number of children who played with them was recorded. The children were free to choose the target activity or any other indoor or outdoor activity. It was found that 80% of the children who had not been explicitly reinforced for their previous puzzle activity spontaneously elected to play with the puzzles; the corresponding figure for the preschoolers who had received extrinsic reinforcement was only 60%, a statistically significant difference. The authors of this research, therefore, believe that "extrinsic incentives may undermine children's intrinsic interest in an activity" (p. 484).

It would appear that the simple use of tokens or other extrinsic reinforcers, such as preferred activities, does not enhance generalization and may even be counter-productive if the reinforcing contingencies are withdrawn. There is, however, a very important qualification to this conclusion. Specifically, in none of the investigations cited did the researchers make any effort to overcome what they considered to be a weakness in their procedures; if generalization is desired then "generalization should be programmed rather than expected or lamented," to quote Baer, Wolf, and Risley (1968, p. 97).

O'Leary and Drabman (1971) offer some advice on additions which may be built into a token economy so that the chances of generalization become greater. Their recommendations, which apply to any extrinsic reinforcement program, hinge upon tying the explicitly reinforced behaviors to naturally-occurring reinforcers. In this way, when the formal program stops, there will still be positive outcomes available to maintain the activity. For example, the giving of tokens or other reinforcers should always be accompanied by social reinforcement, a word of praise or a warm smile. In addition, the subject might also be taught that what he is getting tokens for now, perhaps learning to read, will pay off in the future; he'll be able to enjoy comic books. Drabman, Spitalnik, and O'Leary (1973) found that by encouraging children to self-evaluate their own non-disruptive behavior and academic performance, these token-reinforced behaviors were maintained even during periods of the day when the token program was not in effect.

Self-reinforcement. Self-evaluation has a favorable effect upon generalization which may come about because the subject becomes, in effect, his own dispenser of reinforcements. The idea of self-reinforcement as a primary behavior change strategy has received considerable attention, and the procedure has been relatively successful.

The efficacy of self-reinforcement as a vehicle for promoting weight gain was tested by Gulanick, Woodburn, and Rimm (1975). Twenty-one adult male and female volunteers were procured through newspaper ads announcing a five-week weight gain program. The subjects were randomly assigned to one of three groups. The self-reinforcement treatment consisted of having subjects focus upon desirable eating habits, such as having eggs and bacon every morning. Each week, one such eating goal was set, and the subject was to provide self-reinforcement contingent upon engaging in the target activity. The reinforcements were decided on an individual basis and were selected for their accessibility and subjective potency; watching a favorite TV show can be used as an example. The reinforcement treatment subjects were expected to continue working on those target behaviors introduced in the early weeks as new target behaviors were added. The second treatment involved punishment in the form of self-denials if the subjects engaged in undesirable eating habits. For example, if the subject skipped a meal, he might deprive himself of cigarettes. Each week, a new undesirable habit was added and self-punishment was made contingent upon its occurrence. As with the self-reinforcement treatment, the subjects in the self-punishment group were expected to continue to work on undesirable behaviors that had been targeted earlier in the program. The third group was a discussion-control in which subjects reflected upon desirable and undesirable eating habits with no mention of reinforcements or punishments.

The results of this program were assessed at a sixth session weigh-in, and again at 12 week follow-up. It was found that the self-reinforcement subjects gained an average of 3.5 pounds at post-treatment, and an additional .17 pounds by the follow-up assessment. In contrast, the self-punishment group only added .43 pounds by the end of treatment, and had actually lost a pound from their pre-treatment weight at follow-up; the control group gained .71 pounds during treatment, but at follow-up were found to be at exactly the same mean weight as they were at pre-treatment.

While the magnitude of weight gain is not spectacular for the self-reinforcement group, it is consistent with what might be hoped for over a five week span. The fact that no additional weight was gained subsequent to the termination of active treatment suggests that self-reinforcement, to be effective for weight gain, has to be closely supervised; or, at least, "booster" sessions must be provided subsequent to the termination of the treatment proper.

In a general survey of the weight loss research using behavioral strategies, O'Leary and Wilson (1975) assert that no matter which particular approach is taken, the inclusion of a self-reinforcement component is usually important. The primary reinforcement for very obese people, weight reduction of a magnitude sufficient to affect appearance and physical well being, might not be realized for weeks or even months; self-reinforcement can bridge what may be a long period by helping to keep the individual on his dietary program.

Programmed Instruction. Skinner (1953) sees education as the establishment of new behaviors through the process of conditioning. The educational agency provides reinforcements contingent upon behavior acquisition; these take the form of grades, diplomas, awards, and, hopefully, an occasional kind word from the teacher. In most cases, however, the available reinforcers are not utilized in optimal fashion. They may be offered non-contingently, or contingent upon an "incorrect" response, or only after a considerable period of time has passed since the correct response was emitted; in most classroom situations, a student does not receive an exam grade until days after the exam has been completed.

In order to correct these deficiencies, Skinner developed an educational procedure which is a derivative of operant conditioning principles. The procedure is called *programmed learning* or *programmed instruction* and, in its early applications, involves the utilization of an apparatus known as a *teaching machine*.

The teaching machine has a display which presents a bit of information. This is followed by a relevant, simple question which the student answers. The student then compares his response to the correct one provided by the machine. If the two correspond, a lever is pressed which programs the machine to go on to the next frame. Incorrect frames are repeated. This general teaching strategy has more recently been incorporated into books which follow a programmed routine. When a book format is used, a page flap or an index card is employed to conceal the correct answer until after the student has committed himself. So long as the student does not "cheat" by looking at the correct answer before writing his own response to the question, programmed texts seem to work quite well; and they are much more convenient and considerably less expensive than the machines.

Skinner (1958) believes that programmed instruction takes advantage of the principles of behavior modification extracted from operant conditioning research. Most importantly, correct answers are reinforced immediately. In addition, the answers called for are very discrete, making them comparable to the objective target behaviors which are the focus of operant conditioning. Thirdly, as in any effective shaping program, the educational process unfolds in very small steps; each step is eminently manageable, and once they have all been mastered they collectively comprise an impressive amount of learning.

Programmed instructional material is designed to yield learning without error. In fact, an error rate of less than 5% among students on any given frame is usually considered acceptable. If the rate exceeds this percentage, it probably means that the question is vague, or that the step taken from the previous frame is too large; in either case, program alteration is called for. The net effect of this design is that the student receives a huge amount of reinforcement relative to what would have been earned in the process of acquiring a similar amount of information or skill under traditional classroom procedures. Commenting on programmed instructional material, Lundin notes, "Education becomes fun instead of drudgery for the child. The problem is not one of getting the student to work at the machine [or programmed text] but of keeping him away from it" (1969, p. 162).

As an example of programmed instruction, consider how Skinner teaches the spelling of *manufacture*. First, the child simply copies the word after reading the sentences, "Manufacture means to make or build. Chair factories manufacture chairs." The second frame points out that the words *manufacture* and *factory* are partly the same, both being derived from the old word meaning "to make or build." The student is then asked to fill in the missing letters in m a n u _ _ _ _ u r e. In the third frame, the student reads that part of the word manufacture is like the word manual; both are derived from the old word for hand, and "Many things used to be made by hand." In this frame the student completes _ _ _ _ f a c t u r e. The fourth and fifth frames makes salient the fact that the same letters repeat in the word manufacture. Thus, in frame four the student completes m _ n u f _ c t u r e. In the fifth frame he supplies the missing letters to m a n _ f a c _ u r e. The sixth and last frame requires the student to spell the entire word he has now mastered without the provision of additional aides (1958, p. 972).

In this program and others like it, Skinner sees a shifting emphasis in education from punishment to reinforcement. "In light of our present knowledge, a school system must be called a failure if it cannot induce students to learn except by threatening them for not learning . . ." (1958, p. 977).

Guttman believes that programmed instruction, "singlehandedly" begun by Skinner, "has grown into a thing of immense proportions involving literally thousands of practitioners and further developers whose applications of the concept have now been felt by untold millions of students" (1977, p. 324).

Biofeedback techniques. As a final example of how operant reinforcement may be used for behavior modification, we turn to *autonomic responses,* such as heart rate, blood pressure, and body temperature. Traditionally, these responses have been seen as beyond conscious control. Nevertheless, evidence is accumulating that autonomic activity *is* susceptible to operant conditioning.

In a recent study, Kondo and Canter (1977) treated 20 adults with complaints or histories of "tension" headaches which were believed to be associated with chronically high levels of muscle tension. Electromyographic (EMG) activity in the subjects' frontalis muscles, the forehead, was monitored with a polygraph recorder. The subjects were told that they would hear a tone whose pitch varied with EMG activity; a high tone was correlated with high frontalis tension, and lower tones with low levels of tension. "Their task was to find a way to decrease the pitch of the tone and keep it as low as possible" (p. 94). Half of the subjects heard veridical feedback; the control group did not receive accurate tonal information. Instead, they heard a prepared tone whose pitch gradually lowered over the ten, twenty-minute sessions.

The two groups, experimental and control, did not differ in the frequency with which they suffered from tension headaches prior to their treatments, each averaging about one per day per subject. At the completion of the training, the subjects who had received accurate tonal feedback were only experiencing an average of one tension headache per person per five-day block; members of the false feedback group were suffering an average of three to five headaches per five-day block. This difference at the end of training was significant at the $p < .005$ level. In addition, four of the five accurate-feedback subjects who were contacted one year after training had maintained their gains. The fifth reported some degree of setback, but not to the pre-training level.

This particular investigation is important because it points to the efficacy of autonomic feedback independent of relaxation training, a therapy component which has been routinely administered in conjunction with autonomic feedback in the treatment of tension headaches. However, since Tasto and Hinkle (1973) achieved similar success in relieving tension headaches with relaxation training alone, O'Leary and Wilson (1975) question the necessity of using expensive and highly sophisticated biofeedback equipment.

Autonomic feedback procedures have also been used to effect clinically significant decreases in blood pressure among hypertensive patients, and to increase blood flow to the uncomfortably cold extremities of those suffering from Raynaud's disease. The most successful application of these feedback procedures has been with the modification of cardiac arrhythmias of purely medical origin. O'Leary and Wilson (1975) report that patients have not only been able to manage their heart rates but that this skill has been maintained even after the externally administered feedback was faded out, "indicating that true self-control had been acquired" (p. 283).

Despite these successes, O'Leary and Wilson caution against considering biofeedback a panacea. They point out that insufficient research has been conducted to testify to the generalization of within-laboratory gains. In addition, the effective ingredients of biofeedback procedures have not been fully clarified. Questions remain as to whether the effects are primarily mediated by the provision of information via the feedback, or whether the feedback functions as a reinforcer in a truly operant sense. From an empirical perspective, because the feedback has the effect of increasing specific autonomic behavior upon which it is contingent, it would appear to qualify as a reinforcer in the sense meant by Skinner.

Negative reinforcement

So far, our discussions of reinforcement have primarily used examples which involve positive reinforcement. Much less routinely used in applied settings is negative reinforcement, the offset of an aversive stimulus contingent upon a response. Negative reinforcement procedures are also called *escape conditioning* because the term "escape" so aptly describes what the subject appears to do; for example, an animal learns to press a bar in order to terminate, escape from, receipt of shock.

One of the difficulties encountered in using escape conditioning is that the aversive stimulation tends to produce an agitated subject, making subtle kinds of learning more difficult than they would be with the use of positive reinforcement. Nevertheless successful clinical applications have been reported; Feldman (1966) treated homosexuals by making shock termination contingent upon them voluntarily changing a picture of a nude male to that of a nude female. The description of negative reinforcement procedures involves the defining of shock as a discriminative stimulus which sets the occasion for the response instrumental in bringing about aversion relief. In general, the cumulative response patterns associated with the various schedules of reinforcement outlined earlier are applicable when negative reinforcement procedures are employed.

In another application of escape conditioning, Lovaas, Schaeffer, and Simmons (1965) used shock termination to negatively reinforce the "social behavior" of autistic children. The children were placed on an electrified grid and were asked to approach the experimenter. If no approach was made, shock was administered and continued until the child moved toward the experimenter. The effective ingredient in this strategy is not clear. Was the child's stationary behavior being punished, or was approach behavior being negatively reinforced? Probably there is an ingredient of both. An additional complication was the subsequent use of *avoidance conditioning* to help maintain the approach behavior. This procedure consisted of permitting the child to avoid shock altogether if an approach response was made within five seconds of the verbal request.

Avoidance conditioning seems to have a superficial resemblance to escape conditioning, in that, "successful" behavior ultimately results in "no shock" in both procedures. However, since successful avoidant behavior prevents the occurrence of an aversive event instead of terminating it, what is the reinforcement? One might suggest that, in the Lovaas (1965) research, the experimenter's request functioned as a conditioned stimulus, setting off emotional reactions anticipatory of receiving shock. The avoidant response then serves to reduce this unpleasant emotionality, and it is this reduction which is reinforcing. However, analyses such as this are speculative; Kanfer and Phillips (1970) report that there is no generally accepted explanation for the learning which takes place under an avoidance procedure.

AVERSIVE CONTROL OF BEHAVIOR

Operant attempts to modify behavior are, of course, not restricted to the employment of positive reinforcement or to the use of negative reinforcement. Punishing consequences, involving either the onset of an aversive stimulus or the withdrawal of one which is reinforcing, have been routinely employed to directly inhibit the elicitation of undesirable response patterns.

Bandura (1969) points out that there are two main objections to the use of punishment. Those who believe that unconscious forces, such as instincts, are primary determinants of behavior fear that punishment will dam up these impulses. They will then, theoretically, be forced to find alternative means of expression, perhaps resulting in behavior which is even less appropriate than that which was originally punished. Such concerns become irrelevant if behavior is seen as the product of its consequences. From the operant learning perspective, punishment does not suppress any impulse clamoring for expression, it merely introduces an outcome which is less than neutral. The behavior will then be abandoned in favor of one having a more reinforcing consequence.

The second objection raised against punishment is that it may produce a number of unwanted learned reaction tendencies in addition to the intended inhibition of the target behavior. This concern appears to be justified although the problems are not insurmountable. Because the potential side effects are different for positive and negative punishment, the two will be considered separately.

Presentation of aversive consequences

Positive punishment is exemplified by physical abuse, shock, or receipt of other noxious stimulation contingent upon behavior. Although Skinner would prefer the investigations of positive punishment to be conducted on a purely empirical basis, there have been theoretical explanations presented to account for the noted inhibitory effects.

The *conditioned emotionality* hypothesis suggests that response inhibition due to operant punishment is mediated by classical conditioning. Specifically, it is thought that strong emotional reactions become conditioned to the environmental context of severe punishment. Later, exposure to the same context results in emotional responding which disrupts the behavior previously punished. This line of reasoning is based upon the behavior-suppressing effect of presenting conditioned emotional stimuli. For example, if a green light is paired with shock and becomes capable of eliciting conditioned emotional responses, the presence of the green light will readily suppress eating behavior, even in a food-deprived animal. A variation of this idea put forth by Mowrer (1960) adds that among the contextual stimuli which may become conditioned emotional stimuli are the proprioceptive cues accompanying the punished response. From this point of view, any time the individual begins to make a previously-punished response, the correlated body sensations which have been associated with the past receipt of pain will generate behavior-disrupting emotional arousal. Mowrer's position therefore stresses that the locus of aversive control, at least in part, resides within the individual.

A somewhat more cognitive notion has been called the *discrimination hypothesis* by Holz and Azrin (1961). This stresses that punishment has an informational aspect which permits the individual to anticipate that on future occasions in the same situation the previously-punished response is again likely to result in unwanted aversive consequences.

Potential problems. Bandura (1969) lists five unwanted side effects which may arise from the implementation of positive punishment.

1. Generalization of conditioned inhibition. Recall that whenever a response is classically conditioned to a CS, other similar stimuli also automatically acquire the capacity to provoke the conditioned response, although perhaps to a lesser degree. This we called stimulus generalization. The same phenomenon may occur when emotional responses become conditioned to stimuli associated with punishment. That is, a variety of other stimuli similar to the CS may become capable of eliciting disruptive emotionality. This generalization is most likely to occur when the nature of the response-punishment contingencies are unclear, as when the punishing agent does not indicate exactly what response was instrumental in bringing on punishment. For example, if a parent beats a child for being a "bad boy," the child may come away with only uncertain or vague ideas as to the meaning of "bad"; he doesn't know what particular responses ought to be suppressed in order to circumvent future punishment. Because he is not able to discriminate between punished and non-punished responses, conditioned emotionality might generalize to a wide array of inappropriate situational and/or proprioceptive cues, and large segments of behavior thereby come to be suppressed.

On the presumption that punishment is in fact being administered in some systematic manner — the inconsistent administration of punishment makes discriminations virtually impossible — Bandura suggests that discrimination may be facilitated through the use of "verbal aids" (1969, p. 310). This simply involves articulating the particular responses which lead to punishing consequences and spelling out those which, while they may be similar, do not lead to punishment. For instance, a parent might punish a child for crayoning on the wall but also point out that a coloring book is an appropriate object in which to color. In addition, it would be well for the parent to reinforce appropriate behaviors similar to those which were punished, in order for the child to actually experience the different outcomes. Using such a strategy, the generalization of conditioned inhibition can largely be avoided.

2. Emotional conditioning. It is quite possible for any contextual event or object which is salient at the time of punishment to itself become a conditioned emotional stimulus. For instance, a child who is punished in the bathroom for soiling or wetting may acquire a conditioned emotional response to the very room which one must enter in order to elicit approved toileting behavior. The fear reduction which reinforces avoiding the bathroom then establishes a behavioral pattern which may be more undesirable than the originally punished "accident."

3. *Avoidance of punishing agents.* Just as the child may acquire the habit of avoiding the bathroom if that has come to be associated with punishment, so, too, might there develop an avoidance of the punishing agents. Bandura notes that "to the extent that negative sanctions foster fear and active avoidance of change agents, their opportunities to influence the behavior of others is reduced" (p. 312).

4. *Behavioral inflexibility.* When temporal discontinuities exist with respect to the kinds of consequences which may be expected to follow a behavior pattern, the early use of positive punishment may be, in the long run, counterproductive. In our society there is still a tendency for childhood and adolescent sexuality to be met with parental punishment. The suppressing effect of such sanctions may not be easily lifted when the time comes for sexuality to be a permitted form of expression and enjoyment. Appel (1961) has dramatically illustrated the enduring effects of punishment in animal research. A squirrel, if given a small number of shocks while eating, will thereafter suppress consummatory responses to the point of starving, despite the ready availability of food.

5. *Negative modeling.* Finally, Bandura reminds us that very often punishment is inflicted by parents in an attempt to suppress aggressive behavior in their children; unfortunately, the parent is unwittingly exemplifying the very behavior which is being punished — aggression. In the next chapter we will see the powerful effect which significant models have on our personality. At this time it is sufficient to point out that the child who observes his parents control him through punishment may well go out and employ similar strategies in order to control his peers; and he will probably meet with a level of success.

When punishment fails. There are basically two situations in which the application of aversive contingencies, positive punishment, may fail to suppress unwanted behavior. The first is when the punished response is simultaneously being reinforced. This frequently occurs when a child's disruptive behavior is being positively punished by an adult but is, at the same time, receiving attention from peers in the form of laughter or even admiration. The change agent must then work to either remove the simultaneously-occurring reinforcement or administer punishment of a severity which overrides the reinforcement. If the latter approach is taken, the risk is greater that some of the unwanted side effects of positive punishment, such as emotional conditioning, will arise because especially harsh consequences are being imposed.

The second situation in which the effects of punishment will be, at best, short lived, is when the individual does not possess alternative behavioral skills to obtain the reinforcement previously secured by the punished response. In such a circumstance punishment may have a temporary suppressive effect but, lacking any other vehicle for the gaining of reinforcement, the individual may have little choice but to revert to his old patterns. Bandura observed that, "This is one reason that punishment is ineffective in modifying the anti-social patterns of delinquents and adult offenders who lack alternative pro-social modes of response for acquiring possessions that they value highly" (1969, p. 315).

The very obvious solution to this second dilemma is for the change agent to reinforce alternative ways of behaving at the same time as the old ways are being suppressed through punishment. It is best when the reinforced response is one which is incompatible with that being punished. For example, if a child is disruptive at the dinner table as a vehicle for obtaining parental attention, punishment will be best employed if the parents are prepared to also offer the same reinforcement, attention, for more approved behaviors, such as for eating properly and engaging in polite conversation. In this way the child is not being deprived of that which he seeks; attention is now simply being made contingent upon a response which is incompatible with being punished. The result is that everyone gets what he wants, the child receives attention and the parents do not have to contend with meal-time disturbances.

The clinical use of punishment-reinforcement treatment packages is widespread. For instance, it is common to use positive punishment in order to suppress the severe self-destructive behaviors sometimes manifested by highly-disturbed children, particularly in those cases where irreparable self-mutilation is a distinct possibility. It is usual for the punishment to be employed as an adjunct to reinforcement. In one such case study, Tate and Baroff (1966) treated self-injurious behavior in a partially blind psychotic boy by withdrawing physical contact and stopping conversation whenever a destructive behavior, such as head-banging, was attempted or committed; they were using negative punishment. If no self-injurious act was attempted for three seconds, physical contact and conversation was reinstated, thus providing positive reinforcement. This complex treatment effected a dramatic decrease in the frequency of self-injurious behaviors; these responses dropped from about six per minute to less than one per minute. Subsequently, in an effort to eliminate the head-banging completely, a behavior which threatened further vision loss, Tate and Baroff administered shock contingent upon head banging; they were now using positive punishment. This second phase of treatment also involved a reinforcement component, in that the boy was verbally praised and given affection for appropriate behaviors. Overall, the treatment resulted in the complete elimination of self-destructive behavior. The child, once restrained in bed for periods in order to be protected from himself, was able to fully and freely participate in all activities.

Withdrawal of positive reinforcers

This form of aversive control, negative punishment, is probably much more routinely employed than positive punishment. In general, whenever a response is instrumental in bringing about some deprivation, the procedure of negative punishment is being implemented. Common examples include monetary fines for motor vehicle violations, and denial of TV privileges because of dinner-time histrionics. The suppressive effects of negative punishment accrue because the aversive outcomes override the positive reinforcers which have heretofore been maintaining the behavior. Because of this necessity of "tipping the scales" in the aversive direction, as with positive punishment, negative punishment will be most effective when reinforcing consequences of the punished behavior are discovered and eliminated. Even when behavioral suppression is accomplished, a permanent modification of the behavior pattern is most likely to occur if the change agent can provide the punished individual with alternative behavioral vehicles for acquiring the same reinforcement.

The advantage of negative punishment over positive punishment is that unwanted side effects are unlikely to develop; since the denial of reinforcement does not involve pain or high levels of fear, emotional conditioning will not occur. There will, therefore, be no generalization of conditioned inhibition, and the punished agent is less likely to actively avoid the change agent. In fact, when parents use withdrawal of love or attention as an aversive consequence to a child's unwanted behavior, it is typical for the child to seek out the parent in an attempt to regain what has been temporarily denied.

Probably the most frequently employed negative punishment procedure is some variation of the old-fashioned, but effective, "stand in the corner" routine; psychologists have labeled this "time-out". The basic time-out strategy is to send the punished individual to a place which is as free of social reinforcers as possible. The successful implementation of time-out depends upon three factors, according to Morris (1976). It is crucial that the time-out *not* be inadvertently made too reinforcing. For example, many toys and interesting diversions are usually present in a child's bedroom, so that location for a time-out period is usually a mistake. Alternatively, even when the child is sent to a boring place, such as a stairwell, the consequence may not be aversive to the child if it permits escape from a noxious situation. Many children will happily suffer through time-out if it means they get away with not eating an unpalatable dinner. The second recommendation is that time-out be of short duration, no more than a few minutes for children, and, if possible, its termination should be contingent upon the ceasing of the unwanted behavior. Consistent with this is the statement, "Go to your room and don't come back until you calm down!" With this, the parent is imposing a punishment contingent upon disruptive behavior and lifting the punishment contingent upon quiet behaviors; thus, behaviors incompatible with punished disruptive ones are being simultaneously reinforced. Finally, Morris warns against imposing time-out within an hysterical context. Many children enjoy seeing a parent become agitated and this reinforcement may override any potential suppressive effects of time-out, thereby maintaining the punished behavior. Consequently, time-out should be imposed in a very matter-of-fact way so that the procedure doesn't degenerate into a "three-ring circus." As with any operant behavior modification procedure, favorable results come more easily when efforts are made to tie consequences clearly to specific target behaviors; being sent to the corner for being a "bad boy" is much too imprecise.

EXTINCTION

Reductions in the frequency with which a response is emitted may be accomplished with an *extinction* procedure. In operant conditioning, extinction refers to the repeated elicitation of a response without it being followed by the reinforcement which has been maintaining it. Bandura draws a distinction between the removal of positive reinforcers, such as time-out, and extinction, in the following way: "In extinction, consequences that ordinarily follow the behavior are simply discontinued; in punishment, behavior results in the application of aversive consequences through forfeiture of positive reinforcers" (1969, p. 338).

To this we add that the positive reinforcers which are forfeited in a negative punishment procedure are not those which have been maintaining the punished behaviors; rather, the suppressive effect of aversive forfeiture is pitted against the effect of the reinforcers which otherwise maintain the behavior. When a child disturbs a classroom in order to gain teacher attention, the denial of recess privileges can be seen as negative reinforcement; recess has not been the reinforcement responsible for the behavior disorder. If, on the other hand, the teacher ignores the child's disturbances, those responses are being subjected to extinction because they are not yielding their usual attentional pay-off.

A number of explanations for the effects of extinction procedures have been offered, all of which are irrelevant to Skinner's atheoretical orientation. Hull (1943) proposed a two factor theory in this regard. He hypothesized that repeated non-reinforced response elicitation produces a fatigue-like state which serves to counteract the tendency to respond; this results in a lower response rate. The response-produced inhibition, called *reactive inhibition,* should theoretically dissipate after responding has stopped. Response rates therefore increase subsequent to a period of "rest" following a series of extinction trials. The phenomenon of *spontaneous recovery* is partly supportive of this supposition. Spontaneous recovery refers to the increased strength of a response which has been subject to extinction after the passage of a period of time during which the response is not elicited. For example, if a pigeon learns to peck at a disc at an operant rate of five per second under a VR schedule, the behavior will decrease and finally cease after a string of non-reinforced pecks. If, at this point, the bird is removed from the conditioning chamber for several hours, upon its return the pigeon will again exhibit rapid pecking. If no reinforcements are obtained, the behavior will again fade; another placement in the chamber after some hours will again result in the reinstitution of the pecking behavior. However, each time the bird is returned to the chamber, presumably after the "fatigue" has dissipated, the response rates systematically decline until a point is reached where no spontaneous recovery is observed at all. Hull's notion of reactive inhibition does not account for this fact.

In order to explain the decline of spontaneous recovery effects, Hull also postulated the production of *conditioned inhibition* as a by-product of extinction. It is presumed that reactive inhibition, when high, constitutes an aversive drive state. The response of "stopping responding," therefore, is reinforced since it is followed by the reduction of reactive inhibition. Thus, the organism is learning to "not respond."

While these ideas of Hull are theoretically elegant, they are not able to account for all extinction phenomena. In particular, reactive and conditioned inhibition seem out of place when trying to understand extinction which occurs without responding. A number of investigators have described the phenomenon of *latent extinction,* in which the extinction process is speeded if an animal is first repeatedly exposed to an empty food box before ever being subjected to actual extinction trials. In addition, Bandura (1969) describes the process of "vicarious" extinction, whereby an operant response will extinguish if a person simply has the opportunity to observe someone else undergo extinction trials.

A second major point of view regarding the nature of extinction is known as the *discrimination hypothesis* (Bandura, 1969). This position is much more cognitively-oriented than that of Hull. The discrimination hypothesis asserts that behavior persists for a while, even though reinforcement has been discontinued, "because the subject has failed to recognize that previous reinforcement contingencies are no longer in effect" (p. 360). The different rates of extinction which are typically observed consequent to the various schedules of reinforcement are consistent with this hypothesis. For instance, it is well-documented that behavior which has been maintained by a CRF schedule is least resistant to extinction. Presumably, this is because a shift from continuous reinforcement to no reinforcement at all is so obvious that the responder can hardly fail to notice the change. Intermittent schedules, which all result in behaviors more resistant to extinction than a CRF schedule, also show differences among themselves on this dimension. In particular, all else being equal, VI and VR schedules of reinforcement maintain behaviors which are much more resistant to extinction than behaviors maintained by FI and FR schedules. Consistent wtih the discrimination hypothesis, these phenomena are interpreted to mean that irregular reinforcement is least easily discriminable from the onset of a series of extinction trials. In contrast, FI and FR schedules, which yield reinforcement on a regular basis, are relatively easy to discriminate from extinction. Finally, several investigators have conducted research illustrating how rates of extinction vary as a function of the manipulated discriminability between a reinforcement and an extinction phase. For example, Bridger and Mandel (1965) showed that a response acquired on a partial reinforcement schedule can be made to extinguish more rapidly than one acquired under a CRF schedule if the subject is informed prior to the onset of the extinction trials that reinforcement will no longer be available.

Extinction of positively reinforced behaviors

In order to extinguish a behavior which has resulted in positive reinforcement, all that needs to be done is to discontinue the reinforcement. While this may sound straightforward, in practice it may be rather complicated; the skill of the change agent in the practice of behavioral assessment techniques can be crucial to the success of an extinction program.

One must first discover the context within which the unwanted behavior occurs. A naive observer may say, "He always is aggressive!" However, closer inspection invariably reveals that the behavior is only elicited when specific S^Ds are present. Second, and more important, one must ascertain what reinforcements are instrumental in maintaining the behavior. This can best be done by observing the natural consequences of the behavior. Among these consequences will be found the reinforcement(s).

If such a behavioral analysis incorrectly identifies a consequence as the reinforcement of aggressive behavior, its withdrawal will, of course, not produce extinction.

Assuming that there has been an accurate identification of reinforcers, the conduct of an extinction program may still involve some rough sailing. It is typical, when extinction trials begin, for the target behavior to temporarily become more frequent or extreme in its emission. It is as if the individual is disbelieving of the new outcome, no reinforcement, and feels he must try harder to bring forth that to which he is accustomed. This transient intensification of the target behavior is most pronounced when it has a history of being continually reinforced.

By way of illustration, consider a child who tries to earn parental attention through the prolongation of bedtime activities. This may involve repeated requests for water, blankets, a night light, etc., and ultimately culminate every night in a crying spell to which the parents respond by reading a story. In this case extinction would probably necessitate ignoring all such behaviors; after the child is placed in bed, all requests and crying should be left unattended. At this juncture, the child may think that the parents have not heard his calls, and he may cry more loudly and more frantically than he did previously. The critical point has now been reached. If the parents are firm in their resolve, what has become worse will soon become better. In other words, the child will "get the message" that such bedtime behaviors no longer yield reinforcement and they will rapidly extinguish. If, on the other hand, the parents "give in," the child's extreme behavior is immediately placed on a partial reinforcement schedule, and will be that much more difficult to extinguish should future attempts be made to do so.

Extinction procedures are least likely to be successful when the change agent does not have complete control over reinforcing consequences. For example, if one parent ignores the bedtime antics of a child but the other does not, little behavioral change may occur. At best, the unresponsive parent will come to function as an S^Δ. In addition, even where extinction procedures are successfully utilized with respect to a target behavior, there is no guarantee that the subject will engage in more acceptable behavioral means to gain the lost reinforcement. The change agent may find that the new strategy is worse than that which was extinguished. Thus, as with the use of punishment, overall satisfaction with program results is best assured if an effort is made to provide the reinforcement for desirable behaviors at the same time as extinction is being imposed. In other words, if a child is being deprived of bedtime attention in the service of extinguishing unwanted bedtime activity, it would be best if heavy doses of attention were offered contingent upon other of the child's behaviors at a more appropriate time of the day.

The use of extinction plus reinforcement operant treatment packages in clinical cases is widespread. For instance, lethargy among chronic psychiatric patients is frequently improperly dealt with by staff encouragement to participate in activities.

Schaefer and Martin (1975) demonstrated that these expressions of encouragement may be functioning as reinforcers which actually help to maintain low levels of patient participation. When psychiatric nurses offered attention contingent upon patient participation in activities and ignored non-participation, the level of behavioral involvement by the patients rose dramatically.

Extinction of escape and avoidant behavior

The reduction of behavior which has been maintained by negative reinforcement can be accomplished in a manner similar to that outlined for positively reinforced behaviors. The crucial element is that response elicitation not be followed by the reinforcement.

If a dog is trained to escape shock by pressing a bar, that response will rapidly fade if it no longer results in shock termination. The same holds if the bar press response has been instrumental in avoiding the onset of shock, but no longer functions in that capacity and shock becomes, therefore, unavoidable. At the human level, this extinction procedure can be illustrated by the child who has acquired a repertoire of aggressive behaviors which serve to keep other children from disturbing him. If conditions change, and the child becomes involved with a group of older, stronger, and/or generally very assertive peers, the aggressive responses may no longer function to escape and avoid the annoyances of others. These aggressive patterns may then quickly extinguish (Rachlin, 1976).

The speed with which extinction occurs when using this first procedure can be explained in terms of the ease with which reinforcement trials are distinguishable from extinction trials. When an organism who has been trained to avoid or escape shock by pressing a bar finds that the response is ineffective in terminating or putting off the aversive event, it should be quite obvious that something has changed; the old response is simply not "working" the way it used to.

One of the problems with this method of reducing the frequency of a previously negatively reinforced behavior is that the extinction may involve a very active suppression of the behavior. In fact, it is often quite difficult to reestablish instrumental responding after exposing a subject to a series of extinction trials which consist of inescapable or unavoidable aversive stimulation. Seligman reports that dogs which have been subjected to inescapable shock will lie down and quietly whine instead of trying to terminate the aversive condition. Seligman refers to this phenomenon as *learned helplessness*, "When an organism has experienced trauma it cannot control, its motivation to respond in the face of later trauma wanes" (1975, p. 22). Similarly, a child who finds himself helpless in the face of assertive figures may acquire the habit of just "taking it," believing that nothing he can do will prevent their behavior.

The second way of extinguishing a negatively reinforced behavior is much less rapid, and is only applicable to avoidance behaviors. The procedure involves no longer presenting the aversive stimulus which the animal has worked to avoid. For example, suppose a dog is trained to jump over a barrier in order to avoid shock whenever a light comes on. If the shock is turned off, the jumping behavior will very gradually extinguish. The slowness with which extinction proceeds in this case can again be explained in terms of the discrimination hypothesis. Specifically, on a reinforcement trial the dog jumps and does not get shocked; on an extinction trial precisely the same thing is happening from the animal's perspective. Consequently, it may take considerable time before the animal "realizes" that he no longer has to jump, since there is nothing to be avoided. Similarly, the child who uses aggressive behaviors as a means of avoiding the disturbing intrusions of peers may persist in this interpersonal approach even if he enters a peer group of unassertive children who may be younger than he. So long as the child continues to "bully" these peers, he will never permit himself to find out that they do not present a threat.

COMPARISON OF CLASSICAL AND OPERANT CONDITIONING

There are three dimensions on which Kanfer and Phillips contrasted classical and operant conditioning (1970, p. 97). The first has to do with "locus of control." In classical conditioning, the receipt of reinforcement, the UCS, is *non-contingent* with respect to either the UR or the CR. It does not matter what the organism does, on an acquisition trial the CS will always be followed by the UCS and on an extinction trial the reinforcement is withheld. Thus, outcome is completely controlled by the change agent, and not by the subject. In contrast, the subject in an operant or instrumental conditioning procedure does have control over the outcome because reinforcement is contingent upon a response. If the "correct" response is emitted, reinforcement is the outcome; if the response is not made then there is no reinforcement.

A second dimension on which classical and operant conditioning have been said to differ is that of "the response systems of the organism for which each type of learning can be employed" (p. 99). Historically, classical conditioning has been tied to the modification of S-R bonds involving autonomic or involuntary responses, such as emotional or reflexive responses. In fact, for a considerable time it was believed that the only way in which involuntary responses could be conditioned was via classical procedures. At the same time, operant conditioning was viewed as the method for the modification of voluntary behaviors involving the skeletal-muscular system. These distinctions now appear to have been made prematurely. Today there is no doubt that autonomic responses are susceptible to modification through the application of operant techniques. In addition, we have reviewed evidence showing that the course of acquisition and extinction of classically conditioned autonomic responses is subject to major alteration as a function of subjects' voluntary, cognitive processes.

The third case for distinguishing between classical and operant conditioning rests upon apparent differences in the operations employed. In classical conditioning, behavior modification is based upon making a neutral stimulus capable of response evocation through its repeated pairing with an unconditioned stimulus. This was illustrated by McGuire and Vallance's (1964) treatment of a fetish. You will recall that they had the patient engage in fetishistic fantasies and when his images of the fetish object were clearly visualized, the CS, shock, the US, was administered. Through the repeated pairing of imagined fetishistic stimuli with an unconditioned aversive stimulus, the fetish object acquired the capacity to provoke a CR, avoidance. Thus, classical conditioning was responsible for a successful treatment. However, it would not be difficult to reinterpret the favorable results of McGuire and Vallance's aversive classical conditioning therapy in terms of operant conditioning procedures. Specifically, one can look at what they did from a Skinnerian perspective and see a response, the production of fetishistic fantasies, being followed by positive punishment, shock, on a continuous schedule. This sequence has the expected effect of inhibiting the future occurrence of fetishistic fantasies.

This particular case is not an isolated example of a behavior modification procedure which is not clearly identifiable as either classical or operant conditioning. In fact, because there is usually some time lag between the presentation of a CS and the onset of the US in classical conditioning procedures, it is routine for responses occurring in that interval to become operantly conditioned, with the US serving as the operant reinforcement. One of the responses emitted in the CS-US interval happens to be the CR. Thus, a typical sequence in a classical conditioning experiment is:

$$\text{bell (CS)} \longrightarrow \text{salivation (CR)} \longrightarrow \text{food (US)}$$

$$\text{time} \longrightarrow$$

If one chooses to focus in on the S-R sequence, as Pavlov did, a response, salivation, is seen as being evoked by a stimulus, bell. If one takes an operant perspective and neglects the stimuli which evoke responses, what is left is an S-R sequence; a salivation response is emitted and then followed by positive reinforcement, food.

Kanfer and Phillips point out that "the purity of the instrumental or operant conditioning paradigm is similarly a fiction" (1970, p. 96). Any time a response-consequence sequence repeats itself, it does so within a stimulus context which is referred to as an S^D. Because the S^D is repeatedly associated with the consequence of the response, reinforcement or punishment, it can quickly come to function as a CS. For example, if eating is repeatedly followed by shock, the punishing consequence serves to inhibit the eating response. In addition, all of the stimulus cues surrounding the eating behavior, the presence of food, the conditioning chamber, the sounds of the apparatus, become conditioned emotional stimuli which a considerable body of research has shown to be capable of disrupting eating behavior. Therefore, it would appear that the same procedure can be interpreted from either a classical or an operant conditioning perspective. In summary, modern behaviorists have not arrived at a clear-cut answer to the question of how classical and operant conditioning are different, or how they are the same.

EVALUATION OF SITUATIONISM

There was a period during which behaviorists became vigorously engaged in polemic exchanges with representatives of other schools of thought. The famous Rogers-Skinner debate on the control of human behavior is a case in point (1956).

Despite apparent attention to particular matters, the overriding issue undoubtedly centered on the legitimacy of behaviorism as one of the three primary forces in psychology. That struggle has passed. While articles continue to appear speaking to the relative merits of this or that viewpoint with respect to any number of matters, there is no doubt that behaviorism has "arrived." Today, many of the most influential psychologists would be willing to testify that the strength of contemporary psychology lies in modern behaviorism. Even those who identify with psychoanalytic and phenomenological orientations now find it difficult to remain unimpressed by what the conditioning psychologists have wrought.

The accomplishments of classical and operant conditioning advocates most assuredly derive from their explicit commitment to empiricism. If there is a dogma, it is that the discovery of facts is paramount and that this is to be achieved via the scientific method of investigation. The result has been an incredibly large accumulation of correlations and probability statements which reflect a greater level of control over behavior than has ever before been possible. Nevertheless, strict empiricism in the most conservative behaviorist tradition is not without its drawbacks.

Probably the most serious criticism leveled at behaviorism and at its chief proponent, Skinner, is that operant "learning theory," as it is so often *incorrectly* referred to, is not a theory at all. That is, Skinner is loathe to go beyond the level of description; he will not speculate about what goes on within the organism's head. Why a reinforcement is reinforcing or a punishment is punishing are not given serious attention. Even the issue of causality is ignored; notions of "x causing y" are replaced by straightforward presentations of observed "functional relationships." For example, "A specific change in a schedule of reinforcement is functionally related to a specific change in rate, strength, or form of responding." Rotter has said that, for Skinnerians, "statistical relationships are both the immediate and ultimate goal of science" (1954, p. 6).

Skinner defends his approach by asserting that, "Theories are fun. But it is possible that the most rapid progress toward an understanding of learning may be made by research which is not designed to test theories" (1959, p. 69). The history of psychology reveals that Skinner may be correct in believing that major gains are not always made by becoming prematurely attached to a theoretical position. The great contribution of Pavlov has proven to be his description of a process of conditioning, not his hypothetical neurological explanations which faded from the scene. Similarly, whereas Dollard and Miller's (1950) attempt to translate psychoanalytic theory into a drive reduction conditioning model was once hailed as a major theoretical contribution, there are many today who view their effort as a negligible gain for either psychoanalysis or for Hullian learning theory. In point of fact, neither camp was pleased with the product, so there were few around who made efforts to build upon it. As for Hullian learning theory itself, we have already discussed how it fell from an impressive peak of popularity only to be overshadowed by the influence of operant conditioning which, in many respects, is little more than what Hull had to say and minus the hypothetico-deductive theorizing.

In summary, then, Skinner eschews theory in the sense of "any explanation of an observed fact which appeals to events taking place somewhere else, at some other level of observation, described in different terms, and measured, if at all, in different dimensions" (1959, p. 39). He nevertheless "does not exclude the possibility of theory in another sense. Beyond the collection of uniform relationships lies the need for a formal representation of the data reduced to a minimal number of terms" (p. 69). This kind of "theory," it should be noted, does not arise before experimentation; it develops after the facts have been collected and organized. In addition, such a "theory" is still limited to descriptive generalizations of empirical propositions; explanatory, theoretical propositions, usually considered to be the hallmark of traditional theory, are still shunned. We leave it to the reader to decide whether Skinner is to be faulted for not having sufficient appreciation of the roles of theory as these were presented in Chapter 16, or whether the gains to be had from adopting an atheoretical perspective outweigh the advantages of functioning within a theoretical framework.

Other accusations of weakness in the behaviorist orientation may also be seen as deriving from the penchant for empiricism which abounds among these psychologists. For example, it has been argued that, while classical and operant conditioning principles may be very adequate descriptions of the range of phenomena with which behaviorists deal, this range is unfortunately too limited. In other words, behaviorism is not maximally inclusive; serious considerations of the biological and psychological correlates of learning processes have been omitted. Learning must surely involve neurological and/or biochemical alteration, yet little is said on this matter. Similarly, the importance of cognitive variables are, at most, paid cursory lip service. These gaps exist because, at present, neurological and cognitive phenomena are not as accessible to direct, controlled observation as are overt behaviors and situations. The same can be said of all so-called "internal" determinants of behavior, including instinct, drive, trait, and character. Bowers has commented, "Thus, while the layman may view a person as 'honest,' a situationist is apt to retort that telling the truth is under the control of the circumstances in which it occurs" (1973, p. 309). In other words, the focus is not on what the person is, but on the condition which sets the occasion for a response. In another example of the way in which situationists are thought to be unreasonably biased in their view of human behavior, Bowers asks us to consider the implications of a recent review which revealed that operantly conditioned behaviors return to pre-training levels among patients subsequent to the termination of treatment. "Should this characteristic relapse be attributed to the patient's post-treatment environment (as typically is done by behaviorists), or to some problematic condition of the subject that impairs his ability to function in an environment that does not programmatically reinforce his behavior?" (p. 313).

What empiricism does lead behaviorists to study, and study very well, has not remained unscathed either. Their subject matter has been seen as too simplistic, too molecular, and too trivial. No one doubts at this point that, under controlled laboratory conditions, an organism having a very circumscribed learning history will manifest highly predictable changes in discrete response patterns as a function of specified stimulus variation. But how meaningful are such analyses to the description, if not the understanding, of complex behaviors at the human level? When a person frequently paints, or composes, or plays baseball, is it really possible to understand these activities in terms of chains of discrete responses elicited in the presence of S^Ds and maintained by extrinsic reinforcement? Bowers (1973) takes a more molar, internally-oriented viewpoint. He prefers to think of the person as having a level of skill, interest, and intrinsic enjoyment for the activity. "If it is argued that this account of the matter is simply an explanatory fiction, the very least we can say is that skills, interests, and enjoyment are no more fictional explanations of behavior than is the reinforcement inferred from the occurrence of behavior" (p. 313).

This brings us to another frequent point of contention; namely, the principles of conditioning are not nearly as non-inferential as they may at first appear to be. When an alteration in behavior is noted, it is taken as presumptive evidence that the situation has also become altered. The implicit assumption is that personality change cannot occur within an unchanging environment. On the other hand, when a change agent tries, and fails, to alter the environment in order to effect behavior modification, the inference is drawn that the situation has not really changed. A corollary of this inference is that stable personality characteristics cannot maintain their stability in the face of a changing environment. "In other words, if (truly) changed environments can only be inferred from changed behavior, then the potential circularity of the situationist model becomes actual and viscious" (Bowers, 1973, p. 317).

In terms of some of the more important formal criteria for an adequate theory of personality, atheoretical behaviorism does well. Probably more than in any other approach, there has been an effort to use operational constructs. Consequently, investigation has flourished despite there being no heuristic theoretical underpinning to spur it on.

The level of systematization within the set of principles which comprise classical and operant conditioning is impressive. However, we must keep in mind that the specified relationships are restricted, for the most part, to empirical propositions and do not involve theoretical propositions. This makes for very accurate prediction for situations and behaviors which are similar to those already studied. Prediction becomes far less precise when an attempt is made to deal with a unique circumstance. According to Hall and Lindzey, a strict behaviorist believes that "the laws of behavior can only be extrapolated to instances of the same type of behavior . . . the system contains no theoretical statements that imply more empirical assertions than those on which they have been built" (1970, p. 510).

Systematization also tends to break down when attempts are made to defend therapeutic operations as derivations of conditioning principles. In particular, the still-active debate surrounding the fundamental nature of Wolpe's systematic desensitization procedures exemplifies this problem. The most frequently-voiced objection is that the therapeutic actions do not systematically follow from classical conditioning principles; and, even if in part they do, so many things are going on in addition to a simple conditioning procedure that it has been virtually impossible to pin down the effective ingredients of systematic desensitization. Agreement seems to be unanimous, however, that systematic desensitization does what it claims to do, for whatever reason.

As a final point, we feel it is important to mention that behaviorism, preoccupied as it is with classical and operant conditioning, represents a position in the laboratory which is primarily concerned with process, not with content. The same principles of behavior acquisition and change are observed almost regardless of the specific response in question. In fact, the reponse has been little more than the necessary vehicle for studying process. Paradoxically, when behaviorism moved out of the laboratory and into the therapist's office, attention was paid to content more than in any other approach. While Freud and Rogers present one therapeutic process to be used regardless of the client in question, behaviorists have tailored their treatment programs to the particular behavioral problems presented by the individual client. This was reflected earlier in our presentation of systematic desensitization as the preferred behavior therapy for the alleviation of maladaptive avoidant behavior patterns, and in the prescription of covert sensitization or other aversive counter conditioning procedures for the treatment of maladaptive approach responses. Thus, the treatment process is individualized to the client and the nature of his presenting problem.

SUMMARY

In this second chapter on behaviorism-situationism, we focused upon operant conditioning. From this point of view, the future probability of behavior is a function of consequences which have followed that behavior on previous occasions. Four classes of consequences were described: positive and negative reinforcement, both serving to increase behavior probability; and positive and negative punishment, both associated with behavior inhibition.

The basic schedules of reinforcement were presented and their impact upon behavior detailed. In general, fixed schedules promote behavior which is less resistant to extinction than do variable schedules. Theoretical reasons for this and other operant conditioning phenomena, such as those having to do with superstitious behavior, were discussed. In addition, we briefly reviewed some application areas in which operant techniques have proven to be useful. These included marriage therapy, token economies, and programmed instruction.

Aversive control of behavior, through the presentation of aversive consequences and the withdrawal of reinforcements, was given careful attention. The undesirable side effects of the former procedure were explained. The use of extinction as a third behavior reduction strategy, and the pitfalls associated with it, were also discussed. The chapter concluded with a comparison of operant and classical conditioning and an evaluation of situationism.

TERMS TO KNOW

CHAPTER 21
Cognitive Learning Theory

This chapter is devoted to a presentation of recent major innovations in cognitive personality theorizing. In reviewing the accomplishments of Albert Bandura, Julian Rotter, Walter Mischel, Norman Endler, David Magnusson, and their co-workers the current vitality of personality as a sub-area of psychology will become apparent. By way of introduction, it is important to realize that these psychologists all emphasize the "O" in the S-O-R-C-K model of behavior. The importance of the "person" in personality is again being emphasized; covert processes, such as cognition, and stable personality characteristics, such as needs and traits, are accepted as legitimate topics for scientific personality investigation. It will be seen that each of the theoretical positions which follow reflects this trend in its own way, but the general theme is ever present.

OBSERVATIONAL LEARNING

In 1963, Bandura and Walters presented a "socio-behavioristic" personality theory in their book, *Social Learning and Personality Development*. Although they adopted a classical and operant conditioning perspective, they were critical of these learning processes for failing to account for the rapid acquisition of novel behaviors. For instance, in classical conditioning there are no new responses, only new stimuli capable of eliciting old responses. With operant techniques it is possible to shape novel behavior patterns but only with the speed that, according to Skinner, "a sculptor shapes a lump of clay . . . [and] at no point does anything emerge which is very different from what preceded it" (1953, p. 91).

It is the contention of Bandura and Walters (1963) that "imitation is an indispensable aspect of learning . . . [and that] the process of acquisition can be considerably shortened by the provision of social models" (p. 3). In other words, the process of *observational learning* was invoked to account for the speedy emergence of even very complex behavior patterns, such as that evidenced by a child who suddenly recites a nursery rhyme after having heard it once at some earlier time.

There are three unique features of observational learning which distinguish the process from classical and operant conditioning. First, it is not necessary that an overt response occur for there to be acquisition. Consequently, Bandura (1965a) designates observational learning as "no trial learning," because no overt responses are necessary on the learner's part. Second, acquisition does not depend upon the provision of immediate reinforcement, as is the case with both classical and operant conditioning. Finally, there is an explicit utilization of cognitive processes to theoretically explain the link between exposure to a modeling display and the subsequent imitation of observed behavior. While research in the areas of classical and operant conditioning has revealed that cognitive factors can influence the processes of acquisition and extinction, in neither case is cognition seen as a necessary ingredient for learning.

Bandura presents a "contiguity-mediational" explanation of the observational learning process. He theorizes that "transitory perceptual phenomena produce relatively enduring, retrievable images of modeled sequences of behavior. Later, reinstatement of imaginal mediators serves as a guide for reproduction of matching responses" (1969, p. 133). For example, a child observing her mother prepare a bowl of breakfast cereal may establish an image of the mother's actions which, on some later morning, will be recalled. This "retrieved" image then serves to guide the child in her first attempt at imitating the mother's cereal preparation.

Added to this is the idea that the observer's perceptual responses "become sequentially associated and centrally integrated on the bases of temporal contiguity of stimulation" (p. 133). This means that the discrete images which are established during observational learning maintain a temporal association to each other corresponding to the sequence of the observed events on which they are based. Consequently, the entire image sequence can be invoked, in its proper order, through the presentation of a discrete stimulus corresponding to just one constituent image of the sequence. For example, when we are having difficulty remembering a melody, it is common practice to try to come up with the first two or three notes; once this has been achieved, the entire tune is usually recalled with ease. Similarly, hearing the name of a person may be sufficient to provoke images which correspond to lengthy observational sequences of that person. As a third example, most students know that the recall of long passages of academic material can be easily accomplished if it is verbally coded in some short-hand way. For instance, the mnemonic device of remembering just one long word, each letter standing for the author of a different research project, has assisted many graduate students in examinations. Unfortunately, things do not always go as Bandura says they should and, occasionally, a student may be seen handing in a blank paper and walking out of the room in despair, mumbling "supercalifragilisticexpialidocious."

The contiguity-mediational explanation of observational learning phenomena is theorized to involve four essential observer processes.

Attentional Processes. It is evident that for observational learning to occur the observer must attend to a modeling display. If there is no attention, then there can be no later imitation. Three categories of attention-controlling variables influence attentional processes: *properties of the modeling display itself, observer characteristics,* and *incentive conditions.*

With respect to the first category, properties of the modeling display, complexity is an important component; if a modeling display is too complicated or unfolds too quickly, the observer will be unable to attend to all relevant details. Bandura notes, "Observational learning will necessarily be limited and fragmented" under such conditions (1969, p. 138). Discernability is also thought to be an important property of the modeling display. When the key elements of a display "stand out," they are more likely to become the object of attention than when they are embedded in a complex array of trivial stimuli. For example, in demonstrating how to operate an automobile, the driving teacher may first verbally highlight the crucial elements of driving — two hands on the wheel, right foot on the gas, etc. — because he does not want these points to later become lost in a morass of particulars which might include his posture and other incidental movements. Finally, the personal characteristics of the model have been found to significantly affect attentional processes; models who are deemed attractive and/or competent command our attention more than models who do not possess these qualities.

The second set of attention-controlling variables has to do with *observer characteristics*. Important in this regard is the observer's own reinforcement history. Someone who has been reinforced for matching behaviors tends to pay more attention to a model than one who lacks such a history. Zigler (1966) believes that mental retardates are one group whose social learning history induces a low expectation of favorable outcomes as a function of self-reliant behavior; instead, retardates anticipate a higher likelihood of reinforcement if they imitate the solutions of others. This Zigler refers to as *outer-directed* problem-solving strategy (p. 99). As a consequence, retardates are typically very prone to attend to the behavior of others, presumably in the service of using those behaviors as a guide for their own. In general, people of low self-esteem, low competence, and those who are characterized by dependency are most likely to enthusiastically attend to modeling displays.

Incentive conditions are seen by Bandura as the third category of factors which influence attentional processes. "Persons who are informed in advance that they will later be asked to reproduce a given model's responses and rewarded in terms of the number of elements performed correctly would be expected to pay much closer attention to relevant modeling stimuli than those persons who are exposed to the same modeled events without any predisposition to observe and to learn them" (1969, p. 137). Incentive conditions are most important, and can easily override the influence of both model and observer characteristics.

Retention Processes. The second observer process basic to Bandura's observational learning is the retention of modeled events. "In order to reproduce social behavior without the continued presence of external modeling cues, a person must retain the original observational inputs in some symbolic form" (1969, pp. 138-139).

Retention is thought to depend upon two representational systems, one imaginal and the other verbal. Modeling stimuli may be centrally represented in the form of images, as was previously mentioned; however, the speed of complex observational learning, and the long-term retention of modeling displays, theoretically depend heavily upon *verbal* coding. Bandura (1969) makes the point that most cognitively-regulated complex behavior is mediated by verbal rather than visual guides. Instead of memorizing the picture of a map to my home, guests unfamiliar with its location are simply and efficiently programmed to get there by verbal instructions. In an empirical test of the importance of verbal representations for observational learning, Bandura, Grusec and Menlove (1966) had children observe a complex modeling display under one of three conditions: simple attention, verbalizing novel responses as they were performed by the model, or counting while watching the display. It was found that the children who verbalized novel responses were best able to imitate that which they had observed, while the children who were forced to engage in a competing verbal activity, counting, were the least able.

It has been said that performance is not necessary for observational learning; however, Bandura feels that retention is enhanced if the observer has the opportunity to practice what has been modeled. "Rehearsal operations effectively stabilize and strengthen acquired responses" (1969, p. 139). Rehearsal tends to focus attention more strongly on important elements of the modeling display than passive observation. It also serves to make salient incorrectly coded aspects of the display so that appropriate alterations can be effected. It should be pointed out that effective rehearsal does not have to be overt; when it is inconvenient or impractical to actually practice, covert rehearsal "may likewise enhance the retention of acquired matching responses" (p. 139).

Motor reproduction processes. Motor reproduction processes are the third major component of Bandura's (1969) cognitive mediational explanation of modeling phenomena. It is not enough to attend to a display and then to retain it. The centrally coded material must be eventually utilized as a guide for overt behavior. If the behavior called for simply consists of a new organization of already well-practiced component responses, then the motor reproduction will come easily. If some necessary motor components are novel to the person, then the observation of these elements may have to be repeated before smooth motor reproduction of the entire sequence is possible. In some cases, physical or other limitations make it virtually impossible for the observer to ever behaviorally reproduce a modeling display, despite having paid careful attention and having formed accurate symbolic representations.

Incentive and motivational processes. "A person may acquire and retain modeled events and possess the capabilities for skillful execution of modeled behavior, but the learning may rarely be activated into overt performance if negative sanctions or unfavorable incentive conditions [exist]" (1969, p. 142).

With this statement, Bandura is making the very important distinction between *acquisition* and *performance*. One may never know that observational learning has taken place unless appropriate incentives are offered which make it worthwhile for the individual to manifest that which has been acquired.

In an experiment which clearly illustrates the significance of the distinction between acquisition and performance, Bandura (1965b) had three groups of children observe a film in which a model exhibited four novel aggressive responses. One group saw the filmed model severely punished for his aggressive actions; the second group observed the model receiving verbal approval and food for his behavior; and the third group saw the model's behavior ignored. While viewing the film, the children themselves did not perform the model's responses, nor did they receive any reinforcement. Thus, if learning was to occur it could only be of the "no-trial" sort. After viewing the film, all the children were given the opportunity, although no particular incentive, to exhibit "motor reproduction" of the modeling display. Children who saw the model-punished film exhibited the fewest matching responses, and there were no differences in matching between the model-reinforced and no-consequence treatments.

If the experiment were stopped at this juncture, one might conclude that the model-punished group learned the least. However, the procedure was carried one very important step further. All children were now offered incentives for accurate imitative behavior. This provided sufficient motivation for the children, regardless of treatment group, to attempt motor reproduction of the modeling display. The result was that between-group differences in mean number of matched behaviors disappeared. The children who had seen the model-punished film displayed, on the average, more than 3.5 of the four novel aggressive behaviors which had been depicted on the film, in contrast to a mean of about 1.5 previously found for this group. They thereby equalled the accuracy of matching exhibited by the children who had viewed the model-reinforced and no-consequence films.

Bandura and Walters (1963) conclude from these findings "that the *acquisition* of imitative responses results primarily from the contiguity of sensory events, whereas response consequences to the model or to the observer have a major influence only on the *performance* of imitatively learned responses" (p. 57).

As the influence of incentive and motivational processes upon motoric reproduction are discussed by Bandura, it becomes clear that performance is seen as being under the control of variables which are deemed important in operant conditioning, specifically, reinforcements and punishments. What is unique to Bandura's socio-behavioristic theory is that current consequence expectations are what determines the probability of a response, not the actual punishment-reinforcement history which is so crucial to strict Skinnerians. The person's own history, his observations of the consequences experienced by others, and other available information pertaining to the probable receipt of punishment or reinforcement combine to determine these expectancies for reinforcement and/or punishment as a consequence of imitating a modeling display. In summary, Bandura's theory is much more cognitive than operant conditioning and, with observational learning, Bandura is explaining the origin of emitted operants.

The effects of modeling upon behavior

Viewing a modeling display can have a variety of behavioral outcomes, their nature being determined by the modeled consequences and by the observer's own social learning history. These outcomes are categorized by Bandura (1969) as the *establishment of new response patterns,* also known as *modeling effects, extinction, inhibition, disinhibition,* and *response facilitation.*

Modeling Effects. The previously-discussed research by Bandura (1965b), in which children observed an aggressive model display four novel responses and then exhibited matching behavior, illustrates the fact that new responses can be acquired easily through simple observation.

There is also evidence that the acquisition of more complex behavior patterns are, at least in part, attributable to observational processes. In particular, observational learning is implicated by Bandura in language development: "Children can construct an almost infinite variety of sentences that they have never heard. Consequently, instead of imitating and memorizing specific utterances they have heard, children learn sets of rules, on the basis of which they can generate unlimited number of grammatical sentences" (1969, p. 149). Thus, the acquisition of words and syntaxic structures, but not necessarily the sentences themselves, are seen as rooted in the observation of "verbalizing models."

In an experiment whose findings are supportive of Bandura's position, Liebert, Odon, Hill, and Huff (1969) exposed preschoolers, second graders, and teenagers to a model who was rewarded for talking either in the typical English rule form of preposition-article-noun — "The man was *at the door:*" —, or in the novel form of article-noun-preposition — "The man was *the door at.*" It was found that the oldest children were responsive to having observed the new grammatical rule form, eliciting much higher rates of new-form sentences than did the younger two groups of children.

Naturalistic studies also provide evidence for the role of observational learning in language acquisition. For instance, the speech of young children is typically only partially correct in its grammatical form. Brown and Bellugi (1964) observed that about 30% of the time adults will repeat the child's syntaxically weak sentence in a more complex and correct form, placing stress on those elements of the sentence which were left out or distorted by the child. Thus, it appears that parents go out of their way to provide appropriate verbal displays of grammatically well-formed sentences.

One other illustrative area in which observational learning may play an important role is in the acquisition of *self-controlling* behaviors, including self-reinforcing and self-punishing responses. Bandura and Kupers (1964) had a group of children play a bowling game, in which scores from five to 30 could be earned, with either an adult or a peer model. The children began the game with an accessible supply of candy which they could draw from at will. In one experimental condition, the model made self-approving comments and drew upon the supply of candy whenever his score exceeded 20; the model took no candy and emitted self-punitive comments when his score fell below the apparently self-imposed cut-off. The second experimental treatment was identical, except that the criterion for success established by the model was less demanding, with the cut-off between self-reinforcement and self-punishment set at 10. The control group of subjects played the game in isolation.

Children's patterns of self-reinforcement and punishment tended to mimic those displayed by the model, both with respect to the taking of candy and the reproduction of self-directed verbal comments. In addition, the experimental children were more imitative of an adult than a peer model. The control subjects set no standards and liberally indulged themselves with candy. We can conclude that self-administered reinforcements and punishments by a model can bring about correlated levels of self-control in an observer.

Good evidence exists that observational learning can result in the acquisition of a classically-conditioned response. Bernal and Berger (1976) presented observers with a videotaped display of a model in a simulated eyelid conditioning experiment. The model was shown to develop a CR, an eyeblink, in response to a tone, the CS, which had been paired with an air puff directed at the model's eye, the US. A discrimination learning paradigm was depicted in which two tones were employed; one, CS+ was paired with the air puff; the other tone, CS− was unpaired. The observer's own electromyographic, EMG, eyelid responses were recorded; EMG responses were also recorded from the subject's right arm in order to test for general increases in motor activity due to arousal, as distinct from localized vicariously-conditioned eyelid responses. As predicted, observer EMG responses were established to the CS+ tone, but not to the CS− tone. In addition, the conditioned motor response was, indeed, found to have been localized in the eyelid. Note that the observers in this experiment never experienced an air puff aimed at their own eyes. Thus, classical eyelid conditioning was established *without* the direct administration of a US.

The vicarious conditioning of emotional responses via observational learning is also thought to be a rather common, naturally-occurring process. For instance, people acquire intense emotional reactions to various minority groups such as the mentally ill, even though they may never have experienced any first-hand contacts. Similarly, Bandura and Menlove (1968) noted that fear and avoidant reactions can develop by simply observing someone else undergo painful experiences. Vicarious emotional arousal induced by observing someone else's plight has been referred to as "empathy" in the personality literature. Presumably, the individual experiences this arousal as a result of imagining what the other person is going through. Bandura (1969) feels that high levels of "empathic" arousal are mediated in a somewhat different way. Research by Stotland, Shaver, and Crawford (1966) indicates that "observers reacted more emotionally to the sight of a person undergoing painful stimulation when they were previously asked to imagine how they themselves would feel if they were being hurt than when they were told to imagine how the other person felt during treatment" (p. 171). Bandura, therefore, feels that vicarious emotional arousal may be primarily due to self-induced images of the observer undergoing pain or stress similar to that being experienced by the model.

Vicarious Extinction. Emotional responses, which we indicated could be acquired vicariously, have also been shown to be susceptible to extinction on the same basis. Bandura and Barab had adult snake phobics twice view one of three films. Two of the films presented models fearlessly interacting with a snake. The behaviors depicted ranged from simply looking at it to draping the snake around their necks and letting it slither freely over their bodies. The only difference between these two modeling displays was that one film had adult models, while the other used very young child models. The third film was irrelevant to the subject's phobia; it showed children engaging in fearless activity with dogs. As the films were being viewed, each subject's GSRs were continuously recorded on a polygraph as an index of vicarious fear arousal and extinction. In addition, pre- and post-treatment behavioral and verbal self-report measures were obtained. The behavioral score was based upon the subjects' ability to engage in a series of 29 graded tasks, from approaching a caged snake to allowing it to crawl over their laps.

Bandura and Barab found that both groups who had viewed a phobia-relevant modeling display manifested similarly significant degrees of behavioral improvement. The control subjects who had viewed the irrelevant dog film did not show any re-duction of snake phobic behavior. Of particular interest is that the greatest approach responses produced by the adult form of the snake film were correlated with decreases in levels of expressed fear and with GSR activity. For example, subjects who had the fewest and weakest autonomic responses during the second viewing of the film later proved themselves to be the most behaviorally-improved. These results are inter-preted to mean that vicarious extinction of emotional responses were responsible for the success of the observational treatment. On the other hand, no such correlations emerged for those snake phobics who viewed the child form of the snake film, and who manifested equal degrees of behavioral improvement. "Neither pretest fear measures nor autonomic responsiveness to the modeled displays correlated with treatment outcome" (1973, p. 6). Self-report data obtained from these subjects revealed that many increased their snake-approach behaviors at post-test, not because their fear had been extinguished, but for motivational reasons: "If a little kid isn't afraid, why should I be? . . . It made me feel foolish that I despise handling these things when the little children in the film looked like they didn't mind doing it . . . I figured if the little kids had enough moxie to do it, I should be able to" (1973, p. 4). Thus, it seems that when certain motivational issues become salient, a filmed modeling display can induce behavior change among phobics equal to that obtained with a display that results in correlated vicarious extinction of the anxiety response. It should also be noted that the mediation of approach behavior by incentive motivation among viewers of the child models served to eliminate the stronger observational effects usually found when the model is similar to the observer.

Vicarious extinction of avoidant behaviors has been shown to be facilitated also if, instead of symbolic modeling, a live display is employed. In addition, if the therapist himself performs the duties of a live model and guides the activity of the patient, the treatment package is considered to be a powerful one.

In summary, Bandura conceptualizes vicarious extinction of avoidant behaviors as involving repeated exposure to a fearless model who experiences no adverse consequences. This serves to lower the aversive properties of the phobic object or event to a point where the subject can bring himself to engage in approach behaviors. Direct contact then sets the stage for additional extinction trials. It is Bandura's contention that, without prior vicarious extinction, "the reinstatement of severely inhibited behavior generally requires a tedious and protracted program'' (1969, p. 192).

Response Inhibition. In addition to the vicarious acquisition and extinction of responses, observational experiences can have dramatic effects upon the frequency with which a well-established behavior will be emitted. Inhibitory effects are defined by the reduction of response emission subsequent to viewing a model experience a punishing outcome for the expression of similar behaviors; the observer himself does not directly experience receipt of punishment. Bandura believes that "when the subject witnesses behavior that is subsequently punished, the response-facilitative effects of modeling cues are counteracted by the suppressive effects of adverse outcomes" (1969, p. 192). One can think of response inhibition via observational processes as being an operant punishment effect induced vicariously.

Bandura's (1965b) study in which children at first failed to match the novel aggressive behaviors of a punished model exemplifies response inhibition. In fact, in that study, vicarious punishment resulted in complete suppression of imitative aggressive responses among the girls who, presumably, came into the experiment having an already higher level of inhibition regarding physical aggression than did the boys.

Inhibitory effects also include a reduction in the overall level of responding consequent to observing another receive punishment. This generalization phenomenon is most likely to occur when the response-consequence contingencies are unclear. For example, suppose a child observes an adult hitting children and is not able to tie the observed punishment to specific model responses. The child may then choose to maintain a very low profile and inhibit all responses that would direct the adult's attention at him. This phenomenon is quite analogous to the "generalization of inhibition" previously discussed in the context of "unwanted" side effects of positive punishment. The major difference is that, in this example, the generalized inhibition is a function of vicarious processes instead of the direct receipt of punishment.

Response Disinhibition. When behavioral inhibitions, originally established on the basis of observational process or direct aversive conditioning, are lifted due to new observational experiences, we speak of "disinhibitory" effects. The kind of modeling display necessary for producing disinhibition involves the model performing the prohibited activity without punishment, or with contingent reinforcement, as a consequence.

Bandura notes that "when a model displays punishable behavior, absence of anticipated adverse consequences increases transgressive behavior in observers to the same degree as witnessing the model experience rewarding outcomes ... These findings suggest that non-reaction to formerly prohibited activities may take on, through contrast, positive significance" (1969, p. 195). Thus, one does not have to observe a state trooper congratulate the speeding driver; simply seeing others "get away with it" is usually sufficient reason for drivers to exceed the speed limit. The ease with which such dishibitory effects occur is explained in terms of concurrently available reinforcement. That is, most inhibited behaviors are suppressed for reasons which outweigh the potential gains to be had if they were manifested. As soon as one observes that the expected negative outcomes are not materializing for others, the behavior becomes more purely controlled by anticipated reinforcements.

Response Facilitation. The observation of a modeling display may increase the probability of an already-learned response, one which is socially appropriate and for which the person has not received prior punishment. Thus, facilitation must be distinguished from disinhibition in that only the latter has to do with increases of a previously-suppressed behavior.

Facilitation may theoretically come about through straightforward imitation of what is observed. Alternatively, Bandura says the modeling display may serve an "orienting function" (1969, p. 197) in that it directs the observer's attention toward a stimulus, which is then responded to in a manner similar to that of the model. When spectators in a baseball park put their hands over their heads and crouch down as a baseball descends on them, it may not be so much that each is matching the other's behavior; rather, one person screams and ducks, orienting the others who emit similar response patterns. The orienting function of a modeling display may also elicit behavior which is quite different from that of the model. A child may be bored on a winter day until he sees some children enjoying a snow-ball fight; now oriented toward snow, the observer may proceed to go outside for a sleigh ride.

Sexual Behavior. Mann, Berkowitz, Sidman, Starr, and West (1974) showed either erotic or non-sexual movies once a week for one month to 66 married couples. The couples who viewed the erotic films saw either two weeks of "standard" sexual displays followed by two weeks of "less conventional" films, or the reverse. The unconventional films depicted such activities as oral-genital play. All participant couples kept track of their sexual behavior over the course of the experiment. The effects of the three treatments is presented in Table 9. Two features stand out. First, initial exposure to erotic material produced a powerful eliciting effect upon the likelihood of intercourse on movie nights, but not on non-movie nights; thus, the effect is short-lived. Second, the capacity of erotic material to elicit sexual activity diminishes with re-exposure. For example, subjects in Group I manifest a steady decline in intercourse rates on movie nights over the four weeks. The relatively high rate on the third movie night for Group II is attributable to the arousing power of viewing a highly "novel" sex portrayal for the first time. However, this rate also declines on the fourth night after viewing the unconventional film for the second time. Incidentally, note that there is also a tendency toward higher intercourse rates on movie nights for those in Group III; their self-reports confirm that they, indeed, were in a more romantic mood upon returning home.

The findings of Mann and his colleagues are quite consistent with earlier reports on the eliciting effects of sexually-provocative stimulus displays. For example, Schmidt and Sigusch (1970) found that both males and females reported increases in their frequency of masturbation within 24 hours after viewing sexually-explicit slides and movies. Similarly, in a more general review, the United States Commission on Obscenity and Pornography (1970) finds unquestioned evidence for short-duration elicitation effects of erotica. There does not appear to be evidence that erotic films provoke sexual behaviors not usually carried out by the observers; that is, elicitation and not modeling and/or disinhibition is the primary outcome of pornography.

TABLE 9 Intercourse rates on Movie and Nonmovie Nights

FILM CONDITION	WEEK 1		WEEK 2		WEEK 3		WEEK 4		OVERALL	
	M	NM	M	NM	M	NM	M	NM	M	NM
I. Unconventional sex first	.64	.30	.48	.27	.44	.24	.28	.19	.46	.25
II. Conventional sex first	.67	.22	.24	.24	.58	.18	.36	.19	.46	.21
III. Non-erotic films	.25	.13	.40	.27	.25	.19	.34	.22	.31	.20

Note: M = Movie nights, NM = Non-movie nights. There were 25 couples in each of the sex film treatments, and 16 couples in the non-erotic film treatment. (Mann, J., Berkowitz, L., Sidman, J., Starr, S., and West, S., Satiation of the transient stimulating effect of erotic films. *Journal of Personality and Social Psychology*, 1974, *30*, 729-735. Copyright 1974 by the American Psychological Association. Reprinted by permission.)

Aggressive Behavior. It would be fair to conclude that viewing erotic material does not produce a cathartic effect. The same can be said about the witnessing of violence. Instead of purging the soul of violent tendencies, Berkowitz (1975) concluded that aggressive modeling displays can be expected to elicit aggression in both normal and emotionally-disturbed individuals.

As long ago as 1954, the United States Senate Subcommittee to investigate Juvenile Delinquency concluded that "televised crime and brutality could be potentially harmful to young children" (Murray, 1973, p. 472). The Subcommittee recommended a reduction in the level of television violence. However, survey research conducted in the late 1960s revealed that, while there was some decline in the frequency with which killing was portrayed, the overall level of violence remained unchanged, and violence in programs designed for children actually increased (Gerbner, 1972). Barcus (1971) found that 71% of all segments of Saturday morning children's programming contained at least some elements of human violence, and 33% of the segments were described as being saturated with violence.

In a review of research on the impact of this televised violence upon children, Murray (1973) concludes that "viewing televised violence causes the viewer to become more aggressive" (1973, p. 477). Stein and Friedrich (1972) conducted a study which helped Murray in making this assertion. They found that nursery school children who were fed a diet of "Batman" and "Superman" exhibited more aggressive behavior during their daily activities than did preschoolers who were only permitted to watch neutral or pro-social programming, such as "Mr. Rogers Neighborhood." The aggression-eliciting effects of "Batman" and "Superman" were most pronounced for children who were initially judged to be more aggressive.

In addition, a more recent study by Leyens, Camino, Parke, and Berkowitz arrived at findings compatible with Murray's statement. This research was conducted in an institution for delinquent boys. The treatments consisted of showing aggressive commercial movies every night for one week in two cottages, and neutral commercial movies in two other cottages. Using a behavioral observation, time-sampling procedure, it was found that the violent films immediately elicited higher levels of activity and physical aggression. In one of these cottages, verbal aggression persisted at a higher rate for a week subsequent to the violent film exposure. These behaviors were obtained "in spite of the presence of agents of social control who negatively sanctioned antagonistic behaviors and who could therefore inhibit these behaviors" (1975, p. 357). It is also important to note that elicitation effects were variable across individual subjects. Specifically, already-dominant boys appeared to be most affected by the viewing of violent films. This individual difference effect, combined with that reported by Stein and Freidrich (1972) using preschoolers, suggests that elicitation is most pronounced among those who naturally have the weakest self-control over aggression, but that elicitation effects are certainly not restricted to such individuals.

The findings by Stein and Friedrich (1972) and those of Leyens and his colleagues (1975) are particularly important because they involve natural setting observations. These investigators are, therefore, not subject to the criticism of having limited external validity. However, their findings only deal with relatively short term phenomena. The importance of observational processes to the elicitation of aggressive behavior was studied from a longitudinal perspective by Eron, Heusmann, Lefkowitz, and Walder (1972). In 1960, as part of an investigation on third graders, the television-viewing habits of 427 boys and girls were recorded. In addition, peer aggression ratings were obtained for each of the children. Ten years later the "children," whose modal age was then 19, were again interviewed. Peer ratings for aggression were obtained once again, as were data relevant to TV viewing. A highly significant relationship between boys' preferences for TV violence when in the third grade and the two measures of peer-rated aggression were found. Neither of these correlations was significant for females. Using sophisticated correlational analyses, it was concluded that "the single most plausible causal hypothesis is that a preference for watching violent television in the third grade contributes to the development of aggressive habits (p. 258). . . . these early television habits seem to be more influential than current viewing patterns since a preference for violent television in the thirteenth grade [college] is not at all related to concurrent aggressive behavior, nor are early television habits related to later television habits" (p. 260). Thus, the viewing of violent TV programming is seen as being productive of later aggressive behavior patterns, an effect operating over a 10 year time span. It is not, of course, claimed that television is the only causal antecedent of aggression among teenagers and adults.

Direct Reinforcement

Bandura and Walters made a major contribution to the understanding of personality by focusing attention on vicarious learning and other observational phenomena. Additionally, in Social Learning and Personality Development they integrate previous research on classical and operant conditioning, and arrive at some insightful ideas regarding how these processes influence the development and maintenance of personality characteristics which other theorists deem important. One such area of personality functioning has to do with what might loosely be called "morality," but which is probably best thought of as self-control, or resistance to temptation, and guilt. As we will see, "in neither case is there a need to assume that some inner moral agent or faculty has played a role in regulating behavior" (1963, p. 185).

It is believed that self-control is largely mediated through experiencing previous punishment, the timing of which is crucial. If punishment occurs after an act has been committed, as is most often the case in the natural course of things, conditioned fear will be most strongly associated with the commission of the deviation. However, the behavior may persist because the suppressive effects of punishment can be overridden by the receipt of reinforcements contingent upon the action. In contrast, punishment which comes early in a behavioral sequence, preferably when the person is preparing to engage in the deviation, is much more effective in keeping the person from emitting the unwanted behavior on future occasions. Fear is being conditioned to *preparatory* responses; suppression at this point precludes the unwanted behavior from ever occurring, thereby effectively removing any possibility of competing reinforcements.

Self-punitive statements which are often heard after a transgression — "I shouldn't have done that" or "I'm sorry I was bad" — and which are taken as the behavioral indices of "guilt" by many theorists, are thought to be acquired because they result in reinforcement. That is, they typically bring on either the termination of punishment or negative reinforcement, as when the parent stops rejecting the child, or the receipt of positive reinforcers, as when the parent provides a forgiving hug after the child confesses or makes restitution.

According to Bandura and Walters "there is no necessary relationship between resistance to temptation and guilt as defined in terms of self-punitive responses . . . whereas resistance to temptation involves the classical conditioning of emotional responses, the habit of responding self-punitively appears to result from instrumental conditioning" (1963, p. 203). Research which has investigated both aspects of "morality" has in fact found no consistent relationship between resistance to temptation and verbal expressions of guilt. This, of course, contradicts psychoanalytic theory, which sees both response patterns as being mediated by superego processes.

SOCIAL LEARNING THEORY

Julian Rotter first presented his theory of personality in *Social Learning and Clinical Psychology* (1954). In 1972, Social Learning Theory (SLT) was reformulated by Rotter, Chance, and Phares with only minor revision, but its principles were extended to diverse phenomena on the basis of a massive accumulation of empirical data. Areas of application included personality development, social psychology, assessment, learning theory, psychopathology, and psychotherapy.

Like Bandura's socio-behavioristic theory, Rotter's theory places heavy emphasis upon an empirical law of effect: "any stimulus complex has reinforcing properties to the extent that it influences movement toward or away from a goal" (Rotter et al., 1972, p. 9).

Unfortunately, Rotter chooses to adopt the older nomenclature of Thorndike, describing response consequences as "negative reinforcers" instead of "punishments" if they tend to suppress behavior. The second similarity between Rotter and Bandura lies in the importance accorded cognitive "expectancies" as a determinant of behavior; in SLT the construct "expectancy" is even more formalized and central.

One very important difference between the two positions concerns behavior acquisition. Bandura, of course, invokes the process of observational learning in this regard; Rotter's theory is weak on this very important point. As such, his theory, in the manner of classical and operant conditioning, provides a set of principles which are most useful as a vehicle for analyzing levels, and changes in levels, of already-existing behaviors.

Basic Assumptions

Social Learning Theory entertains four assumptions about the nature of permeability. First, personality is learned on the basis of the individual's interactions with his meaningful environment. Therefore, in order to truly understand an individual, the antecedent events in his life must be known. As a corollary of this assumption, it is asserted that accurate prediction and postdiction are difficult "without systematic recourse to the environment or the situation" (1972, p. 4).

The second assumption stresses the unity of personality. Specifically, "a person's experiences (or his interactions with his meaningful environment) influence each other . . . New experiences are a partial function of acquired meanings, and old acquired meanings or learnings are changed by new experiences" (1954, p. 94). This assumption implies that personality stabilizes with age, since the new experiences which a person encounters become increasingly dictated by the ever-growing fund of previous experiences. Rotter recognizes that this implication is consistent with psychoanalytic theory, but cautions against believing in "the fixity of behavior or in arbitrarily cutting off the developmental picture in the belief that the major structure of personality is completed by the time the individual is six (or five or seven) years old . . ." (1954, p. 96).

Rotter's third basic assumption about the nature of personality is that "behavior . . . has a directional aspect. It may be said to be goal-directed" (1954, p. 97). The directional quality of human functioning is inferred from the impact of positive and negative reinforcers upon behavior. Simply put, we seek to maximize rewards and minimize punishments. In a discussion of motivation, Rotter points out that when we focus upon the environmental events which accompany increased behavior we speak of goals or reinforcements; when attention shifts to the individual himself as determining the directionality of behavior, needs are invoked. However, "the distinction between *goals* and *needs* is a semantic convenience . . . (since) both are inferred from the same referents — the interaction of the person with his meaningful environment" (1972, p. 10).

The final assumption of SLT is that "the occurrence of a behavior of a person is determined not only by the nature or importance of goals or reinforcements but also by the person's anticipation or expectancy that these goals will occur . . . In short, one needs a concept other than simple value of reinforcement to account for human behavior" (1972, p. 11).

Basic Constructs

In SLT, four basic constructs are used to explain and predict behavior: *behavior potential, expectancy, reinforcement value,* and the *psychological situation.*

Behavior Potential. Behavior potential is defined as, ". . . the potentiality of any behavior's occurring in any given situation or situations as calculated in relation to any single reinforcement or set of reinforcements" (1954, p. 105). Thus, behavior potential (*BP*) is a relativistic notion; it has meaning only in terms of other available behaviors in the same situation which may be used to achieve the same goal. This construct is readily operationalizable in terms of simply counting the relative frequency of behaviors. If a child is observed to cry more frequently than to call for recognition in the service of gaining parental attention in a given situation, it is concluded that the behavior potential for crying is greater than that for calling.

There are two points which may be made about the kinds of behaviors for which potential may be measured. First, no guidelines are provided regarding unit size; a meaningful behavioral unit can be anything from a minor movement or brief verbal utterance to a complex chain of movements or utterances, depending upon the interests and purposes of the investigator. Second, the *BP* of covert behaviors, such as attitudes, can be measured only indirectly by recording the *BP* of a theoretically-correlated overt response. The validity of this strategy depends upon establishing that the observable behavior varies in a way which is consistent with the theory. For example, one may theoretically predict that certain interpersonal encounters increase the probability of hostile thoughts toward others. If one observes an increase in aggressive interpersonal behavior, that may be taken as presumptive evidence for the higher BP of the hostile thoughts.

Reinforcement Value. Rotter defines his second major construct as ". . . the degree of preference for any reinforcement to occur if the possibilities of this occurring were all equal" (1954, p. 107). For example, if a child is told that he can earn a dime or a candy bar if he cleans his room, by definition the one selected has a higher reinforcement value (*RV*). Reinforcement value may, therefore, be measured by simply observing which goals a person pursues, assuming that all goals are equally obtainable; one must hold the expectancy for obtaining the various reinforcements equal in order to assess RV on the basis of choice behavior. Alternatively, verbal report can be employed by having the individual rate or rank-order potential reinforcers, again assuming that all are equally obtainable. A variation of this is to present the individual with choice-pairs and have him select which pair member is the more preferred goal: "Would you rather have teachers like you or believe that you are bright?" If being liked by a teacher is consistently chosen in preference to being thought of as bright by the teacher, it is assumed that the former reinforcement is more valued than the latter. Of course, because this measurement approach involves verbal self-report it is subject to all of the sources of error inherent in the process, such as social desirability and response sets.

While the notion is accepted that the value of a reinforcement may have arisen because of its previous association with primary reinforcers such as food, this is accorded only minor significance. "Instead, it is argued that psychological goals, needs, or reinforcements acquired during the individual's life depend upon other reinforcements for their value. The value of any given reinforcement depends upon its association or pairing with other reinforcements" (1972, p. 18). The following general formula may be used to predict the value of a reinforcement:

$$1. \quad RV_{a,s_1} = f\,[E_{Ra \rightarrow R(b-n),s_1} \,\&\, RV_{(b-n),s_1}].$$

This says that the value of reinforcement a in situation $s1$ is a function of the expectancy (E) that reinforcement a will lead to reinforcements b through n in situation 1, and the values of reinforcements b through n in situation 1. It should be noted that, in this and other formulae, Rotter uses the sign "&" to indicate a mathematical relationship between constructs, in this case E and RV. This is done "to avoid, for the time being, a more precise mathematical formulation because of an insufficient amount of experimental data" (1954, p. 108).

In an experiment cited by Rotter which illustrates the principle formalized above, Dunlap (1953) varied the consequences of obtaining valued reinforcers. Specifically, he found that primary school children's preferences for toys rose when playing with them was followed by social reinforcement; the RV of the toys declined when they were associated with receipt of social punishment.

It is difficult to predict what will happen to the value of reinforcement a if a person finds that it is not associated with or does not lead to reinforcement b. On the one hand, it is possible that the RV of a will fall if it is associated with the unpleasantness of not obtaining b. Alternatively, RV of a can increase if the person engages in "imaginative rehearsal of additional reinforcements obtainable through later success" (Rotter et al., 1972, p. 19). For example, the value of a dollar does not necessarily diminish if we go to a store and find it does not have what we wish to purchase; the dollar may become psychologically more valued as we anticipate using it to purchase the desired item b in the future.

Expectancy. This is defined as "the probability held by the individual that a particular reinforcement will occur as a function of a specific behavior on his part in a specific situation or situations" (Rotter, 1954, p. 107).

Stressed here are subjective probabilities held by the person regarding behavioral outcomes. While these expectancies are, no doubt, substantially influenced by the objective reinforcement history, SLT emphasizes "a principle of internal expectancy as its major intervening variable or construct" (1954, p. 107).

The term "subjective" does not mean that the assessment of expectancies (Es) is precluded. If a crude measure is sufficient, one can observe choice behavior when reinforcement value is controlled. In a given stiuation, that behavior will be emitted which the individual expects will most likely result in reinforcement. For instance, of all the possible strategies which may be adopted when playing a board game, the one which the person expects will most probably result in winning, the reinforcement, is the one which will be followed. Other measurement techniques depend upon verbalizations by the subject who, in one form or another, is asked to express beliefs about the probability of specific outcomes as a function of particular behaviors in a given situation. The subject may be requested to submit a probability statement, which could range from zero to 100%, regarding the likelihood of a behavior consequence; or a number of different outcomes can be rank-ordered in terms of their expected probability of occurrence as a function of a given behavior. Alternatively, subjects can rank different behaviors with respect to their likelihood of leading to a given reinforcement. Again, these approaches are prone to the sources of error inherent in verbal self-report measurement.

A given behavior-reinforcement expectancy, such as the winning of a game of tennis, emerges from two component expectancies. The first component is notated E' and refers to behavior-reinforcement expectancies which are specific to the very behavior, reinforcement, and situation in question. For example, part of the tennis player's expectation for winning derives from the fact that he has been victorious over the same person on the tennis court on previous occasions. The second component of a given expectancy is notated GE, for *generalized expectancy*. Generalized expectancies derive from previous experience with similar, but not the same, behavior-reinforcement-situation complexes. For instance, the anticipation of winning held by our tennis player derives in part from his perception of himself as generally having come out on top in most of his previous athletic competitions.

More formally, the above principles take the following form:

$$2. \quad E_{s1} = f(E'_{s1} \ \& \ GE).$$

This reads: Expectancy for reinforcement in situation *1* is a function of a specific expectancy based upon previous experience in the same situation (E'_{s1}) and expectancies generalized from experience in related situations (GE). The terms "same" and "related" in the above sentence are not meant to be objective; we are speaking from the individual's subjective frame of reference.

Generally speaking, the more novel the situation, the less important is E'_{s1} and the more our expectancy is determined by GE. For example, the first time one tries to do something in order to reach a goal, the only data upon which to base an expectancy for success is to consider previous behavior-reinforcement sequences in related circumstances (GE). One can't use E'_{s1} because, not having had previous experience in the given situation, E'_{s1} does not yet exist. This principle, which takes into account the novelty of the situation as a factor in determining expectancies, results in the following modification of formula 2:

$$3. \quad E_{s1} = f \ \frac{(E'_{s1} \ \& \ GE)}{N_{s1}}.$$

In this formula N stands for the number of past experiences in situation *1*. The effect of varying values of N upon E_{s1} can be noted. When N is large it denotes that the person has had considerable experience in the same situation with the behavior-reinforcement sequence in question, and the relative magnitude of the fraction containing *GE* diminishes; when the value of *N* is small, that fraction increases in magnitude. When $N=0$, the hypothetical mathematical value of GE/N_{s1} becomes infinity. In more psycholgical terms, this means that, lacking prior experience in the specific situation, *GE* becomes the all-important determinant of E_{s1}.

Changes in subjectively-held expectancies for behavior-reinforcement sequences occur all the time. When a behavior is emitted, but fails to be followed by reinforcement, we would expect E_{s1} to decline; and we would expect it to increase if reinforcement occurred on the last "trial." The magnitude of specific expectancy change ($\Delta E'$) is thought to be a function of two variables. First, there is the surprise value of the consequence; that is, regardless of whether there is reinforcement, or no reinforcement, $\Delta E'$ is greater if the outcome is unexpected. By "unexpected" Rotter means the difference between the observed outcome (*O*) and the previously-held expectancy for that outcome (*E*). When the expected outcome actually occurs, the value of *O* becomes 1.00; its value is zero when the expected outcome does not materialize. The second variable which influences the magnitude of expectancy changes ($\Delta E'$) is the number (*N*) of previous experiences in the same situation; "with a lot of experience in a given situation, a recent, inconsistent experience will have little effect on our expectancies (unless cues present suggest that the situation itself has changed)" (1972, p. 29).

The formal statement of this principle is as follows:

$$4. \quad \Delta E' = f\left(\frac{O-E}{N}\right).$$

Suppose a student, after earning grades of A in two summer school courses prior to starting full-time college ($N=2$), entertains very high hopes for the receipt of future grades of A; in fact, he's 92% certain that he'll be able to earn As in his courses ($E=.92$). At the end of his first semester, a grade card is received and, sure enough, there is an A on it ($O=1.00$). Therefore,

$$\Delta E' = f\left(\frac{1.00-.92}{2}\right)$$

$$= f(+.04).$$

According to these figures, the student will now become even more certain of his capacity to earn As. That is, *E* will rise from .92 to .96 (.92 + .04 = .96). Notice, however, that this expectancy change is relatively minor because of the substantial similarity between the values of *O* and *E*.

Now imagine that the second grade card received at the end of the first semester does not have an A on it. In this case, the actual observed value (*O*) equals zero:

$$\Delta E' = f\left(\frac{.00-.96}{3}\right)$$

$$= f(-.32).$$

Staying strictly with the obtained numbers, we find the value of $\Delta E'$ to be $-.32$ which, in combination with an initial E of .96, results in a subjectively-held probability for earning As of only $+.64$ ($.96 - .32 = .64$). The substantial decline in expectancy is due to the surprise value of not earning an A; there is a large discrepancy between the value of O, which turned out to be zero, and E, which was .96.

Finally, let us see what happens to the student who, after earning 20 consecutive grades of A and who, therefore, is completely certain of his ability to obtain As in future coursework ($E = 1.00$), finally gets his first B. Even though the discrepancy between O and E in this case is as great as it can be, the surprise value cannot be more substantial; the effect of not receiving an A at this point will not have nearly the impact upon expectancies that the receipt of the B did for the previously considered student:

$$\Delta E' = f \left(\frac{.00 - 1.00}{20} \right)$$

$$= f (-.05).$$

Thus, strictly in terms of the numbers alone, the student's expectancy for receiving grades of A will drop only from 1.00 to $+.95$.

Of course, it is very important to keep in mind that these mathematical illustrations are only presented to highlight some points. In fact, changes in E' would not occur quite so neatly. The formula contains f to indicate that $\Delta E'$ is *some function* of the values of $O, E,$ and N, *not* that it is *equal* to the value of the fraction of which $O, E,$ and N are components. Variables, such as the length of time since the situation was first experienced, the schedule of previous reinforcement, and the degree to which the person saw the unexpected event as being just a chance happening, may all interact in complex ways to determine actual changes in subjective expectancies.

The belief that outcomes are due to "chance," as opposed to factors under one's own control, defines a generalized expectancy regarding *internal vs. external control of reinforcement*. This generalized expectancy, and others like it, such as the belief that the written and spoken words of others can be relied upon, *trust vs. distrust,* form a special group of *GEs* independent of particular behavior-reinforcement sequences. They can best be equated with "social attitudes," (Rotter et al., 1972, p. 39) or with beliefs about the nature of the world in general.

Expecting to be in control of reinforcement, having an "internal locus of control," or anticipating that people are not to be trusted rests upon defining situations as members of broad categories which cut across the particular responses emitted in them, or the reinforcements which might therein be obtained. For example, if one has the expectancy that he can win at a game, but defines the game situation as one in which opponents are likely to cheat, then the resultant expectancy for victory might be quite low. Similarly, an individual, who would otherwise have high expectations for winning a game, may lower his hopes for success if the "game situation" is defined as one in which luck determines the outcome instead of skill.

Rotter and his collaborators have developed personality inventories which are designed to assess where a person stands on these expectancy dimensions of "locus of control" and "interpersonal trust." Their format and utility will be discussed later in this section. For now, we will move on to the fourth major construct in SLT.

The Psychological Situation. Behavior does not take place independently of a context. At all times Rotter's theorizing implicitly takes the situation into account; he considers the situation to be one of the major determinants of behavior. This view falls midway between theorists who hypothesize core motives, such as instincts and "the actualizing tendency," as the prime movers and the purely situational perspective of strict operant and classical conditioning behaviorists.

Intuitively, it is easy to appreciate how the situation interacts with Rotter's other main constructs, E, and RV. For example, an adolescent male might have high expectations for physically affectionate outcomes should he engage in certain amorous advances toward his girlfriend; those very behaviors directed at his math teacher would hardly be expected to produce the same consequences. Even if they did, it is reasonable to assume that the RV of physical affection from his girlfriend is much greater than that which might conceivably be received from the teacher. Even receipt of affectionate expression from the same person changes in value as a function of the situation. A little boy might want to be held and kissed by his mother at bedtime, but would avoid such advances with vigor when his peers were around.

Despite the fact that situations are so important, there have been very few attempts to arrive at a meaningful taxonomy of them. Frederiksen makes a plea for the development of such a taxonomic system, believing that it would facilitate the study of person by situation interactions — the very focus of Rotter's SLT. Frederiksen believes that it is possible to develop such a system and suggests that "a possible criterion for use in empirically developing a taxonomy of situations is the similarity of situations with regard to the behaviors they elicit" (1972, p. 123). Rotter et al. (1972) also suggest that this would be a reasonable basis for categorization. Thus, situations provocative of achieving behavior are "achievement" situations; those in which hostility is observed to occur are "hostile" situations. In addition, Rotter suggests that situations might be categorized profitably either in terms of the actual reinforcements which they have to offer, or with respect to the reinforcements which people typically expect to obtain in them. The fourth suggested strategy involves noting the frequency with which a type of behavior occurs in an array of situations and then using reinforcement to modify the behavior rate in one of the situations. To the degree that rate changes are also observed to occur in other situations, they may be construed as similar to the first. In other words, the taxonomy would be based upon the empirical determination of generalization effects.

The Basic Formula

Rotter relates the four basic constructs to each other in the following way:

5. $BP_{x,s_1,R_a} = f\ (E_{x,R_a s, 1}\ \&\ RV_{a,s_1})$.

"The potential for behavior x to occur in situation 1 in relation to reinforcement a is a function of the expectancy of the occurrence of reinforcement a following behavior x in situation 1 and the value of reinforcement a" (1954, p. 108). This formula is only concerned with one behavior (x) in one situation (1) with respect to one reinforcement (a). It is more typical for psychologists to be concerned with the potential for a group of functionally related behaviors to occur in a range of situations with respect to a range of reinforcements. This broader prediction can be formulated as follows:

$$6. \quad BP_{(x-n),\, s_{(1-n)},\, R_{(a-n)}} = f\,[\, E_{(x-n),\, s_{(1-n)},\, R_{(a-n)}} \;\&\; RV_{(a-n),\, s_{(1-n)}}\,].$$

"This may be read: The potentiality of the functionally related behaviors x to n to occur in the specified situations 1 to n in relation to potential reinforcements a to n is a function of the expectancies of these behaviors leading to these reinforcements in these situations and the value of these reinforcements" (1954, p. 110).

Broader Constructs

No doubt the reader finds formula 6 complicated, but we trust it is understandable. The principles contained in it have been translated into a much more molar formula which departs from the details of formula 6. In order to make this translation, a number of terms have to be redefined.

Need Potential *(NP)*. This is the more general analogue of behavior potential. "The difference is that need potential refers to groups of functionally related behaviors rather than single behaviors. Functional relatedness of behaviors exists when several behaviors all lead to, or are directed toward, obtaining the same or similar reinforcements" (Rotter et al., 1972, p. 30). The inclusiveness of the group of functionally related behaviors dealt with by the construct *NP* can vary; one can speak of need potential for recognition, which is more inclusive than need potential for recognition in academic situations. "Need potential, then, describes the mean potentiality of a group of functionally related behaviors directed at obtaining the same or a set of similar reinforcements, occurring in any segment of the individual's life" (1972, p. 31).

Need Value. Rotter defines Need Value (NV) as the "mean preference value of a set of functionally related reinforcements. Where reinforcement value indicates preference for one reinforcement over others, need value indicates preference for one set of functionally related reinforcements over another set" (1972, p. 33). Need value may be assessed by having people indicate preferences for sample reinforcements derived from an array of reinforcement sets. In effect, subjects are required to do just this in Liverant's Goal Preference Inventory (1958), the only test designed to measure *NV* as described in SLT. The Inventory lists pairs of behaviors, with each member of a pair indicating an activity in which a student might engage if he were acting on a need, "academic recognition" or "social love and affection," for example. By calculating the number of times behaviors reflecting one need are chosen over those reflecting another need, the relative strengths of several needs are assessed. A more complete description of the Goal Preference Inventory can be found in Chapter 13.

Freedom of Movement. "This is defined as, the mean expectancy of obtaining positive satisfactions as a result of a set of related behaviors directed toward obtaining a group of functionally related reinforcements" (Rotter et al., 1972, p. 34). In other words, when an individual fully expects to be able to procure any or all of a group of reinforcements on the basis of certain exhibited behaviors he is said to have high Freedom of Movement *(FM)*. For example, the person might be confident that attention from others, the reinforcements, can be obtained by behaving in dependent ways. *FM* is low when the individual does not expect to be able to obtain a category of reinforcements by behaving in certain ways. It is possible to have high *FM* with respect to one group of behaviors leading to a category of reinforcements, and low *FM* regarding another class of behavior leading to the same reinforcements. An individual may learn that attention from others is obtainable via dependent behaviors, and this results in high *FM*; the individual may also learn that a hostile manner will not bring the kind of attention he seeks, and so this sequence is correlated with low *FM*.

When a person has low expectations for the fulfillment of highly-valued needs, or low *FM* combined with high *NV,* a condition of conflict exists in which valued goals seem out of reach. "Forced" attempts to obtain the prized reinforcements may then be made. For example, the neglected child who craves attention might become a behavior problem at home or in school in a desperate move to satisfy his need for attention. When such measures fail or when they result in punishing consequences, the anxiety which becomes associated with real world attempts to gain reinforcement might be avoided by resorting to "irreal" or "symbolic" response patterns (Rotter et al., 1972, p. 36); the person might fantasize about the satisfactions instead of trying to procure them in reality.

Low *FM* is thought to come about in a variety of ways. The person may simply not have learned social behaviors which are necessary for need satisfaction; he doesn't know how to relate to others in a way which encourages them to offer attention. In other cases, low *FM* derives from a person valuing a need which others refuse to fulfill; instead of providing satisfaction they offer punishment. When such punishments come early in life, perhaps as a child he was rejected by his parents, the adult may persist in generalizing from previous experiences and come to the expectation that even now people will be rejecting.

Related to the construct *FM* is that of *minimum goal level.* This is "the lowest goal in a continuum of potential reinforcements for some life situation which will be perceived by the person as satisfactory to him. . . . The point along this dimension at which reinforcements change from positive to negative in value for the person is his minimal goal level" (1972, p. 36).

When a person establishes an unreasonably high minimal goal level for himself, he is setting himself up for failure and low *FM*. Too high minimal goal levels may derive from an early history in which a need, perhaps for attention, was indulged, leading to a situation in which realistic levels of satisfaction are experienced as insufficient. Other cases reveal that individuals set excessively high standards because they erroneously believe that subsequent reinforcements will not be available unless that high level is reached. The pre-med student, frantically struggling to keep from academically "sinking," and believing that unless he becomes a doctor his life will be empty, is an example of someone with an unreasonably high minimum goal level.

At the other extreme is the person who is content with very low levels of goal attainment. Such an individual may appear unmotivated to others and, in academic circles, is often called an "underachiever."

The Broader Formula

The molar constructs *NP, NV,* and *FM,* relate to each other in a way analogous to the theoretical relationships described between *BP, RV,* and *E.* The broader formula basic to SLT is therefore:

$$NP = f \, (FM \, \& \, NV)$$

This reads, Need Potential is some function of Freedom of Movement and Need Value. That is, the potential for engaging in a set of functionally related behaviors *(NP)* is determined by the mean expectancy that these behaviors will lead to related reinforcements *(FM)* and the value of those reinforcements *(NV).* In this formula, the situation is left implicit.

Applications of Social Learning Theory

Rotter's theory has been applied to diverse areas of interest to psychology. Because of the operationality of its constructs, SLT has generated a massive volume of research. In this section we will consider two major areas of research and application; personality assessment and psychotherapy. In so doing, other issues to which SLT has been applied will be dealt with in passing.

Personality Assessment. Rotter (1960) is critical of many assessment procedures because neither the tests themselves nor their administration and scoring take the subjects' needs and expectations into account. The situational context of testing is routinely neglected as a source of test score variation. Rotter believes that the prediction of behavior from test responses would be improved if subjects' test-taking behavior were interpreted with respect to these important SLT variables.

With regard to needs, it is pointed out that "what we call faking is only our recognition of the fact that the S[subject] is taking the test with a different purpose or goal than the one the examiner wants him to have" (1972, p. 309). For example, the examiner typically wants the test-taker to respond in an honest fashion, while the subject may prefer to suspend honesty in the service of gaining interpersonal approval; he answers questionnaire items in a socially-desirable manner in order to create a favorable self-image. In Chapters 11 and 13 Crowne and Marlowe's (1960) Social

Desirability (SD) Scale was described as a measure of the strength of a need for approval. Recently, test constructors have routinely correlated their own measures with the SD scale in order to give users some idea of how susceptible their instruments are to social desirability response sets.

Similarly, behavior-reinforcement expectancies, if taken into consideration, can greatly enhance the predictive efficiency of a test. This point is illustrated by research which reveals that aggressive theme counts on the TAT correlate with overt indices of aggression only for certain subjects. Those who came from a background in which aggression has been punished appear to inhibit the expression of aggressive themes in their TAT projections. Mussen and Naylor (1954) and Kagan (1956) found that subjects not having this expectation for punishment consequent to aggression produce aggressive TAT themes more freely, and at a level which accurately mirrors what is overtly expressed.

Finally, the testing situation itself is crucial to the interpretation of test behavior, because it is so influential in determining the needs and expectancies which will be salient during evaluation. In order for valid conclusions to be drawn, many test constructors make elaborate efforts to communicate the nature of the "standard testing situation" which must accompany the administration of their instrument. It might be very productive if information were also provided regarding the impact which test situation variability has upon test behavior. Situational variables, such as the sex of the examiner and the testing location, home, school or hospital, undoubtedly influence the kinds of responses which a subject is likely to produce; knowing their probable effect can only serve to increase predictive power. Clark (1952), in research bearing on this point, showed that expression of sexuality does not appear on the TAT, even if subjects are sexually aroused, when the testing situation contains cues which, from the subject's perspective, "prohibit" themes having sexual content. Also, Henry and Rotter (1956) revealed that the context within which the Rorschach is administered significantly affects the number and quality of projections.

In addition to providing insights into how other assessment tools might best be employed and interpreted, SLT has been responsible for the development of several personality measures; the aforementioned Social Desirability Scale is just one example. Questionnaires also exist which are designed to measure generalized expectancies — Rotter's (1966) *Internal versus External Control of Reinforcement (I-E)* Scale, and his *Interpersonal Trust Scale* (1967).

I-E Scale. This is a 29 item, forced-choice instrument on which the subject chooses which member of a pair of statements reflects the world as he understands it. On 23 of the paired items, one member reflects a belief in internal control of reinforcement, for example, "What happens to me is my own doing"; and the other reflects a belief in external control, "There's not much use in trying too hard to please people, if they like you, they like you." The remaining six items are "fillers" which have been added to the test in an attempt to disguise its purpose. A person's score is simply the number of times he responds in an external direction; high scores reflect a generalized expectancy for control of reinforcement by fate, luck, and other factors beyond one's control.

The I-E scale has been used to predict an incredibly broad array of behaviors, including the use of birth control techniques (MacDonald, 1970) and political activism (Gore and Rotter, 1963; Strickland, 1965). Rotter himself is critical of much of this research because the investigators failed to fully utilize SLT constructs *other* than "generalized expectancy for locus of control" in their work. He points out that prediction would be greatly enhanced if RV were also taken into account. For instance "an internal person may *not* protest, be a member of a protest group, or sign a petition, simply because he does not believe in the cause . . ." (1975, p. 59).

Rotter's second criticism pertains to the typical neglect of the situation in studies which use the I-E scale for predictive purposes. Researchers seem to lose sight of the fact that I-E scale scores derive from items which cover a broad range of situations in which the locus of control dimension might be relevant, including academic, vocational, political, governmental and social situations. It is unreasonable to anticipate high levels of prediction from this measure of generalized locus of control to specific situations, such as political activism, since only a very few I-E scale items deal with any one area. In addition, someone might obtain an overall internal I-E scale score, and, therefore, be seen as a likely prospect for political activism, yet he may have responded in an external direction on all of the politically relevant items. Consistent with these concerns, Gootnick (1974) used the I-E scale, a measure of generalized expectancy, and another locus of control scale, Coan and Fairchild's Personal Opinion Survey, to predict political activity. The Personal Opinion Survey differs from Rotter's I-E scale in that its 120 items are designed to cover many content areas and provide sub-scores on dimensions such as "self-control over internal processes," and "successful planning and organization." One of the Personal Opinion Survey subscales, "control over large-scale social and political events," was found to correlate with student voter registration at a highly significant level ($r = .32$; $p < .001$). In comparison, the correlation between registration and Rotter's I-E scale scores was insignificant ($r = .02$). These findings, of course, support the idea that the locus of control dimension would be more predictive if situational distinctions were made in the measurement process. That is, we should be trying to assess expectancies for locus of control in categories of situations.

Interpersonal Trust Scale. This questionnaire is designed to measure the degree to which one believes in the written and spoken words of others. In its final form, the scale contains 40 items to which the subject indicates agreement or disagreement on a 5 point dimension. Fifteen of the items are "fillers," and of the remaining 25 items, half are keyed in the "agree" direction and half in the "disagree" direction in order to minimize the effect of acquiescence. In addition, in order for items to be included, they had to have shown low correlations with the Marlowe-Crowne Social Desirability Scale, thereby also reducing the effect of the SD response set on Trust scale scores.

As with the I-E scale, Rotter's Interpersonal Trust scale has been utilized to predict behavior in a broad range of situations. In his 1970 presidential address to the Division of Personality and Social Psychology of the American Psychological Association, Rotter (1971) highlighted some of the research that had been conducted. In one study, that of Hamsher, Geller, and Rotter (1968), a strong relationship was found between Trust scale scores and the degree to which students believed the Warren Commission Report on the assassination of President Kennedy. Specifically, low-scoring students tended to view the Report as part of a cover-up conspiracy. Other research has established that low Trust scale scores are associated with maladjustment as measured by the Rotter Incomplete Sentences Blank (1950), a validated measure of psychological well-being.

Sometimes it is important to know not just what a scale can predict but its limitations as well. In this regard, Aronson (1970) and Stein (1970) have revealed that low Trusting scorers are not necessarily secretive. In another investigation, MacDonald, Kessel, and Fuller (1970) did not find any relationship between Trust scores and performance in a competitive game situation. Rotter has said that the Trust Scale measures "an expectancy that communications can be believed, not a willingness or desire to speak out about private matters to strangers or belief in the benevolence of others in competitive situations" (1967, p. 448).

Psychotherapy. From a Social Learning Theory perspective, psychotherapy is construed as a learning situation in which behavior change emerges from a problem-solving perspective. As such, there is considerable emphasis upon cognitive "work," looking for alternative vehicles for goal attainment, exploring the consequences of one's behavior, building discriminations between life situations, and trying to better understand *other* people's needs and attitudes. This last point of emphasis particularly distinguishes this psychotherapy from traditional long term approaches in which the patient is encouraged to meditate about his own predicament and subjective reactions. According to Rotter (1970), this may only serve to maintain an egocentricity and an ignorance of others which must be circumvented if improvement is to occur. Sensitivity training group experiences are judged useful in this regard because they often serve to increase participants' awareness of others and encourage insights into how others view them.

At a more specific level, a Social Learning psychotherapy might become very pedagogical in tone. This can happen when one of the mutually-set goals is a modification of the patient's minimal goal level. The problem may then become one of changing expectancies for subsequent reinforcements. For instance, it is quite common for people to insist upon striving for unreasonably high levels of immediate reinforcement in the belief that long term goals are unobtainable. It is also common for such individuals *not* to appreciate the unwanted, long term consequences of preoccupation with high levels of immediate gratification. A husband, for instance, may have to be alerted to the destructive effects that his excessive demands for moment-to-moment attention have upon his wife's attitudes toward him.

In cases where the patient's minimal goal level is reasonable but he nevertheless has low freedom of movement, it is often incumbent upon the therapist to provide social reinforcement and directly alter the patient's expectations. The therapist may satisfy interpersonal needs by offering approval, attention, and recognition. In addition, the therapist can help the patient by going over the circumstances surrounding the development of low freedom of movement. For example, he might review a history of paternal rejection and point out how such expectations, based as they are on situations which have long since past, are no longer appropriate.

When low freedom of movement is attributed to an inadequate social skill repertoire, direct instruction may be appropriate. In a recently-developed psychotherapeutic approach called Structured Learning Therapy, Goldstein (1973) tries to improve basic social skills by providing skill-deficient patients with a modeling display which depicts starting a conversation, expressing appreciation, apologizing, responding to anger, negotiating, making requests, and many others. The patients are then asked to role play what they observed in the presence of the therapist, who provides feedback regarding the quality of skill execution. In addition, in order to facilitate transfer to the "real world," the patients are encouraged to try out their newly-enhanced interpersonal skills in their own life situations. From the perspective of Rotter's SLT, this modeling-role play-feedback approach is an excellent way to raise freedom of movement among those who have a history of inadequate training in social skills.

Principles of SLT have also been employed to predict the effectiveness of other behavior modification techniques through the identification of particularly receptive patients. O'Conner (1969, 1972) and Evers and Schwarz (1973) found that social withdrawal among preschoolers can be reduced if the children are exposed to a filmed modeling display depicting youngsters happily interacting with each other. Nevertheless, considerable individual differences in treatment outcome were found; some children remained primarily asocial, while others developed high rates of peer interaction.

On the assumption that unresponsive children simply may not care to interact with peers, the reinforcement value of peers for a group of 16 isolate preschoolers was assessed by Evers-Pasquale, and Sherman (1975). A forced-choice procedure was used in which two cartoons depicting a play activity, such as riding a bicycle, were presented. One illustrated a child engaging in the activity alone, and the other showed him in the company of a peer; altogether, 11 activities of this general nature were pictured. The children were simply shown the pair of illustrations and asked; "Would you rather ride a bike by yourself, or with someone your own age?" (p. 183). Isolates were defined as being "peer-oriented," or as having a high NV with respect to peer interaction, if they tended to select the interactive cartoons over the isolate cartoons. It was assumed that the peer-oriented isolates would profit most from the modeling treatment used by O'Conner (1969, 1972). They want to interact, but do not do so simply because of low expectations for reinforcement; the filmed display would provide an opportunity for increasing these expectations. In contrast, those isolates who were found to devalue peer interaction on the forced choice measure were expected to show much smaller increases in their rates of interactive play subsequent to viewing O'Conner's modeling film.

The results of this investigation strongly support the hypothesis. Specifically, it was found that peer-oriented isolates increased their rates of interaction after viewing the modeling film, raising it to a level which equalled that of the most interactive children in the nursery school. In fact, the percentage of time spent interacting with peers rose from a mean pre-treatment level of 9.4%, using a time sampling procedure, to a post-treatment high of 63.7%. In comparison, the gains of the isolate children diagnosed as *not* valuing peer interactions were significantly less. These children interacted only 27.4% of the time after treatment, in comparison to a pretreatment percentage of 10.2%. A control group of seven isolates who viewed an animal film manifested no significant increases in their rates of peer interaction. These results support the idea that a modeling therapy may be selectively beneficial as a function of the value which subjects place upon the goal of treatment. The investigation, therefore, also illustrates the utility of SLT as a vehicle for generating prescriptive therapeutic predictions.

One prediction which is particularly important in clinical settings where the therapists are over-burdened is that of identifying premature terminators. It is usually a waste of both the therapist's and the client's time when the patient "disappears" after only a few sessions. On the assumption that the potential for prolonged treatment, as any other behavior, is a function of expectancy and reward value, these variables were assessed in a group of patients by Piper, Wogan, and Getter (1972). The expectancy assessment involved giving incoming patients to the Mental Health Clinic of the University of Connecticut Health Service a list of symptoms; they were asked to check those which applied to themselves, and then to rate the degree to which they anticipated symptomatic relief as a consequence of therapy. The mean expectancy rating was taken as each patient's "expectancy for improvement." In addition, the patients had to rate how important it was for them to solve each problem which they had checked. The mean of these ratings was the operational index of "reinforcement value of improvement." Using therapist judgments as to whether a patient did or did not prematurely terminate his therapy contacts as the dependent measure, both the expectancy and reinforcement value indices were highly predictive. Patients who valued and expected improvement tended to remain in treatment, while those whose expectancies for gain were low, and who did not especially value symptom relief, were most likely to drop out of therapy at an early stage.

The role which patient expectancies play in the actual success of psychotherapy has been extensively discussed by Goldstein (1962). In a recent investigation, Efran and Marcia sought to determine the therapeutic efficacy of inducing high expectancies for successful treatment among phobic patients, as compared to an active systematic desensitization procedure styled after that of Wolpe. The group of phobics, who feared either snakes or spiders and whose treatment consisted of expectancy elevation procedures, were exposed to a so-called "T-scope therapy" (1972, p. 529). These subjects were met by a therapist and a "white coated GSR technician" who told them that phobic stimuli would be presented tachistiscopically, "too fast for the conscious mind to perceive, yet perceptible to the unconscious" (p. 529). These subliminal stimuli would ostensibly provoke unconscious phobic reactions which would allegedly be recorded on a polygraph. Each subject's reaction was followed by the administration of mild electric shock. Subjects were placed in a soundproof chamber and actually viewed blank cards presented for very brief durations. Each session involved 100 tachistiscopic presentations and 16 shocks. At the end of the sessions, the subject was shown false polygraph data by the technician and told how they revealed "improvement." Actual improvement was assessed by obtaining statements from the subjects regarding their own opinions on improvement, and by recording how close they could come to the snake or spider at the end of a 15-foot runway. Significant improvement was shown for both systematic desensitization and "T-scope therapy." Subjects who received no treatment or "T-scope" procedures presented without explanation showed no improvement. Furthermore, systematic desensitization was not found to be superior to the expectancy-elevating "T-scope therapy."

Efran and Marcia conclude that much of the reported therapeutic efficacy of systematic desensitization may not be due to either relaxation training or to counter-conditioning. Instead, they believe that "systematic desensitization may be viewed most adequately as a method of modifying beliefs and attitudes by the use of social influence" (p. 532). This conclusion does not necessarily follow from the experiment conducted; it is possible that systematic desensitization and "T-scope therapy" were efficacious for very different reasons. However, it is hard to argue with the suggestion that there is usefulness in "turning our attention to the design of more varied and efficient means of modifying cognitions, rather than continuing to focus primarily on the *conditioning* parameters of behavior therapy techniques like systematic desensitization" (p. 532).

COGNITIVE SOCIAL LEARNING THEORY

Rotter's Social Learning Theory and Bandura's socio-behaviorism have proven themselves to be immensely important catalysts for a movement away from the strict behaviorism of Watson and Skinner. Emphasis upon expectancies, reinforcement values, and observational learning have placed the focus of personality theory once again upon internal determinants of behavior, without losing the importance of situational variables. In the words of Mahoney (1977), the trend of the 1950s and 1960s has now become something of a "revolution . . . in the sense that cognitive processes have become a very popular topic."

Several advocates of behavioral psychology have been influenced by, and have contributed to, the flourish of cognitive personality theorizing which characterizes this decade. Of these, probably the most significant is Walter Mischel who published an important paper reconceptualizing "social learning (social behavior) theories" (1973b, p. 252). The product, *Cognitive Social Learning Theory,* represents a new integration of recent research and concepts. However, because it is an incipient effort, the theory in no way achieves the comprehensiveness of those presented by Freud and Rogers. Nevertheless, it clearly articulates directions for future development.

Person-Variables

Mischel proposes a set of *person-variables* reflecting what people *"do* — behaviorally and cognitively — in relation to the psychological conditions in which they do it" (p. 265). This contrasts with the behaviorists' emphasis upon how behavior is "acquired, evoked, maintained, and modified" (p. 265). It also is to be distinguished from a focus which concentrates on what the person already *has* in the form of traits, etc. Many of the ideas associated with Mischel's cognitive social learning person-variables should sound familiar in that they "are a synthesis of seemingly promising constructs in the area of cognition and social learning" (p. 265), many of which have been previously discussed in this and other chapters.

In all, he speaks of five general person-variables. The first deals with the individual's *competencies* to generate, or construct, diverse behaviors and cognitions when the situation calls for them. The second person-variable relates to the way in which the individual *categorizes* events and cognitively processes, or encodes, incoming information. *Expectancies* for outcomes, and the *subjective values* of these outcomes, are the third and fourth person-variables. The fifth person-variable deals with *self-regulatory systems and plans.*

Cognitive and Behavioral Construction Competencies. On the basis of direct experience and observational learning, we all acquire the potential to engage in diverse cognitive and behavioral activity. For instance, we learn to conduct ourselves in terms of a gender identity; we gain insights about the nature and workings of the physical and social world, and we develop problems solving strategies. All of these "psychological acquisitions" (p. 266) are included in the concept of cognitive and behavioral construction competencies.

The use of the word "construction" emphasizes the fact that our experience is not merely a function of what we have perceived, retained, and recalled. Cognitive operations are performed on this storehouse of data in such a way that the products of learning "involve a novel, highly organized synthesis of information rather than a photocopy of specific observed response" (p. 266).

Of course, people manifest individual differences in their range and quality of cognitive and behavioral construction competencies. If we expose a poet and a retardate to the same modeling display, the former will use the newly-acquired information very differently from the retardate. The individual assessment of cognitive and behavioral construction competencies is much like achievement testing, in that one tries to determine not typical behavior which is the focus of much personality assessment, but behavioral *potential,* which is the limit of one's capacity. In many ways, intelligence testing approaches the assessment of competence as spoken of by Mischel; this is particularly true of individually-administered scales, such as the Stanford-Binet which require the examinee to "do things." One's Stanford-Binet IQ is, therefore, largely determined by the quality of thinking and motor functioning revealed. In fact, IQ scores have repeatedly been shown to be excellent predictors of "later adjustment," and this adjustment is thought to depend upon high levels of construction competencies.

Encoding Strategies and Personal Constructs. The manner in which perceivers categorize, interpret, and bring meaning to what is seen, greatly influences what they subsequently learn and can do. Kelly has developed a substantive theory of personality whose fundamental postulate reads: "A person's processes are psychologically channeled by the ways in which he anticipates events" (1955, p. 46). What one does cognitively and behaviorally is a function of the way in which the world is construed. Kelly emphasizes that individual differences in personality merely reflect the uniqueness of each individual's set of personal constructs. While one's constructs are largely based upon real world experience, this experience, in turn, can only be understood in terms of one's constructs. For instance, a person might have come to construe people as generally hostile. To some degree this understanding dictates future meanings which will be imposed upon interpersonal encounters, as well as the behavior which will be exhibited: "Since people are hostile, this person walking toward me probably is ill-intentioned; I'd better make a hasty retreat." In contrast, when one holds the view that people are friendly, the same situation might result in the following reaction: "Since people are friendly, this person walking toward me probably intends to offer assistance; I'll go up to greet him." In summary, Kelly suggests that "man looks at his world through transparent patterns or templates (constructs) which he creates and then attempts to fit over the realities of which the world is composed" (1955, pp. 8-9). The similarity between the assumptions of Kelly and Mischel is apparent when the latter asserts that "people can readily perform *cognitive transformations* on stimuli, focusing on selected aspects of the objective stimulus (e.g., the taste versus the shape of a food object): such selective attention, interpretation, and categorization substantially alter the impact the stimulus exerts on behavior" (1973b, p. 267).

Behavior-Outcome and Stimulus-Outcome Expectancies. The first two person-variables, those concerned with construction capacities and constructs, really deal with potential behaviors. Like Rotter, Mischel invokes the notion of expectancies to explain why behavior appears as it does in specific situations. These expectancies regarding environmental contingencies are thought to develop "on the basis of direct experience, instructions, and observational learning" (1973b, 269).

Mischel argues for a distinction between two kinds of expectancies. He defines *behavior-outcome* expectancies as those which involve anticipations about outcomes of alternative behaviors. This meaning of "expectancy" is analogous to that of Rotter (1954) and presumably derives from one's vicarious and direct history of response-contingent reinforcements and punishments. In fact, Mischel makes the claim that the effectiveness of operant reinforcements "rests on their ability to modify behavior-outcome expectancies. When information about the response pattern required for reinforcement is conveyed to the subject by instructions, 'conditioning' tends to occur much more readily than when the subject must experience directly the reinforcing contingencies actually present in the operant training situation" (1973b, p. 270).

Expectancies for *stimulus-outcome* relations are thought to be more related to classical conditioning phenomena. Specifically, the CS is construed by Mischel as a sign, or cue, which enables the person to predict that other events are forthcoming. Pavlov's dogs learned that light is predictive of shock; the subject in an eyelid-conditioning experiment develops the expectation that a sound will be followed by a puff of air. This interpretation is supported by research showing that "any information which negates that expectancy will eliminate the conditioned response" (p. 271). For instance, our eyelid-conditioning subject will rapidly manifest extinction if, prior to the onset of extinction trials, he is told that no more puffs of air will be forthcoming. Of course, the speed of extinction may be related to the subject's constructs regarding the experimenter as a believable source of information.

Although not mentioned by Mischel, it seems that the functioning of discriminative stimuli (S^Ds) in operant conditioning paradigms can also be explained in terms of the expectancies they generate regarding stimulus-outcome relations. For instance, a person who undergoes avoidance conditioning learns that when the light (S^D) comes on, shock will follow unless the appropriate response is emitted. The outcome which is expected in this case is complex in that its nature is contingent upon the making of a response.

Subjective Stimulus Values. With this person-variable, Mischel is essentially re-naming the dimensions referred to by Rotter (1954) as reward value or need value. Mischel believes that the particular cognitive and behavioral constructions one engages in are a function of the value placed upon the expected consequences of these constructions.

Self-Regulatory Systems and Plans. The fifth and last of Mischel's suggested person-variables represents an acknowledgment of his belief that "the individual also regulates his own behavior by self-imposed goals (standards) and self-produced consequences" (1973b, p. 273). Our behavior is not just governed by the imposition of extrinsically imposed contingencies.

The notion of a self-imposed standard was previously discussed with reference to Rotter's construct of minimal goal level, but Mischel carries the point further. He suggests that people adopt contingency rules "that guide behavior in the absence of, and sometimes in spite of, immediate external situational pressures" (1973b, p. 274). These rules involve the specification of kinds and qualities of behaviors and their consequences. We saw, for example, that children establish cut-off scores for a bowling game, and provide verbal and tangible self-reinforcements only when their performances exceed the self-imposed minimal goal level. Failure to reach their performance goal is typically followed by statements of self-condemnation (Bandura and Kupers, 1964).

The word "plans" in the title of this person-variable is intended to convey the idea that people construct outlines for themselves regarding intended sequences of activities. These sequences may project far into the future and involve behaviors such as going to college, studying hard, going to medical school, etc. Each plan consists of an ordered series of sub-routines which appear to exercise considerable control over cognition and behavior.

In summary, with these five person-variables for a cognitive social learning theory of personality, Mischel believes he has made a beginning. "The selections should be seen as suggestive and open to progressive revision rather than as final. . . . But these variables should serve to demonstrate that a social behavior approach to persons does not suggest an empty organism" (1973b, p. 265).

The interaction between the person and environment.

From the perspective of Mischel's cognitive social learning theory, behavior is seen as being the outcome of the person in interaction with a situation. Situations are not seen to directly affect behavior; they exert influence only insofar as they have an impact upon a person's construction competencies, construct system, expectancies, reinforcement values, ability to generate plans, and other self-controlling mechanisms.

Mischel points out that situations are powerful when they induce everyone to construe things in the same way, and to develop similar expectancies, etc. The outcome will then be inter-individual behavioral stereotypy of the kind usually observed in well-controlled classical and operant conditioning experiments. Conversely, when the situation does not generate uniform cognitive effects across individuals, the behavioral outcome will be highly variable. In fact, projective tests are designed to take advantage of this very phenomenon; they are intentionally ambiguous with respect to their demands. To the degree they accomplish this, responses are more influenced by personal than by situational conditions.

Many instances consistent with Mischel's ideas can be found in everyday life. A classroom provides all sorts of cues which affect expectancies and reinforcement values in a way which is quite similar across students. For instance, the behavioral prerequisites for teacher reinforcement are usually common knowledge; consequently, one observes considerable behavioral stereotypy in this setting. In more relaxed social situations, where the range of expectations regarding response-reinforcement sequences is much broader, individual differences in observed behavior patterns are marked.

TRANSACTIONISM

Bandura, Rotter, and other social learning theorists have brought attention to what may be called *unidirectional interactionism*. Behavior is seen as the outcome of an interaction between situational and person-variables: Situation X person → behavior. Lately, Endler and Magnusson have popularized a more complex conceptualization of interactionism which involves *reciprocal causation* and takes the following form: Situation X person ⇄ behavior. This means that while situational and person-variables combine to affect behavior, behavior in turn affects the situation and person-variables. Endler and Magnussen suggest the term "transaction" for this reciprocal causation model to distinguish it from the simple conception of interactionism (1976, p. 969).

According to Endler and Magnusson a transactional personality theory is, in many ways, similar to Mischel's cognitive social learning theory. For instance, the situation is understood to be important only in terms of its psychological meaning to the perceiver. As for person-variables as determinants of behavior, they also focus on cognition. In addition, a main point of a transactional theory is that the individual is seen as being "an intentional active agent in this interaction process" (p. 969). Mischel deals with this issue when he emphasizes "self-regulatory systems and plans" as important person-variables.

The central feature of transactional personality theory is that "actual behavior is a function of a continuous process or multidirectional interaction (feedback) between the individual and the situation that he or she encounters" (p. 968). Mischel reveals himself to be quite sympathetic to a transactional viewpoint, although he employs the word "interaction" in this regard: ". . . some of the most striking differences between persons may be found . . . by analyzing their selection and construction of stimulus conditions . . . The person continuously influences the 'situations' in his life as well as being affected by them in a mutual, organic, two-way interaction" (1973, pp. 277-278). Mischel cites relevant research on this point by Raush to remind us that when naturalistic, ongoing interactions are investigated, "the major determinant of an act was the immediately preceding act. Thus, if you want to know what child B will do, the best single predictor is what child A did to child B the moment before" (Raush, 1965, p. 492). In other words, A has in part determined for himself the nature of the interpersonal situation to which he must now respond. Mischel concludes that "in a sense, the person is generating his own conditions" (1973b, p. 278).

Endler and Magnusson see transactional personality theory as "the model of behavior that . . . is most functional and realistic" and an ever-growing number of psychologists agree with them. (1976, p. 769), However, the complexities which are raised by transactional theory represent a considerable challenge to personality investigators, in that mutual dynamic interactionism is "an area for which we have not yet developed the necessary methodological and analytical tools" (p. 970).

EVALUATION

The cognitive trend in personality theory is the most significant current development in this area of psychology. One has only to follow the career of Mischel to see that a rapprochement between cognitive theory and behaviorism involves more than a cautious flirtation between two historically competitive positions. The "hybrid" which has arisen, and been given the generic title "cognitive-learning theory" by Mahoney (1977), appears to be here to stay.

While cognitive-learning theory may be a relatively strong vehicle for the analysis of personality, it is certainly not without its drawbacks. Most significantly, there has as yet been no systematic, inclusive personality theory developed from this point of view. Rotter has probably accomplished the most in this regard; however his 1954 statement remains substantially unchanged, and neither reflects the more comprehensive ideas regarding person-variables put forth by Mischel, nor those which pertain to transactionism.

A second major deficit has to do with what may be an inadequate language for scientific description. In particular, the word "cognition" has varied behavioral referents. Mahoney asks: ". . . What is a cognition? What differentiates a cognitive process from a non-cognitive one? What is the difference between a *process,* a *construct,* and an *event?"* (1977, p. 9). Fuzzy answers to these questions do not necessarily rule out the promise of cognitive-learning theory; nevertheless, some consensus on these points would certainly be of benefit. At the very least, one psychologist could then be clear on what another was saying.

Skinner has always maintained that a scientific psychology must deal only with observable events. Cognitive person-variables are non-observables which must be inferred from an external referent, such as overt behavior. This is acceptable as long as the magnitude or quality of the cognitive variable is inferred from some referent *other* than the one it is alleged to effect. Mahoney notes that, if one conducts research on the effects of fearful imagery upon autonomic arousal, "one cannot use the measures of arousal as indices of the imagery; that is, one cannot argue that highly-aroused subjects experienced the imagery but less aroused ones did not. This would be logically circular . . ." (1977, p. 10). Such tautologous inference is avoided if the investigator uses self-report or some other index independent of autonomic arousal as the measure of the inferred cognitive process in question.

Mahoney lists several other pitfalls which might impede the development of cognitive learning theory. It has inadequate tools to assess cognitive phenomena, and substantial ignorance regarding the development and change of cognitive person-variables. However, these concerns are raised in a constructive spirit, one which derives from a belief that "critical scrutiny is not just a technical amenity. It is a crucially important component in scientific growth" (p. 9).

SUMMARY

In this final chapter we sketched in the highlights of four actively growing theoretical positions. They each combine principles of learning theory with a ready acceptance of cognitive variables.

Our survey began with Bandura's observational learning. His major contribution was the introduction of a process, observational learning, which can readily account for the rapid acquisition of complex novel responses. In combination with principles of classical and operant conditioning, observational learning theory was shown to be a powerful explanatory tool.

More than any other cognitive theorist, Rotter, in his Social Learning Theory, has succeeded in operationalizing his major constructs of BP, RV, and E, and has formalized the relationships thought to exist among them. This resulted in an outpouring of research which, after more than two decades, remains unabated.

More recently, Mischel has integrated many of the ideas of Bandura and Rotter with those of cognitively-oriented personologists, such as George Kelly, and has presented an important new statement thrusting person-variables back into the center stage of personality theory. This trend is being carried one step further by transactional theorists, who view person-variables as not only important in their own right, but as being themselves determiners of the situation to which the person reacts.

502   Personality: Inquiry and Application

TERMS TO KNOW

	Page No.		Page No.
acquisition-performance distinction	470	no trial learning	468
attentional processes	468	observational learning	467
behavioral construction competency	496	outer-directed problem solving	469
behavior outcome expectancy	497	personal constructs	496
behavior potential (BP)	481	person-variables	495
cognitive construction competency	496	reinforcement values (RV)	481
Δ E'	484	response disinhibition	475
encoding strategy	496	response facilitation	476
expectancy (E)	482	response inhibition	475
freedom of movement (FM)	488	retention processes	469
generalized expectancy (GE)	483	self-regulatory systems and plans	498
I-E scale	490	Social Learning Theory	479
Interpersonal Trust Scale	491	specific expectancy (E')	483
locus of control	485	stimulus outcome expectancy	497
minimal goal level	488	subjective stimulus value	498
modeling effect	472	T-scope therapy	494
need potential (NP)	487	transactionism	499
need value (NV)	487	unidirectional interactionism	499
		vicarious extinction	473

References   503

REFERENCES

Aborn, M. The influence of experimentally induced failure on the retention of material acquired through set and incidental learning. *Journal of Experimental Psychology,* 1953, *45,* 225-231.

Adcock, C.J. Review of the MMPI. In O.K. Buros (Ed.) *Sixth mental measurements yearbook.* Highland Park, N.J.: Gryphon Press, 1965. Pp. 313-316.

Allen, K.E., Hart, B.M., Buell, J.S., Harris, F.R., & Wolf, M.M. Effects of social reinforcement on isolate behaviors of a nursery school child. *Child Development,* 1964, *35,* 511-518.

Allport, G.W. *Personality: A psychological interpretation.* New York: Holt, Rinehart & Winston, 1937.

Allport, G.W. *Patterns and growth in personality.* New York: Holt, Rinehart & Winston, 1961.

Allport, G.W., & Odbert, H.S. Trait names: A psycholexical study. *Psychological Monographs,* 1936, *47,* (Whole No. 211).

Altshuler, K.Z. Comments on recent sleep research related to psychoanalytic theory. *Archives of General Psychiatry,* 1966, *15,* 235-239.

American Psychological Association. *Ethical principles in the conduct of research with human participants.* Washington, D.C.: American Psychological Association, 1973.

American Psychological Association, *Standards for educational and psychological tests.* Washington, D.C.: American Psychological Association, 1974.

Amrine, M. The 1965 Congressional inquiry into testing: A commentary. *American Psychologist,* 1965, *20,* 859-870.

Anastasi, A. *Psychological testing (3rd ed.).* New York: Macmillan, 1968.

Appel, J.B. Punishment in the squirrel monkey Saimiri sciurea. *Science,* 1961, *133,* 36.

Aronson, E., & Carlsmith, J.M. Experimentation in social psychology. In G. Lindzey & E. Aronson (Eds.). *Handbook of social psychology (Vol. 2).* Reading, Mass.: Addison-Wesley, 1968.

Aronson, S.R. A comparison of cognitive vs. focused activities techniques in sensitivity group training. Unpublished doctoral dissertation, University of Connecticut, 1970.

Asch, S.E. *Social psychology.* Englewood Cliffs, N.J.: Prentice Hall, 1952.

Ash, P. Reliability of psychiatric diagnosis. *Journal of Abnormal and Social Psychology,* 1949, *44,* 272-277.

Atkinson, J.W., & Litwin, G.H. Achievement motive and test anxiety conceived as motive to approach success and motive to avoid failure. *Journal of Abnormal and Social Psychology,* 1960, *60,* 52-63.

Ayer, A.J. *Language, truth and logic.* New York: Dorien Pub., 1946.

Ayllon, T., & Azrin, H.H. The measurement and reinforcement of behavior of psychotics. *Journal of Experimental Analysis of Behavior,* 1965, *8,* 357-383.

Baer, D.M., Wolf, M.M., & Risley, T. Some current dimensions of applied behavior analysis. *Journal of Applied Behavioral Analysis,* 1968, *1,* 91-97.

Bandura, A. Vicarious processes: A case of no-trial learning. In L. Berkowitz (Ed.), *Advances in experimental social psychology. Vol. II.* New York: Academic Press, 1965. Pp. 1-55 (a).

Bandura, A. Influence of models' reinforcement contingencies on the acquisition of imitative responses. *Journal of Personality and Social Psychology,* 1965, *1,* 589-595 (b).

Bandura, A. *Principles of behavior modification.* New York: Holt, Rinehart & Winston, 1969.

Bandura, A., & Barab, P.G. Processes governing disinhibitory effects through symbollic modeling. *Journal of Abnormal Psychology,* 1973, *82,* 1-9.

Bandura, A., Grusec, J.E., & Menlove, F.L. Observational learning as a function of symbolization and incentive set. *Child Development,* 1966, *37,* 499-506.

Bandura, A., & Kupers, C.J. The transmission of patterns of self-reinforcement through modeling. *Journal of Abnormal and Social Psychology,* 1964, *69,* 1-9.

Bandura, A., & Menlove, F.L. Factors determining vicarious extinction of avoidance behavior through symbolic modeling. *Journal of Personality and Social Psychology,* 1968, *8,* 99-108.

Bandura, A., & Walters, R.H. *Social learning and personality development.* New York: Holt, Rinehart & Winston, 1963.

Barber, T.X., & Silver, M.J. Fact, fiction and the experimenter bias effect. *Psychological Bulletin Monograph,* 1968, *70,* 1-29.

Barcus, F.E. *Saturday children's television: A report on TV programming and advertising on Boston commercial television.* Boston: Action for Children's Television, 1971.

Bardwick, J.M. *Psychology of women.* New York: Harper & Row, 1971.

Barnes, E.H. The relationship of biased test responses to psychopathology. Unpublished doctoral dissertation, Northwestern University, 1954.

Baron, R.A., & Bell, P.A. Aggression and heat: The influence of ambient temperature, negative affect, and a cooling drink on physical aggression. *Journal of Personality and Social Psychology,* 1976, *3,* 245-255.

Barthell, C.N. & Holmes, D.S. High school yearbooks: A nonreactive measure of social isolation in graduates who later become schizophrenic. *Journal of Abnormal Psychology,* 1968, *73,* 313-316.

Barton, E.S., Guess, D., Garcia, E., & Baer, D.M. Improvement of retardates' mealtime behaviors by time-out procedures using multiple baseline techniques. *Journal of Applied Behavior Analysis,* 1970, *3,* 77-84.

Battle, E.S., & Rotter, J.B. Children's feelings of personal control as related to social class ethnic group. *Journal of Personality,* 1963, *3,* 482-490.

Bechtoldt, H.P. Selection. In S.S. Stevens (Ed.) *Handbook of Experimental Psychology.* New York: Wiley, 1951. Pp. 1237-1267.

Becker, W.C. Comments on Cattell's paper on "perturbations" in personality structure research. *Psychological Bulletin,* 1961, *58,* 175.

Bentler, P.M., Jackson, D.N., & Messick, S. Identification of content and style: A two dimensional interpretation of acquiescence. *Psychological Bulletin,* 1971, *76,* 186-204.

Berg, I.A. Response bias and personality: The deviation hypothesis. *Journal of Psychology,* 1955, *40,* 61-72.

Berg, I.A. Deviant responses and deviant people. *Journal of Counseling Psychology,* 1957, *4,* 154-161.

Berg, I.A., & Hunt, W.A. *The Perceptual Reaction Test.* Evanston, Ill.: 1949.

Berg, I.A. & Rapaport, G.M. Response bias in an unstructured questionnaire. *Journal of Psychology,* 1954, *38,* 475-481.

Bergmann, G., & Spence, K.W. Operationism and theory in psychology. *Psychological Review,* 1941, *48,* 1-14.

Berkowitz, L. The effects of observing violence. In *Scientific American. Psychology in progress.* San Francisco: W.H. Freeman, 1975. Pp. 303-309.

Bernal, G., & Berger, S.M. Vicarious eyelid conditioning. *Journal of Personality and Social Psychology,* 1976, *34,* 62-68.

Bieri, J. Cognitive complexity and predictive behavior. *Journal of Abnormal and Social Psychology,* 1955, *51,* 263-268.

Black, J.D. The interpretation of MMPI profiles of college women. Doctoral dissertation, University of Minnesota, 1953. Reprinted in part in Welsh, G.S. & Dahlstrom, W.G. (Eds.) *Basic reading on the MMPI in psychology and medicine.* Minneapolis: University of Minnesota Press, 1956.

Block, J. *The Q-Sort method in personality assessment and psychiatric research.* Springfield, Ill.: Charles C. Thomas, Publisher, 1961.

Block, J. On further conjectures regarding acquiescence. *Psychological Bulletin,* 1971, *76,* 205-210.

Blum, G.S. *The Blacky pictures.* New York: Psychological Corporation, 1950.

Blum, G.S., & Miller, D.R. Exploring the psychoanalytic theory of the "oral character." *Journal of Personality,* 1952, *20,* 287-304.

Bouchard, T.J. Review of the 16 PF. In O.K. Buros (Ed) *Seventh Mental Measurement Yearbook* (Vol. 1). Highland Park, N.J.: Gryphon Press, 1972. Pp. 329-332.

Bowers, K.S. Situationism in psychology. *Psychological Review,* 1973, *80,* 307-336.

Braddock, J.H. Radicalism and alienation among black college students: A comparison of black students' attitudes at Florida Agricultural and Mechanical University and Florida State University. Unpublished master's thesis, Florida State University, 1972.

Brady, J.V. Ulcers in "executive monkeys." *Scientific American,* 1958, *199,* 95-100.

Braginsky, B.M., & Braginsky, D.O. Schizophrenic patients in the psychiatric interview: An experimental study of their effectiveness at manipulation. *Journal of Consulting Psychology,* 1967, *31,* 543-547.

Braginsky, B., Braginsky, D., & Ring, K. Methods of Madness: The mental hospital as a last resort. New York: Holt, Rinehart & Winston, 1969.

Braginsky, B., Grosse, M., & Ring, K. Controlling outcomes through impression management: an experimental study of the manipulative tactics of mental patients. *Journal of Counseling Psychology,* 1966, *30,* 295-300.

Bramel, D. A dissonance theory approach to defensive projection. *Journal of Abnormal and Social Psychology,* 1962, *64,* 121-129.

Braun, J.R. Effects of "typical neurotic" and "after therapy" set on Personal Orientation Inventory scores. *Psychological Reports,* 1966, *19,* 1282.

Brayfield, A. About special privilege—and special responsibility. *American Psychologist,* 1965, *20,* 857.

Breger, L. Function of dreams. *Journal of Abnormal Psychology Monograph,* 1967, *72* (Whole No. 641).

Brenner, C. *An elementary textbook of psychoanalysis.* Garden City, N.Y.: Doubleday, 1957.

Bridger, W.H., & Mandel, I.J. Abolition of the PRE by instructions in GSR conditioning. *Journal of Experimental Psychology,* 1965, *69,* 476-482.

Brody, N., & Oppenheim, P. Methodological differences between behaviorism and phenomenology in psychology. *Psychological Review,* 1967, *74,* 330-334.

Brown, R., & Bellugi, U. Three processes in the child's acquisition of eyntax. *Harvard Educational Review, 1964, 34,* 133-151.

Buhler, C. Basic theoretical concepts of humanistic psychology. *American Psychologist,* 1971, *26,* 378-386.

Burdock, E.I., & Hardesty, A.S. Psychological test for psychopathology. *Journal of Abnormal Psychology.,* 1968, *73,* 62-69.

Butcher, J.N. *Objective Personality Assessment.* New York: General Learning Press, 1971.

Butcher, J.N., & Tellogen, A. Objections to MMPI items. *Journal of Consulting Psychology,* 1966, *30,* 527-534.

Butler, J.M., & Haigh, G.V. Changes in the relation between self-concepts and ideal concepts consequent upon client-centered counseling. In C.R. Rogers & R. Dymond (Eds.), *Psychotherapy and personality change.* Chicago: University of Chicago Press, 1954. Pp. 55-75.

Campbell, D.T., & Fiske, D.W. Convergent and discriminant validation by the multi-trait multi method matrix. *Psychological Bulletin,* 1959, *56,* 81-105.

Campbell, D.T., Cruskal, W.H., & Wallace, W.P. Seating segregation as an index of attitude. *Sociometry,* 1966, *29,* 1-15.

Campbell, D.T., & Stanley, J.C. *Experimental and quasi-experimental designs for research.* Chicago: Rand McNally, 1963.

Cannon, W.Z. *The way of an investigator.* New York: Norton, 1945.

Cattell, R.B., Eber, H.W., & Tatsuoka, M.M. *Handbook for the Sixteen Personality Factor Questionnaire* (3rd Ed.). Champaign, Ill.: Institute for Personality and Ability Testing, 1970.

Cautela, J.R. Treatment of compulsive behavior by covert sensitization. *Psychological Record,* 1966, *16,* 33-34.

Clark, R.A. Projective measurement of sexual motivation. *Journal of Experimental Psychology,* 1952, *44,* 391-399.

Coan, R.W., & Fairchild, M.T. The personal opinion survey. Unpublished Manuscript, University of Arizona, undated.

Coffin, T.E. Some conditions of suggestion and suggestibility. *Psychological Monographs,* 1941,*53,* No. 4, Chapter 4.

Cohen, L.H. Imagery and its relation to schizophrenic symptoms. *Journal of Mental*

Science, 1938, *84*, 248-346.

Combs, A.W., & Snygg, D. *Individual behavior: A new frame of reference for psychology*. New York: Harper & Brothers, 1949.

Combs, A.W., & Snygg, D. *Individual behavior: A perceptual approach to behavior*. New York: Harper & Brothers, 1959.

Conger, J.J. The effects of alcohol on conflict behavior in the albino rat. *Quarterly Journal of Studies on Alcoholism*, 1951, *12*, 1-29.

Conrad, H.S. Clearance of questionnaires with respect to "invasion of privacy" public sensitivities, ethical standards, etc. *American Psychologist*, 1967, *22*, 356-359.

Couch, A., & Keniston, K. Yeasayers and Naysayers: Agreeing response set as a personality variable. *Journal of Abnormal and Social Psychology*, 1960, *60*, 151-174.

Cox, B., & Sargent, H. TAT responses of emotionally disturbed and emotionally stable children: Clinical judgement vs. normative data. *Journal of Projective Techniques*, 1950, *14*, 60-74.

Craig, K.D. Physiological arousal as a function of imaginal, vicarious and direct stress experiences. *Journal of Abnormal Psychology*, 1968, *73*, 513-520.

Cronbach, L.J. Coefficient alpha and the internal structure of tests. *Psychometrikea*, 1951, *16*, 297-334.

Cronbach, L.J. *Essentials of psychological testing*. New York: Harper and Row, 1970.

Cronbach, L.J., & Meehl, P.E. Construct validity in psychological tests. *Psychological Bulletin*, 1955, *52*, 281-302.

Crowne, D.P., & Marlowe, D. A new scale of social desirability independent of psychopathology. *Journal of Consulting Psychology*, 1960, *24,* 349-354.

Crowne, D.P., Marlowe, D. *The approval motive: Studies in evaluative dependence*. New York: Wiley, 1964.

Culbert, S.A., Clark, J.U., & Bobele, H.K. Measures of change toward selfactualization in two sensitivity training groups. *Journal of Counseling Psychology*, 1968, *15*, 53-57.

Cumming, J., & Cumming, E. On the stigma of mental illness. *Community Mental Health Journal*, 1965, *1*, 135-143.

Dahlstrom, W.G., & Welsh, G.S. *An MMPI handbook: A guide to use in clinical practice and research*. Minneapolis: University of Minnesota Press, 1960.

Dahlstrom, W.G., Welsh, G.S., & Dahlstrom, L.E. *An MMPI handbook (Vol.1)*. Minneapolis: University of Minnesota Press, 1972.

Datel, W.E., & Gengerelli, J.A. Reliability of Rorschach interpretations. *Journal of Projective Techniques*, 1955, *19*, 372-381.

Davis, C. Studies in the self-selection diet by young children. *American Journal of Diseases of Children*, 1933, *46*, 743-750.

Davis, W.E., & Jones, M.H. Negro versus caucasian psychological test performance revisited. *Journal of Consulting and Clinical Psychology*, 1974, *42*, 675-679.

Davison, G.C., & Wilson, G.T. Goals and strategies in behavioral treatment of homosexual pedophilia: Comments on a case study. *Journal of Abnormal Psychology*, 1974, *83*, 196-198.

de Charms, R., Morrison, A.W., Reitman, W., & McClelland, D.C. Behavioral corre-lates of directly and indirectly measured achievement motivation, In D.C. McClel-land (Ed.), *Studies in motivation*. New York: Appleton-Century-Crofts, 1955.

Depue, R.A., & Fowles, D.C. Electrodermal activity as an index of arousal in schizo-phrenics. *Psychological Bulletin*, 1973, *79*, 233-238.

Doll, E.A. *Vineland Social Maturity Scale: Manual of directions* (Rev. ed.). Min-neapolis: American Guidance Service, 1965.

Dollard, J. & Miller, N.E. *Personality and psychotherapy*. New York: McGraw-Hill, 1950.

Doob, A.N., & Gross, A.E. Status of frustration as an inhibitor of horn-honking response. *Journal of Social Psychology*, 1968, *76*, 213-218.

Drabman, R.S., Spitalnik, R.S., & O'Leary, K.D. Teaching self-control to disruptive children. *Journal of Abnormal Psychology*, 1973, *82*, 10-16.

Drake, L.E., & Otting, E.R. *An MMPI codebook for counselors*. Minneapolis: Univer-sity of Minnesota Press, 1959.

DuBrin, A.J. The Rorschach "eyes" hypothesis and paranoid schizophrenia. *Journal of Clinical Psychology*, 1962, *18*, 468-471.

Dunlap, R.L. Changes in children's preferences for goal objects as a function of differences in expected social reinforcements. Unpublished doctoral dissertation, Ohio State University, 1953.

Dymond, R. Adjustment changes over therapy from self-sorts. In C.R. Rogers & R. Dymond (Eds.), *Psychotherapy and personality change*. Chicago: University of Chicago Press, 1954. Pp. 76-84.

D'Zurilla, T. Recall efficiency and mediating cognitive events in "experimental repres-sion." *Journal of Personality and Social Psychology*, 1965, *3*, 253-256.

Edwards, A.L. The relationship between the judged desirabilities of a trait and the probability that the trait will be endorsed. *Journal of Applied Psychology*, 1953, *37*, 90-93 (a).

Edwards, A.L. *Manual for Edwards Personal Preference Schedule*. New York: Psychological Corporation, 1953 (b).

Edwards, A.L. *The social desirability variable in personality assessment and research*. New York: Dryden Press, 1957.

Edwards A.L. *Manual for Edwards Personal Preference Schedule* (Revised). New York: Psychological Corporation, 1959.

Edwards, A.L. Social desirability or acquiescence in the MMPI? A case study with the SD scale. *Journal of Abnormal and Social Psychology*, 1961, *63*, 351-359.

Edwards, A.L. Social desirability and performance on the MMPI. *Psychometrika*, 1964, *29*, 295-308.

Efran, J.D., & Marcia, J.E. Systematic desensitization and social learning. In J.B. Rotter, J.E. Chanee, & E.J. Phares (Eds.) *Applications of a social learning theory of personality*. New York: Holt, Rinehart, & Winston, 1972. Pp. 524-532.

Eichler, R.M. Experimental stress and alleged Rorschach indices of anxiety. *Journal of Abnormal and Social Psychology*, 1951, *46*, 344-355.

Eisler, R.M. Thematic expression of sexual conflict under varying stimulus conditions.

Journal of Consulting and Clinical Psychology, 1968, *32*, 216-220.

Elion, V.H., & Megargee, E.I. Validity of the MMPI *Pd* scale among Black males. *Journal of Consulting and Clinical Psychology*, 1975, *43*, 166-172.

Endler, N.S., & Hunt, J.McV. Sources of behavioral variance as measured by the S-R Inventory of anxiousness. *Psychological Bulletin*, 1966, *65*, 336-346.

Endler, N.S., Hunt, J.McV., & Rosenstein, A.J. An S-R Inventory of anxiousness. *Psychological Monographs*, 1962, *76*, 1-33.

Endler, N.S., & Magnusson, D. Toward an interactional psychology of personality. *Psychological Bulletin*, 1976, *83*, 956-974.

Endler, N.S., & Okada, M. A multi-dimensional measure of trait anxiety: The S-R Inventory of general trait anxiousness. *Journal of Consulting and Clinical Psychology*, 1975, *43*, 319-329.

Epstein, S. Some theoretical considerations on the nature of ambiguity and the use of stimulus dimensions in projective tests. *Journal of Consulting Psychology*, 1966, *30*, 183-192.

Eron, L.D. A normative study of the Thematic Apperception Test. *Psychological Monographs*, 1950, *64*, (Whole No. 315).

Eron, L.D., Huesmann, L.R., Lefkowitz, M.M., & Walder, L.O. Does television violence cause violence? *American Psychologist*, 1972, *27*, 253-263.

Ervin, S.J. Why Senate hearings on psychological tests in government? *American Psychologist,* 1965, *20,* 879-880.

Evans, G.W., & Howard, R.B. Personal space. *Psychological Bulletin*, 1973, *80*, 334-344.

Evers, W.L., & Schwarz, J.C. Modifying social withdrawal in preschoolers: The effects of filmed modeling and teacher reinforcement. *Journal of Abnormal Child Psychology*, 1973, *1*, 248-256.

Evers-Pasquale, W., & Sherman, M. The reward value of peers: A variable influencing the efficacy of filmed modeling in modifying social isolation in pre-schoolers. *Journal of Abnormal Child Psychology*, 1975, *3*, 179-189.

Exner, J.E. *The Rorschach: A comprehensive system.* New York: Wiley, 1974.

Eysenck, H.J., & Eysenck, S.B.G. *The Eysenck Personality Inventory*. San Diego, CA: Educational and Industrial Testing Service, 1963.

Eysenck, H.J., & Rachman, S. *The causes and cures of neurosis*. London: Routledge, & Kegan Paul, 1965.

Fancher, R.E., & Strahan, R.F. Galvanic skin response and the secondary revision of dreams: A partial disconfirmation of Freud's dream theory. *Journal of Abnormal Psychology*, 1971, *77*, 308-312.

Farber, I.E. The things people say to themselves. *American Psychologist*, 1963, *18*, 185-197.

Farina, A., Hagelauer, H.D., & Holzberg, J.D. Influence of psychiatric history on physicians' response to a new patient. *Journal of Consulting and Clinical Psychology*, 1976, *44*, 499.

Farina, A., Holland, C., & Ring K. Role of stigma and set in interpersonal interaction. *Journal of Abnormal Psychology*, 1966, *71*, 421-428.

Farr, J., & Seaver, W.B. Stress and discomfort in psychological research: subject perceptions of experimental procedures. *American Psychologist*, 1975, *30*, 770-773.

Faschinghauer, T. A short written form of the group MMPI. Unpublished doctoral dissertation,-University of North Carolina, 1973.

Feldman, M.P. Aversion therapy for sexual deviations: A critical review. *Psychological Bulletin*, 1966, *65*, 65-79.

Fenichel, O. *The psychoanalytic theory of neurosis*. New York: Norton, 1945.

Ferster, C.R., & Skinner, B.F. *Schedules of reinforcement*. New York: Appleton-Century-Crofts, 1957.

Findley, J.D., & Brady, J.V. Facilitation of large ratio performance by use of a conditioned reinforcement. *Journal of the Experimental Analysis of Behavior*, 1965, *8*, 125-129.

Fisher, S., & Cleveland, S.E. *Body image and personality*. New York: Van Nostrand, 1958.

Ford, D.H., & Urban, H.B. *Systems of psychotherapy*. New York: Wiley, 1963.

Forer, B.B. The fallacy of personal validation: A classroom demonstration of gullibility. *Journal of Abnormal and Social Psychology*, 1949, *44*, 118-123.

Foreyt, J.O., & Hagen, R.L. Convert sensitization: Conditioning or suggestion? *Journal of Abnormal Psychology*, 1973, *82*, 17-23.

Foulds, M.L., & Warehime, R.G. Effects of a "fake good" response set on a measure of self-actualization. *Journal of Counseling Psychology*, 1971, *18*, 279-280.

Foxx, R.M. & Azrin, N.H. Dry pants: A rapid method of toilet training children. *Behavior Research and Therapy*, 1973, *11*, 435-442.

Frank, L. Projective methods for the study of personality. *Journal of Psychology*, 1939, *8*, 389-413.

Frederiksen, N. Toward a taxonomy of situations. *American Psychologist* 1972, *27*, 114-123.

Freud, A. *The ego and the mechanisms of defense*. New York: International University Press, Inc., 1936.

Freud, S. *The problem of anxiety*. New York: Norton, 1936.

Freud, S. *An outline of psychoanalysis*. New York: Norton, 1949.

Freud, S. *Psychopatholgy of everyday life*. New York: New American Library, 1951.

Freud, S. *A general introduction to psychoanalysis*. New York: Washington Square Press, 1952(a).

Freud, S. *On Dreams*. New York: Norton, 1952(b).

Freud, S. *The interpretation of dreams*. New York: Basic Books, 1955(a).

Freud, S. *Standard edition of the complete psychological works of Sigmund Freud*. (James Strachey, Ed.) Vol. X *Two case histories: "Little Hans" and the "Rat Man."* London: Hogarth Press, 1955(b).

Freud, S. *A general selection from the works of Sigmund Freud*. (J. Richman, Ed.) New York: Doubleday, 1957.

Freud, S. *Jokes and their relation to the unconscious*. New York: Norton, 1960(a).

Freud, S. *The ego & the id*. New York: Norton, 1960(b).

Freud, S. *Therapy and technique*. New York: Collier Books, 1963.

Freud, S. *New introductory lectures on psychoanalysis*. New York: Norton, 1965.

Freud, S. *On the historyof the psyhchoanalytic movement*. New York: Norton, 1966.

Freund, K. A laboratory method for diagnosing predominence of home and hetero-erotic interest in the male. *Behavior Research and Therapy*, 1963, *1*, 85-93.

Freund, K. Diagnosing heterosexual pedophilia by means of a test for sexual interest. *Behavior Research and Therapy*, 1965, *3*, 229-234.

Friedman, H. Perceptual regression in schizophrenia: An hypothesis suggested by the use of the Rorschach test. *Journal of Genetic Psychology*, 1952, *81*, 63-98.

Friedman, H. Perceptual regression: An hypothesis suggested by the use of the Rorschach test. *Journal of Projective Techniques*, 1953, *17*, 171-185.

Fromer, R. & Berkowitz, L. Effect of sudden and gradual shock onset on the conditioned fear response. *Journal of Comparative and Physiological Psychology*, 1964, *8*, 169-170.

Fromm, E. *Man for himself*. New York: Holt, Rinehart, & Winston, 1947.

Fromm, E. *Sigmund Freud's mission: An analysis of his personality and influence*. New York: Harper & Row, 1959.

Gage, N.L. Accuracy of social perception and effectiveness in interpersonal relationships. *Journal of Personality*, 1953, *22*, 128-141.

Gallagher, C.E. Why House hearings on invasion of privacy? *American Psychologist*, 1955, *20*, 881-882.

Garfield, S.L. Values: An issue in psychotherapy: Comments on a case study. *Journal of Abnormal Psychology*, 1974, *83*, 202-203.

Garmezy, N. Children at risk: The search for the antecedents of schizophrenia. Part II: Ongoing research programs, issues, and intervention. *Schizophrenia Bulletin*, 1974, *No. 9*, 55-125.

Geer, J.H. The development of a scale to measure fear. *Behavior Research and Therapy*, 1965, *3*, 45-53.

Gerbner, G. Violence in television drama: Trends and symbolic functions. In G.A. Comstock and E.A. Rubenstein (Eds.) *Television and social behavior* (Vol. I.) *Media content and control*. Washington, D.C.: U.S. Government Printing Office, 1972.

Gibby, R.G., Miller, D.R., & Walker, E.L. The examiner's influence on the Rorschach protocol. *Journal of Consulting Psychology*, 1953, *17*, 425-428.

Gilberstadt, H. & Duker, J. *A handbook for clinical and acturial MMPI interpretation*. Philadelphia: Saunders, 1965.

Ginott, H. *Between parent and teenager*. New York: Avon Books, 1969.

Glatt, C.T., & Karon, B.P. A Rorschach validation study of the ego regression theory of psychopathology. *Journal of Consulting and Clinical Psychology*, 1974, *42*, 569-576.

Goffman, E. *Stigma: Notes on the management of spoiled identity*. Englewood Cliffs, N.J.: Prentice-Hall, 1959.

Goldberg, L.R. Simple models or simple processes? Some research on clinical judgements. *American Psychologist*, 1968, *23*, 483-491.

Goldberg, L.R. Review of the CPI. In O.K. Buros (Ed.). *Seventh Mental Measurement Yearbook,* (Vol. 1). Highland Park, N.J.: Gryphon Press, 1972. Pp. 94-96.

Goldfried, M.R., & Kent, R.N. Traditional vs. behavioral personality assessment: A comparison of methodological and theoretical assumptions. *Psychological Bulletin,* 1972, *77,* 409-420.

Goldfried, M.R., & Sprafkin, J.N. *Behavioral personality assessment.* Morristown, N.J.: General Learning Press, 1974.

Goldstein, A.P. *Therapist-patient expectancies in psychotherapy.* New York: Pergamon Press, 1962.

Goldstein, A.P. *Structured learning therapy: Toward a psychotherapy for the poor.* New York: Academic Press, 1973.

Goldstein, A.P., Heller, K., & Sechrest, L.B. *Psychotherapy and the psychology of behavior change.* New York: Wiley, 1966.

Goldstein, A.P., & Stein, N. *Prescriptive psychotherapy.* New York: Pergamon Press, 1976.

Goldwater, B.C. Psychological significance of pupilary movements. *Psychological Bulletin,* 1972, *77,* 340-355.

Goodfellow, L.D. The human element in probability. *Journal of General Psychology,* 1940, *33,* 201-205.

Gootnick, A.T. Locus of control and political participation of college students: A comparison of unidimensional and multidimensional approaches. *Journal of Consulting and Clinical Psychology,* 1974, *42,* 54-58.

Gore, R., & Rotter, J.B. A personality correlate of social action. *Journal of Personality,* 1963, *31,* 58-64.

Gorman, B.S. An observation of altered locus of control following political disappointment. *Psychological Reports,* 1968, *33,* 582-589.

Gottman, J.M. N-of-one and N-of-two research in psychotherapy. *Psychological Bulletin,* 1973, *80,* 93-105.

Gough, H.G. *California Psychological Inventory.* Palo Alto, CA.: Consulting Psychologists Press, 1956-1960.

Greenspoon, J. The reinforcing effects of two spoken words on the frequency of two responses. *American Journal of Psychology,* 1955, *68,* 409-416.

Grings, W.W. Verbal-perceptual factors in the conditioning of autonomic responses. In W. F. Prokasy (Ed.), *Classical conditioning: A symposium.* New York: Appleton-Century-Crofts, 1965. Pp. 71-89.

Grings, W.W., & Lockhart, R.A. Effects of "anxiety-lessening" instructions and differential set development on the extinction of GSR. *Journal of Experimental Psychology,* 1963, *66,* 292-299.

Gross, L.R. Effects of verbal and nonverbal reinforcement in the Rorschach. *Journal of Consulting Psychology,* 1959, *53,* 66-68.

Grossberg, J.M., & Wilson, H.K. Physiological changes accompanying the visualization of fearful and neutral situations. *Journal of Personality and Social Psychology,* 1968, *10,* 124-133..

Gulanick, N., Woodburn, L.T., & Rimm, D.C. Weight gain through self-control procedures. *Journal of Consulting and Clinical Psychology,* 1975, *43,* 536-539.

Guttmann, N. On Skinner and Hull: A reminiscence and projection. *American Psychologist,* 1977, *32,* 321-328.

Gynther, M.D. White norms and black MMPIs: A prescription for discrimination? *Psychological Bulletin,* 1972, *78,* 386-402.

Haase, W. The role of socioeconomic class in examiner bias. In F. Russman, J. Cohen, & A. Pearl (Eds.), *Mental health of the poor.* New York: Free Press of Glencoe, 1964.

Hall, C.S. *A Primer of Freudian Psychology.* New York: Mentor, 1954.

Hall, C.S., & Lindzey, G. *Theories of personality.* New York: Wiley, 1957.

Hall, C.S., & Lindzey, G. *Theories of personality (2nd Ed.).* New York: Wiley, 1970.

Hall, C., & Van de Castle, R.L. An empirical investigation of the castration complex in dreams. *Journal of Personality,* 1965, *33,* 20-29.

Hamsher, J.H., Geller, J.D., & Rotter, J.B. Interpersonal trust, internal-external control, and the Warren Commission report. *Journal of Personality and Social Psychology,* 1968, *9,* 210-215.

Hanley, C. Social desirability and responses to items from three MMPI scales: D, Sc, and K. *Journal of Applied Psychology,* 1956, *40,* 324-328.

Harlow, H.F. The nature of love. *American Psychologist,* 1958, *13,* 673-685.

Harré, R., & Secord, P.F. *The explanation of social behavior.* Oxford: Basil, Blackwell & Mott, 1972.

Harris, S., & Masling, J. Examiner sex, subject sex, and Rorschach productivity. *Journal of Consulting and Clinical Psychology,* 1970, *34,* 60-63.

Harrison, R.H., & Kass, E.H. Differences between Negro & white pregnant women on the MMPI. *Journal of Consulting Psychology,* 1967, *31,* 454-463.

Harrison, R.H., & Kass, E.H. MMPI correlates of Negro acculturation in a northern city. *Journal of Personality and Social Psychology,* 1968, *10,* 262-270.

Hartshorne, H., & May, M.A. *Studies in the nature of character: Studies in deceit.* New York: Macmillan, 1928.

Hathaway, S.R. A coding system for MMPI profile classification. *Journal of Consulting Psychology,* 1947, *11,* 334-337.

Hathaway, S.R. Seminar to graduate clinical psychology trainees and residents in neuropsychiatry, 1957.

Hathaway, S.R. MMPI: Professional use by professional people. *American Psychologist,* 1964, *19,* 204-210.

Hathaway, S.R., & McKinley, J.C. *Manual for the Minnesota Multiphasic Personality Inventory.* Minneapolis: University of Minnesota Press, 1943.

Hathaway, S.R., & Meehl, P.E. *An atlas for the clinical use of the MMPI.* Minneapolis: University of Minnesota Press, 1951.

Hathaway, S.R., & Monachesi, E.D. *An atlas of juvenile MMPI profiles.* Minneapolis: University of Minnesota Press, 1961.

Hebb, D.O. The motivating effects of exteroceptive stimulation. *American Psychologist,* 1958, *13,* 109-113.

Hedlund, J.L., Cho, D.W., & Powell, B.J. Use of MMPI short forms with psychiatric patients. *Journal of Consulting and Clinical Psychology,* 1975, *43,* 924.

Heilbrun, A.B. Revision of the MMPI *K* correction procedure for improved detection of maladjustment in a normal population. *Journal of Consulting Psychology,* 1963, *27,* 161-165.

Heilbrun, A.B. Social learning theory, social desirability, and the MMPI. *Psychological Bulletin,* 1964, *61,* 377-387.

Hendrick, I. *Facts and theories of psychoanalysis.* New York: Delta, 1958.

Henry, E.M., & Rotter, J.B. Situational influences on Rorschach responses. *Journal of Consulting Psychology,* 1956, *20,* 457-462.

Hersh, J.B. Effects of referral information on testers. *Journal of Consulting and Clinical Psychology,* 1971, *37,* 116-122.

Hess, E.H. Attitude and pupil size. *Scientific American,* 1965, *212,* 46-54.

Hess, E.H., & Polt, J.M. Pupil size as related to interest value of visual stimuli. *Science,* 1960, *132,* 349-350.

Hess, E.H., & Polt, J.M. Pupil size in relation to mental activity during simple problem solving. *Science,* 1964, *143,* 1190-1192.

Hess, E.H., Seltzer, A.C., & Shlien, J.M. Pupil response of hetero- and homosexual males to pictures of men and women: A pilot study. *Journal of Abnormal Psychology,* 1965, *70,* 165-168.

Hoffman, N.G., & Butcher, J.N. Clinical limitations of three Minnesota Multiphasic Personality Inventory short forms. *Journal of Consulting and Clinical Psychology,* 1975, *43,* 32-39.

Holmes, D. Dimensions of projection. *Psychological Bulletin,* 1968, *69,* 248-268.

Holmes, D. The conscious control of thematic projection. *Journal of Consulting and Clinical Psychology,* 1974, *42,* 323-329(a).

Holmes, D.S. Investigations of repression: Differential recall of material experimentally or naturally associated with ego threat. *Psychological Bulletin,* 1974, *81,* 632-653(b).

Holz, W.C., & Azrin, N.H. Discriminative properties of punishment. *Journal of the Experimental Analysis of Behavior,* 1961, *4,* 225-232.

Holzmàn, P. *Psychoanalysis and psychopathology.* New York: McGraw-Hill, 1970.

Horowitz, M.J. A study of clinicians' judgments from projective test protocols. *Journal of Consulting Psychology,* 1962, *26,* 251-256.

Horowitz, I.A., & Rothschild, B.H. Conformity as a function of deception and role playing. *Journal of Personality and Social Psychology,* 1970, *14,* 224-226.

Hull, C.L. *Principles of behavior.* New York: Appleton-Century-Crofts, 1943.

Humphreys, L. *Tearoom trade.* Chicago: Aldine, 1970.

Hutt, M.L., & Gibby, R.G. *Patterns of abnormal behavior.* Boston: Allyn & Bacon, 1957.

Ilardi, R.L., & May, W.T. A reliability study of Shostrom's Personal Orientation Inventory. *Journal of Humanistic Psychology,* 1968, *8,* 68-72.

Insko, C.A., & Oakes, W.F. Awareness and the "conditioning" of attitudes. *Journal of Personality and Social Psychology,* 1966, *4,* 487-496.

Irvine, M.J., & Gendreau, P. Detection of the fake "good" and "bad" response on the sixteen personality factor inventory in prisoners and college students. *Journal of Consulting and Clinical Psychology,* 1974, *42,* 465-466.

Ives, V., Grant, M.Q., & Ranzoni, J.H. The "neurotic" Rorschachs of normal adolescents. *Journal of Genetic Psychology,* 1953, *83,* 31-61.

Jackson, D.N., & Messick, S. Content and style in personality assessment. *Psychological Bulletin,* 1958, *55,* 243-251.

Jacobson, E. *Progressive relaxation.* Chicago: University of Chicago Press, 1938.

Jacobson, N.S. Problem solving and contingency contracting in the treatment of marital discord. *Journal of Consulting and Clinical Psychology,* 1977, *45,* 92-100.

Jacobson, N.S., & Martin, B. Behavioral marriage therapy: Current status. *Psychological Bulletin,* 1976, *83,* 540-556.

James, W.H., Woodruff, A.B., & Werner, W. Effect of internal and external control upon changes in smoking behavior. *Journal of Consulting Psychology,* 1965, *29,* 127-129.

Janda, L.H., & Rimm, D.C. Covert sensitization in the treatment of obesity. *Journal of Abnormal Psychology,* 1972, *80,* 37-42.

Janis, I.L., Mahl, G.F., Kagan, J., and Holt, R.R. *Personality: Dynamics, development and assessment.* New York: Harcourt, Brace & World, 1969.

Jensen, A. Review of the Rorschach. In O.K. Buros (Ed.) *Sixth Mental Measurement yearbook.* Highland Park, N.H.: Gryphon Press, 1965. P. 238.

Johnson, W. *People in quandries.* New York: Harper & Bros., 1946.

Jones, E. *The life and work of Sigmund Freud (Vol. 1).* New York: Basic Books, 1953.

Jones, M.C. A behavior study of fear: The case of Peter. *Journal of Genetic Psychology,* 1924, *31,* 508-515.

Jones, M.C. Albert, Peter & John B. Watson. *American Psychologist,* 1974, *29,* 581-583.

Jung, C. The association method. *American Journal of Psychology,* 1910, *21,* 219-269.

Kagan, J. The measurement of overt aggression from fantasy. *Journal of Abnormal and Social Psychology,* 1956, *52,* 390-393.

Kanfer, F.H., & Phillips, J.S. *Learning foundation of behavior therapy.* New York: Wiley, 1970.

Kanfer, F.H., & Saslow, G. Behavioral analysis: An alternative to diagnostic classification. *Archives of General Psychiatry,* 1965, *12,* 529-538.

Kazdin, A.E., & Wilcoxin, L.A. Systematic desensitization and nonspecific treatment effects: A methodological evaluation. *Psychological Bulletin,* 1976, *83,* 729-758.

Kelly, G. *The psychology of personal constructs.* New York: Basic Books, 1955.

Kelly, G. *Theory of personality.* New York: Norton, 1963.

Kelman, H.C. Human use of subjects: The problem of deception in social psychological experiments. *Psychological Bulletin,* 1967, *67,* 1-11.

Kent, G.H., & Rosanoff, A.J. A study of association in insanity. *American Journal of Insanity,* 1910, *67,* 37-96, 317-390.

Kessler, P., & Neale, J.M. Hippocampal damage and schizophrenia: A critique of Mednick's theory. *Journal of Abnormal Psychology,* 1974, *83,* 91-96.

Kiesler, D.J. Some myths of psychotherapy research and the search for a paradigm. *Psychological Bulletin,* 1966, *65,* 110-136.

Kincannon, J.C. Prediction of the standard MMPI scale scores from 71 items: The Mini-Mult. *Journal of Consulting and Clinical Psychology,* 1968, *32,* 319-325.

Klavetter, R.E., & Mogar, R.E. Stability and internal consistency of a measure of self-actualization. *Psychological Reports,* 1967, *21,* 422-424.

Kleinmuntz, B. *Personality measurement.* Homewood, Ill.: Dorsey Press, 1967.

Klopfer, B., Ainsworth, M.D., Klopfer, W.G., & Holt, R.R. *Developments in the Rorschach technique: Technique and theory (Vol. 1).* New York: Harcourt Brace and World, 1954.

Klopfer, B., & Davidson, H.H. *The Rorschach technique: An introductory manual.* New York: Harcourt, Brace & World, 1962.

Knapp, R.R. Relationship of a measure of self-actualization to neuroticism and ex-traversion. *Journal of Consulting Psychology,* 1965, *29,* 168-172.

Knowles, E.S., & Johnson, P.K. Intrapersonal consistency in interpersonal distance. *JSAS: Catalogue of Selected Documets in Psychology,* 1974, *4,* 124.

Kohlenberg, R.J. Treatment of a homosexual pedophiliac using *in vivo* desensitization: A case study. *Journal of Abnormal Psychology,* 1974, *83,* 192-195.

Kondo, C., & Canter, A. True and false electromyographic feedback: Effect on tension headaches. *Journal of Abnormal Psychology,* 1977, *86,* 93-95.

Koscherak, S., & Masling, J. Noblisse oblige effect: The interpretation of Rorschach responses as a function of ascribed social class. *Journal of Consulting and Clinical Psychology,* 1972, *39,* 415-419.

Kostlan, A. A method for the empirical study of psychodiagnoses. *Journal of Consulting and Clinical Psychology,* 1954, *18,* 83-88.

Kroger, R.O., & Turnbull, W. Invalidity of validity scales: The case of the MMPI. *Journal of Consulting and Clinical Psychology,* 1975, *43,* 48-55.

Kuder, G.F., & Richardson, M.W. The theory of estimation of test reliability. *Psychometrika,* 1937, *2,* 151-160.

Lachar, D. Accuracy and generalizability of an automated MMPI interpretation system. *Journal of Consulting and Clinical Psychology,* 1974, *42,* 267-273.

Lang, P.J., Melamed, B.G., & Hart, J.A. A psychophysiological analysis of fear modification using an automated desensitization procedure. *Journal of Abnormal Psychology,* 1970, *76,* 220-234.

Lanyon, R.I., & Goodstein, L.D. *Personality assessment.* New York: Wiley, 1971.

Lashley, K.J., & Colby, K.M. An exchange of views on psychic energy and psychoanalysis. *Behavioral Science,* 1957, *2,* 231-240.

Lavin, N.I., Thorpe, J.G., Boucker, J.C., Blakemore, C.B., & Conway, G.G. Behavior therapy in a case of transvestism. *Journal of Nervous and Mental Disease,* 1961, *133,* 346-353.

Lazarus, R.S. *Adjustment and personality.* New York: McGraw-Hill, 1961.

Leitenberg, H. The use of single-case methodology in psychotherapy research. *Journal of Abnormal Psychology,* 1973, *82,* 87-101.

Lentz, T.F. Acquiescence as a factor in the measurement of personality. *Psychological Bulletin,* 1938, *35,* 659.

Lepper, M.R., & Greene, D. Turning play into work: Effects of adult surveillance and extrinsic rewards on children's intrinsic motivation. *Journal of Personality and Social Psychology,* 1975, *31,* 479-486.

Lesser, G.S. The relationship between overt and fantasy aggression as a function of maternal response to aggression. *Journal of Abnormal and Social Psychology,* 1957, *55,* 218-221.

Levine, F.M., & Fasnacht, G. Token rewards may lead to token learning. *American Psychologist,* 1974, *29,* 816-820.

Levonian, E. A statistical analysis of the 16 Personality Factor Questionnaire. *Educational and Psychological Measurement,* 1961, *21,* 589-596.

Lewinsohn, P.M., & Libet, J. Pleasant events, activity schedules, and depressions. *Journal of Abnormal Psychology,* 1972, *79,* 291-295.

Leyens, J., Camino, L., Parke, R.D., & Berkowitz, L. Effects of movie violence on aggression in a field setting as a function of group dominance and cohesion. *Journal of Personality and Social Psychology,* 1975, *32,* 346-360.

Lieb, J.W., & Snyder, W.V. Achievement and positive mental health: A supplementary report. *Journal of Counseling Psychology,* 1968, *15,* 388-389.

Liebert, R.M., Odon, R.D., Hill, J.H., & Huff, R.L. The effects of age and rule familiarity on the production of modeled language constructions. *Developmental Psychology,* 1969, *1,* 108-112.

Little, K.B., & Shneidman, E.S. The validity of MMPI interpretation. *Journal of Consulting Psychology,* 1954, *18,* 425-428.

Little, K.B., & Shneidman, E.S. The validity of thematic projective technique interpretations. *Journal of Personality,* 1955, *23,* 285-294.

Liverant, S. The use of Rotter's social learning theory in developing a personality inventory. *Psychological Monographs,* 1958, *72,* (2) Whole No. 455.

Loevinger, J. Three principles for a psychoanalytic psychology. *Journal of Abnormal Psychology,* 1966, *71,* 432-443.

Lord, E. Experimentally induced variations in Rorschach performance. *Psychological Monographs,* 1950, *64,* (10) Whole No. 316.

Lovaas, O.I., Schaeffer, B., & Simmons, J.Q. Building social behavior in autistic children by use of electric shock. *Journal of Experimental Research in Personality,* 1965, *1,* 99-109.

Lundin, R.W. *Personality: A behavioral analysis.* London: Macmillan, 1969.

Lykken, D.T. Neurophysiology and psychophysiology in personality research. In Edgar Borgatta and William Lambert (Eds.), *Handbook of personality theory and research.* Chicago: Rand McNally, 1968, pp. 413-509.

MacDonald, A.P. Internal-external locus of control and the practice of birth control. *Psychological Reports,* 1970, *27,* 206.

MacDonald, A.P., Kessel, V.S., & Fuller, J.B. Self-disclosure and two kinds of trust. Unpublished manuscript, Rehabilitation, research and training center, West Virginia University, 1970.

MacPhillamy, D.J., & Lewinsohn, P.M. Measuring reinforcing events. In: *Proceedings of the 80th Annual Convention,* American Psychological Association, 1972.

Maddi, S.R. *Personality theories: A comparative analysis* (3rd ed.). Homewood, Ill.: Dorsey, 1976.

Magnussen, M.G. Verbal and nonverbal reinforcers in the Rorschach situation. *Journal of Clinical Psychology,* 1960, *16,* 167-169.

Mahoney, M.J. Reflections on the cognitive-learning trend in psychotherapy. *American Psychologist,* 1977, *32,* 5-13.

Mann, J., Berkowitz, L., Sidman, J., Starr, S., & West, S. Satiation of the transient stimulating effect of erotic films. *Journal of Personality and Social Psychology,* 1974, *30,* 729-735.

Mariotto, M.J., & Paul, G.P. A multimethod validation of the Inpatient Multidimensional Psychiatric Scale with chronically institutionalized patients. *Journal of Consulting and Clinical Psychology,* 1974, *42,* 497-508.

Marlowe, D. Need for approval and the operant conditioning of meaningful verbal behavior. *Journal of Consulting Psychology,* 1962, 26, 79-83.

Marlowe, D., & Crowne, D.P. Social desirability and response to perceived situational demands. *Journal of Consulting Psychology,* 1961, *25,* 109-115.

Masling, J. Differential indoctrination of examiners and Rorschach responses. *Journal of Consulting and Clinical Psychology,* 1965, *29,* 198-201.

Masling, J., & Harris, S. Sexual aspects of TAT administration. *Journal of Consulting Psychology,* 1969, *33,* 166-169.

Maslow, A.H. *Toward a psychology of being.* Princeton, N.J.: D. Van Nostrand, 1962.

Maslow, A.H. *Motivation and personality (2nd ed.).* New York: Harper & Row, 1970.

Masters, W.H., & Johnson, V.E. *Human sexual response.* Boston: Little, Brown, 1966.

Masters, W., & Johnson, V. *Human sexual inadequacy.* Boston: Little, Brown, 1970.

McArthur, C.C. Review of the Rorschach. In O.K. Buros, (Ed.) *Seventh mental measurement yearbook* (Vol. 1). Highland Park, N.J.: Gryphon Press, 1972. Pp. 329-332.

McBride, G., King, M.G., & James, J.W. Social proximity effects on galvanic skin responsiveness in adult humans. *Journal of Psychology,* 1965, *61,* 153-157.

McClelland, D.C. Opinions predict opinions: So what else is new? *Journal of Consulting and Clinical Psychology,* 1972, *38,* 325-326.

McFall, R.M. Effects of self-monitoring on normal smoking behavior. *Journal of Consulting and Clinical Psychology,* 1970, *35,* 135-142.

McFall, R.M., & Hammen, C.L. Motivation, structure and self-monitoring: Role of nonspecific factors in smoking reduction. *Journal of Consulting and Clinical Psychology,* 1971, *37,* 80-86.

McFall, R.M., & Lillisand, D.B. Behavior rehearsal with modeling and coaxing in assertion training. *Journal of Abnormal Psychology,* 1971, *77,* 313-323.

McFall, R.M., & Marsten, A.R. An experimental investigation of behavior rehearsal in assertive training. *Journal of Abnormal Psychology,* 1970, *76,* 295-303.

McFall, R.M., & Twentyman, G.T. Four experiments on the relative contributions of rehearsal, modeling and coaching to assertion training. *Journal of Abnormal Psychology,* 1973, *81,* 199-218.

McGraw, M., & Molloy, L. The pediatric anamnesis: Inaccuracies in eliciting developmental data. *Child Development,* 1941, *12,* 255-265.

McGuire, R.J., & Vallance, M. Aversion therapy by electric shock: A simple technique. *British Medical Journal,* 1964, *1,* 151-153.

McKinley, J.C., & Hathaway, S.R. The Minnesota Multiphasic Personality Inventory V, hysteria, hypomania, and psychopathic deviate. *Journal of Applied Psychology,* 1944, *28,* 1-17.

Meehl, P.E. Wanted — A good cookbook. *American Psychologist,* 1956, *11,* 263-272.

Meehl, P.E., & Hathaway, S.R. The K factor as a suppressor variable in the Minnesota Multiphasic Personality Inventory. *Journal of Applied Psychology,* 1946, *30,* 525-564.

Menges, R.J. Openess and honesty versus coercion and deception in psychological research. *American Psychologist,* 1973, *28,* 1030-1034.

Merrill, R. The effect of pre-experimental and experimental anxiety on recall efficiency. *Journal of Experimental Psychology,* 1954, *48,* 167-172.

Middlemist, R.D., Knowles, E.S., & Matter, C.F. Personal space invasions in the laboratory: Suggestive evidence for arousal. *Journal of Personality and Social Psychology,* 1976, *33,* 541-546.

Milgrim, S. Behavioral study of obedience. *Journal of Abnormal and Social Psychology,* 1963, *67,* 371-378.

Milgrim, S. Issues in the study of obedience: A reply to Baumrind. *American Psychologist,* 1964, *19,* 848-852.

Milgrim, S. Liberating effects of group pressure. *Journal of Personality and Social Psychology,* 1965, *1,* 127-134.

Miller, A.G. Role playing: An alternative to deception? A review of the evidence. *American Psychologist,* 1972, *27,* 623-636.

Mischel, W. *Personality and assessment.* New York: Wiley, 1968.

Mischel, W. Toward a cognitive social learning reconceptualization of personality. *Psychological Review,* 1973, *80,* 252-283(a).

Mischel, W. On the empirical dilemmas of psychodynamic approaches: Issues and alternatives. *Journal of Abnormal Psychology,* 1973, *82,* 335-344(b).

Mooney, R.L., & Gordon, L.V. *Mooney problem checklist: 1950 revision.* New York: Psychological Corporation, 1950.

Morris, R.J. *Behavior modification with children: A systematic guide.* Cambridge, Mass.: Winthrop, 1976.

Morris, R., & Suckerman, K. The importance of the therapeutic relationship in systematic desensitization. *Journal of Consulting and Clinical Psychology,* 1974, *42,* 148.

Mowrer, O.H. *Learning theory and behavior.* New York: Wiley, 1960.

Murray, H.A. The effects of fear upon estimates of the maliciousness of other personalities. *Journal of Social Psychology,* 1933, *4,* 310-329.

Murray, H.A. (Ed.) *Explorations in personality.* New York: Oxford University Press,

1938.

Murray, H.A. *Thematic apperception test manual.* Cambridge, Mass.: Harvard University Press, 1943.

Murray, H.A. Uses of the Thematic Apperception Test. *American Journal of Orthopsychiatry,* 1951, *21,* 577-581.

Murray, H.A. *Explorations in personality.* New York: Science Editions, 1962.

Murray, J.P. Television and violence. Implementation of the Surgeon General's research program. *American Psychologist,* 1973, *28,* 472-478.

Murstein, B. *Theory and research in projective techniques (emphasizing the TAT).* New York: Wiley, 1963.

Murstein, B. The stimulus. In Bernard Murstein (Ed.), *Handbook of projective techniques.* New York: Basic Books, 1965. Pp. 509-546.

Mussen, P.H., & Naylor, H.K. The relationship between overt and fantasy aggression. *Journal of Abnormal and Social Psychology,* 1954, *49,* 235-239.

Mussen, P.H., & Scodel, A. The effects of sexual stimulation under varying conditions on TAT sexual responsiveness. *Journal of Consulting Psychology,* 1955, *19,* 90.

Neale, J.M., & Liebert, R.M. *Science and behavior: An introduction to methods of research.* Englewood Cliffs, N.J.: Prentice Hall, 1973.

Nowicki, S., & Strickland, B.R. A locus of control scale for children. *Journal of Consulting and Clinical Psychology,* 1973, *40,* 148-154.

Nunnally, J.C., Jr. *Popular conceptions of mental health.* New York: Holt, Rinehart & Winston, 1961.

O'Conner, R.D. Modification of social withdrawal through symbolic modeling. *Journal of Applied Behavior Analysis,* 1969, *2,* 15-22.

O'Conner, R.D. Relative efficacy of modeling, shaping, and the combined procedures for modification of social withdrawal. *Journal of Abnormal Psychology,* 1972, *79,* 327-334.

Olds, J. Pleasure centers in the brain. *Scientific American,* 1956, *195,* 108-116.

Olds, J. Satiation effects on self-stimulation of the brain. *Journal of Comparative and Physiological Psychology,* 1958, *51,* 675-678.

Olds, J., & Milner, P. Positive reinforcement produced by electrical stimulation of the septal area and other regions of the rat brain. *Journal of Comparative and Physiological Psychology,* 1954, *47,* 419-427.

O'Leary, K.D., & Drabman, R. Token reinforcement programs in the classroom. *Psychological Bulletin,* 1971, *75,* 379-398.

O'Leary, K.D., & Kent, R.N. Behavior modification for social action: Research tactics and problems. In L. Hamerlynck and collaborators (Eds.), *Critical issues in research and practice.* Champaign, Ill.: Research Press, 1973.

O'Leary, K.D., & Wilson, G.T. *Behavior therapy: Application and outcome.* Englewood Cliffs, N.J.: Prentice-Hall, 1975.

Orne, M., & Schiebe, K.E. The contribution of non-deprivation factors in the production of sensory deprivation effects: The psychology of the "panic button." *Journal of Abnormal Psychology,* 1964, *68,* 3-12.

Osgood, C.E., Luria, Z., Jeans, R.F. & Smith, S.W. The three faces of Evelyn: A case report. *Journal of Abnormal Psychology,* 1976, *85,* 247-286.

Overall, J., & Gomez-Mont, F. MMPI-168 for psychiatric screening. *Educational and Psychological Measurement,* 1974, *34,* 315-319.

Overmann, S.R. Dietary self-selection by animals. *Psychological Bulletin,* 1976, *83,* 218-235.

Paul, L.L. *Insight vs. desensitization in psychotherapy.* Stanford: Stanford University Press, 1966.

Paul, G.L. Outcome of systematic desensitization II: Controlled investigations of individual treatment, technique variations, and current status. In C.M. Franks (Ed.), *Behavior therapy: Appraisal and status.* New York: McGraw-Hill, 1969. Pp. 105-159.

Pavlov, I.P. *Conditioned reflexes.* (G.V. Anrel, trans.) London: Oxford University Press, 1927.

Pervin, L. *Personality: Theory, assessment and research (2nd edition).* New York: Wiley, 1975.

Piliavin, I.M., Rodin, J., & Piliavin, J.A. Good samaritanism: An underground phenomenon? *Journal of Personality and Social Psychology,* 1969, *13,* 289-299.

Piper, W.E., Wogan, M., & Getter, H. Social learning theory predictors of termination in psychotherapy. In J.B. Rotter, J.E. Chance, & E.J. Phares (Eds.). *Applications of a social learning theory of personality.* New York: Holt, Rinehart & Winston, 1972. Pp. 548-553.

Premack, D. Toward empirical behavior laws: I. Positive reinforcement. *Psychological Review,* 1959. *66,* 219-233.

Purcell, K. The Thematic Apperception Test and antisocial behavior. *Journal of Consulting Psychology,* 1956, *20,* 449-456.

Pyles, M., Stolz, H. & Macfarlane, J. The accuracy of mothers' reports on birth and developmental data. *Child Development,* 1935, *6,* 165-176.

Rabin, A., Nelson, W., & Clark, M. Rorschach content as a function of perceptual experience and sex of examiner. *Journal of Clinical Psychology,* 1954, *10,* 188-190.

Rachlin, H. *Introduction to modern behaviorism. (2nd ed.)* San Francisco: W.H. Freeman, 1976.

Rachman, S. Sexual fetishism: An experimental analogue. *Psychological Record,* 1966, *16,* 293-296.

Rankin, R.J. Analysis of items perceived as objectionable in the Minnesota Multiphasic Personality Inventory. *Perceptual and Motor Skills,* 1968, *27,* 627-633.

Raush, H.L. Interaction sequences. *Journal of Personality and Social Psychology,* 1965, *2,* 487-499.

Redfield, J., & Paul, G.L. Bias in behavioral observation as a function of observer familiarity with subjects and typicality of behavior. *Journal of Consulting and Clinical Psychology,* 1976, *44,* 156.

Rehm, L.P., & Marston, A.R. Reduction of social anxiety through modification of self-reinforcement. *Journal of Consulting and Clinical Psychology,* 1968, *32,* 565-574.

Reid, J.B. Reliability assessment of observation data: A possible methodological problem. *Child Development,* 1970, *41,* 1143-1150.

Reitan, R. Neurological and physiological bases of psychopathology. *Annual Review of Psychology,* 1976, *27,* 189-216.

Rescorla, R.A. Pavlovian conditioned inhibition. *Psychological Bulletin,* 1969, *72,* 77-94.

Ring, K. Experimental social psychology: Some sober questions about some frivolous values. *Journal of Experimental Social Psychology,* 1967, *3,* 113-123.

Ring, K., & Farina, A. Personal adjustment as a determinant of aggressive behavior toward the mentally ill. *Journal of Consulting and Clinical Psychology,* 169, *33,* 683-690.

Ring, K., Wallston, K., & Corey, M. Mode of debriefing as a factor affecting subjective reaction to a Milgrim-type obedience experiment: An ethical inquiry. *Representative Research in Social Psychology,* 1970, *1,* 67-88.

Robbins, L.C. The accuracy of parental recall of aspects of child development and of child rearing practices. *Journal of Abnormal and Social Psychology,* 1963, *60,* 261-270.

Rodgers, D.A. Review of the MMPI. In O.K. Buros, (Ed.) *Seventh mental measurement yearbook.* Highland Park, N.J.: Gryphon Press, 1972.

Rogers, C.R. Significant aspects of client centured therapy. *American Psychologist,* 1946, *1,* 415-422.

Rogers, C.R. *Client-centered therapy.* Boston: Houghton Mifflin, 1951.

Rogers, C.R. A process conception of psychotherapy. *American Psychologist* 1958, *13,* 142-149.

Rogers, C.R. A theory of therapy, personality and interpersonal relationships as developed in the client-centered framework. In S. Koch (Ed.) *Psychology: A study of a science* (vol. 3). New York: McGraw Hill, 1959.

Rogers, C.R. *Carl Rogers on encounter groups.* New York: Harper & Row, 1970.

Rogers, C.R. In retrospect: Forty-six years. *American Psychologist,* 1974, *29,* 115-123.

Rogers, C.R., Kiesler, D., Gendlin, E.T., & Truax, C.B. *The therapeutic relationship and its impact: A study of psychotherapy with schizophrenics.* Madison: University of Wisconsin Press, 1965.

Rogers, C.R., & Skinner, B.F. Some issues concerning the control of human behavior: A symposium. *Science,* 1956, *124,* 1057-1066.

Romanczyk, R.G., & Goren, E.R. Severe self-injurious behavior: The problem of clinical control. *Journal of Consulting and Clinical Psycholgy,* 1975, *43,* 730-739.

Romanczyk, R.G. Kent, R.N., Diament, C.F., & O'Leary, K.D. Measuring the reliability of observational data: a reactive process. *Journal of Applied Behavioral Analysis,* 1973, *6,* 175-184.

Rorer, L.G. The great response style myth. *Psychological Review,* 1965, *63,* 129-156.

Rorer, L.G., & Goldberg, L.R. Acquiescence in the MMPI? *Educational and Psychological Measurement,* 1965, *25,* 801-817.

Rorschach, H. *Psychodiagnostik.* Leipzig: Ernest Bucher Verlag, 1921.

Rosenthal, R. *Experimenter bias in behavior.* New York: Appleton-Century-Crofts, 1966.

Rosenthal, R. Covert communication in the psychological experiment. *Psychological Bulletin,* 1967, *67,* 356-367.

Rosenthal, R., & Fode, K.L. The effect of experimenter bias on the performance of the albino rat. *Behavioral Science,* 1963, *8,* 183-189.

Rotter, J.B. *Manual for the Cotter Incomplete Sentences Blank.* New York: The Psychological Corporation, 1950.

Rotter, J.B. *Social learning and clinical psychology.* Englewood Cliffs, N.J.: Prentice-Hall, 1954.

Rotter, J.B. Some implications of a social learning theory for the prediction of goal-directed behavior from testing procedures. *Psychological Review,* 1960, *67,* 301-316.

Rotter, J.B. Generalized expectancies for internal vs. external control of reinforcement. *Psychological Monographs,* 1966, *80,* (Whole No. 609).

Rotter, J.B. A new scale for the measurement of interpersonal trust. *Journal of Personality,* 1967, *35,* 651-665.

Rotter, J.B. Some implications of a social learning theory for the practice of psychotherapy. In D.J. Levis (Ed.), *Learning approaches to therapeutic behavior change.* Chicago: Aldine, 1970.

Rotter, J.B. Generalized expectancies for interpersonal trust. *American Psychologist,* 1971, *26,* 443-452.

Rotter, J.B. Some problems and misconceptions related to the construct of internal vs. external control of reinforcement. *Journal of Consulting and Clinical Psychology,* 1975, *43,* 56-67.

Rotter, J.B., Chance, J.E., & Phares, E.J. *Application of a social learning theory of personality.* New York: Holt, Rinehart & Winston, 1972.

Rotter, J.B., & Wickens, D.D. The consistency and generality of ratings of "social aggressiveness" made from observations of role-playing situations. *Journal of Consulting Psychology,* 1948, *12,* 234-239.

Rozin, P. Are carbohydrates and protein intakes separately regulated? *Journal of Comparative and Physiological Psychology,* 1968, *65,* 23-29.

Rychlak, J.F. *A philosophy of science of personality theory.* Boston: Houghton Mifflin, 1968.

Rycroft, C. Cause and meaning. In S.G.M. Lee and M. Herbert (Eds.), *Freud and psychology.* Middlesex, England: Penguin Books, 1970. Pp. 323-335.

Sahakian, S.S. (Ed.). *Psychology of personality: Readings in theory.* Chicago: Rand McNally, 1965.

Salzinger, K. *Schizophrenia: Behavioral aspects.* New York: Wiley, 1973.

Sanders, R., & Cleveland, S.E. The relationship between certain examiner personality variables and subjects' Rorschach scores. *Journal of Projective Techniques,* 1953, *17,* 34-50.

Sarason, I.G. The effects of anxiety and threat on the solution of a difficult task. *Journal of Abnormal and Social Psychology,* 1961, *62,* 165-168.

Sarason, I.G. *Personality: An objective approach* (2nd ed.). New York: Wiley, 1966.

Sarason, I.G. Experimental approaches to test anxiety. In C.D. Spielberger (Ed.), *Anxiety: Current trends in theory and research* (Vol. 2). New York: Academic Press, 1972.

Sarnoff, I., & Corwin, S.M. Castration anxiety and the fear of death. *Journal of Personality*, 1959, *27*, 374-385.

Schactel, E.G. Subjective definitions of the Rorschach test situation and their effect on performance. *Psychiatry*, 1950, *13*, 419-448.

Schaefer, H.H., & Martin, P.L. *Behavioral therapy*. New York: McGraw Hill, 1975.

Schmidt, G., & Sigusch, V. Sex differences in response to psychosexual stimulation by films and slides. *Journal of Sex Research*, 1970, *6*, 268-283.

Schmidt, H.O., & Fonda, C.P. The reliability of psychiatric diagnosis? A new look. *Journal of Abnormal and Social Psychology*, 1956. *52*, 262-267.

Schofield, W., & Balian, L. A comparative study of the personal histories of schizophrenic and nonpsychiatric patients. *Journal of Abnormal and Social Psychology*, 1959, *59*, 216-225.

Schroeder, H.E., & Rich, A.R. The process of fear reduction through systematic desensitization. *Journal of Consulting and Clinical Psychology*, 1976, *44*, 191-199.

Schubert, D.S.P., & Wagner, M.E. A sub-cultural change of MMPI norms in the 1960s due to adolescent role confusion and glamorization of alienation. *Journal of Abnormal Psychology*, 1975, *84*, 406-411.

Schultz, D.P. The human subject in psychological research. *Psychological Bulletin*, 1969, *72*, 214-228.

Schwarz, C. Comment on high school yearbooks: A nonreactive measure of social isolation in graduates who later become schizophrenic. *Journal of Abnormal Psychology*, 1970, *75*, 317-318.

Seligman, M.E. *Helplessness: On depression, development and death*. San Francisco: W.H. Freeman, 1975.

Shah, S.A. Privileged communication, confidentiality and privacy: Privileged communications. *Professional Psychology*, 1969, *1*, 56-69.

Shah, S.A. Privileged communications, confidentiality and privacy: Confidentiality. *Professional Psychology*, 1970(a), *1*, 159-164.

Shah, S.A. Privileged communication, confidentiality and privacy: Privacy. *Professional Psychology*, 1970(b), *1*, 243-252.

Shapiro, D. *Neurotic styles*. New York: Basic Books, 1965.

Sheldon, W.H. *The varieties of human physique: An introduction to constitutional psychology*. New York: Harper, 1940.

Sherfey, M.J. The evaluation and nature of female sexuality in relation to psychoanalytic theory. *Journal of the American Psychoanalytic Association*, 1966, *14*, 28-128.

Sherman, M., Trief, P., & Sprafkin, R. Impression management in the psychiatric interview: Quality, style, and individual differences. *Journal of Consulting and Clinical Psychology*, 1975, *43*, 867-871.

Shontz, F.C. Research methods in personality. New York: Appleton-Century-Crofts, 1965.

Shostrom, E. *Personal Orientation Inventory (POI): A test of self-actualization.* San Diego, Calif: Educational and Industrial Testing Service, 1963.

Sidman, M. *Tactics of scientific research.* New York: Basic Books, 1960.

Silverman, L.H. Psychoanalytic theory: "The reports of my death are greatly exaggerated." *American Psychologist,* 1976, *31,* 621-637.

Silverman, L.H., Kwawer, J.S., Wolitzky, C., & Coron, M. An experimental study of aspects of the psychoanalytic theory of male homosexuality. *Journal of Abnormal Psychology,* 1973, *82,* 178-188.

Skinner, B.F. *Science and human behavior.* New York: The Free Press, 1953.

Skinner, B.F. Teaching machines. *Science,* 1958, *128,* 969-977.

Skinner, B.F. *Cumulative record.* New York: Appleton-Century-Crofts, 1959.

Skinner, B.F. *Behavior of Organisms.* Englewood Cliffs, N.J.: Prentice Hall, 1966.

Smith, M.B. A phenomenological approach in personality theory: Some critical remarks. *Journal of Abnormal and Social Psychology,* 1950, *45,* 516-522.

Snyder, W.V., & Cohen, L.H. Validity of imagery testing in schizophrenia. *Character and Personality,* 1944, *9,* 35-43.

Sommer, R. *Personal space: The behavioral bases of design.* Englewood Cliffs, N.J.: Prentice Hall, 1969.

Spock, B. *Baby and child care.* New York: Park Books, 1957.

Stein, A., & Friedrich, L.K. Television content and young children's behavior. In J.P. Murray, E.A. Rubenstein, and G.A. Comstock (Eds.), *Television and social learning.* Washington, D.C.: U.S. Government Printing Office, 1972.

Stein, D.K. Expectation and modeling in sensitivity groups. Unpublished doctoral dissertation, University of Connecticut, 1970.

Stephenson, W. *The study of behavior.* Chicago: University of Chicago Press, 1953.

Stotland, E., Shaver, K., & Crawford, R. Empathizing with pain and with pleasure, perceived similarity and birth order. Unpublished manuscript, University of Washington, 1966.

Strickland, B.R. The prediction of social action from a dimension of internal-external control. *Journal of Social Psychology,* 1965, *66,* 353-358.

Strupp, H.H. Some observations on the fallacy of value-free psychotherapy and the empty organism: Comments on a case study. *Journal of Abnormal Psychology,* 1974, *83,* 199-201.

Stuart, R.B. Operant-interpersonal treatment for marital discord. *Journal of Consulting and Clinical Psychology,* 1969, *33,* 675-682.

Suinn, R.M., Osborne, D., & Winfree, P. The self-concept in accuracy of recall of inconsistent self-related information. *Journal of Clinical Psychology,* 1962, *18,* 473-474.

Sullivan, D.S., & Decker, T.E. Subject-experimenter perceptions of ethical issues in human research. *American Psychologist,* 1973, *28,* 587-591.

Sullivan, H.S. *The interpersonal theory of psychiatry.* New York: Norton, 1953.

Sullivan, H.S. *The psychiatric interview.* New York: Norton, 1954.

Sullivan, H.S. *Clinical studies in psychiatry.* New York: Norton, 1956.

Tallent, N. On individualizing the psychologist's clinical evaluation. *Journal of Clinical Psychology,* 1958, *14,* 243-244.

Tasto, D.L., & Hinkle, J.E. Muscle relaxation treatment for tension headaches. *Behavior Research and Therapy,* 1973, *11,* 347-350.

Tate, B.G., & Baroff, G.S. Aversive control of self-injurious behavior in a psychotic boy. *Behavior Research and Therapy,* 1966, *4,* 281-287.

Thigpen, C.H. & Cleckley, H. A case of multiple personality. *Journal of Abnormal and Social Psychology,* 1954, *49,* 139-151.

Thorndike, E.L. *Animal intelligence: Experimental studies.* New York: Macmillan, 1911.

Thorndike, R.L. Review of the California Psychological Inventory. In O.K. Buros (Ed.), *Fifth mental measurements yearbook.* Highland Park, N.J.: Gryphon Press, 1959. Pp. 99.

Tompkin, S.S. *The Thematic Apperception Test.* New York: Grune & Stratton, 1947.

Tribich, D., & Messer, S. Psychoanalytic character type and status of authority as determinants of suggestibility. *Journal of Consulting and Clinical Psychology,* 1974, *42,* 842-848.

Truax, C.B. Reinforcement and nonreinforcement in Rogerian psychotherapy. *Journal of Abnormal Psychology,* 1966, *71,* 1-9.

Turner, R.H., & Vanderlippe, R.H. Self-ideal congruence as an index of adjustment. *Journal of Abnormal and Social Psychology,* 1958, *57,* 202-206.

Ullmann, L.P., & Krasner, L. *A psychological approach to abnormal behavior.* Englewood Cliffs, N.J.: Prentice Hall, 1969.

Underwood, B.J. *Psychological research.* New York: Appleton-Century-Crofts, 1957.

United States Commission on Obscenity and Pornography. *The report of the commissioners on obscenity and pornography.* New York: Bantam, 1970.

United States Riot Commission. *Report of the national advisory commission on civil disorders.* New York: Bantam, 1968.

Venables, P.H., & Wing, J.K. Level of arousal and the subclassification of schizophrenia. *Archives of General Psychiatry,* 1962, *7,* 114-119.

Vernon, P.E. The matching method applied to investigations of personality. *Psychological Bulletin,* 1936, *33,* 149-177.

Wachtel, P.L. Psychodynamics behavior therapy and the implacable experimenter: An inquiry into the consistency of personality. *Journal of Abnormal Psychology,* 1973, *82,* 324-334.

Walker, A.M., Rablen, R.A. & Rogers, C.R. Development of a scale to measure process changes in psychotherapy. *Journal of Clinical Psychology,* 1960, *16,* 79-85.

Wallace, J. What units shall we employ? Allport's question revisited. *Journal of Consulting Psychology,* 1967, *31,* 56-64.

Walsh, J.A. Review of the CPI. In O.K. Buros (Ed.), *Seventh mental measurement yearbook* (Vol. 1). Highland Park, N.J.: Gryphon Press, 1972.

Watson, J.B. Psychology as the behaviorist views it. *Psychological Review,* 1913, *20,* 158-177.

Watson, J.B. *Behaviorism.* New York: People's Institute, 1924.

Watson, J.B., & Raynor, R. Conditioned emotional reactions. *Journal of Experimental Psychology,* 1920, *3,* 1-14.

Webb, E.J., Campbell, D.T., Schwartz, R.D., & Sechrest, L. *Unobtrusive measures: Nonreactive research in the social sciences.* Chicago: Rand McNally, 1970.

Werner, H. *Comparative psychology of mental development* (Rev. ed). Chicago: Follett, 1948.

Werner, H. The concept of development from a comparative and organismic point of view. In D.B. Harris (Ed.), *The concept of development.* Minneapolis, Minn.: University of Minnesota Press, 1957, Pp. 125-148.

Wernimont, P.F., & Campbell, J.P. Signs, samples and criteria. *Journal of Applied Psychology,* 1968, *52,* 372-376.

West, S., Whitney, G., & Schnedler, R. Helping a motorist in distress: The effects of sex, race, and neighborhood. *Journal of Personality and Social Psychology,* 1975, *31,* 691-698.

Wickes, T.A., Jr. Examiner influence in a testing situation. *Journal of Consulting Psychology,* 1956, *20,* 23-26.

Wittenborn, J.R., & Holzberg, J.D. The Rorschach and descriptive diagnoses. *Journal of Consulting Psychology,* 1951, *15,* 460-463.

Wolpe, J. *Psychotherapy by reciprocal inhibition.* Stanford, Ca.: Stanford University Press, 1958.

Wolpe, J. *The practice of behavior therapy.* New York: Pergamon Press, 1969.

Wolpe, J., & Lang, P.J. A fear survey schedule for use in behavior therapy. *Behavior Research and Therapy,* 1964, *2,* 27-30.

Wolpe, J., & Rachman, S. Psychoanalytic "evidence": A critique based on Freud's case of Little Hans. *Journal of Nervous and Mental Disease,* 1960, *130,* 135-148.

Woods, W.L. Language study in schizophrenia. *Journal of Nervous and Mental Diseases,* 1938, *87,* 290-316.

Woodworth, R.S. *Personal data sheet.* Chicago: Stoelting, 1920.

Zeller, A. An experimental analogue of repression. I. Historical Summary. *Psychological Bulletin,* 1950, *47,* 39-51(a).

Zeller, A. An experimental analogue of repression: II. The effect of individual failure and success on memory measured by relearning. *Journal of Experimental Psychology,* 1950, *40,* 411-422(b).

Zigler, E. Research on personality structure in the retardate. In N.R. Ellis (Ed.), *International review of research in mental retardation.* New York: Academic Press, 1966.

Zigler, E., & Phillips, L. Psychiatric diagnosis and symptomatology. *Journal of Abnormal and Social Psychology,* 1961, *63,* 69-75.

Zuckerman, M. Physiological measures of sexual arousal in the human. *Psychological Bulletin,* 1971, *75,* 297-329.

SUBJECT INDEX

AUTHOR INDEX

About the Author

After earning his Ph.D. at the University of Connecticut, Mark Sherman joined the Clinical Psychology Training Program at Syracuse University as Associate Professor. In 1978 Dr. Sherman joined the staff of United States International University where he is currently Assistant Coordinator of Clinical Training and Associate Professor of Clinical Psychology. He has published numerous research articles dealing with the stigma of mental illness, malingering among psychiatric patients, and behavioral therapy.

TITLES IN THE PERGAMON GENERAL PSYCHOLOGY SERIES (Continued)